cpt®

Reference of Clinical Examples

Official scenarios for correct coding

AMA
AMERICAN MEDICAL ASSOCIATION

Executive Vice President, Chief Executive Officer: Michael D. Maves, MD, MBA
Chief Operating Officer: Bernard L. Hengesbaugh
Senior Vice President, Publishing and Business Services: Robert A. Musacchio, PhD
Vice President, Business Products: Anthony J. Frankos
Director, Editorial and Operations: Mary Lou White
Senior Acquisitions Editor: Elise Schumacher
Director, CPT Editorial and Information Services: Michael Beebe
Director, CPT Product Development: Dan Reyes
Coding Specialist: Jennifer Trajkovski
Coding Specialist: Martha Espronceda
Director, Physician Payment Policy and Systems: Sherry L. Smith
Senior Policy Analyst, Physician Payment Policy and Systems: Roseanne Fischoff
Senior Policy Analyst, Physician Payment Policy and Systems: Susan Clark
RBRVS Data and Methods Manager: Todd Klemp
Director, Production and Manufacturing: Jean Roberts
Manager, Developmental Editing: Nancy C. Baker
Senior Production Coordinator: Rosalyn Carlton
Senior Production Coordinator: Boon Ai Tan
Senior Print Coordinator: Ronnie Summers
Director of Marketing, Business Marketing and Communication: Pam Palmersheim
Director of Sales, Business Products: J.D. Kinney
Manager, Marketing and Strategic Planning: Erin Kalitowski
Marketing Manager: Leigh Bottiger

ISBN: 978-1-57947-874-2
OP153907

AC38:06-P-045:03/07

Table of Contents

Using the Book

This book is designed to serve as a reference guide to the CPT® codebook and related CPT products, and is not intended to replace the *CPT® Professional* or *Standard* editions. *CPT® Reference of Clinical Examples: Official Scenarios for Correct Coding* should be used as an aid in understanding the application of some of the most commonly reported and often misunderstood codes. The clinical examples will greatly benefit users of CPT who are accustomed to working from operative reports.

The book follows the same organizational structure as the main CPT codebook, making it easy to locate the placement of code information. Over 470 codes were selected based on a review of the most frequently reported codes according to Medicare claims data and information obtained from the American Medical Association's CPT Information Services, which fields inquiries from users of CPT. In addition, third-party payer reporting practices may differ.

The CPT references within the body of this book contain the:

- CPT code
- CPT description
- Clinical example
- Illustrations and coding tips (when appropriate)
- *CPT® Assistant* newsletter references
- *Clinical Examples in Radiology* newsletter references
- *CPT® Changes: An Insider's View* references
- Add-on code symbol
- Modifier 51 exempt symbol
- Moderate sedation symbol

Also included are data generated from the Centers for Medicare and Medicaid Services and the RBRVS (Resource-Based Relative Value Scale) process, including:

- Global Period
- Work Value
- Five-Year Review

Clinical Examples

The clinical examples included in this text represent the typical situation for which a code would be reported. It is important to note that these clinical scenarios do not suggest limiting the use or reporting of a code, but only represent the typical patient and service/procedure. They do not describe the universe of patients for whom the service/procedure would be appropriate. These clinical examples richly illustrate detailed case histories providing a framework for understanding code selection. Each chosen CPT code not only includes the clinical scenario but also the descriptions of physician work. CPT physician work may consist of the physician activities involved in the procedure in the preservice, intraservice, and postservice time-periods.

Preservice Period

The preservice period includes physician services provided from the day before the operative procedure until the time of the operative procedure and may include the following:

- Hospital admission work-up.
- The preoperative evaluation may include the procedural work-up, review of records, communicating with other professionals, patient and family, and obtaining consent.

- Other preoperative work may include dressing, scrubbing, and waiting before the operative procedure, preparing patient and needed equipment for the operative procedure, positioning the patient and other non "skin-to-skin" work in the operating room.

The following services are *not included*:

- Consultation or evaluation at which the decision to provide the procedure was made (reported with modifier 57).
- Distinct evaluation and management services provided in addition to the procedure (reported with modifier 25).
- Mandated services (reported with modifier 32).

Intraservice Period

The intraservice period includes the work involved in actually providing a service or performing a procedure. For office visits, the intraservice period is defined as patient encounter time; for hospital visits, it is the time spent on the patient's floor; and for surgical procedures, it is the period from initial incision to the closure of the incision (ie, "skin-to-skin" time).

Postservice Period

The postservice period includes services provided on the day of the procedure, and services within 90 days of the procedure, and may include care on the day of the procedure (immediate postservice time) and any subsequent visit on the day of the operative procedure. Immediate postservice time may also include non-"skin-to-skin" work in the operating room, patient stabilization in the recovery room or special unit, communicating with the patient and other professionals including written and telephone reports and orders.

Coding Tips

The coding tips provide exclusive information and guidance obtained from the American Medical Association's CPT Editorial Panel meetings and minutes.

Work RVU

A relative value scale is a list of physicians' services ranked according to "value," with the value defined with respect to the basis for the scale. The relative value units on the Medicare Physician Fee schedule relate to the value of the service in relation to all other services. The factors used to determine physician work include the time it takes to perform the service; the technical skill and physical effort; the required mental effort and judgment; and stress due to the potential risk to the patient. The physician work relative values are updated each year to account for changes in medical practice.

Annual updates to the physician work relative values are based on recommendations from a committee involving the American Medical Association (AMA) and national medical specialty societies. The AMA/Specialty Society RVS Update Committee (RUC) was formed in 1991 to make recommendations to the Centers for Medicare and Medicaid Services (CMS) on the relative values to be assigned to new or revised codes in the *Current Procedural Terminology (CPT)* book. Over 8,000 procedure codes are defined in CPT, and the relative values in the RBRVS were originally developed to correspond to the procedure definitions in CPT. The RUC submits recommendations to the Centers for Medicare and Medicaid Services (CMS) based on CPT coding changes to be included in the Medicare payment schedule. Since inception, the RUC has submitted more than 3,000 relative value recommendations for new and revised codes for the Resource Based Relative Value Scale (RBRVS) updates. In addition, Section 1848(C)2 (B) of the Omnibus Budget Reconciliation Act of 1990, enacting the RBRVS requires the Centers for Medicare and Medicaid Services (CMS) to comprehensively review the whole scale at least every five years and make any needed adjustments.

Global Periods

A global surgical package for major surgical procedures refers to a payment policy of bundling payment for the various services associated with an operation into a single payment covering the operation and other services such as postoperative hospital visits. It is common practice among surgeons to bill for such global surgical packages, which generally include the immediate preoperative care, the operation itself, and the normal, uncomplicated follow-up care.

The global periods refer to the number of postservice days of care that are included in the payment for the service as determined by the CMS for Medicare payment purposes. Categories of global period:

090 90 days of postservice care are included in the work RVU

010 10 days of postservice care are included in the work RVU

000 0 days of postservice care are included in the work RVU

ZZZ Code related to another service and is always included in the global period of the other service
Note: Physician work is associated with intraservice time and in some instances the pre- and post-service time.

XXX A global period does not apply to the code and evaluation and management and other diagnostic tests or minor services performed may be reported separately on the same day.

RBRVS Five-Year Review Process

In addition to annual updates reflecting changes in CPT, every five years CMS comprehensively reviews all physician work relative values and makes any changes to the values based on anomalies or changes in medical practice. Codes included in this book that were part of the most recent Five-Year Review have been tagged with the ❺ symbol. It should be understood that the Five-Year Review process is limited to physician work relative values only.

List of Symbols

This book uses some of the coding conventions that appear in the CPT codebook. An additional symbol was added to the text of this book only to indicate if a selected code was part of the most recent Five-Year Review. **Note:** The Five-Year Review symbol does not appear in the CPT codebook.

- ✚ Indicates a CPT add-on code
- ⊘ Indicates a code that is exempt from the use of modifier 51 but is not designated as a CPT add-on procedure/service
- ⊙ Indicates a code that typically includes moderate sedation
- ❺ Five-Year Review
- ➲ Indicates there is an article in the *CPT® Assistant* or *Clinical Examples in Radiology* newsletters that discusses the referenced code. The symbol may also indicate that the code is discussed in a past edition of the book, *CPT® Changes: An Insiders View.* For more information about or to purchase products, go to www.amabookstore.com.

The CPT® Process

The CPT Editorial Panel is responsible for maintaining the CPT nomenclature. This panel is authorized to revise, update, or modify the CPT codes. The Panel is comprised of 17 members. Of these, 11 are physicians nominated by the AMA; one physician each nominated from the Blue Cross and Blue Shield Association, the Health Insurance Association of America, the American Hospital Association, and the Centers for Medicare and Medicaid Services (CMS), and the co-chair and a representative of the Health Care Professionals Advisory Committee. The AMA's Board of Trustees appoints the Panel members. Of the eleven AMA seats on the panel, seven are regular seats, having a maximum tenure of two 4-year terms, or a total of eight years for any one individual. One of these seats is designated for a physician who can represent the managed care viewpoint. The four remaining seats, called rotating seats, have one four-year term. These rotating seats allow for diverse specialty input.

Five members of the Editorial Panel serve as the panel's Executive Committee. The Executive Committee includes the Editorial Panel chairman and co-chairman, and three panel members-at-large, as elected by the entire panel. One of the three members-at-large of the Executive Committee must be a third-party payer representative.

Supporting the CPT Editorial Panel in its work is a larger body of CPT advisors, the CPT Advisory Committee. The members of this committee are primarily physicians nominated by the national medical specialty societies represented in the AMA House of Delegates. Currently, the Advisory Committee is limited to national medical specialty societies seated in the AMA House of Delegates and to the AMA Health Care Professionals Advisory Committee (HCPAC), organizations representing limited-license practitioners and other allied health professionals. Additionally, a group of individuals, the Performance Measures Advisory Committee (PMAC), who represent various organizations concerned with performance measures, also provide expertise. The Advisory Committees' primary objectives are to:

- serve as a resource to the CPT Editorial Panel by giving advice on procedure coding and appropriate nomenclature as relevant to the member's specialty or practice;
- provide documentation to AMA staff and the CPT Editorial Panel regarding the appropriateness of various medical and surgical procedures under consideration as CPT codes;
- suggest revisions to the CPT nomenclature (the Advisory Committee meets annually to discuss items of mutual concern and to keep informed on current issues in coding and nomenclature);
- assist in the review and further development of relevant coding issues and in the preparation of technical education material and articles pertaining to CPT coding;
- promote and educate its membership on the use and benefits of CPT coding via recommendations from the AMA Health Care Professionals Advisory Committee (HCPAC)

Category I CPT Codes

In developing new and revised regular CPT codes the Advisory Committees and the Editorial Panel require that the:

- service/procedure has received approval from the Food and Drug Administration (FDA) for the specific use of devices or drugs;
- suggested procedure/service is a distinct service performed by many physicians/practitioners across the United States;
- clinical efficacy of the service/procedure is well established and documented;

- suggested service/procedure is neither a fragmentation of an existing procedure/service nor currently reportable by one or more existing codes; and
- suggested service/procedure is not requested as a means to report extraordinary circumstances related to the performance of a procedure/service already having a specific CPT code.

Category II CPT Codes Performance Measurement

Category II CPT codes are a set of supplemental tracking codes intended to facilitate data collection about quality of care by coding certain services and/or test results that support performance measures and that have been agreed upon as contributing to good patient care. These codes describe components that are typically included in an evaluation and management service or test results that are part of the laboratory test/procedure. Consequently, since the aggregate service has already been valued, the Category II codes do not have a relative value associated with them and will not be referred to the RUC for valuation. The use of tracking codes for performance measurement will decrease the need for record abstraction and chart review, and thereby minimize administrative burden on physicians and other health care professionals. The use of these codes is optional for tracking performance measurement. The codes are not required for correct coding and may not be used as a substitute for Category I codes. Category II Performance Measurement Codes are located in a separate section of CPT, following the Medicine section, and assigned a five digit numeric-alpha identifier (ie, four numbers followed by the letter 'F'). These digits are not intended to reflect the placement of the code in the regular (Category I) part of CPT.

Requests for Category II CPT codes will be reviewed by the CPT/HCPAC Advisory Committee just as requests for Category I CPT codes are reviewed. In developing new and revised Performance Measurement Codes, the CPT Advisory Committees and the Editorial Panel will be assisted by the Performance Measure Advisory Group (PMAG). The PMAG is interested in:

- measurements that have been developed and tested by a national organization;
- evidence-based measurements with established ties to health outcomes;
- measurements that address clinical conditions of high prevalence, high risk or high cost; and
- well-established measurements that are currently used by large segments of the health care industry.

Category II codes are published twice a year on January 1, and July 1. The most current listing can be reviewed at www.ama-assn.org/go/cpt.

Category III CPT Codes Emerging Technology

Category III CPT codes are a temporary set of tracking codes for new and emerging technologies. These codes are intended to facilitate data collection on and assessment of new services and procedures. The Category III codes are intended for data collection purposes in the FDA approval process or to substantiate widespread usage. As such, the Category III codes may not conform to the usual CPT code requirements that:

- services/procedures are performed by many health care professionals across the country;
- FDA approval is documented or imminent within a given CPT cycle;
- the service/procedure has proven clinical efficacy; and
- the service/procedure must have relevance for research, either ongoing or planned.

These codes will be assigned a numeric-alpha identifier (eg, 1234T). These codes will be located in a separate section of CPT, following the "Category II" section. Introductory language in this code section explains the purpose of the Category III codes. Since Category III CPT codes are intended to be used for data collection purposes to substantiate widespread usage or in the FDA approval process, they are not intended for services/procedures that are not accepted by the Editorial Panel because the proposal was incomplete, more information is needed, or the Advisory Committee did not support the proposal.

Once approved by the Editorial Panel, the newly added Category III CPT codes are made available on a semi-annual basis (January 1 or July 1) via electronic distribution at *www.ama-assn.org/go/cpt*. The full set of Category III codes is included in the next published edition for that CPT cycle.

Category III CPT codes are not referred to the AMA /Specialty RVS Update Committee (RUC) for valuation because no relative value units (RVUs) will be assigned. Payment for these services/procedures is based on the policies of payers and not on a yearly fee schedule.

These codes will be archived five years from the date of implementation, if the code has not been accepted for placement in the Category I section of CPT, unless demonstrated that a Category III code is still needed. These codes will not be reused.

When Are CPT Codes Implemented?

For federal programs, January 1 of each year is generally the effective date for using the new CPT Category I codes. The AMA prepares each annual update so that the new CPT books are available in late fall of each year preceding their implementation.

Category I vaccine product codes, Category II, and Category III codes are typically "early released" for reporting either January 1 or July 1 of a given CPT cycle. In order to comply with HIPAA requirements, the effective implementation dates for these codes have been altered to become effective six months subsequent to the date of release following code set updates.

AMA/Specialty Society RVS Update Committee (RUC) Process

Throughout this book there are references to Global Period, Work Value, and the Five-Year Review. This information is a subset of data derived from the AMA/Specialty Society RVS Update Committee (RUC) process. The following provides a brief history of the RUC process and the RBRVS system.

Introduction to the Medicare RBRVS

In 1992, Medicare significantly changed the way it pays for physicians' services. Instead of basing payments on charges, the federal government established a standardized physician payment schedule based on a resource-based relative value scale (RBRVS). In the RBRVS system, payments for services are determined by the resource costs needed to provide them. The cost of providing each service is divided into three components: physician work, practice expense and professional liability insurance. Payments are calculated by multiplying the combined costs of a service by a conversion factor (a monetary amount that is determined by the Centers for Medicare and Medicaid Services). Payments are also adjusted for geographical differences in resource costs.

The physician work component accounts, on average, for 52% of the total relative value for each service. The initial physician work relative values were based on the results of a Harvard University study. The factors used to determine physician work include the time it takes to perform the service; the technical skill and physical effort; the required mental effort and judgment; and stress due to the potential risk to the patient. The physician work relative values are updated each year to account for changes in medical practice. Also, the legislation enacting the RBRVS requires the Centers for Medicare and Medicaid Services (CMS) to review the whole scale at least every five years.

The practice expense component of the RBRVS accounts for an average of 44% of the total relative value for each service. Practice expense relative values were initially based on a formula using average Medicare approved charges from 1991 (the year before the RBRVS was implemented) and the proportion of each specialty's revenues that is attributable to practice expenses. However, in January 1999, CMS began a transition to resource-based practice expense relative values for each CPT code that differs based on the site of service. In 2002, the resource-based practice expenses were fully transitioned.

On January 1, 2000, CMS implemented the resource-based professional liability insurance (PLI) relative value units. The PLI component of the RBRVS accounts for an average of 4% of the total relative value for each service. With this implementation and final transition of the resource-based practice expense relative units on January 1, 2002, all components of the RBRVS are resource-based.

The RBRVS Updating Process

Annual updates to the physician work relative values are based on recommendations from a committee involving the American Medical Association (AMA) and national medical specialty societies. The AMA/Specialty Society RVS Update Committee (RUC) was formed in 1991 to make recommendations to CMS on the relative values to be assigned to new or revised codes in the *Current Procedural Terminology* (CPT) book.

Over 8,000 procedure codes are defined in CPT, and the relative values in the RBRVS were originally developed to correspond to the procedure definitions in CPT.

CPT is maintained by the CPT Editorial Panel. This seventeen-member panel is authorized to revise, update, or modify CPT. Eleven of the seats on the Editorial Panel are nominated by the AMA and the remaining seats are nominated by the Blue Cross and Blue Shield Association, the Health Insurance Association of America, the Centers for Medicare and Medicaid Services and the American Hospital Association. A representative from managed care and two members of the CPT HCPAC (an advisory committee representing non-MD/DO health professionals) serve as part of the eleven AMA appointed seats in CPT necessitate annual updates to the RBRVS for the new and revised codes.

The RUC represents the entire medical profession, with 23 of its 29 members appointed by major national medical specialty societies including those recognized by the American Board of Medical Specialties, those with a large percentage of physicians in patient care, and those that account for high percentages of Medicare expenditures. Three seats rotate on a two-year basis, with two reserved for an internal medicine subspecialty and one for any other specialty. The RUC Chair, the Co-Chair of the RUC HCPAC Review Board, and representatives of the American Medical Association, American Osteopathic Association, the Chair of the Practice Expense Review Committee (PERC) and CPT Editorial Panel hold the remaining six seats.

RVS Update Committee (RUC)

Chair

American Medical Association

CPT Editorial Panel

American Osteopathic Association

Health Care Professionals Advisory Committee

Practice Expense Review Committee:

Anesthesiology	Ophthalmology
Cardiology	Orthopaedic Surgery
Dermatology	Otolaryngology
Emergency Medicine	Pathology
Family Medicine	Pediatrics
General Surgery	Plastic Surgery
Geriatric Medicine*	Psychiatry
Internal Medicine	Radiology
Neurology	Spine Care*
Neurosurgery	Thoracic Surgery
Obstetrics/Gynecology	Urology
Oncology*	

* Indicates rotating seat

Advisory Committee

One physician representative is appointed from each of the 114 specialty societies seated in the AMA House of Delegates to serve on the *Advisory Committee* to the RUC. Specialty societies that are not in the House of Delegates also may be invited to participate in developing relative values for coding changes of particular relevance to their members. Advisory committee members designate an *RVS Committee* for their specialty, which is responsible for generating relative value recommendations using a survey method developed by the RUC. The Advisors attend the RUC meeting and present their societies' recommendations, which the RUC evaluates. Specialties represented on both the RUC and the Advisory Committee are required to appoint different physicians to each committee to distinguish the role of advocate from that of evaluator.

Practice Expense Refinement

The AMA continues to participate and monitor all phases of the refinement of the new practice expense relative values and continues to advocate that they be based on valid physician practice expense data. Since there is not a single universally accepted cost allocation methodology, it is especially important that CMS base its methodology on actual practice expense data. The decisions reached by CMS have enormous implications for physicians and all their patients, not just those on Medicare. Since many other payment systems use the Medicare RBRVS, the change to resource-based practice expense relative values has broad implications for the entire health care system. Due to the significance of this issue, the RUC established a special subcommittee called the Practice Expense Advisory Committee (PEAC) to monitor this process. The PEAC was charged with the review of direct expense inputs (clinical labor activities, medical supplies, and equipment) used to calculate practice expense relative values, and made code-specific recommendations to the RUC. The RUC then made the final recommendation to CMS. The PEAC specifically reviewed the practice expense inputs of essentially the entire Medicare Fee Schedule by making recommendations on over 6,500 medical procedures. The composition of the PEAC mirrored the RUC with additional representation from nursing. The PEAC review process was similar to the RUC process, relying on specialty societies to make recommendations that were reviewed by a panel of medical experts and then forwarded to CMS. The PEAC concluded its work in March 2004. The RUC continues to work closely with specialty societies and CMS to maintain the practice expense component of the RBRVS. The RUC has formed a committee that continues to address any existing code refinement issues that arise. This group, the Practice Expense Review Committee (PERC) also assists the RUC in its review of practice expense inputs for new and revised codes.

The RUC Health Care Professionals Advisory Committee (HCPAC)

The HCPAC was formed to allow for participation of limited license practitioners and allied health professionals in the RUC process. All of these professionals use CPT to report the services they provide independently to Medicare patients, and they are paid for these services based on the RBRVS physician payment schedule. The 11 organizations seated on the HCPAC represent physician assistants, chiropractors, nurses, occupational therapists, optometrists, physical therapists, podiatrists, psychologists, audiologists, speech pathologists, social workers and registered dieticians. The HCPAC members together with three physician members of the RUC comprise the *RUC HCPAC Review Board*, which is responsible for developing relative value recommendations to CMS for new and revised codes that are reported principally by non-MD/DO professionals. The Co-Chair of the Review Board also serves as a member of the RUC.

RUC Cycle and Methodology

The RUC's annual cycle for developing recommendations is closely coordinated with both the CPT Editorial Panel's schedule for annual code revisions and the CMS schedule for annual updates in the Medicare Payment Schedule. The Editorial Panel meets three times a year to consider coding changes for the next year's edition. The RUC meets after the Editorial Panel meetings to consider relative value codes that are changed or added by the Editorial Panel.

The CPT Editorial Panel's yearly cycle must be completed in February of each year so that the RUC can submit its recommendations to CMS in May. CMS publishes the annual update to the Medicare RVS in the *Federal Register* every year, at about the same time that the AMA publishes the new *CPT* book for the coming year. The updated CPT codes and relative values go into effect annually on January 1. Due to the close coordination between RUC and CPT and the timely submission of recommendations to CMS, physicians have the benefit of organized medicine's input into relative values for new codes in the same year that the coding changes appear in CPT.

The RUC Process

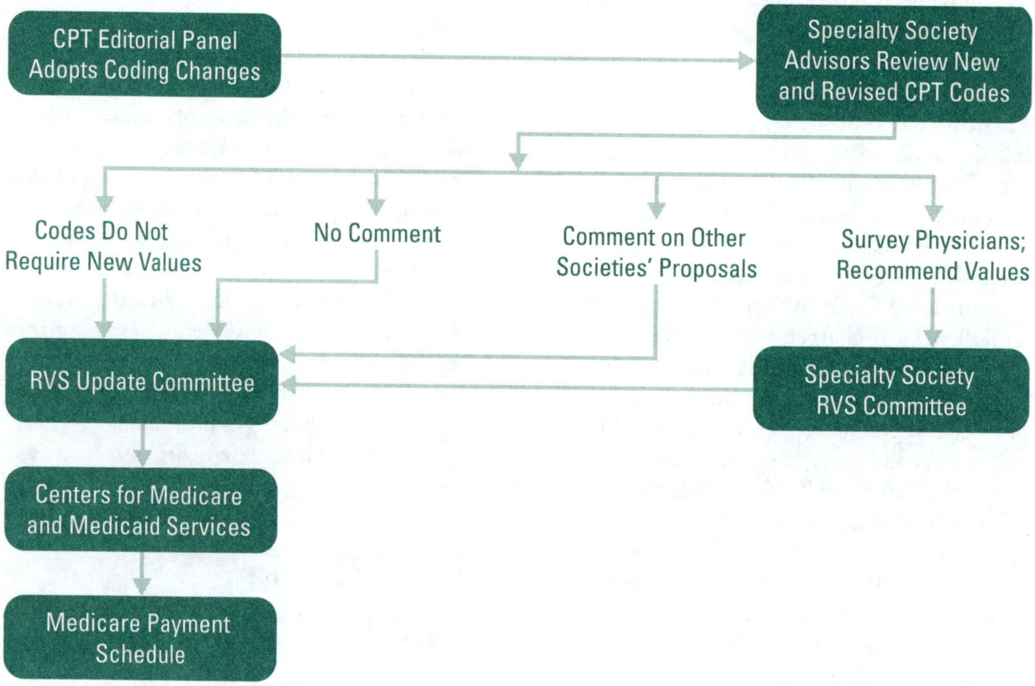

The RUC process for developing relative value recommendations is as follows:

Step 1. The CPT Editorial Panel's new or revised codes are transmitted to the RUC staff, who then prepare a "Level of Interest" form. This form summarizes the panel's coding actions.

Step 2. Members of the RUC Advisory Committee and specialty society staff review the summary and indicate their societies' level of interest in developing a relative value recommendation. The societies have several options: (1) they can survey their members to obtain data on the amount of work involved in a service and develop recommendations based on the survey results; (2) they can comment in writing on recommendations developed by other societies; (3) in the case of revised codes, they may decide that the coding change does not require action because it does not significantly alter the nature of the service; or (4) they may take no action because the codes are not used by physicians in their specialty.

Step 3. AMA staff distributes survey instruments for the specialty societies. The societies are required to survey at least 30 practicing physicians. The RUC survey instrument asks physicians to use a list of 15 to 25 services as reference points that have been selected by the specialty RVS committee. Physicians receiving the survey are asked to evaluate the work involved in the new or revised code relative to the reference points. The survey data may be augmented by analysis of Medicare claims data and information from other studies of the procedure, such as the Harvard RBRVS study.

Step 4. The specialty RVS committees conduct the surveys, review the results, and prepare their recommendations to the RUC. When two or more societies are involved in developing recommendations, the RUC encourages them to coordinate their survey procedures and develop a consensus recommendation. The written recommendations are disseminated to the RUC before the meeting and consist of physician work, time, and practice expense recommendations.

Step 5. The specialty Advisors present the recommendations at the RUC meeting. The Advisory Committee members' presentations are followed by a thorough question-and-answer period during which the Advisors must defend every aspect of their proposal(s).

Step 6. The RUC may decide to adopt a specialty society's recommendation, refer it back to the specialty society, or modify it before submitting it to CMS. Final recommendations to CMS must be adopted by a two-thirds majority of the RUC members. Recommendations that require additional evaluation by the RUC are referred to a Facilitation Committee.

Step 7. The RUC's recommendations are forwarded to CMS in May of each year. CMS Medical Officers and Contractor Medical Directors review the RUC's recommendations.

Step 8. The Medicare Physician Payment Schedule, which includes CMS's review of the RUC recommendations, is published in late fall.

Annual RBRVS Updates: 1993-2007

The RUC has submitted approximately 3,100 relative value recommendations for new and revised codes for the 1993-2007 RBRVS annual updates. In addition, the RUC submitted more than 300 recommendations to CMS for carrier priced or non-covered services, including preventive medicine visits. A major reason for evaluating these non-covered codes using the RBRVS system is the widespread adoption of the Medicare payment system by state Medicaid programs and other insurance programs covering pediatric populations. Each year CMS has relied heavily upon these recommendations when establishing interim values for new or revised CPT codes. CMS's acceptance rate for the RUC's recommendations is more than 90% annually.

The RBRVS Five-Year Review Process

In addition to annual updates reflecting changes in CPT, Section 1848(C)2 (B) of the Omnibus Budget Reconciliation Act of 1990 requires CMS to comprehensively review all relative values at least every five years and make any needed adjustments. The changes resulting from the first Five-Year Review of the RBRVS became effective January 1, 1997. Relative value changes from the second Five-Year Review of the RBRVS were implemented on January 1, 2002. The success of the RUC's role in the annual updates led CMS to seek assistance from the RUC in both Five-Year Review processes. The RUC is currently playing a key role in the third Five-Year Review which began in 2005 and will conclude with the CMS implementation of new values on January 1, 2007. Because a separate process is ongoing to develop and refine new resource-based practice expense relative values, the Five-Year Review processes have been limited to the physician work relative values.

To allow identification of codes to be included in the initial review, CMS asked the RUC to develop a list of reference services spanning multiple specialties, types of service, and the full range of relative value units. Reference services provide a way of comparing the physician work involved in a service to the work involved in another service, which has an established relative value. For example, a surgical procedure might be identified as misvalued in comparison to another procedure if the first service required two hours more intraoperative work but had a lower relative value than the reference procedure. In response to CMS's request, the RUC developed and has maintained a list of more than 300 services, which could provide standard points of comparison for misvalued services.

Each Five-Year Review presents an unprecedented opportunity to improve the accuracy of the physician work component of the RBRVS, as well as a significant challenge to the medical community. All of the codes on the Medicare Physician Payment Schedule were open for public comment as part of each Five-Year Review. The initial Five-Year Review included the development of relative values for pediatric services. The Social Security Amendments Act of 1994 required that RVUs be developed for the full range of pediatric services, as well as determining whether significant variations existed in the work required to furnish similar pediatric patient services.

During the public comment period for the initial Five-Year Review, CMS received nearly 500 letters identifying about 1,100 CPT codes for review. The Carrier Medical Directors, the American Academy of Pediatrics (AAP) and special studies conducted for three specialty societies identified additional codes for review. Following an initial review in late February 1995, CMS referred to the RUC comments on about 3,500 codes.

The second Five-Year Review was initiated in March 2000 when CMS shared comments submitted by 30 specialties on more than 870 codes. The third Five-Year Review was initiated in February 2005 when CMS provided public comments from forty-four specialty societies related to 556 codes. In addition, CMS requested that the RUC review an additional 168 codes, selected principally because they were high volume codes that had not been reviewed since the initial implementation of the RBRVS in 1992.

Methods and Procedures Used in the Five-Year Review

The RUC's process for each Five-Year Review involved the same basic methodology as the annual update process, with some important innovations. First, a modified survey instrument was developed. Because the Five-Year Review involved evaluating the work of established codes with established relative values instead of new codes, specialties had to offer evidence that the established relative value was incorrect in addition to showing why the recommended value was correct.

To help gather evidence to support such arguments, in addition to comparing the total physician work involved in the services under review to key reference services, survey respondents were asked to provide a detailed comparison of the pre-, intra-, and postservice time involved, to that of key reference services. Survey questions were also added regarding the other elements of work besides time, as well as the extent to which the service has changed over the last five years. If they believed the service had changed over the past five years, they were asked whether: the service represents new technology that has become more familiar; patients requiring the service are more or less complex; and, if the usual site of service has changed.

Another innovation was the collection of information besides that which is developed by the specialty societies to facilitate evaluation of the comments. In addition to the specialty recommendation forms, the AMA assembled data from several sources into a supplemental report on each code. The report included recent trends in claims frequency and site of service; specialties that provide the service; and information from the Harvard RBRVS study on physician time.

The RUC developed "Guidelines for Compelling Evidence" for the 2005 Five-Year Review. These guidelines were created specifically for this Five-Year Review and were used in the comment process as well as in the review of individual codes to justify new valuations. The argument for a change was required to meet the compelling evidence standards, including:

- Documentation in the peer-reviewed literature or other reliable data that there have been changes in physician work.
- An anomalous relationship between the code and multiple key reference services.
- Evidence that technology has changed physician work.
- Analysis of other data on time and effort measures.
- Evidence that incorrect assumptions were made in the previous valuation of the service, as documented.

Results of the Five-Year Review

Year 1995 Five-Year Review

In September 1995, the RUC submitted to CMS relative value recommendations for more than 1,000 individual codes for the first Five-Year Review. Of the 1,000 codes evaluated individually, the majority of the recommendations made by the RUC were to maintain the current relative work values. However, the RUC recommended increasing the value for about 300 services, which addressed long-standing concerns about several major groups of services. The data gathered on the work involved in the evaluation and management, gynecology, and vascular surgery services, for example, supported the commenter's' contention that these services were originally valued too low, and the RUC recommended significant increases. These data tended to show that the work involved in the services had increased since the Harvard study was conducted and that the services had been undervalued relative to key reference services since the RBRVS was originally implemented. The recommendations may be summarized as follows:

- For 296 codes, the RUC recommended that the relative value be increased.
- For 650 codes, the RUC recommended that the current relative value be maintained.
- For 107 codes, the RUC recommended that the relative value be decreased.
- The RUC referred 65 codes to the CPT Editorial Panel to consider coding changes prior to further consideration of the relative value.

CMS's proposed RVU changes were published in a May 1996 *Federal Register*. Overall, CMS accepted nearly 96% of the RUC's recommendations, including 100% acceptance for several specialties. Following a public comment period, final decisions were announced in the November 22, 1996, *Federal Register*.

Year 2000 Five-Year Review

In October 2000, the RUC submitted recommendations on 870 individual CPT codes to CMS. The RUC recommended increases to many surgical services, primarily to address vascular and general surgery procedures that have been historically undervalued. The recommendations may be summarized as follows:

- For 469 codes, the RUC recommended that the relative values be increased.
- For 311 codes, the RUC recommended that the current relative value be maintained.
- For 27 codes, the RUC recommended that the relative values be decreased.
- The RUC referred 63 codes to the CPT Editorial Panel to consider coding changes prior to consideration of the work relative value.

On November 1, 2001, CMS published a Final Rule in the *Federal Register* with refined work relative value units. CMS accepted 98% of the RUC's recommendations. The relative value changes were implemented on January 1, 2002.

Year 2005 Five-Year Review

In October 2005 and February 2006, the RUC submitted recommendations on 723 individual CPT codes to CMS. The RUC has recommended improvements to the work RVUs for numerous services including the Evaluation and Management Services, for both stand alone visits and those perform in the post-operative period of surgical procedures. The recommendations may be summarized as follows:

- For 266 codes, the RUC recommended that the relative values be increased.
- For 288 codes, the RUC recommended that the current relative value be maintained.
- For 30 codes, the RUC recommended that the relative values be decreased.
- The RUC referred 139 codes to the CPT Editorial Panel to consider coding changes prior to consideration of the work relative value.

The CMS published a *Proposed Notice* on June 29, 2006, and a *Final Rule* on December 1, 2006, stating that 95% of these recommendations were accepted and would be implemented on January 1, 2007. The following details some of the key changes announced by CMS:

Evaluation and Management Services

This Five-Year Review included 35 evaluation and management (E/M) services. The RUC agreed that incorrect assumptions were made in the previous valuation of E/M services. The RUC recommended and CMS approved an increase in work RVUs for 28 services and maintained work RVUs for seven services. Furthermore, the RUC also recommended and CMS accepted that the full increase of the E/M service be incorporated into the surgical global periods for each CPT code with global periods of 010 and 090.

Dermatology and Plastic Surgery

Three significant dermatological issues—the excision of lesions, the destruction of lesions, and Mohs surgery—were addressed by the RUC during the Five-Year Review. For these three groups of services, various issues had to be addressed including new Medicare coverage policies, the difference in work between treating a malignant or benign lesion, and potential changes in descriptors to reflect accurately where the service is being performed. The RUC reaffirmed the relativity in payment for the excision of lesion codes and persuaded CMS that there is a difference in postoperative work in the excision of a benign and malignant lesion. The RUC recommended relative value changes for destruction of lesion codes to reflect the change in the modality used. The CPT Editorial Panel considered major revisions to the Mohs surgery section prior to RUC review and development of recommendations. One hundred percent of the RUC recommendations for these dermatology and plastic surgery codes were accepted by CMS.

Orthopaedic Surgery

The orthopaedic surgery community presented recommendations on 108 services that were identified as misvalued due to changes in the patient population and rank order anomalies. Of these services, 86 were referred to the CPT Editorial Panel to address various issues, eg, the differentiation between benign and malignant tumors, assignment of modifier 51, and clarification of any subjective terms within the existing descriptors. The RUC recommendations for the remaining procedures were all approved by CMS. This included a RUC recommendation to retain relativity within the total joint codes (27130, 27236, and 27447).

Gynecology, Urology, and Neurosurgery

The RUC reviewed codes from gynecology, urology, and neurosurgery due to changes in the patient population, changes in technology, or an anomalous relationship between the code being valued and other codes. Of these 32 procedures, CMS will implement increases to 19 procedures. For example, the RUC agreed that craniotomies with elevation of bone flap for lobectomy, temporal lobe with and without electrocorticography during surgery had, during the last five years, required additional physician work due to a change in the complexity of patient population.

Radiology, Pathology, and Other Miscellaneous Services

The RUC reviewed various procedures pertaining to radiology including maxillofacial X rays, radiation therapy, and general X rays. Of all of the radiological procedures addressed by the RUC during the Five-Year Review, 50 of these 80 procedures' work values were recommended by the RUC and approved by CMS to be maintained.

Cardiothoracic Surgery

The RUC recommended increases to nine congenital cardiac surgery codes and 72 adult cardiac and general thoracic surgery codes, largely due to the increased complexity of the patient population to receive these services. CMS accepted 100% of the RUC's recommendations for cardiothoracic surgery.

General Surgery, Colorectal Surgery, and Vascular Surgery

The RUC reviewed 116 recommendations for procedures predominately performed by general, colorectal, and vascular surgeons. These codes were identified to be a part of the Five-Year Review based on flawed crosswalk assumptions, rank-order anomalies, and, in the case of vascular surgery, the services were historically undervalued dating back to the original Harvard Studies. The RUC recommended and CMS will implement increases in work RVUs associated with 58 out of 86 of the general surgical and vascular surgical services. CMS requested that new survey data for the colorectal surgery codes be reviewed by the RUC at its February 2006 meeting.

Otolaryngology and Ophthalmology

There were two major issues identified by the RUC pertaining to otolaryngology and ophthalmology. For otolaryngology, CMS identified a procedure—removal impacted cerumen—that had never been evaluated by the RUC. The RUC recommended and CMS will implement a maintenance of the current value associated with this service as the RUC felt the current value was justified based on a specialty society survey that indicated that 94% of respondents felt that the work in performing this service has not changed in the past five years. For ophthalmology, CMS identified cataract surgery as a procedure to be reviewed in the Five-Year Review based on the fact that this procedure has experienced advances in technology that have likely resulted in a modification to the physician work. The RUC recommended a slight decrease in physician work related to the intraservice portion of the procedure; however, the increase in the E/M component of the global period provided an overall increase to the physician work for this service.

List of Illustrations

Evaluation and Management

The Evaluation and Management (E/M) Services codes were introduced into Current Procedural Terminology (CPT®) nomenclature in 1992. These codes describe services provided by physicians to evaluate patients and manage their care. Prior to the establishment of the E/M codes, "visit" codes were used to describe services generally as, for example, a brief visit, intermediate, or comprehensive. The E/M services codes are widely reported by physicians of all specialties and describe a large portion of the medical care provided to patients.

The levels of Evaluation and Management (E/M) services include examinations, evaluations, consultations, treatments, conferences, counseling with patients and/or family, preventive pediatric and adult health supervision, adult and pediatric critical and intensive care, and emergency department. Also, included are home, nursing home care, and similar medical services, such as the determination of the need and/or location for appropriate care.

Although specific codes will be addressed throughout this E/M section, it is important to note that this text should be used with the current edition of the CPT codebook to reference E/M guidelines as well as the entire E/M code family.

The basic format of the E/M codes are as follows:

- A unique code number is listed
- The place or type of service is specified (eg, office or other outpatient setting)
- The content of the service is defined (eg, a problem-focused history; a problem-focused examination; straightforward medical decision making)
- Counseling and/or coordination of care with other providers or agencies is included when an E/M service is reported, if appropriate
- The nature of the presenting problem(s) usually associated with a given level is described
- The time typically required to provide the service is specified in many codes

Office or Other Outpatient Services

New Patient

⑤ 99201 Office or other outpatient visit for the evaluation and management of a new patient, which requires these three key components:

- **A problem focused history;**
- **A problem focused examination;**
- **Straightforward medical decision making.**

Counseling and/or coordination of care with other providers or agencies are provided consistent with the nature of the problem(s) and the patient's and/or family's needs.

Usually, the presenting problem(s) are self limited or minor. Physicians typically spend 10 minutes face-to-face with the patient and/or family.

Work Value: 0.45 // Global Period: XXX

➲ *CPT Assistant* Winter 91: 11, Spring 92: 13, 24, Summer 92: 1, 24, Spring 93: 34, Summer 93: 2, Fall 93: 9, Spring 95: 1, Summer 95: 4, Fall 95: 9, Jul 98: 9, Sep 98: 5, Jun 99: 8, Feb 00: 3, 9, 11, Aug 01: 2, Oct 04: 11, Mar 05: 11, Apr 05: 1, May 05: 1, Jun 05: 11, Dec 05: 10, Feb 06: 14

Clinical Example

Initial office visit for a 25-year-old out-of-town patient for refill of a topical prescription medication.

Preservice

Review the medical history form completed by the patient and vital signs obtained by the clinical staff.

Intraservice

Obtain a problem-focused history. Perform a problem-focused examination. Formulate a diagnosis and develop a treatment plan (straightforward medical decision making). Discuss the diagnosis and treatment options with the patient. Discuss the need for preventive health care with the patient. Reconcile medication(s) as necessary. Write prescription(s) as necessary.

Postservice

Complete the medical record documentation. Handle (with the help of clinical staff) any treatment failures or adverse reactions to medications that may occur after the visit. Provide necessary care coordination, telephonic or electronic communication assistance, and other necessary management related to this office visit.

99202 Office or other outpatient visit for the evaluation and management of a new patient, which requires these three key components:

- **An expanded problem focused history;**
- **An expanded problem focused examination;**
- **Straightforward medical decision making.**

Counseling and/or coordination of care with other providers or agencies are provided consistent with the nature of the problem(s) and the patient's and/or family's needs.

Usually, the presenting problem(s) are of low to moderate severity. Physicians typically spend 20 minutes face-to-face with the patient and/or family.

Work Value: 0.88 // Global Period: XXX

➲ *CPT Assistant* Winter 91: 11, Spring 92: 13, 24, Summer 92: 1, 24, Spring 93: 34, Summer 93: 2, Fall 93: 9, Spring 95: 1, Summer 95: 4, Fall 95: 9, Jul 98: 9, Sep 98: 5, Feb 00: 11, Aug 01: 2, Apr 02: 14, Oct 04: 10, Apr 05: 1, 3, Jun 05: 11, Dec 05: 10

Clinical Example

This is an initial office visit for a 42-year-old female patient with a history and rash consistent with poison ivy who is not responding to over-the-counter medication.

Preservice

Review the medical history form completed by the patient and vital signs obtained by clinical staff.

Intraservice

Obtain an expanded problem focused history. Perform an expanded problem focused examination. Formulate a diagnosis and develop a treatment plan (straight forward medical decision making). Discuss diagnosis and treatment options with the patient. Address the preventive health care needs of the patient. Reconcile medication(s), write prescription(s), order and arrange diagnostic testing or referral as necessary.

Postservice

Complete the medical record documentation. Handle (with the help of clinical staff) any treatment failures or adverse reactions to medications that may occur after the visit. Provide necessary care coordination, telephonic or electronic communication assistance, and other necessary management related to this office visit. Receive and respond to any interval testing results or correspondence. Revise treatment plan(s) and communicate with the patient, as necessary.

---

⑮ 99203 Office or other outpatient visit for the evaluation and management of a new patient, which requires these three key components:

- **A detailed history;**
- **A detailed examination;**
- **Medical decision making of low complexity.**

Counseling and/or coordination of care with other providers or agencies are provided consistent with the nature of the problem(s) and the patient's and/or family's needs.

Usually, the presenting problem(s) are of moderate severity. Physicians typically spend 30 minutes face-to-face with the patient and/or family.

Work Value: 1.34 // Global Period: XXX

➲ **_CPT Assistant_ Winter 91: 11, Spring 92: 14, 24, Summer 92: 1, 24, Spring 93: 34, Summer 93: 2, Fall 93: 9, Spring 95: 1, Summer 95: 4, Fall 95: 9, Jul 98: 9, Sep 98: 5, Feb 00: 11, Aug 01: 2, Apr 02: 14, Oct 04: 10, Feb 05: 9, Apr 05: 1, 3, Jun 05: 11, Dec 05: 10**

Clinical Example

Initial office visit for a 63-year old female with hypertension presents for a pre-employment physical after moving to the area. Her blood pressure has been adequately controlled with her current medication and home blood pressure monitoring.

Preservice

Review the medical history form completed by the patient and vital signs obtained by clinical staff. Communicate with other health professionals.

Intraservice

Obtain a detailed history. Perform a detailed examination. Consider relevant data, options, and risks and formulate a diagnosis and develop a treatment plan (low complexity medical decision making). Discuss diagnosis and treatment options with the patient. Address the preventive health care needs of the patient. Reconcile medication(s). Write prescription(s). Order and arrange diagnostic testing or referral as necessary.

Postservice

Complete the medical record documentation. Handle (with the help of clinical staff) any treatment failures or adverse reactions to medications that may occur after the visit. Provide necessary care coordination, telephonic or electronic communication assistance, and other necessary management related to this office visit. Receive and respond to any interval testing results or correspondence. Revise treatment plan(s) and communicate with patient, as necessary.

⑤ 99204 Office or other outpatient visit for the evaluation and management of a new patient, which requires these three key components:

- **A comprehensive history;**
- **A comprehensive examination;**
- **Medical decision making of moderate complexity.**

Counseling and/or coordination of care with other providers or agencies are provided consistent with the nature of the problem(s) and the patient's and/or family's needs.

Usually, the presenting problem(s) are of moderate to high severity. Physicians typically spend 45 minutes face-to-face with the patient and/or family.

Work Value: 2.30 // Global Period: XXX

➲ *CPT Assistant* **Winter 91: 11, Spring 92: 14, 24, Summer 92: 1, 24, Spring 93: 34, Summer 93: 2, Fall 93: 9, Spring 95: 1, Summer 95: 4, Fall 95: 9, Jul 98: 9, Sep 98: 5, Feb 00: 11, Aug 01: 2, Apr 02: 14, May 02: 1, Oct 04: 10, Apr 05: 1, 3, Jun 05: 11, Dec 05: 10**

Clinical Example

Initial office visit for a 60-year-old female who has a history of hypertension, osteoarthritis, and morbid obesity. She is complaining of heart palpitations with occasional dizziness. Past medical history includes total abdominal hysterectomy 15 years previously for dysfunctional uterine bleeding. She has had no follow-up for 5 years.

Preservice

Review the medical history form completed by the patient and vital signs obtained by the clinical staff. Communicate with other health care professionals.

Intraservice

Obtain a comprehensive history. Perform a comprehensive examination. Consider relevant data, options, and risks and formulate a diagnosis and develop a treatment plan (moderate-complexity medical decision making). Discuss the diagnosis and treatment options with the patient. Address the preventive health care needs of the patient. Reconcile medication(s). Write prescription(s). Order and arrange diagnostic testing or referral as necessary.

Postservice

Complete the medical record documentation. Handle (with the help of clinical staff) any treatment failures or adverse reactions to medications that may occur after the visit. Provide necessary care coordination, telephonic or electronic communication assistance, and other necessary management related to this office visit. Receive and respond to any interval testing results or correspondence. Revise treatment plan(s) and communicate with the patient as necessary.

⑤ 99205 Office or other outpatient visit for the evaluation and management of a new patient, which requires these three key components:

- **A comprehensive history;**
- **A comprehensive examination;**
- **Medical decision making of high complexity.**

Counseling and/or coordination of care with other providers or agencies are provided consistent with the nature of the problem(s) and the patient's and/or family's needs.

Usually, the presenting problem(s) are of moderate to high severity. Physicians typically spend 60 minutes face-to-face with the patient and/or family.

Work Value: 3.00 // Global Period: XXX

➲ *CPT Assistant* **Winter 91: 11, Spring 92: 14, 24, Summer 92: 1, 24, Spring 93: 34, Summer 93: 2, Fall 93: 9, Spring 95: 1, Summer 95: 4, Fall 95: 9, Jul 98: 9, Sep 98: 5, Feb 00: 11, Aug 01: 2, Apr 02: 2, May 02: 1, Oct 04: 10, Apr 05: 1, 3, Jun 05: 11, Dec 05: 10**

Clinical Example

Initial office visit for a 63-year-old male with type II diabetes mellitus, coronary artery disease, osteoarthritis, chronic bronchitis, hypertension, gastroesophageal reflux, and hyperlipidemia who presents with a 20 pound weight loss, dysphagia, and abdominal pain. He is on multiple medications and has not seen a physician for 18 months.

Preservice

Review the medical history form completed by the patient and vital signs obtained by clinical staff. Communicate with other health professionals.

Intraservice

Obtain a comprehensive history. Perform a comprehensive examination. Consider relevant data, options, and risks and formulate a diagnosis and develop a treatment plan (high complexity medical decision making). Discuss diagnosis and treatment options with the patient. Address the preventive health care needs of the patient. Reconcile medication(s). Write prescription(s). Order and arrange diagnostic testing or referral as necessary.

Postservice

Complete the medical record documentation. Handle (with the help of clinical staff) any treatment failures or adverse reactions to medications that may occur after the visit. Provide necessary care coordination, telephonic or electronic communication assistance, and other necessary management related to this office visit. Receive and respond to any interval testing results or correspondence. Revise treatment plan(s) and communicate with patient, as necessary.

Coding Tip for 99201-99205

A new patient is one who has not received any professional services from the physician or another physician of the same specialty who belongs to the same group practice within the past 3 years.

Established Patient

❺ **99211** **Office or other outpatient visit** for the evaluation and management of an established patient, that may not require the presence of a physician. Usually, the presenting problem(s) are minimal. Typically, 5 minutes are spent performing or supervising these services.

Work Value: 0.17 // Global Period: XXX

➲ *CPT Assistant* **Winter 91: 11, Spring 92: 14, 24, Summer 92: 1, 24, Spring 93: 34, Summer 93: 2, Fall 93: 9, Spring 95: 1, Summer 95: 4, Fall 95: 9, Oct 96: 10, Feb 97: 9, May 97: 4, Jul 98: 9, Sep 98: 5, Oct 99: 9, Feb 00: 11, Aug 01: 2, Jan 02: 2, Oct 04: 10, Feb 05: 15, Mar 05: 11, Apr 05: 1, 3, May 05: 1, Jun 05: 11, Nov 05: 1, Dec 05: 10, Feb 06: 14**

Clinical Example

Office visit for a 58-year-old male, established patient, presenting for a blood pressure check. The blood pressure is 130/83. His blood pressure is acceptable.

Intraservice

Provide supervision to the clinical staff, review any data of concern, answer any questions that arise, and provide guidance to the clinical staff as necessary.

Postservice

Provide necessary care coordination, telephonic or electronic communication assistance, and other necessary management related to this office visit. Receive and respond to any interval testing results or correspondence. Revise treatment plan(s) and communicate with the patient, as necessary.

---

❺ **99212** **Office or other outpatient visit** for the evaluation and management of an established patient, which requires at least two of these three key components:

- **A problem focused history;**
- **A problem focused examination;**
- **Straightforward medical decision making.**

Counseling and/or coordination of care with other providers or agencies are provided consistent with the nature of the problem(s) and the patient's and/or family's needs.

Usually, the presenting problem(s) are self limited or minor. Physicians typically spend 10 minutes face-to-face with the patient and/or family.

Work Value: 0.45 // Global Period: XXX

➲ *CPT Assistant* **Winter 91: 11, Spring 92: 14, 24, Summer 92: 1, 24, Spring 93: 34, Summer 93: 2, Fall 93: 9, Spring 95: 1, Summer 95: 4, Fall 95: 9, Jul 98: 9, Sep 98: 5, Feb 00: 11, Jun 00: 11, Aug 01: 2, Jan 02: 2, May 02: 3, Apr 04: 14, Oct 04: 10, Apr 05: 1, 3 Jun 05: 11, Dec 05: 10**

Clinical Example

Office visit for a mildly symptomatic 20-year-old female, established patient, with upper respiratory complaints consistent with an upper respiratory tract infection.

Preservice

Review the medical history form completed by the patient and vital signs obtained by the clinical staff.

Intraservice

Obtain a problem-focused history (which includes reviewing information about the patient's response to treatment at her last visit and reviewing interval correspondence or medical records received).* Perform a problem-focused examination.* Consider relevant data, options, and risks; formulate a diagnosis; and develop a treatment plan (straightforward medical decision making).* Discuss the diagnosis and treatment options with the patient. Address the preventive health care needs of the patient. Reconcile medication(s). Write prescription(s). Order and arrange diagnostic testing or referral as necessary.

*Two of these three components required.

Postservice

Complete the medical record documentation. Handle (with the help of clinical staff) any treatment failures or adverse reactions to medications that may occur after the visit. Provide necessary care coordination, telephonic or electronic communication assistance, and other necessary management related to this office visit. Receive and respond to any interval testing results or correspondence. Revise treatment plan(s) and communicate with the patient as necessary.

---

❺ 99213 Office or other outpatient visit for the evaluation and management of an established patient, which requires at least two of these three key components:

- **An expanded problem focused history;**
- **An expanded problem focused examination;**
- **Medical decision making of low complexity.**

Counseling and coordination of care with other providers or agencies are provided consistent with the nature of the problem(s) and the patient's and/or family's needs.

Usually, the presenting problem(s) are of low to moderate severity. Physicians typically spend 15 minutes face-to-face with the patient and/or family.

Work Value: 0.92 // Global Period: XXX

➲ *CPT Assistant* **Winter 91: 11, Spring 92: 14, 24, Summer 92: 1, 24, Spring 93: 34, Summer 93: 2, Fall 93: 9, Spring 95: 1, Summer 95: 4, Fall 95: 9, Jan 97: 10, Jul 98: 9, Sep 98: 5, Aug 01: 2, May 02: 3, Oct 03: 5, Apr 04: 14, Oct 04: 10, Mar 05: 11, Apr 05: 1, 3, Jun 05: 11, Dec 05: 10**

Clinical Example

Office visit for a 55-year-old male, established patient, with a history of hypertension and hyperlipidemia who presents for follow up.

Preservice

Review the medical history form completed by the patient and vital signs obtained by clinical staff.

Intraservice

Obtain an expanded problem focused history (including response to treatment at last visit and reviewing interval correspondence or medical records received)*. Perform an expanded problem focused examination*. Consider relevant data, options, and risks and formulate a diagnosis and develop a treatment plan (low complexity medical decision making)*. Discuss diagnosis and treatment options with the patient. Address the preventive health care needs of the patient. Reconcile medication(s). Write prescription(s). Order and arrange diagnostic testing or referral as necessary.

*Two of these three components required.

Postservice

Complete the medical record documentation. Handle (with the help of clinical staff) any treatment failures or adverse reactions to medications that may occur after the visit. Provide necessary care coordination, telephonic or electronic communication assistance, and other necessary management related to this office visit. Receive and respond to any interval testing results or correspondence. Revise treatment plan(s) and communicate with patient, as necessary.

---

⑮ **99214** **Office or other outpatient visit** for the evaluation and management of an established patient, which requires at least two of these three key components:

- **A detailed history;**
- **A detailed examination;**
- **Medical decision making of moderate complexity.**

Counseling and/or coordination of care with other providers or agencies are provided consistent with the nature of the problem(s) and the patient's and/or family's needs.

Usually, the presenting problem(s) are of moderate to high severity. Physicians typically spend 25 minutes face-to-face with the patient and/or family.

Work Value: 1.42 // Global Period: XXX

➲ ***CPT Assistant*** **Winter 91: 11, Spring 92: 15, 24, Summer 92: 1, 24, Spring 93: 34, Summer 93: 2, Fall 93: 9, Spring 95: 1, Summer 95: 4, Fall 95: 9, May 97: 4, Jul 98: 9, Sep 98: 5, Aug 01: 2, Jan 02: 2, May 02: 1-2, Oct 03: 5, Apr 04: 14, Oct 04: 10, Apr 05: 1, 3, Jun 05: 11, Dec 05: 10**

Clinical Example

Office visit for a 45-year-old male carpenter, established patient, with rheumatoid arthritis, hypertension, and hyperlipidemia. His joint disease has been stable in the past, but in the last 3 weeks he has noticed increasing pain and has developed redness in several joints. He has had a low-grade fever for the past week.

Preservice

Review the medical history form completed by the patient and vital signs obtained by the clinical staff.

Intraservice

Obtain a detailed history (which includes reviewing information about the patient's response to treatment at the last visit and reviewing interval correspondence or medical records received).* Perform a detailed examination.* Consider relevant data, options, and risks; formulate a diagnosis; and develop a treatment plan (moderate-complexity medical decision making).* Discuss diagnosis and treatment options with the patient. Address the preventive health care needs of the patient. Reconcile medication(s). Write prescription(s). Order and arrange diagnostic testing or referral as necessary.

*Two of these three components required.

Postservice

Complete the medical record documentation. Handle (with the help of clinical staff) any treatment failures or adverse reactions to medications that may occur after the visit. Provide necessary care coordination, telephonic or electronic communication assistance, and other necessary management related to this office visit. Receive and respond to any interval testing results or correspondence. Revise treatment plan(s) and communicate with the patient as necessary.

⑤ 99215 Office or other outpatient visit for the evaluation and management of an established patient, which requires at least two of these three key components:

- **A comprehensive history;**
- **A comprehensive examination;**
- **Medical decision making of high complexity.**

Counseling and/or coordination of care with other providers or agencies are provided consistent with the nature of the problem(s) and the patient's and/or family's needs.

Usually, the presenting problem(s) are of moderate to high severity. Physicians typically spend 40 minutes face-to-face with the patient and/or family.

Work Value: 2.00 // Global Period: XXX

➲ *CPT Assistant* Winter 91: 11, Spring 92: 15, 24, Summer 92: 1, 24, Spring 93: 34, Summer 93: 2, Fall 93: 9, Spring 95: 1, Summer 95: 4, Fall 95: 9, Jan 97: 10, Jul 98: 9, Sep 98: 5, Aug 01: 2, Jan 02: 2, May 02: 1, 3, Apr 04: 14, Oct 04: 10, Mar 05: 11, Apr 05: 1, 3, Jun 05: 11, Dec 05: 10

Clinical Example
Office visit for a 63-year-old male, established patient, with type II diabetes mellitus (with neuropathy and nephropathy), congestive heart failure, hyperlipidemia, and chronic anxiety. He presents with blurred vision, frequency of urination, high blood sugars, and left leg pain and swelling.

Preservice
Review the medical history form completed by the patient and vital signs obtained by the clinical staff.

Intraservice
Obtain a comprehensive history (including response to treatment at last visit and reviewing interval correspondence or medical records received).* Perform a comprehensive focused examination.* Consider relevant data, options, and risks; formulate a diagnosis; and develop a treatment plan (high-complexity medical decision making).* Discuss diagnosis and treatment options with the patient. Address the preventive health care needs of the patient. Reconcile medication(s). Write prescription(s). Order and arrange diagnostic testing or referral as necessary.

*Two of these three components required.

Postservice
Complete the medical record documentation. Handle (with the help of clinical staff) any treatment failures or adverse reactions to medications that may occur after the visit. Provide necessary care coordination, telephonic or electronic communication assistance, and other necessary management related to this office visit. Receive and respond to any interval testing results or correspondence. Revise treatment plan(s) and communicate with the patient as necessary.

Coding Tip for 99211-99215
An established patient is one who has received professional services from the physician or another physician of the same specialty who belongs to the same group practice within the past 3 years.

Hospital Observation Services

Observation Care Discharge Services

99217 Observation care discharge day management (This code is to be utilized by the physician to report all services provided to a patient on discharge from "observation status" if the discharge is on other than the initial date of "observation status." To report services to a patient designated as "observation status" or "inpatient status" and discharged on the same date, use the codes for Observation or Inpatient Care Services [including Admission and Discharge Services, 99234-99236 as appropriate.])

Work Value: 1.28 // Global Period: XXX

➲ *CPT Assistant* Nov 97: 2, Mar 98: 1, May 98: 3, Sep 98: 5, Sep 00: 3, May 05: 1, Nov 05: 10

Clinical Example

At 9 pm, a 22-year-old primigravida presents to the labor and delivery unit at 38 weeks' gestation with contractions every 4 minutes, but no cervical dilation. She is sedated and when she awakens, the contractions have stopped. The patient is discharged from observation the following morning.

Coding Tip for 99217

This code is intended to be reported for the observation care discharge day management, which includes the following: conducting a final examination of the patient, discussing the hospital stay with the patient, providing the patient with instructions for continuing care, and preparing the discharge records. For observation or inpatient hospital care including the admission and discharge of the patient on the same date, see codes 99234-99236 as appropriate.

Hospital Inpatient Services

Initial Hospital Care

New or Established Patient

99221 **Initial hospital care,** per day, for the evaluation and management of a patient, which requires these three key components:

- **A detailed or comprehensive history;**
- **A detailed or comprehensive examination; and**
- **Medical decision making that is straightforward or of low complexity.**

Counseling and/or coordination of care with other providers or agencies are provided consistent with the nature of the problem(s) and the patient's and/or family's needs.

Usually, the problem(s) requiring admission are of low severity. Physicians typically spend 30 minutes at the bedside and on the patient's hospital floor or unit.

Work Value: 1.88 // Global Period: XXX

Clinical Example

A 43-year-old male is admitted to the hospital with low back pain after failing outpatient treatment. A recent MRI of the lumbar spine demonstrated minimal bulging discs without nerve root compromise, stenosis or lumbar spine structural abnormality. There is no significant past medical history and he is on no medications. The patient did not complain of any lower extremity numbness or weakness and denied any difficulty with bladder or bowel control.

Preservice

Review data not available on the unit (eg, diagnostic and imaging studies). Communicate with other professionals and with the patient and/or the patient's family. Obtain and review necessary past results or records not available on the unit. Perform evaluation/management in other sites of service earlier the same day.

Intraservice

Review medical records and data available on the unit. Obtain a detailed or comprehensive history. Perform a detailed or comprehensive physical exam. Consider relevant data, options, and risks and formulate a diagnosis and develop a treatment plan (straightforward or low complexity medical decision making). Discuss diagnosis and treatment options with the patient and/or family. Consider discharge needs of patient. Communicate with other health care professionals. Write/review admission orders including ordering/arranging for necessary diagnostic testing, consultation and therapeutic intervention(s). Complete medical record documentation.

Postservice

Address interval data obtained and changes in condition reported. Communicate results and further care plans to other health care professionals and to the patient and/or family.

99222 Initial hospital care, per day, for the evaluation and management of a patient, which requires these three key components:

- **A comprehensive history;**
- **A comprehensive examination; and**
- **Medical decision making of moderate complexity.**

Counseling and/or coordination of care with other providers or agencies are provided consistent with the nature of the problem(s) and the patient's and/or family's needs.

Usually, the problem(s) requiring admission are of moderate severity. Physicians typically spend 50 minutes at the bedside and on the patient's hospital floor or unit.

Work Value: 2.56 // Global Period: XXX

Clinical Example

A 55-year-old male is admitted to the hospital with progressive shortness of breath over the past week. He feels more short of breath than ever before. His history reveals many years of hypertension and several years of congestive heart failure. He has been taking his diuretic every other day to save money.

Preservice

Review data not available on the unit (eg, diagnostic and imaging studies). Communicate with other professionals and with the patient and/or patient's family. Obtain and review necessary past results or records not available on the unit. Perform evaluation/management in other sites of service earlier the same day.

Intraservice

Review medical records and data available on the unit. Obtain a comprehensive history. Perform a comprehensive physical exam. Consider relevant data, options, and risks and formulate a diagnosis and develop a treatment plan (moderate complexity medical decision making). Discuss diagnosis and treatment options with the patient and/or family. Consider discharge needs of patient. Communicate with other health care professionals. Write/review admission orders including ordering/arranging for necessary diagnostic testing, consultation and therapeutic intervention(s). Complete medical record documentation.

Postservice

Address interval data obtained and changes in condition reported. Communicate results and further care plans to other health care professionals and to the patient and/or family.

---

❺ **99223 Initial hospital care,** per day, for the evaluation and management of a patient, which requires these three key components:

- **A comprehensive history;**
- **A comprehensive examination; and**
- **Medical decision making of high complexity.**

Counseling and/or coordination of care with other providers or agencies are provided consistent with the nature of the problem(s) and the patient's and/or family's needs.

Usually, the problem(s) requiring admission are of high severity. Physicians typically spend 70 minutes at the bedside and on the patient's hospital floor or unit.

Work Value: 3.78 // Global Period: XXX

➲ *CPT Assistant* Winter 91: 11, Spring 92: 14, 24, Summer 92: 10, 24, Fall 92: 1, Spring 93: 34, Spring 95: 1, Fall 95: 9, Jul 96: 11, Sep 96: 10, Nov 97: 2, Mar 98: 1, Sep 98: 5, Jan 02: 2-3, Apr 03: 26, Apr 04: 14, Aug 04: 11

Clinical Example

A 75-year-old female is admitted to the hospital with cellulitis around a right great toe ulcer. She has a history of type II diabetes mellitus, ischemic cardiomyopathy, atherosclerotic peripheral vascular disease, hypertension, chronic renal insufficiency and dementia. She is a widow living in a nursing home.

Preservice
Review data not available on the unit (eg, diagnostic and imaging studies). Communicate with other professionals and with patient or patient's family. Obtain and review necessary past results or records not available on the unit. Perform evaluation/management in other sites of service from earlier the same day.

Intraservice
Review medical records and data available on the unit. Obtain a comprehensive history. Perform a comprehensive physical exam. Consider relevant data, options, and risks and formulate a diagnosis and develop a treatment plan (high complexity medical decision making). Discuss diagnosis and treatment options with the patient and/or family. Consider discharge needs of patient. Communicate with other health care professionals. Write/review admission orders including ordering/arranging for necessary diagnostic testing, consultation and therapeutic intervention(s). Complete medical record documentation.

Postservice
Address interval data obtained and changes in condition reported. Communicate results and further care plans to other health care professionals and to the patient and/or family.

Subsequent Hospital Care

⑤ **99231 Subsequent hospital care,** per day, for the evaluation and management of a patient, which requires at least two of these three key components:

- **A problem focused interval history;**
- **A problem focused examination;**
- **Medical decision making that is straightforward or of low complexity.**

Counseling and/or coordination of care with other providers or agencies are provided consistent with the nature of the problem(s) and the patient's and/or family's needs.

Usually, the patient is stable, recovering or improving. Physicians typically spend 15 minutes at the bedside and on the patient's hospital floor or unit.

Work Value: 0.76 // Global Period: XXX

➲ ***CPT Assistant*** **Winter 91: 11, Spring 92: 14, 24, Summer 92: 10, 24, Fall 92: 1, Spring 93: 34, Spring 95: 1, Fall 95: 16, Nov 97: 2, Sep 98: 5, Jan 99: 10, Nov 99: 5, Aug 01: 2, Jan 02: 2-3, Apr 04: 14, Aug 04: 11, Mar 05: 11, May 05: 1**

Clinical Example
Subsequent hospital visit for a 43-year-old male who presented to the hospital with low back pain after failing outpatient treatment. A recent magnetic resonance imaging scan of the lumbar spine demonstrated minimal bulging discs without nerve root compromise, stenosis, or lumbar spine structural abnormality. The patient did not complain of any lower extremity numbness or weakness and denied any difficulty with bladder or bowel control. The patient's pain has improved with medical management, but is not controlled on oral medications nor is ready for discharge home.

Preservice
Review data not available on the unit (eg, diagnostic and imaging studies). Communicate with other professionals and with the patient and/or the patient's family.

Intraservice
Review the medical records and data available on the unit. Obtain a problem-focused history.* Perform a problem-focused physical exam.* Consider relevant data, options, and risks and formulate/revise diagnosis and treatment plan(s) (straightforward or low-complexity medical decision making).* Discuss diagnosis and treatment options with the patient and/or the patient's family. Consider the discharge needs of patient. Communicate with other health care professionals. Write/review orders including

ordering/arranging for necessary diagnostic testing, consultation, and therapeutic intervention(s). Complete the medical record documentation.

Postservice
Address interval data obtained and changes in the condition reported. Communicate results and further care plans with other health care professionals and with the patient and/or the patient's family.

---

⑤ **99232 Subsequent hospital care,** per day, for the evaluation and management of a patient, which requires at least two of these three key components:

- **An expanded problem focused interval history;**
- **An expanded problem focused examination;**
- **Medical decision making of moderate complexity.**

Counseling and/or coordination of care with other providers or agencies are provided consistent with the nature of the problem(s) and the patient's and/or family's needs.

Usually, the patient is responding inadequately to therapy or has developed a minor complication. Physicians typically spend 25 minutes at the bedside and on the patient's hospital floor or unit.

Work Value: 1.39 // Global Period: XXX

➲ *CPT Assistant* **Winter 91: 11, Spring 92: 14, 24, Summer 92: 10, 24, Fall 92: 1, Spring 93: 34, Spring 95: 1, Fall 95: 16, Nov 97: 2, Sep 98: 5, Jan 99: 10, Nov 99: 5, Jan 00: 11, Aug 01: 2, Apr 04: 14, Aug 04: 11**

Clinical Example
Subsequent hospital visit for a 63-year-old male with type II diabetes mellitus, diabetic neuropathy and nephropathy, hypertension, and hyperlipidemia, who was admitted with a diabetic foot infection and hyperglycemia, is seen for subsequent hospital care. The patient continues to be febrile with no improvement in his foot despite parenteral antibiotics.

Preservice
Review data not available on the unit (eg, diagnostic and imaging studies). Communicate with other professionals and with the patient and/or the patient's family.

Intraservice
Review medical records and data available on the unit. Obtain a problem-focused history.* Perform a problem-focused physical exam.* Consider relevant data, options, and risks and formulate/revise diagnosis and treatment plan(s) (straightforward or low-complexity medical decision making).* Discuss diagnosis and treatment options with the patient and/or the patient's family. Consider the discharge needs of the patient. Communicate with other health care professionals. Write/review orders including ordering/arranging for necessary diagnostic testing, consultation, and therapeutic intervention(s). Complete the medical record documentation.

*Two of these three components required.

Postservice
Address interval data obtained and changes in the condition reported. Communicate results and further care plans with other health care professionals and with the patient and/or the patient's family.

99233 Subsequent hospital care, per day, for the evaluation and management of a patient, which requires at least two of these three key components:

- **A detailed interval history;**
- **A detailed examination;**
- **Medical decision making of high complexity.**

Counseling and/or coordination of care with other providers or agencies are provided consistent with the nature of the problem(s) and the patient's and/or family's needs.

Usually, the patient is unstable or has developed a significant complication or a significant new problem. Physicians typically spend 35 minutes at the bedside and on the patient's hospital floor or unit.

Work Value: 2.00 // Global Period: XXX

➲ *CPT Assistant* Winter 91: 11, Spring 92: 14, 24, Summer 92: 10, 24, Fall 92: 1, Spring 93: 34, Spring 95: 1, Fall 95: 16, Nov 97: 2, Sep 98: 5, Jan 99: 10, Nov 99: 5, Aug 01: 2, Apr 04: 14, Aug 04: 11

Clinical Example

This is a subsequent hospital visit for a 75-year-old female admitted with cellulitis around a right great toe ulcer. She has type II diabetes mellitus, ischemic cardiomyopathy, atherosclerotic peripheral vascular disease, hypertension, and chronic renal insufficiency. Her cellulitis is better, but non-invasive blood flow measurements show significantly reduced flow to the foot, blood sugars are over 200, and she is newly delirious.

Preservice

Review data not available on the unit (eg diagnostic and imaging studies). Communicate with other professionals and with patient and/or patient's family.

Intraservice

Review medical records and data available on the unit. Obtain a problem focused history.* Perform a problem focused physical exam.* Consider relevant data, options, and risks and formulate/revise diagnosis and treatment plan(s) (straightforward or low complexity medical decision making).* Discuss diagnosis and treatment options with the patient and/or family. Consider discharge needs of patient. Communicate with other health care professionals.

Write/review orders including ordering/arranging for necessary diagnostic testing, consultation and therapeutic intervention(s). Complete medical record documentation.

*Two of these three components required

Postservice

Address interval data obtained and changes in condition reported. Communicate results and further care plans to other health care professionals and to the patient and/or family.

Coding Tip for 99231-99233

All levels of subsequent hospital care include reviewing the medical record and reviewing the results of diagnostic studies and changes in the patient's status (ie, changes in history, physical condition, and response to management) since the last assessment by the physician.

Observation or Inpatient Care Services (Including Admission and Discharge Services)

99234 **Observation or inpatient hospital care,** for the evaluation and management of a patient including admission and discharge on the same date which requires these three key components:

- **A detailed or comprehensive history;**
- **A detailed or comprehensive examination; and**
- **Medical decision making that is straightforward or of low complexity.**

Counseling and/or coordination of care with other providers or agencies are provided consistent with the nature of the problem(s) and the patient's and/or family's needs.

Usually the presenting problem(s) requiring admission are of low severity.

Work Value: 2.56 // Global Period: XXX

➲ *CPT Assistant* Nov 97: 2, Mar 98: 2, May 98: 1, Sep 98: 5, Jan 00: 11, Sep 00: 3, Jan 02: 2, Jun 02: 10, Jan 03: 10, May 05: 1, Nov 05: 10

Clinical Example

A 19-year-old pregnant patient (9 weeks' gestation) presents to the emergency department complaining of persistent vomiting for 1 day.

Intraservice

A detailed history is taken. The patient provides no history consistent with infection, but does recall a similar occurrence during her previous pregnancy. She also complains of some dizziness upon standing. A detailed examination is performed and elicits findings associated with moderate dehydration, including postural hypotension. Intravenous therapy and antiemetics are initiated. Diagnostics are consistent with dehydration. The patient is placed on observation status and periodic reassessments are made. Following cessation of postural hypotension and after demonstrating the ability to retain p.o. fluids, the patient is discharged 9 hours after initial presentation, with instructions and a prescription for antiemetic medication.

99235 Observation or inpatient hospital care, for the evaluation and management of a patient including admission and discharge on the same date which requires these three key components:

- **A comprehensive history;**
- **A comprehensive examination; and**
- **Medical decision making of moderate complexity.**

Counseling and/or coordination of care with other providers or agencies are provided consistent with the nature of the problem(s) and the patient's and/or family's needs.

Usually the presenting problem(s) requiring admission are of moderate severity.

Work Value: 3.41 // Global Period: XXX

➲ *CPT Assistant* Nov 97: 2, Mar 98: 2, May 98: 1, Sep 98: 5, Jan 00: 11, Sep 00: 3, Jan 02: 2, Jun 02: 10, Jan 03: 10, Nov 05: 10

Clinical Example

An 18-year-old patient presents to the emergency department with respiratory compromise.

Intraservice

A comprehensive history is obtained with some difficulty because the patient is unable to speak complete sentences. The patient has a history of asthma and has been hospitalized twice for this condition, but not recently. A comprehensive multisystem examination is performed and elicits that the patient has labored breathing, is using accessory muscles, and has muffled wheezing in all lung fields. Coincident with obtaining blood samples, treatment is initiated with oxygen, aerosol bronchodilators, intravenous (IV) fluids, and IV steroids. After two additional, but only partially successful, courses of therapy over a 2-hour period, the patient is placed on observation status. Additional diagnostics are ordered and respiratory therapy is continued based on periodic reassessments by the physician. Following cessation of wheezing and the demonstration of an acceptable peak flow rate, the patient is discharged 10 hours after initial presentation, with instructions and a modified prescription regimen.

99236 Observation or inpatient hospital care, for the evaluation and management of a patient including admission and discharge on the same date which requires these three key components:

- **A comprehensive history;**
- **A comprehensive examination; and**
- **Medical decision making of high complexity.**

Counseling and/or coordination of care with other providers or agencies are provided consistent with the nature of the problem(s) and the patient's and/or family's needs.

Usually the presenting problem(s) requiring admission are of high severity.

Work Value: 4.26 // Global Period: XXX

➲ *CPT Assistant* Nov 97: 2, Mar 98: 2, May 98: 1, Sep 98: 5, Jan 00: 11, Sep 00: 3, Jan 02: 2, Jun 02: 10, Jan 03: 10, Nov 05: 10

Clinical Example

A 62-year-old patient brought to the emergency department because of dyspnea and chest pressure.

Intraservice

A comprehensive history is obtained, which elicits increasing exertional dyspnea over the past few days, known coronary artery disease, a myocardial infarction 2 years prior, and two episodes of congestive heart failure last year. A comprehensive multisystem examination is performed. Diagnostics reveal nonspecific ST changes inferiorly, congestive heart failure, and high normal creatine kinase with a normal index. Oxygen, nitrates, and diuretics are initiated. Two hours post admission to the emergency department, the patient's chest pressure has resolved, but the dyspnea remains. The patient is placed on observation status. Additional diagnostics are ordered, and therapy is continued based on periodic reassessments by the physician. Following cessation of dyspnea, and with no change in serial electrocardiogram and CK-MBs, the patient is discharged 12 hours after presenting to the emergency department.

Coding Tip for 99234-99236

When observation status is initiated in the course of an encounter in another site of service (eg, hospital emergency department, physician's office, nursing facility), all evaluation and management services provided by the supervising physician in conjunction with initiating observation status are considered part of the initial observation care when performed on the same date. The observation care level of service should include the services related to initiating observation status provided in the other sites of service as well as in the observation setting when provided by the same physician.

Hospital Discharge Services

⑤ **99238 Hospital discharge day management;** 30 minutes or less

Work Value: 1.28 // Global Period: XXX

➲ ***CPT Assistant*** **Fall 92: 1, Spring 93: 4, Nov 97: 4, Mar 98: 3, 11, May 98: 2, Jan 99: 10, Jan 02: 2, Aug 04: 11, May 05: 1**

Clinical Example

A final visit with a 55-year-old male admitted with a community-acquired pneumonia is seen in preparation for discharge from the hospital. He is euvolemic, afebrile, asymptomatic, and his oxygen saturations are normal.

Preservice

Review data not available on the unit (eg diagnostic and imaging studies). Communicate with other professionals and with the patient and/or patient's family.

Intraservice

Review medical records and data available on the unit. Obtain an interval history. Perform a physical exam. Consider relevant data, options, and risks and formulate/revise diagnosis and treatment plan(s) including making the decision for discharge. Discuss aftercare treatment with the patient, family and other healthcare professionals. Provide care coordination for the transition including instructions for aftercare to caregivers. Order/arrange for post discharge follow-up professional services and testing. Reconcile medications with attention to pre-admission therapy, inpatient therapy and outpatient formulary and write prescriptions. Complete discharge and aftercare forms. Inform the primary care or referring physician of discharge plans. Complete medical record documentation.

Postservice

Complete discharge records. Handle (with the help of clinical staff) any treatment failures or adverse reactions to medications that may occur after discharge. Provide necessary care coordination, telephonic or electronic communication assistance, and other necessary management related to this hospitalization. Receive and respond to any interval testing results or correspondence, including obtaining any results pending at discharge. Revise treatment plan(s) and communicate with the patient and/or caregiver, as necessary.

Coding Tip for 99238 and 99239

The hospital discharge day management codes are to be used to report the total duration of time spent for final hospital discharge of a patient.

⑤ **99239 Hospital discharge day management more than 30 minutes**

Work Value: 1.90 // Global Period: XXX

➲ *CPT Assistant* Nov 97: 4, Mar 98: 3, 11, May 98: 2, Jan 99: 10, Jan 02: 2, Aug 04: 11

Clinical Example

A 75-year-old female who required a below the knee amputation for an infected non-healing ulcer on her right foot is seen in preparation for discharge from the hospital. She has type II diabetes mellitus, ischemic cardiomyopathy, atherosclerotic peripheral vascular disease, hypertension, chronic renal insufficiency and dementia. She is no longer delirious, her blood sugars are well controlled, and she is at her baseline weight. She is being discharged back to the nursing home.

Preservice

Review data not available on the unit (eg diagnostic and imaging studies). Communicate with other professionals and with patient and/or patient's family.

Intraservice

Review medical records and data available on the unit. Obtain an interval history. Perform a physical exam. Consider relevant data, options, and risks and formulate and revise diagnosis and treatment plan(s) including making the decision for discharge. Discuss aftercare treatment with the patient, family and other healthcare professionals. Provide care coordination for the transition including instructions for aftercare to caregivers. Order and arrange for post discharge follow-up professional services and testing. Reconcile medications with attention to pre-admission therapy, inpatient therapy and outpatient formulary and write prescriptions. Complete discharge and aftercare forms. Inform the primary care or referring physician of discharge plans. Complete medical record documentation.

Postservice

Complete discharge records. Handle (with the help of clinical staff) any treatment failures or adverse reactions to medications that may occur after discharge. Provide necessary care coordination, telephonic or electronic communication assistance, and other necessary management related to this hospitalization. Receive and respond to any interval testing results or correspondence, including obtaining any results pending at discharge. Revise treatment plan(s) and communicate with the patient and/or caregiver, as necessary.

Consultations

Office or Other Outpatient Consultations

New or Established Patient

⑤ **99241 Office consultation** for a new or established patient, which requires these three key components:

- **A problem focused history;**
- **A problem focused examination; and**
- **Straightforward medical decision making.**

Counseling and/or coordination of care with other providers or agencies are provided consistent with the nature of the problem(s) and the patient's and/or family's needs.

Usually, the presenting problem(s) are self limited or minor. Physicians typically spend 15 minutes face-to-face with the patient and/or family.

Work Value: 0.64 // Global Period: XXX

➲ *CPT Assistant* Winter 91: 11, Spring 92: 4, 23-24, Summer 92: 12, Spring 93: 4, Spring 95: 1, Oct 97: 1, Sep 98: 5, Jun 99: 10, Apr 00: 10, Aug 01: 3, Jan 02: 2, Jul 02: 2, Sep 02: 11, May 05: 1, Dec 05: 10, Jan 06: 46

Clinical Example

A 21-year-old female was seen for an office consultation for rectal bleeding. She has had prior sigmoidoscopy within 1 year, which showed only internal hemorrhoids. She has recently become constipated, and while straining, saw scant blood on the tissue.

Preservice
Review the patient's referral records. Review the medical history form completed by the patient and vital signs obtained by the clinical staff. Communicate with other health care professionals.

Intraservice
Obtain a problem-focused history. Perform a problem-focused examination. Consider relevant data, options, and risks; formulate a diagnosis; and develop a treatment plan (straightforward medical decision making). Discuss diagnosis and treatment options with the patient. Address the preventive health care needs of the patient. Write prescription(s) and order and arrange diagnostic testing or referral as necessary.

Postservice
Complete the medical record documentation. Handle (with the help of clinical staff) any treatment failures or adverse reactions to medications that may occur after the visit. Provide necessary care coordination, telephonic or electronic communication assistance, and other necessary management related to this office visit. Receive and respond to any interval testing results or correspondence. Revise treatment plan(s) and communicate with the patient as necessary. Provide ongoing consultation to the referring health care professional.

---

⑮ **99242 Office consultation** for a new or established patient, which requires these three key components:

- **An expanded problem focused history;**
- **An expanded problem focused examination; and**
- **Straightforward medical decision making.**

Counseling and/or coordination of care with other providers or agencies are provided consistent with the nature of the problem(s) and the patient's and/or family's needs.

Usually, the presenting problem(s) are of low severity. Physicians typically spend 30 minutes face-to-face with the patient and/or family.

Work Value: 1.34 // Global Period: XXX

➲ ***CPT Assistant*** **Winter 91: 11, Spring 92: 4, 23-24, Summer 92: 12, Spring 93: 2, 34, Spring 95: 1, Oct 97: 1, Sep 98: 5, Aug 01: 3, Jan 02: 2, Jul 02: 2, Sep 02: 11, Dec 05: 10;** ***CPT Changes: An Insider's View*** **2000**

Clinical Example
A 30-year-old male is seen for an office consultation for heartburn. He is otherwise healthy but describes episodic burning substernal pain with typical provocative meals, eating late, or excessive coffee. He experiences relief with antacids and has no symptoms suggesting serious disease.

Preservice
Review the patient's referral records. Review the medical history form completed by the patient and vital signs obtained by the clinical staff. Communicate with other health care professionals.

Intraservice
Obtain an expanded history. Perform an expanded examination. Consider relevant data, options, and risks; formulate a diagnosis; and develop a treatment plan (straightforward medical decision making). Discuss diagnosis and treatment options with the patient. Address the preventive health care needs of the patient. Write prescription(s) and order and arrange diagnostic testing or referral as necessary.

Postservice
Complete the medical record documentation. Handle (with the help of clinical staff) any treatment failures or adverse reactions to medications that may occur after the visit. Provide necessary care coordination, telephonic or electronic communication assistance, and other necessary management related to this office visit. Receive and

respond to any interval testing results or correspondence. Revise treatment plan(s) and communicate with the patient as necessary. Provide ongoing consultation to the referring health care professional.

---

❺ **99243** **Office consultation** for a new or established patient, which requires these three key components:

- **A detailed history;**
- **A detailed examination; and**
- **Medical decision making of low complexity.**

Counseling and/or coordination of care with other providers or agencies are provided consistent with the nature of the problem(s) and the patient's and/or family's needs.

Usually, the presenting problem(s) are of moderate severity. Physicians typically spend 40 minutes face-to-face with the patient and/or family.

Work Value: 1.88 // Global Period: XXX

➲ **_CPT Assistant_ Winter 91: 11, Spring 92: 4, 23-24, Summer 92: 12, Spring 93: 2, 34, Spring 95: 1, Oct 97: 1, Sep 98: 5, Aug 01: 3, Jan 02: 2, Jul 02: 2, Sep 02: 11, Oct 03: 5, Dec 05: 10**

Clinical Example

A 24-year-old male is seen for an office consultation for throbbing headaches associated with nausea. Headaches are throbbing in character and usually, but not always, associated with visual 'floaters' in the left visual field. These headaches occur usually 2-3 times per month and are precipitated by sleep deprivation or red wine.

Preservice

Review the patient's referral records. Review the medical history form completed by the patient and vital signs obtained by the clinical staff. Communicate with other health care professionals.

Intraservice

Obtain a detailed history. Perform a detailed examination. Consider relevant data, options, and risks; formulate a diagnosis; and develop a treatment plan (low-complexity medical decision making).

Discuss diagnosis and treatment options with the patient. Address the preventive health care needs of the patient. Write prescription(s) and order and arrange diagnostic testing or referral as necessary.

Postservice

Complete the medical record documentation. Handle (with the help of clinical staff) any treatment failures or adverse reactions to medications that may occur after the visit. Provide necessary care coordination, telephonic or electronic communication assistance, and other necessary management related to this office visit. Receive and respond to any interval testing results or correspondence. Revise treatment plan(s) and communicate with the patient as necessary. Provide ongoing consultation to the referring health care professional.

---

❺ **99244** **Office consultation** for a new or established patient, which requires these three key components:

- **A comprehensive history;**
- **A comprehensive examination; and**
- **Medical decision making of moderate complexity.**

Counseling and/or coordination of care with other providers or agencies are provided consistent with the nature of the problem(s) and the patient's and/or family's needs.

Usually, the presenting problem(s) are of moderate to high severity. Physicians typically spend 60 minutes face-to-face with the patient and/or family.

Work Value: 3.02 // Global Period: XXX

➲ **_CPT Assistant_ Winter 91: 11, Spring 92: 3, 23-24, Summer 92: 12, Spring 93: 2, 34, Spring 95: 1, Oct 97: 1, Sep 98: 5, Aug 01: 3, Jan 02: 2, Jul 02: 2, Sep 02: 11, Oct 03: 5, Dec 05: 10**

Clinical Example

A 60-year-old female is seen for an office consultation for the evaluation of complaints of heart palpitations with occasional dizziness and abdominal pain. She has a past history of hypertension, osteoarthritis, and morbid obesity. Past medical history includes total abdominal hysterectomy 15 years previously for dysfunctional uterine bleeding. She has had no follow-up for 15 years.

Preservice

Review the patient's referral records. Review the medical history form completed by the patient and vital signs obtained by the clinical staff. Communicate with other health care professionals.

Intraservice

Obtain a comprehensive history. Perform a comprehensive examination. Consider relevant data, options, and risks; formulate a diagnosis; and develop a treatment plan (moderate-complexity medical decision making). Discuss diagnosis and treatment options with the patient. Address the preventive health care needs of the patient. Write prescription(s) and order and arrange diagnostic testing or referral as necessary.

Postservice

Complete the medical record documentation. Handle (with the help of clinical staff) any treatment failures or adverse reactions to medications that may occur after the visit. Provide necessary care coordination, telephonic or electronic communication assistance, and other necessary management related to this office visit. Receive and respond to any interval testing results or correspondence. Revise treatment plan(s) and communicate with the patient as necessary. Provide ongoing consultation to the referring health care professional.

Coding Tip for 99241-99244, 99251-99255

When a consultation is mandated by a third-party payer, modifier 32, *Mandated services,* should be appended to the consultation code reported.

---

⑤ **99245** **Office consultation** for a new or established patient, which requires these three key components:

- **A comprehensive history;**
- **A comprehensive examination; and**
- **Medical decision making of high complexity.**

Counseling and/or coordination of care with other providers or agencies are provided consistent with the nature of the problem(s) and the patient's and/or family's needs.

Usually, the presenting problem(s) are of moderate to high severity. Physicians typically spend 80 minutes face-to-face with the patient and/or family.

Work Value: 3.77 // Global Period: XXX

➲ *CPT Assistant* **Winter 91: 11, Spring 92: 4, 23-24, Summer 92: 12, Spring 93: 2, 34, Spring 95: 1, Oct 97: 1, Sep 98: 5, Aug 01: 2, Jan 02: 2, Jul 02: 2, Sep 02: 11, Dec 05: 10**

Clinical Example

A 63-year-old male is seen for an office consultation for a 20-lb weight loss, dysphagia, and abdominal pain. He has a history of coronary artery disease, osteoarthritis, chronic bronchitis, hypertension, gastroesophageal reflux disease, and hyperlipidemia and type II diabetes mellitus. He is on multiple medications.

Preservice

Review the patient's referral records. Review the medical history form completed by the patient and vital signs obtained by the clinical staff. Communicate with other health care professionals.

Intraservice

Obtain a comprehensive history. Perform a comprehensive examination. Consider relevant data, options, and risks; formulate a diagnosis; and develop a treatment plan (high-complexity medical decision making). Discuss diagnosis and treatment options with the patient. Address the preventive health care needs of the patient. Write prescription(s) and order and arrange diagnostic testing or referral as necessary.

Postservice

Complete the medical record documentation. Handle (with the help of clinical staff) any treatment failures or adverse reactions to medications that may occur after the visit. Provide necessary care coordination, telephonic or electronic communication assistance, and other necessary management related to this office visit. Receive and respond to any interval testing results or correspondence. Revise treatment plan(s) and communicate with the patient as necessary. Provide ongoing consultation to the referring health care professional.

Inpatient Consultations

New or Established Patient

❺ **99251** **Inpatient consultation** for a new or established patient, which requires these three key components:

- **A problem focused history;**
- **A problem focused examination; and**
- **Straightforward medical decision making.**

Counseling and/or coordination of care with other providers or agencies are provided consistent with the nature of the problem(s) and the patient's and/or family's needs.

Usually, the presenting problem(s) are self limited or minor. Physicians typically spend 20 minutes at the bedside and on the patient's hospital floor or unit.

Work Value: 1.00 // Global Period: XXX

➲ *CPT Assistant* Winter 91: 11, Spring 92: 16, 23-24, Summer 92: 12, Spring 93: 34, Spring 95: 1, Oct 97: 1, Sep 98: 5, Aug 01: 3, Sep 02: 11, May 05: 1

Clinical Example

Initial inpatient consultation for a 45-year-old female admitted with unrelenting low back pain for 2 days. There is no significant past medical history and she is on no medications. The neurological exam is normal.

Preservice

Review data not available on the unit (eg, diagnostic and imaging studies). Communicate with other professionals and with the patient and/or the patient's family. Obtain and review necessary past results or records not available on the unit.

Intraservice

Review medical records and data available on the unit. Obtain a problem-focused history. Perform a problem-focused physical exam. Consider relevant data, options, and risks; formulate a diagnosis; and develop a treatment plan (straightforward medical decision making). Discuss diagnosis and treatment options with the patient and/or the patient's family. Communicate with other health care professionals. Write/review admission orders including ordering/arranging for necessary diagnostic testing, consultation, and therapeutic intervention(s). Complete the medical record documentation.

Postservice

Address interval data obtained and changes in the condition reported. Communicate results and further care plans with other health care professionals and with the patient and/or the patient's family. Provide ongoing consultation to the referring health care professional.

❺ **99252** **Inpatient consultation** for a new or established patient, which requires these three key components:

- **An expanded problem focused history;**
- **An expanded problem focused examination; and**
- **Straightforward medical decision making.**

Counseling and/or coordination of care with other providers or agencies are provided consistent with the nature of the problem(s) and the patient's and/or family's needs.

Usually, the presenting problem(s) are of low severity. Physicians typically spend 40 minutes at the bedside and on the patient's hospital floor or unit.

Work Value: 1.50 // Global Period: XXX

➲ *CPT Assistant* **Winter 91: 11, Spring 92: 16, 23-24, Summer 92: 12, Summer 93: 34, Spring 95: 1, Oct 97: 1, Sep 98: 5, Aug 01: 4, Sep 02: 11**

Clinical Example

Initial inpatient consultation for a 76-year-old female admitted for evaluation and treatment of a painful and swollen shoulder and hand. She has well controlled hypertension.

Preservice

Review data not available on the unit (eg, diagnostic and imaging studies). Communicate with other professionals and with the patient and/or the patient's family. Obtain and review necessary past results or records not available on the unit.

Intraservice

Review medical records and data available on the unit. Obtain an expanded history. Perform an expanded physical exam. Consider relevant data, options, and risks; formulate a diagnosis; and develop a treatment plan (straightforward medical decision making). Discuss diagnosis and treatment options with the patient and/or the patient's family. Communicate with other health care professionals. Write/review admission orders including ordering/arranging for necessary diagnostic testing, consultation, and therapeutic intervention(s). Complete the medical record documentation.

Postservice

Address interval data obtained and changes in the condition reported. Communicate results and further care plans with other health care professionals and with the patient and/or the patient's family. Provide ongoing consultation to the referring health care professional.

Coding Tip for 99241-99244, 99251-99255

A consultation initiated by a patient and/or the patient's family, and not requested by a physician or other appropriate source (eg, physician assistant, nurse practitioner, doctor of chiropractic, physical therapist, occupational therapist, speech-language pathologist, psychologist, social worker, lawyer, or insurance company), is not reported using the consultation codes but may be reported using the office visit, home service, or domiciliary/rest home care codes.

---

❺ **99253** **Inpatient consultation** for a new or established patient, which requires these three key components:

- **A detailed history;**
- **A detailed examination; and**
- **Medical decision making of low complexity.**

Counseling and/or coordination of care with other providers or agencies are provided consistent with the nature of the problem(s) and the patient's and/or family's needs.

Usually, the presenting problem(s) are of moderate severity. Physicians typically spend 55 minutes at the bedside and on the patient's hospital floor or unit.

Work Value: 2.27 // Global Period: XXX

➲ *CPT Assistant* **Winter 91: 11, Spring 92: 16, 23-24, Summer 92: 12, Summer 93: 34, Spring 95: 1, Oct 97: 1, Oct 97: 1, Sep 98: 5, Aug 01: 4, Sep 02: 11**

Clinical Example

Initial inpatient consultation for a 75-year-old white female with a status post right hip fracture with a history of hypertension and well-controlled type II diabetes mellitus. A consultation is requested for surgical clearance.

Preservice

Review data not available on the unit (eg, diagnostic and imaging studies). Communicate with other professionals and with the patient and/or patient's family. Obtain and review necessary past results or records not available on the unit.

Intraservice

Review medical records and data available on the unit. Obtain a detailed history. Perform a detailed physical exam. Consider relevant data, options, and risks and formulate a diagnosis and develop a treatment plan (low complexity medical decision making). Discuss diagnosis and treatment options with the patient and/or family. Communicate with other health care professionals. Write/review admission orders including ordering/arranging for necessary diagnostic testing, consultation and therapeutic intervention(s). Complete medical record documentation.

Postservice

Address interval data obtained and changes in condition reported. Communicate results and further care plans to other health care professionals and to the patient and/or family. Provide ongoing consultation to referring healthcare professional.

---

❺ **99254** **Inpatient consultation** for a new or established patient, which requires these three key components:

- **A comprehensive history;**
- **A comprehensive examination; and**
- **Medical decision making of moderate complexity.**

Counseling and/or coordination of care with other providers or agencies are provided consistent with the nature of the problem(s) and the patient's and/or family's needs.

Usually, the presenting problem(s) are of moderate to high severity. Physicians typically spend 80 minutes at the bedside and on the patient's hospital floor or unit.

Work Value: 3.29 // Global Period: XXX

➲ *CPT Assistant* **Winter 91: 11, Spring 92: 16, 23-24, Summer 92: 12, Summer 93: 34, Spring 95: 1, Oct 97: 1, Sep 98: 5, Aug 01: 4, Sep 02: 11**

Clinical Example

Initial inpatient consultation for a 75-year-old female admitted with cellulitis around a right great toe ulcer. She has a history of type II diabetes mellitus, ischemic cardiomyopathy, atherosclerotic peripheral vascular disease, hypertension, and chronic renal insufficiency. She is a widow living in a nursing home. She has developed a fever and a hot, swollen painful left knee.

Preservice

Review data not available on the unit (eg, diagnostic and imaging studies). Communicate with other professionals and with the patient and/or the patient's family. Obtain and review necessary past results or records not available on the unit.

Intraservice

Review medical records and data available on the unit. Obtain a comprehensive history. Perform a comprehensive physical exam. Consider relevant data, options, and risks; formulate a diagnosis; and develop a treatment plan (moderate-complexity medical decision making).

Discuss diagnosis and treatment options with the patient and/or the patient's family. Communicate with other health care professionals. Write/review admission orders including ordering/arranging for necessary diagnostic testing, consultation, and therapeutic intervention(s). Complete the medical record documentation.

Postservice

Address interval data obtained and changes in the condition reported. Communicate results and further care plans with other health care professionals and with the patient and/or the patient's family. Provide ongoing consultation to the referring health care professional.

⊕ **99255 Inpatient consultation** for a new or established patient, which requires these three key components:

- **A comprehensive history;**
- **A comprehensive examination; and**
- **Medical decision making of high complexity.**

Counseling and/or coordination of care with other providers or agencies are provided consistent with the nature of the problem(s) and the patient's and/or family's needs.

Usually, the presenting problem(s) are of moderate to high severity. Physicians typically spend 110 minutes at the bedside and on the patient's hospital floor or unit.

Work Value: 4.00 // Global Period: XXX

➲ ***CPT Assistant*** **Winter 91: 11, Spring 92: 16, 23-24, Summer 92: 12, Summer 93: 34, Spring 95: 1, Oct 97: 1, Sep 98: 5, Aug 01: 4, Sep 02: 11**

Clinical Example

Initial inpatient consultation for a 75-year-old female admitted with cellulitis around a right great toe ulcer. She has a history of type II diabetes mellitus, ischemic cardiomyopathy, atherosclerotic peripheral vascular disease, hypertension, and chronic renal insufficiency. She is a widow living in a nursing home. She is delirious and febrile.

Preservice

Review data not available on the unit (eg, diagnostic and imaging studies). Communicate with other professionals and with the patient and/or the patient's family. Obtain and review necessary past results or records not available on the unit.

Intraservice

Review the medical records and data available on the unit. Obtain a comprehensive history. Perform a comprehensive physical exam. Consider relevant data, options, and risks; formulate a diagnosis; and develop a treatment plan (high-complexity medical decision making). Discuss diagnosis and treatment options with the patient and/or the patient's family. Communicate with other health care professionals. Write/review admission orders including ordering/arranging for necessary diagnostic testing, consultation, and therapeutic intervention(s). Complete the medical record documentation.

Postservice

Address interval data obtained and changes in the condition reported. Communicate results and further care plans with other health care professionals and with the patient and/or the patient's family. Provide ongoing consultation to the referring health care professional.

Coding Tip for 99251-99255

Codes 99251-99255 are used to report physician consultations provided to hospital inpatients, residents of nursing facilities, or patients in a partial hospital setting. Only one consultation should be reported by a consultant per admission. Subsequent services performed during the same admission are reported with the Subsequent Hospital Care codes (99231-99233) or the Subsequent Nursing Facility Care codes (99307-99310), including those services performed to complete the initial consultation, monitor progress, revise recommendations, or address a new problem.

Emergency Department Services

New or Established Patient

⊕ **99281 Emergency department visit** for the evaluation and management of a patient, which requires these three key components:

- **A problem focused history;**
- **A problem focused examination; and**
- **Straightforward medical decision making.**

Counseling and/or coordination of care with other providers or agencies are provided consistent with the nature of the problem(s) and the patient's and/or family's needs.

Usually, the presenting problem(s) are self limited or minor.

Work Value: 0.45 // Global Period: XXX

➲ *CPT Assistant* Winter 91: 11, Spring 92: 24, Summer 92: 18, Spring 93: 34, Spring 95: 1, Feb 96: 3, Sep 98: 5, Jan 00: 11, Feb 00: 11, Sep 00: 3, Apr 02: 14, Jul 02: 2, May 05: 1, Nov 05: 10, Feb 06: 14

Clinical Example

A patient presents to the emergency department for suture removal status post repair of a forearm laceration by a different provider in another different location. There are no complaints and the wound appears well healed.

Intraservice

Intraservice work includes preparing to see the patient; reviewing records; communicating with other professionals; evaluating the patient, which includes obtaining a problem-focused history, performing a problem-focused exam, and straightforward decision making; documenting the medical record; and coordinating patient care after discharge from the emergency department.

Coding Tip for 99281-99285

No distinction is made between new and established patients. The reason for this is that many different physicians staff emergency departments, and the service they provide is unscheduled and episodic. Also, previous information about a patient may not be readily available to physicians in the emergency department.

---

❺ **99282 Emergency department visit** for the evaluation and management of a patient, which requires these three key components:

- **An expanded problem focused history;**
- **An expanded problem focused examination; and**
- **Medical decision making of low complexity.**

Counseling and/or coordination of care with other providers or agencies are provided consistent with the nature of the problem(s) and the patient's and/or family's needs.

Usually, the presenting problem(s) are of low to moderate severity.

Work Value: 0.88 // Global Period: XXX

➲ *CPT Assistant* Winter 91: 11, Spring 92: 24, Summer 92: 18, Spring 93: 34, Spring 95: 1, Summer 95: 1, Feb 96: 3, Sep 98: 5, Jan 00: 11, Feb 00: 11, Sep 00: 3, Apr 02: 14, Jul 02: 2, Nov 05: 10, Feb 06: 14

Clinical Example

A patient presents to the emergency department complaining of a pruritic rash on both legs of 1 day duration. She walked through brush and sat on grass the night before while attending an outdoor concert. She is noted to have an erythematous, vesicular rash.

Intraservice

Intraservice work includes preparing to see the patient; reviewing records; communicating with other professionals; evaluating the patient, which includes obtaining an expanded problem-focused history, performing an expanded problem-focused exam, and medical decision making of low complexity; documenting the medical record; coordinating patient care, and communicating with the patient, the patient's family, and other health care professionals associated with the delivery of care to this patient after the patient is discharged from the emergency department.

Coding Tip for 99281-99285

When the Emergency Department codes are reported, all three key components must meet or exceed the requirements stated in the code descriptor to qualify for a particular level of service.

⑤ 99283 Emergency department visit for the evaluation and management of a patient, which requires these three key components:

- **An expanded problem focused history;**
- **An expanded problem focused examination; and**
- **Medical decision making of moderate complexity.**

Counseling and/or coordination of care with other providers or agencies are provided consistent with the nature of the problem(s) and the patient's and/or family's needs.

Usually, the presenting problem(s) are of moderate severity.

Work Value: 1.34 // Global Period: XXX

➲ *CPT Assistant* Winter 91: 11, Spring 92: 24, Summer 92: 18, Spring 93: 34, Spring 95: 1, Summer 95: 1, Feb 96: 3, Sep 98: 5, Jan 00: 11, Feb 00: 11, Sep 00: 3, Apr 02: 14, Jul 02: 2, Nov 05: 10, Feb 06: 14

Clinical Example

A previously well 8-year-old girl presents to the emergency department with fever, diarrhea, and crampy-type abdominal pain. She appears to be hydrated, and there are no complaints of vomiting, dysuria, or frequency. Her abdominal examination is not consistent with a surgical condition.

Intraservice

Intraservice work includes preparing to see the patient; reviewing records; communicating with other professionals; evaluating the patient, which includes obtaining an expanded problem-focused history, performing an expanded problem-focused exam, and medical decision making of moderate complexity; considering alternative diagnostic and treatment modalities; reevaluating the patient as indicated; reconsidering the likelihood of a surgical condition; reviewing any diagnostics previously obtained and now available; formulating and discussing a postdischarge plan with the patient and the patient's family, which includes a discussion of the initiation of medications, dietary modifications, and follow-up with the patient's established physician; documenting the medical record; coordinating patient care, and communicating with the patient, the patient's family, and other health care professionals associated with the delivery of care to this patient after the patient is discharged from the emergency department.

Coding Tip for 99281-99285

Generally, when more than one physician provides E/M services to the same patient in the emergency department, only the emergency department physician should report his/her E/M services with the codes in this series. The other physician(s) would report his/her services with the appropriate level of office or other outpatient services code, or with an office or other outpatient consultation code, as appropriate.

⑤ 99284 Emergency department visit for the evaluation and management of a patient, which requires these three key components:

- **A detailed history;**
- **A detailed examination; and**
- **Medical decision making of moderate complexity.**

Counseling and/or coordination of care with other providers or agencies are provided consistent with the nature of the problem(s) and the patient's and/or family's needs.

Usually, the presenting problem(s) are of high severity, and require urgent evaluation by the physician but do not pose an immediate significant threat to life or physiologic function.

Work Value: 2.56 // Global Period: XXX

➲ *CPT Assistant* Winter 91: 11, Spring 92: 24, Summer 92: 18, Spring 93: 34, Spring 95: 1, Summer 95: 1, Feb 96: 3, Sep 98: 5, Jan 00: 11, Feb 00: 11, Sep 00: 3, Apr 02: 14, Jul 02: 2, Nov 05: 10, Feb 06: 14

Clinical Example

A 4-year-old boy presents to the emergency department after sustaining a fall from his bicycle and hitting his head. He was observed to have a brief loss of consciousness and has vomited twice. He has a scalp hematoma, postconcussive behavior, and no evidence of other injuries.

Intraservice

Intraservice work includes preparing to see the patient; reviewing patient records; communicating with other professionals including emergency medical services personnel, as appropriate; performing an evaluation of the patient, which includes obtaining a detailed history (portions of which may have to be deferred or obtained from someone other than the patient due to patient's head injury and age), performing a detailed examination, and decision making of moderate complexity; considering alternative treatment modalities and implementing a course of treatment; considering possible diagnostics including imaging options and obtaining those deemed appropriate; reconsidering the likelihood of a surgical condition; reevaluating the patient after the initial evaluation course of observation and/or treatment for head injury has been completed, which includes obtaining supplemental history, new subjective elements, and a reexamination; considering further diagnostics and obtaining those deemed appropriate; reconsidering alternative treatment modalities and implementing a revised course of treatment as indicated by additional information; formulating and discussing with the patient and the patient's family a postdischarge plan and follow-up with the patient's established physician; documenting the medical record; coordinating patient care, and communicating with the patient, the patient's family, and other health care professionals associated with the delivery of care to this patient after the patient is discharged from the emergency department.

Coding Tip for 99281-99285

For critical care services provided in the emergency department, see Critical Care guidelines and 99291, 99292.

---

❺ **99285 Emergency department visit** for the evaluation and management of a patient, which requires these three key components within the constraints imposed by the urgency of the patient's clinical condition and/or mental status:

- **A comprehensive history;**
- **A comprehensive examination; and**
- **Medical decision making of high complexity.**

Counseling and/or coordination of care with other providers or agencies are provided consistent with the nature of the problem(s) and the patient's and/or family's needs.

Usually, the presenting problem(s) are of high severity and pose an immediate significant threat to life or physiologic function.

Work Value: 3.80 // Global Period: XXX

➲ ***CPT Assistant*** **Winter 91: 11, Spring 92: 24, Summer 92: 18, Spring 93: 34, Spring 95: 1, Summer 95: 1, Feb 96: 3, Aug 98: 8, Sep 98: 5, Nov 99: 23, Jan 00: 11, Feb 00: 11, Sep 00: 3, Apr 02: 14, Jul 02: 2, Sep 02: 11, Mar 05: 11, Nov 05: 10, Feb 06: 14;** ***CPT Changes: An Insider's View*** **2000**

Clinical Example

A 45-year-old male presents to the emergency department via ambulance with the acute onset of chest pain compatible with cardiac ischemia. He has several cardiac risk factors. He appears anxious, has a sinus tachycardia and is mildly short of breath.

Intraservice

Intraservice work includes preparing to see the patient; reviewing patient records, communicating with other professionals including EMS personnel, as appropriate;

performing an evaluation of the patient, which includes obtaining a comprehensive history (portions of which may have to be obtained from, or verified by, someone other than the patient due to patient clinical condition), a comprehensive examination, and decision making of high complexity; considering possible etiologies given the patient's age, medical history, and current medications; considering possible diagnostics and obtaining those deemed appropriate; serial re-evaluation of the patient including new subjective elements and physical examinations; reviewing electronically available medical records including any diagnostics previously obtained and now available; considering further diagnostics and obtaining those deemed appropriate and review of such further diagnostics when available. Consideration of patient's eligibility for immediate time sensitive management options such as cardiac catheterization or aggressive medical treatment and of other specialty consultation; discussing with patient's established physician and obtaining other consultations as appropriate, formulatind and discussing post-ED plan with patient and/or family.

Coding Tip for 99285

Note that code 99285 is unique in that it indicates that the three key components are required within the constraints imposed by the urgency of the patient's clinical condition and/or mental status. This means that code 99285 may be reported when the patient's condition requires this level of service, but the physician is unable to complete a comprehensive level of history or examination due to the nature of the patient's clinical condition and/or mental status (eg, comatose patient). When this circumstance occurs, documentation should be used to specify the imposing constraints of the patient's clinical condition, and the diagnosis codes reported should be indicative.

Pediatric Critical Care Patient Transport

99289 Critical care services delivered by a physician, face-to-face, during an interfacility transport of critically ill or critically injured pediatric patient, 24 months of age or less; first 30-74 minutes of hands on care during transport

Work Value: 4.79 // Global Period: XXX

➲ *CPT Assistant* May 05: 1; *CPT Changes: An Insider's View* 2002, 2003

Clinical Example

A previously healthy patient is struck by a vehicle while crossing a busy street. The patient is not run over, but is thrown and impacts the road 15 ft from the point of the accident. The patient is taken by emergency medical services to the nearest hospital, a non-trauma facility. During initial stabilization, the emergency department (ED) physician finds significant injuries to the head, chest, and abdomen requiring trauma specialty care that is unavailable at her facility. After consultation with the receiving trauma center, a specialized transport team consisting of a physician, nurse, respiratory therapist, and paramedic is dispatched to the local hospital.

At the local hospital, the transport physician reviews the patient's history, clinical progress, labs and radiographs, with the ED physician, and assists in further stabilization of the patient, including endotracheal intubation (following rapid sequence induction), and the placement of central lines and a chest tube. The patient has unstable vital signs, but requires the trauma center's services. The patient is moved to the transport unit where he is placed on continuous heart, respiratory, blood pressure, pulse oximetry, and end-tidal carbon dioxide monitors. All intravenous lines and medications are on electronic monitoring pumps. The patient is placed on a transport ventilator. The physician remains at the patient's side in continuous attendance providing direct care and directing the activities of the team. The transport unit has limited space and resources. Bedside blood tests are used to adjust respiratory and medical treatment. The vehicle is in constant motion and patient observation and intervention is challenging.

Upon arrival at the trauma center, there has been no further deterioration in the patient's condition. Care is transferred to the trauma service after review of the patient's records from the transferring facility and events that occurred and care that was provided during the transport.

Preservice
Preservice work includes discussing the patient's diagnosis and present status with the referring hospital to determine the most appropriate mode of transport, contacting the transport communication center to arrange for the team and vehicle, traveling in the transport vehicle to the referring hospital, discussing the patient's status with the treating team, and reviewing the patient's records and lab results.

Intraservice
Intraservice work includes caring for the critically ill patient during transport.

Postservice
Postservice work includes communicating patient information to the receiving hospital, completing the transport forms, communicating with the referring hospital, and providing an update on the patient's condition.

Coding Tip for 99289
Code 99289 is used to report the first 30-74 minutes of direct face-to-face time with the transport pediatric patient and should be reported only one time on a given date.

+ 99290 Critical care services delivered by a physician, face-to-face, during an interfacility transport of critically ill or critically injured pediatric patient, 24 months of age or less; each additional 30 minutes (List separately in addition to code for primary service)

Work Value: 2.40 // Global Period: ZZZ

➲ *CPT Changes: An Insider's View* 2002

Clinical Example
A previously healthy patient is struck by a vehicle while crossing a busy street. The patient is not run over, but is thrown and impacts the road 15 ft from the point of the accident. The patient is taken by emergency medical services to the nearest hospital, a non-trauma facility. During initial stabilization, the emergency department (ED) physician finds significant injuries to the head, chest, and abdomen requiring trauma specialty care that is unavailable at her facility. After consultation with the receiving trauma center, a specialized transport team consisting of a physician, nurse, respiratory therapist, and paramedic is dispatched to the local hospital.

At the local hospital, the transport physician reviews the patient's history, clinical progress, labs and radiographs, with the ED physician, and assists in further stabilization of the patient, including endotracheal intubation (following rapid sequence induction), and the placement of central lines and a chest tube. The patient has unstable vital signs, but requires the trauma center's services. The patient is moved to the transport unit where he is placed on continuous heart, respiratory, blood pressure, pulse oximetry, and end-tidal carbon dioxide monitors. All intravenous lines and medications are on electronic monitoring pumps. The patient is placed on a transport ventilator. The physician remains at the patient's side in continuous attendance providing direct care and directing the activities of the team. The transport unit has limited space and resources. Bedside blood tests are used to adjust respiratory and medical treatment. The vehicle is in constant motion and patient observation and intervention is challenging.

Upon arrival at the trauma center, there has been no further deterioration in the patient's condition. Care is transferred to the trauma service after review of the patient's records from the transferring facility and events that occurred and care that was provided during the transport.

Intraservice

Intraservice work includes caring for the critically ill patient during transport.

Coding Tip for 99289 and 99290

Code 99290 is used to report each additional 30 minutes beyond the first 74 minutes of direct face-to-face time with the transport pediatric patient provided on a given date. Face-to-face services less than 30 minutes should not be reported with codes 99289 and 99290.

Critical Care Services

⑮ **99291 Critical care, evaluation and management** of the critically ill or critically injured patient; first 30-74 minutes

Work Value: 4.50 // Global Period: XXX

➲ ***CPT Assistant*** **Summer 92: 18, Summer 93: 1, Summer 95: 1, Jan 96: 7, Apr 97: 3, Dec 98: 6, Nov 99: 3, Apr 00: 6, Sep 00: 1, Dec 00: 15, Jul 02: 2, Feb 03: 15, Oct 03: 2, Aug 04: 7, 10, Oct 04: 14, May 05: 1, Jul 05: 15, Nov 05: 10**

Clinical Example

A 65-year-old female who, following a hysterectomy, suffers an onset of severe dyspnea. Time spent 30 to 74 minutes. Services included in 99291 are: interpretation of cardiac output measurements (93561, 93562), chest Xrays (71010, 71015, 71020), pulse oximetry (94760, 94761, 94762), blood gases, and information data stored in computers (eg, ECGs, blood pressure, hematologic data (99090); gastric intubation (43752, 91105); temporary transcutaneous pacing (92953); ventilatory management (94002–94004, 94660, 94662); and vascular access procedures (36000, 36410, 36415, 36540, 36600). Any services not listed are reported separately.

Preservice

The patient is critically ill. Review assessment and integration of available data from multiple databases (eg, {not all inclusive} telemetry, central venous/intra-cardiac measurements of blood gases, and other diagnostic laboratory, radiological and nuclear medicine data in correlation with the patient's signs, symptoms and reactions to therapeutic interventions) and reading of films, rhythm strips, etc. Explanation of procedure(s)/service(s) bundled into critical care and not separately billable to patient and/ or family members, outlining risks and benefits.

Intraservice

Patient is examined assessing all body systems. Consultations are made with nurses, respiratory therapists, nutritionists, physical therapists, pharmacists and other physicians. Adjustments to ventilator settings; titration of fluid replacement; calculation of needed parenteral nutritional support; titration of amounts of vasoactives to maintain patient's blood pressure, and determining need for blood and volume expanders. Any necessary procedures are performed, and those not included in the list above may be reported separately and the time to perform those procedures is NOT counted in critical care time. End-of-life discussions with surrogate decision-makers.

Postservice

A note is written describing the patient's critical illness, the critical care service provided including any procedures performed (bundled into critical care, and not separately billable), and the time (total time or start-stop time) spent. Notes may include explanations of interpretations of data and the planned course of action. Discussions with nurses, respiratory therapists, nutritionists, physical therapists, pharmacists and other physicians are often noted. Detailed instructions and orders are written for staff. Consultations with family members or surrogate decision makers are more frequent and complex than in other E/M services because of the severity of the patient's condition. High probability of imminent or life threatening deterioration in the patient's condition. Medically significant decisions for next 24 hours on-call, or until next subsequent hospital visit.

Coding Tip for 99291

Code 99291 is used to report the first 30-74 minutes of critical care provided on a given date. It should be used only once per date even if the time spent by the physician is not continuous on that date. Critical care of less than 30 minutes in total duration on a given date should be reported with the appropriate evaluation and management code.

+⑤ 99292 Critical care, evaluation and management of the critically ill or critically injured patient; each additional 30 minutes (List separately in addition to code for primary service)

Work Value: 2.25 // Global Period: ZZZ

➲ ***CPT Assistant*** **Summer 92: 18, Summer 93: 1, Summer 95: 1, Jan 96: 7, Apr 97: 3, Dec 98: 6, Nov 99: 3, Apr 00: 6, Sep 00: 1, Dec 00: 15, Feb 03: 15, Oct 03: 2, Aug 04: 10, Oct 04: 14, Jul 05: 15, Nov 05: 10**

Clinical Example

A 65-year-old female who, following hysterectomy, suffers an onset of severe dyspnea. She requires a 30 minute segment of critical care time beyond the first 74 minutes.

Intraservice

Same intraservice work as 99291, but of longer duration. The patient is examined and all body systems are assessed. Nurses, respiratory therapists, nutritionists, physical therapists, pharmacists, and other physicians are consulted. Adjustments to ventilator settings are made. Fluid replacement is titrated. Needed parenteral nutritional support is calculated. The amount of vasoactives needed to maintain the patient's blood pressure is titrated, and the need for blood and volume expanders is determined. Any necessary procedures are performed. Those procedures not included in the previous list may be reported separately and the time to perform those procedures is not counted in the critical care time.

Coding Tip for 99292

Code 99292 is used to report additional block(s) of time up to 30 minutes each beyond the first 74 minutes.

Inpatient Pediatric Critical Care

99293 Initial inpatient pediatric critical care, per day, for the evaluation and management of a critically ill infant or young child, 29 days through 24 months of age

Work Value: 15.98 // Global Period: XXX

➲ ***CPT Assistant*** **Feb 03: 15, Oct 03: 2, Aug 04: 7, 10, May 05: 1, Nov 05: 10;** ***CPT Changes: An Insider's View*** **2003, 2004, 2005**

Clinical Example

A 6-month-old female, a former 28-week gestational-age premature infant, now with chronic lung disease (bronchopulmonary dysplasia) following her neonatal course, is admitted to the pediatric intensive care unit (PICU) from home with respiratory distress and impending respiratory failure. She had been stable on a low flow of nasal oxygen until 2 days prior to admission when she developed a fever, cough, and increased oxygen requirement. She gradually developed tachypnea, wheezing, and retractions despite increased bronchodilator therapy at home (in addition to her daily diuretics, supplemental oxygen and maintenance bronchodilator therapy for her chronic lung disease).

In the emergency room she was found to have an oxygen saturation of 83% on 1L of nasal cannula oxygen. An arterial blood gas test revealed acute and chronic hypercarbia and hypoxia. A chest X ray revealed bilateral diffuse pneumonia, as well as hyperinflation. She was transferred to the PICU for evaluation and management by the pediatric intensivist. Despite aggressive therapy to treat her pulmonary disease, she progressed to respiratory failure requiring intubation and mechanical ventilation. Central venous and arterial access was obtained by the pediatric intensivist after numerous attempts at peripheral arterial and venous catheterization were unsuccessful due to scarring from line placement during her stay in the neonatal intensive care unit. Arterial blood pressure and central venous pressure monitoring revealed hypotension and intravascular volume depletion. Blood, urine, and respiratory cultures were obtained and broad-spectrum antibiotic coverage was instituted for presumed sepsis. The patient's hypotension responded to treatment with fluid boluses and low doses of pressors.

Her respiratory failure worsened and she developed acute respiratory distress syndrome, circulatory failure, and fluid and electrolyte disturbances that required high frequency oscillatory ventilation and increased inotropic support for 7 days. She was eventually converted back to conventional ventilation and weaned to extubation. The pediatric intensivist spent many hours throughout the child's admission coordinating the activities of other subspecialists, nursing staff, respiratory therapists, nutritionists, and social workers involved, as well as providing daily communications to the patient's family and the patient's primary care physician.

Preservice

Preservice work includes obtaining and reviewing the results of any lab work and/or radiologic studies, reviewing the care flow sheet, discussing the patient's status with the bedside nurse, and communicating with other health care professionals as appropriate.

Intraservice

Intraservice work includes performing a complete examination of the head, eyes, nose, mouth, chest, lungs, heart, abdomen, genitals, rectum, joints, spine, and extremities, and performing a neurologic appraisal of movement, reflexes, cranial nerves, and degree of arousal and activity. All attached monitors and tubes are checked for secure placement and proper function.

Postservice

Postservice work includes all coordination of care, documentation, and telephone calls with the patient, family members, or other health care professionals. Postservice also includes writing the daily total parenteral nutrition orders after recovery and/or writing new feeding orders, ordering daily laboratory and imaging studies as necessary, documenting care changes in the patient's chart and verbally with the nursing staff, speaking with the family in person or by telephone, and updating the referring physician.

99294 Subsequent inpatient pediatric critical care, per day, for the evaluation and management of a critically ill infant or young child, 29 days through 24 months of age

Work Value: 7.99 // Global Period: XXX

➲ ***CPT Assistant*** **Feb 03: 15, Oct 03: 2, Aug 04: 7, Nov 05: 10;** ***CPT Changes: An Insider's View*** **2003, 2004, 2005**

Clinical Example

A 1½-year-old male, who was in his usual state of health, presents with acute respiratory distress to the emergency department. The patient's ongoing medications included home nebulized bronchodilator therapy and low-dose steroids for significant reactive airway disease. After evaluation and failure to clear with bronchodilator therapy in the emergency department, he was admitted to the pediatric intensive care unit with increasing respiratory distress and impending respiratory failure. Over the next few hours he demonstrated increasing oxygen requirements, tachypnea, cough, and a mild rash. He was placed on bronchodilator therapy, constant cardiopulmonary, blood pressure, and oxygen saturation monitoring, intravenous (IV) infusions, antibiotics, chest radiographs, blood gases, and intravenous steroids. He was placed on a 100% nonrebreather mask and multiple laboratory examinations for bacterial and viral studies were performed.

His response to therapy was variable over the first 12 hours and he then gradually deteriorated. The patient's deteriorating clinical state was discussed extensively with the family including the need to intubate the patient for ventilatory support. He required endotracheal intubation and mechanical ventilation for respiratory failure. His chest X ray at that time showed a diffuse, interstitial pattern consistent with progressive diffuse alveolar disease. The patient was placed on IV continuous sedation of fentanyl and midazolam to assist with ventilator/patient asynchrony. The patient's family and primary care physician were contacted daily for updates and therapeutic planning.

The patient continued to show a deteriorating state of oxygenation and ventilation over the first 48 hours, and increasing lung congestion consistent with noncardiogenic pulmonary edema. Initially this was treated with diuretic therapy and increasing the mechanical ventilatory support with positive expiratory pressure. The patient had associated glucose and electrolyte abnormalities, which were treated with additional diuretic therapy and changes in intravenous solutions. Nutritional support was provided in the form of hyperalimentation.

Over the next 72 hours he continued to require increased nasal cannula oxygen to 80% and increasing ventilatory support resulting in high airway pressures, necessitating his placement on high frequency oscillatory ventilation. Due to the child's unstable condition he required 1:1 nursing care. An arterial line and central venous pressure monitoring line were placed to closely monitor the patient's hemodynamics and his intravascular fluid status. During the course of high frequency oscillation, progressive anemia from blood obtained for laboratory tests and from hemodilution was treated with packed red blood cell transfusions.

Over the course of the first week of high frequency oscillation the patient developed improvement of his chest radiograph and decrease in oxygen requirements to less than 50%. By the end of the second week his respiratory status had improved and he was transferred to conventional mechanical ventilation with moderate settings on pressure-regulated volume control. The family was given daily updates and discussion about his progress. His primary physician received daily calls during which clinical changes were discussed. At this time the patient was taken off paralysis and sedation was weaned down to minimum ventilator and oxygen levels. By the end of the third week, the patient had been successfully weaned down to continuous positive airway pressure and subsequently extubated to a nasal cannula. His clinical condition was no longer considered critical, but he continued to require close observation and evaluation.

Preservice

Preservice work includes obtaining and reviewing the results of any lab work and/or radiologic studies, reviewing the care flow sheet and discussing the patient's status with the bedside nurse, and communicating with other health care professionals as appropriate.

Intraservice

Intraservice work includes performing a complete examination of the head, eyes, nose, mouth, chest, lungs, heart, abdomen, genitals, rectum, joints, spine, and extremities, and performing a neurologic appraisal of movement, reflexes, cranial nerves, and degree of arousal and activity. All attached monitors and tubes are checked for secure placement and proper function.

Postservice

Postservice work includes all coordination of care, documentation, and telephone calls with the patient, family members, or other health care professionals. Postservice also includes writing the daily total parenteral nutrition orders after recovery and/or writing new feeding orders, ordering daily laboratory and imaging studies as necessary, documenting care changes in the patient's chart and verbally with the nursing staff, speaking with the family in person or by telephone, and updating the referring physician.

Inpatient Neonatal Critical Care

99295 Initial inpatient neonatal critical care, per day, for the evaluation and management of a critically ill neonate, 28 days of age or less

Work Value: 18.46 // Global Period: XXX

➲ *CPT Assistant* Summer 93: 1, Nov 97: 4-5, Mar 98: 11, Nov 99: 5-6, Dec 00: 14, Feb 03: 15, Oct 03: 1, May 05: 1, Nov 05: 10; *CPT Changes: An Insider's View* 2000, 2003, 2004, 2005

Clinical Example

Under the care of the attending physician, either personally or by direct supervision, a 900 gram male 28 week gestation infant is admitted. The infant is examined and determined to have respiratory distress syndrome. The infant is intubated and placed on a ventilator. Umbilical artery and vein catheters are placed. Blood culture is obtained and antibiotics started. The infant is placed on continuous cardiovascular, respiratory and blood pressure monitoring. The mother's record is reviewed and she is interviewed for her history. A family history is obtained from the father. Arterial blood gases, X-ray, and laboratory results are reviewed. Surfactant is administered. Parents are counseled as to diagnoses, prognoses, and appropriate informed consent is obtained. Throughout the first 24 hours, the infant is examined repeatedly and arterial blood gases, X-rays, and laboratory values are evaluated repeatedly. This infant is given volume expansion and started on dopamine. An additional dose of surfactant is given. Medical records including history, physical assessment, plan orders, and progress notes are prepared. Parents are informed and counseled as to the infant's condition, progress and prognosis.

99296 Subsequent inpatient neonatal critical care, per day, for the evaluation and management of a critically ill neonate, 28 days of age or less

Work Value: 7.99 // Global Period: XXX

➲ *CPT Assistant* Summer 93: 1, Nov 97: 4-5, Mar 98: 11, Nov 99: 5-6, Dec 00: 14, Feb 03: 15, Oct 03: 1, Nov 05: 10; *CPT Changes: An Insider's View* 2000, 2003, 2004, 2005

Clinical Example

A 3-day-old infant is under the care and direct supervision of the attending physician. The infant remains intubated and on intermittent mandatory ventilation. The infant has both umbilical artery and view catheters in place and is on continuous cardiac, respiratory, and blood pressure monitoring. Blood pressure is being supported with dopamine. Hyperalimentation has been started. After evaluation, indomethacin has been started for a patent ductus arteriosus. Evaluation for intraventricular hemorrhage with ultrasound has been completed. A packed red blood cell transfusion is given. The infant is examined repeatedly and laboratory, X rays, and arterial blood gasses are repeatedly evaluated. The parents are informed and counseled as to the infant's condition and prognosis. Medical records are maintained including orders and progress notes. Fluids and ventilator changes are made frequently as required.

Continuing Intensive Care Services

99298 Subsequent intensive care, per day, for the evaluation and management of the recovering very low birth weight infant (present body weight less than 1500 g)

Work Value: 2.75 // Global Period: XXX

➲ *CPT Assistant* Nov 98: 2-3, Nov 99: 5-6, Aug 00: 4, Dec 00: 15, Oct 03: 2, May 05: 1, Nov 05: 10; *CPT Changes: An Insider's View* 2000, 2003

Clinical Example

A 1100-g, 30-week preterm infant is now 3 weeks of age and weighs 1200 g. The child was ventilated from birth and received two doses of surfactant. By 7 days of age, the neonate was extubated and is now on a nasal cannula of 1/4 L oxygen. His umbilical venous and arterial catheter were removed at 10 days of age. A percutaneous central venous line was then placed for total parenteral nutrition. Feedings began at 10 days of age and he is now receiving 75% of his total calorie requirement by the enteral route. He has been moved from a radiant warmer to an isolette for continued heat maintenance. He was maintained on antibiotics for the first 7 days of life. All cultures were subsequently negative. His initial ultrasound examination on day 3 detected a grade 1 subependymal bleed; a repeat study on day 7 showed progression into the ventricles with dilation on the right side. His most recent chest radiograph is compatible with mild chronic lung disease. He has completed a single short course of steroids. His first eye examination demonstrated grade 1 retinopathy of prematurity. The infant continues with recurrent episodes of apnea and was placed on caffeine therapy. His family lives 60 miles from the neonatal intensive care unit and visits 2-3 times weekly. A review of the child's flow sheet, discussion with the nursing staff, a complete physical examination, a review of laboratory and medical imaging data, and conversations with the family occur daily. The referring physician is updated by telephone twice a week.

Preservice

Preservice work includes obtaining and reviewing the results of any lab work and/or radiologic studies, reviewing the intensive care flow sheet and discussing the patient's status with the bedside nurse, and communicating with other professionals as appropriate.

Intraservice

Intraservice work includes performing a complete examination of the head, eyes, nose, mouth, chest, lungs, heart, abdomen, genitals, rectum, joints, spine, and extremities, and performing a neurologic appraisal of movement, reflexes, cranial nerves, and degree or arousal and reactivity. All attached monitors and tubes are checked for secure placement and proper function.

Postservice

Postservice work includes all coordination of care, documentation, and telephone calls with the patient, family members, or other health care professionals. Postservice also includes writing the daily total parenteral nutrition orders after recovery and/or writing new feeding orders, ordering daily laboratory and imaging studies as necessary, documenting care changes in the patient's chart and verbally with the nursing staff, speaking with the family in person or by telephone, and updating the referring physician.

99299 **Subsequent intensive care,** per day, for the evaluation and management of the recovering low birth weight infant (present body weight of 1500-2500 g)

Work Value: 2.50 // Global Period: XXX

➲ *CPT Assistant* Oct 03: 2, Nov 05: 10; *CPT Changes: An Insider's View* 2003

Clinical Example

A neonate, now weighing 2080 g, is 9 days of age. He was born at 35 weeks' gestation and weighed 2000 g. His mother presented to the hospital with a temperature of 103.5°F. Membranes had been ruptured for 6 hours. The fetal monitoring strip was nonreassuring with a tachycardia and persistent variable declarations. The mother received one dose of penicillin and delivery via cesarean section was performed. Cervical culture was positive for Group B streptococcus. The infant was flaccid at birth. Apgar scores were 2, 4, and 7 at 1, 5, and 10 minutes, respectively. The infant was intubated and needed 5 days of conventional ventilation. Chest X ray was consistent with pneumonia and the baby was started on a 10-day course of antibiotics. He was weaned to nasal continuous positive airway pressure on day 6 and nasal cannula oxygen on day 7. Hyperalimentation was begun on day 3 and gavage feedings on day 7. He currently is on nasal cannula oxygen (30%-½ l) and 50% total parenteral nutrition (TPN) through a peripherally inserted central catheter (PICC) line. There is no apnea but there are 2-3 brief desaturation episodes per day that are self-resolving. X ray results show improvement but are still not normal. He remains in an isolette on cardiorespiratory and oxygen saturation monitoring.

Preservice
Preservice work includes obtaining and reviewing the results of any lab work and/or radiologic studies, reviewing the care flow sheet and discussing the patient's status with the bedside nurse, and communicating with other health care professionals as appropriate.

Intraservice
Intraservice work includes performing a complete examination of the head, eyes, nose, mouth, chest, lungs, heart, abdomen, genitals, rectum, joints, spine, and extremities, and performing a neurologic appraisal of movement, reflexes, cranial nerves, and degree of arousal and activity. All attached monitors and tubes are checked for secure placement and proper function.

Postservice
Postservice work includes all coordination of care, documentation, and telephone calls with the patient, family members, or other health care professionals. Postservice also includes writing the daily TPN orders after recovery and/or writing new feeding orders, ordering daily laboratory and imaging studies as necessary, documenting care changes in the patient's chart and verbally with the nursing staff, speaking with the family in person or by telephone, and updating the referring physician.

99300 Subsequent intensive care, per day, for the evaluation and management of the recovering infant (present body weight of 2501-5000 g)

Work Value: 2.40 // Global Period: XXX

➲ *CPT Changes: An Insider's View* 2006

Clinical Example
A 3500-g neonate is recovering from bacteremia and pneumonia following intrapartum acquisition of Group B streptococcus organisms from his mother. He had severe pneumonia, pulmonary hypertension, neutropenia, thrombocytopenia, and septic shock requiring prolonged mechanical ventilation including nitric oxide, oscillatory ventilation, surfactant, and large pressor doses to maintain perfusion and blood pressure. He is now on low-flow nasal cannula oxygen. His umbilical lines have been removed and a peripherally inserted central catheter (PICC) line is being placed to complete antibiotic therapy and for use in providing bridging parenteral nutrition until he is tolerating all enteral feeds.

Preservice
In the morning, the patient's chart is reviewed and the flowsheet viewed and discussed with the bedside nurse. The online laboratory results are obtained from yesterday as well as early morning values that are back in the chart. Any recent radiographs are reviewed through the picture archiving and communication system available in the intensive care unit. His complete blood count is reviewed to assure continued recovery of the low platelet and neutrophil count.

Intraservice
The patient is examined with particular attention paid to overall cardiovascular stability, neurological function, pulmonary status post extubation, and gastrointestinal function. Comprehensive evaluations of these organ systems are completed. The PICC line site is carefully evaluated for any signs of cellulitis. The lungs are carefully evaluated for any evidence of postextubation atelectasis. The gastrointestinal tract is evaluated for any sign of mucosal or transmural injury leading to feeding intolerance, malabsorption, or perforation. The patient is evaluated neurologically to determine whether physical therapy or occupational therapy would be indicated. The patient is visited throughout the day and evening to ensure that he continues to tolerate feedings and that there has been no

change in his pulmonary, cardiovascular, or neurologic function.

Postservice

The results of the history, laboratory, and imaging work are discussed at the bedside with the resident, nurse practitioner, bedside primary nurse, nutritionist, social worker, and respiratory therapist. The plan of care is agreed to and discussions around the opportunity to transport the patient back to the home nursery and/or the potential home care needs for the child are conducted. After bedside rounds, the patient's condition and plans are discussed with the patient's parents and extended family. Later in the day, any obtained laboratory work or medical imaging studies are checked and any additional orders are completed.

Coding Tip for 99298-99300

Codes 99298-99300 are used to report services subsequent to the day of admission provided by a physician directing the continuing intensive care of the low birth weight (LBW, 1500-2500 g present body weight) infant, very low birth weight (VLBW, less than 1500 g present body weight) infant, or normal weight (2501-5000 g present body weight) newborn who do not meet the definition of critically ill but continue to require intensive observation, frequent interventions, and other intensive services.

Nursing Facility Services

Initial Nursing Facility Care

New or Established Patient

99304 Initial nursing facility care, per day, for the evaluation and management of a patient which requires these three key components:

- **A detailed or comprehensive history;**
- **A detailed or comprehensive examination; and**
- **Medical decision making that is straightforward or of low complexity.**

Counseling and/or coordination of care with other providers or agencies are provided consistent with the nature of the problem(s) and the patient's and/or family's needs.

Usually, the problem(s) requiring admission are of low severity.

Work Value: 1.20 // Global Period: XXX

➲ *CPT Changes: An Insider's View* 2006

Clinical Example

An 80-year-old Alzheimer's patient with associated bowel and bladder incontinence plus controlled glaucoma, hypertension, and moderate osteoarthritis arrives for an admission visit because he is no longer able to be maintained at an assisted living facility and requires nursing facility placement. He is presently on a topical eye medication, a mild analgesic, and a cholinesterase inhibitor but no psychotropics.

Preservice

Preservice work includes preparing to see the patient, procuring and reviewing previous medical records, and communicating with facility professionals as appropriate.

Intraservice

Intraservice work includes obtaining a detailed history of dietary and fluid intake; reviewing the patient's chronic but stable vision, mild hearing loss, general arthritis, and chronic constipation; reviewing medications; and gathering a health history from the patient's wife, the previous assisted living staff, and his previous medical care providers. Intraservice also includes performing a detailed physical exam and noting vital signs; inspecting the skin for ulceration or pre-ulceration; noting oral hygiene; performing cardiovascular, pulmonary, abdominal, and genitourinary exams, paying special attention to any evidence of obstructive urinary retention and fecal impaction; and assessing the patient's ability to communicate and gait safety.

Postservice

Postservice work includes communicating with the facility regarding diagnostic findings and the postservice coordination of care, documentation, and interaction with facility health care professionals associated with the delivery of care to this patient until the next face-to-face physician encounter. Discussion with family and/or surrogate decision maker regarding preferred intensity of care/do not resuscitate is also included.

99305 Initial nursing facility care, per day, for the evaluation and management of a patient which requires these three key components:

- **A comprehensive history;**
- **A comprehensive examination; and**
- **Medical decision making of moderate complexity.**

Counseling and/or coordination of care with other providers or agencies are provided consistent with the nature of the problem(s) and the patient's and/or family's needs.

Usually, the problem(s) requiring admission are of moderate severity.

Work Value: 1.61 // Global Period: XXX

➲ *CPT Changes: An Insider's View* 2006

Clinical Example

An 88-year-old, cognitively intact patient who suffered a hip fracture from a mechanical fall while living at home presents for a skilled nursing facility (SNF) admission. While in the hospital for treatment of the fracture, he developed a urinary tract infection and a stage 1 heel pressure ulcer. Prior to the fracture, he was known to have multiple health problems including controlled chronic heart failure and hypertension, chronic constipation, benign prostatic hyperplasia, osteoarthritis, old cerebrovascular accident, and depression. He was also known to have peripheral perfusion compromise.

Preservice

Preservice work includes preparing to see the patient; procuring and reviewing the hospital records, labs and diagnostic findings; and communicating with facility professionals as appropriate.

Intraservice

The SNF admission includes a review of the patient's intake and hydration status; the postoperative course and initial rehabilitation results; the recent urosepsis and the development of the pressure ulcer; plus an evaluation of the status of the patient's multiple chronic health problems. A comprehensive physical exam is performed to assess the recent surgical site, the potential return of function, the need for the continued indwelling catheter, and the status of the pressure sore. Additionally, an examination of the patient's vision and hearing (especially in relation to rehabilitation potential), overall cardiovascular status in regard to stamina, plus a general abdominal, genitourinary, mental status, and neurological examination are performed and documented. A multidisciplinary plan of care is developed that includes physical therapy and occupational therapy services, initiation of a pressure wound care program, adjustments in diet, weaning off of the catheter, retitration of medications, evaluation of dietary and fluid intake, and monitoring for mental status changes due to changes in environment.

Postservice

Postservice work includes communicating with the patient's orthopedist and with the facility regarding diagnostic findings and the postservice coordination of care, documentation, and interaction with facility health care professionals associated with the delivery of care to this patient until the next face-to-face physician encounter. Discussion with family and/or surrogate decision maker regarding preferred intensity of care/do not resuscitate is also included.

99306 Initial nursing facility care, per day, for the evaluation and management of a patient, which requires these three key components:

- **A comprehensive history;**
- **A comprehensive examination; and**
- **Medical decision making of high complexity.**

Counseling and/or coordination of care with other providers or agencies are provided consistent with the nature of the problem(s) and the patient's and/or family's needs.

Usually, the problem(s) requiring admission are of high severity.

Work Value: 2.01 // Global Period: XXX

➲ *CPT Changes: An Insider's View* 2006

Clinical Example

A 72-year-old diabetic patient who previously lived at the same skilled nursing facility (SNF) is now being admitted posthospitalization to the SNF for aspiration pneumonitis, blood sugars running in the 300+ range, chronic heart failure, and delirium associated with an ongoing history of dementia. She also suffers from chronic atrial fibrillation, constipation, stress incontinence, and a recent vertebral compression fracture associated with osteoporosis. She returns on intravenous (IV) hydration, antibiotics, oxygen, and new psychotropics. She also requires continued titration of her diabetes and diuretic regimen, control of her pain (which is reducing her inspiratory effort), rehabilitation of swallowing and respiratory function, and stabilization of her cardiovascular and mental status.

Preservice

Preservice work includes preparing to see the patient; procuring and reviewing the hospital records, labs and diagnostic findings; and communicating with facility professionals as appropriate.

Intraservice

The SNF admission includes a comprehensive history including a review of the hospital records, labs, and diagnostic findings; the patient's intake and hydration status; plus a review of the sliding scale insulin and psychotropic regimen. Additionally, there is a discussion with the patient's formal and informal care providers regarding a symptom review of the patient's multiple, still unstable, health problems. The comprehensive physical exam involved assessment of the current status of cardiopulmonary function, swallowing and mobility function, and cognitive function. Lab review includes assessing oxygenation, hydration, white count, cardiac rhythm, and glucose level trends. Orders are initiated for oxygen, IV fluids, antibiotics, pain control, and rehabilitation and diagnostic testing to assess status. Also, included in the multidisciplinary plan of care is physical therapy, respiratory therapy, and speech services; titration off of the insulin sliding scale; adjustments in diet and hydration; retitration of psychotropic and analgesic medications; and monitoring for mental status changes.

Postservice

Postservice work includes communicating with the facility regarding diagnostic findings and the postservice coordination of care, documentation, and interaction with facility health care professionals associated with the delivery of care to this patient until the next face-to-face physician encounter. Discussion with family and/or surrogate decision maker regarding preferred intensity of care/do not resuscitate is also included.

Subsequent Nursing Facility Care

99307 Subsequent nursing facility care, per day, for the evaluation and management of a patient, which requires at least two of these three key components:

- **A problem focused interval history;**
- **A problem focused examination;**
- **Straightforward medical decision making.**

Counseling and/or coordination of care with other providers or agencies are provided consistent with the nature of the problem(s) and the patient's and/or family's needs.

Usually, the patient is stable, recovering, or improving.

Work Value: 0.60 // Global Period: XXX

➲ *CPT Changes: An Insider's View* 2006

Clinical Example

An 88-year-old demented, nondiabetic patient with a previously evaluated stage 4 sacral pressure sore with peripheral, localized inflammation is seen in follow-up to evaluate the wound's response to the present plan of care.

Preservice

Preservice work includes preparing to see the patient, reviewing records of previously attempted interventions, communicating with facility professionals as appropriate, and reviewing the suggestions of the facility dietitian and consultant pharmacist.

Intraservice

The visit includes an interval history that reveals ongoing poor dietary intake and urinary incontinence in a patient who cannot cooperate in pressure relief activities because of cognitive impairment. Intraservice also includes a focused physical exam that reveals an improving lesion with no peripheral inflammation and no evidence of systemic involvement. The topical regimen is altered, a new nutritional program is ordered, and a support surface is authorized.

Postservice

Postservice work includes communicating with facility staff regarding the coordination and documentation of care as indicated associated with the delivery of care to this patient until the next face-to-face physician encounter.

99308 Subsequent nursing facility care, per day, for the evaluation and management of a patient, which requires at least two of these three key components:

- **An expanded problem focused interval history;**
- **An expanded problem focused examination;**
- **Medical decision making of low complexity.**

Counseling and/or coordination of care with other providers or agencies are provided consistent with the nature of the problem(s) and the patient's and/or family's needs.

Usually, the patient is responding inadequately to therapy or has developed a minor complication.

Work Value: 1.00 // Global Period: XXX

➲ *CPT Changes: An Insider's View* 2006

Clinical Example

During a nursing facility visit for the evaluation and management of an acute urinary tract infection (UTI) in a 35-year-old male with multiple sclerosis with an indwelling catheter, the patient presents with a new intermittent hematuria and fever.

Preservice

Preservice work includes preparing to see the patient, reviewing records, and communicating with other facility professionals as appropriate.

Intraservice

The visit includes an expanded history review including intake and hydration information, discussion of the suprapubic-localizing discomfort and muscle spasm, and a psychosocial review of the patient's coping with his underlying disease. An expanded physical examination notes no evidence of dehydration, further gross hematuria, or focal neurological findings, but increased depression is detected. After necessary labs are ordered, he is treated for the UTI and started on an antidepressant.

Postservice

Postservice work includes communicating with facility social services and activities programming, communicating with the nursing facility regarding titration of the antidepressant, reviewing the confirming diagnostic lab data, and following up on antibiotic effectiveness. Postservice also includes all coordination of care, documentation, and interaction with facility health care professionals associated with the delivery of care to this patient until the next face-to-face physician encounter.

99309 Subsequent nursing facility care, per day, for the evaluation and management of a patient, which requires at least two of these three key components:

- **A detailed interval history;**
- **A detailed examination;**
- **Medical decision making of moderate complexity.**

Counseling and/or coordination of care with other providers or agencies are provided consistent with the nature of the problem(s) and the patient's and/or family's needs.

Usually, the patient has developed a significant complication or a significant new problem.

Work Value: 1.42 // Global Period: XXX

➲ *CPT Changes: An Insider's View* 2006

Clinical Example

A 72-year-old patient with chronic obstructive pulmonary disease (COPD), hypertension, peripheral vascular disease, gastroesophageal reflux disease (GERD), chronic constipation, bladder stress incontinence, osteoarthritis, osteoporosis, dementia, and hypothyroidism on more than nine medications is seen for interval disease management of her chronic health issues and also to evaluate the status of a recent upper respiratory infection (URI), increased constipation, new behavioral changes, and a skin tear that has occurred since the last medical visit.

Preservice

Preservice work includes preparing to see the patient; reviewing the telephone orders associated with the recently reported URI; reviewing the changes in the dietary, bowel, and psychotropic regimens; and reviewing the treatment of the noninfected skin tear reported by the nursing staff since last medical visit. Preservice also includes communicating with facility professionals as appropriate.

Intraservice

The visit includes a detailed interval history review of each involved organ system that has an acute or active medical problem. This includes the status of the recent URI complicating her underlying COPD, any associated cardiovascular complication or decline, the status of the GERD, bowel and bladder function, and the recent change in mental status associated with the patient's dementia. Also included in the history is

1) a review of the patient's multiple medications for indication and efficacy;

2) recent lab and diagnostic data ordered to evaluate her recent respiratory compromise;

3) the updated nursing plan of care. A detailed physical exam reveals a 'frailer' more confused patient with normal vitals, resting comfortably in bed with a dry oral mucosa, 'clear' lung fields, regular rhythm with no change in her AS murmur, no pedal edema, a vaguely tender abdomen, no lateralizing neurological signs, and a noninflamed skin tear.

Postservice

Postservice work includes evaluating additional diagnostic testing to determine the patient's hydration and pulmonary status and further changes in the patient's psychotropic regimen, and communicating with the facility staff. Postservice also includes all coordination of care, documentation, and interaction with facility health care professionals associated with the delivery of care to this patient until the next face-to-face physician encounter.

99310 Subsequent nursing facility care, per day, for the evaluation and management of a patient, which requires at least two of these three key components:

- **A comprehensive interval history;**
- **A comprehensive examination;**
- **Medical decision making of high complexity.**

Counseling and/or coordination of care with other providers or agencies are provided consistent with the nature of the problem(s) and the patient's and/or family's needs.

The patient may be unstable or may have developed a significant new problem requiring immediate physician attention.

Work Value: 1.77 // Global Period: XXX

➲ *CPT Changes: An Insider's View* **2006**

Clinical Example

A 69-year-old, long-time resident of a nursing facility with a long history of multiinfarct dementia, non-insulin-dependent diabetes mellitus, hypertension, and chronic renal insufficiency develops an acute decline in mental status with decreased intake and vague right-sided weakness. The family requests that she not be transferred to the hospital but receive treatment at the facility. Her blood pressure is 188/102, pulse 92/regular, and respirations are 20/minutes off oxygen. Physical examination reveals a dry mucosa and decreased skin turgor, no cyanosis, reduced lung sounds, no pedal or sacral edema, a soft, nondistended abdomen, and a slight right hemiparesis. Lab values drawn just prior to visit reveal blood glucose 352, Na 152, BUN 78, creatinine 2.8, Hct 32, Hb10.1, a white blood cell count of 18, oxygen saturation of 87% on room air, and a portable chest X ray that "cannot rule out" left lower lobe pneumonia.

Preservice

Preservice work includes preparing to see the patient, reviewing the medical record and previously ordered diagnostic labs, and communicating with facility professionals as appropriate.

Intraservice

The visit includes a comprehensive history including the evaluation of hydration and intake, ability to swallow, cardiopulmonary status, abdominal bowel and bladder function, mental status, and sensorimotor function. The multifactorial etiologies and their effect on multiple, additional comorbidities require a comprehensive physical examination involving virtually every organ system. The resultant multidisciplinary care planning includes intravenous hydration and antibiotic therapy; nursing instructions regarding the monitoring of respiratory, mental, functional, and diabetic status; a respiratory therapy and physical therapy assessment with treatment as indicated; and further lab monitoring to track the effectiveness of the treatment.

Postservice

Postservice work includes evaluating additionally ordered lab and diagnostic testing, communicating with the facility to adjust interventions as indicated, discussing with the patient's family updating the patient's end of life issues, coordinating all care, writing documentation, and interacting with facility health care professionals associated with the delivery of care to this patient until the next face-to-face physician encounter.

Nursing Facility Discharge Services

99315 Nursing facility discharge day management; 30 minutes or less

Work Value: 1.13 // Global Period: XXX

➲ *CPT Assistant* **Nov 97: 5-6, Sep 98: 5, May 02: 19, Nov 02: 11, May 05: 1**

Clinical Example

This is the final nursing facility day for a 72-year-old female with community acquired pneumonia who spent two days at an acute level and then transferred to skilled nursing unit with the need for continued IV antibiotic, breathing treatments and inability to care for herself. She is improving and able to switch to oral antibiotics. The discharge history and exam are problem focused, the medical decision making straight forward and the patient requires a written prescription for antibiotic, and simple instructions for medication, follow-up and complications to be alert to. A brief chart note and short written or dictated discharge summary is prepared. Approximate physician time of service is 20 minutes.

Intraservice

The nursing facility discharge day management codes are to be used to report the total duration of time spent by a physician for the final nursing facility discharge of a patient. The codes include, as appropriate, final examination of the patient, discussion of the nursing facility stay, even if the time spent by the physician on that date is not continuous. Instructions for continuing care to all relevant caregivers, and preparation of discharge records, prescriptions and referral forms.

99316 Nursing facility discharge day management; more than 30 minutes

Work Value: 1.50 // Global Period: XXX

➔ *CPT Assistant* Nov 97: 5-6, Sep 98: 5, May 02: 19, Nov 02: 11

Clinical Example

This is the final nursing facility day for an 84-year-old male who entered the nursing facility after suffering a cerebrovascular accident with hemiparesis, complicating diabetes (which now requires insulin management), hypertension, and a prior myocardial infarction with prior congestive heart failure. A gastrostomy feeding tube was placed. The discharge day history and exam are extended to verify that all systems are stable and that medical decision making is moderate. The home health agency and the patient's family will be involved with home care with physical and occupational therapy visits and periodic nursing assessments. Multiple medications and insulin instructions are prescribed. Prescriptions must be phoned to the local pharmacy and separate written prescriptions prepared for a mail-away pharmacy. The home health agency referral sheet, a discharge note, a lengthy discharge summary, instructions to the nursing staff, and complex verbal and written instructions to family are prepared. Approximate physician time of service is 50 minutes.

Intraservice

The nursing facility discharge day management codes are to be used to report the total duration of time spent by a physician for the final nursing facility discharge of a patient. The codes include, as appropriate, the final examination of the patient and discussion of the nursing facility stay, even if the time spent by the physician on that date is not continuous. Providing instructions for continuing care to all relevant caregivers, and preparing discharge records, prescriptions, and referral forms are also included.

Other Nursing Facility Services

99318 Evaluation and management of a patient involving an annual nursing facility assessment, which requires these three key components:

- **A detailed interval history;**
- **A comprehensive examination; and**
- **Medical decision making that is of low to moderate complexity.**

Counseling and/or coordination of care with other providers or agencies are provided consistent with the nature of the problem(s) and the patient's and/or family's needs.

Usually, the patient is stable, recovering, or improving.

Work Value: 1.20 // Global Period: XXX

➔ *CPT Changes: An Insider's View* 2006

Clinical Example

An annual nursing facility history, physical exam and MDS/RAI evaluation for a two-year nursing facility resident who is an 84-year-old female with multiple chronic health problems, including stable controlled hypertension, chronic constipation, osteoarthritis, and moderated stable dementia.

Preservice

Preservice work includes preparing to see the patient, procuring previous medical records over the past year, and communicating with facility professionals as appropriate.

Intraservice

Intraservice work includes reviewing the interval history for the occurrence and resolution of intercurrent episodes of illness or injury and for signs and symptoms of progression of the chronic conditions that justify continued nursing facility services. (A review of systems may include an assessment of dietary and fluid intake, noting any dental concerns or changes in appetite; a review of worsening sensory impairments such as vision or hearing loss; changes in functional level, especially related to mobility or continence, that might be amenable to therapy; a medication review with attention to the accumulation of therapies no longer needed and that screening tests for toxicity, side-effects, and efficacy have been performed; and a review of any noted behavioral changes or changes in affect.) Intraservice also includes ensuring compliance with routine specialty follow-up care and ensuring that health maintenance measures have been provided; performing a comprehensive physical exam, taking care to note vital signs, including the patient's weight over the previous year; carefully inspecting the skin for ulceration; noting any evidence of sensory impairments and the status of oral hygiene; performing cardiovascular, pulmonary, abdominal, and genitorurinary exams, paying special attention to evidence of urinary retention and fecal impaction; assessing the patient's ability to communicate and gait safety; performing short-form evaluations of interval changes in cognitive functioning and a screen for affective changes as indicated; and assessing the patient's and family's goals for care and their preferences for medical interventions in light of the prognosis derived from the review of the chart, the interval history, and physical examination.

Postservice

Postservice work includes communicating with the family and the facility regarding diagnostic findings and the postservice coordination of care, documentation, and interaction with the facility health care professionals associated with the delivery of care to this patient until the next face-to-face physician encounter. A reassessment of the advance directives and updates of contact information for surrogate decision makers is included.

Coding Tip for 99318

Do not report code 99318 on the same date of service as nursing facility services codes 99304-99316.

Domiciliary, Rest Home (eg, Boarding Home), or Custodial Care Services

New Patient

99324 Domiciliary or rest home visit for the evaluation and management of a new patient, which requires these three key components:

- **A problem focused history;**
- **A problem focused examination; and**
- **Straightforward medical decision making.**

Counseling and/or coordination of care with other providers or agencies are provided consistent with the nature of the problem(s) and the patient's and/or family's needs.

Usually, the presenting problem(s) are of low severity. Physicians typically spend 20 minutes with the patient and/or family or caregiver.

Work Value: 1.01 // Global Period: XXX

➲ *CPT Assistant* Jan 06: 1; *CPT Changes: An Insider's View* 2006

Clinical Example

An 84-year-old male with advanced osteoarthritis, which has rendered him wheelchair-bound, complains of a rash and itching involving the plantar surface of the foot.

Preservice

Preservice work includes preparing to see the patient, reviewing records, and communicating with other professionals.

Intraservice

Intraservice work includes the time in which the physician obtains the history, performs an evaluation, and counsels the patient.

Postservice

Postservice work includes arranging for further services, reviewing the results of studies, and communicating further with the patient, the patient's family, and other health care professionals (including providing written and telephone reports).

99325 Domiciliary or rest home visit for the evaluation and management of a new patient, which requires these three key components:

- **An expanded problem focused history;**
- **An expanded problem focused examination; and**
- **Medical decision making of low complexity.**

Counseling and/or coordination of care with other providers or agencies are provided consistent with the nature of the problem(s) and the patient's and/or family's needs.

Usually, the presenting problem(s) are of moderate severity. Physicians typically spend 30 minutes with the patient and/or family or caregiver.

Work Value: 1.52 // Global Period: XXX

➲ ***CPT Assistant*** **Jan 06: 1;** ***CPT Changes: An Insider's View*** **2006**

Clinical Example

An 84-year-old male with advanced osteoarthritis and peripheral vascular disease, which has rendered him wheelchair-bound, is followed for vascular insufficiency ulcers that have healed after treatment with custom shoes and topical wound care.

Preservice

Preservice work involves preparing to see the patient, reviewing records, and communicating with other professionals.

Intraservice

Intraservice work includes the time in which the physician obtains the history, performs an evaluation, and counsels the patient.

Postservice

Postservice work includes arranging for further services, reviewing the results of studies, and communicating further with the patient, the patient's family, and other health care professionals (including providing written and telephone reports).

99326 Domiciliary or rest home visit for the evaluation and management of a new patient, which requires these three key components:

- **A detailed history;**
- **A detailed examination; and**
- **Medical decision making of moderate complexity.**

Counseling and/or coordination of care with other providers or agencies are provided consistent with the nature of the problem(s) and the patient's and/or family's needs.

Usually, the presenting problem(s) are of moderate to high severity. Physicians typically spend 45 minutes with the patient and/or family or caregiver.

Work Value: 2.27 // Global Period: XXX

➲ ***CPT Assistant*** **Jan 06: 1;** ***CPT Changes: An Insider's View*** **2006**

Clinical Example

A 77-year-old female with aortic valve replacement is maintained on warfarin. Her past medical history includes atrial fibrillation and insulin dependent diabetes. She has had several falls recently. Anti-coagulation and diabetic management have been in good control through close monitoring by the nurse in the assisted living facility.

Preservice

Preservice work includes preparing to see the patient, reviewing records, and communicating with other professionals.

Intraservice

Intraservice work includes the time in which the physician obtains the history, performs an evaluation, and counsels the patient.

Postservice

Postservice work includes arranging for further services, reviewing the results of studies, and communicating further with the patient, the patient's family, and other health care professionals (including providing written and telephone reports).

99327 Domiciliary or rest home visit for the evaluation and management of a new patient, which requires these three key components:

- **A comprehensive history;**
- **A comprehensive examination; and**
- **Medical decision making of moderate complexity.**

Counseling and/or coordination of care with other providers or agencies are provided consistent with the nature of the problem(s) and the patient's and/or family's needs.

Usually, the presenting problem(s) are of high severity. Physicians typically spend 60 minutes with the patient and/or family or caregiver.

Work Value: 3.03 // Global Period: XXX

➔ ***CPT Assistant* Jan 06: 1; *CPT Changes: An Insider's View* 2006**

Clinical Example

A family refers a 73-year-old female patient to a physician for evaluation and management. Despite having been moved to an assisted living facility, she has had progressive weight loss, social withdrawal and intermittent agitation over the past two months. She refuses to leave her room for visits to her physicians. Her meals are brought to her, but she eats sparingly. The patient has been followed through with telephonic conversations between the nurse and the primary care physician, who has been ordering psychotropic medications to control her behavior, and a cardiologist for management of her ischemic heart disease, for which she takes four medications. She has seen neither physician for over a year.

Preservice

Preservice work includes preparing to see the patient, reviewing records, and communicating with other professionals.

Intraservice

Intraservice work includes the time in which the physician obtains the history, performs an evaluation, and counsels the patient.

Postservice

Postservice work includes arranging for further services, reviewing the results of studies, and communicating further with the patient, the patient'ss family, and other professionals (including providing written and telephone reports).

99328 Domiciliary or rest home visit for the evaluation and management of a new patient, which requires these three key components:

- **A comprehensive history;**
- **A comprehensive examination; and**
- **Medical decision making of high complexity.**

Counseling and/or coordination of care with other providers or agencies are provided consistent with the nature of the problem(s) and the patient's and/or family's needs.

Usually, the patient is unstable or has developed a significant new problem requiring immediate physician attention. Physicians typically spend 75 minutes with the patient and/or family or caregiver.

Work Value: 3.78 // Global Period: XXX

➲ *CPT Assistant* Jan 06: 1; *CPT Changes: An Insider's View* 2006

Clinical Example

An 83-year-old male presents with a history of schizophrenia and progressive neurologic degeneration with dementia, emphysema from smoking, osteoporosis with vertebral fractures and kyphosis, non-insulin-dependent diabetes mellitus, and osteoarthritis of the back, hips and knees. He now has a fever of 101.5 degrees a productive cough, tachypnea, and delirium. Oral intake has dropped sharply for the past two days. His family does not want him to be hospitalized, accepts that this may be a terminal event, but wants to take all available measures to help him recover at the group home. The resident counselor is willing to participate in providing intravenous therapies.

Preservice

Preservice work includes preparing to see the patient, reviewing records, and communicating with other professionals.

Intraservice

Intraservice work includes the time in which the physician obtains the history, performs an evaluation, and counsels the patient.

Postservice

Postservice work includes arranging for further services, reviewing the results of studies, and communicating further with the patient, the patient's family, and other health care professionals (including providing written and telephone reports).

Established Patient

99334 Domiciliary or rest home visit for the evaluation and management of an established patient, which requires at least two of these three key components:

- **A problem focused interval history;**
- **A problem focused examination;**
- **Straightforward medical decision making.**

Counseling and/or coordination of care with other providers or agencies are provided consistent with the nature of the problem(s) and the patient's and/or family's needs.

Usually, the presenting problem(s) are self-limited or minor. Physicians typically spend 15 minutes with the patient and/or family or caregiver.

Work Value: 0.76 // Global Period: XXX

➲ *CPT Assistant* Jan 06: 1; *CPT Changes: An Insider's View* 2006

Clinical Example

A 74-year-old male with hypertension and peripheral vascular disease has lived in a board and care home for two years following a stroke, resulting in right-sided hemiparesis. The patient is seen routinely for hypertension monitoring, medication refills and preventive care.

Preservice

Preservice work includes preparing to see the patient, reviewing records, and communicating with other professionals.

Intraservice

Intraservice work includes the time in which the physician obtains the history, performs an evaluation, and counsels the patient.

Postservice

Postservice work includes arranging for further services, reviewing the results of studies, and communicating further with the patient, the patient's family, and other health care professionals (including providing written and telephone reports).

99335 Domiciliary or rest home visit for the evaluation and management of an established patient, which requires at least two of these three key components:

- **An expanded problem focused interval history;**
- **An expanded problem focused examination;**
- **Medical decision making of low complexity.**

Counseling and/or coordination of care with other providers or agencies are provided consistent with the nature of the problem(s) and the patient's and/or family's needs.

Usually, the presenting problem(s) are of low to moderate severity. Physicians typically spend 25 minutes with the patient and/or family or caregiver.

Work Value: 1.26 // Global Period: XXX

➲ *CPT Assistant* Jan 06: 1; *CPT Changes: An Insider's View* 2006

Clinical Example

A 78-year-old male with Alzheimer's disease was difficult to control for two weeks due to agitation caused by hallucinations. Psychotropic medications were initiated with partial resolution of the agitation. The aides at the assisted living facility assure his safety, but are worried that he might fall.

Preservice

Preservice work includes preparing to see the patient, reviewing records, and communicating with other professionals.

Intraservice

Intraservice work includes the time in which the physician obtains the history, performs an evaluation, and counsels the patient.

Postservice

Postservice work includes arranging for further services, reviewing the results of studies, and communicating further with the patient, the patient's family, and other health care professionals (including providing written and telephone reports).

99336 Domiciliary or rest home visit for the evaluation and management of an established patient, which requires at least two of these three key components:

- **A detailed interval history;**
- **A detailed examination;**
- **Medical decision making of moderate complexity.**

Counseling and/or coordination of care with other providers or agencies are provided consistent with the nature of the problem(s) and the patient's and/or family's needs.

Usually, the presenting problem(s) are of moderate to high severity. Physicians typically spend 40 minutes with the patient and/or family or caregiver.

Work Value: 2.02 // Global Period: XXX

➲ *CPT Assistant* Jan 06: 1; *CPT Changes: An Insider's View* 2006

Clinical Example

A 78-year-old male patient with insulin-dependent diabetes mellitus and chronic obstructive pulmonary disease, requiring continuous home oxygen, complains of worsening symptoms of peripheral vascular disease. He is becoming progressively more dependent on assistance with transfers and bathing. He complains of increasing left leg pain at night due to nocturnal ischemic claudication.

Preservice

Preservice work includes preparing to see the patient, reviewing records, and communicating with other professionals.

Intraservice

Intraservice work includes the time in which the physician obtains the history, performs an evaluation, and counsels the patient.

Postservice

Postservice work includes arranging for further services, reviewing the results of studies, and communicating further with the patient, the patient's family, and other health care professionals (including providing written and telephone reports).

99337 Domiciliary or rest home visit for the evaluation and management of an established patient, which requires at least two of these three key components:

- **A comprehensive interval history;**
- **A comprehensive examination;**
- **Medical decision making of moderate to high complexity.**

Counseling and/or coordination of care with other providers or agencies are provided consistent with the nature of the problem(s) and the patient's and/or family's needs.

Usually, the presenting problem(s) are of moderate to high severity. The patient may be unstable or may have developed a significant new problem requiring immediate physician attention. Physicians typically spend 60 minutes with the patient and/or family or caregiver.

Work Value: 3.03 // Global Period: XXX

➲ *CPT Assistant* Jan 06: 1; *CPT Changes: An Insider's View* 2006

Clinical Example

An 89-year-old female with a history of multi-infarct dementia due to hypertension and insulin-dependent diabetes mellitus. The patient's chronic renal insufficiency has worsened with difficult to control hypertension and progressively more fatigue, but her nephrologist is reluctant to offer dialysis. Approximately one year ago, she became wheelchair bound and non-verbal and for four months has been unable to feed herself. Last month, she began to "pocket" her medications and solid foods in her cheek, and was found to spit them out later. She has lost weight over the past three months, associated with several episodes of hypoglycemia and she recently developed a stage 3 pressure ulcer at her coccyx. Her family has been undecided as to resuscitation status.

Preservice

Preservice work includes preparing to see the patient, reviewing records, and communicating with other professionals.

Intraservice

Intraservice work includes the time in which the physician obtains the history, performs an evaluation, and counsels the patient.

Postservice

Postservice work includes arranging for further services, reviewing the results of studies, and communicating further with the patient, the patient's family, and other health care professionals (including providing written and telephone reports).

Coding Tip for 99324-99337

Codes 99324-99337 are used to report evaluation and management services in a facility that provides room, board, and other personal assistance services, generally on a long-term basis. These codes are also used to report evaluation and management services in an assisted living facility.

Domiciliary, Rest Home (eg, Assisted Living Facility), or Home Care Plan Oversight Services

99339 Individual physician supervision of a patient (patient not present) in home, domiciliary or rest home (eg, assisted living facility) requiring complex and multidisciplinary care modalities involving regular physician development and/or revision of care plans, review of subsequent reports of patient status, review of related laboratory and other studies, communication (including telephone calls) for purposes of assessment or care decisions with health care professional(s), family member(s), surrogate decision maker(s) (eg, legal guardian) and/or key caregiver(s) involved in patient's care, integration of new information into the medical treatment plan and/or adjustment of medical therapy, within a calendar month; 15-29 minutes

Work Value: 1.25 // Global Period: XXX

➔ ***CPT Assistant*** **Jan 06: 1;** ***CPT Changes: An Insider's View*** **2006**

Clinical Example

Pediatrics: A 21-year-old male with Down syndrome is transitioning from home care and public special education to a sheltered work program operated by the community service agency. He is moderately mentally retarded with ongoing medical problems including hypothyroidism and sensorineural hearing loss. Over the past two months his behavior has become progressively disruptive. The care plan previously developed for him included assessment of active medical, educational/vocational problems with ongoing adjustments made based on feedback from family members, health care professionals and service providers. His primary care physician (internal medicine, family physician, pediatrician) delivers primary care services and manages and coordinates care plan activities. The physicians typical ongoing care plan oversight activities will include: review of reports including a new audiology assessment and endocrine consultation report; a telephone call to the audiologist regarding results of the most recent hearing assessment and recommendations to provide hearing amplification to the patient; completion of medical forms for the vocational program, listing medical problems, general cognitive and physical abilities, and recommendations for behavior management; discussion by telephone with family members of the patient's recent appetite and weight gain noted after the patient begins a new behavior medication and a subsequent call to the psychiatric nurse practitioner at the mental health center who recommends a dose change and a dietary consultation; review of endocrine recommendations to increase the thyroid dosage, with an ensuing phone call to the family and the pharmacy to prescribe a different dose form of levothyroxine sodium. The physician documents the relevant information in the record that summarizes the above activities.

Geriatrics: The patient is an 84-year-old female who lives with her daughter. She has advanced Alzheimer's disease and is dependent in all instrumental activities of daily living (IADL) and most activities of daily living (ADL). She is becoming increasingly agitated. She could not cooperate sufficiently to be brought to the office for evaluation so a home visit was made (reported separately). Over the next month the physician will need to review the care of the patient assessing progress and the effects of the interventions. This requires contact with the caregiver to review impacts and to support the caregiver to avoid hospitalization and the likely cycle of delirium and nursing home placement that would result. Between 15 and 29 minutes are spent and documented in these activities.

Preservice

Preservice work includes reviewing subsequent reports of patient status, related laboratory reports, and other studies.

Intraservice
Intraservice work includes communicating with health care professional(s), family member(s), and/or key caregivers(s) for the purposes of assessment or care decisions; and developing or revising a care plan.

Postservice
Postservice work includes integrating new information into the patient chart.

Preventive Medicine Services

New Patient

99381 Initial comprehensive preventive medicine evaluation and management of an individual including an age and gender appropriate history, examination, counseling/anticipatory guidance/risk factor reduction interventions, and the ordering of appropriate immunization(s), laboratory/diagnostic procedures, new patient; infant (age younger than 1 year)

Work Value: 1.19 // Global Period: XXX

➲ *CPT Assistant* Winter 91: 11, Spring 93: 14, 34, Spring 95: 1, Aug 97: 1, Jul 98: 9, Sep 98: 5, Nov 98: 3-4, May 02: 1, May 05: 1, Aug 05: 15; *CPT Changes: An Insider's View* 2002

Clinical Example
A 6-month-old female is brought in by her mother for the first time for health supervision and evaluation. Her complete past medical, family, social, religious, and cultural history is reviewed. A complete review of systems is done. A complete physical is performed. Growth, development, and behavior are assessed. Immunizations are reviewed. Anticipatory guidance is given to the parents regarding the prevention of injuries, good parenting practices, nutrition, and sleep practices. Risk factors are identified and interventions are discussed. Medically appropriate lab tests are ordered.

Preservice
Preservice work includes reviewing the patient's chart.

Intraservice
Intraservice work includes obtaining a comprehensive history; performing a comprehensive exam; taking growth measurements; performing a sensory screening; performing a developmental/behavioral assessment; identifying risk factors and discussing interventions; providing anticipatory guidance; and ordering medically necessary lab tests and immunizations.

Postservice
Postservice work includes completing forms as necessary, updating the medical record, updating the patient record, and indicating the next appointment date.

99382 Initial comprehensive preventive medicine evaluation and management of an individual including an age and gender appropriate history, examination, counseling/anticipatory guidance/risk factor reduction interventions, and the ordering of appropriate immunization(s), laboratory/diagnostic procedures, new patient; early childhood (age 1 through 4 years)

Work Value: 1.36 // Global Period: XXX

➲ *CPT Assistant* Winter 91: 11, Spring 93: 14, 34, Spring 95: 1, Aug 97: 1, Jul 98: 9, Sep 98: 5, Nov 98: 3-4, May 02: 1, Aug 05: 15

Clinical Example
A woman brings her healthy 3-year-old son to the office for the first time for health supervision and evaluation. His complete past medical, family, social, religious, and cultural history is reviewed. A complete review of systems is done. A complete physical is performed. Speech and blood pressure are checked. Growth, development, and behavior are assessed. Immunizations are reviewed. Anticipatory guidance is given to the parents regarding the prevention of injuries in this age group, good parenting practices, nutrition, discipline, and dental care. Risk factors are identified and interventions are discussed. Medically appropriate lab tests are ordered.

Preservice
Preservice work includes reviewing the patient's chart.

Intraservice
Intraservice work includes obtaining a comprehensive history; performing a comprehensive exam; taking growth measurements; performing a sensory screening; performing a developmental/behavioral assessment; identifying risk factors and discussing interventions; providing anticipatory guidance; and ordering medically necessary lab tests and immunizations.

Postservice
Postservice work includes completing forms as necessary, updating the medical record, updating the patient record, and indicating the next appointment date.

99383 Initial comprehensive preventive medicine evaluation and management of an individual including an age and gender appropriate history, examination, counseling/anticipatory guidance/risk factor reduction interventions, and the ordering of appropriate immunization(s), laboratory/diagnostic procedures, new patient; late childhood (age 5 through 11 years)

Work Value: 1.36 // Global Period: XXX

➲ *CPT Assistant* Winter 91: 11, Spring 93: 14, 34, Spring 95: 1, Aug 97: 1, Jul 98: 9, Sep 98: 5, Nov 98: 3-4, May 02: 1, Aug 05: 15

Clinical Example
A 9-year-old male presents for the first time to the office for health supervision and evaluation. His complete medical, family, social, religious, and cultural history is reviewed. A complete review of systems is done. A complete physical is performed. Speech and blood pressure are checked. Growth, development, and behavior are assessed. Immunizations are reviewed. Anticipatory guidance is given to the child regarding good health habits and self-care. Anticipatory guidance is given to the parents about good parenting practices. Risk factors are identified and interventions are discussed. Medically appropriate lab tests are ordered.

Preservice
Preservice work includes reviewing the patient's chart.

Intraservice
Intraservice work includes obtaining a comprehensive history; performing a comprehensive exam; taking growth measurements; performing a sensory screening; performing a developmental/behavioral assessment; identifying risk factors and discussing interventions; providing anticipatory guidance; and ordering medically necessary lab tests and immunizations.

Postservice
Postservice work includes completing forms as necessary, updating the medical record, updating the patient record, and indicating the next appointment date.

99384 Initial comprehensive preventive medicine evaluation and management of an individual including an age and gender appropriate history, examination, counseling/anticipatory guidance/risk factor reduction interventions, and the ordering of appropriate immunization(s), laboratory/diagnostic procedures, new patient; adolescent (age 12 through 17 years)

Work Value: 1.53 // Global Period: XXX

➲ *CPT Assistant* Winter 91: 11, Spring 93: 14, 34, Spring 95: 1, Aug 97: 1, Jul 98: 9, Sep 98: 5, Nov 98: 3-4, May 02: 1, Aug 05: 15

Clinical Example
A 16-year-old female presents to the office for the first time for health supervision and evaluation. Her complete past medical, family, social, religious, and cultural history is reviewed. A complete review of systems is completed. A complete physical is performed. Speech, blood pressure, and fitness are checked. A scoliosis screen and pelvic examination are performed. Growth, development, and behavior are assessed. Immunizations are reviewed. Anticipatory guidance is given

to the patient regarding good health habits and self-care, including problems with drugs, alcohol, and tobacco, and driving responsibly. Guidance is also given about sexual activity and the importance of educational activities and social interaction. Anticipatory guidance is given to the patient's parents regarding good parenting practices. Risk factor problems are identified and interventions are discussed. Medically appropriate lab tests are ordered.

99385 Initial comprehensive preventive medicine evaluation and management of an individual including an age and gender appropriate history, examination, counseling/anticipatory guidance/risk factor reduction interventions, and the ordering of appropriate immunization(s), laboratory/diagnostic procedures, new patient; 18-39 years

Work Value: 1.53 // Global Period: XXX

➲ **_CPT Assistant_ Winter 91: 11, Spring 93: 14, 34, Spring 95: 1, Aug 97: 1, Jul 98: 9, Sep 98: 5, Nov 98: 3-4, May 02: 1, Aug 05: 15**

Clinical Example

A 28-year-old female presents to the office for the first time for a complete health evaluation and physical exam. Her complete past medical, family, and social history is reviewed. A complete review of systems is completed. A complete physical is performed, which includes a pelvic exam, Pap smear, breast exam, and blood pressure check. Counseling is provided regarding diet and exercise, substance use, sexual activity, and dental health. Risk factors are identified and interventions are discussed. Medically appropriate lab tests are ordered.

99386 Initial comprehensive preventive medicine evaluation and management of an individual including an age and gender appropriate history, examination, counseling/anticipatory guidance/risk factor reduction interventions, and the ordering of appropriate immunization(s), laboratory/diagnostic procedures, new patient; 40-64 years

Work Value: 1.88 // Global Period: XXX

➲ **_CPT Assistant_ Winter 91: 11, Spring 93: 14, 34, Spring 95: 1, Aug 97: 1, Jul 98: 9, Sep 98: 5, Nov 98: 3-4, May 02: 1, Aug 05: 15**

Clinical Example

A 52-year-old female presents to the office for the first time for a complete health evaluation and physical exam. Her complete past medical, family, and social history is reviewed. A complete review of systems is completed. A complete physical is performed, which includes a pelvic exam, Pap smear, breast exam, digital rectal exam, and blood pressure check. Counseling is provided regarding diet and exercise, sexual activity, and dental health. Risk factors are identified and interventions are discussed. Medically appropriate lab tests are ordered.

99387 Initial comprehensive preventive medicine evaluation and management of an individual including an age and gender appropriate history, examination, counseling/anticipatory guidance/risk factor reduction interventions, and the ordering of appropriate immunization(s), laboratory/diagnostic procedures, new patient; 65 years and older

Work Value: 2.06 // Global Period: XXX

➲ **_CPT Assistant_ Winter 91: 11, Spring 93: 14, 34, Spring 95: 1, Aug 97: 1, Jul 98: 9, Sep 98: 5, Nov 98: 3-4, May 02: 1, Aug 05: 15**

Clinical Example

A 70-year-old female presents to the office for the first time for a complete health evaluation and physical exam. Her complete past medical, family, and social history is reviewed. A complete review of systems is completed. A complete physical is performed, which includes a pelvic exam, Pap smear, breast exam, digital rectal exam, and blood pressure check. Counseling is provided regarding diet and exercise, injury prevention, and dental health. Risk factors are identified and interventions are discussed. Medically appropriate lab tests are ordered.

Established Patient

99391 Periodic comprehensive preventive medicine reevaluation and management of an individual including an age and gender appropriate history, examination, counseling/anticipatory guidance/risk factor reduction interventions, and the ordering of appropriate immunization(s), laboratory/diagnostic procedures, established patient; infant (age younger than 1 year)

Work Value: 1.02 // Global Period: XXX

➲ ***CPT Assistant*** **Winter 91: 11, Spring 93: 14, 34, Spring 95: 1, Aug 97: 1, Jul 98: 9, Sep 98: 5, Nov 98: 3-4, May 02: 1, May 05: 1, Aug 05: 15;** ***CPT Changes: An Insider's View*** **2002**

Clinical Example

A 6-month-old female, established patient, is brought in by her mother for health supervision and evaluation. Her interval past medical, family, social, and religious, and cultural history is reviewed. A complete review of systems is done. A complete physical is performed. Growth, development, and behavior are assessed. Immunizations are reviewed. Anticipatory guidance is given to the parents regarding the prevention of injuries, good parenting practices, nutrition, and sleep practices. Risk factors are identified and interventions are discussed.

Preservice

Preservice work includes reviewing the patient's chart.

Intraservice

Intraservice work includes obtaining a comprehensive history; performing a comprehensive exam; taking growth measurements; performing a sensory screening; performing a developmental/behavioral assessment; identifying risk factors and discussing interventions; providing anticipatory guidance to the extent that it has not been given in previous visits; and ordering medically necessary lab tests and immunizations.

Postservice

Postservice work includes completing forms as necessary, updating the medical record, updating the patient record, and indicating the next appointment date.

99392 Periodic comprehensive preventive medicine reevaluation and management of an individual including an age and gender appropriate history, examination, counseling/anticipatory guidance/risk factor reduction interventions, and the ordering of appropriate immunization(s), laboratory/diagnostic procedures, established patient; early childhood (age 1 through 4 years)

Work Value: 1.19 // Global Period: XXX

➲ ***CPT Assistant*** **Winter 91: 11, Spring 93: 14, 34, Spring 95: 1, Aug 97: 1, Jul 98: 9, Sep 98: 5, Nov 98: 3-4, May 02: 1, Aug 05: 15**

Clinical Example

A woman brings her healthy 3-year-old son, established patient, to the office for health supervision and evaluation. His interval past medical, family, social, religious, and cultural history is reviewed. A complete review of systems is done. A complete physical is performed. Speech and blood pressure are checked. Growth, development, and behavior are assessed. Immunizations are reviewed. Anticipatory guidance is given to the parents regarding prevention of injuries in this age group, good parenting practices, nutrition, discipline, and dental care. Risk factors are identified and interventions are discussed. Medically appropriate lab tests are done.

Preservice

Preservice work includes reviewing the patient's chart.

Intraservice
Intraservice work includes obtaining a comprehensive history; performing a comprehensive exam; taking growth measurements; performing a sensory screening; performing a developmental/behavioral assessment; identifying risk factors and discussing interventions; providing anticipatory guidance to the extent that it has not been given in previous visits; and ordering medically necessary lab tests and immunizations.

Postservice
Postservice work includes completing forms as necessary, updating the medical record, updating the patient record, and indicating the next appointment date.

99393 Periodic comprehensive preventive medicine reevaluation and management of an individual including an age and gender appropriate history, examination, counseling/anticipatory guidance/risk factor reduction interventions, and the ordering of appropriate immunization(s), laboratory/diagnostic procedures, established patient; late childhood (age 5 through 11 years)

Work Value: 1.19 // Global Period: XXX

➲ *CPT Assistant* **Winter 91: 11, Spring 93: 14, 34, Spring 95: 1, Aug 97: 1, Jul 98: 9, Sep 98: 5, Nov 98: 3-4, May 02: 1, Aug 05: 15**

Clinical Example
A 9-year-old male, established patient, presents to the office for health supervision and evaluation. His interval past medical, family, social, religious, and cultural history is reviewed. A complete physical is performed. Speech and blood pressure are checked. Growth, development, and behavior are assessed. Immunizations are reviewed. Anticipatory guidance is given to the child regarding good health habits and self-care. Anticipatory guidance is given to the parents about good parenting practices. Risk factors are identified and interventions are discussed. Medically appropriate lab tests are ordered.

Preservice
Preservice work includes reviewing the patient's chart.

Intraservice
Intraservice work includes obtaining a comprehensive history; performing a comprehensive exam; taking growth measurements; performing a sensory screening; performing a developmental/behavioral assessment; identifying risk factors and discussing interventions; providing anticipatory guidance to the extent that it has not been given in previous visits; and ordering medically necessary lab tests and immunizations.

Postservice
Postservice work includes completing forms as necessary, updating the medical record, updating the patient record, and indicating the next appointment date.

99394 Periodic comprehensive preventive medicine reevaluation and management of an individual including an age and gender appropriate history, examination, counseling/anticipatory guidance/risk factor reduction interventions, and the ordering of appropriate immunization(s), laboratory/diagnostic procedures, established patient; adolescent (age 12 through 17 years)

Work Value: 1.36 // Global Period: XXX

➲ *CPT Assistant* **Winter 91: 11, Spring 93: 14, 34, Spring 95: 1, Aug 97: 1, Jul 98: 9, Sep 98: 5, Nov 98: 3-4, May 02: 1, Aug 05: 15**

Clinical Example
A 16-year-old female, established patient presents to the office for health supervision and evaluation. Her interval past medical, family, social, religious, and cultural history is reviewed. A complete review of systems is completed. A complete physical is performed and speech, blood pressure, and fitness are checked. A scoliosis screen and pelvic examination are performed. Growth, development, and behavior are assessed. Immunizations are reviewed. Anticipatory guidance is given to the patient regarding good health habits and self-care, including problems with drugs,

alcohol, and tobacco, and driving responsibly. Guidance also given about sexual activity and the importance of educational activities and social interaction. Anticipatory guidance is given to the patient's parents regarding good parenting practices. Risk factor problems are identified and interventions are discussed. Medically appropriate lab tests are ordered.

99395 Periodic comprehensive preventive medicine reevaluation and management of an individual including an age and gender appropriate history, examination, counseling/anticipatory guidance/risk factor reduction interventions, and the ordering of appropriate immunization(s), laboratory/diagnostic procedures, established patient; 18-39 years

Work Value: 1.36 // Global Period: XXX

➲ ***CPT Assistant*** **Winter 91: 11, Spring 93: 14, 34, Spring 95: 1, Aug 97: 1, Jul 98: 9, Sep 98: 5, Nov 98: 3-4, May 02: 1, Aug 05: 15**

Clinical Example

A 28-year-old female, established patient presents to the office for a complete health evaluation and physical examination. Her interval past medical, family, and social history is reviewed. A complete review of systems is completed. A complete physical is performed, which includes a pelvic examination, Pap smear, breast exam, and blood pressure check. Counseling is provided regarding diet and exercise, substance use, sexual activity, and dental health. Risk factors are identified and interventions are discussed. Medically appropriate lab tests are ordered.

99396 Periodic comprehensive preventive medicine reevaluation and management of an individual including an age and gender appropriate history, examination, counseling/anticipatory guidance/risk factor reduction interventions, and the ordering of appropriate immunization(s), laboratory/diagnostic procedures, established patient; 40-64 years

Work Value: 1.53 // Global Period: XXX

➲ ***CPT Assistant*** **Winter 91: 11, Spring 93: 14, 34, Spring 95: 1, Aug 97: 1, Jul 98: 9, Sep 98: 5, Nov 98: 3-4, May 02: 1, Aug 05: 15**

Clinical Example

A 52-year-old female, established patient presents to the office for a complete health evaluation and physical exam. Her interval past medical, family, and social history is reviewed. A complete physical is performed, which includes a pelvic exam, Pap smear, breast exam, digital rectal exam, and blood pressure check. Counseling is provided regarding diet and exercise, sexual activity, and dental health. Risk factors are identified and interventions are discussed. Medically appropriate lab tests are ordered.

99397 Periodic comprehensive preventive medicine reevaluation and management of an individual including an age and gender appropriate history, examination, counseling/anticipatory guidance/risk factor reduction interventions, and the ordering of appropriate immunization(s), laboratory/diagnostic procedures, established patient; 65 years and older

Work Value: 1.71 // Global Period: XXX

➲ ***CPT Assistant*** **Winter 91: 11, Spring 93: 14, 34, Spring 95: 1, Aug 97: 1, Jul 98: 9, Sep 98: 5, Nov 98: 3-4, May 02: 1, Aug 05: 15**

Clinical Example

A 70-year-old female, established patient presents to the office for a complete health evaluation and physical exam. Her interval past medical, family, and social history is reviewed. A complete review of systems is completed. A complete physical is performed, which includes a pelvic exam, Pap smear, breast exam, digital rectal exam, and blood pressure check. Counseling is provided regarding diet and exercise, injury prevention, and dental health. Risk factors are identified and interventions are discussed. Medically appropriate lab tests are ordered.

Coding Tip for 99381-99397
Codes 99381-99397 include counseling, anticipatory guidance, and risk factor reduction interventions that are provided at the time of the initial or periodic comprehensive preventive medicine examination.

Newborn Care

99431 History and examination of the normal newborn infant, initiation of diagnostic and treatment programs and preparation of hospital records. (This code should also be used for birthing room deliveries.)

Work Value: 1.17 // Global Period: XXX

➲ *CPT Assistant* Apr 97: 10, Nov 97: 9, Sep 98: 5, Apr 04: 14, May 05: 1

Clinical Example
A full-term newborn male is delivered to a 23-year-old primigravida mother. The mother's and infant's charts are reviewed, and a complete examination of the infant is performed. The findings are reviewed with both parents. Issues discussed with the parents include feeding, circumcision, immunizations, car safety, early discharge, and utilization of the health care system.

Preservice
Preservice work includes reviewing the charts of both the mother and infant.

Intraservice
Intraservice work includes obtaining a comprehensive history; performing a comprehensive examination; taking measurements; performing a sensory screening; ordering medically necessary lab tests; and reviewing the utilization of the health care system.

Postservice
Postservice work includes completing forms as necessary, updating the medical record, updating the patient record, and indicating the next appointment date.

99432 Normal newborn care in other than hospital or birthing room setting, including physical examination of baby and conference(s) with parent(s)

Work Value: 1.26 // Global Period: XXX

➲ *CPT Assistant* Sep 98: 5, May 99: 11, Apr 04: 14

Clinical Example
A full-term newborn female is delivered by a nurse midwife at home to a 20-year-old gravida 3 mother. Later that day, the mother presents the infant at the office for her first check-up. Prenatal, family, and social histories are reviewed, and a complete examination of the infant is performed. Issues discussed include routine feeding, immunizations, car safety, and utilization of the health care system.

Preservice
Preservice work includes reviewing the charts of both the mother and infant.

Intraservice
Intraservice work includes obtaining a comprehensive history; performing a comprehensive examination; taking measurements; performing a sensory screening; ordering medically necessary lab tests; and reviewing the utilization of the health care system.

Postservice
Postservice work includes completing forms as necessary, updating the medical record, updating the patient record, and indicating the next appointment date.

99433 Subsequent hospital care, for the evaluation and management of a normal newborn, per day

Work Value: 0.62 // Global Period: XXX

➲ *CPT Assistant* Sep 98: 5, Apr 03: 27

Clinical Example
A full-term newborn male is in his second day of his hospital stay. His general health status is assessed and a physical exam is

performed. The findings are reviewed with the parents. Issues discussed with the parents include feeding, jaundice, circumcision, cord care, sleep pattern, newborn behavior, peeling of skin, bowel movements, crying, response to tactile stimulation, safety issues, and the parents' needs for rest.

Preservice
Preservice work includes reviewing the patient's chart.

Intraservice
Intraservice work includes obtaining a comprehensive interval history; performing a comprehensive examination; taking measurements; performing a sensory screening; ordering medically necessary lab tests; and providing relevant counseling to the parents.

Postservice
Postservice work includes completing forms as necessary, updating the medical record, updating the patient record, and indicating the next appointment date.

99435 **History and examination** of the normal newborn infant, including the preparation of medical records. (This code should only be used for newborns assessed and discharged from the hospital or birthing room on the same date.)

Work Value: 1.50 // Global Period: XXX

➲ *CPT Assistant* Sep 98: 5, Apr 04: 14

Clinical Example
A full-term newborn male is delivered to a 28-year-old gravida 2 mother. The mother and infant's charts are reviewed, and a complete examination of the infant is performed. The findings are reviewed with both parents. Issues discussed with the parents include feeding, jaundice, circumcision, cord care, sleep pattern, newborn behavior, peeling of skin, bowel movements, crying response to tactile stimulation, safety issues, immunizations, the parents' need for rest, early discharge, and utilization of the health care system. The infant and mother are discharged from the hospital later that same day. Hospitalization and discharge records are completed.

Preservice
Preservice work includes obtaining and reviewing the results of diagnostic and other studies before the physician is present on the patient's hospital unit or floor.

Intraservice
Intraservice work includes reviewing the mother's and infant's charts; obtaining a history from the parent(s) and examining the infant; discussing with the parents issues including feeding, jaundice, circumcision, cord care, sleep pattern, newborn behavior, peeling of the skin, bowel movements, crying, response to tactile stimulation, safety issues, immunizations, the parents' need for rest, early discharge, and utilization of the health care system; and documenting the medical records and providing instructions for continuing care to all relevant caregivers while the physician is present on the patient's hospital unit or floor.

Postservice
Postservice work includes providing instructions for continuing care to all relevant caregivers and preparing the medical records after the physician has left the patient's hospital unit or floor.

Coding Tip for 99435
This code is reported for discharge services provided to newborns admitted and discharged on the same date.

99436 **Attendance** at delivery (when requested by delivering physician) and initial stabilization of newborn

Work Value: 1.50 // Global Period: XXX

➲ *CPT Assistant* Nov 97: 9-10, Sep 98: 5, Nov 99: 5-6, Aug 00: 3, Aug 04: 9, Nov 05: 15

Clinical Example
A physician is requested by the obstetrician to attend the delivery of the 37-week gestation infant whose 32-year-old mother arrived at the hospital with spontaneous rupture

of her membranes at home. The physician arrives at the hospital, changes into scrubs clothes, scrubs, and enters the delivery room suite. The physician commences introductions with the family, obtains the maternal and fetal histories from the obstetrician, and reviews the mother's chart and labor records. Attention is then turned to the equipment for neonatal care. The radiant warmer is checked, wall oxygen turned on and connected to the self-inflating resuscitation bag, the laryngoscope light is checked and an appropriate-sized blade chosen, wall suction is adjusted, an appropriate-sized endotracheal tube is chosen, and the availability of medication team who are present is confirmed. The physician then gowns and scrubs and prepares to receive the newborn from the obstetrician after delivery and cord cutting. Shortly after admission, the mother demonstrates the onset of vaginal bleeding with painful contractions associated with intermittent fetal tachycardia interspersed with deep variable deceleration. The obstetrician decides on a cesarean section, which is done under general anesthesia. The physician is present during the birth of the child and provides any necessary assistance required to maintain the health of the child during the birthing process. The neonate is handed to the physician blue with a weak cry and a large amount of oral/nasal secretion. The child's initial heart rate is 100. The child is dried, stimulated, and the nasopharynx and oropharynx are suctioned and the blow by oxygen provided. A visual inspection of the child is provided and the child appears consistent with 37 weeks of gestation with no other apparent anomalies. The 1-minute Apgar score is 5 but increases to 8 by 5 minutes. Blow by oxygen is discontinued at 8 minutes. The lungs are still moist but breath sounds are present in all lobes. The child begins to cry vigorously and color remains pink. The child is then wrapped in a blanket and given to the parents to hold. The parental concerns regarding the health of the newborn are addressed and any questions relating to the continuing care of the infant are answered. The physician completes the delivery room attendance, resuscitation record, and the Apgar form.

Preservice

Preservice work includes changing into scrub clothes, scrubbing hands, reviewing maternal prenatal and labor history, reviewing studies of newborn well being, preparing the radiant warmer, adjusting wall suction, checking the ambu bag, turning on wall oxygen, checking the laryngoscope blade and light, and ensuring the availability of medications.

Intraservice

Intraservice work includes receiving the newborn from the delivery physician, placing the child under the overhead warmer, drying the child, stimulating the child, bulb suctioning the nose and mouth, visually inspecting the child, obtaining a heart rate and respiratory rate, providing blow by oxygen as necessary, and assigning 1 and 5 minutes Apgar scores.

Postservice

Postservice work includes discussing the care of the child with the obstetrician or the delivering physician and the parents as well as completing the delivery room attendance form and the Apgar scoring sheet.

Coding Tip for 99436

Code 99436 should not be reported in conjunction with code 99440.

99440 Newborn resuscitation: provision of positive pressure ventilation and/or chest compressions in the presence of acute inadequate ventilation and/or cardiac output

Work Value: 2.93 // Global Period: XXX

➲ ***CPT Assistant*** **Summer 93: 3, Mar 96: 10, Nov 97: 9, Sep 98: 5, Nov 99: 5-6, Aug 00: 3, Oct 03: 3, Aug 04: 9**

Clinical Example

The physician is called in to attend a cesarean section delivery of a full-term multiparous female with fetal bradycardia recorded on the monitors and meconium found in the amniotic fluid. An infant female is delivered with an Apgar score of 2 at 1 minute. Meconium is suctioned from the cords. Bag and mask resuscitation is applied with external cardiac compressions. At 3 minutes, the heart rate is 120/minute and spontaneous respirations begin with a vigorous cry. The 5-minute Apgar score is 9. No further resuscitative efforts are required, and the infant is taken to the nursery in good condition.

Preservice
Preservice work includes reviewing chart.

Intraservice
Intraservice work includes attending the cesarean section delivery, resuscitating the newborn, providing direct care to the newborn, and stabilizing the newborn.

Postservice
Postservice work includes updating the medical record and communicating with the parents.

Anesthesia

Coding for the administration of anesthesia services (reported by codes 00100-01999) represent a unique challenge to the user of the CPT® code set. For example, in many instances any additional procedures/services may appear to be straightforward; however, varying payer reporting requirements can add complexity to coding for both categories of services.

Careful consideration should be applied to claims for separate procedures/services, as they may be denied, bundled into anesthesia administration, or require special payer-specific modifiers. Therefore, it is critical for the CPT user to familiarize themselves with the anesthesia guidelines of the CPT codebook.

Neck

00326 Anesthesia for all procedures on the larynx and trachea in children younger than 1 year of age

Work Value: 7

➲ *CPT Changes: An Insider's View* 2003

Clinical Example

The patient is a 4 month-old, 5 kg infant noted to have noisy breathing worsening on excitement. The patient was born at 35 weeks gestational age. The patient was discharged home on day four after bilirubin levels were noted to be decreasing. Stridor was noted to be present on inspiration when crying and has become worse in the past two weeks. The baby is noted to be of normal color and has a mild suprasternal notch tug on quiet inspiration. When crying there is inspiratory stridor associated with significant chest retractions. A laryngoscopy and rigid bronchoscopy are planned.

Preservice

There is no significant family history for congenital diseases or adverse anesthesia reactions. The patient is on iron fortified formula and takes no medications. There are no known allergies. The patient weighs 5 kg. Vital signs are appropriate for age. The baby is noted to be of normal color and has a mild suprasternal notch tug on quiet inspiration. When crying there is inspiratory stridor associated with significant chest retractions. No change in color is noted. The airway is noted to be of normal appearance. The breath sounds are clear bilaterally. The heart is auscultated with normal rate and rhythm. No murmur is heard. No other obvious congenital abnormalities are noted. Significant laboratory results include a hematocrit of 32%. After discussion of the anesthetic options, the parents agree to a general anesthetic with induction by mask. Anesthesia risk with particular attention to the heightened risk of respiratory complications in this particular case are discussed and informed consent is obtained. Before initiating anesthesia, anesthetic drugs are prepared and the anesthesia machine is checked for correct operation following the manufacturer's guidelines.

Intraservice

An intramuscular injection of atropine is administered. The baby is transported to the operating room where monitors are placed. A forced air mattress is in place as are heating lamps. Anesthesia is gradually induced by volatile agent through a mask. Intravenous access is secured. The anesthetic is slowly deepened with careful attention to blood pressure. When the baby is sufficiently anesthetized, laryngoscopy is performed and topical local anesthesia is sprayed in the trachea and on the larynx. The airway is again secured by mask, vital signs are checked. Caffeine 10 mg/kg is intravenously administered.

The baby is turned to the bronchoscopist with careful attention to the patency of the airway. The mask is removed and the bronchoscopist performs laryngoscopy and placement of a rigid bronchoscope into the trachea. The anesthesia circuit is attached to the bronchoscope and adequate ventilation is determined by carbon dioxide monitoring, chest excursion with positive pressure ventilation and auscultation of breath sounds. Pulse oximetry and end tidal carbon dioxide are continuously and closely monitored throughout the procedure. An endotracheal tube is placed by the anesthesiologist after bronchoscopy ends. During the direct laryngoscopy, the anesthesiologist evaluates the airway for trauma and edema. If either is present in significant amount, the anesthesiologist must determine whether the patient needs to remain intubated in the post-operative period. Due to the very small tracheal diameter of the neonate and infant, even small amounts of edema, secretions or airway trauma can significantly increase the patient's work of breathing, leading to potential respiratory failure. In this case, trauma and edema are minimal thus the anesthetic gases are discontinued. Emergence from anesthesia ensues.

When the infant demonstrates sufficient strength and awareness by opening the eyes, the endotracheal tube is removed and the patient observed for air movement with inspiration. The patient is carefully evaluated for increased work of breathing as evidenced by stridor, sternal and intercostal retraction, and tachypnea. Pulse oximetry and end tidal carbon dioxide are verified. When the patient is stable, transport to recovery with monitors and supplemental oxygen takes place.

Postservice

The anesthesiologist provides a report to the post-anesthesia nurse, covering the patient's history and anesthetic course. Vital signs are obtained and the anesthesiologist provides orders for oxygen therapy, analgesia and nausea treatment. The anesthesiologist remains available to the PACU nurse by pager, until the patient is discharged from the recovery area. The patient is monitored for a prolonged period in the recovery room prior to transfer to the inpatient unit. The infant is placed on continuous pulse oximetry and respiratory monitors. When the baby has been stable for a period of at least six hours, with no evidence of apnea, discharge to home occurs.

Intrathoracic

00528 Anesthesia for closed chest procedures; mediastinoscopy and diagnostic thoracoscopy not utilizing one lung ventilation

Work Value: 8

➲ ***CPT Assistant*** **Nov 99:7;** ***CPT Changes: An Insider's View*** **2000, 2003, 2004**

Clinical Example

A 60-year old male with a 30-year history of smoking, coronary artery disease and mild COPD presents with large perihilar masses on chest radiograph and CT. No distinct masses are present in the lungs. Lung washings are non-diagnostic. The patient has well-controlled hypertension and no recent angina. Current medications include an antihypertensive agent and a bronchodilator. ECG shows evidence of an old infarction but no acute changes. Hemoglobin is slightly elevated and electrolytes are within normal limits. He is scheduled for a diagnostic mediastinoscopy with biopsy under general anesthesia.

Preservice

Pre-operative visit and evaluation of cardiovascular, neurological and pulmonary systems.

Review surgeon's history and physical and any notes from consultants.

Review of pulmonary function tests, ECG, laboratory tests, medications, allergies and past medical and surgical history.

Explain anesthetic options and risks to patient, answer questions and obtain consent.

Prepare anesthetic drugs.

Check anesthesia machine is operating per manufacturer's guidelines.

Intraservice

Obtain intravenous access

Transport patient to OR, apply routine monitors and confirm placement after patient is positioned on OR table.

Preoxygenation by mask.

Induction of anesthesia with intravenous lidocaine, fentanyl, propofol and a neuromuscular blocking agent.

Insertion of endotracheal tube – confirm position and secure with tape.

Protection of eyes, extremities, and pressure points.

Delivery of inhalational and intravenous anesthetics:

- constant attention to vital signs
- constant monitoring of oxygenation and respiratory status and degree of neuromuscular block
- intervention to maintain normothermia, regulation of depth of anesthesia and control of BP and cardiac output. IV fluids given to maintain hydration and treat hypotension

Prepare for emergence:

- inhalation agents withdrawn and residual neuromuscular blockage reversed using anticholinesterase and anticholinergic drugs;
- extubate trachea after determining adequacy of spontaneous ventilation;

Patient moved to stretch and transferred with supplemental oxygen by facemask to PACU.

Postservice

Vital signs checked and level of consciousness is determined.

Assessment of airway maintenance; patient's ability to handle secretions and adequacy of ventilation.

Additional analgesics ordered as needed.

History of procedure and patient's history provided to PACU nurse.

Determine when patient is fit to be turned over to PACU care.

00529 Anesthesia for closed chest procedures; mediastinoscopy and diagnostic thoracoscopy utilizing one lung ventilation

Work Value: 11

➲ *CPT Assistant* Jun 04:3; *CPT Changes: An Insider's View* 2004

Clinical Example

A 65-year old man presents with six-month history of lower lateral chest wall pain and shortness of breath. Chest X-ray shows pleural thickening of the entire lateral chest wall. He is taken to the operating room for diagnostic thoracoscopy under general anesthesia, which reveals mesiothelioma.

Preservice

Pre-operative visit and evaluation of cardiovascular, neurological, and pulmonary systems.

Review of surgeon's history and physical and any notes from consultants.

Review of pulmonary function tests, ECG, laboratory tests, medications, allergies and past medical and surgical history.

Explain anesthetic options and risks to patient, answer questions and obtain consent.

Prepare anesthetic drugs.

Check anesthesia machine is operating per manufacturer's guidelines.

Prepare equipment and supplies for endobronchial intubation including fiberoptic bronchoscope.

Intraservice

Obtain intravenous access.

Administer pre-medication (sedation, anti-aspiration, anti-asthmatic drugs, etc).

Transport patient to OR, apply routine monitors and confirm placement after patient is positioned on or table.

Preoxygenation by mask.

Induction of anesthesia with intravenous lidocaine, fentanyl, propofol and a neuromuscular blocking agent.

Insertion of endobronchial tube – confirm position with fiberoptic bronchoscope and auscultation and secure with tape.

Protection of eyes, extremities and pressure points.

Position in lateral decubitus position.

Reconfirm endobronchial tube placement with fiberoptic bronchoscopy and auscultation. Adjust ventilation parameters as required by change in patient position.

Delivery of inhalational and intravenous anesthetics:

- constant attention to vital signs;
- constant monitoring of oxygenation and respiratory status and degree of neuromuscular block;
- initiate single lung ventilation, adjust ventilator settings, assure normoxia and normocarbia. Application of CPAP and/or PEEP as needed.

- intervention to maintain normothermia, regulation of depth of anesthesia and control of BP and cardiac output. IV fluids given to maintain hydration and treat hypotension.

Prepare for emergence:

- resume two-lung ventilation, manage atelectasis;
- inhalation agents withdrawn and residual neuromuscular blockage reversed using anticholinesterase and anticholinergic drugs;
- extubate trachea after determining adequacy of spontaneous ventilation;

Patient moved to stretcher and transferred with supplemental oxygen by facemask to PACU.

Postservice

Vital signs checked and level of consciousness is determined.

Assessment of airway maintenance; patient's ability to handle secretions and adequacy of ventilation.

Additional analgesics ordered as needed.

History of procedure and patient's history provided to PACU nurse.

Determine when patient is fit to be turned over to PACU care.

00539 Anesthesia for tracheobronchial reconstruction

Work Value: 18

➲ *CPT Changes: An Insider's View* 2003

Clinical Example

A 47-year-old woman is scheduled to undergo tracheal resection and reconstruction for tracheal stenosis. The patient sustained chest and abdominal trauma from a motor vehicle accident 5 years ago. As a result of the injuries, she had a prolonged hospitalization complicated by ARDS, sepsis and renal failure. The patient required mechanical ventilatory support for 6 weeks. During that hospitalization the patient underwent tracheotomy to facilitate long term mechanical ventilation and bronchopulmonary hygiene. Since removal of the tracheotomy tube, the patient has had clinical evidence of severe tracheal stenosis and several episodes of severe stridor.

Preservice

The patient requiring tracheobronchial reconstruction has known abnormalities of the airways, necessitating a more thorough preoperative evaluation and more careful planning for airway management at the time of surgery. The evaluation includes review of neck and chest radiographs, cine-radiographs and CT or MRI scans to assess the caliber of the airway and the degree of tracheomalacia. This assessment is essential in order to determine the most appropriate approach to tracheal intubation and airway management during the procedure. Because of the known tracheal abnormalities, the patient is also at increased risk for infection and aspiration, necessitating preoperative preparation with medications to reduce the likelihood of respiratory failure.

Preservice work includes the pre-operative visit and evaluation of the patient's cardiovascular, neurological and pulmonary systems with special attention to pulmonary function. Pre-service work also includes the review of appropriate pulmonary function tests, ECG, ABGs, other laboratory tests, medications, allergies, past medical and surgical history, and available reports from consultants. Alternatives to anesthesia management and associated risks are explained and discussed with the patient. Questions are answered. Consent for anesthesia is obtained. On the day of surgery, the patient is identified, the surgical and anesthesia consents are verified, and the site of surgery is confirmed. The chart is reviewed with particular attention to the vital signs relevant laboratory tests and other pre-operative studies. The medical and surgical history is again briefly reviewed with the patient. Discussion of the options for anesthesia care, including relative risks and advantages, is again explained. In addition IV access is secured and suitable monitoring equipment (arterial pressure, CVP or

Swan-Ganz monitoring transducers) is setup and calibrated. Before initiating anesthesia, anesthetic drugs are prepared and the anesthesia machine is checked for correct operation following the manufacturer's guidelines.

Intraservice

In order to provide the surgical conditions necessary to complete the tracheal reconstruction, the surgeon and anesthesiologist must carefully coordinate the intraoperative management of the patient's airway, ventilation and gas exchange. Since both the surgeon and anesthesiologist are sharing the airway during tracheobronchial reconstruction, the anesthesiologist and surgeon must coordinate the manipulation of the trachea and artificial airway to allow the surgical procedure to be completed without loss of airway integrity or life-threatening compromise in ventilation and oxygenation. The anesthesiologist must carefully coordinate mechanical ventilation, hand ventilation and airway suctioning to ensure that the airway remains clear of blood and secretions that would be aspirated into the lungs. The endotracheal tube position must be frequently adjusted to provide surgical conditions that facilitate the repair of the trachea and ensure ventilation and oxygenation of the patient. Because of the blood and secretions in the surgical field, the anesthesiologist must provide regular suctioning of the airway and repositioning of the endotracheal tube. After completion of the surgical repair, the anesthesiologist must ensure that the airway is properly positioned to protect the airway from aspiration, ensure gas exchange and prevent pressure necrosis on surgical suture lines.

Intraservice work includes: transporting patient to OR; positioning of patient on OR table; and application of routine monitors (ECG, BP cuff, pulse oximeter); connection and calibration of arterial line and central venous catheter or PA catheter; preoxygenation by mask; induction of anesthesia with intravenous lidocaine, fentanyl, propofol and a neuromuscular blocking agent; laryngoscopy and insertion of an endotracheal tube; confirmation of correct endotracheal tube position and securing the endotracheal tube; protection of eyes; delivery of inhalational and intravenous anesthetics; intervening to assure normothermia, constant attention to vital signs; constant monitoring of oxygenation and respiratory status and degree of neuromuscular block; regulation of depth of anesthesia and control of blood pressure and cardiac output. The patient remains paralyzed and her ventilation controlled throughout the procedure. During the case, ABG's are obtained and respiratory parameters changed as needed to ensure patient stability and homeostasis. Increased oxygen concentrations and hand ventilation may be necessary during surgical manipulation to maintain adequate oxygenation of the patient. Intravenous fluids are given to maintain hydration and treat hypotension. Following completion of the surgical procedure, the inhalation agents are withdrawn and residual neuromuscular blockade is reversed using anticholinesterase and anticholinergic drugs. If ventilation, oxygenation, and restoration of neuromuscular function are satisfactory, and if emergence from anesthesia is apparent, the patient is then moved to a stretcher and transferred with supplemental oxygen by endotracheal tube to the post-anesthesia care unit.

Postservice

The patient who undergoes tracheal resection requires meticulous management after the surgical procedure to ensure that the suture line remains intact and that there is no compromise in tracheal blood flow. The initial goal is to remove the endotracheal tube as soon as possible, after the procedure, while also ensuring that the patient has a clear airway. After the tracheal resection, mucociliary clearance is impaired, necessitating intensive respiratory care and careful suctioning of pulmonary secretions to optimize bronchopulmonary hygiene without disrupting the tracheal anastomosis. Pain relief is carefully titrated to achieve patient comfort.

On admission to PACU, vital signs are checked, and level of consciousness is determined. Adequacy of ventilation, maintenance of airway, and ability to handle secretions are again assessed. Cardiovascular and respiratory status is closely monitored. A brief summary of the procedure and the patient's medical history is conveyed to the PACU nurse and the patient's immediate care is transferred to the recovery room personnel. The anesthesiologist orders analgesics, anti-emetics, and respiratory treatments as indicated. The patient's condition is reported frequently to the anesthesiologist who makes appropriate medical decisions regarding: control of pain, adequacy of respiration, and discharge to the intensive care unit. Interpretation of ABG's and regulation of blood pressure and circulation are required in this immediate post-op period. After the patient's vital signs are stable, after an appropriate level of consciousness has returned, after oxygenation is adequate, and after the analgesic needs are satisfied, the patient is extubated and discharged from the PACU to the intensive care unit.

The patient is seen on a post-op visit the first post-op day and evaluated for any post-anesthesia problems. The patient's questions and concerns about the anesthetic are addressed by the anesthesiologist.

00561 Anesthesia for procedures on heart, pericardial sac, and great vessels of chest; with pump oxygenator, younger than one year of age

Work Value: 25

➲ *CPT Changes: An Insider's View* 2005

Clinical Example

This infant was noted to have trisomy 21 and a heart murmur at birth. Subsequent studies determined the presence of an atrioventicular (AV) canal defect. The patient was followed closely after starting digoxin and furosemide by mouth. At his six month check-up the infant was noted to have tachypnea and failure to gain weight. The oxygen saturation was noted to be 88 % (a decrease from previous measurements), and radiologic examination of the chest noted signs consistent with cardiac failure. The repair of the congenital heart defect under cardio-pulmonary bypass was scheduled.

Preservice

The day prior to the scheduled surgery the infant was seen in the pre-anesthetic clinic. Prior to entering the examination room the medical chart was reviewed with special attention to the cardiology notes and laboratory investigations including the results of cardiac catheterizations and ultrasonic evaluations. The electrocardiogram demonstrated sinus tachycardia and ventricular hypertrophy. Increased lung markings were noted on the chest x-ray. A detailed history including prenatal care and birth history was completed. On questioning the parents were unaware of any defects in any other body system. Past history revealed no previous anesthetics or significant events. Family history and review of systems were unremarkable.

A small-for-age crying infant was noted on examination. He appeared cachectic and slightly dusky in color. The cry was weak. There were mild retractions noted throughout the thorax, and tachypnea with a respiratory rate of 45 breaths per minute was observed. There were no other associated defects noted that would indicate the presence of a congenital syndrome. Examination of the airway was normal for this age and condition. The auscultation of the lungs noted rhonci throughout and possibly some rales in the bases; however, the patient was not cooperative enough and did not stop crying long enough for a complete examination. As noted earlier intercostal and suprasternal retractions were observed as was an occasional inspiratory grunt. Examination of the heart noted a rate greater than 170 beats per minute. A loud 4/6 systolic murmur was evident throughout the precordium.

Blood was drawn for a complete blood count, electrolytes, and type and cross-match.

The process of anesthesia including intramuscular injection of anesthetic agents for induction, monitors, vascular access including peripheral and subclavian venous access and arterial access likely at the wrist were described. The maintenance of anesthesia and the plan to maintain endotracheal intubation into the post-operative period were discussed. The number of 'tubes' entering and exiting the infant was mentioned as was the likelihood of generalized edema especially noticeable on the face post-operatively. The possibility of using nitric oxide for pulmonary vascular dilation was noted. Lastly, plans for pain management in the postoperative period were discussed with the parents. After discussing the total anesthetic plan the parents were given the opportunity to have any questions they may have answered.

The following morning the patient's chart was reviewed for additional information including the results of the previous day's blood tests. Both the complete blood count and electrolyte panel were normal for age. The anesthesiologist confirmed four units of blood were available in the operating room. The patient was examined with no interval changes noted. The parents were given the opportunity to again ask questions and all were answered to their satisfaction.

The operating room was prepared for administration of general anesthesia. This includes preparing the anesthesia machine, as well as medications and airway and monitoring equipment including preparation of pressure transducers for arterial and central venous pressure monitoring. A tower of intravenous medication pumps was prepared for the administration of cardio- and vaso-active medications as well as aprotinin for aid in hemostasis. The nitric oxide delivery equipment and airway circuit were assembled and checked.

A final chart review was performed to confirm the presence of required documentation and consent forms.

Intraservice

Ketamine and atropine doses were calculated based on weight and administered intramuscularly after sterile preparation into the deltoid muscle. Once the infant was noted to be under the influence of the anesthetic he was transferred to the operating room. Monitors were placed for five lead electrocardiogram, pulse oximetry and blood pressure. A saphenous vein was cannulated with a 20 gauge catheter and intravenous narcotic anesthesia and muscle relaxation were infused. Manual ventilation with 100% oxygen was begun. After appropriate demonstration of paralysis with a nerve blockade monitor, the trachea was intubated with the appropriate age calculated sized endotracheal tube. Auscultation of breath sounds and capnography confirmed the correct tube placement. The endotracheal tube was secured with waterproof tape so as not to be disturbed by placement of the transesophageal echo probe (separately reported).

A radial artery was cannulated with a 22 gauge catheter and a left subclavian 5 French double lumen central line was placed under sterile conditions (both reported separately). Both lines were connected to the pressure transducers after zeroing as recommended. Blood samples were drawn for blood gas analysis and activated clotting time (ACT). A 1 ml test dose of aprotinin was administered and after noting no adverse reaction the continuous infusion started. The remaining cardioactive infusion drugs were connected to the central line but not started.

Intravenous medications to prevent infection and inflammation were administered. Anesthesia charting was performed. Ventilation was adjusted as indicated by the blood gas results.

Surgery commenced and ventilation was momentarily stopped during sternotomy. Intermittent blood gas analysis and ACT were measured throughout the surgery. Narcotics and muscle relaxants were intermittently administered as necessary and blood pressure was titrated with inhaled isoflurane.

After the surgeons adequately dissected the great vessels, heparin was administered intravenously and the activated clotting time was measured to be over 400 seconds. Cardiopulmonary bypass commenced soon after cannulation of the aorta and right atrium, and ventilation was discontinued. During bypass the anesthesiologist in conjunction with the perfusionist administered anesthetic agents and relaxants as appropriate. Surgical repair of the atrio-ventricular canal ensued with graft closure of the septal defects and suture repair of the valvular insufficiency. The anesthesiologist and the surgeon worked together to assure venting of air from the heart prior to release of the aortic cross-clamp. Near the anticipated end of bypass and after adequate re-warming, ventilation was restarted and inotropic cardiac support was begun with infusions of dopamine and dobutamine. Afterload reduction was produced by an infusion of milrinone. Heating the infant was partially accomplished with forced warm air mattress controlled by the anesthesiologist.

After discontinuing bypass, the pulmonary artery was cannulated by the surgeon and the pressure line was passed to the anesthesiologist for connection to a transducer. As is typically seen with AV canal repair in children less than one year of age, the pulmonary artery pressure was discovered to be high and inhaled nitric oxide gas was added to the inspiratory anesthetic circuit. Flows were adjusted to obtain the correct concentration as measured in the inspiratory limb. Once cardiac and pulmonary parameters were stabilized the heparin anticoagulation was reversed with intravenous protamine and the ACT was measured as normal. Blood gases were intermittently checked. Due to the patient's weight and the effects of cardiopulmonary bypass on the coagulation system, coagulopathies are commonly seen after discontinuation from bypass.

After the conclusion of surgery a portable monitor and ventilation circuit were connected to the patient for transport of the baby to the intensive care unit. The nitric oxide circuit was tested to ensure adequate delivery of the vasodilator during transport. The infusion pumps delivering cardiovascular medications were checked for proper function prior to transport. On arrival to the intensive care unit, hemodynamic and respiratory monitors were transferred to the unit's system. Ventilation was transferred to a bedside ventilator and parameters adjusted to satisfaction. The continued administration of nitric oxide was confirmed. Vital signs were monitored.

Postservice

A full report was given to the physician assuming care and the assigned nurse. Finally, the anesthetic record was completed and filed. The anesthesiologist then met with the infant's family and discussed the course of the anesthetic and anticipated issues during the initial period of recovery. The anesthesiologist visited the patient on the first post-operative day to assess recovery from anesthesia and document adverse events associated with the procedure. An entry in the medical record was made.

Spine and Spinal Cord

00640 Anesthesia for manipulation of the spine or for closed procedures on the cervical, thoracic or lumbar spine

Work Value: 3

➲ *CPT Changes: An Insider's View* 2003

Clinical Example

The typical patient is a middle-aged, moderately obese male with lumbar back pain secondary to a workplace injury. The patient has been treated by multiple practitioners, including a chiropractor, whose office manipulations of the lumbar spine have failed to relieve the pain syndrome. The patient is unable to work, his activities are restricted and he resists further office therapy because of the pain involved. He is receiving multiple medications, including an oral opioid and an antihypertensive, with only moderate pain relief. He is scheduled for manipulation of his lumbar spine under general anesthesia. He does not have any medical allergies and does not smoke.

Preservice

The patient is evaluated one week prior to the procedure by the anesthesiologist. A medical history is taken and a systems review is conducted along with a physical examination to determine the presence of coexisting medical illness. Special emphasis is given to current drug therapy that may affect the conduct of anesthesia. For example, the use of non-steroidal anti-inflammatory drugs may interfere with coagulation, which has implications for anesthetic management. The patient is questioned about previous allergic reactions to drugs. A surgical and family history is obtained to determine if there have been any previous anesthetic complications. A history of hypertension was elicited and his antihypertensive medications were reviewed. He was instructed to take his medications on the day of surgery. Physical examination included airway evaluation, cardiopulmonary exam, and a brief neurological evaluation. Blood pressure was normal. Diagnostic studies reviewed included an EKG, electrolytes, and complete blood count. At this point the patient is counseled about the plans for general anesthesia and the risks and benefits of the anesthetic are explained. Alternative anesthetic techniques are described as well. Instructions relating to the anesthetic, including the appropriate period of time for fasting prior to the surgery, are given. An informed consent is obtained. On the day of the procedure, the patient is re-evaluated by the anesthesia provider who starts a peripheral intravenous line and begins an infusion of lactated ringers. The anesthesia providers will have ensured themselves that all equipment and drugs necessary for resuscitation are available and working.

Intraservice

The patient is placed on the operating room table, monitoring devices are applied (ECG, NIBP, pulse oximetry) and baseline values are obtained. Intravenous anesthetics, usually propofol, a benzodiazepine and an opioid are most commonly used. Supplemental oxygen is administered and a patent airway is maintained throughout the procedure. Maintenance of the airway is especially important and sometimes difficult during manipulation of the cervical spine. Additional intravenous medication is given as required. Hemodynamic and ventilatory variables are monitored every 3-5 minutes or more frequently if indicated. As the procedure nears its conclusion, anesthetic agents are withdrawn to prepare the patient for awakening. Hemodynamic stability, adequacy of ventilation, and level of consciousness are evaluated, and if these parameters are acceptable, the patient is transferred to the post anesthesia care unit. The procedure usually takes approximately 30 minutes. The anesthesia provider maintains a complete record.

Postservice

In the post anesthesia care unit, the patient is recovered according to ASA guidelines. Any side effects of anesthesia, such as nausea and vomiting, are assessed and treated if necessary. The patient is evaluated to see whether he meets the criteria for discharge such as appropriate level of consciousness, adequate respiratory function, the ability to ambulate without assistance and the availability of an escort. Discharge instructions are given. Discharge criteria are documented in the patient's record.

Pelvis (Except Hip)

01173 Anesthesia for open repair of fracture disruption of pelvis or column fracture involving acetabulum

Work Value: 12

➲ *CPT Assistant* Jun 04:3-4; *CPT Changes: An Insider's View* 2004

Clinical Example

A 29-year-old male involved in a motor vehicle accident 36 hours previously presents to the operating room for open repair of an acetabular wall dislocation fracture. Such patients are typically multiply injured; thoracic and abdominal injuries add to the complexity of the anesthetic management. Associated injuries include a recently repaired ipsilateral tib/fib fracture, recently sutured facial lacerations, a pulmonary contusion and a ruptured spleen. He has already received four units of packed red blood cells, 20 units of platelets and 2 units of fresh frozen plasma for stabilization of continually dropping hemoglobin and correction of coagulopathy. He is currently in a neck collar as cervical spine stability is still uncertain. He is receiving oxygen by facemask, is oriented to person, and is receiving intravenous morphine sulfate for analgesia.

Preservice

The patient is transferred to the pre-op holding area from the intensive care unit where the RN gives a report to the anesthesiologist. The patient's recent clinical course and vital signs are reviewed. The anesthesiologist reviews the medical record and the anesthetic record and progress notes from the previous evening. Neither neurosurgery or orthopedic surgery is able to adequately determine cervical spine stability. In addition, the recent notes by the trauma surgeon as well as the consulting orthopedic, plastic and general surgeons are reviewed. Current laboratory data and imaging studies are noted. A directed physical exam is performed with special attention to pulmonary, cardiac and mental status. Plans, risks, and expectations are reviewed with the patient and his family and all questions are answered as consent is obtained for the planned anesthetic care.

Intraservice

Venous access sites are examined and a new 14 gauge peripheral intravenous line is placed. A radial artery is cannulated (separately reported). In addition, a central venous pressure monitor (separately reported) is placed into the jugular or subclavian veins to assess volume status during the periods of rapid blood loss. At this time, topicalization for the patient's airway has begun, both by local anesthetic spray and a translaryngeal injection. The patient is transferred to the operating room with oxygen being continued by face mask. Additional intravenous analgesics are administered prior to carefully moving the patient to the operating table. ECG, non-invasive blood pressure, and pulse oximetry monitoring are established. Prior to inducing general anesthesia, further topical anesthesia and intravenous sedation are provided and gas analysis including end tidal CO_2 monitoring is initiated. An endotracheal tube is placed and after confirming correct positioning with auscultation and end tidal CO_2 analysis, the endotracheal tube is secured and mechanical ventilation commenced. Mild hypotension post induction is corrected pharmacologically with agents that had been prepared in advance. Inhalational anesthetics are added to maintain anesthesia. A high flow fluid warmer with IV fluids is attached to the recently placed 14 gauge IV. A forced- air warming blanket is placed and an esophageal stethoscope/temperature probe is inserted orally in order to attempt to maintain normothermia. Careful attention is given to positioning and padding, as the potential for a prolonged surgery exists. Inhalational anesthetics and intravenous narcotics are carefully titrated to maintain anesthesia and hemodynamic stability. Neuromuscular blockade is regularly monitored using peripheral nerve stimulation and additional paralytic agents administered to maintain adequate surgical relaxation. Intravenous fluids are administered at a rapid rate to replace substantial insensible losses and surgical blood loss. Urinary output and temperature are monitored. Throughout the duration of the procedure, assessment and treatment of surgical blood loss and maintenance of stable hemodynamics are undertaken. This assessment and treatment is generally quite complex as there is often massive bleeding. Retroperitoneal hematoma is often present. Shock is always a concern. Intermittent analysis of arterial blood gases and continual evaluation of the central venous pressure are evaluated and any abnormalities are addressed. As the surgical procedure nears completion, adequacy of neuromuscular function is determined, inhalational anesthetics are gradually reduced and the patient is attempted to be weaned from mechanical ventilation. Depending of the various intraoperative conditions, the patient may begin to breathe spontaneously and morphine is titrated intravenously to provide for analgesia yet allow for planned extubation at the conclusion of the procedure. The patient's level of consciousness, ventilatory efforts, capnogram and oximetry are assessed to determine the adequacy of spontaneous respiration. If these parameters appear satisfactory, the patient is extubated and mask oxygen administered. Otherwise the patient will remain on full ventilatory support and taken directly to the ICU. The patient is then transported to the PACU with continuous oxygen by mask or transported directly to the Intensive Care Unit on full ventilatory support.

Postservice

In either the ICU or PACU, a patient history and synopsis of intraoperative events, including fluids administered, blood loss, urinary output, drugs administered, and vital sign trends is provided to the nursing staff. The anesthesiologist continues to participate in the management of postoperative analgesia, fluid balance and respiratory care while the patient is cared for in the PACU. When the patient is stable, the anesthesiologist discharges the patient from the post anesthesia care unit. The patient is seen again the next day to evaluate the patient's recovery from anesthesia and determine if any anesthesia related complications occurred.

Obstetric

01958 Anesthesia for external cephalic version procedure

Work Value: 5

➲ *CPT Assistant* Jun 04:5-6; *CPT Changes: An Insider's View* 2004

Clinical Example

A 31-year old woman, Gravida 2 Para 1, is 38 weeks and 5 days pregnant. Her first pregnancy was uncomplicated and she delivered vaginally on her estimated due date. She received a neuraxial analgesic (a continuous epidural, CPT code 01967) for relief of pain during labor and delivery. With this pregnancy, her clinical examination at 32 weeks suggested a breech presentation, which was confirmed by transabdominal ultrasound examination. Subsequent sonographic examinations continued to show a frank breech presentation. After considering the options, the patient and her obstetrician, both desiring a vaginal delivery, elected to attempt an external cephalic version (ECV). For the attempt at ECV, the patient and obstetrician requested pain relief. A neuraxial analgesic consisting of epidural catheter and local anesthesia combined with narcotic supplementation was recommended.

Preservice

The next day, the patient was admitted to the labor and delivery floor at 0630 hrs, having had no oral intake for nine hours. The anesthesiologist reviewed the admission history and physical and the pre-anesthesia questionnaire. An anesthetic history and physical was obtained, focusing on allergies, medications, previous anesthetic experiences, family history of anesthetic complications as well as a systems review emphasizing the airway, cardiac, respiratory, neurological, hepatic and renal systems. The anesthesiologist examined the airway, performed cardiac and pulmonary auscultation and examined the spine. An 18 gauge intravenous catheter was inserted in a dorsal hand vein, blood was sent to the laboratory for a complete blood count and a 'type and screen' was sent to the hospital blood bank. Prior to initiating the attempt at ECV, the obstetrician and anesthesiologist reviewed the analgesic/anesthetic and delivery options with the patient and her husband, and informed consent was obtained. The delivery options discussed included:

1) if the ECV is successful and the fetus showed no untoward effects, she would be sent home to await the onset of spontaneous labor;

2) if unsuccessful, and the fetus remained stable, an elective cesarean delivery would be performed later that day;

3) if unsuccessful and the fetus showed signs of distress, a cesarean delivery would be performed immediately. In the event of a cesarean section, the options of utilizing the indwelling epidural with more potent anesthetic agents or proceeding to general anesthesia were discussed. The risks of the planned anesthetic were discussed with the patient and her questions were answered.

Intraservice

In order to minimize the likelihood of labor resulting from the version manipulations, a tocolytic, terbutaline, was administered on the order of the obstetrician and the patient was given 30cc of sodium citrate orally. With the mother being monitored with electrocardiogram, pulse oximetry and non-invasive blood pressure cuff and external fetal monitors in place, the patient was placed in the sitting position. After sterile preparation of the lumbar spine region and under local anesthesia, an epidural needle was advanced into the lumbar epidural space and a catheter was advanced approximately 4 cm into the epidural space. The epidural needle was removed; 3 cc of 2% lidocaine with 1:200.000 epinephrine as a 'test-dose' was injected via the catheter. After one minute there was no change in the mother's pulse or blood pressure and no evidence of a subarachnoid injection, so 12 ml of .25% bupivicaine and 100 mcg. of fentanyl were injected in divided doses. The patient was repositioned in the supine position and a roll place under the patient's right hip to create left uterine displacement. Vital signs were carefully monitored with particular attention to blood pressure. With adequate analgesia, and under ultrasound guidance, the obstetrician began the ECV attempt. The external rotation was successful as demonstrated by physical assessment and by ultrasound examination.

Postservice

The epidural infusion was discontinued and the catheter was removed. On examination, the catheter was noted to be intact. The patient was monitored in the birthing room for vital signs and neurologic function. An external monitor for the fetus was continued. Two hours after the procedure, once the patient was able to ambulate without assistance and able to urinate, she was discharged home. The anesthesiologist evaluated the patient before discharge and recorded a note in the medical record.

01965 Anesthesia for incomplete or missed abortion procedures

Work Value: 4

➲ *CPT Changes: An Insider's View* 2006

Clinical Example

A 24-year-old female presents with a positive pregnancy test and heavy vaginal bleeding which started one day prior. By the last menstrual period, she should be 10-weeks pregnant. She denies passing tissue but has had large clots. On exam, she has a dilated cervical os with tissue at the os. The patient undergoes surgical treatment of incomplete abortion.

Preservice

The patient was seen in the pre-operative holding area after being admitted through the emergency department. She was a healthy appearing young woman who was pale and somewhat anxious. Her past medial history was unremarkable; she was on no medications and had no known drug allergies. She had never had a general anesthetic, and knew of no family history of problems with anesthesia. Her last oral intake was 7 hrs earlier. She weighed 60 kg, and her airway was a Mallampati Class I. Her vital signs demonstrated tachycardia at 106 and a blood pressure of 90/60. Her hemoglobin was slightly low at 10.1. The anesthetic options and risks were discussed as well as the remote possibility of blood transfusions. She chose to have a general anesthetic. Consent was obtained for the anesthesia procedure.

Intraservice

An 18 gauge intravenous (IV) catheter was inserted in her left forearm. After a fluid bolus of crystalloid fluid, which corrected her tachycardia, she was given 2 mg of midazolam and 10mg of metoclopramide and taken to the operating room (OR). After moving to the OR table, EKG, non-invasive blood pressure and pulse oximetry monitors were attached. She breathed 100% oxygen by mask, and anesthesia was induced with 100 mcg of fentanyl and 150 mg of propofol. Desflurane was added to the inspired oxygen, and she was ventilated by hand. After approximately 60 seconds, a laryngeal mask airway (LMA) was inserted. Proper positioning was ensured by chest movement and a satisfactory wave form and numerical value on the end-tidal CO_2 monitor. The patient was gently ventilated by hand for an additional 4 to 5 minutes before spontaneous respirations resumed.

The patient was put in the lithotomy position, and after a vaginal prep, the procedure commenced. At the request of the surgeon, 20 units of pitocin were added to the Ringer's Lactate solution that was infusing via the IV.

Also, as prophylaxis against nausea, 4 mg of ondansetron was given IV.

The procedure lasted 20 minutes. Estimated blood loss was 150 cc. At the conclusion of the procedure, the patient was taken out of the lithotomy position. The desflurane had been discontinued as the surgeon announced that she was through; the patient was still breathing spontaneously and the LMA was removed a minute or two later.

The patient was moved to a recovery stretcher and taken to the Post Anesthesia Care Unit (PACU). Report was given to the PACU nurse as the monitors were being applied. After ensuring that the patient's condition was satisfactory, the anesthesiologist transferred care to the PACU nurse. A hemoglobin was obtained, demonstrating a slight additional drop to 9.5. After discussion with the surgeon, the decision was made to manage the patient's anemia conservatively.

Postservice

The patient was seen approximately an hour and a half later in the second stage recovery area. She was awake, alert and oriented, and except for some mild cramping, she had no complaints. She was judged ready for discharge.

01966 Anesthesia for induced abortion procedures

Work Value: 4

➲ *CPT Changes: An Insider's View* 2006

Clinical Example

A 30-year-old female is pregnant. At thirteen weeks gestation, an ultrasound reveals that her fetus has anencephaly. She consults her obstetrician about a termination of pregnancy. Except for some seasonal reactive airway disease, she is in otherwise good health.

Preservice

The patient was seen in the pre-operative holding area of an out patient day surgery center before surgery. She was a healthy appearing young woman who was somewhat anxious. Her past medial history was unremarkable; she was on no medications and had no known drug allergies. She had never had a general anesthetic, and knew of no family history of problems with anesthesia. Her last oral intake was at 2200 hrs the previous day. She weighed 60 kg, and her airway was a Mallampati Class I. The anesthetic options and risks were discussed, and she chose to have a general anesthetic. Consent was obtained for the anesthesia service.

Intraservice

An 18 gauge intravenous (IV) catheter was inserted in her left forearm; she was given 2 mg of midazolam and 10 mg of metoclopramide and taken to the operating room (OR). After moving to the OR table, EKG, non-invasive blood pressure and pulse oximetry monitors were attached. She breathed 100% oxygen by mask, and anesthesia was induced with 100 mcg of fentanyl and 150 mg of propofol. Desflurane was added to the inspired oxygen, and she was ventilated by hand. After approximately 60 seconds, a #3 laryngeal mask airway (LMA) was inserted. Proper positioning was ensured by chest movement and a satisfactory wave form and numerical value on the end-tidal CO_2 monitor. The patient was gently ventilated by hand for an additional 4 to 5 minutes before spontaneous respirations resumed.

The patient was put in the lithotomy position, and after a vaginal prep, the procedure commenced. At the request of the surgeon, 20 units of pitocin were added to the Ringer's Lactate solution that was infusing via the IV. Also, as prophylaxis against nausea, 4 mg of ondansetron was given IV.

The procedure lasted 20 minutes; at the conclusion of the procedure, the patient was taken out of the lithotomy position. The desflurane had been discontinued as the surgeon announced that she was through; the patient was still breathing spontaneously and the LMA was removed a minute or two later, when the patient began to respond to verbal stimuli.

The patient was moved to a recovery stretcher and taken to the Post Anesthesia Care Unit (PACU). Report was given to the PACU nurse as the monitors were being applied. After ensuring that the patient's condition was satisfactory, the anesthesiologist transferred care to the PACU nurse.

Postservice

The patient was seen approximately an hour and a half later in the second stage recovery area. She was awake, alert and oriented, and except for some mild cramping, she had no complaints. She was judged ready for discharge.

Surgery

It is essential for users of the CPT® code set to familiarize themselves with the subsections of service and take the time to achieve an understanding of the common layout of the Surgery section and its subsections.

For example, there is a "head-to-toe" arrangement of procedures and services in the musculoskeletal system subsection. Then, within each heading, there is a consistent theme of the types of procedures or services described. Generally, there are codes to describe procedures involving the following:

Incision

Excision

Introduction or Removal

Repair, Revision, and/or Reconstruction

Fracture and/or Dislocation

Arthrodesis

Amputation

A similar "head-to-toe" format is repeated throughout the other Surgery subsections as well. By developing an understanding of the general layout of the CPT codebook, users will be able to locate the appropriate code(s) for reporting the procedures performed and the services provided.

General

10021 Fine needle aspiration; without imaging guidance

Work Value: 1.27 // Global Period: XXX

➲ *CPT Assistant* Aug 02:10, Mar 05:11; *CPT Changes: An Insider's View* 2002

Clinical Example

1) A 55-year-old female presents with a palpable breast mass. Attempted aspiration reveals that it is not cystic. Fine needle aspiration biopsy is performed.

2) A patient presents with a thyroid nodule discovered during a routine physical examination. A thyroid-stimulating hormone (TSH) test is performed and the results show normal thyroid function. A fine needle aspiration biopsy of the thyroid nodule is performed.

Preservice

Obtain a clinical history. Perform a physical examination of both breasts. Review the current and previous mammograms if available. Explain the procedure and its purpose to the patient, including potential complications. Obtain informed consent.

Intraservice

Clean the biopsy site with disinfectant. Inject local anesthesia (optional). Insert a 21-23 gauge needle with attached syringe into the mass and perform numerous short up and down excursions while applying negative pressure to the syringe. Withdraw the needle and express material onto slides or into a fixative. Repeat this process once. Apply compression.

Postservice

Dictate a report of the procedure to the referring physician. When results are received, dictate an addendum to report. If the results are positive, provide the report to the referring physician.

Coding Tip for 10021 and 10022

A fine-needle aspiration is performed when fluid or tissue is aspirated with a long slender needle and the cells are examined cytologically. This is in contrast to a biopsy, during which a small piece of tissue is taken and examined for histologic architecture.

10022 Fine needle aspiration; with imaging guidance

Work Value: 1.27 // Global Period: XXX

➲ *CPT Changes: An Insider's View* 2002

Clinical Example

1) A 49-year-old female has a nonpalpable mass identified on a screening mammogram. An ultrasound exam reveals that the mass is not a simple cyst. Fine-needle aspiration biopsy of the mass is performed under ultrasonic guidance. (Radiologic guidance is separately reportable.)

2) A patient is referred for a thyroid scan because of diffuse thyroid enlargement. A cold nodule is identified on the scan. The nodule is not palpable. The patient is referred for a thyroid ultrasound exam and the nodule is shown to be noncystic. Fine-needle aspiration biopsy is performed under ultrasound guidance. (Radiologic guidance is separately reportable.)

Preservice

Obtain a clinical history. Perform a physical examination of both breasts. Review any available current and previous mammograms. Explain the procedure and its purpose to the patient, including potential complications. Obtain informed consent.

Intraservice

Clean the breast with disinfectant. Clean the ultrasound transducer with disinfectant. Inject local anesthesia (optional). Localize the mass under ultrasound. Insert a 21-23 gauge needle with attached syringe into mass under ultrasound guidance. Perform numerous short up and down excursions while applying negative pressure to the syringe. Withdraw the needle and express the material onto slides or into a fixative. Repeat the process. Apply compression.

Postservice

Dictate a report of the procedure to the referring physician. When results are received, dictate an addendum to the report. If the results are positive, call the report to the referring physician.

Coding Tip for 10022

For the evaluation of a fine-needle aspirate, see codes 88172 and 88173.

Integumentary System

Skin, Subcutaneous and Accessory Structures

Incision and Drainage

10040 Acne surgery (eg, marsupialization, opening or removal of multiple milia, comedones, cysts, pustules)

Work Value: 1.19 // Global Period: 010

Clinical Example

A 16-year-old female presents with stage 3–4 acne inclusive of multiple open comedones, inflammatory papules, pustules, and some small cysts. Acne surgery is indicated. This is done by extraction of comedones, and by gentle lancing and drainage of the pustular component of acne lesions. The site of the treatment is cleaned. A follow-up visit is scheduled.

Excision—Debridement

11005 Debridement of skin, subcutaneous tissue, muscle and fascia for necrotizing soft tissue infection; abdominal wall, with or without fascial closure

Work Value: 14.24 // Global Period: 000

➲ *CPT Changes: An Insider's View* 2005

Clinical Example

A 43-year-old male is 10 days status-post repair of colon wound, secondary to a shotgun injury to the abdomen. The patient has a fever of 103.2°F and appears dehydrated and toxic. His partially opened abdominal midline wound has areas of full thickness skin necrosis with surrounding erythema and crepitus involving large areas of the abdominal wall skin, subcutaneous tissue, fascia, and muscle. His white blood cell count is 25,000. He was started on fluid resuscitation and intravenous antibiotics. Because he has fulminating necrotizing fasciitis, he requires immediate debridement. At operation, complete debridement of all involved skin, subcutaneous tissue, fascia, and muscle is carried out. The wounds are packed, dressed, and the fascia is partially reapproximated.

Preservice

Write preoperative orders for perioperative medications. Review preoperative work-up, paying particular attention to the microbiology reports. Review the surgical procedure, postoperative recovery in and out of the hospital, and expected outcome(s) with the patient and the patient's family. Answer the patient's and the family's questions and obtain informed consent. Begin and ensure adequate fluid resuscitation and cardiovascular stability. Review the planned incisions and procedure. Change into scrub clothes. Review with the anesthesiologist the induction/intraoperative plan for maintaining circulatory flow and possible transfusions. Review the length and type of anesthesia with the anesthesiologist. Review the planned procedure and the positioning and draping of the patient. Verify that all necessary surgical instruments and supplies are readily available in the operative suite. Monitor the patient's positioning and draping, and assist with positioning as needed. Scrub and gown.

Intraservice

Open the skin in its entirety. Open the fascia along the necrotic portion. Debride the necrotic skin, subcutaneous tissue, fascia, and underlying muscle of the rectus abdominus and external oblique by sharp dissection. Enter and drain multiple abscesses. Carry out the debridement cephalad, caudal, and laterally until healthy muscle and subcutaneous tissue is reached and all of the necrotic/abscessed tissue is removed and all areas of hemorrhage are controlled. Irrigate all wound areas with copious amounts of saline and then antibiotic solution. Place multiple drains in all wound sites and pack the wound beds with saline-soaked gauze. Partially reapproximate the abdominal fascia with sutures to help prevent evisceration of bowel and to protect exposed viscera in areas without peritoneum.

Postservice

Apply dressings. Write orders for postoperative labs, films, medications, diet, and patient activity. Review recovery room care and medications with the staff. Discuss the outcome of the procedure with the patient's family, Discuss the outcome of the procedure with the patient after the patient emerges from anesthesia. Dictate a postoperative report. Discuss the outcome of the procedure with the referring physician. Dictate the procedure outcome and an expected recovery letter for the referring physician and/or insurance company. Examine the patient, checking wounds and the patient's progress. Review with the nursing and/or other staff the patient's chart notes. Answer the patient's and the family's questions. Answer the nursing and/or other staff's questions. Write orders for following day's labs, films, medications, diet, and patient activity. Chart patient progress notes.

Debridement of Abdominal Wall
11005

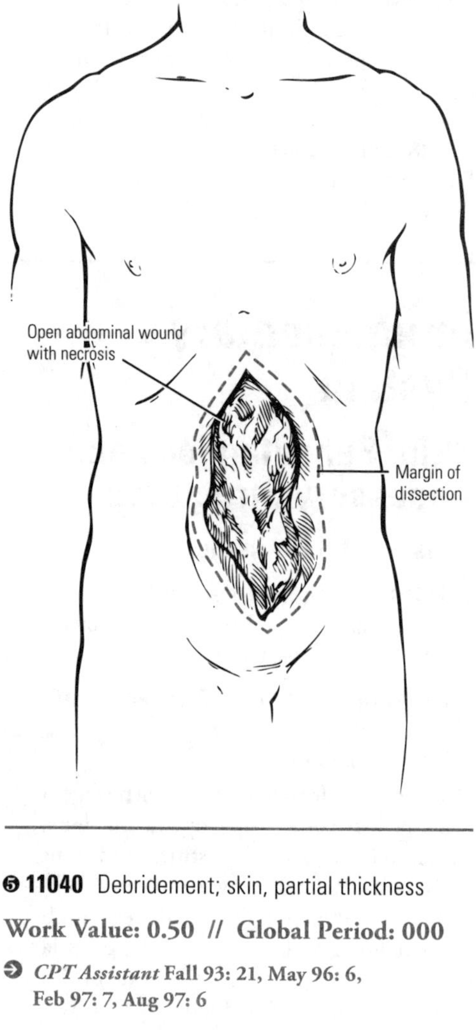

❺ 11040 Debridement; skin, partial thickness

Work Value: 0.50 // Global Period: 000

➲ *CPT Assistant* Fall 93: 21, May 96: 6, Feb 97: 7, Aug 97: 6

Clinical Example

A 68-year-old male with non-insulin-dependent diabetes presents with a 4×4-cm noninfected partial thickness skin ulceration of the plantar aspect of the fourth and fifth metatarsal heads. The decision is made to debride the wound.

Preservice

Review and update the chart with general medical and surgical history, including current medications and allergies. Conduct a physical examination that includes evaluating the neurological and vascular status of the patient. Conduct a dermatologic and musculoskeletal examination, paying particular attention to deformities in the area of the ulcer. Review the treatment options and consult with the referring physician and other health care professionals, if necessary. Communicate with the patient (and/or the patient's family) to explain the procedure and possible complications or sequelae.

Intraservice

Inspect and palpate the ulcer for size, location, functional risks, and depth. Debride the ulcer to viable tissue. Ensure adequate hemostasis. Measure the ulcer and record its size. Apply appropriate topical medication and dressing. Determine the type of padding and specific material needed to offload the ulcer area. Cut the pad to properly remove pressure. Apply padding.

Postservice

Instruct the patient and/or the patient's caregiver on the appropriate home care, the proper selection and sizing of footwear, and the importance of controlling concomitant medical conditions. Discuss the future management of the condition. Complete the medical record and communicate the findings to the primary care physician.

---

❺ 11042 Debridement; skin, and subcutaneous tissue

Work Value: 0.80 // Global Period: 000

➲ ***CPT Assistant*** **Winter 92: 10, May 96: 6, Feb 97: 7, Aug 97: 6**

Clinical Example

A 74-year-old male with insulin-dependent diabetes presents with a 4 × 4-cm noninfected ulceration involving the skin and subcutaneous tissue of the plantar aspect of the right heel. The decision is made to debride the wound.

Preservice

Review and update the chart with general medical and surgical history, including current medications and allergies. Conduct a physical examination that includes evaluating the neurological and vascular status of the patient. Conduct a dermatologic and musculoskeletal examination, paying particular attention to deformities in the area of the ulcer. Review the treatment options. Consult with the referring physician and other health care professionals, if necessary. Communicate with the patient and/or the patient's family to explain the procedure and possible complications or sequelae.

Intraservice

Inspect and palpate the ulcer for size, location, functional risks, and depth. Debride the ulcer to viable tissue. Ensure adequate hemostasis. Measure the ulcer and record its size. Apply the appropriate topical medication and dressing. Determine the type of padding and specific material needed to offload the ulcer area. Cut the pad to properly remove pressure. Apply padding.

Postservice

Instruct the patient and/or the patient's caregiver on the appropriate home care, the proper selection and sizing of footwear, and the importance of controlling concomitant medical conditions. Discuss the future management of the condition. Complete the medical record and communicate the findings to the primary care physician.

Coding Tip for 11040 and 11042

Codes 11040 and 11042 may be used more than one time for a single patient encounter when multiple sites are debrided. For each site, select the appropriate code on the basis of the intensity of the wound and append modifier 59, *Distinct procedural service,* to the secondary code(s).

Paring or Cutting

11056 Paring or cutting of benign hyperkeratotic lesion (eg, corn or callus); two to four lesions

Work Value: 0.61 // Global Period: 000

➲ ***CPT Assistant*** **Nov 97: 11, Jan 99: 11**

Clinical Example

A 69-year-old rheumatoid arthritic diabetic female presents with chronic recurring corns on the dorsolateral aspect of both fifth toes, and a callus beneath her second metatarsal head on her right foot. The patient unsuccessfully self-treated the lesion with an emery board and over-the-counter foot remedies. The hyperkeratotic lesions are pared, 1/8-in felt aperture pads are cut and applied to the toes, and a 1/4-in felt aperture pad is applied to the bottom of the right foot.

Preservice

Conduct a preservice evaluation. Review and update the chart with general medical history, including current medications and allergies. Review the treatment options. Review the procedure with the patient and discuss possible complications or sequelae. Prepare instruments, including disposable surgical blade, blade handle, tissue nippers, antiseptic, drapes, gloves, lighting, padding material, and scissors. Communicate with the patient's family or caregiver.

Intraservice

Inspect and palpate the lesion for size, location, functional risks, and depth. Pare the lesion. Apply antiseptic to the skin. Determine the type of padding and specific material needed to shield the toe. Cut the pad to fit the toe and properly remove the pressure point.

Postservice

Instruct the patient and/or the patient's caregiver on the appropriate home care, the proper selection and sizing of footwear, and the importance of controlling concomitant medical conditions. Discuss the future management of the condition. Complete the medical record and communicate the findings to the primary care physician.

Coding Tip for 11056

Code 11056 is used to report the paring or cutting of two to four benign hyperkeratotic lesions such as corns or calluses.

Biopsy

❺ **11100** Biopsy of skin, subcutaneous tissue and/or mucous membrane (including simple closure), unless otherwise listed; single lesion

Work Value: 0.81 // Global Period: 000

➲ ***CPT Assistant*** **Fall 94: 20, Mar 97: 12, Jun 97: 12, Apr 00: 7, Nov 02: 6, Jul 04: 5, Oct 04: 4**
CPT Changes: An Insider's View **2004**

Clinical Example

A 58-year-old female presents with an indurated patch on the forehead. The differential includes a morpheaform basal cell carcinoma and a granuloma of unknown etiology.

Preservice

Prior to biopsying the lesion, obtain pertinent history from the patient that includes information about previous skin cancer and prior treatment and sun protection. Discuss with the patient the following: the indication for biopsy procedure, risks, and benefits; a description of the biopsy procedure method; and the expected results and/or possible scarring. Obtain the patient agreement/informed consent and advise staff of the preparation of the patient and the necessary anesthetic, supplies, and instruments.

Intraservice

Inspect and palpate the lesion to assess its depth and to select the most representative site to obtain a specimen. Cleanse the biopsy site with suitable antiseptic. Inject the appropriate local anesthetic. Apply sterile drapes. Obtain skin specimen with scalpel, skin punch, or suitable instrument depending on the depth and amount of tissue needed. Collect specimen in a labeled formalin container. Undermine wound edges as needed to facilitate repair. Suture to approximate wound edges or achieve hemostasis with pressure, chemical, or electrocautery, or by applying topical hemostatic agents. Apply antibiotic ointment and sterile dressing.

Postservice

Instruct the patient and/or the patient's family on postoperative wound care, dressing changes, and follow-up. Advise the patient on how to recognize significant complications (eg, bleeding) or an allergic reaction to antibiotic ointment or adhesive dressings. Advise the patient when the results will be available and how they will be communicated. Complete the medical record and communicate the results to the referring physician as appropriate.

+ 11101 Biopsy of skin, subcutaneous tissue and/or mucous membrane (including simple closure), unless otherwise listed; each separate/additional lesion (List separately in addition to code for primary procedure)

Work Value: 0.41 // Global Period: ZZZ

➲ *CPT Assistant* Fall 94: 20, Apr 00: 6, Apr 00: 7, Nov 02: 6, Jul 04: 5, Oct 04: 4

Clinical Example

A 44-year-old male is referred for a dermatologic evaluation with a 3-month history of recurring, very pruritic, pink, grouped papules on his elbows, extensor forearms, knees, and occasionally on his lower back, buttocks, and waist. Eruption was not controlled with topical steroids prescribed by a family physician. The dermatologist, after obtaining a history and performing a complete skin exam, makes a presumptive clinical diagnosis of dermatitis herpetiformis. The need for pathologic confirmation of the diagnosis with a skin biopsy prior to instituting a systemic treatment is discussed and the patient agrees. A representative, recent, typical skin lesion near the elbow is identified and anesthetized. A 4-mm punch biopsy is obtained from this lesion including underlying fat. The wound edges are undermined with scissors and approximated along skin tension lines with nylon sutures and dressed with elastic skin closures and waterproof dressing. The patient is instructed on wound care. The specimen is submitted to pathology. (This service is the same clinical presentation and procedure as described for CPT® code 11100.) During a complete skin exam, the dermatologist discovers an ill-defined, scar-like, grayish, firm, flat, 9-mm lesion on the patient's nose/cheek junction. The patient denies symptoms, but thinks the lesion has been present for one to two years. Suspecting a fibrosing basal cell cancer, the dermatologist recommends a biopsy of the lesion for confirmation of suspected skin cancer. After suitable discussion, the patient agrees to a second biopsy procedure on the same date of service. The patient's face is prepared for a sterile procedure, the lesion is anesthetized and draped, and a small punch biopsy is obtained from the nose/cheek junction. A 6-0 nylon suture is placed to control bleeding and a sterile dressing is applied. The specimen is submitted separately to pathology.

Preservice

This separate lesion, unless of the same nature as the first lesion biopsed, will usually require additional pertinent patient history including previous skin cancer, prior treatment history and sun protection history, beyond that which is required for the other presenting problem. Discuss with the patient probable diagnoses and that indications are usually different from that of the first biopsy procedure. Discuss with the patient indication for biopsy procedure, risks and benefits; description of biopsy procedure method, and expected result or scar. In addition, a patient agreement/informed consent must be obtained and staff must be advised for preparation of patient and necessary anesthetic, supplies, and instrument tray preparation.

Intraservice

Intraservice work can include inspecting and palpating the lesion to assess depth and to select the most representative lesion or site to obtain a specimen; cleansing the biopsy site with a suitable antiseptic; injecting the appropriate local anesthetic; scrubbing and gloving by the physician; applying sterile drapes; obtaining the skin specimen with a scalpel, skin punch, or suitable instrument depending on the depth and amount of tissue needed; collecting the specimen in a labeled formalin container; undermining the wound edges as needed to facilitate repair; suturing when necessary to approximate the wound edges; achieving hemostasis with pressure, chemical, or electrocautery, or applying topical hemostatic agents; and applying elastic skin closures or antibiotic ointment and a sterile dressing.

Postservice

The patient and/or family must be instructed on postoperative wound care, dressing changes, and follow-up; advise the patient on how to recognize significant complications, eg, bleeding or allergic reaction to antibiotic ointment or adhesive dressings. The patient should be advised when results will be available and how they will be communicated. Complete medical record and communicate results to referring physician as appropriate.

Coding Tip for 11100 and 11101

Codes 11100 and 11101 are general codes reported for the biopsy of skin, subcutaneous tissue, and/or mucous membrane. These codes include simple closure when such closures are performed.

Removal of Skin Tags

11200 Removal of skin tags, multiple fibrocutaneous tags, any area; up to and including 15 lesions

Work Value: 0.79 // Global Period: 010

➲ *CPT Assistant* Winter 90: 3, Nov 97: 11-12, Nov 02: 11

Clinical Example

A 66-year-old female presents with complaints of growing skin lesions on her neck. They are irritated by her collar and sometimes catch in her necklace, causing bleeding on one occasion. She has a family history of similar lesions. On examination there are 12 lesions from 3 to 6 mm in size on the anterior and sides of the neck, all typical for the diagnosis of skin tags. Removal is recommended because they are symptomatic. The procedure is described and informed consent is obtained. After cleansing the area with alcohol, each tag is anesthetized with 1% lidocaine. The smaller neck lesions are removed with scissors excision and aluminum chloride solution is applied topically for hemostasis. The larger neck lesions are electrodessicated at their base to facilitate hemostasis prior to the scissors excision. Topical bacitracin ZN/polymyxin B is applied along with a bandage for the larger neck surgical sites.

Preservice

Review pertinent data in the patient's medical records. Discuss the choice of treatment or service options with the patient. Review the medical risks, such as syncope, bleeding, pain, edema, infection, headache, delayed healing, scarring, pigmentation, recurrence, and paresthesias with the patient. Obtain informed consent. Provide the necessary instructions to the patient and staff. Prepare the electrosurgical equipment and disposable supplies including cautery tips, masks, and gloves. Ensure appropriate lighting and draping if necessary. Prepare the nondisposable equipment including scissors and forceps. Prepare for cryosurgery, including transferring liquid nitrogen to an application container (eg, a cup with cotton-tipped application, a cryospray unit, or a cryoprobe). Obtain protective shields and perform a clean preparation.

Intraservice

Inspect and palpate the lesion for size, location, functional risks, and depth. Administer local anesthesia. Perform the electrosurgical destruction of the lesion and the scissor removal of the lesion. Control bleeding with aluminum chloride.

Postservice

Apply antibiotic ointment. Apply dressing, when appropriate. Instruct the patient on wound care, functional risks, and follow-up. Instruct the staff to schedule a one-month follow-up postsurgical visit. Communicate with the patient and the patient's family on postoperative care and follow-up. Complete the medical record chart, including dictating the operative report and communicating with the referring physicians, if appropriate.

+ 11201 Removal of skin tags, multiple fibrocutaneous tags, any area; each additional ten lesions (List separately in addition to code for primary procedure)

Work Value: 0.29 // Global Period: ZZZ

➲ *CPT Assistant* Winter 90: 3, Nov 97: 11-12, Nov 02: 11

Clinical Example

A 66-year-old female presents with complaints of growing skin lesions on her neck and axillary areas. She has a family history of similar lesions. The tags on her neck are irritated by her collars and catch in her necklaces. The tags in the axillae itch in warm weather and with exercise. On examination there are 12 pedunculated papules on the sides of the neck, 3 to 5 mm in size, and 11 tags that are 2 to 6 mm in size in the axillary areas. They are all typical for the diagnosis of skin tags. Because the tags are symptomatic, removal is recommended. The procedure is described to the patient and informed consent is obtained. After cleansing the area with alcohol, each tag is anesthetized with 1% lidocaine. The bases of the tags are electrodessicated and the larger tags are removed by scissors excision. Aluminum chloride is applied as needed topically for hemostasis. The larger sites are covered with topical bacitracin ZN/polymyxin B and bandages.

Preservice

Review pertinent data in the patient's medical records. Discuss the choice of treatment or service options with the patient. Review the medical risks, such as syncope, bleeding, pain, edema, infection, headache, delayed healing, scarring, pigmentation, recurrence, and paresthesias with the patient. Obtain informed consent. Provide the necessary instructions to the patient and staff. Prepare the electrosurgical equipment and disposable supplies including cautery tips, masks, and gloves. Ensure appropriate lighting and draping if necessary. Prepare the nondisposable equipment including scissors and forceps. Prepare for cryosurgery, including transferring liquid nitrogen to an application container (eg, a cup with cotton-tipped application, a cryospray unit, or a cryoprobe). Obtain protective shields and perform a clean preparation.

Intraservice

Inspect and palpate lesion for size, location, functional risks, and depth. Administer local anesthesia. Perform the electrosurgical destruction of the lesion and the scissor removal of the lesion. Control bleeding with aluminum chloride.

Postservice

Apply antibiotic ointment. Apply dressing, when appropriate. Instruct the patient on wound care, functional risks, and follow-up. Instruct the staff to schedule a one-month follow-up postsurgical visit. Communicate with the patient and the patient's family on postoperative care and follow-up. Complete the medical record charting, including dictating the operative report and communicating with the referring physicians, if appropriate.

Removal of Skin Tags
11200, 11201

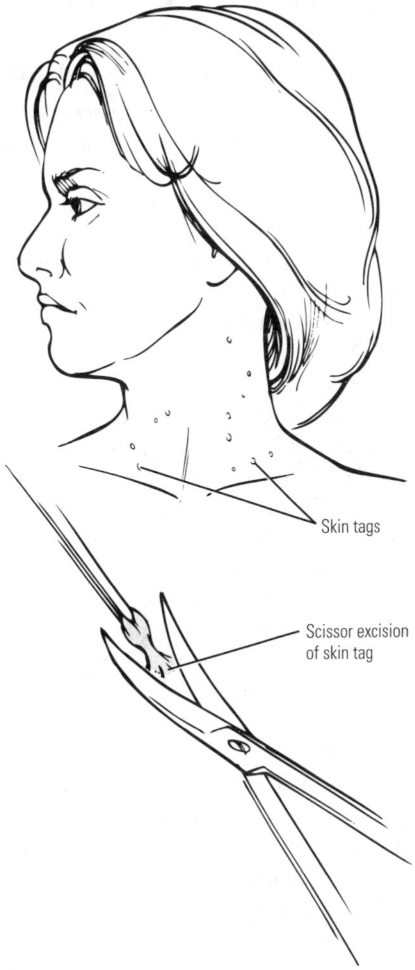

Coding Tip for 11200 and 11201

Codes 11200 and 11201 are reported for the removal of skin tags from any area of the body. These codes represent the removal of skin tags by scissoring or any sharp method, ligature strangulation, electrosurgical destruction, or a combination of treatment modalities including the chemical or electrocauterization of a wound.

Excision—Benign Lesions

❺ 11400 Excision, benign lesion including margins, except skin tag (unless listed elsewhere), trunk, arms or legs; excised diameter 0.5 cm or less

Work Value: 0.87 // Global Period: 010

➲ *CPT Assistant* Summer 92: 22, Fall 93: 7, Fall 95: 3, May 96: 11, Aug 00: 5, Nov 02: 5, 7; *CPT Changes: An Insider's View* 2003

Clinical Example

A 35-year-old male presents for removal of an atypical pigmented nevus on the waistline with excised diameter of 0.45 cm.

Preservice

The benefits, risks, and alternatives to removal are explained to the patient. The procedure is explained, and the healing period with restrictions is reviewed. Dates for probable suture removal are discussed. A fresh history of medications taken, including aspirin, vitamin E, and/or other blood thinners, is reviewed along with pertinent problems that may have arisen since the scheduling visit. Consent is obtained.

Intraservice

The physician cleanses the area with dermalogical surgery scrub. With a sterile surgical marker, the physician delineates the extent of the excision, including appropriate margins. The physician then injects the site with a local anesthetic. The patient is re-prepped and draped, lights are positioned, and a scalpel is used to incise along the borders of the lesion. The excision is carried through the dermis into the subcutaneous fat. Hemostasis is achieved with either cautery and/or suture. Suture material is used to close the wound. The area is cleansed, dried, and a pressure bandage is applied.

Postservice

Wound care; instructions for problems such as bleeding, pain, or dehiscence; and restrictions on motion and activities are reviewed with the patient. Prescriptions for pain and antibiotics, if needed, are given.

❺ 11406 Excision, benign lesion including margins, except skin tag (unless listed elsewhere), trunk, arms or legs; excised diameter over 4.0 cm

Work Value: 3.47 // Global Period: 010

➲ *CPT Assistant* Summer 92: 22, Fall 93: 7, Fall 95: 3, May 96: 11, Nov 02: 5, 7; *CPT Changes: An Insider's View* 2003

Clinical Example

A 35-year-old male presents for removal of a biopsy-proven, atypical pigmented nevus on the waistline with an excised diameter of 4.6 cm.

Preservice

Review the preoperative work up, paying special attention to the pathology report. Meet with the patient to review the planned procedure and postoperative management. Review and obtain informed consent with the patient and witness. Verify that all required instruments and supplies are available. Monitor/assist with the positioning of the patient. Mark the site and side of the proposed skin incision and confirm with the patient. Indicate the area of skin to be prepped and draped. Trim hair with scissors over and around the lesion. Scrub and gown. Perform surgical "time out." Administer a local anesthetic using a field block technique and wait for it to take effect.

Intraservice

Make an elliptical incision around the entire lesion (excisional biopsy) with a 2-mm margin of normal skin. (The dissection is full thickness and includes some subcutaneous fat.) Use electrocautery to obtain hemostasis, paying attention to not destroy the tissue architecture. Place a suture in the edge of the specimen before it is removed from the body (ie, at 12 o'clock). Note the original position of the suture with a drawing on the pathology specimen form. Close the skin with interrupted nylon sutures or skin staples.

Postservice

Day of Procedure: Apply a sterile dressing. Discuss the procedure, discharge instructions, and outcome with the patient. Write prescriptions for postdischarge medications as needed. Dictate the operative report and supply a copy to the referring physician(s) along with a letter outlining plans for long-term management. Complete all appropriate medical records, discharge summary, and insurance forms.

In Office After Procedure: Review the pathology report and the patient's chart. Talk with the patient and the patient's family. Check the wound and remove sutures/staples. Advise the patient on sun exposure risks, the need for monthly self examinations, the need for follow-up care to detect the occurrence of other lesions, and the potential risk of FAMMM (genetic syndrome). Answer the patient's and family's questions. Dictate progress notes for medical records and communicate with the referring/family physician.

Coding Tip for 11406

To report an unusual or complicated excision, append modifier 22, *Unusual procedural service,* to the procedure code.

---

⑤ 11440 Excision, other benign lesion including margins, except skin tag (unless listed elsewhere), face, ears, eyelids, nose, lips, mucous membrane; excised diameter 0.5 cm or less

Work Value: 1.02 // Global Period: 010

➲ ***CPT Assistant*** **Summer 92: 22, Fall 95: 3, May 96: 11; *CPT Changes: An Insider's View* 2003**

Clinical Example

A 35-year-old male presents for removal of an atypical pigmented nevus on the left zygomatic area of the cheek with excised diameter of 0.45 cm.

Preservice

The benefits, risks, and alternatives to removal are explained to the patient. The procedure is explained, and the healing period with restrictions is reviewed. Dates for probable suture removal are discussed. A fresh history of medications taken, including aspirin, vitamin E, and/or other blood thinners, is reviewed along with pertinent problems that may have arisen since the scheduling visit. Consent is obtained.

Intraservice

The physician cleanses the area with a dermalogical surgery scrub, and with a sterile surgical marker delineates the extent of the excision including appropriate margins. The physician then injects the area with a local anesthetic. The patient is reprepped and draped, lights are positioned, and a scalpel is used to incise along the borders of the lesion. The excision is carried through the dermis into the subcutaneous fat. Hemostasis is achieved with either cautery and/or suture. Suture material is used to close the wound. The area is cleansed, dried, and a pressure bandage is applied.

Postservice

Wound care is reviewed with the patient. Instructions for problems such as bleeding, pain, or dehiscence, and restrictions on motion and activities are reviewed with the patient. Prescriptions for pain and antibiotics, if needed, are given.

---

⑤ 11446 Excision, other benign lesion including margins, except skin tag (unless listed elsewhere), face, ears, eyelids, nose, lips, mucous membrane; excised diameter over 4.0 cm

Work Value: 4.75 // Global Period: 010

➲ ***CPT Assistant*** **Summer 92: 22, Fall 95: 3, May 96: 11; *CPT Changes: An Insider's View* 2003**

Clinical Example

A 35-year-old patient presents for removal of a biopsy-proven atypical pigmented nevus on the left zygomatic area of the cheek with an excised diameter of 4.6 cm.

Preservice

The benefits, risks, and alternatives to removal are explained to the patient. The procedure is explained, and the healing period with restrictions is reviewed. Dates for probable suture removal are discussed. A fresh history of medications taken, including aspirin, vitamin E, and/or other blood thinners, is reviewed along with pertinent problems that may have arisen since the scheduling visit. Consent is obtained.

Intraservice

The physician cleanses the area with an antiseptic, and with a sterile surgical marker delineates the extent of the excision. The physician then injects the area with a local anesthetic. The patient is reprepped and draped, lights are positioned, and a scalpel is used to incise along the borders of the lesion. The excision is carried through the dermis into the subcutaneous fat. Hemostasis is achieved with either cautery and/or suture. Undermining is preformed as necessary to ease wound tension. The wound is closed in one layer with a nonabsorbable suture. The area is cleansed, dried, and a pressure bandage is applied.

Postservice

Wound care is reviewed with the patient. Instructions for problems such as bleeding, pain, or dehiscence, and restrictions on motion and activities are reviewed with the patient. Prescriptions for pain and antibiotics, if needed, are given.

Coding Tip for 11400, 11406, 11440, and 11446

Excision is defined as full-thickness (through the dermis) removal of a lesion, including margins, and includes simple (nonlayered) closure when performed. It is appropriate to report separately each benign lesion excised. Code selection is determined by measuring the greatest clinical diameter of the apparent lesion plus that margin required for complete excision (ie, the lesion diameter plus the most narrow margins required equals the excised diameter). The margins refer to the most narrow margin required to adequately excise the lesion based on the physician's judgment. The measurement of lesion plus margin is made prior to excision. The excised diameter is the same whether the surgical defect is repaired in a linear fashion or reconstructed (eg, with a skin graft).

Excision—Malignant Lesions

❺ 11600 Excision, malignant lesion including margins, trunk, arms, or legs; excised diameter 0.5 cm or less

Work Value: 1.58 // Global Period: 010

➲ *CPT Assistant* **Fall 95: 3, May 96: 11, Nov 02: 5;** *CPT Changes: An Insider's View* **2003**

Clinical Example

A 55-year-old male presents for removal of a biopsy-proven squamous cell carcinoma on the upper back with excised diameter of 0.45 cm.

Preservice

The patient is taken to the surgical room and gowned. The benefits, risks, and alternatives to removal are explained. Sun exposure is discussed. The procedure is explained, and the healing period with restrictions is reviewed. Probable dates for suture removal are discussed. A fresh history of medications taken, including aspirin, vitamin E, and/or other blood thinners, is reviewed along with pertinent problems that may have arisen since the scheduling visit.

Intraservice

The patient is placed on the surgical table and positioned for access. The area is cleansed with a dermalogical surgery scrub. A sterile surgical marker is used to delineate the extent of the planned excision including appropriate margins. Lidocaine is injected. The patient is reprepped and draped, lights are positioned, and a scalpel is used to incise along the planned borders of the excision.

The excision is carried through the dermis into and through the subcutaneous fat. With manual and visual inspection, the specimen and wound margin are examined to ascertain that no clinically visible or palpable tumor is left behind. The specimen is then oriented and marked with sutures to facilitate the report of accurate margins by the pathology laboratory. Hemostasis is achieved with either cautery and/or suture. The wound is closed with suture material. The area is cleansed, dried, and a pressure bandage is applied.

Postservice

Wound care is reviewed with the patient. Instructions for problems such as bleeding, pain, or dehiscence, and restrictions on motion and activities are reviewed with the patient. Prescriptions for pain and antibiotics, if needed, are given.

Excision Malignant Lesion
11600

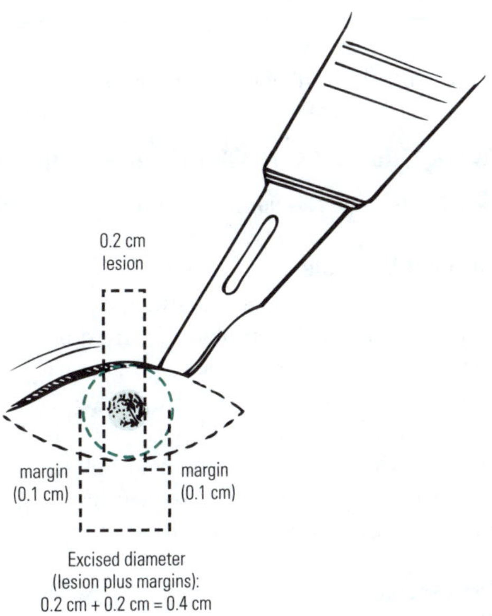

⑤ 11602 Excision, malignant lesion including margins, trunk, arms, or legs; excised diameter 1.1 to 2.0 cm

Work Value: 2.22 // Global Period: 010

➲ ***CPT Assistant*** **Fall 95: 3, May 96: 11, Nov 02: 5;** ***CPT Changes: An Insider's View*** **2003**

Clinical Example

A 55-year-old male presents for removal of a biopsy-proven squamous cell carcinoma on the upper back with excised diameter of 1.6 cm.

Preservice

The patient is taken to the surgical room and gowned. The benefits, risks, and alternatives to removal are explained. Sun exposure is discussed. The procedure is explained, and the healing period with restrictions is reviewed. Probable dates for suture removal are discussed. A fresh history of medications taken, including aspirin, vitamin E, and/or other blood thinners, is reviewed along with pertinent problems that may have arisen since the scheduling visit.

Intraservice

The patient is placed on the surgical table and positioned for access. The area is cleansed with a dermalogical surgery scrub. A sterile surgical marker is used to delineate the extent of the planned excision including appropriate margins. Lidocaine is injected. The patient is reprepped and draped, lights are positioned, and a scalpel is used to incise along the planned borders of the excision. The excision is carried through the dermis into and through the subcutaneous fat. With manual and visual inspection, the specimen and wound margin are examined to ascertain that no clinically visible or palpable tumor is left behind. The specimen is then oriented and marked with sutures to facilitate the report of accurate margins by the pathology laboratory. Hemostasis is achieved with either cautery and/or suture. The wound is closed with suture material. The area is cleansed, dried, and a pressure bandage is applied.

Postservice

Wound care is reviewed with the patient. Instructions for problems such as bleeding, pain, or dehiscence, and restrictions on motion and activities are reviewed with the patient. Prescriptions for pain and antibiotics, if needed, are given.

Nails

11719 Trimming of nondystrophic nails, any number

Work Value: 0.17 // Global Period: 000

➲ *CPT Assistant* Nov 97: 12, Dec 02: 4

Clinical Example

A 67-year-old obese diabetic female presents with 10 hypertrophied nails. All 10 nails are trimmed.

Preservice

Conduct a preservice evaluation. Review and update the chart with medical history, including current medications and allergies. Review treatment options. Review the procedure with the patient and discuss possible complications. Prepare instruments, including nail nippers, nail rasp, curette, antiseptic, drapes, gloves, and lighting.

Intraservice

Inspect length and thickness of nails and periungual tissue. Trim all toenails. Apply antiseptic to nails and periungual tissue.

Postservice

Instruct the patient and/or the patient's caregiver on appropriate home care and the importance of controlling concomitant medical conditions. Discuss future management of the condition. Communicate with the patient's primary care physician.

11720 Debridement of nail(s) by any method(s); one to five

Work Value: 0.32 // Global Period: 000

➲ *CPT Assistant* Nov 96: 3, Dec 02: 4

Clinical Example

A 67-year-old female presents with four painful toenails. The problems started to develop 10 years ago and have progressively worsened so that these nails are thickened, dystrophic, and painful. There is yellowish discoloration of each deformed nail plate with subungual debris. The patient has difficulty wearing normal shoes and walking.

Preservice

Review the patient's medical records. Communicate with other professionals. Communicate with the patient and/or the patient's family. Prepare the patient and instruments.

Intraservice

Using a combination of surgical hand instruments and power rotating burr, debride the nails to reduce the size and girth of the abnormal nail plates, short of avulsion.

Postservice

Apply the appropriate topical medication and dressing as necessary. Provide appropriate prescriptions. Communicate with the patient, the patient's family, and other professionals as appropriate. Complete the patient's medical record.

11721 Debridement of nail(s) by any method(s); six or more

Work Value: 0.54 // Global Period: 000

➲ *CPT Assistant* Nov 96: 3, Dec 02: 4

Clinical Example

A 67-year-old female presents with eight painful toenails. The problems started to develop 10 years ago and have progressively worsened so that these nails are thickened, dystrophic, and painful. There is yellowish discoloration of each deformed nail plate with subungual debris. The patient has difficulty wearing normal shoes and walking.

Preservice

Review the patient's medical records. Communicate with other professionals. Communicate with the patient and/or the patient's family. Prepare the patient and instruments.

Intraservice

Using a combination of surgical hand instruments and power rotating burr, debride the nails to reduce the size and girth of the abnormal nail plates, short of avulsion.

Postservice

Apply the appropriate topical medication and dressing as necessary. Provide appropriate prescriptions. Communicate with the patient, the patient's family, and other professionals as appropriate. Complete the medical record.

Lateral Nail View
11719, 11720, 11721

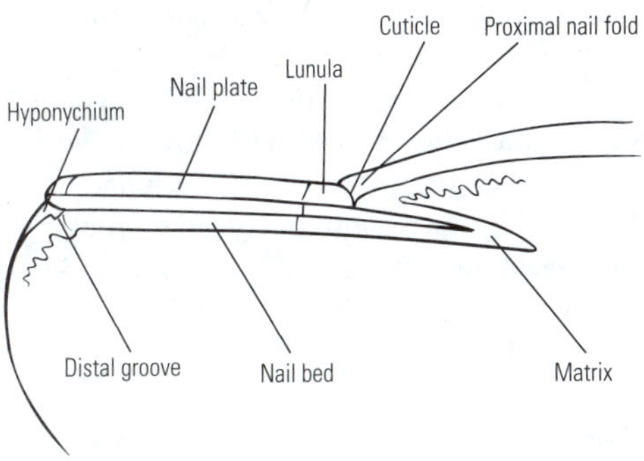

Dorsal Nail View
11719, 11720, 11721

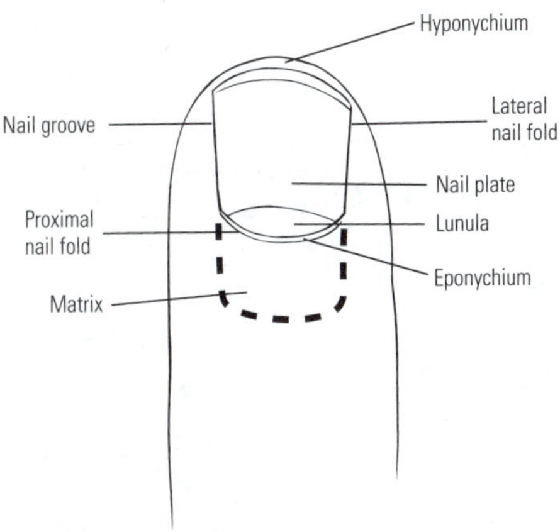

Repair (Closure)

Repair Intermediate

⑤ **12052** Layer closure of wounds of face, ears, eyelids, nose, lips and/or mucous membranes; 2.6 cm to 5.0 cm

Work Value: 2.81 // Global Period: 010

➲ ***CPT Assistant*** **Feb 00: 10, Aug 00: 9, Jan 02: 10**

Clinical Example

A 40-year-old male requires closure of a surgical wound of the lower left cheek resulting in a defect measuring 2.4 cm × 0.8 cm. The defect extends to subcutaneous tissue with a large subcutaneous dead space. The wound is under significant tension.

Preservice

Preservice work begins with assessing the patient and taking a history; reviewing current prescriptions; obtaining and reviewing current imaging and laboratory studies; communicating with other health care professionals; ordering preoperative antibiotics; and communicating with the patient and/or patient's family to explain the operative risks and benefits and to obtain informed consent. Other preoperative services include dressing; scrubbing; supervising the positioning, prepping, and draping of the patient; and ensuring that the necessary surgical instruments and supplies are present.

Intraservice

Intraservice work includes injecting local anesthetic for anesthesia and hemostasis; waiting for adequate anesthesia; prepping and draping the area; performing any closure the defect may require; removing any additional wound debris; irrigation; and performing electrocauterization for hemostasis. Sutures are placed in the superficial fascia to close the dead space and approximate the tissues. Suturing of the skin is performed as a separate layer. The area is cleansed and a sterile dressing is applied.

Postservice

Postservice work begins with monitoring patient stabilization postprocedure. An operative report is dictated and orders are written. The physician communicates with the patient's family and other health care professionals (including providing written and oral reports). Discharge management includes the surgeon's final examination of the patient, which includes a discussion of home care and follow up; completing the discharge forms and prescriptions; reconciling preprocedure prescriptions; and communicating with other health care providers and the patient's family.

Adjacent Tissue Transfer or Rearrangement

⑤ **14040** Adjacent tissue transfer or rearrangement, forehead, cheeks, chin, mouth, neck, axillae, genitalia, hands and/or feet; defect 10 sq cm or less

Work Value: 8.44 // Global Period: 090

➲ *CPT Assistant* Jul 99: 3, Jul 00: 10, Jan 06: 47

Clinical Example

A 63-year-old male with an excised basal cell carcinoma on the left medial cheek leaves a defect through the subcutaneous plane that is 1.4 cm in diameter and involves the lower part of the left lower eyelid. To prevent ectropion, reconstruction via adjacent tissue transfer is performed.

Preservice

Preservice begins with assessing the patient and taking a history, reviewing current prescriptions, obtaining and reviewing current imaging and laboratory studies, communicating with other health care professionals, ordering preoperative antibiotics, and communicating with the patient and/or patient's family to explain the operative risks and benefits and to obtain informed consent. Other preoperative services include dressing, scrubbing, and waiting to begin the operation; supervising the positioning, prepping, and draping of the patient; and ensuring that the necessary surgical instruments and supplies are present and available in the operative suite.

Intraservice

Skin markings are made to outline the excision of the lesion and the appropriate margin. Local anesthetic is injected. After an adequate hemostatic wait, the lesion is excised. The lesion is oriented and marked with sutures. Hemostasis is obtained. Care is taken to determine the availability of adjacent tissue for closure and the possibility of functional impairment or anatomic distortion of adjacent structures. An adjacent flap is designed. The flap is incised and raised at the appropriate level. The flap is rotated into the defect. Tension is assessed and additional dissection is performed as necessary. Drains may be placed. The flap is sutured into position. A sterile dressing is applied.

Postservice

Postservice begins with monitoring the stabilization of the patient in the operating and recovery rooms. The operative report is dictated and orders are written. The physician communicates with the family and other health care professionals (including providing written and oral reports). Discharge management is completed, which includes the surgeon's final examination of the patient, a discussion of home care and follow-up with the patient, completion of the discharge forms and prescriptions, reconciliation of preprocedure prescriptions, and communication with other health care providers and the patient's family.

Adjacent Tissue Repairs
14040

Repair of primary and secondary defects. Assign code based upon repair location and approximate description (as demonstrated below) of area repaired.

A. Advancement Flap

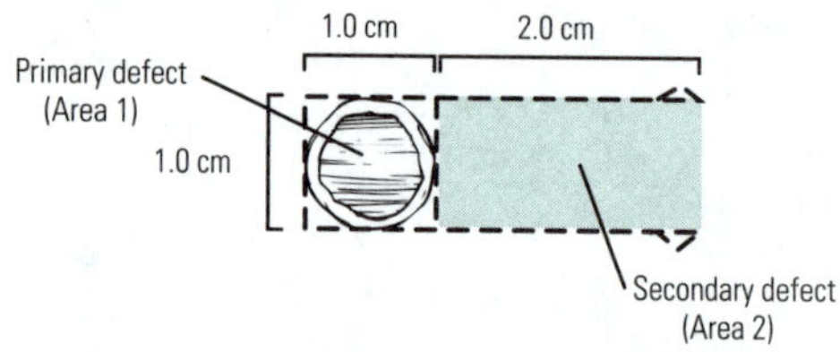

Area 1: 1.0 cm x 1.0 cm = 1.0 sq cm
Area 2: 1.0 cm x 2.0 cm = 2.0 sq cm
(Area 1) + (Area 2) = 1.0 sq cm + 2.0 sq cm = 3.0 sq cm

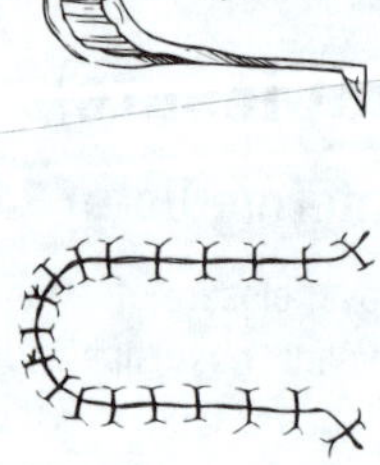

B. Rotation Flap
14040

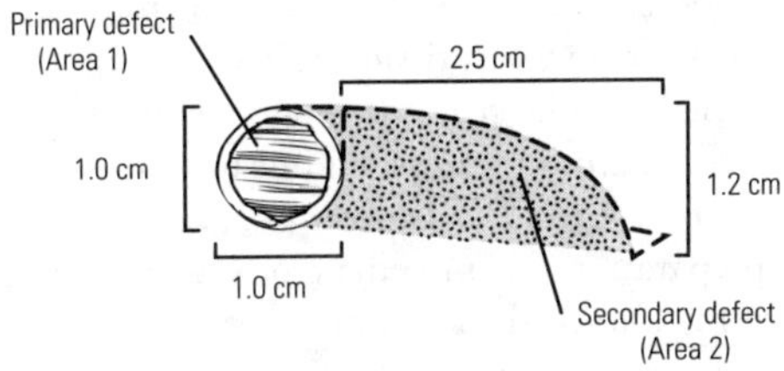

Area 1: 1.0 cm x 1.0 cm = 1.0 sq cm
Area 2: 2.5 cm x 1.2 cm = 3.0 sq cm
(Area 1) + (Area 2) = 1.0 sq cm + 3.0 sq cm = 4.0 sq cm

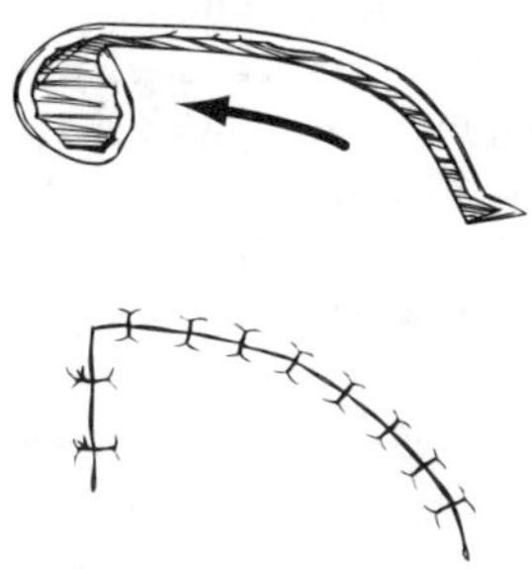

Coding Tip for 14040 and 14060

Codes 14040 and 14060 are reported for the excision (including lesion) and/or repair by adjacent tissue transfer or rearrangement (eg, Z-plasty, W-plasty, V-Y plasty, rotation flap, advancement flap, double pedicle flap).

---

❺ **14060** Adjacent tissue transfer or rearrangement, eyelids, nose, ears and/or lips; defect 10 sq cm or less

Work Value: 9.07 // Global Period: 090

➲ ***CPT Assistant*** **Fall 93: 7, Jul 99: 3, Dec 99: 10, Jan 06: 47**

Clinical Example

A 63-year-old male with an excised basal cell carcinoma on the lower left lateral sidewall of the nose presents with a defect through the subcutaneous plane that is 1.4 cm in diameter and involves the lower part of the left lower eyelid. In order to prevent ectropion, reconstruction via adjacent tissue transfer is performed.

Preservice

Preservice work begins with assessing the patient and taking a history; reviewing current prescriptions; obtaining and reviewing current imaging and laboratory studies; communicating with other health care professionals; ordering preoperative antibiotics; and communicating with the patient and/or patient's family to explain the operative risks and benefits and obtain informed consent. Other preoperative services include dressing, scrubbing, and waiting to begin the operation; supervising the positioning, prepping, and draping of the patient; and ensuring that the necessary surgical instruments and supplies are present and available in the operative suite.

Intraservice

Skin markings are made to outline the excision of the lesion and the appropriate margin. Local anesthetic is injected. After an adequate hemostatic wait, the lesion is excised. The lesion is oriented and marked with sutures. Hemostasis is obtained. Care is taken to determine the availability of adjacent tissue for closure and the possibility of functional impairment or anatomic distortion of adjacent structures. An adjacent flap is designed. The flap is incised and raised at the appropriate level. The flap is rotated into the defect. Tension is assessed and additional dissection performed as necessary. Drains may be placed. The flap is sutured into position. A sterile dressing is applied.

Postservice

Postservice work begins with monitoring patient stabilization in the operating and recovery room. An operative report is dictated and orders are written. The physician communicates with the patient's family and other health care professionals (including providing written and oral reports). Discharge management includes the surgeon's final examination of the patient, which includes discussing home care and follow up; completing the discharge forms and prescriptions; reconciling the preprocedure prescriptions; and communicating with other health care providers and the patient's family.

Skin Replacement Surgery and Skin Substitutes

Surgical Preparation

15002 Surgical preparation or creation of recipient site by excision of open wounds, burn eschar, or scar (including subcutaneous tissues), or incisional release of scar contracture, trunk, arms, legs; first 100 sq cm or 1% of body area of infants and children

Work Value: 3.65 // Global Period: 000

➲ ***CPT Assistant*** **Fall 93: 7, Apr 97: 4, Aug 97: 6, Sep 97: 2, Nov 98: 5, Jan 99: 4, Apr 99: 10, May 99: 10, Nov 02: 7, Aug 03: 14;** ***CPT Changes: An Insider's View*** **2007**

Clinical Example

A 27-year-old cook was admitted to the burn center with grease scald burns involving the left shoulder, chest, and arm. A total of 25% body surface area was burned full thickness. Under general anesthesia, the left shoulder, arm and chest burns were excised down to viable subcutaneous tissue; the first 100 sq cm of a planned total of 500 sq cm was excised.

Preservice

Preservice work includes taking an interval history and performing a physical exam; reviewing the previous work-up and preoperative laboratory test results; consulting with the referring physician, if necessary, and other health care professionals; and communicating with the patient and/or the patient'ss family to explain the operative risks and benefits and obtain informed consent. Other preoperative services include performing a type crossmatch for blood to be administered during the procedure; administering preoperative antibiotics; dressing, scrubbing, and waiting to begin the operation; supervising the positioning, prepping, and draping of the patient; and ensuring that the necessary surgical instruments and supplies are present and available in the operative suite.

Intraservice

After the induction of anesthesia, the subcutaneous tissue beneath the full-thickness burn is infiltrated with crystalloid solution containing epinephrine in order to minimize blood loss. The eschar is excised down to viable subcutaneous tissue. Hemostasis is obtained with electrocautery, epinephrine-soaked laparotomy pads, and/or topical thrombin. A total of 100 sq cm is excised in preparation for immediate or staged skin grafting and/or the application of a skin substitute/replacement.

Postservice

Postservice work begins after the application of the wound dressing in the operating room and includes monitoring the patient's stability in the recovery room; writing orders; communicating with the patient's family and other health care professionals (including providing written and oral reports and orders); and all hospital visits and services performed by the surgeon in the intensive care unit or on a suitable nursing floor. Discharge management includes the surgeon's final examination of the patient, which includes providing instructions for continuing care of the operative sites, and preparing the discharge records.

Coding Tip for 15002

Code 15002 is reported for initial wound recipient site preparation.

Grafts

15340 Tissue cultured allogeneic skin substitute; first 25 sq cm or less

Work Value: 3.76 // Global Period: 010

➲ ***CPT Changes: An Insider's View*** **2006**

Clinical Example

A 68-year-old male with type II diabetes presents with a 3 cm × 3 cm noninfected full-thickness chronic ulceration of the plantar aspect of the right heel. The decision is made to debride the wound and proceed with application of a tissue-cultured allogeneic skin substitute.

Preservice

Preservice work includes taking an interval history and performing a physical exam; reviewing the previous work-up; consulting with the referring physician, if necessary, and other health care professionals; and communicating with the patient and/or the patient's family to explain the operative risks and benefits and obtain informed consent. Other preoperative services include dressing, scrubbing, and waiting to begin the operation; supervising the positioning, prepping, and draping of the patient; and ensuring that the necessary surgical instruments and supplies, including appropriate graft material, are present and available in the operative suite.

Intraservice

The wound is debrided and after adequate hemostasis has been achieved and the administration of anesthesia has occurred, graft materials are obtained. The wound is measured. Approximately 25 sq cm of tissue cultured allogeneic skin substitute is fenestrated and then grafted to the excised surface and secured with interrupted sutures.

Postservice

Postservice work begins after skin closure in the operating room and includes the application of a low adherent dressing that is reinforced with absorbent and compressive dressings. Postservice work also includes monitoring the patient's stability in the recovery room; writing orders; and communicating with the family and other health care professionals (including providing written and oral reports and orders). Discharge management includes the surgeon's final examination of the patient, which includes providing instructions for continuing care of the operative sites, and preparing the discharge records. In addition, all postdischarge office visits for this procedure for 10 days after the day of the operation are considered part of the postservice work for this procedure including the removal of sutures, dressing changes, and antibiotic and pain medication adjustments.

Coding Tip for 15340

Code 15340 should not be reported in conjunction with codes 11040-11042 and codes 15002-15005. A tissue-cultured allogeneic skin substitute is defined as cultured allogeneic skin with both a dermal and epidermal layer.

15400 Xenograft, skin (dermal), for temporary wound closure, trunk, arms, legs; first 100 sq cm or less, or 1% of body area of infants and children

Work Value: 4.38 // Global Period: 090

➲ *CPT Assistant* **Apr 97: 4, Sep 97: 3, Nov 98: 6, Jan 99: 4, Apr 01: 10, Nov 03: 15, Jan 06: 1;** *CPT Changes: An Insider's View* **2006**

Clinical Example

A 22-year-old mechanic suffered burns of the left shoulder and arm from a radiator scald injury. The burns involved 10% of his body surface. These burns were deep partial thickness. During the first operative session, the patient underwent surgical preparation of the burn on the left shoulder and arm by excision down to viable dermis (reported separately). After adequate hemostasis had been achieved in the excised surface, 100 sq cm of xenograft skin was then grafted to the excised surface and secured with interrupted sutures. The graft was dressed with a low adherent dressing and reinforced with absorbent dressing and secured with net dressing.

Preservice

Preservice work includes taking an interval history and performing a physical exam; reviewing the previous work-up and preoperative laboratory test results; consulting with the referring physician, if necessary, and other health care professionals; and communicating with the patient and/or the patient's family to explain the operative risks and benefits and obtain informed consent. Other preoperative services include administering preoperative antibiotics; dressing, scrubbing, and waiting to begin the operation; supervising the positioning, prepping, and draping of the patient; supervising the preparation of the acellular dermal replacement; and ensuring that the necessary surgical instruments and supplies are present and available in the operative suite.

Intraservice

Hemostasis of the debrided/excised graft site is obtained. Xenograft skin (dermal) is obtained from the tissue bank. A total of 100 sq cm is applied to the left shoulder and arm and secured to the excised wound with interrupted sutures or surgical staples. The wound is then covered with gauze dressings and secured with a bulky dressing to prevent mechanical shear.

Postservice

Postservice work begins after the application of the wound dressing in the operating room and includes monitoring the patient's stability in the recovery room; writing orders; communicating with the patient's family and other health care professionals (including providing written and oral reports and orders); and all hospital visits and services performed by the surgeon in the intensive care unit or on a suitable nursing floor. Discharge management includes the surgeon's final examination of the patient, which includes providing instructions for continuing care of the operative sites, and preparing the discharge records. In addition, all postdischarge office visits for this procedure for 90 days after the day of the operation are considered part of the postservice work for this procedure including the removal of sutures, dressing changes, and antibiotic and pain medication adjustments.

Xenograft, Skin
15400

Application of a porcine skin graft following excision of the burn wound and/or surgical preparation of the site.

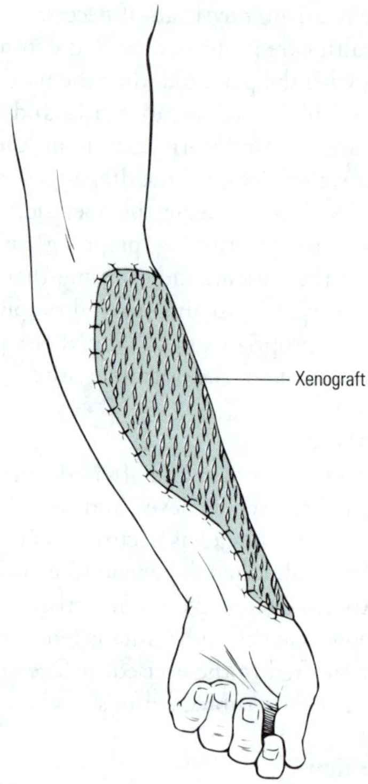

Coding Tip for 15400

Code 15400 is reported for the application of a nonhuman skin graft or biologic wound dressing (eg, porcine tissue or pigskin) to a part of the recipient's body following the debridement of the burn wound or area of traumatic injury, a soft tissue infection and/or tissue necrosis, or surgery. A xenogeneic dermis is defined as a nonhuman dermis for temporary wound closure.

Flaps (Skin and/or Deep Tissues)

15732 Muscle, myocutaneous, or fasciocutaneous flap; head and neck (eg, temporalis, masseter muscle, sternocleidomastoid, levator scapulae)

Work Value: 19.70 // Global Period: 090

➲ *CPT Changes: An Insider's View* 2002

Clinical Example

A 77-year-old smoker develops a carcinoma of the palate, which is resected with a loss of approximately one half of the soft and hard palate. This defect is then reconstructed with a temporalis muscle flap. A separate operative approach must be made to harvest the temporalis muscle. A scalp incision is made and the muscle is separated from its origins in the temporal fossa. A dissection of the deep temporal artery is made and this vascular pedicle must carefully be preserved. The muscle is then tunneled deep to the zygomatic arch into the oral cavity. The donor site is closed primarily. The muscle flap is inset into the palatal defect, reconstructing the palate unilaterally.

Preservice

Begin preservice on the day before the surgery. Obtain and review preprocedural laboratory and imaging studies. Review findings from the prior operation. Consult with the referring physician and if necessary, other health care professionals. Communicate with the patient and/or patient's family to explain operative risks and benefits and to obtain informed consent. Additional preoperative services include dressing, scrubbing, and waiting for surgery; supervising the positioning, prepping, and draping of the patient; and ensuring that surgical instruments and supplies that are necessary are present and available in the operative suite.

Intraservice

After the ablative part of the procedure has been completed, obtain appropriate measurements of the defect and plan for the size of the flap. Make an incision over the ipsilateral temporalis muscle. Dissect to the temporal fascia, which is opened widely and the appropriate amount of muscle dissected from the temporal fossa. Isolate this muscle on the deep temporal artery and its accompanying vein and assess the surrounding anatomic relationships. Create a tunnel deep to the zygomatic arch, taking care not to disturb existing intact arteries and nerves. Open this tunnel into the oral cavity and enlarge it to accommodate the muscle flap. Transpose the flap and reassess the vascular pedicle. Inset the flap into the palatal defect and suture in place. Because of its anatomic setting, no dressings are appropriate.

Postservice

Communicate with the patient's family and other health care professionals (including providing written and oral reports and orders). All hospital visits and services are performed by the surgeon, including monitoring and caring for the incision; monitoring, caring for, and removing drains, if used; and prescribing antibiotic and pain medication, examining the patient, discussing the hospital stay, providing instructions for continuing care, and preparing the discharge records. Additionally, all postdischarge office visits for this procedure for 90 days after the day of the operation are considered part of the postoperative work, including removal of sutures; evaluation of periodic imaging, pathology, and laboratory reports, if needed; and antibiotic and pain medication adjustments.

➒ 15734 Muscle, myocutaneous, or fasciocutaneous flap; trunk

Work Value: 19.62 // Global Period: 090

Clinical Example

A 55-year-old female with a history of breast cancer treated with mastectomy followed by radiation therapy presents with a large non-healing radiation ulcer of the left lateral chest. The excision of the radiation ulcer results in the exposure of several ribs. The defect is reconstructed with a pedicled latissimus muscle flap. The entire latissimus muscle is harvested through a separate incision and then tunneled through the axilla to reach the defect. The muscle is secured to the chest wall with interrupted sutures and the donor site is closed primarily. The muscle is covered with a split thickness skin graft. The excision and the skin graft are coded separately.

Preservice

Begin preservice work on the day before the surgery. Obtain and review preprocedural laboratory and imaging studies. Review findings at the prior operation. Consult with the referring physician and if necessary, other health care professionals. Communicate with the patient and/or patient's family to explain operative risks and benefits and to obtain informed consent. Additional preoperative services include dressing, scrubbing, and waiting for surgery; supervising the positioning, prepping, and draping of the patient; and ensuring that surgical instruments and supplies that are necessary are present and available in the operative suite.

Intraservice

After the ablative part of the procedure has been completed, obtain appropriate measurements of the defect and plan for the size of the flap. Make an incision over the ipsilateral latissimus muscle. Dissect to the fascia, which is elevated off the muscle. Expose the anterior and posterior borders of the muscle and continue the dissection inferiorly until enough length is obtained to reach the defect. Divide the inferior portion of the muscle. Elevate the muscle off the chest wall and isolate it on the thoracodorsal vascular pedicle. Create a tunnel subcutaneously to reach the defect and enlarge it to accommodate the muscle flap. Transpose the flap and reassess the vascular pedicle. Inset the flap into the chest wall defect and suture in place after placing a closed suction drain. Close the donor site primarily over the suction drains. Harvest a split-thickness skin graft from the ipsilateral thigh and mesh and secure it to the muscle. Apply a bolster dressing over the skin graft. Cover the skin graft donor site with an occlusive dressing.

Postservice

Communicate with the patient's family and other health care professionals (including providing written and oral reports and orders). All hospital visits and services are performed by the surgeon, including monitoring and caring for the incision; monitoring, caring for, and removing drains, if used; and prescribing antibiotic and pain medication as well as examining the patient, discussing the hospital stay, providing instructions for continuing care, and preparing the discharge records. Additionally, all postdischarge office visits for this procedure for 90 days after the day of the operation are considered part of the postoperative work, including the removal of sutures; the evaluation of periodic imaging, pathology, and laboratory reports, if needed; and antibiotic and pain medication adjustments.

Coding Tip for 15732 and 15734

Procedure codes 15732 and 15734 do not include extensive immobilization. (Large plaster casts and other immobilizing devices are considered additional separate procedures.)

Destruction

Destruction, Benign or Premalignant Lesions

❺ **17000** Destruction (eg, laser surgery, electrosurgery, cryosurgery, chemosurgery, surgical curettement), premalignant lesions (eg, actinic keratoses); first lesion

Work Value: 0.62 // Global Period: 010

➲ ***CPT Assistant*** **Winter 90: 3, Nov 97: 12, Jun 99: 10;** ***CPT Changes: An Insider's View*** **2002, 2007**

Clinical Example

A 72-year-old Caucasian female presents with a scaly, 6 × 5-mm erythematous papule, adjacent to the lateral canthus, of four months duration. Inspection and palpation of the lesion is compatible with the diagnosis of a hypertrophic actinic keratosis. Medication and allergy history is reviewed. The risks and benefits of various treatment options are discussed and informed consent given. Liquid nitrogen is obtained from the central dispenser and poured into a disposable transfer cup. A small cotton tip applicator is used to apply the liquid nitrogen directly to the skin using a droplet technique without application of pressure. The application of liquid nitrogen is timed (based on the thickness of the lesion) so that once the ice ball forms it has a thaw time of 20 to 30 seconds. The patient is instructed on wound care. A blister and crust form that require cleansing with hydrogen peroxide and the application of antibiotic ointment for approximately 7 to 10 days.

Preservice
Conduct a preoperative evaluation that includes a review of pertinent data in the patient's medical records. Discuss treatment or service options. Review medical risks, such as syncope, bleeding, pain, edema, infection, headache, delayed healing, scarring, pigmentation, recurrence, and paresthesias. Obtain informed consent. Provide necessary instructions to the patient and staff. Prepare electrosurgical equipment and disposable supplies including electrocautery tips, masks, gloves, appropriate lighting, and drape, if necessary. Prepare non-disposable equipment including curette and scissors. Communicate with the patient's family. For cryosurgery, prepare equipment and supplies including transferring liquid nitrogen to an application container such as a cup with a cotton-tipped application, cryo spray unit, or cryo probe. Obtain protective shields and perform a clean preparation.

Intraservice
Inspect and palpate lesion for size, location, functional risks, depth. Administer local anesthetic, if needed. Destruction of lesion is to include multiple freeze/thaw cycles with appropriate lateral margins and depth into papillary dermis, or similar margins via other destructive modalities. Control bleeding as needed.

Postservice
Apply antibiotic ointment. Apply dressing, when appropriate. Instruct the patient on wound care, functional risks, risk of recurrence, and follow-up. Instruct staff to schedule follow-up postsurgical visit. Communicate with the patient and the patient's family on postoperative care and follow-up. Complete medical record charting, including dictating the operative report and communicating the report to the referring physician, if appropriate.

Coding Tip for 17000, 17003, and 17004
Destruction means the ablation of benign, premalignant, or malignant tissues by any method, with or without curettement, including local anesthesia, and not usually requiring closure.

+ ❺ 17003 Destruction (eg, laser surgery, electrosurgery, cryosurgery, chemosurgery, surgical curettement), premalignant lesions (eg, actinic keratoses); second through 14 lesions, each (List separately in addition to code for first lesion)

Work Value: 0.07 // Global Period: ZZZ

➲ *CPT Assistant* **Nov 97: 12, Jun 99: 10**

Clinical Example
A 72-year-old Caucasian female presents with a scaly, 6 x 5 mm, erythematous papule adjacent to the lateral canthus, and three additional 5 x 7 mm lesions, one each on the face, cheek, and forehead, of 4 month duration. Inspection and palpation of the lesions are compatible with the diagnosis of hypertrophic actinic keratosis.

Intraservice
Inspect and palpate the lesion for size, location, functional risks, and depth. Administer a local anesthetic. Destroy the lesion with electrosurgery. Apply a dermal curette to the lesion, two or more times. Control bleeding with additional destruction to the lesion base using an electrocautery unit as needed.

Coding Tip for 17003
Code 17003 must be reported in conjunction with code 17000.

⊘ ❺ 17004 Destruction (eg, laser surgery, electrosurgery, cryosurgery, chemosurgery, surgical curettement), premalignant lesions (eg, actinic keratoses), 15 or more lesions

Work Value: 1.82 // Global Period: 010

➲ *CPT Assistant* **Nov 97: 12, Nov 98: 7, Jun 99: 10, Mar 03: 21;** ***CPT Changes: An Insider's View*** **2002, 2007**

Clinical Example

A 65-year-old Caucasian male presents with 15 or more rough scaling patches scattered over the face, scalp, and ears.

Preservice

Review pertinent data in the patient's medical records. Discuss the choice of treatment or service options with the patient. Review the medical risks, such as syncope, bleeding, pain, edema, infection, headache, delayed healing, scarring, pigmentation, recurrence, and paresthesias with the patient and obtain informed consent. Provide necessary instructions to the patient and staff. Prepare the equipment and disposable supplies (eg, masks, gloves) for the procedure, and ensure appropriate lighting and draping. Transfer liquid nitrogen to an application container. Obtain protective shields and perform a clean preparation.

Intraservice

Inspect and palpate the lesions for size, location, functional risks, and depth. Administer a local anesthetic, if needed. Perform the destruction of the lesions, which includes multiple freeze/thaw cycles with appropriate lateral margins and depth into papillary dermis, or similar margins via other destructive modalities. Control bleeding as needed.

Postservice

Apply antibiotic ointment. Apply dressing, when appropriate. Instruct the patient on wound care, functional risks, risk of recurrence, and follow-up. Instruct the staff to schedule a follow-up post-surgical visit. Communicate with the patient and the patient's family on postoperative care and follow-up. Complete the medical record charting. Dictate the operative report and communicate with the referring physician, if appropriate.

Destruction, Benign or Premalignant Lesions
17004

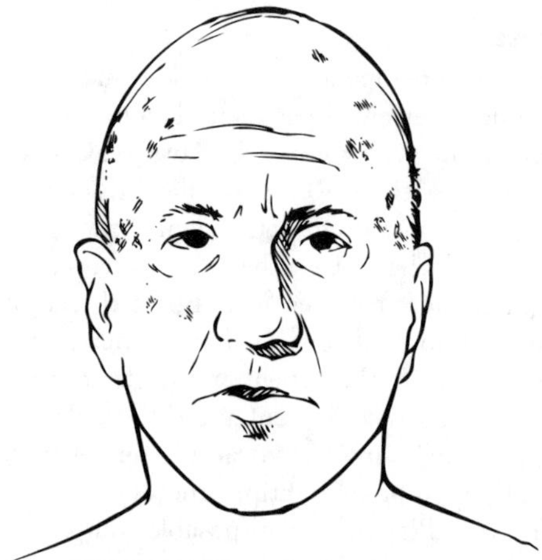

Rough scaling patches scattered over the face, scalp and ears. Lesions are destroyed by cryosurgery or other surgical means.

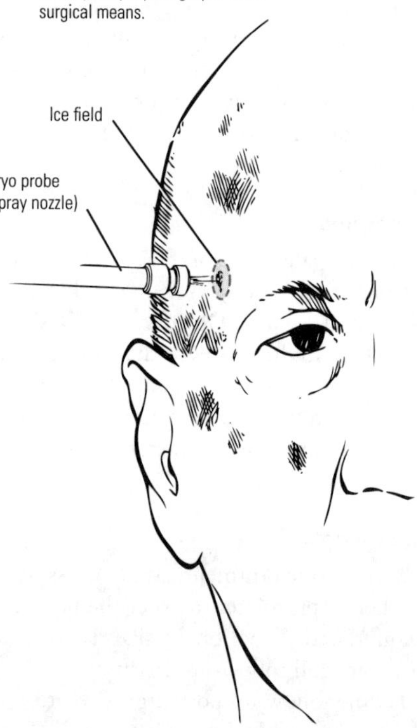

Coding Tip for 17004

Do not report code 17004 in conjunction with codes 17000-17003.

Breast

Excision

19120 Excision of cyst, fibroadenoma, or other benign or malignant tumor, aberrant breast tissue, duct lesion, nipple or areolar lesion (except 19300), open, male or female, one or more lesions

Work Value: 5.84 // Global Period: 090

➲ *CPT Assistant* Feb 96: 9, Nov 97: 14, Jan 01: 8, May 01: 10, Apr 05: 6, 13; *CPT Changes: An Insider's View* 2001, 2007

Clinical Example

A 55-year-old female presents with a 0.75-CEM stellate density in the upper outer quadrant of the right breast containing macrocalcification by mammography. On physical examination, this is palpable 1 cm superior and lateral to the areola. She is taken to the operating room the following day and, under local anesthesia, undergoes excision of this lesion. Frozen section diagnosis is consistent with infiltrating ductal carcinoma.

Preservice

Preservice begins after the decision to operate is made until the time of the procedure. This activity includes obtaining and reviewing previous laboratory and imaging studies, paying special attention to mammograms and ultrasounds of the breast; communicating with the patient and/or the patient's family to explain the operative risks and benefits; and obtaining informed consent. Other preoperative services include dressing, scrubbing, and waiting to begin the operation; supervising the positioning, prepping, and draping of the patient; and ensuring that the necessary surgical instruments and supplies are present and available in the operative suite.

Intraservice

The incisional site is identified and injected with local anesthetic. (Additional anesthesia is injected as needed during the operation.) The skin is incised. The lesion is identified and dissected with instruments and electrocautery. The biopsy specimen is removed and the surgeon ensures that the proper history is transmitted to the pathologist, along with the specimen. Intraoperative consultation with the pathologist is accomplished and further excision is performed, as needed. Drains are placed as appropriate and the wound is closed in layers.

Postservice

Postservice begins after skin closure in the operating room and includes applying sterile dressing; monitoring the patient's stability; communicating with the patient's family and other health care professionals (including providing written and oral reports and orders); and all hospital visits and services performed by the surgeon, including monitoring and caring for the incision; monitoring, caring for, and removing drains, if used; and prescribing antibiotic and pain medication. Discharge day management includes the surgeons final examination of the patient, discussing the hospital stay, providing instructions for continuing care, and preparing the discharge records. Additionally, all postdischarge office visits for this procedure for 90 days after the day of the operation are considered part of the postoperative work for this procedure, including the removal of sutures; the evaluation of periodic mammographic, imaging, pathology, and laboratory reports, as needed; and antibiotic and pain medication adjustments.

Coding Tip for 19120

Although the code descriptor language for code 19120 states male or female, code 19120 is the only code in this section that references the sex of the patient. The majority of codes may be applicable to either male or female patients, dependent on the disease process present.

19125 Excision of breast lesion identified by preoperative placement of radiological marker, open; single lesion

Work Value: 6.59 // Global Period: 090

➲ *CPT Assistant* Fall 94: 18, Mar 98: 10, Jan 01: 8, Apr 05: 6; *CPT Changes: An Insider's View* 2001

Clinical Example

A 65-year-old female presents with a 7-mm aggregate of macrocalcification that is 3-cm deep to the left nipple and 4-cm superior to the left nipple in the outer quadrant of the left breast. The identifying marker is 7-mm medical and 3-mm deep to the lesion. A marker is placed by the radiologist 30 minutes prior to the operation.

Coding Tip for 19125

If procedure code 19125 is performed bilaterally, it is appropriate to append modifier 50, *Bilateral procedure.*

Repair and/or Reconstruction

19318 Reduction mammaplasty

Work Value: 15.91 // Global Period: 090

➲ ***CPT Assistant*** **Jan 03: 7, Apr 05: 6**

Clinical Example

A 30-year-old female presents with excessively large breasts and symptoms of pain and discomfort in her back and neck. She demonstrates notching of the subcutaneous tissue over both shoulders underneath the normal location of her bra straps. She also described intermittent submammary intertriginous dermatitis in warm weather. She also indicates the fact that her lifestyle is restricted and she avoids sports that require jogging or running and does not participate in aerobics. She wears a size 38DD bra and is approximately 15 lbs overweight. At operation, a reduction mammaplasty is performed, utilizing an inferior pedicle technique. (Ratings of relative work for this operation are for one breast [unilateral] reduction only.)

Preservice

Preservice begins on the day before the surgery until the time of the procedure. This includes obtaining and reviewing preprocedural laboratory and imaging studies, paying special attention to mammograms and ultrasounds of the breast; communicating with other health care professionals; communicating with the patient and/or the patient's family to explain the operative risks and benefits; and obtaining informed consent. Other preoperative services include personal preparation, patient marking, skin preparation, supervising the positioning and draping of the patient, and ensuring that surgical instruments and supplies that are necessary are present and available in the operative suite.

Intraservice

After the satisfactory induction of general endotracheal anesthesia, the previously applied markings for surgery (done in the standing position prior to surgery) are scratched on the skin with a needle. The final skin preparation and draping is done. (The skin markings are critical to ensure proper positioning of the nipple/areolar complex in the completed reduction.) The operation commences with deep epithelization of the inferior-based pedicle. Extreme care must be taken to suture an adequate base for the pedicle so the blood supply to the nipple/areola complex is maintained. The medial and lateral triangular wedges of skin, subcutaneous tissue, fat, and breast gland are excised. Hemostasis must be meticulous to prevent excessive blood loss. The remaining breast skin and gland are undermined to the clavicle and excess gland is removed from this flap to provide a uniformly thin flap. The medial and lateral segments are approximated and the closure completed in layers. The nipple/areolar complex is likewise sutured into place. Drains are placed as indicated. A bulky dressing, simulating a brassiere, is fabricated and applied over topical antibiotic cream and antiseptic gauze and secured in place.

Postservice

Postservice begins after skin closure in the operating room and includes the frequent monitoring of the areolar complex to ensure viability; monitoring patient stabilization; communicating with the patient's family and other health care professionals (including providing written and oral reports and orders); and all hospital visits and services performed by the surgeon, including monitoring and caring for the incision; monitoring, caring for, and removing drains, if used; and prescribing antibiotic and pain medication. Discharge day management includes the surgeons final examination of the patient, discussing the hospital stay, providing instructions for continuing care, and preparing the discharge records. Additionally, all postdischarge office visits for this procedure for 90 days after the day of the operation are considered part of the postoperative work for this procedure; including the removal of sutures; the evaluation of periodic imaging and laboratory reports, if needed; and antibiotic and pain medication adjustments.

Coding Tip for 19318

If procedure code 19318 is performed bilaterally, it is appropriate to append modifier 50, *Bilateral procedure.*

19357 Breast reconstruction, immediate or delayed, with tissue expander, including subsequent expansion

Work Value: 20.57 // Global Period: 090

➲ *CPT Assistant* Winter 91: 2, Apr 05: 6, Aug 05: 1

Clinical Example

A 67-year-old female presents with a newly diagnosed breast carcinoma. She is 5 ft 6 in tall, weighs 185 lbs, and wears a size C bra cup. She is in good health with no previous surgery. After discussion, she wishes to proceed with unilateral breast reconstruction utilizing a prosthetic implant. Following her mastectomy, a subpectoral tissue expander is placed and filled with 100 cc of saline. The skin is closed primarily. Subsequent expansions are performed in the office without complications.

Preservice

The day before surgery, write the preoperative orders for perioperative medications. Review preoperative work-up including the patient's history and physical examination; Re-examine breasts and chest. Review laboratory results (complete blood count, electrolytes, renal function). Review biopsies, pathology reports, and mammograms related to cancer staging. Review previous operative reports. Discuss patient status and the status of previous oncologic procedures with the general surgeon. Review the planned incisions and procedure. Mark the patient's inframammary folds and other breast landmarks.

On the day of the surgery, change into scrub clothes. Check with the lab on the availability of blood and/or cross match. Review the surgical procedure, postoperative recovery in and out of the hospital, and expected outcome(s) with the patient and the patient's family. Mark the patient's inframammary folds and other breast landmarks if not previously done or if previous markings have faded. Answer the patient's and family's questions. Obtain the patient's informed consent. Review the length and type of anesthesia with the anesthesiologist. Review the planned procedure and the positioning and draping of patient. Verify that antibiotics and prophylaxis for deep venous thrombosis/pulmonary embolus are provided (eg, subcutaneous heparin administration, placement of support stockings, or sequential compression devices on lower extremities). Place padding and support beneath the patient's head/neck. Place padding/pillows beneath the patient, particularly extremities, to prevent neuropraxia. Verify that all necessary surgical instruments, supplies, and devices are available in the operative suite. Monitor the patient's positioning and draping and assist with positioning as needed. Scrub and gown.

Intraservice

If immediate reconstruction is performed, the general surgery team performs the mastectomy, lymph node dissection, and any other procedures related to the breast cancer treatment. The plastic surgeon may assist with the placement of incisions for the mastectomy and lymph node dissection. After the mastectomy is completed, the plastic surgeon assesses the viability of the mastectomy skin flaps and excises any obviously non-viable tissue. If a delayed reconstruction is being performed, the previous mastectomy scar is excised and sent for permanent pathological examination. The mastectomy skin flaps are elevated off the pectoralis major muscle until the lateral border of the muscle is reached.

Elevation of the pectoralis major muscle off the chest wall is then performed. This is started by dissecting along the lateral edge of the muscle, and developing a plane of dissection beneath the muscle using blunt dissection and electrocautery. The pectoralis minor muscle is identified and separated from the pectoralis major, leaving it attached to the chest wall. Perforating vessels from the chest wall to the muscle are divided. The dissection is carried superiorly to the level of the clavicle, inferiorly to the origin of the muscle, and medially to the lateral sternal border. A lighted retractor is used to better visualize the perforating vessels as dissection proceeds medially. Care must be taken to avoid tearing or injuring these vessels before they can be clipped or cauterized because significant bleeding in the field may result. The medial row of perforating vessels supplying the pectoralis muscle can usually be preserved, though one or two may need to be divided to enlarge the pocket medially. At the lateral border of the pectoralis muscle, the serratus anterior muscle is incised and elevated off the chest wall for a short distance. The width of the subpectoral pocket is measured, and the proper sized tissue expander is chosen. It is opened and rinsed with antibiotic irrigation. The air is removed from the expander and it is filled with 100-200 cc of sterile saline. The subpectoral pocket is rinsed with antibiotic irrigation and meticulous hemostasis is achieved. The tissue expander is placed in the pocket making sure the orientation is correct and that it lays flat against the chest wall with minimal wrinkling. If a remote port is used a separate subcutaneous pocket is developed. The remote port is attached and secured to the tissue expander. The port is placed in the separate pocket and secured with sutures to prevent its migration.

The lower lateral border of the pectoralis muscle is then sutured to the previously elevated edge of the serratus anterior muscle to completely cover the expander with care not to puncture it. If an immediate reconstruction is being performed, one or two drains are placed in the wound and brought out through separate stab incisions and secured with sutures. The mastectomy skin flaps are evaluated again with regard to viability and any clearly non-viable skin is removed. The skin edges are then closed in layers, again with care not to injure the underlying expander. The skin is closed with an interrupted subdermal layer and then a final surface skin layer. The skin flaps are assessed for tension during and after final skin closure, and additional sterile saline may be added or removed from the expander if deemed necessary. The wounds are cleansed and sterile dressings are applied. The patient is taken to the recovery area.

Postservice

Apply sterile dressings to the incisions and inspect the suction drains to ensure that adequate suction is in place and working. Dictate an operative note for the patient's chart. Sign operating room forms, indicating pre- and postoperative diagnoses and the operation performed. Write orders for postoperative labs, medications, diet, and patient activity. Write a brief operative note for the patient's chart, documenting in the daily progress notes pre- and postoperative diagnoses, the operation performed, findings, blood loss, intraoperative intravenous fluids administered, complications, specimens sent to pathology, and the condition of the patient at the end of the procedure. Discuss the outcome of the procedure with the patient's family. Discuss the outcome of the procedure with the patient after the patient emerges from anesthesia. Discuss the outcome of the procedure with the referring physician. Coordinate care with other physicians if needed. Dictate a letter describing the outcome of the procedure and the expected recovery for the referring physician and/or insurance company. Revisit the patient to assess progress, pulmonary function, pain control, and status of dressings.

After the patient is discharged from recovery, examine the patient, checking wounds and patient progress. Review patient chart notes from the nursing and/or other staff. Answer the patient's and/or family's questions. Answer the nursing and/or other staffs questions. Write orders for the following days labs, films, medications, diet, and patient activity. Chart patient progress notes.

Starting on the first postoperative day until the patient is discharged from the hospital, examine and talk with the patient. Encourage ambulation and vigorous pulmonary physiotherapy. Check wounds and patient progress. Discuss patient progress with the referring physician (verbal and written). Coordinate care with other physicians (eg, general surgery, oncology). Review nursing/other staff patient chart notes. Answer the patient's and/or family's questions. Answer the nursing and/or other staffs questions (verbal and written). Answer the insurance staffs questions. Write orders for postoperative labs, films, medications, diet, and patient activity. Chart patient progress notes.

On discharge day, examine and talk with the patient. Check the final pathology, lab, and film reports and discuss the findings with the patient. Carefully explain to the patient and a family member dietary management, activities permitted, bathing, handling of wound or any drains, return appointment to office, and so on. Check wounds and patient progress. Coordinate care with other physicians (eg, general surgery, oncology). Coordinate postoperative physical therapy. Review chart notes from the nursing and/or other staff. Review postdischarge wound care and activity limitations with the patient. Answer the patient's and/or the family's questions. Answer the nursing and/or other staff's questions. Answer the insurance staff's questions. Write orders for postdischarge labs, films, and medications. Chart patient discharge notes.

After the patient is discharged from hospital and through 90 days after surgery, examine and talk with the patient. Check wounds and patient progress. Begin serial expansion of tissue expander after adequate healing of wounds. Perform expansion by localizing the port by palpation, or, in the case of an incorporated port, by using a handheld magnetic localizer. Access the port percutaneously with a needle and syringe. Confirm proper positioning by withdrawing fluid to confirm the withdrawal of expander fluid. Inject saline, constantly assessing the skin overlying the implant for blanching to ensure the vascularity is not compromised. Re-evaluate the patient to determine pain tolerance and discomfort. Assess the skin again for blanching. If the pain is too intense or the skin appears compromised, the port may need to be reaccessed for removal of fluid until symptoms resolve. Repeat this process until the breast is symmetrical with contralateral side. Assess patient tolerance of expansion at prior office visit and adjust volume of current expansion accordingly. Answer the patient's and/or the family's questions. Answer the insurance staffs questions. Discuss patient progress with the referring physician (verbal and written). Coordinate care with other physicians. Write orders for medications. Review postdischarge labs and films. Discuss progress with the patient and the patient's family. Remove sutures and drains. Dictate patient progress notes for the patient's medical chart.

Musculoskeletal System

General

Introduction or Removal

20550 Injection(s); single tendon sheath, or ligament, aponeurosis (eg, plantar "fascia")

Work Value: 0.75 Global Period: 000

➲ ***CPT Assistant*** **Jan 96: 7, Jun 98: 10, Mar 02: 7, Aug 03: 14, Sep 03: 13, Dec 03: 11** ***CPT Changes: An Insider's View*** **2002, 2003, 2004**

Clinical Example

1) A 50-year-old female presents with stenosing tenosynovitis of the right index finger, which is treated with a steroid injection into its flexor tendon sheath.

2) A 46-year-old female diagnosed with plantar fasciitis, who has failed to respond to nonsteroidal anti-inflammatory drugs, modifications in shoe gear, and stretching exercises, presents with plantar fasciitis of the right foot, which is treated with a steroid injection into the plantar fascia.

Preservice

1) Place the patient's involved hand on a sterile barrier and prep. The physician gloves.

2) Communicate with other professionals. Review treatment options. Review X rays. Review procedure with the patient. Discuss possible complications. Obtain patient consent. Communicate with the patient's family. Prepare injection by mixing a local anesthetic with a steroid. Place the patient's involved foot on a sterile barrier and prep.

Intraservice

1) Locate the proximal edge of the A-1 pulley of the right index finger. Provide the injection in the flexor tendon sheath.

2) Palpate the medial and lateral tubercles of the calcaneus and identify the point of maximum tenderness. Localize the medial and central bands of the plantar fascia. Using a medial approach, provide the injection superficial to the plantar fascia.

Postservice

1) Cleanse the injection area and apply a bandage. Monitor the patient for any potential complications from the injection.

2) Cleanse the injection area and apply a bandage. Monitor the patient for any potential complications from the injection. Instruct the patient and/or the patient's caregiver on the appropriate activities and home care. Discuss future management of the condition. Complete the patient's medical record.

20551 Injection(s); single tendon origin/insertion

Work Value: 0.75 // Global Period: 000

➲ *CPT Assistant* **Mar 02: 7, Sep 03: 13;** *CPT Changes: An Insider's View* **2002, 2004**

Clinical Example

1) A 35-year-old male is treated for lateral epicondylitis with an injection into the origin of the extensor carpi radialis brevis (ECRB) on the lateral epicondyle.

2) A 35-year-old male is treated for peroneus brevis tendonitis of the left foot with an injection into the insertion of the peroneus brevis tendon at the base of the fifth metatarsal.

Preservice

1) The patient's involved elbow is placed on a sterile barrier and prepped. The physician gloves.

2) Communicate with other professionals; review treatment options; review X rays; review the procedure with the patient; discuss possible complications; obtain patient consent; and communicate with patient's family. Prepare the injection by mixing a local anesthetic with a steroid. The patient's involved foot is placed on a sterile barrier and prepped.

Intraservice

1) The region of the insertion of the ECRB on the lateral epicondyle is localized and injected.

2) The region of the insertion of the peroneus brevis tendon on the base of the fifth metatarsal is localized and injected.

Postservice

1) The injection area is cleansed and a bandage is applied. The patient is monitored for any potential complications from the injection.

2) The injection area is cleansed and a bandage is applied. The patient is monitored for any potential complications from the injection. The patient and/or care giver is instructed on appropriate activities and home care. Future management of the condition is discussed. The medical record is completed.

Coding Tip for 20550 and 20551

Codes 20550 and 20551 are used to report single or multiple injections per single anatomic tendon sheath or ligament. Therefore, multiple injections to the same tendon would be reported only one time while injections to multiple tendon sheaths, ligaments, tendon origins, or tendon insertions would be reported one time for each injection.

20552 Injection(s); single or multiple trigger point(s), one or two muscle(s)

Work Value: 0.66 // Global Period: 000

➲ *CPT Assistant* Mar 02: 7, May 03: 19, Sep 03: 11; *CPT Changes: An Insider's View* 2002, 2003, 2004

Clinical Example

A 60-year-old female presents with a 3-month history of pain in the lower-left back above the posterior iliac crest with radiation of pain into the left buttock. Muscle relaxants, nonsteroidal anti-inflammatory drugs, and physical therapy have been ineffective in relieving her pain. She undergoes injection of the trigger point in the multifidus muscle left of the L5 spinous process.

Preservice

Position the patient prone and prep and drape in a sterile manner the lower back around the spine.

Intraservice

After identifying the trigger point in the multifidus muscle left of the L5 spinous process by palpation, insert a 1.5- to 2-in 25-gauge needle through the skin into the muscle. Advance the needle a short distance, approximately 2 to 4 cm, observing for any complaints of paresthesias but searching for the area of maximum tenderness. If any complaints or paresthesias are encountered, withdraw the needle slightly until they stop. Infiltrate the injectant solution in a fanwise method into the trigger point after aspiration is negative for blood.

Postservice

Cleanse the injection area and apply a bandage. Monitor the patient for any potential complications from the injection.

Coding Tip for 20552 and 20553

Codes 20552 and 20553 are used to report trigger point injections. These codes are intended to be reported once per session, regardless of the number of trigger points or muscles injected.

20553 Injection(s); single or multiple trigger point(s), three or more muscle(s)

Work Value: 0.75 // Global Period: 000

➲ *CPT Assistant* Mar 02: 7, May 03: 19, Sep 03: 11; *CPT Changes: An Insider's View* 2002, 2003

Clinical Example

A 40 year-old male presents with chronic left neck and right upper back pain resulting from cervical degenerative disk disease and myofascial pain syndrome. The patient has already completed a trial of physical therapy and NSAID therapy without relief of his pain. He undergoes injection of the trigger points in the left multifidus muscle, the left trapezius muscle, and the right levator scapular muscle.

Preservice

The patient is placed in a sitting position and the shoulders and posterior neck are prepped and draped in a sterile manner.

Intraservice

After identification of the three trigger points by palpation, a 1.5-2.0 inch 25 gauge needle is inserted through the skin into the muscles. The needle is advanced a short distance, about 1 to 3 centimeters, observing for any complaints of paresthesias, but searching for the areas of maximum tenderness. If any complaints or paresthesias are encountered the needle is withdrawn slightly until they stop. Next 1 to 3 cc of the injectant solution is infiltrated in a fanwise method into the trigger points after aspiration is negative for blood.

Postservice

The injection area is cleansed and a bandage is applied. The patient is monitored for any potential complications from the injection.

Trigger Point Injection(s)
20552, 20553

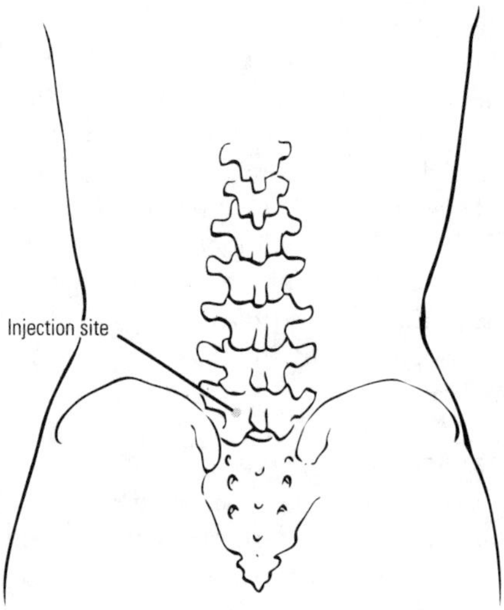

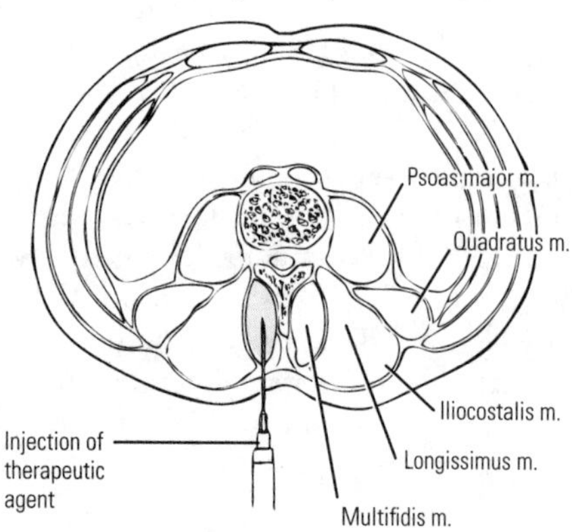

⑤ 20600 Arthrocentesis, aspiration and/or injection; small joint or bursa (eg, fingers, toes)

Work Value: 0.66 // Global Period: 000

➲ *CPT Changes: An Insider's View* 2003

Clinical Example

1) Upper extremity: A 50-year-old male with joint inflammation is treated by aspiration and injection of the metacarpophalangeal joint with a fine needle.

2) Lower extremity: A 50-year-old male with joint inflammation is treated by aspiration and injection of the metatarsophalangeal joint with a fine needle.

Preservice

Review the procedure with the patient; discuss possible complications; obtain patient consent; prepare injection. Place the patient's involved hand or foot on a sterile barrier and prep. The physician gloves.

Intraservice

Aspirate the joint and after positive identification that the needle is inserted inside the joint, perform the aspiration and/or injection.

Postservice

Cleanse the injection area and apply a bandage. Monitor the patient for any potential complications from the injection. Instruct the patient and/or the patient's caregiver on the appropriate activities and home care.

⑤ 20610 Arthrocentesis, aspiration and/or injection; major joint or bursa (eg, shoulder, hip, knee joint, subacromial bursa)

Work Value: 0.79 Global Period: 000

➲ *CPT Assistant* **Spring 92: 8, Mar 01: 10, Apr 04: 15**

Clinical Example

A 55-year-old female with acute inflammation has a hip joint aspirated to collect fluid for a culture.

Arthrocentesis
20610

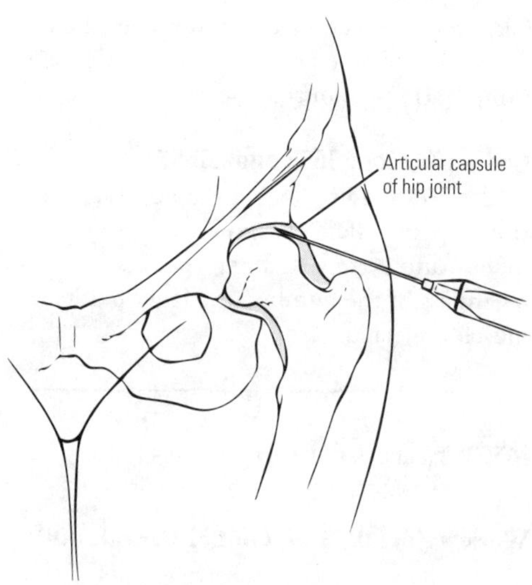

Coding Tip for 20610
If imaging guidance is performed, see codes 76942, 77002, 77012, and 77021, as appropriate.

20664 Application of halo, including removal, cranial, 6 or more pins placed, for thin skull osteology (eg, pediatric patients, hydrocephalus, osteogenesis imperfecta), requiring general anesthesia

Work Value: 9.86 Global Period: 090

➲ *CPT Assistant* Nov 97: 14

Clinical Example

A 5-year-old female presents with fixed rotary atlantoaxial subluxation, which has not reduced in preliminary halter traction. The patient is to be place in a halo for purposes of attempted reduction and immobilization with fusion if indicated. (General anesthesia will be used.) Her age is predictive of the skull osteology necessitating a preoperative computed tomography (CT) scan for halo pin placement determination.

Preservice

Preservice work that occurs within 24 hours of the procedures is divided into five areas:

1) Because of the psychological impact of the placement of pins in the skull, the patient and the patient's family are counseled about the need for the halo as opposed to alternate methods of treatment and the specifics of cranial halo placement. The counseling process is repeated just before surgery and additional questions are answered.

2) The patient is evaluated and prepared for anesthesia. The physician evaluates the patient and writes appropriate orders and consults with the anesthesiologist about any unusual aspects of the case and/or procedure.

3) The physician performs a cranial evaluation of the patient. Because the patient's age is predictive of a thin skull that may allow penetration of the halo pins, the physician orders and reviews a CT scan of the patient's skull before surgery. The purpose of the review is to identify areas of skull thinness that may preclude the placement of halo pins and to identify alternate pin placement sites as necessary. All potential pin placement sites are evaluated on the appropriate CT sections.

4) The patient's skull is sized preoperatively to make sure an appropriate halo ring is available. This involves measuring the skull, noting any abnormalities in shape, and obtaining all potentially necessary sizes. In addition, appropriate halo pins are requested, and all equipment is reviewed before surgery.

5) The patient is brought into the operating suite and the anesthesiologist prepares to anesthetize the patient. The surgeon prepares the operating table for placement of the halo. This often involves the use of an extension board for careful placement of the skull to allow halo placement. After induction of anesthesia, the patient's head is brought into the appropriate position off the superior aspect of the operating table and held carefully in position by the surgeon. (The use of a support board underneath the skull does not preclude holding the skull in place by the physician.) The appropriate halo ring is then applied to make sure that there is adequate clearance in all areas of the skull. The skull is then prepped by shaving the appropriate areas to allow halo pin placement. At least six halo pins are used, and sometimes as many as ten. After shaving the appropriate sites, the sites are then thoroughly prepped while the surgeon holds the skull.

Intraservice

With the patient appropriately under anesthesia, the skull is prepped and the halo ring is placed around the skull just above the ears and superorbital ridge. The 6–10 halo pins are then placed through the halo in a sterile manner and opposing pins are sequentially tightened. In this example, sequential tightening of the pins occurs until approximately 3–4 lbs of pressure is documented on the torque screwdrivers. Repeated evaluation of the placement of the ring and skull clearance is made while the halo pins are tightened. Local anesthesia is then injected at each of the pin sites. In this example, the patient is then replaced on the operating table and awakened from anesthesia while her head is held in place.

Postservice

The patient is returned to the recovery area. In this example, the patient is placed in cervical traction using the cranial halo. Operative and postoperative notes are dictated and postoperative orders are written. Care is made to make sure the traction is appropriate. X rays of the cervical spine are taken to confirm the position of the neck in traction. The procedure is then reviewed with the patient's family. Following recovery from anesthesia, the patient is monitored in the postanesthesia area to make sure the halo pins are tolerated. The physician, often assisted by the nursing staff, instructs the family in regards to cleansing the halo pins. The halo pins are again tightened (usually in the presence of sedation) 24–48 hours after surgery. The second episode of tightening may occur as per the preference of the physician. Daily evaluation of the halo pins occurs while the patient is hospitalized. In this example, the patient would be in the hospital for several days of traction before a decision to place the patient in a halo vest for operative or nonoperative care. As the vest is placed, careful evaluation of the position of the cervical spine is made by the physician. The physician is in attendance during the placement of the thoracic vest attached to the cranial halo. Placement X rays are then made to make sure the cervical spine is held in the appropriate position. Daily evaluation of the pin sites by the physician occurs. The family is reinstructed in pin-site care.

Following discharge from the hospital, the patient is seen in 1 week for re-evaluation of the cranial halo pins as well as the underlying cervical problem. In this 5-year-old patient, the patient is seen at least every 3 weeks for evaluation of the pin sites in addition to any other necessary medical care. Should any of the pins become infected, the pin may be removed and, if necessary, placed in an alternate site in the cranial halo ring. Placement of the pin in an alternate pin site will require general anesthesia.

Removal of the cranial halo may occur within a 90-day global period. The cranial halo is removed in the physician's office after appropriate counseling of the patient and the patient's family. Sedation of the patient may be necessary. After detaching the halo from the vest, the halo pins are sequentially loosened and the halo is removed. Each of the halo pin sites is surgically scrubbed and antibiotic ointment is often applied. Counseling of the patient and the patient's family reoccurs in regards to the cosmetic significance of the pin sites. The patient is seen in several days to re-evaluate the pin sites.

Halo Application for Thin Skull Osteology

20664

A cranial halo is placed on the head of a child whose skull is unusually thin due to congenital or developmental problems.

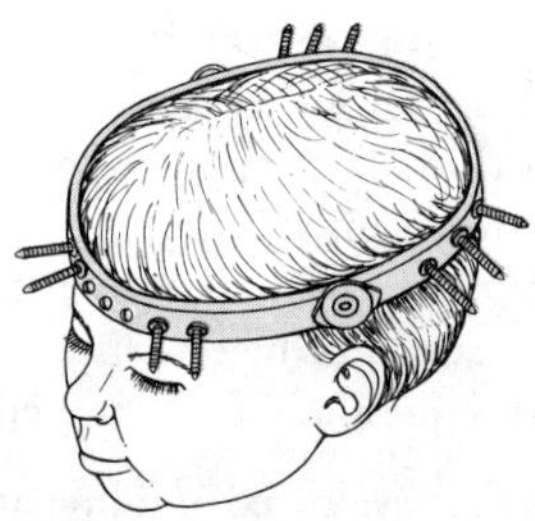

---

❺ **20680** Removal of implant; deep (eg, buried wire, pin, screw, metal band, nail, rod or plate)

Work Value: 5.90 // Global Period: 090

➲ *CPT Assistant* Spring 92: 11

Clinical Example

A 35-year-old ironworker who sustained a fracture of the femur treated by closed intramedullary nailing 18 months ago now undergoes removal of intramedullary nail. (Consider only the work involved in removing the intramedullary nail.)

Preservice

Preservice begins after the decision to remove the intramedullarly nail has been made and occurs from the day before the surgery until the time of the procedure. It includes reviewing the radiology images of the femur to assess the position of the implant in the bone, its relationship to bony landmarks, and the features of the implant. The surgeon must observe the presence and location of locking screws. Appropriate equipment for removal of the implant must be available, including extraction equipment to lock into the top of the rod and appropriate screw drivers for screw removal. This might necessitate identifying and calling a representative from a local manufacturer to have this equipment available. On the day of the surgery, the surgeon must meet with the patient and the patient's family to explain operative risks and benefits and to obtain informed consent. The involved limb must be marked. A history and physical may need to be updated. The range of motion of the hip and knee and neurovascular status must be assessed. The exact location of all previous surgical scars must be identified. On radiographs, the presence of overlying, overgrown, or entopic bone must be assessed. Preoperative work will also include scrubbing, supervising prepping, draping the patient, and again checking that all of the necessary equipment is available on the operating table. The surgeon must ensure that C-arm fluoroscopy equipment is available during the procedure.

Intraservice

Based on preoperative planning, the first step is to identify the location of screws that lock the nail to the bone. Once they have been identified, incisions are made in the appropriate places and carried through superficial and deep layers down to the level of the bone. The screws then need to be removed with the appropriate screwdriver. Usually, soft tissues have ingrown around the screw that need to be removed with sharp instruments and bleeding controlled. Occasionally, the heads of the screws have become buried in bone or overgrown with new bone. When this happens, osteotomes and other bone-cutting instruments are required to expose them. If they are extremely difficult to find, C-arm fluoroscopy must be brought in and the area of the bone where there is underlying screws identified. Bony instruments are then directed in this direction. Occasionally, screws are stripped and will only back out with a positive capture mechanism or when another instrument is applied to the head of the screw to help extract it. Occasionally, there are broken screws. When this happens, it may be necessary to make a counter incision on the far side of the screw and use a high-speed burr, fluoroscopy, and other cutting instruments to expose the far end of the broken screw and remove it. As many as three or four screws may need to be removed through two or three separate incisions. These incisions are then closed in layers. The incision over the tip of the intramedullarly nail is then opened and deepened in layers. Surface landmarks and palpation are used to identify the tip of the intramedullarly nail. Similar to the screws, this may be difficult and scar tissue may need to be removed with a series of sharp instruments. Occasionally, when overgrown with bone, osteotomies and other bone instruments are necessary. When the nail cannot be identified, C-arm fluoroscopy is used to direct cutting instruments in the correct direction through the bone. When the nail tip is exposed, soft tissue and bone elements are curetted from the entry hole into the nail. Typically, a screw-in mechanism will fit onto the top of the nail. The nail is removed with back slapping onto an out rigger of this screw and instrument. The wound is then irrigated and closed in layers.

Postservice

The postservice begins after skin closure in the operating room and includes applying a sterile dressing to the wounds. Postoperative work may also include reviewing X rays that are made after hardware removal to make sure there has been no intraoperative fracture. The surgeon will go over discharge instructions with the patient and the patient's family, including instruction on care of the incision, pain medication management, the use of crutches, and weight-bearing. Typically, the patient will be seen for an office visit 2 weeks after the procedure for assessment of the wound, removal of sutures, and assessment of joint range of motion. Generally, the patient's activities are progressed at this stage and one final postoperative visit will be required during the 90-day global period prior to discharge.

Grafts (or Implants)

⊘ **20931** Allograft for spine surgery only; structural

Work Value: 1.81 // Global Period: ZZZ

➲ *CPT Assistant* **Feb 96: 6, Feb 02: 6, Feb 05: 15**

Clinical Example

A patient undergoes an anterior spine fusion utilizing a tibial strut graft obtained from a bone bank.

Intraservice

Measurements are taken by caliper and other devices to provide the dimensions recorded from the recipient site and to assess the integrity and state of readiness of the graft. Using a bone-suiting instrument, the graft is trimmed to fit the recipient site. A trial fit is made and the proper orientation is selected. Additional fashioning of the graft for exact fit is accomplished. The fit is made under distraction and/or with impaction. The graft is checked for adequacy of contact, stability, and absence of interference with surrounding soft tissues. More time is required to fashion the graft if more than one level is to be filled.

⊘ **20937** Autograft for spine surgery only (includes harvesting the graft); morselized (through separate skin or fascial incision)

Work Value: 2.79 // Global Period: ZZZ

➲ *CPT Assistant* **Feb 96: 6, Sep 97: 8, Dec 99: 2, Feb 02: 6**

Clinical Example

A patient undergoes a laminectomy and fusion of the lumbar spine for spinal stenosis that requires the use of a bone graft harvested from the iliac crest through a separate incision in the fascia.

Intraservice

Attention is given during positioning and draping to be sure that there is sterile access to the proposed donor site intraoperatively. The recipient area is evaluated to assess the volume and type of the graft needed. The length of the incision and amount of subperiosteal reflection are planned accordingly. The soft tissue dissection and retraction of the recipient area is evaluated to determine whether a separate skin incision is needed to access the donor site or whether it can be approached through a fascial incision. The proper skin and/or fascial incision is made. Muscles are reflected subperiosteally over the donor site and held with retractors. With bone-cutting instruments, the cortex is removed to expose the cancellous bone. If needed, osteotomes or power devices are used to cut corticocancellous strips; bone-cutting instruments are used to remove cancellous bone. In the case of iliac grafting, care is taken to avoid deep penetration of the inner table or the sacroiliac joint; bleeding from adjacent muscles is carefully controlled. If necessary, a drainage tube is placed deep in the wound and brought out through a separate stab wound. The fascia over the bone is closed with heavy sutures. Subcutaneous tissues and skin are closed in layers.

⊘ **20938** Autograft for spine surgery only (includes harvesting the graft); structural, bicortical or tricortical (through separate skin or fascial incision)

Work Value: 3.02 // Global Period: ZZZ

➲ *CPT Assistant* **Feb 96: 6, Mar 96: 5, Sep 97: 8, Feb 02: 6**

Clinical Example

A patient undergoes a multilevel anterior cervical fusion utilizing a tibial strut graft harvested from the patient's own tibia. The graft is internally fixed, either separately or by the use of spinal instrumentation.

Intraservice

Special attention is given to positioning and draping to allow sterile and convenient access intraoperatively without compromising the operation in progress on the recipient area. For tribal or fibular strut grafts, a tourniquet is applied to the extremity. A longitudinal incision is made over the proposed donor area. The muscles and fascia are removed by subperiosteal reflection from the bone. Data are obtained by caliper or other measurement technique from X rays of the exposed recipient area. The donor site is evaluated to select the ideal site considering the thickness and curvature of the cortex, the quality and thickness of the underlying cancellous bone, and the residual integrity of the donor site. Bone-cutting instruments are used to cut through the cortex of the donor bone and then completed deep within the bone, using angled cuts or curved instruments. The donor graft is removed and a trial fit to the recipient area is made. Additional shaping and modeling of the donor bone is carried out until the fit is exact under distraction and by impaction. The graft is then applied and tested for fit and stability. Any protruding portions of the bone that threaten the overlying soft tissue are removed with bone-cutting instruments.

Spine (Vertebral Column)

Fracture and/or Dislocation

+ 22328 Open treatment and/or reduction of vertebral fracture(s) and/or dislocation(s), posterior approach, one fractured vertebrae or dislocated segment; each additional fractured vertebrae or dislocated segment (List separately in addition to code for primary procedure)

Work Value: 4.60 Global Period: ZZZ

➲ *CPT Assistant* Feb 96: 6

Clinical Example

A 35-year-old male, who was in an automobile accident, presents with a dislocation at more than one level of the cervical, thoracic, and/or lumbar spine. Using a posterior approach to the spine, after reduction of one dislocated segment, a similar reduction procedure is carried out on an additional dislocated segment in the same region through the same incision.

Intraservice

The skin, fascial, and muscle dissection are extended as necessary to provide safe exposure of the additional injured vertebra and segment. The extent of muscle, ligament, bone, theca, and nerve injury is assessed at the additional injury site. The bone is resected as necessary to protect theca or neural tissue. Bone grasping and leveling instruments and/or adjustment of table position are employed to effect a reduction. (Instrumentation and grafting, if used, are coordinated with the reduction and are coded separately.) The added incision into the muscle, fascia, and skin are sutured.

Arthrodesis

Anterior or Anterolateral Approach Technique

⊛ 22554 Arthrodesis, anterior interbody technique, including minimal discectomy to prepare interspace (other than for decompression); cervical below C2

Work Value: 17.54 // Global Period: 090

➲ *CPT Assistant* Spring 93: 36, Sep 97: 8, Sep 00: 10, Jan 01: 12, Feb 02: 4

Clinical Example

A 50-year-old female presents with neck pain radiating to the right hand with numbness, tingling and weakness. Six weeks of nonoperative treatment are unsuccessful and imaging studies identify C 5/6 spondylosis. The patient undergoes anterior excision of the C 5/6 disc and preparation of the end plates for arthrodesis. Postoperative hospital care and office visits are conducted as necessary through the 90 day global period. [Instrumentation, decompression and/or bone grafting would be reported separately using the appropriate code(s).]

Preservice

Review preperative lab work-up; write preoperative orders for perioperative medications; locate, review, and place MRI and/or other spinal imaging studies on the view box in the operating room; review planned incisions and procedure; greet patient in holding area and review the surgical procedure, postop recovery in and out of the hospital, and expected outcome(s) with patient and family; sign and mark operative site; obtain informed consent; verify that all necessary surgical instruments, supplies, and devices are available in the operative suite; review length and type of anesthesia with anesthesiologist; monitor initial patient positioning for induction of anesthesia; following the induction of anesthesia, assist with repositioning of patient; verify/assist with padding of the patient to prevent pressure on neurovascular structures; scrub and gown; mark the incisions and supervise prepping/draping of the patient.

Intraservice

A transverse incision is made anteriorly over the level of the proposed arthrodesis. The platysma muscle is cut in line with the skin incision. The interval between the sternocleidomastoid and carotid sheath laterally and the trachea and esophagus medially is developed and the prevertebral fascia cleared from the front of the spine. The disc between the vertebrae to be fused is identified and the level confirmed by x-ray. The longus colli muscles are mobilized along their medial edges. Lateral and longitudinal self retaining traction devices are inserted. The anterior longitudinal ligament and anterior anulus are removed by sharp dissection. The disc and cartilaginous end-plates are removed by curettage. With the disc space under distraction, the bone graft (coded separately) is inserted into the disc space. The traction is released and the graft checked for security. Any protruding parts of the graft are trimmed to avoid esophageal compression. A drain is placed in the wound as desired. The platysma muscle, subcutaneous tissue, and skin are sutured. Sterile dressings and a collar or brace are applied.

Postservice

Hospital: When anesthesia has been reversed, transfer the patient to the recovery room; write an OP note in the patient's record; examine the patient, check wound(s) and patient progress, monitor for abnormal neurological findings; sign operating room forms, including pre- and postoperative diagnosis, operations performed; discuss procedure outcome with the patient's family; dictate postoperative report; discuss procedure outcome with the referring physician; dictate procedure outcome and expected recovery letter for referring physician and/or insurance company; order and review films to check alignment of cervical spine; write orders daily, as necessary, for medications, diet, and patient activity; examine the patient daily, check wounds and patient progress; review nursing andother staff patient chart notes; chart patient progress notes; discuss the patient's progress with the referring physician (verbal and written); answer patient/family questions, nursing/other staff questions (verbal and written), insurance staff questions; at discharge, review post-discharge wound care, use and proper fit of collar, and activity limitations, including planned physical therapy; answer patient/family questions, nursing/other staff questions; write orders for post-discharge films, and medications; chart patient discharge notes.

Office: Write orders for medications and follow-up films; review post-discharge films; examine the patient and perform periodic neurological exams; monitor wounds and remove sutures/staples; review use and proper fit of collar with patient; review physical therapy progress and revise orders as needed; dictate patient progress notes for medical chart; answer patient/family questions, insurance staff questions; discuss patient progress with the referring physician (verbal and written).

Anterior Approach for Cervical Fusion
22554

An example of an exposure technique used to reach anterior cervical vertebrae for spinal procedures (eg, diskectomy, arthrodesis, spinal instrumentation).

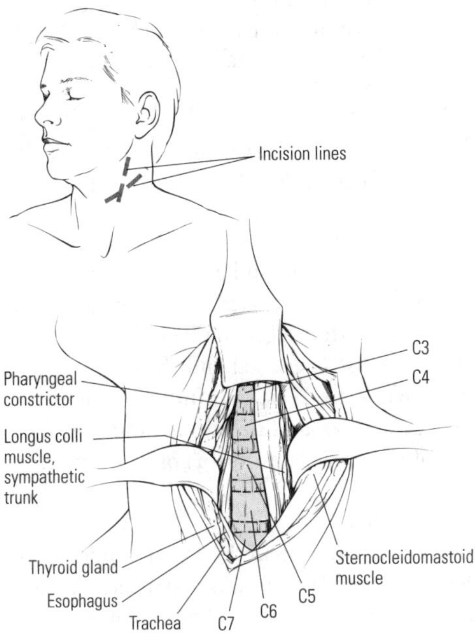

22558 Arthrodesis, anterior interbody technique, including minimal discectomy to prepare interspace (other than for decompression); lumbar

Work Value: 23.33 // Global Period: 090

➲ *CPT Assistant* **Spring 93: 36, Mar 96: 6, Jul 96: 7, Sep 97: 8, Sep 00: 10, Feb 02: 4**

Clinical Example

A 50-year-old male undergoes anterior arthrodesis of the lumbar spine for degenerative disease. Using a retroperitoneal approach, excision of the disc and preparation of the end plates for fusion is performed. (Instrumentation and/or bone grafting is reported separately using the appropriate code[s].)

Preservice

Preservice includes obtaining and reviewing hospital admission roentgenograms and laboratory studies, taking care to review radiographic and surface anatomy landmarks in preparation for the intraoperative location of the desired level to be fused; communicating with the referring physician and other health care professionals; and communicating with the patient to explain the operative risks and benefits and to obtain informed consent. Preservice also includes preoperative scrubbing, and positioning, prepping, and draping the patient.

Intraservice

For the fusion of L2-L3, L3-L4, or L4-L5, a transverse or oblique skin incision is made over the site of the abdomen and flank. The external and internal oblique muscles and fascia are dissected and incised by electrocautery. The transversalis fascia is dissected and opened. The peritoneum is separated with an effort to preserve its integrity. With care to protect the ureter, genitofemoral nerve, and sympathetic chain, the retroperitoneal soft tissues are mobilized. The segmental vessels are ligated and cut to mobilize the great vessels. (Alternatively, for L1-L2 exposure, a thoracolumber 10th rib resection retroperitoneal approach with attention to the diaphragm and pleura may be necessary. For lumbosacral arthrodesis, an anterior paramedian retroperitoneal or transperitoneal approach with attention to iliac vessels, parasympathetic nerves, and middle sacral artery may be needed.) The front of the psoas muscles are exposed and the medial edges reflected from the front of the spine. The disc at the center of the proposed fusion is identified and confirmed by X ray. The anterior longitudinal ligament and anterior fibers of the anulus are removed by sharp dissection. The nuclear and cartilaginous end plates are removed by curettage. The bony end plates are removed by bone-cutting instruments and the cancellous bone of the vertebral bodies above and below is exposed. With the space under distraction, the graft (coded separately) is placed and the distraction is released. The graft is checked for stability and for absence of protrusion against surrounding soft tissues. The wound is drained through a separate stab wound. When necessary, the peritoneum and/or diaphragm are repaired. The transversalis fascia, abdominal muscles, subcutaneous tissues, and skin are sutured in layers. Sterile dressings are applied.

Postservice

Postservice includes stabilizing the patient, communicating with the patient's family and the referring physician (including written and telephone reports and orders), and removing the drain. Discharge day management includes the surgeon's final examination of the patient, discussing the hospital stay, providing instructions for continuing care, and preparing the discharge records. In addition, all hospital visits and postdischarge office visits for this procedure for 90 days after the day of the operation are considered part of the postoperative work for this procedure, including the evaluation of periodic laboratory reports and medication adjustments.

Anterior Approach for Lumbar Fusion (Anterior Retroperitoneal Exposure)
22558

An example of an exposure technique used to reach anterior lumbar vertebrae for spinal procedures (eg, diskectomy, arthrodesis, spinal instrumentation).

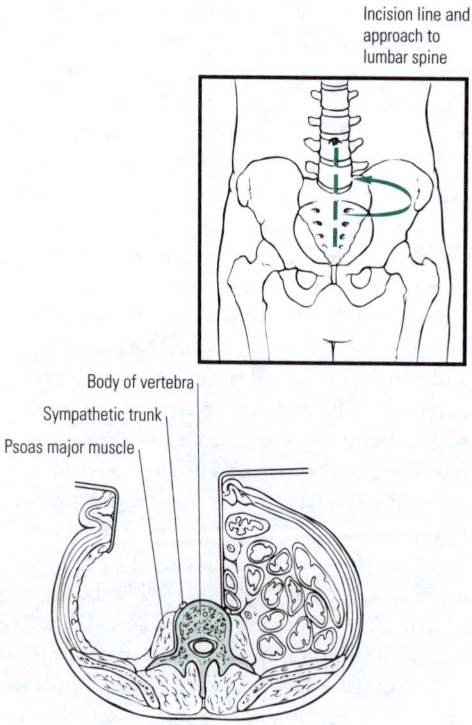

+22585 Arthrodesis, anterior interbody technique, including minimal discectomy to prepare interspace (other than for decompression); each additional interspace (List separately in addition to code for primary procedure)

Work Value: 5.52 // Global Period: ZZZ

➲ *CPT Assistant* Spring 93: 36, Feb 96: 6, Mar 96: 6, Sep 97: 8, Sep 00: 10, Feb 02: 4

Clinical Example

A 50-year-old male undergoes anterior arthrodesis of the cervical, thoracic, and/or lumbar spine for degenerative disc disease. After one disc is excised and the end plates are prepared for fusion, a similar excision procedure of an additional disc and preparation of the end plates for fusion is performed.

Intraservice

The incision and dissection of superficial muscles are extended to accommodate additional retraction of deep tissues. Additional segmental vessels are ligated and cut to provide further reflection of the great vessels. Muscle attachments to the anteromedial edges of the vertebral bodies are reflected over the additional segment and retractors are repositioned. The periosteum is reflected from the bone of the additional segments. A marker is placed at the disc to confirm by X ray whether there is any question as to the location. The anterior longitudinal ligament and anterior fibers of the annulus are removed by sharp dissection. The nucleus and cartilaginous end plates are removed by curettage. The bony end plates are removed by bone-cutting instruments. The cancellous bone of the vertebral bodies is exposed with the prepared site under distraction, and with the space stability and absence of protrusion against surrounding soft tissues.

Coding Tip for 22554, 22558 and 22585

Procedure codes 22554 and 22558 are reported for a single interspace. To report additional interspaces, report code 22585. A vertebral interspace is the nonbony compartment between two adjacent vertebral bodies that contains the intervertebral disc and includes the nucleus pulposus, annulus fibrosus, and two cartilagenous endplates.

Posterior, Posterolateral or Lateral Transverse Process Technique

22600 Arthrodesis, posterior or posterolateral technique, single level; cervical below C2 segment

Work Value: 17.20 // Global Period: 090

➲ *CPT Assistant* Spring 93: 36, Sep 97: 8

Clinical Example

A 50-year-old male undergoes posterior fusion of C4–C5 for post-traumatic instability. Using a posterior approach to the cervical spine, preparation of the lamina of C4 and C5 for the bone graft is performed. Bone graft material is applied to the prepared bony surfaces. After the wound is closed, a brace or cast is applied.

Preservice

Preservice work includes obtaining and reviewing hospital admission roentgenograms and laboratory studies; communicating with the referring physician and other health care professionals; and communicating with the patient to explain the operative risks and benefits and obtain informed consent. Preservice work also includes preoperative scrubbing and positioning, prepping, and draping the patient. Intraoperative spinal cord function monitoring is arranged.

Intraservice

An incision is made in the midline and carried through the subcutaneous tissue. The ligamentum nuchae is identified and the exposure deepened through it as the paraspinal muscles are retracted laterally. Identification of the level is confirmed to avoid subperiosteal dissection beyond the limit chosen for arthrodesis. The muscles are subperiosteally stripped from the spinous process and posterior lamina out to the mid-portion of the facet joints. Decortication is performed with bone cutting instruments. (Instrumentation and/or bone harvesting, if used, are coordinated at this point, and are coded separately.) The bone graft material is applied over the prepared bony surfaces. The paraspinal muscles and ligamentum nuchae are sutured. The subcutaneous tissues and skin are closed in layers over a drain, if necessary. Sterile dressings and an external immobilizing device are applied.

Postservice

Postservice work includes stabilizing the patient; communicating with the patient's family and the referring physician (including providing written and telephone reports and orders); monitoring and adjusting the external immobilization device; and performing discharge day management. In addition, all hospital visits and postdischarge office visits for the procedure for 90 days after the day of the operation are considered part of the post-service work for this procedure, including evaluating periodic laboratory reports and making medication adjustments.

Coding Tip for 22600

A vertebral segment describes the basic constituent part into which the spine may be divided. It represents a single complete vertebral bone with its associated articular processes and laminae.

---

⑮ **22612** Arthrodesis, posterior or posterolateral technique, single level; lumbar (with or without lateral transverse technique)

Work Value: 23.38 // Global Period: 090

➲ *CPT Assistant* Spring 93: 36, Mar 96: 7, Sep 97: 8, 11

Clinical Example

A 45-year-old male has a 1-year history of progressive low back pain that is unresponsive to conservative treatment. Imaging studies identify L5/S1 spondylolisthesis. He undergoes posterolateral fusion of L5 to S1. Postoperative hospital care and office visits are conducted as necessary through the 90-day global period. (Instrumentation and/or bone preparation or harvesting is reported separately using the appropriate code[s].)

Preservice

Review the preoperative lab work-up. Write preoperative orders for perioperative medications. Locate, review, and place magnetic resonance imaging and/or other spinal imaging studies on the view box in the operating room. Review the planned incisions and procedure. Greet the patient in the holding area and review the surgical procedure, postoperative recovery in and out of the hospital, and expected outcome(s) with the patient and the patient's family. Sign and mark operative site. Obtain the patient's informed consent. Verify that all necessary surgical instruments, supplies, and devices are available in the operative suite. Review the length and type of anesthesia with anesthesiologist. Monitor initial patient positioning for induction of anesthesia. Following the induction of anesthesia, assist with repositioning the patient. Verify and assist with padding the patient to prevent pressure on neurovascular structures. Scrub and gown. Mark the incisions. Supervise the prepping and draping of the patient.

Intraservice

Make a mid-line incision over the spinous processes of the vertebrae to be fused plus one or more segments above and below to provide for adequate retraction and safe exposure of the bone to be prepared. Strip the paraspinal muscles and fascia from the lateral surfaces of the spinous processes and the posterior surfaces of the laminae by subperiosteal dissection. Remove the capsules of the facet joints to be fused and remove cartilage from the joint surfaces. Strip the muscle attachments and periosteum from the posterior cortices of the transverse processes of the vertebra to be fused and from the lateral edge of the pars interarticularis and pedicles posterior to the transverse process. (Instrumentation and/or bone harvesting, if used, are coordinated at this point, and are coded separately.) Apply the bone graft material over the prepared surfaces of the bone (decorticated transverse processes and lateral facets) and in the intervals between. Suture the muscles and fascia. Place one or more drains through separate stab wounds if desired. Close the subcutaneous tissue and skin in layers. Apply sterile dressings. (Alternatively, the posterolateral fusion can be accomplished through muscle splitting incisions on each side of the spine with exposure of the transverse process and facet joints through two posterolateral approaches.)

Postservice

Turn the patient into the supine position. When anesthesia is reversed, transfer the patient to the recovery room. Write a postoperative note in the patient's record. Examine the patient, check wound(s) and patient progress. Monitor for abnormal neurological findings. Sign operating room forms, including pre- and postoperative diagnosis and operations performed. Discuss the outcome of the procedure with the patient's family. Dictate the postoperative report. Discuss the outcome of the procedure with the referring physician. Dictate a letter describing the outcome of the procedure and the expected recovery for the referring physician and/or insurance company. Order and review films to check alignment of lumbar spine. Write orders daily, as necessary, for medications, diet, and patient activity. Examine patient, check wounds, and patient progress daily. Review patient chart notes from the nursing and/or other staff. Chart patient progress notes. Discuss patient progress with the referring physician (verbal and written). Answer the patient's and the familys questions, the nursing and/or other staffs questions (verbal and written), and the insurance staffs questions. At discharge, review with the patient postdischarge wound care, use and proper fit of brace, and activity limitations, including planned physical therapy. Answer the patient's and the familys questions and the nursing and/or other staffs questions. Write orders for postdischarge films and medications. Chart patient discharge notes.

In the office, write orders for medications and follow-up films; review postdischarge films; examine the patient, including performing periodic neurological exams; monitor wounds and remove sutures and/or staples; review the use and proper fit of brace with the patient; review the progress of physical therapy and revise orders as needed; dictate patient progress notes for the patient's medical chart; answer the patient's and familys questions and the insurance staffs questions; discuss patient progress with the referring physician (verbal and written).

22630 Arthrodesis, posterior interbody technique, including laminectomy and/or discectomy to prepare interspace (other than for decompression), single interspace; lumbar

Work Value: 21.89 // Global Period: 090

➲ *CPT Assistant* **Spring 93: 36, Sep 97: 8, Nov 99: 11, Dec 99: 2, Jan 01: 12;** ***CPT Changes: An Insider's View*** **2000**

Clinical Example

A 48-year-old male with a history of previous diskectomy and posterolateral fusion of L4-L5, presents with pseudarthrosis, minimal signs of nerve root dysfunction, and intractable back pain that improves with recumbency or back bracing. Using a posterior approach to L4-L5, the canal and roots are exposed, the dural sac is mobilized, the disk interspace is evacuated, and the vertebral end plates are prepared for fusion. (Instrumentation and/or bone preparation or harvesting is reported separately using the appropriate code[s].)

Preservice

Preservice includes obtaining and reviewing hospital admission roentgenograms and laboratory studies; communicating with the referring physician and other health care professionals; and communicating with the patient to explain the operative risks and benefits and to obtain informed consent. Preservice also includes preoperative scrubbing, and positioning, prepping, and draping the patient. Care is taken to position the patient to reduce intra-abdominal pressure and to provide for intraoperative radiographs.

Intraservice

An incision is made in the midline and carried through the subcutaneous tissue to the spinous processes. Muscles and fascia are removed from both sides of the spinous process and the posterior surface of the lamina out over the facets of the segment to be fused. The ligamentum flavum and/or scar are removed from between the laminae of the vertebrae to be fused. Bone-cutting tools are used to remove as much of the lamina above and below and as much of the medial edges of the facets as is necessary for adequate decompression and for safe exposure of the disk space. The nerve root is carefully mobilized from adhesions and/or peridural membrane. Epidural veins are cauterized and cut. The nerve root is protected by packing and retraction. The anulus is incised and an ample section of it removed by sharp dissection. The nucleus is removed within the disk space with rongeurs and curettes. Bone-cutting instruments are used to remove cartilaginous and subchondral end plates of the vertebrae above and below the disc to be fused. The bone dissection is fashioned to accept the graft in a way that will provide for adequate contact and maintenance of the disc space height and stability. (Instrumentation and/or bone harvesting, if used, are coordinated at this point and are coded separately.) The graft(s) is impacted into the recipient site. From the other side of the table, the entire exposure, bone preparation, and graft insertion and impaction are repeated on the other side. The nerve roots are inspected to confirm that they are free of any impingement over the graft site or in the forearm. Interposition membrane, as by free fat graft, is used to cover the exposed dura and nerve root. Muscles and fascia are sutured. A drain is inserted through a separate stab wound. The subcutaneous tissues and skin are closed and sterile dressings are applied.

Postservice

Postservice includes stabilizing the patient, communicating with the patient's family and the referring physician (including providing written and telephone reports and orders), and removing the drain. Discharge day management includes the surgeons final examination of the patient, discussing the hospital stay, providing instructions for continuing care, and preparing the discharge records. In addition, all hospital visits and postdischarge office visits for this procedure for 90 days after the day of the operation are considered part of the postoperative work for this procedure, including the evaluation of periodic laboratory reports and medication adjustments.

Spine Deformity (eg, Scoliosis, Kyphosis)

22812 Arthrodesis, anterior, for spinal deformity, with or without cast; 8 or more vertebral segments

Work Value: 34.00 Global Period: 090

➲ *CPT Assistant* Feb 02: 4

Clinical Example

An 18-year-old male presents with thoracic hypnoses, second to Steersman's disease. Using a transthoracic, thoracoabdominal, or retroperitoneal approach, ostomies are performed (8 or more vertebral segments) and vertebrae are prepared to accept graft.

Preservice

Preservice work includes obtaining and reviewing preoperative and hospital admission roentgenograms and laboratory studies; arranging for autologous blood donation; communicating with the referring physician and other health care professionals; and communicating with the patient to explain the operative risks and benefits and obtain informed consent. Preservice work also includes preoperative scrubbing and positioning, prepping, and draping the patient. Preparation is necessary for intraoperative cell saver and monitoring of neurologic functions and intraoperative x-ray assessment. Preoperative X rays are analyzed to select the site of the incision and rib to be excised.

Intraservice

The skin and muscles are incised to expose the rib(s) chosen for excision. After rib resection, pleura is divided and the lung is collapsed. If necessary, the diaphragm is incised and detached from the chest wall. The intercostal and/or lumbar vessels are clamped, neurologic functions monitored, and, if stable, ligated as close to the aorta as possible. The aorta and vena cava are displaced. Periosteal and muscle attachments are mobilized from the anterior surfaces of the spine in the area to be fused. The level is confirmed by X ray. The annulus is removed from the anterior portion of the disks of the segments to be fused. The nucleus is evacuated from the disc space. Bone-cutting instruments are used to remove the cartilaginous end plates and bony end plates of the vertebrae above and below in a fashion to accept the proposed grafting material. (Instrumentation and/or bone grafting, if used, are coordinated at this point, and are coded separately.) The bone graft is inserted and impacted into the disc spaces. (Alternatively, bone-cutting instruments may be used to prepare the sites for the graft within the bodies of the vertebrae to be fused, and strut grafts impacted across the proposed fusion area and supplemented with cancellous bone packing.) Impaction of the graft is coordinated with manipulation of the vertebrae so that stability of the graft is insured. The stability of the graft, the integrity of the great vessels, and homeostasis are confirmed. The pleura is repaired. The muscles of the chest and/or abdominal wall are closed in layers. A chest tube is inserted and sutured. The subcutaneous tissues and skin are sutured. Sterile dressings are applied. If needed in the immediate postoperative period, casting or another external immobilization device is applied.

Postservice

Postservice work includes stabilizing the patient and monitoring of neurologic status; communicating with the patient's family and the referring physician (including providing written and oral reports and orders); caring for and removing the chest tube and drain; monitoring chest radiographs; monitoring the patient's tolerance of the immobilization device and ambulatory functions; and performing discharge day management, including providing instructions to the patient on wearing and care of the immobilization device. In addition, all hospital visits and postdischarge office visits for this procedure for 90 days after the day of the operation are considered part of the postservice work for this procedure, including the evaluation of periodic radiographs, laboratory reports, and medication adjustments.

Spinal Instrumentation

⊘ ❺ **22840** Posterior non-segmental instrumentation (eg, Harrington rod technique, pedicle fixation across one interspace, atlantoaxial transarticular screw fixation, sublaminar wiring at C1, facet screw fixation)

Work Value: 12.52 // Global Period: ZZZ

➲ *CPT Assistant* **Feb 96: 6, Jul 96: 10, Sep 97: 8, Nov 99: 12, Feb 02: 6;** ***CPT Changes: An Insider's View*** **2000**

Clinical Example

A 56-year-old female falls, sustaining a posteriorly-displaced Type II odontoid fracture without spinal cord injury. Computed tomographic imaging shows adequate pars interarticularis diameter with normal vertebral artery anatomy through the atlanto-axial region. Following a posterior cervical arthrodesis, transarticular screw placement is performed.

Intraservice

Fluoroscopy is used to assess the alignment of C1 and C2. A separate incision is made caudally for the entry point of the trocar to insert the C1-C2 transarticular screw. (If computer-assisted neuronavigation is used, report it separately.) The angle is checked with fluoroscopy with the starting point at the inferior portion of the C2 facet and the angle such that the tip of the screw will end at the C1 arch on the lateral fluoroscopy. The obturator is removed from the trocar and a hole is slowly drilled with fluoroscopic imaging in multiple projections to the appropriate depth. A cannulated screw of the appropriate length is placed over the drill bit or the drill bit is removed and a screw is placed across the C1-C2 joint again under fluoroscopic guidance. The procedure is then repeated on the opposite side. A C1-C2 arthrodesis is then performed (reported separately).

Non-Segmental Spinal Instrumentation
22840

Fixation at each end of the construct.

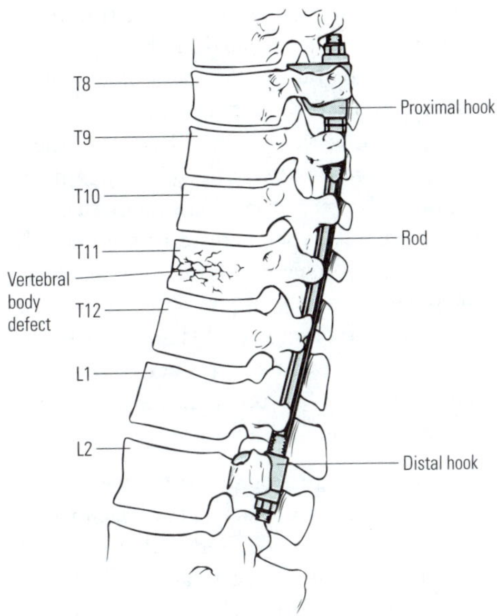

⊘ **22842** Posterior segmental instrumentation (eg, pedicle fixation, dual rods with multiple hooks and sublaminar wires); 3 to 6 vertebral segments

Work Value: 12.56 // Global Period: ZZZ

➲ *CPT Assistant* **Feb 96: 6, Mar 96: 7, Sep 97: 8, Feb 02: 6**

Clinical Example

A 50-year-old male undergoes a posterior lumbar arthrodesis of L3-L5 for degenerative disc disease. After the dissection and preparation of the lamina for the bone graft, screws are placed in both of the pedicles of L3, L4, and L5. X rays confirm the proper positioning of the screws. The screws are attached to rods fashioned to fit the contours of the spine.

Intraservice

After a detailed plan for the instrumentation is drawn on the radiograph or on paper, each of the two to six vertebrae to be fused are completely cleaned of soft tissue attachments from the posterior elements. Those vertebrae selected for segmental fixation are prepared by removing those portions of the ligamentum flavum and bone that would interface with the proper seating of the fixation device. For pedicle fixation at certain levels, the posterior cortex directly posterior to the pedicle is drilled or removed with bone-cutting tools. Entry into the central portion of the pedicle is confirmed by biplane or C-arm X ray. A pathway for a screw is prepared through the pedicle and into the vertebral body and the depth measured. (Alternatively, the ligament flavum is dissected from the undersurface of the lamina at each segment to be segmentally fixed and a passageway for sublaminar wires is prepared with careful protection of the underlying dura and neural elements. Or, laminae and/or transverse processes and/or spinous processes are prepared for multiple segmental fixation with wires or hooks.)

Screws are placed through the pedicle into the vertebral body on each side of each vertebra to be segmentally fixed. (Alternatively, wires are placed under each lamina centrally and separated so that a wire is under each side of each lamina; hooks or claws are placed about the transverse processes and laminae at the chosen vertebrae; or, button and wire devices are placed through both sides of each spinous process.) (Decortication and other preparation for arthrodesis and/or bone graft preparation, coded separately if used, are coordinated at this point.) The rod or plate device to be fixed by the segmental fixation is bent to contour to the spine and to achieve the desired posture of the intrumented segments. The rods or plates are then attached to the segmental fixation by applying nuts or other devices unique to the chosen instrumentation. Correction of the deformity is achieved by sequentially compressing or distracting between appropriate hooks or screws. Wires are carefully tightened around the rods with care to provide secure fixation without over stressing the wires or the bone.

All components of the instrumentation are carefully checked for secure positioning and freedom from impingement against dura or neural structures. Spinal cord monitoring is checked. Radiographic confirmation of the placement of the devices and spinal posture is obtained. Hook or wire rod position is monitored on each postoperative radiograph and compared with the prior radiograph.

Segmental Spinal Instrumentation
22842

Fixation at each end of the construct and at least one additional interposed bony attachment.

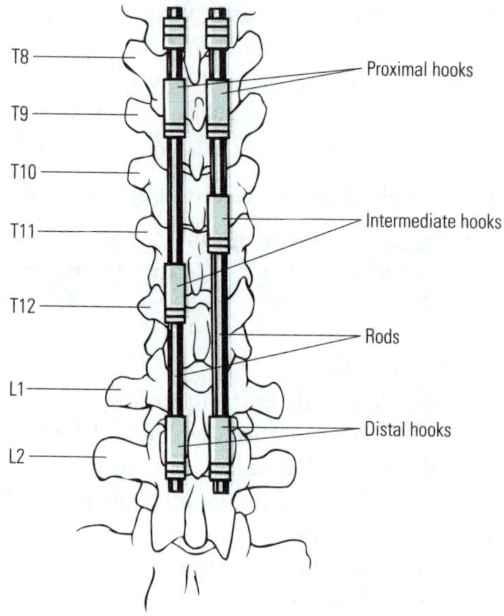

⊘ **22845** Anterior instrumentation; 2 to 3 vertebral segments

Work Value: 11.94 // Global Period: ZZZ

➲ ***CPT Assistant*** **Feb 96: 6, Mar 96: 10, Jul 96: 7, 10, Sep 97: 8, Feb 02: 6**

Clinical Example

A 20-year-old male presents with congenital scoliosis secondary to hemivertebrae over a short segment. After the diskectomy and preparation of the end plates for fusion, screws are placed in the vertebral bodies and attached to a plate spanning three vertebral segments.

Intraservice

The sites of diskectomy over the two to three vertebral segments to be fixed by instrumentation are checked to be certain that the end plates have been removed back to the posterior longitudinal ligaments and that their orientation is accurate. A depth gauge is placed across the disc space to determine the depth and ideal angle of inclination of the fixation screw. A passageway for the screw through the vertebral body is prepared in accordance with the protocol for the selected device.

Screws are placed in each vertebral body to be internally fixed. Care is taken that the portions of the device that will remain external to the bone do not create pressure upon the great vessels and that there is no impingement of dura and neural tissues at the depth of the device. The plate, rod, or cable as selected is secured to the screws by the technique according to the protocol of the particular device. Alternatively, hooks or other devices may be used to anchor to the anterior elements and methacrylate can be added to supplement the fixation. The chosen device is contoured to produce the desired posture of the spine or is adjusted in situ, depending upon the type of instrumentation is used.

⊘ **22848** Pelvic fixation (attachment of caudal end of instrumentation to pelvic bony structures) other than sacrum

Work Value: 5.99 // Global Period: ZZZ

➲ ***CPT Assistant*** **Feb 96: 6, Sep 97: 8, Feb 02: 6**

Clinical Example

A 13-year-old female undergoes correction of a lumbar scoliosis that includes the lumbosacral joint. After the lamina is prepared, Luque rods are inserted. The distal end of the rod is fashioned to be placed into the wing of the ilium down to the sciatic notch. X rays confirm the proper position of the fixation.

Intraservice

Pelvic fixation is an extension of multisegment fixation of the spine (coded separately), which provides stabilization to the pelvis. The rods used for the multisegment fixation must be specially contoured in multiple planes to provide for fit and correction of the spinal deformity and for placement between the tables of the iliac crest. Alternatively, separate rods are fashioned to fit between the tables of the iliac crest and to be apposed to the caudad end of the multisegment fixation rods where the two rods are linked together with a cross-fixation device. The midline exposure of the spine is extended to expose the posterior superior iliac spines, the wings of the ilium being exposed by dissection between the erector spinae fascia and the subcutaneous fat. The ilium is exposed from the posterior superior iliac spine to the mid portion of the iliac wing and to the sciatic notch. A guide pin is inserted inside the wing of the ilium next to the posterior surface of the sacrum, taking care to avoid the sacroiliac joint. The surgeon places a finger in the sciatic notch to direct the positioning of the guide pin. A similar procedure is performed on the other side. The guide pins are then used as reference to contour the rods. The rods must be contoured to conform to pelvic, sacral, and spinal segments. The pelvic guide pin is removed with a vice grip and extractor. The pelvic section of the rod is introduced into the iliac insertion hole and tapped into the wing of the ilium with a rod pusher and mallet. The spinal section is rotated to fit into the prepared multisegmented spine fixation or alongside the rod to which it is to be connected. Segmental fixation (coded separately) to the spine is accomplished or the pelvic fixation device is linked to the spinal rod by cross-linking instruments. Identical procedures are performed on both sides of the pelvis.

⊘ **22851** Application of intervertebral biomechanical device(s) (eg, synthetic cage(s), threaded bone dowel(s), methylmethacrylate) to vertebral defect or interspace

Work Value: 6.70 // Global Period: ZZZ

➲ ***CPT Assistant*** **Feb 96: 6, Sep 97: 8, Nov 99: 12, Dec 99: 2, May 00: 11, Mar 01: 2, Feb 02: 6, Feb 05: 14-15; *CPT Changes: An Insider's View* 2002**

Clinical Example

A 50-year-old male undergoes an anterior fusion of L5-S1 for degenerative disease. A retroperitoneal incision is made and an arthrodesis is performed using a BAK cage. A distractor is placed in the interspace, a hole is drilled in the interspace, and the BAK cage is placed in the hole. The spacer is removed and replaced with another BAK cage. Both cages are filled with bone graft.

Intraservice
The exposed disc space and adjacent vertebrae are prepared with bone-cutting instruments for acceptance of the prosthetic device. Preparation of the recipient site is made according to the protocol of the particular device. If methylmethacrylate is to be used, a screw or pin is inserted into the adjacent vertebral surfaces to anchor the methylmethacrylate. Provision is made for the cooling of adjacent tissues and the protection of heat-sensitive tissue from the exothermic reaction of the curing of the methylmethacrylate. For cages, the recipient site is prepared by bone dissection and a trial fit with the device or a spacer or template as indicated by the protocol is inserted and removed for any final modifications of the recipient site. The prosthetic device is then screwed, impacted, or injected into place according to the protocol for this particular device. (Additional fixation, other provision for arthrodesis, or bone grafting are coordinated with the placement of the prosthetic device and are coded separately.) For devices that incorporate graft material, the material is appropriately placed into the device prior to its final insertion.

Spinal Prosthetic Devices
22851

Application of prosthetic device.

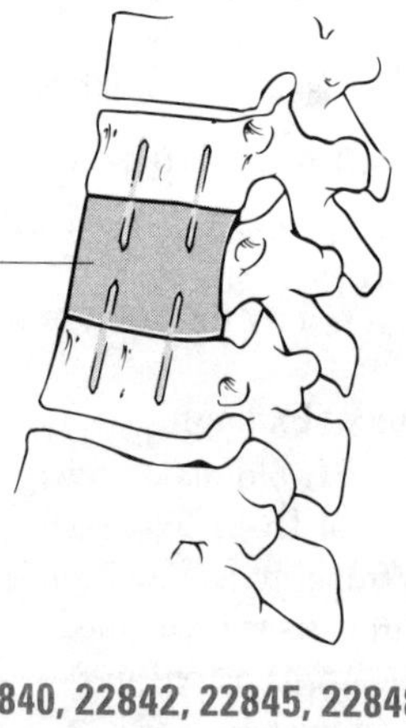

Coding Tip for 22840, 22842, 22845, 22848, and 22851
Instrumentation procedure codes 22840, 22842, 22845, 22848, and 22851 are reported in addition to the definitive procedure(s) without modifier 51, *Multiple procedures,* appended.

Shoulder

Repair, Revision, and/or Reconstruction

23420 Reconstruction of complete shoulder (rotator) cuff avulsion, chronic (includes acromioplasty)

Work Value: 14.75 // Global Period: 090

➲ *CPT Assistant* Feb 02: 11, Oct 05: 23

Clinical Example
A 70-year-old male with a two-month history of a painful shoulder and the inability to raise his arm undergoes a repair of a chronic rotator cuff tear.

Preservice
Preservice work begins after the decision to operate is made, from the day before the surgery until the time of the procedure. Preservice includes obtaining and reviewing preprocedural imaging, pathology, and laboratory studies, paying special attention to shoulder X rays, arthrogram, or magnetic resonance imaging studies; consulting with the referring physician, if necessary, and other health care professionals; and communicating with the patient and/or patient's family to explain the operative risks and benefits and obtain informed consent. Preoperative work also includes preoperative scrubbing; supervising the positioning, prepping and draping of the patient; and ensuring that the necessary surgical instruments and supplies are available in the operative suite.

Intraservice
Under general anesthesia, in a sitting position, the patient's shoulder is incised over the acromion near the acromioclavicular joint. The incision is carried down over the proximal aspect of the deltoid in its raffe for approximately 2 to 3 cm. The anterior acromionectomy is performed with an osteotome, while smoothing the undersurface of the acromion and exposing the torn cuff for inspection. The supraspinatus, infraspinatus, and teres minor are found retracted in chronic avulsions and must be carefully

mobilized. Injury to the supraspinous nerve must be avoided when dissection superior to the rotator cuff. The capsule us usually contracted superiorly and must be released from the superior glenoid without injuring the superior biceps tendon-labrum complex. The greater tuberosity is prepared and the cuff is sutured to the greater tuberosity with a permanent suture. The attachment is done by freshening a trough in the bone of the greater tuberosity lateral to the articular surface of the humeral head. Sutures passed through drill holes in bone or using Sutter anchors allows firm attachment of the rotator cuff to bone. Completion of the cuff repair is accomplished using number one polydioxanone suture material. Then, the fascia of the deltoid and trapezius muscle are reattached, the subcutaneous tissue is approximated using a 4-0 chromic suture, and the skin is closed with a stainless steel staple.

Postservice

Postservice work begins after skin closure in the operating room and includes the application of sterile dressings and an abduction support, as required. Postoperative work also includes monitoring patient stabilization in the recovery room; communicating with the patient's family and other health care professionals (including providing written and oral reports and orders); and all hospital visits and services performed by the surgeon, including monitoring physiotherapy, assessing range of motion progress, and antibiotic and pain medication management. The physician supervises and directs the beginning of early passive assistive range of motion to achieve full range of passive motion within 4–6 weeks of the surgery is critical to the success of this operation. Discharge day management includes the surgeon's final examination of the patient, which includes providing instructions for continuing care, and preparing the discharge records. In addition, all postdischarge office visits for this procedure for 90 days after the day of the operation are considered part of the postoperative work for this procedure; including the evaluation of periodic imaging reports; assessment of physiotherapy progress; and antibiotic and pain medication adjustments.

Forearm and Wrist

Repair, Revision, and/or Reconstruction

⑤ **25447** Arthroplasty, interposition, intercarpal or carpometacarpal joints

Work Value: 10.95 // Global Period: 090

➲ *CPT Assistant* Nov 98: 8, Jan 05: 8, 11-12

Clinical Example

A 55-year-old female undergoes excision of the trapezium with interposition of local tissue between the scaphoid and base of the first metacarpal.

Preservice

Write pre-admission orders for preoperative medications. Review the results of preadmission testing including labs, X rays, computed tomography scans, and/or magnetic resonance imaging scans. Consult with the referring physician and other health care professionals. Reexamine the patient to make sure that the patient's physical findings have not changed and update the patient's History and Physical. Meet with patient and the patient's family to review the planned procedure and postoperative management. Obtain informed consent. Verify that all required instruments and supplies are available. Monitor/assist with patient positioning, padding of bony prominences, and the application of thermal regulation drapes. Assess the position of the extremities and head and adjust as needed. Place the patient's arm on the hand surgery table. Indicate the areas of skin to be prepped and mark surgical incisions. Apply a tourniquet to the proximal arm. Prep and drape the arm and hand. The arm is elevated and exsanguinated. Inflate the pneumatic tourniquet. Scrub and gown. Perform a surgical "time out" with the operating surgical team.

Intraservice

Make an incision over the base of the first metacarpal and trapezium. Carry out careful dissection, taking care to protect the branches of the superficial branch of the radial nerve. Elevate the periosteum over the trapezium and identify and open the first carpometacarpal joint and scaphotrapezio-trapezoid joint. Expose the trapezium via subperiosteal resection, taking care to protect the radial artery. Excise the trapezium piecemeal using osteotomes and a rongeur, taking care to protect the flexor carpi radialis. Clear the base of the first metacarpal of any osteophytes. Identify the flexor carpi radialis in the wound, split it longitudinally, and harvest the radial 1/2–2 transverse incisions of the forearm. Roll the radial one half of the flexor carpi radialis onto itself, sew it together, and then suture it to the soft tissues in the depths of the void created by the trapeziectomy. Hold the first ray in a somewhat adducted position and then pass a Kirschner wire through the first metacarpal into the second metacarpal. Thoroughly irrigate the wound. Repair the capsule in a vest-over-pants fashion. Approximate the skin in layers.

Postservice

In Hospital Work: Apply the dressing and splint. Monitor patient stabilization in the recovery room. Consult with the patient's family and the patient regarding the surgery and postoperative regimen. Communicate with health care professionals, including providing written and oral reports and orders. Coordinate the postoperative care with the recovery room nursing staff. Check the patient's vital signs. Assess the circulation, sensation, and motor function of the operated extremity. Review postoperative imaging studies and labs. Discuss home restrictions (ie, activity, bathing) with the patient and the patient's family. Write prescriptions for medications needed postdischarge. Complete all appropriate medical records, including the discharge summary, discharge instructions, and insurance forms. Dictate an operative report. Write a procedure note in the patient's chart.

In Office Work: Examine and talk with patient. Answer the patient's and family's questions. Remove the splint/dressings. Assess the surgical wound. Remove sutures. Assess the circulation, sensation, and motor function of the operated extremity. Redress the wound. Order occupational therapy. Supervise rehabilitation. Order/review radiographs. Discuss progress with the patient's primary care physician (verbal and written). Write medication prescriptions. Dictate progress notes for the patient's medical record.

Hand and Fingers

Repair, Revision, and/or Reconstruction

26340 Manipulation, finger joint, under anesthesia, each joint

Work Value: 2.62 // Global Period: 090

➲ *CPT Assistant* Nov 02: 10; *CPT Changes: An Insider's View* 2002

Clinical Example

A 30-year-old female is treated for a post-traumatic flexion contracture of the PIP joint with closed manipulation of the joint.

Preservice

Imaging studies are carefully reviewed, including X rays, computed tomography scans, and magnetic resonance imaging scans. Preoperative laboratory tests are reviewed. Consultation is completed with the referring physician and other health care professionals. The patient and the patient's family are apprised of the proposed surgery. The risks and complications associated with the surgery are discussed with the patient's family. Informed consent is obtained. The surgeon goes to the operating room and verifies that all appropriate equipment is available. The patient is brought to the operating room and placed on the operating table in the supine position. The position of the extremities and head are checked and adjusted. The patient's involved arm is prepped and draped. A tourniquet is applied to the proximal arm.

Intraservice

The finger joint is gently taken through a full range of motion from the maximum amount of flexion to the maximum amount of extension allowable. Care is taken to avoid applying excessive force. The manipulation of the joint is repeated as needed until the maximum range of motion is achieved.

Postservice

In Hospital Work: Dressing and a splint are applied. The patient's stabilization in the recovery room is monitored. The patient and the patient's family is consulted regarding the surgery and the postoperative regimen. The physician communicates with health care professionals, including providing written and oral reports and orders. Postoperative care is coordinated with the recovery room nursing staff. The patient's vital signs are checked. The circulation, sensation, and motor function of the operated extremity are assessed. Postoperative imaging studies are reviewed. Postoperative laboratory studies are reviewed. Discharge records are prepared.

In Office Work: The circulation, sensation, and motor function of the operated extremity are assessed. The splint is removed. Physical/occupational therapy is ordered. The physician supervises rehabilitation. Radiographs are reviewed and ordered. The physician provides pain medication management. Laboratory reports are evaluated. The physician communicates with other health care professionals, the patient, and the patient's family regarding the patient's progress. All postdischarge office visits for this procedure for 90 days after the day of the operation are considered part of the postoperative work for this procedure.

26356 Repair or advancement, flexor tendon, in zone 2 digital flexor tendon sheath (eg, no man's land); primary, without free graft, each tendon

Work Value: 10.22 // Global Period: 090

➲ *CPT Assistant* Nov 98: 8, Dec 98: 9; *CPT Changes: An Insider's View* 2002, 2004

Clinical Example

A 30-year-old housewife cut the volar aspect of her middle finger with a knife while slicing a bagel. The laceration severed the flexor tendons, both sublimis and profundus, just proximal to the sublimis insertion. The patient was evaluated in the emergency room where a history was taken and a physical examination was performed. The patient was then taken to the operating room where primary tendon repair was performed. Under general anesthesia, the laceration site was opened proximally and distally and the retracted tendons brought into the wound from the palm. The digital nerves were inspected under loupe magnification and found not to be injured. Both tendons were then repaired with core sutures and the epitenon suture technique. The patient was then placed in a dorsal protective splint with a rubber band attached through a pulley mechanism to the nail of the long finger. For the postoperative period, the 90-day global visit rule is in effect.

Preservice

Preservice work includes assessing the patient in the emergency department; taking a history as to the incident; obtaining and reviewing emergency department admission imaging and laboratory studies; communicating with other health care professionals; ordering preoperative antibiotics; and communicating with the patient and/or the patient's family to explain operative risks and benefits and obtain informed consent. Other preoperative services include supervising the positioning and prepping of the hand; draping the patient; and ensuring that surgical instruments and supplies that are necessary are present and available in the operative suite.

Intraservice

After the patient has been positioned, the tourniquet applied, and the patient anesthetized, the protective dressing can be removed and the hand prepped and draped. The tourniquet is applied. The laceration site is opened and extended in a zig-zag fashion. The tendon lacerations are evaluated and the integrity of the neurovascular bundles are rechecked. The tendon ends are approximated and repaired. The sublimis tendon is repaired with interrupted sutures. The profundus tendon is repaired with a deep interlocking suture (modified Kessler) and running superficial suture (Kleinert). The tendon sheath is repaired. The skin is closed with interrupted sutures. A sterile dressing is applied and a restraining dorsal splint is fabricated and applied. A rubber band is attached to the nail of the middle finger and led through a pulley mechanism to allow early motion to be started in the early postoperative period.

Postservice

Postservice work begins with monitoring patient stabilization; communicating with the patient's family and other health care professionals (including providing written and oral reports and orders); and all hospital visits and services performed by the surgeon, including monitoring and caring for the incision and antibiotic and pain medication management. Discharge management includes the surgeon's final examination of the patient, which includes a discussion of the hospital stay, instructions for planned therapy, and preparation of discharge records. In addition, all postdischarge office visits for this procedure for 90 days after the day of the operation are considered part of the postoperative work for this procedure, including frequent monitoring of planned active extension and passive flexion exercises; removing the sutures and traction device; reviewing periodic imaging and therapist reports; and making antibiotic and pain medication adjustments.

Pelvis and Hip Joint

Introduction or Removal

27096 Injection procedure for sacroiliac joint, arthrography and/or anesthetic/steroid

Work Value: 1.40 // Global Period: 000

➲ *CPT Assistant* Nov 99: 12, Apr 03: 8, Apr 04: 15; *CPT Changes: An Insider's View* 2000

Clinical Example

A 42-year-old male with history of prior lumbosacral fusion presents with severe chronic low back, buttock, and groin pain. Imaging studies of the spine, pelvis, and sacroiliac joints are unremarkable, showing a solid lumbosacral fusion. Patient undergoes diagnostic and therapeutic sacroiliac arthrogram to study intrinsic joint anatomy and to assess, by means of monitoring the joint blockade, whether or not the joint is the major source of his clinical pain.

Preservice

The patient's prior pelvic imaging studies (radiographs, computed tomography scans, magnetic resonance imaging scans, nuclear bone scans, and so on) are reviewed to familiarize the physician with the patient's anatomy, including anatomic variants and any pathology present. The procedure with its risks, potential benefits, and alternatives are explained to the patient and informed consent obtained. A brief history is obtained, including the exclusion of bleeding diathesis.

Intraservice

Initially, the skin is marked over the most caudal aspect of the sacroiliac joint. Flouroscopic guidance is used. (The use of fluoroscopic guidance is separately codeable and should not be considered in the work or practice expense of this code.) Using a sterile technique, the skin is then prepped and draped. Thereafter, a sterile 22-gauge spinal needle is passed through the skin into the inferior aspect of the joint. Then, under flouroscopic observation, a test injection of contrast is made to confirm the presence or absence of an intra-articluar injection. If contrast is noted to be within the joint, without venous opacification or periarticular leakage, non-irritating, nonionic low osmolar contrast is then injected into the joint to a volume of approximately 0.5 to 1 cc. This amount of contrast generally fills a non-inflamed joint adequately to delineate integrity or lack thereof of articular cartilage, as well as morphologic features of the joint in space and capsule. Films are then obtained in at least two projections. (The performance and interpretation of these films are a separate procedure and separately codeable and should not be included in the evaluation of work or practice expense for this code.) In many cases, 13 cc of pure local anesthetic (12% lidocaine, 12% novicain, or 0.5% marcaine) is then injected into the joint. Occasionally, a mixture of local anesthetic (any of the preceding) mixed with water-soluble steroid is injected into the joint. These therapeutic injections are used to block the joint for either immediate or potentially lasting pain relief.

Postservice

The patient is carefully monitored for the therapeutic response to the joint blockade. A report is dictated for the patient's medical records. Results of the procedure are discussed with the referring physician.

Repair, Revision, and/or Reconstruction

❺ **27130** Arthroplasty, acetabular and proximal femoral prosthetic replacement (total hip arthroplasty), with or without autograft or allograft

Work Value: 21.61 // Global Period: 090

➲ *CPT Assistant* Spring 92: 8; *CPT Changes: An Insider's View* 2002

Clinical Example

A 67-year-old obese female (body mass index greater than 30) with osteoarthritis of the lumbar spine and chronic low back pain presents with severe left hip pain affecting activities of daily living. She is hypertensive and a non-insulin-dependent diabetic. At operation, she undergoes a conventional total left hip arthroplasty.

Preservice

Preservice work includes obtaining and reviewing preprocedural imaging, pathology, and laboratory studies, taking care to review the radiographs and scaled radiographs that were used for sizing and ordering special implants or allografts, if necessary. Preservice work also includes reviewing the preoperative laboratory test; consulting with the referring physician, if necessary, and other health care professionals; communicating with the patient and/or patient's family to explain the operative risks and benefits; and obtaining informed consent. The case is templated, which includes taking a leg-length measurement, and assessing the center of rotation of the hip, the proper height for the femoral neck cut, as well as the proper sizing of the components. Preservice work also includes scrubbing, arranging for an intraoperative cell saver, positioning the patient, assessing leg length before the patient is placed in the lateral position, marking the patient for the planned incision, supervising the prepping and draping of the patient, as well as ensuring that the surgical instruments and implants that are necessary are present and available in the operative suite.

Intraservice

After incising the skin and the fascia, the glutei are taken off the femur one at a time. Once this is completed, leg length assessment is done by placing markers in the pelvis and in the femur as well as by checking through the drapes. After assessing leg length and doing a capsulectomy, the femoral head is dislocated and a femoral neck osteotomy is performed at the proper height. This is then followed by finding the femoral canal and then doing sequential raspings with the broaches until the correct rotational and axial stability is achieved. The calcar planer is then used to plane down the neck.

The appropriate dissection and releases are then performed to expose the socket. The appropriate retractors are placed anteriorly as well as posteriorly, and all excess capsule and redundant labrum is removed with a knife. All osteophytes are carefully removed using each of the osteotomes, starting with a 1/2-in osteotome all the way up to a 1-in osteotome. After removing the osteophytes, the base of the acetabulum is found with a small reamer. Once the reamer is carefully placed all the way down to the medial wall of the acetabulum, sequential reamers in 1-mm increments are used all the way up to the correct size. The correct size is determined by the axial and off-center loading of the reamers. Once this is completed, trial implants are seated and stability and leg-length measurements are done. Once the proper sizing and stability issues are determined, the socket is seated. The drill is then placed over the holes for the socket to insert the screws. (Usually, two screws are depth gaged and then inserted.) The central hole sealer is placed in situ and the liner is placed and tapped after cleaning all of the soft tissue.

Once this is completed, trial reduction with the rasp is done again to check stability and range of motion for impingement or dislocation. Redundant capsule is then removed from the posterior aspect. The implant is opened up, checked, and then placed and tapped in situ. Once this is completed, copious irrigation is done. Leg length is assessed again with trial necks. The real head/neck is placed and tapped in situ. The hip is then reduced. An X ray is taken to verify the position of the components. Sponge and needle counts are done and a deep drain is placed. The closure is performed in multilayers, taking care to reattach the muscles to the proper structures.

Postservice

The patient's leg is splinted. Postoperative work also includes monitoring the patient's stabilization in the recovery room; communicating with the patient's family and other health care professionals (including providing written and oral reports and orders); and all hospital visits and services performed by the surgeon, including monitoring lab reports, caring for and removing drains and dressings, supervising physical or occupational therapy, ordering and reviewing postoperative X rays, and managing antibiotic, anticoagulant, and pain medication. Arrangements are made with the case manager and the patient's family for discharge to an inpatient rehabilitation facility or a skilled nursing facility or home. Discharge day management includes the surgeons final examination of the patient, providing instructions to the patient or the patient's family for continuing care including home health care, and preparing the discharge records. In addition, all postdischarge office visits for this procedure for 90 days after the day of the operation are considered part of the postoperative work for this procedure, including removing sutures; evaluating periodic imaging and laboratory reports, if needed; reviewing anticoagulation laboratory values; making appropriate medication adjustments; and managing antibiotic and pain medication. Great attention to the possibility of postoperative hip dislocation must be given with this procedure by careful supervision of postoperative in-hospital care as well as the direction of physical therapy of postoperative exercise and recovery of activity.

Total Hip Replacement
27130

The femoral head is excised, osteophytes are removed, and acetabulum is reamed out before replacement is inserted in the femoral shaft.

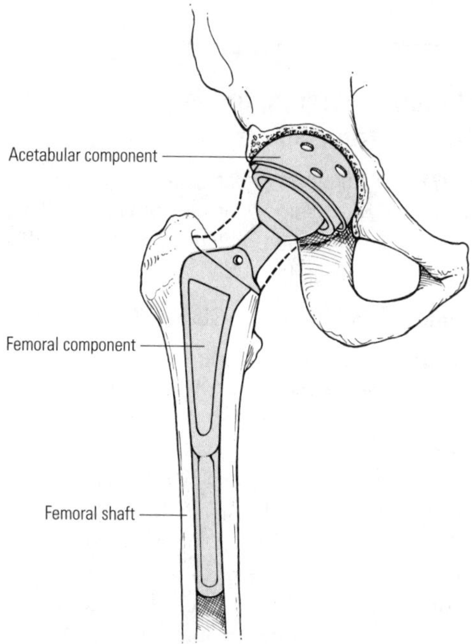

Femur (Thigh Region) and Knee Joint

Repair, Revision, and/or Reconstruction

➎ 27447 Arthroplasty, knee, condyle and plateau; medial AND lateral compartments with or without patella resurfacing (total knee arthroplasty)

Work Value: 23.04 // Global Period: 090

➲ *CPT Changes: An Insider's View* 2002

Clinical Example

A 69-year-old obese female (body mass index greater than 30) with bilateral osteoarthritis of the knee joint presents with increased varus of the right knee affecting activities of daily living. She is hypertensive and a non-insulin-dependent diabetic. At operation, she undergoes a conventional total right knee arthroplasty.

Preservice

Preservice include obtaining and reviewing preprocedural imaging, pathology, and laboratory studies, taking care to review of radiographs and scaled radiographs that were used for sizing and ordering special implants or allografts, if necessary. Preservice also includes reviewing the preoperative laboratory test; consulting with the referring physician, if necessary, and other health care professionals; communicating with the patient and/or patient's family to explain the operative risks and benefits; and obtaining informed consent. Preoperative work also includes templating the case, scrubbing, arranging for an intraoperative cell saver, positioning the patient, marking the patient for the planned incision, supervising the prepping and draping of the patient, and ensuring that the surgical instruments and implants that are necessary are present and available in the operative suite.

Intraservice

After the tourniquet is elevated following exsanguination, an acceptable surgical incision is used to expose the joint. After everting the patella, appropriate soft tissue elevation and removal is performed to expose and visualize the joint. Care and attention is used to evaluate the ligament balance of the knee and appropriate soft tissue releases are performed to restore balance to the joint. The remnant meniscal tissue and overlying osteophytes are removed and if indicated, the cruciate ligaments are released. Next, attention is turned to the patella. The patella is measured and then the articular surface is resected at the appropriate depth. The optimal component size is selected and the fixation holes drilled. Next, attention is turned to the distal femur. The intramedulary canal is drilled and the distal femoral cutting block is applied. The alignment of the block is confirmed and the distal femoral resection is made. The anteroposterior and mediolateral size of the distal femur is evaluated and the appropriate implant size is selected. The remaining chamfer and AP bone cuts of the distal femur are then made. The remainder of the posterior cruciate ligament is excised to expose everything back to the capsule. This tissue is resected, taking care to leave the collateral ligaments intact and to protect the neurovascular structures. The tibia is subluxed forward and the tibial cutting guide is applied. The optimal position in all planes is confirmed and the bone cut is made. The tibia is then sized for the appropriate implant and the bone is prepared. Next, the trial components are inserted and a trial reduction of the prosthetic knee is performed. Overall limb alignment, soft tissue and ligamentous balance, and prosthetic interactions are assessed. Further refinement of the soft tissue balance, the bone resections for alignment, and the prosthetic implant interaction are performed as indicated to optimize the prosthetic longevity. The polyethylene is inserted into place onto the tibial prosthesis. Knee stability, range of motion, and alignment are again confirmed. Having completed all of the preparations, the tourniquet is released, hemostasis obtained, a deep drain placed, and the wound closed in layers.

Postservice

Postservice begins after skin closure in the operating room and includes applying sterile dressing and extension splint or continuous passive motion apparatus. Postoperative work also includes monitoring patient stabilization in the recovery room; communicating with the patient's family and other health care professionals (including providing written and oral reports and orders); and all hospital visits and services performed by the surgeon, including monitoring lab reports; caring for and removing drains and dressings; supervising physical or occupational therapy; ordering and reviewing postoperative X rays; and managing antibiotic, anticoagulation, and pain medication. Discharge day management includes the surgeons final examination of the patient, instructing the patient on continuing care including home health care, and preparing the discharge records. Additionally, all postdischarge office visits for this procedure for 90 days after the day of the operation are considered part of the postoperative work for this procedure, including the removal of sutures; the evaluation of periodic imaging and laboratory reports, if needed; the review of anticoagulation laboratory values; and antibiotic and pain medication adjustments. Supervising the recovery of range of motion as well as ambulatory status is most important during the postoperative course and involves the oversight of in-hospital therapy as well as home or outpatient care physical therapy.

27486 Revision of total knee arthroplasty, with or without allograft; one component

Work Value: 20.92 // Global Period: 090

Clinical Example

A 56-year-old female with a painful loose total knee arthroplasty undergoes a total knee revision of one of the components.

Preservice

Preservice work begins after the decision to operate is made, from the day before the surgery until the time of the procedure. This includes obtaining and reviewing preprocedural imaging, pathology, and laboratory studies, paying special attention to radiographs and scaled radiographs, if necessary, that were used for sizing and ordering special implants or allografts; reviewing the hip aspiration/arthrogram and preoperative laboratory tests; consulting with the referring physician, if necessary, and other health care professionals; and communicating with the patient and/or patient's family to explain operative risks and benefits and obtain informed consent. Preoperative work also includes scrubbing; arranging for intraoperative cell saver; positioning the patient; marking the patient for the planned incision; supervising the prepping and draping of the patient; and ensuring that the surgical instruments and implants that are necessary are present and available in the operative suite.

Intraservice

After the tourniquet is elevated following exsanguination, the old median parapatellar scar is used to expose the joint. After everting the patella, initially, a synovectomy is performed to expose and visualize the joint. In doing this, tissue is removed that is underlying the implant that had violated the bone and interface. Having completed this and irrigated the joint, attention can be turned to extracting the tibial component. The tibia is cut from its interlock and taken out of the insert. The broken piece is then visualized in back and lifted out. The tibial surface is resected, removing bone in order to obtain a stable edge peripherally for supporting the implant. All remaining cement is excised with hand and power tools. The hole is reamed for the central peg. This leaves a sclerotic surface throughout. A right-angle bur is then brought in and many small perforations are made in this sclerotic surface for engaging the cement. The entire top surface was previously burred to remove all fibrous tissue. At this point, the knee is irrigated completely and exsanguinated for tourniquet elevation. The remaining bone surfaces are prepared, first using a bur to go over all of the exposed cortical type surfaces to be sure all fibrous tissue have been removed, and then using right-angle bur to bur small perforation in the sclerotic areas. After a trial reduction, attention is returned to the tibia, removing further bone to flex the bone cut, drop the posterior edge to allow this to seat completely at the top edge of the fibular tibial joint laterally and below that on the medial side but with good coverage and good stability. Components are selected to give complete extension and good tension. Having made all of the decisions, prepared the allograft (as needed), and made all of the cuts for the bone, cementing is begun. The tibia is cemented using pressure inject bone cement loaded with tobramycin sulfate into the tibial metaphyseal surface but not into the diaphysis and inserting the modular base. The tourniquet is released, hemostasis is obtained, a deep drain placed, and the wound closed in layers.

Postservice

Postservice work begins after skin closure in the operating room and includes the application of sterile dressing and an extension splint or continuous passive motion apparatus. Postoperative work also includes monitoring patient stabilization in the recovery room; communicating with the patient's family and other health care professionals (including providing written and oral reports and orders); and all hospital visits and services performed by the surgeon, including monitoring lab reports; caring for and removing drains and dressings (Note: Careful inspection of the operative wound is critical because anterior skin slough with secondary infection is a definite complication.); supervising physical or occupational therapy; ordering and reviewing postoperative X rays; and managing antibiotic and pain medication. Discharge day management includes the surgeon's final examination of the patient, which includes providing instructions for continuing care and home health care, and preparing the discharge records. In addition, all postdischarge office visits for this procedure for 90 days after the day of the operation are considered part of the postoperative work for this procedure, including the removal of sutures, the evaluation of periodic imaging and laboratory reports, if needed, and the adjustment of antibiotic and pain medication. Supervising the recovery of range of motion as well as ambulatory status is most important during the postoperative course and involves not only oversight of in-hospital therapy but home care therapy as well.

Application of Casts and Strapping

Lower Extremity

Strapping—Any Age

⑤ **29580** Strapping; Unna boot

Work Value: 0.55 // Global Period: 000

➲ *CPT Assistant* **Feb 96: 3, Jul 99: 10, Apr 02: 13**

Clinical Example

A 70-year-old male with non-insulin-dependent diabetes presents with edema of the right lower extremity secondary to venous insufficiency. The decision is made to apply a strapping using a compression, zinc-impregnated bandage (Unna boot).

Preservice

Preservice includes reviewing and updating the patient's chart with general medical and surgical history, including current medications and allergies. The existing Unna boot is removed and the area cleansed. A physical examination is conducted, which includes evaluating the neurological and vascular status of the patient, along with a dermatologic and musculoskeletal examination of the foot, ankle, and lower leg where the Unna boot will be applied, as well as an examination of the ulcer. (Proper patient screening has been done to exclude those with deep infection, excessive edema, or excessively fragile skin.) Treatment options are reviewed. Consultation with the referring physician and other health care professionals occurs, if necessary, and communication occurs with the patient and/or the patient's family to explain the procedure, including the possible risks and complications.

Intraservice

The patient is placed supine with an assistant holding the foot with the ankle in neutral position and the knee is flexed at 90 degrees. The Unna boot is applied beginning proximal to the toes and extending proximally to the mid-calf region. (Extreme care must be taken to smooth out any wrinkles in the compression bandage with each compressive wrap.) A figure-of-eight wrap occurs around the ankle. Frequent checks occur to ensure that the neutral position of the foot to the ankle is maintained. Once the entire bandage has been applied, additional smoothing must occur. The bandage is allowed to set while the foot is maintained neutral with the ankle. An Ace wrap or elastic bandage is applied over the Unna boot.

Postservice

A surgical shoe is fitted on the patient. The patient's neurovascular status is evaluated and stabilized. The patient is instructed on the care of the Unna boot.

Endoscopy/Arthroscopy

29806 Arthroscopy, shoulder, surgical; capsulorrhaphy

Work Value: 14.95 // Global Period: 090

➲ *CPT Changes: An Insider's View* 2002

Clinical Example

A 17-year-old high school wrestler falls on the wrestling mat, forcing his arm into abduction and external rotation. The dislocation is reduced at matside, and follow-up X rays rule out an associated fracture. He is treated conservatively with a sling, ice, and anti-inflammatory medication. A gentle program of forward flexion is begun but abduction and external rotation are restricted. After 4 weeks, the restrictions are lifted and an aggressive rotator cuff and shoulder girdle strengthening program is begun. After returning to wrestling, there are several episodes during which his shoulder attempts to redislocate, and a recurrent dislocation takes place during a subsequent match that cannot be reduced matside. After reviewing nonsurgical and surgical options with his orthopaedist, the patient elects to undergo an arthroscopic capsulorrhaphy.

Preservice

Review preoperative work-up including the preprocedural imaging and laboratory studies, taking care to review the magnetic resonance imaging results. Consult with the referring physician and other health care professionals, as necessary. Answer the patient's and familys questions. Obtain informed consent if not already obtained. Review the surgical procedure, the length and type of anesthesia, postoperative procedures, and expected outcome(s) with the patient and the patient's family. Change into scrub clothes. Mark the operative site. Review the planned procedure and the positioning and draping of the patient and the positioning of monitors and laparoscopic/video equipment. Position the patient supinely and apply a shoulder boom to support the arm and allow the appropriate amount and angle of traction. Roll the patient into the lateral decubitus position and place pads to protect areas from pressure. Ensure that the necessary surgical instruments and supplies are present and available in the operative suite. Scrub and gown. The arthroscopic equipment is positioned to allow an unobstructed view of the monitor. The arm is examined for stability, and then prepped and draped

Intraservice

After induction of general anesthesia, create a posterior arthroscopy portal. Once the bloody effusion is irrigated, perform an inspection of the intra-articular structures including the entire articular surface, the biceps tendon, the subscapularis, the superior and middle glenohumeral ligaments, the anterior and posterior inferior glenohumeral ligaments, the labrum, the inferior pouch, the bare area, and the infraspinatus and supraspinatus tendons and associated recesses. Evaluate for a Hill Sachs lesion. Avulse the anterior inferior glenohumeral ligament (AIGHL) from the anterior glenoid. Avulse the labrum with the ligament as it will need to be incorporated in the repair. In this case, the articular surface is intact and no evidence of a Hill-Sachs lesion is identified.

Create an anterior portal with an inside-out or outside-in technique. Place a plastic canula with a rubber damn anteriorly to allow access, but not allow extravasations. Create the original anterior portal in a high position to allow a second anterior portal to be made above the subscapularis tendon. Release the adhesions of the AIGHL from the glenoid. Release all attachments of the ligament to the subscapularis to allow the ligament to shift back to its original or to a slightly advanced position. Burr the anterior glenoid neck to a bleeding surface without injuring the articular surface.

Once the neck is abraded, insert a drill into the lower large bore anterior canula. (This lower position will allow a more perpendicular approach to the glenoid rim.) Create a drill hole for the placement of a bone anchor. The bone anchor has one or two sutures. Carefully pass the sutures through the AIGHL in such a fashion as to advance/shift the ligament when the knots are tied. Repeat this sequence of steps for one or two more bone anchors: place the drill guide, create the drill hole, place the bone anchor, pass and tie the sutures. When these tasks are completed and the AIGHL is tightly held against the glenoid, the stabilization is complete. Remove the arthroscope from the glenohumeral joint and place it in the subacromial space to rule out concomitant pathology in this location. Suture the portal incisions.

Postservice

Postoperative work begins after the skin closure in the operating room and includes applying sterile dressings and a shoulder immobilizer. Postoperative work also includes monitoring the patient's stabilization in the recovery room, taking care to monitor the neurovascular status and function of the arm; and communicating with the patient's family and other health care professionals (including providing written and oral reports and orders). Discharge plans include instructing the patient on continuing care, ordering post-operative pain medication and antibiotics, physiotherapy, and preparing the discharge records. Additionally, all postdischarge office visits for this procedure for 90 days after the day of the operation are considered part of the postoperative work for this procedure, including the removal of sutures; the periodic assessment and adjustment of the splint; direct patient physiotherapy instruction by the surgeon; the assessment of adjunctive physiotherapy progress; and pain medication adjustments.

29807 Arthroscopy, shoulder, surgical; repair of SLAP lesion

Work Value: 14.48 // Global Period: 090

➲ *CPT Changes: An Insider's View* 2002

Clinical Example

A 35-year-old construction worker grabs a support to prevent a fall, but feels a pulling, tearing sensation in the shoulder. Emergency room X rays show no sign of fracture. Despite a program of anti-inflammatory medication, thermal modalities, and gentle physical therapy, after 3 weeks, he is still unable to elevate his arm past shoulder level, especially with the palm facing the ceiling. A magnetic resonance imaging (MRI) scan identifies a superior labrum anterior/posterior (SLAP) tear. An arthroscopic SLAP lesion repair is scheduled.

Preservice

Review the preoperative work-up, including the preprocedural imaging and laboratory studies, paying special attention to the MRI. Consult with the referring physician and other health care professionals, as necessary. Answer the patient's and family's questions. Obtain informed consent if not already obtained. Review the surgical procedure, length and type of anesthesia, postoperative procedures, and expected outcome(s) with the patient and the patient's family. Change into scrub clothes. Mark the operative site. Review the planned procedure and the positioning and draping of the patient, and the positioning of monitors and laparoscopic/video equipment. Position the patient supinely and apply a shoulder boom to support the arm and allow the appropriate amount and angle of traction. Roll the patient into the lateral decubitus position and place pads to protect areas from pressure. Ensure that the necessary surgical instruments and supplies are present and available in the operative suite. Scrub and gown. Position the arthroscopic equipment to allow an unobstructed view of the monitor. Examine the arm for stability and then prep and drape.

Intraservice

A posterior portal is made for insertion of the arthroscope. The intraarticular structures are evaluated. An anterior portal is then made and a probe is inserted. The probe is used to palpate these structures. Care and patience must be taken to closely evaluate every intraarticular structure to determine the often present, comorbid condition. Once assured of the isolated pathology, the superior labrum is thoroughly investigated. The biceps/labral complex is avulsed from the superior glenoid. A shaver is introduced to debride and abrade the superior glenoid, down to bone to provide a bleeding bed. The undersurface of the biceps/labral complex is also debrided. A second anterior portal is made through the rotator cuff interval after needle localization. A large bore cannula with a rubber damn is placed into this portal to allow access but prevent extravasation. A drill is placed through this portal and a drill hole is created on the extraarticular surface of the superior glenoid. Great care is taken to prevent angling the drill toward the articular surface. Once the hole is made, a bone anchor is placed into the hole. The bone anchor has at one or two sutures attached (two or four suture ends, respectively). Each of these sutures is passed through the biceps/labral complex. Once on the nonarticular side of the complex, the sutures are tied arthroscopically. The arthroscopic knots must be accurately tied and tightly to hold the complex against the bleeding surface of the superior glenoid. After tying, the sutures are cut and any loose edges are debrided. The arthroscope is then removed from the glenohumeral joint and placed in the subacromial space. The rotator cuff, acromion, coracoacromial ligament, and the undersurface of the acromion are closely inspected. Pathology found in this area may also require specific treatment. All arthroscopic instrumentation is removed and the portal incisions are sutured.

Postservice

Postservice work begins after the skin closure in the operating room and includes the application of sterile dressings and a shoulder immobilizer. Postservice work also includes monitoring patient stabilization in the recovery room, paying special attention to the neurovascular status and function of the arm, and communicating with the patient's family and other health care professionals (including providing written and oral reports and orders). Discharge plans include instructions for continuing care and orders for postoperative pain medication, antibiotics, and physiotherapy. Discharge records are prepared. In addition, all postdischarge office visits for this procedure for 90 days after the day of the operation are considered part of the postservice work for this procedure, including the removal of sutures; periodic assessment and adjustment of the splint; direct patient physiotherapy instruction by the surgeon; ordering and assessing adjunctive physiotherapy progress; and pain medication adjustments.

29824 Arthroscopy, shoulder, surgical; distal claviculectomy including distal articular surface (Mumford procedure)

Work Value: 8.82 // Global Period: 090

➲ *CPT Changes: An Insider's View* 2002

Clinical Example

A 35-year-old weightlifter presents with pain located over the acromioclavicular (AC) joint region of his right shoulder. On physical examination there is tenderness located at the AC joint. The results of a cross arm adduction stress test are positive. The pain is reproduced by abduction of the shoulder to 180°. X rays show osteolysis of the distal clavicle. The patient is treated with rest and nonsteroidal anti-inflammatory medications. His symptoms persist with weight lifting. A local injection of anesthetic and steroid into his right AC joint yields immediate relief of his pain. The cross arm adduction stress test and abduction to 180° are painless. The patient's pain is temporarily relieved but recurs again with resumption of weight lifting. The results of a bone scan are positive at the AC joint. The patient undergoes arthroscopic resection of the distal 1 cm of the clavicle.

Preservice

The day before surgery, write preoperative orders for perioperative medications. Review the preoperative work-up, including the patient's history and physical examination. Review laboratory results (complete blood count, electrolytes, renal function). Review appropriate X ray, magnetic resonance imaging, and computed tomographic scans. Review the planned incisions and procedure.

The day of surgery, change into scrub clothes. Review the surgical procedure, postoperative recovery in and out of the hospital, and expected outcome(s) with the patient and the patient's family. Answer the patient's and the familys questions. Obtain informed consent if not already obtained. Review the length and type of anesthesia with the anesthesiologist. Review the planned procedure and the positioning and draping of the patient. Verify that all necessary surgical instruments, supplies, and devices are available in the operative suite. Monitor the patient's positioning and draping and assist with positioning as needed. Monitor and assist with the application of longitudinal skin traction to the upper extremity.

Intraservice

Insert the arthroscope posteriorly. Establish the anterior working portal in the interval between the biceps tendon and the subscapularis. Inspect and palpate the intra-articular contents of the shoulder. Closely inspect the articular surface of the rotator cuff. Remove the arthroscope from the glenohumeral joint and place it into the subacromial bursa via the same posterior portal. Establish the anterior subacromial portal just lateral to the coracoacromial ligament, and place an anterior cannula through this portal into the subacromial space. Inspect the subacromial space for signs of impingement, such as abrasion of the periosteum on the undersurface of the acromion or tearing of the bursal surface of the rotator cuff. Assuming neither of these is found, proceed with the distal claviculectomy.

Remove the periosteum on the undersurface of the acromion. (This requires defining the anterior and medial edges of the acromion and the margins of the AC joint.) Remove the joint capsule from the inferior aspect of the AC joint. (To gain a good view of the AC joint, it is often necessary to remove some of the anterior and medial acromion adjacent to the AC joint. It is also necessary to remove the soft tissue attachments, joint capsule, and periosteum circumferentially around the distal end of the clavicle to define the margins. Removal of soft tissue requires the use of a motorized soft tissue resector and an electrothermal soft tissue ablation device to provide hemostasis.)

Following adequate exposure of the distal end of the clavicle, introduce a motorized burr through the anterior portal and remove approximately 8 to 10 mm of the distal end of the clavicle circumferentially. Obtain an intraoperative X ray to ensure the distal clavicle has been adequately resected. Inject the subacromial space and the area of the resected AC joint with mixture of bupivacaine HCl and morphine. Close the portal sites with one or two stitches.

Postservice

Apply sterile dressings to the incisions; remove traction. Apply a sling to the upper extremity. Sign operating room forms, indicating pre- and postoperative diagnoses and the operation performed. Write orders for postoperative labs, chest X ray, medications, diet, and patient activity. Write brief operative note for the patient's chart, documenting in the daily progress notes pre- and postoperative diagnoses, operation performed, findings, blood loss, intraoperative intravenous fluids administered, complications, specimens sent to pathology, and condition of patient at the end of the procedure. Discuss the outcome of the procedure with the patient's family. Discuss the outcome of the procedure with the patient after the patient emerges from anesthesia. Dictate the postoperative report. Discuss the outcome of the procedure with the referring physician. Coordinate care with other physicians. Dictate a letter describing the outcome of the procedure and the expected recovery for the referring physician and/or insurance company. Revisit the patient to assess the patient's progress and pulmonary, cardiac, and renal function, and assess the status of the dressings. Check the patient's wounds. Review the patient chart notes from the nursing and/or other staff. Answer the patient's and family's questions. Answer the nursing and/or other staff's questions.

After the patient is discharged from the hospital and through the 90-day global period, examine and talk with the patient. Check the wounds and the patient's progress. Write orders for and coordinate care with physical therapy. Answer the patient's and family's questions. Answer the insurance staffs questions. Discuss patient progress with the referring physician (verbal and written).

Coordinate care with other physicians. Write orders for medications. Review postdischarge labs and films. Discuss progress with the patient and the patient's family. Remove sutures and drains. Dictate patient progress notes for the patient's medical chart.

Arthroscopy, Shoulder, Distal Claviculectomy (Mumford Procedure)

29824

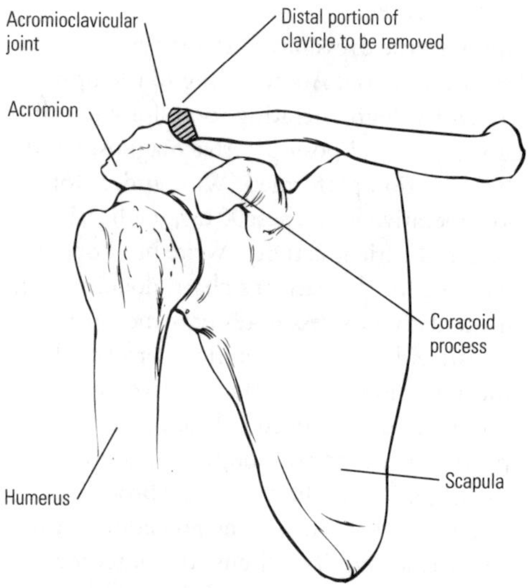

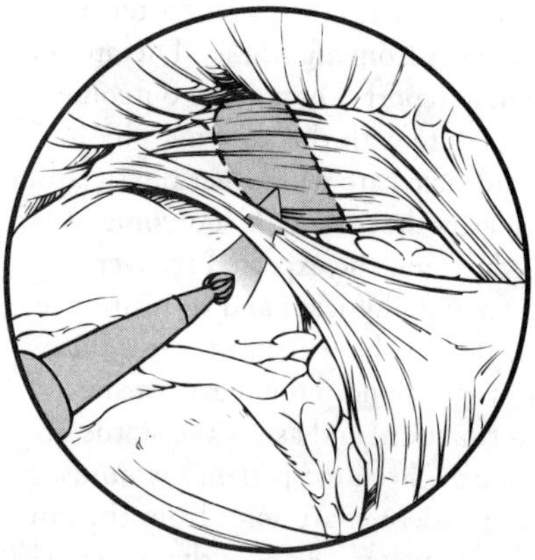

Respiratory System

Nose

Repair

30420 Rhinoplasty, primary; including major septal repair

Work Value: 16.62 // Global Period: 090

Clinical Example

The patient is an 18-year-old male who has fractured his nose several times playing football. His nose is crooked and he cannot breathe out of one side. Service includes exposure of the nasal septum to correct the nasal obstruction as well as exposure of the nasal skeleton to allow removal of a dorsal hump, lateral osteotomies, and resection of the alar cartilages, and may include a possible augmentation graft.

Preservice

Preservice work includes talking with the patient about a reasonable outcome, obtaining consent for the service, marking the face and prepping the skin, applying topical anesthesia internasally, and infiltrating local anesthesia.

Intraservice

Incisions are made (internal and external) to expose lower lateral nasal cartilages. The surgeon resects and/or modifies the lower lateral cartilages and possibly places cartilage tip grafts. The internasal and skin incisions are then closed and nasal packs are inserted. A nasal splint is applied.

Postservice

Postservice work includes applying nasal dressing, discussing follow-up care with the patient and the patient's family, prescribing medication, and dictating a procedure report. In the 90-day global period, the nasal packing, sutures, and nasal dressing are removed.

Coding Tip for 30420

It is appropriate to report a rhinoplasty or a septoplasty in addition to a turbinectomy when performed at the same operative session.

30465 Repair of nasal vestibular stenosis (eg, spreader grafting, lateral nasal wall reconstruction)

Work Value: 12.20 // Global Period: 090

➲ *CPT Changes: An Insider's View* 2001

Clinical Example

A 67-year-old male with compensated congestive heart failure presents with complaints of progressive nasal obstruction because the nasal vestibules are severely narrowed both by ptosis of the thickened nasal tip and by collapse of the flaccid lateral nasal walls. He requires repair of nasal vestibular stenosis. At operation, cartilage grafts are placed in the lateral nasal walls, and the nasal tip is elevated. Excessive dorsal nasal skin is resected directly with horizontal closure. The patient is followed by the surgeon, as necessary, postoperatively through the 90-day global period.

Preservice

Day Before Surgery: Write preoperative orders for perioperative medications. Review the preoperative work-up, paying particular attention to medical status and potential complications. Review the diagnostic evaluation and choice of procedures to select the appropriate treatment plan. Review the planned incisions and procedure.

Day of Surgery: Change into scrub clothes. Review the surgical procedure, postoperative recovery in and out of the hospital, and expected outcome(s) with the patient and the patient's family, especially the likely negative cosmetic change attendant on surgery. Answer the patient's and family's questions and obtain informed consent. Review the length and type of anesthesia with the anesthesiologist. Review the planned procedure and the positioning and draping of the patient. Verify that all necessary surgical instruments and supplies are readily available in the operative suite. Monitor patient positioning and draping, and assist with positioning as needed. (Note: If graft is used, patient may have to be repositioned, prepped, and draped again after harvesting [harvesting is separately billable]).

Intraservice

Anesthetize the operative site. Make incisions. Isolate and define the nasal structure to be manipulated. Separate the upper lateral cartilage from the septal dorsum to place spreader grafts. Isolate the cephalic margins of the lower lateral cartilage to place tip suspension/dilation sutures. Separate the medial crura of the lower lateral cartilage and create an intercrural pocket for the placement of a columellar strut graft. Create subcutaneous pockets in the lateral nasal walls via intercartilaginous incisions for lateral wall batten grafts. Prepare graft(s) to proper size and shape (if used). Place and secure the graft(s). Place the suspension/flaring sutures. Secure the tip support (eg, with septocolumellar sutures). Close wounds.

Postservice

Same Day Work, Through Discharge From Recovery: Apply dressings/splint, as indicated. Write orders for postoperative labs and medications. Review recovery room care and medications with the staff. Discuss the outcome of the procedure with the patient's family. Discuss the outcome of the procedure with the patient after the patient emerges from anesthesia. Answer the patient's and family's questions. Dictate the postoperative report. Discuss the outcome of the procedure with the referring physician. Dictate the outcome of the procedure and expected recovery letter for the referring physician and/or insurance company. Review instructions for postdischarge wound care and home care with the patient and the patient's family. Answer the insurance staff's questions. Write orders for postdischarge medications. Chart the patient's discharge notes.

Office Work, After Discharge From Hospital: Examine and talk with the patient. Check wounds and the patient's progress. Answer the patient's and family's questions. Discuss the patient's progress with the patient's referring physician. Write orders for medications. Discuss progress with the patient and the patient's family. Dictate patient progress notes for the patient's medical chart. Dictate a procedure outcome letter for the patient's referring physician.

Surgical Repair of Vestibular Stenosis
30465

An incision is made in the upper lateral cartilage and continued as an osteotomy of the medial aspect of the nasal bones. The spreader graft is placed to widen the nasal vestibule.

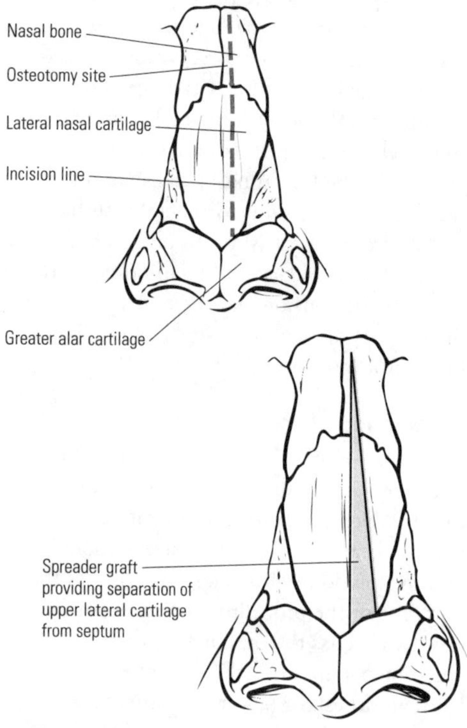

Coding Tip for 30465
Code 30465 is reported for a bilateral procedure. If a unilateral procedure is performed, modifier 52, *Reduced services,* should be appended.

---

⑤ **30520** Septoplasty or submucous resection, with or without cartilage scoring, contouring or replacement with graft

Work Value: 6.85 // Global Period: 090

➲ ***CPT Assistant*** **Oct 97: 11, Dec 02: 10**

Clinical Example
A 30-year-old male who has a prior history of nasal trauma presents complaining of nasal obstruction on both sides. Examination reveals a septal deviation obstructing the left side anteriorly and the right side posteriorly. He is scheduled for a septoplasty.

Preservice
The history and physical exam is reviewed along with other pertinent office notes. Preoperative X-ray studies and nasal endoscopy results are reviewed. The patient is counseled in the preoperative area and surgical consent is obtained. Final questions from the patient and/or the patient's family are answered. The interval history and physical are documented in the patient's record. Airway management is discussed with the anesthesiologist. The availability of necessary surgical equipment and instrumentation are varified. The physician changes into scrub clothes and supervises the positioning of the patient and the administration of necessary preoperative medications. The time out procedure is performed with the operating room personnel to confirm the correct patient and operative site.

Intraservice
The nose is examined and cleaned with nasal vibrissae trimmed. The septum is then injected with lidocaine containing epinephrine and topical anesthesia and vasoconstrictors are applied. The physician then scrubs and supervises the draping of the patient. An anterior septal incision is made and mucoperichondrial flaps are elevated on both sides of the septum. (This exposes the cartilaginous and bony septum along with the floor of the nose.) Care is taken to avoid creating a tear in the flap. Then, the cartiginous and/or bony defect is removed, repositioned, or scored to position the septum in the midline. Care is taken to leave an adequate dorsal and caudal cartilage framework to prevent future collapse. (If necessary, some of the previously removed cartilage/bone can be altered and repositioned between the septal flaps.) The septum is stabilized and the flaps are closed with dissolvable suture. The patient is observed for bleeding and when hemostasis is achieved, nasal packing or splints are placed and secured. The physician is present for extubation, in case airway problems develop.

Postservice

The physician accompanies the patient to the recovery room and observes the patient for airway and bleeding. Postoperative notes and orders are written and the patient's prescriptions are written. The operative note and note to referring physician are dictated. The family is counseled regarding the results of the surgery, expected postoperative course, and postoperative instructions. Questions from the nursing staff are answered. The patient returns to the office on the second or third postoperative day to have the splints and packing removed. The patient is examined and the operative and postoperative courses are discussed, following the removal of the packing and an assessment of the airway. Any questions are answered. Office notes and a letter to the referring physician are dictated.

The patient returns for a second visit between the 7th and 10th postoperative day. At that visit, the nose is cleaned and the healing and the patency and symmetry of the airway are assessed. Any minor adjustments are made. The appropriate office notes are dictated. Instructions are given and medications reviewed.

The patient returns again, usually around 5 to 6 weeks postoperatively for a check on healing and a general exam. Appropriate notes are dictated and instructions given.

A final visit between the 10th and 12th postoperative week occurs to assess the final healing and airway. Notes are dictated and instructions given.

Coding Tip for 30520

It may be appropriate to report code 30930, *Fracture nasal inferior turbinate(s), therapeutic,* in addition to code 30520, *Septoplasty or submucous resection, with or without cartilage scoring, contouring or replacement with graft,* and code 31255, *Nasal/sinus endoscopy, surgical; with ethmoidectomy, total (anterior and posterior),* when performed at the same operative session by the same physician.

Accessory Sinuses

Endoscopy

31231 Nasal endoscopy, diagnostic, unilateral or bilateral (separate procedure)

Work Value: 1.10 // Global Period: 000

➲ *CPT Assistant* Winter 93: 22, Jan 97: 4

Clinical Example

A patient is referred for evaluation of rhinorrhea, nasal obstruction, intermittent epistaxis, and recurrent sinusitis. Because the patient has not responded to prior medical therapy, following a history and physical examination, the patient undergoes a diagnostic nasal endoscopy. The pre- intra- and postservice work components include explaining the procedure to the patient, applying topical decongestants and anesthetics, performing the nasal endoscopy, explaining the findings to the patient (often by the use of the procedure videotape), dictating the procedure note, and relaying the findings to relevant parties. Also included in this code are patients who have had previous nasal endoscopy (thereby requiring no procedure explanation) but are having persistent symptoms and may require re-evaluation with endoscopically directed culture; children in whom cooperation for comprehensive nasal endoscopy may be difficult; and patients requiring a brief follow-up examination.

Coding Tip for 31231

Code 31231 for diagnostic evaluation refers to employing a nasal/sinus endoscope to inspect the interior of the nasal cavity and the middle and superior meatus, the turbinates, and the sphenoethmoid recess. Any time a diagnostic evaluation is performed all of these areas are inspected and a separate code is not reported for each area.

31255 Nasal/sinus endoscopy, surgical; with ethmoidectomy, total (anterior and posterior)

Work Value: 6.95 // Global Period: 000

➲ *CPT Assistant* Winter 93: 23, Jan 97: 4, Dec 02: 10, May 03: 5

Clinical Example

This patient will have chronic (or recurrent acute) sinusitis or purulent rhinitis (possibly with polyps) in the anterior and posterior ethmoid cells with possible mild involvement of the ipsilateral maxillary and sphenoid sinuses and/or associated anatomic abnormalities of the middle turbinate. In this procedure, an attempt is made to open all of the ethmoid cells back to the anterior wall of the sphenoid sinus, including the sphenoethmoidal recess, polyps, OMC, and concha bullosa.

31276 Nasal/sinus endoscopy, surgical with frontal sinus exploration, with or without removal of tissue from frontal sinus

Work Value: 8.84 // Global Period: 000

➲ *CPT Assistant* Winter 93: 24, Jan 97: 4

Clinical Example

A typical patient with acute or chronic frontal sinusitis characterized by frontal pain, purulent frontal sinus drainage, and frontal sinus/frontal recess obstruction who might otherwise have an osteoplastic frontal sinus obliteration. This patient may have had recurrent/persistent frontal sinus disease requiring revision surgery, but have little remaining nasal anatomy and few normal landmarks. The procedure includes a review of computed tomography anatomy in the operating room, decongestion of the nose prior to anesthesia, application of topical/injectable anesthetics, and preparation of the patient. The procedure also includes delicate removal of obstructing frontal recess cells, polyps, or scar tissue and intersinus septae from the dome of the ethmoid and skull base. It may include removal of osteitic bone between the frontal sinus and a supraorbital ethmoid cell. The skull base is at significant risk for perforation resulting in a cerebrospinal fluid (CSF) leak or intracranial bleeding. Hemostasis with bipolar cautery, topical agents, or sponge insertion may be required. Insertion of stents or packing, writing postoperative orders, discussion of postoperative results, dictation of a operative report, and postoperative discharge planning are also a part of the procedure. The surgeon may then communicate with the referring physician.

Preservice

Preservice work includes the decongestion of the nose prior to anesthesia, the application of topical/injectable anesthetics, and preparation of the patient.

Intraservice

Intraservice work includes reviewing computed tomography anatomy in the operating room and obstructing frontal recess cells, polyps, or scar tissue. Intersinus septae from the dome of the ethmoid and skull base are delicately removed. Intraservice may also include removing osteitic bone between the frontal sinus and a supraorbital ethmoid cell. The skull base is at significant risk for perforation resulting in a CSF leak or intracranial bleeding. Insertion of stents or packing is also involved.

Postservice

Postservice work includes writing postoperative orders, discussing the postoperative results, dictating the operative report, and postoperative discharge planning. The surgeon may also communicate with the referring physician.

Sinus Endoscopy

31231-31294

The physician uses an endoscope for visualizing and magnifying the internal structure of the sinuses.

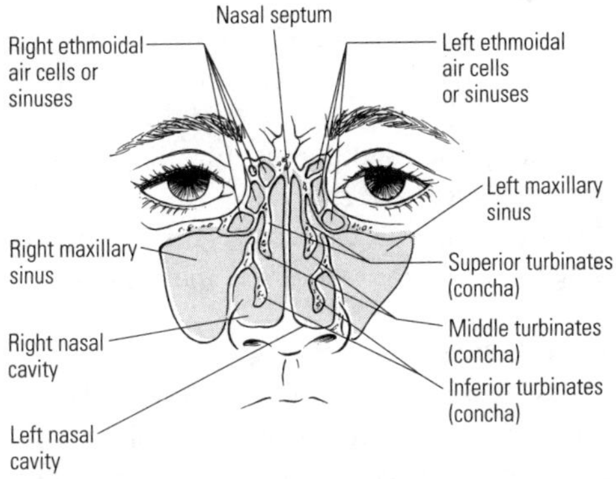

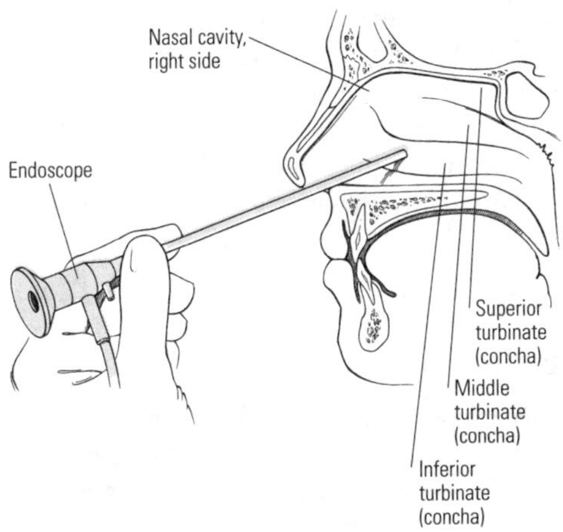

Larynx

Endoscopy

31575 Laryngoscopy, flexible fiberoptic; diagnostic

Work Value: 1.10 // Global Period: 000

Clinical Example

A 49-year-old smoker presents with a 6-week history of persistent hoarseness. A flexible laryngoscopy is done to fully evaluate the hypopharynx and the larynx.

Preservice

The patient's records are reviewed with particular attention paid to sinonasal, breathing, vocal, and swallowing history. The anatomy is reviewed. Any radiographic studies or nasal endoscopic findings are noted. The procedure is discussed with the patient and the patient's family, and questions are answered. Permission is obtained and the equipment checked. The patient is positioned. The physician's hands are scrubbed and gloved.

Intraservice

The nose is vasoconstricted and topically anesthetized. Adequate time is allowed for the medications to work (usually 5 minutes). The flexible laryngoscope is then passed through the selected nostril and any nasal abnormality noted. The nasopharynx is examined with particular attention paid to the fossa of Rosenmueller bilaterally on the posterior wall looking for masses or abnormal adenoid size, palatal elevation and closure, and lateral wall movement. The oropharynx is then examined, looking at palatal/uvular length, tonsillar size, any masses present, and airway competency. The hypopharynx is examined next, looking at the base of tongue, lateral pharyngeal walls, piriform sinuses, laryngeal elevation, and postcricoid area at rest, during phonation, and during swallowing. Particular attention is paid to any masses or abnormality in motion or sensation. The larynx is examined, first looking at the epiglottis for shape, motion, and any masses present. The endolarynx is examined, looking at the petiole of the epiglottis, the false vocal folds, the ventricles, the true vocal folds, the subglottic region, and the upper trachea. Examination is done at rest, during phonation, and swallowing. Vocal fold appearance, mucus consistency and amount, vocal fold mobility, sensation, glottic competence, and the posterior glottic mucosa are assessed. The scope is removed and the patient observed for respiration and epistaxis.

Postservice

The findings are discussed with the patient and the patient's family and treatment options are reviewed and implemented. A procedure note and a letter to the referring physician are dictated. Appropriate referrals, testing, and follow-up are arranged.

Trachea and Bronchi

Incision

31600 Tracheostomy, planned (separate procedure);

Work Value: 7.17 // Global Period: 000

Clinical Example

A 65-year-old male with a history of chronic obstructive pulmonary disease requires a tracheostomy. After a sigmoid resection and colostomy for a diverticular abscess was performed 2 weeks ago, he had gram-negative sepsis and remained respirator-dependent and hypoxia on room air. Total partial nutrition had been started. Preoperatively, once a decision has been made to operate, the surgeon reviews laboratory and X ray/imaging studies to plan the operative approach, discusses the procedure with the patient, and obtains informed consent. Medical and anesthesiology consults are requested. The patient is then transferred to the operating room with a team required to maintain the ventilation and manage his other tubes. After general anesthesia is induced and the wound prepped, a transverse incision is made and the strap muscles are split. The isthmus of the thyroid is divided. An underlying tracheal ring is cleared and segment removed. The tracheal tube is inserted and secured. A team is utilized to transfer the patient back to the intensive care unit. Postoperatively, the wound is monitored for infection and possible dislodgement. Discussions are conducted with the patient, the patient's family, and other health care providers with respect to further care of the patient.

Preservice

Preservice work begins after the decision to operate is made and may include performing the procedural work-up, discussing the procedure with the patient and the patient's family, obtaining informed consent, discussing patient comorbidities with anesthesia, dressing for the operating room, accompanying the patient (who is respiratory-dependent) during the transfer to the operating room, ensuring that all necessary equipment is present, positioning the patient, scrubbing, gowning, and prepping and draping the patient.

Intraservice

After general anesthesia is induced, a transverse incision is made, dissecting through the layers of cervical fascia, and dividing or dissecting the strap musculature. The isthmus of the thyroid is divided. An underlying tracheal ring is cleared and segment removed. The tracheal tube is inserted and secured.

Postservice

Dressings are applied; postoperative orders are written; the transfer of the patient, who is respirator-dependent, back to the intensive care unit is supervised; and a postoperative note is dictated. The outcome of the procedure is discussed with the patient and the patient's family. The wound is monitored for infection or dislodgement. Chart X rays are reviewed. The outcome of the procedure is discussed with the referring physician.

Endoscopy

⊙ ❺ **31622** Bronchoscopy, rigid or flexible, with or without fluoroscopic guidance; diagnostic, with or without cell washing (separate procedure)

Work Value: 2.78 // Global Period: 000

➲ ***CPT Assistant*** **Jul 96: 11, Nov 98: 12, Dec 98: 8, Mar 99: 3, Apr 00: 10, Jun 01: 10, Jan 02: 10, Sep 04: 8, 12, Aug 05: 4;** ***CPT Changes: An Insider's View*** **2004**

Clinical Example

A 72-year-old male undergoes a diagnostic fiberoptic bronchoscopy for evaluation of hemoptysis. The results from his chest X ray were normal.

Preservice

Preservice begins with hospital admission and pre-procedural work-up, review of records, communication with other professionals, and the patient and/or the patient's family.

Obtain an informed consent from the patient. Dress and don a lead apron (in the event a fluoroscopy is required), and estimate waiting time before the procedure. Prepare and position the patient and equipment. The physician examines the patient to verify that the patient can undergo the procedure and verifies the identity of the patient and the procedure to be performed in accord with JCAHO regulations.

Intraservice

The patient is placed on supplemental oxygen in the endoscopy suite which has resuscitative equipment in place. An IV is started and the physician supervises the nebulized administration of inhaled topical anesthesia. The physician next applies local topical anesthesia to the propharynx and nasopharanx and then supervises administration of moderate sedation while a registered nurse or physician assistant properly monitors the pulse, blood pressure, Spo_2, and ECG. Next the physician inserts the bronchoscope through the upper airways noting any abnormalities. The vocal cords are visualized and the structure and function are noted. The bronchoscope is advanced into the tracheobronchial tree. The patient has mild erythema throughout the tracheobronchial tree. In the right lower lobe, blood is seen coming from the right posterior basilar segment. Sterile saline washings of this bronchus are obtained and sent for culture and cytologic examination.

Postservice

The physician examines the patient post-endoscopy and pre-discharge from the facility to ascertain that no complications, such as bleeding, plugging, or shortness of breath have occurred.

The physician explains the findings from the bronchoscopy to the patient and/or family. The physician again reinforces previous instructions about postprocedure complications. The physician communicates results to the referring physician.

Coding Tip for 31622

Code 31622 may also include obtaining diagnostic specimens as part of the examination.

⊙ 31624 Bronchoscopy, rigid or flexible, with or without fluoroscopic guidance; with bronchial alveolar lavage

Work Value: 2.88 // Global Period: 000

➲ ***CPT Assistant*** **Nov 98: 12, Feb 99: 9, Mar 99: 3, 11, Jan 02: 10, Sep 04: 8, Aug 05: 4**

Clinical Example

A 50-year-old male with acquired immunodeficiency syndrome has persistent pneumonia requiring a definitive etiologic diagnosis.

Preservice

The physician examines the patient to verify that the patient can under go the procedure. The patient is then placed on supplemental oxygen in the endoscopy suite, which has resusciative equipment in place. An intravenous line is started. The physician supervises the administration of conscious sedation while the patient receives inhaled topical anesthesia. The patient is monitored for pulse, blood pressure, pulse oximetry, and electrocardiogram results.

Intraservice

The physician inserts the bronchoscope through the upper airway, noting any abnormalities. The vocal cords are visualized and the structure and function are noted. The bronchoscope is advanced into the tracheobronchial tree and all airways are visualized. A catheter is passed through the bronchoscope. Once there is assurance that the catheter is in the infiltrated area, the catheter's seal is broken and an uncontaminated brush is used to collect specimens for culture and sensitivity. (Alternatively, an unprotected brush is used to take samples for cytology and microscopic examination.) Several passes of the unprotected brush are made into the area of infiltrate.

Postservice

The physician examines the patient postendoscopy and predischarge from the facility to ascertain that no complications such as bleeding, plugging, or shortness of breath have occurred. The findings from the bronchoscopy are explained to the patient and the patient's family. The results are communicated to the referring physician.

Coding Tip for 31624

If a bronchial alveolar lavage is performed bilaterally, modifier 50, *Bilateral procedure,* should be appended.

+31637 Bronchoscopy, rigid or flexible, with or without fluoroscopic guidance; each additional major bronchus stented (List separately in addition to code for primary procedure)

Work Value: 1.58 // Global Period: ZZZ

➲ *CPT Assistant* Aug 05: 4;
CPT Changes: An Insider's View 2005

Clinical Example

A patient with stage 4 (metastatic) adenocarcinoma of the left lower lobe develops shortness of breath and left lower lobe atelectasis from progressive endobronchial tumor growth, seen in serial chest computed tomography (CT) scans. It was elected to proceed with bronchoscopy with dilation and stenting of the left lower lobe bronchus. At bronchoscopy, it becomes evident that the right main bronchus is circumferentially involved and nearly obstructed by tumor; therefore, a decision was made to dilate and stent also the right main bronchus.

Intraservice

The CT scan is reviewed to premeasure and ascertain the size of the stent to be deployed. Proper stent sizing is critical. The stent length should exceed the length of the lesion to some degree to ensure patency. If the stent is too small in diameter, it may migrate; conversely, if it is too large, it may not open upon deployment or may cause stress on the airway wall. Following removal of the bronchoscope after deploying the first stent, the bronchoscope is inserted into the right main bronchus and is advanced to the obstruction in the right bronchus, where the bulky tumor is visualized both through the bronchoscope and by fluoroscopy extending down to where a small opening is seen through a tumor mass into the right main bronchus. A dilation catheter is placed through the bronchoscope into the small opening in the tumor mass, and threaded through the tumor mass into the right lower lobe bronchus under fluoroscopic guidance. Then, under fluoroscopic guidance, the obstructed endobronchial area is dilated. The dilating catheter is removed and repositioned more proximally in the right mainstem where a repeat dilation is performed under fluoroscopy. Next, a guide wire is inserted through the bronchoscope into the now patent right lower lobe. Then, the bronchoscope is removed, leaving the guide wire in place, and the stent catheter is manipulated over the guide wire into the right lower lobe bronchus. Two metal markers (eg, paper clips) are taped to the external chest wall under fluoroscopy. The stent is then deployed, using both of the markers for fluoroscopic guides and under direct vision by the physician using the bronchoscope. The two metal markers are repositioned and taped to the external chest wall under fluoroscopy to mark the carina and left mainstem bronchus. Care must be taken to ensure overlap between the distal end of the proximal stent and the proximal end of the distal stent.

Bronchoscopy
31622–31656

A rigid or flexible bronchoscope is inserted through the oropharynx, vocal cords and beyond the trachea into the right/left bronchi.

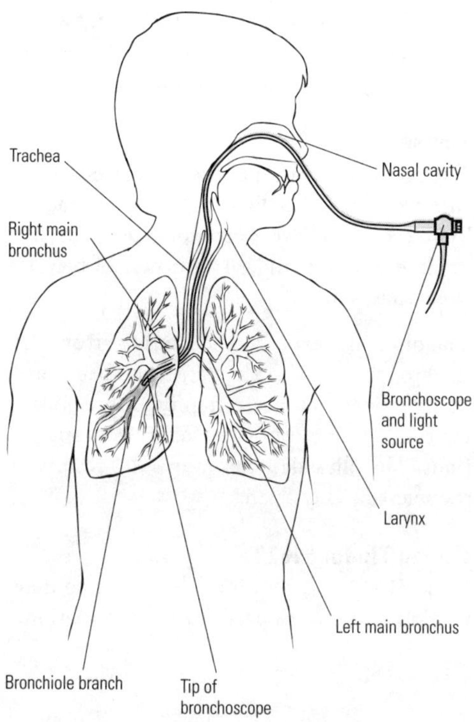

Coding Tip for 31622, 31624, and 31637

Codes 31622, 31624, and 31637 include fluoroscopic guidance, when performed. A separate code should not be reported for fluoroscopy used in conjunction with bronchoscopy.

Lungs and Pleura

Endoscopy

32655 Thoracoscopy, surgical; with excision-plication of bullae, including any pleural procedure

Work Value: 16.09 // Global Period: 090

CPT Assistant Fall 94: 1, 6, Aug 05: 15

Clinical Example

A 45-year-old patient presents with his second ipsilateral episode of spontaneous pneumothorax.

Preservice

Write preoperative orders for perioperative medications. Review preoperative work-up including laboratory results (eg, complete blood count, electrolytes, renal and liver function), chest X rays, and chest computed tomography scan. Review the antibiotic regimen. Assess pulmonary function. Perform a pulmonary function test and arterial blood gas test. Arrange for a surgical assistant. Review the patient's prior history and physical. Perform an interval history and physical exam. Review the planned incisions and procedure. Change into scrub clothes. Review the surgical procedure, postoperative recovery in and out of the hospital, and expected outcome(s) with the patient and the patient's family. Answer the patient's and family's questions. Obtain/review informed consent. Identify the patient and mark the "correct site." Review the length and type of anesthesia and postoperative analgesic strategy (eg, epidural, PCA, intravenous medications) with the anesthesiologist. Review the planned procedure and the positioning and draping of the patient. Verify that perioperative drugs (eg, antibiotics, heparin) have been administered. Verify the availability of blood products and/or crossmatch. Perform a "time out" as required by the Joint Commission on Accreditation of Healthcare Organizations. Place a bladder catheter. Place rolls and towels appropriate to the patient's position in order to avoid pressure injury. Carefully pad the extremities to prevent pressure injury. Prep and drape the chest, abdomen, and neck. Check for and prepare the appropriate operative instruments and imaging equipment. Monitor or assist with prepping and draping the patient.

Intraservice

Assure that all equipment necessary for thoracoscopy (eg, thoracoscope, fiberoptic light cord, video camera, cautery cord) is placed in the field, assembled, and fixed to the drapes; that the ends of the camera, light, and cautery cords are passed off in sterile fashion to the circulating nurse to attach the light, video, and cautery equipment; and that the equipment is activated and the settings adjusted appropriately (eg, focus, light settings, cautery settings). Instruct the anesthesiologist to institute single-lung ventilation. Remove the indwelling chest tube and anesthetize the site with local anesthetic. Introduce the thoracoscope. Anesthetize the site for all other trochar incisions with a local anesthetic. Fashion one to three additional trochar incisions using sharp, cautery and blunt dissection until the pleural cavity is breached at each site. Place access ports at each site for the passage of instruments. Insert the thoracoscope and grasping instruments through the trochars. Actively compress the lung to promote deflation and allow for adequate visualization. Inspect the entire surface of the lung (including fissures and diaphragmatic surface) to identify blebs or bullae.

Once the "suspect" bleb/bulla is identified, reexpand the lung under direct vision to assess for air leak. Identify the "culprit" bleb/bulla and excise with single or multiple firings of an endoscopic stapler reinforced with a buttress (eg, commonly bovine pericardium or polytetrafluoroethylene). Apply additional fibrin sealant to the staple closure as necessary. Instill saline into the pleural cavity and reexpand the lung underwater to identify and quantitate any continuing air leak. (Deal with new air leaks in identical fashion as described earlier). Once all the leaking sites have been treated, place one or more (up to three) chest tubes within the thoracic cavity to assure adequate drainage and complete lung expansion. (Commonly, trochar sites are used as chest tube sites.) Fix chest tubes to the skin with fixation sutures and connect the tubes themselves to chest drainage units. Perform a multilevel intercostal block using a local anesthetic in order to encompass the trochar sites. Remove trochars and inspect the chest wall thoracoscopically at each site to rule out bleeding secondary to trochar placement. Inflate the lung while visualizing with the scope to ensure complete reexpansion. Upon reexpansion of the lung, check the chest drainage units for vigorous air leaks to be certain reexploration is not required. Close the trochar sites that do not contain a chest tube in two layers.

Postservice

Same Day Work Through Discharge From Recovery: Apply sterile dressings to the chest tube sites and all remaining trochar sites. Assist/monitor patient repositioning to supine. Monitor patient stabilization. Await extubation. Write operative note for the patient's chart documenting pre- and postoperative diagnoses, operation performed, findings, blood loss, intraoperative intravenous fluids administered, complications, and specimens sent to microbiology. Sign the operating room forms, indicating pre- and postoperative diagnoses and the operation performed. Sign the pathology and pharmacy forms. Assist/monitor in the transfer of the patient to a gurney. Accompany the patient during transport to the recovery room/intensive care unit. Write postoperative orders for care, labs, films, medications, diet, and activity. Review the recovery room care and medications with staff. Write orders for postoperative chest X ray to assess expansion of the lungs and placement of the chest tubes. Discuss the outcome of the procedure with the patient's family. Discuss the outcome of the procedure with the patient after the patient emerges from anesthesia. Dictate an official operative note. Call and discuss the outcome of the procedure with the referring primary and/or specialist physician. Coordinate care with other physicians. Dictate the outcome of the procedure and expected recovery letter for the referring physician(s) and/or insurance company. Revisit and examine the patient to assess postoperative chest X ray and clinical status.

Same Day Work After Discharge From Recovery: Take an interval history. Assess the patient's cardiovascular and neurologic status. Assess the patient's fluid status and urinary output. Adjust intravenous tube and revise orders, as needed. Assess the patient's respiratory status. Check wound dressings. Check tube drainage/air leak. Review the nursing and/or other staff patient chart notes. Answer the patient's and family's questions. Answer the nursing and/or other staff's questions. Write orders for following day's labs, films, medications, diet, and patient activity. Chart the patient's progress.

Other Hospital Work; Beginning Postoperative Day 1 Until Discharge Day: Complete daily rounds (morning), which include examining and interviewing the patient and taking an interval history. Assess the patient's cardiovascular, fluid (intake and output), neurologic, respiratory (bronchodilators, oxygen, percussion, postural drainage, pulse oximetry, incentive spirometry), and nutritional status (oral and/or enteral). Check the wound dressings and chest tube(s) for drainage and air leak. Check pathology results. Encourage ambulation and vigorous pulmonary physiotherapy. Manage chest tube(s) as appropriate to include discontinuing suction, removing tube(s), and placing a Heimlich valve. Review the patient's chest radiograph daily. Treat cardiac arrhythmias (in up to 20% of patient's). Discuss the patient's progress with the referring physician (verbal and written). Coordinate care with other physicians. Review the nursing and/or other staff patient chart notes. Answer the patient's questions. Answer the nursing and/or other staff's questions (verbal and written). Answer the ancillary staff's (eg, respiratory, pharmacy, dietary, physical therapy) questions. Write orders for postoperative labs, films, medications, diet, and patient activity.

Chart patient progress notes. Complete daily rounds (afternoon), which include taking a brief assessment of the patient's cardiovascular, respiratory, and nutritional status; checking lab and test results; communicating the results/progress to the patient and the patient's family; answering the family's questions; and answering the hospital staff's questions.

Discharge Work: Perform a final predischarge assessment of the patient's respiratory status, wounds, and nutrition/diet. Review the nursing and/or other staff's patient chart notes. Check final lab/film reports. Fill out discharge forms and orders for outpatient labs and X rays. Fill out prescriptions. Explain to the patient and the patient's family the suggested home activities regarding the management of Heimlich valve if present, dietary management, activities permitted/restricted, the management of wound sites, and the need for a return appointment in the office. Coordinate care with other physicians. Coordinate home health needs with the home health service. Answer the patient's and family's questions. Answer nursing and/or other staff's questions. Answer the insurance staff's questions. Write the discharge day note. Dictate clinical resume.

Office Work; After Discharge From Hospital: Take interval histories and perform physical exams. Review postdischarge labs/films. Check wounds and the patient's progress. Remove sutures. Check the Heimlich valve for leakage and manage the chest tube accordingly. Discuss the management of analgesics and other medications. Write prescriptions for new medications/doses. Discuss the patient's progress with the patient and the patient's family. Answer the patient's and family's questions regarding further perioperative care. Answer the insurance staff's questions. Discuss the patient's progress with the referring physician (verbal and written). Coordinate care with other physicians. Dictate/write patient progress notes for medical chart.

Cardiovascular System

Heart and Pericardium

Pacemaker or Pacing Cardioverter-Defibrillator

⊙ **33212** Insertion or replacement of pacemaker pulse generator only; single chamber, atrial or ventricular

Work Value: 5.51 // Global Period: 090

➲ ***CPT Assistant*** **Summer 94: 10, 18, Fall 94: 24, May 04: 15**

Clinical Example

A 92-year-old male is undergoing replacement of his previously implanted ventricular pulse generator that was implanted 10 years ago because of battery depletion. There has been no evidence of lead malfunction. Following the surgical removal of the old pulse generator (reported separately), the pulse generator is set aside for explant analysis and testing during the procedure to confirm the apparent battery depletion. The lead is tested with a pacing system analyzer to make certain that sensing and pacing thresholds are acceptable, that lead impedance is within an acceptable range, and that no untoward effects of pacing at high outputs occur. After ascertaining that the lead is acceptable for continued use, it is connected to a new pulse generator that has also been tested during the procedure to make certain that it is within specifications. The pacemaker and lead are placed in the pacemaker pocket with care taken to place the lead beneath the pacemaker pocket. The pacemaker pocket is then closed with appropriate suture material.

Preservice

The patient is evaluated in the Pacemaker Clinic. The pacemaker is reprogrammed and interrogated to determine battery status, appropriate sensing, and appropriate capture. The pacemaker is inhibited to determine underlying rhythm and the requirement for a temporary transvenous pacemaker and the risk of asystole during disconnection of the pacemaker. The patient's overall cardiovascular status is evaluated for stability. A brief history and physical are obtained. Arrangements are made for the cardiovascular, laboratory, and/or fluoroscopy in the operating room. A complete blood cell count and coagulation panel are obtained. The patient is admitted to the hospital. The procedure and its risks and potential complications are discussed with the patient and patient's family. If required, arrangements are made for a temporary transvenous pacemaker. The Cardiac Catheterization Laboratory and operating room are scheduled, as well as an X-ray technician, cardiovascular technician, and nurse. A reliable intravenous line is established.

Intraservice

The patient is sedated per the instructions of the physician. Continuous electrocardiographic, blood pressure, and oxygen saturation monitoring is established. The patient is prepped and draped. The areas are infiltrated with local anesthesia. A cutdown is made over the existing pocket, and dissection is carried down to the old pulse generator, which is freed up and disconnected from the endocardial lead system. The pacemaker pocket is sterilized with a topical antiseptic agent and lavage, and the temporary electrode is then tediously freed up from entrapping scar. Chronic threshold testing is carried out with respect to the underlying rhythm, sensing, and capture threshold. The pacemaker pocket is lavaged and revised if necessary. After appropriate threshold measurements, if the electrode is reliable, a new pulse generator is connected to the chronic electrode. It is inserted in the pocket. The pocket is then sutured with two layers of subcutaneous suture and one layer of subcuticular skin closure. A dry sterile dressing is applied. The patient is returned to the monitoring area.

Postservice

After monitoring the patient's vital signs and obtaining a chest X ray and an electrocardiogram, the patient is discharged to be followed in the Pacemaker Clinic where appropriate pacemaker sense and capture are again determined. The wound is assessed with respect to appropriate healing. The dressing is removed. Any required antibiotics or analgesic medications are prescribed. The patient is then established on a schedule for periodic appropriate appointments.

Coding Tip for 33212

It is appropriate to report the removal of the pulse generator (codes 33233 and 33241) in addition to the code for the insertion of the new generator (code 33212), as it is not considered an inclusive component.

⊙ **33213** Insertion or replacement of pacemaker pulse generator only; dual chamber

Work Value: 6.36 // Global Period: 090

➲ *CPT Assistant* **Summer 94: 10, 18, Oct 96: 10, Feb 98: 11**

Clinical Example

A 74-year-old male with a dual-chamber pacing system previously implanted for a third-degree atrioventricular block is in need of a pulse generator replacement due to battery depletion. There has been no evidence of lead malfunction.

Preservice

The pacemaker site is examined for any evidence of local device complications, infection, or twitching. The lead system hardware is reviewed for compatibility with the replacement generator.

Intraservice

Following removal of the old pulse generator (reported separately), the pacemaker is disconnected from the leads and tested to confirm battery depletion. The atrial and ventricular leads are then both tested for sensing and pacing threshold characteristics as well as for lead impedance. Testing at high outputs on both leads is accomplished. The leads are connected to a new pulse generator, which has also been evaluated for appropriate activity. The pacemaker and leads are once again placed within the fibrous capsule of the pacemaker and the pocket is closed with appropriate suture material.

Postservice

After monitoring the vital signs and obtaining a chest X ray and an electrocardiogram, the patient is discharged to be followed in the Pacemaker Clinic where appropriate pacemaker sense and capture are again determined. The wound is assessed with respect to appropriate healing. The dressing is removed. Any required antibiotics or analgesic medications are prescribed. The patient is then established on a schedule for periodic appropriate Pacemaker Clinic visits, as well as transtelephonic monitoring.

⊙ 33214 Upgrade of implanted pacemaker system, conversion of single chamber system to dual chamber system (includes removal of previously placed pulse generator, testing of existing lead, insertion of new lead, insertion of new pulse generator)

Work Value: 7.78 // Global Period: 090

➲ ***CPT Assistant*** **Summer 94: 10, 18, Fall 94: 24**

Clinical Example

A 63-year-old male, incapacitated with what appears to be pacemaker syndrome, is undergoing an upgrade of his previously implanted ventricular transvenous pacing system to a dual-chamber system.

Preservice

The pacemaker site is examined for any evidence of local device complications, infection, or twitching. The lead system hardware is reviewed for compatibility with the replacement generator.

Intraservice

The skin is surgically prepared and a local anesthetic agent is infiltrated over the previous infraclavicular pacemaker pocket. The pacemaker pocket is opened using sharp and blunt dissection, with care taken to avoid cutting the pacemaker lead lying within the pocket. The lead and pulse generator are dissected free of adhesions and both are removed from the pocket and disconnected. The pulse generator is set aside for explant evaluation. The lead is tested with a pacing system analyzer (sensing thresholds, pacing thresholds, and impedance) to make certain that it is acceptable for continued use in a dual-chamber system. Under fluoroscopic guidance through the upper aspect of the pacemaker pocket, an 18-gauge needle is inserted into the left subclavian vein with care taken to avoid puncturing the ventricular lead. Using the Seldinger technique, the new atrial lead is advanced into the central venous circulation. The lead is positioned into several different areas of the right atrium before acceptable electrical parameters are accomplished after the injury current is allowed to abate. This new atrial lead is secured to the underlying fibrous capsule of the pacemaker pocket using the sleeve and suture material. Pacing at high outputs is accomplished to make certain that right diaphragmatic (phrenic nerve) stimulation is not present. Ventriculoatrial conduction is tested by pacing on the ventricular lead and sensing on the atrial lead. The pacemaker pocket is enlarged using sharp and blunt dissection inferomedially to accommodate the new, larger pacemaker and leads are placed in the pacemaker pocket with the leads coiled deep to the pacemaker. The wound is then closed with appropriate suture materials in several layers.

Postservice

After monitoring the vital signs and obtaining a chest X ray and an electrocardiogram, the patient is discharged to be followed in the Pacemaker Clinic where appropriate pacemaker sense and capture are again determined. The wound is assessed with respect to appropriate healing. The dressing is removed. Any required antibiotics or analgesic medications are prescribed. The patient is then established on a schedule for periodic appropriate Pacemaker Clinic visits, as well as transtelephonic monitoring.

Implanted Pacemaker
33212, 33213, 33214

A. In 33212, a pacemaker pulse generator is inserted or replaced in a single chamber.

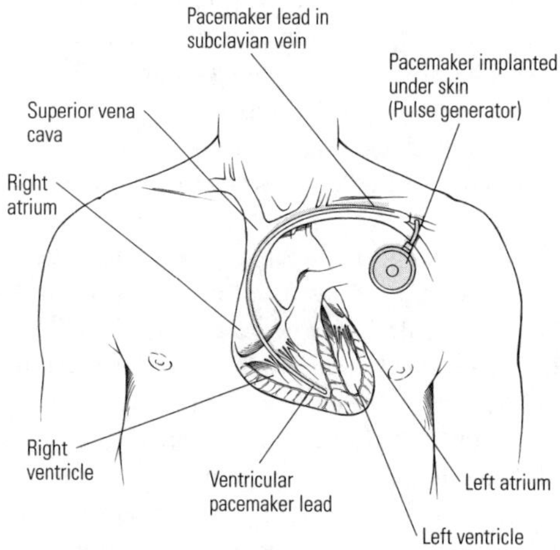

B. In 33213, a pacemaker pulse generator is inserted or replaced in two chambers. In 33214, an upgrade to an existing pacemaker system is done.

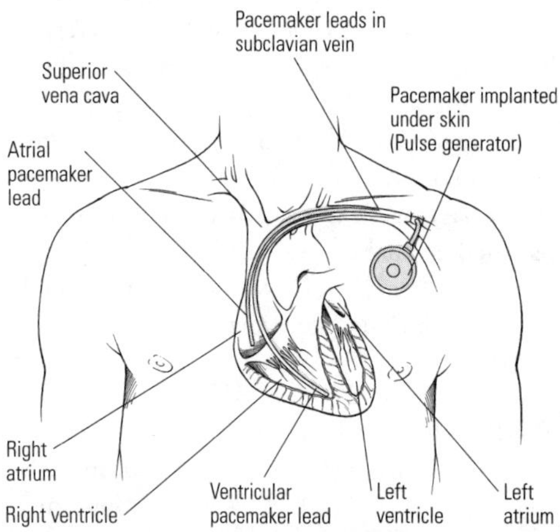

⊙ **33241** Subcutaneous removal of single or dual chamber pacing cardioverter-defibrillator pulse generator

Work Value: 3.26 // Global Period: 090

➲ *CPT Assistant* **Summer 94: 40, Nov 99: 16-17;** *CPT Changes: An Insider's View* **2000**

Clinical Example

A 64-year-old male with a history of coronary artery disease and an old myocardial infarction approximately 3–4 years ago with depressed left ventricular function and a left ventricular ejection fraction of 34%. The patient presented with sudden cardiac arrest 3 years ago and underwent cardiac catheterization and electrophysiological evaluation. An implantable pacemaker-cardioverter-defibrillator pulse generator and lead system were inserted by thoracotomy. During the past 3 years the patient has used both the antitachycardia pacing and shock therapy function of the device and has been followed in the defibrillator clinic. In the previous month the battery charge has declined below specified end-of-life values.

The patient was admitted on the evening prior to the procedure. A brief admission history and physical examination is performed to assess wound site and a chest X ray is taken to assess lead system integrity. The wound site is inspected for any infection of effusion. The surgical procedure requires induction of general anesthesia and preparation of the abdomen, or in the future thoracic pulse generator pocket site. The pocket is opened and the lead system is carefully dissected free. The generator is disconnected and removed.

Preservice

Preservice work includes taking a brief admission history; performing a physical examination to assess the wound site; taking a chest X ray to assess lead system integrity; and inspecting the wound for any infection or effusion.

Intraservice

The surgical procedure requires the induction of general anesthesia and preparation of the abdominal thoracic pulse generator pocket site. The pocket is opened and the lead system is carefully dissected free. The generator is disconnected and removed. Determination of the stimulation threshold and lead system integrity is made.

Postservice

The patient is maintained in the hospital after recovering from general anesthesia. Chest X ray and abdominal film are performed to evaluate and record the presence of a new device and the patient is discharged from the hospital on the day after the operative procedure.

⊙ 33249 Insertion or repositioning of electrode lead(s) for single or dual chamber pacing cardioverter-defibrillator and insertion of pulse generator

Work Value: 15.02 // Global Period: 090

➲ *CPT Assistant* **Summer 94: 21, Nov 99: 16-17, Apr 04: 6;** ***CPT Changes: An Insider's View*** **2000**

Clinical Example

A 66-year-old self-employed grocer with coronary artery disease and a history of myocardial infarction (2 years ago) presents with a left ventricular ejection fraction of 38% with recurrent sustained ventricular tachycardia. His clinical state is further complicated by frequent episodes of paroxysmal atrial fibrillation and atrial flutter requiring therapy. In the presence of antirhythmic agents he also demonstrates symptomatic bradycardia episodes consistent with drug-aggravated sick sinus syndrome. Insertion of an implantable cardioverter-defibrillator system using nonthoractomy leads including an atrial lead to provide dual chamber physiological pacing and enhanced tachycardia detection is indicated.

Preservice

A pertinent history is taken and a physical examination is performed. All laboratory tests, including blood tests, chest X ray, and electrocardiogram (ECG) are reviewed. The risks and benefits of and alternatives to the procedure are discussed with the patient and informed consent is obtained. The pertinent history and physical examination and subsequent discussion are documented in the patient's records. Consultation is made with the patient's primary physician, and the decision to proceed with surgery is made.

Intraservice

The procedure is performed under ECG, intraarterial blood pressure, and pulse oximetry monitoring. The patient is prepped, given intravenous antibiotic prophylaxis, and placed under conscious sedation or general anesthesia. Local anesthetic is injected into the region where the incision is made (unless the patient is under general anesthesia), and an incision is then made in the prepectoral region below either the right or left clavicle. Subcutaneous dissection is performed, and the implantable cardioverter-defibrillator (ICD) leads are inserted into the subclavian or cephalic vein and passed into the right ventricle and right atrium. The leads are positioned, and adequate pacing, sensing, and impedance characteristics are confirmed with a pacing system analyzer. The leads may require repositioning to ensure adequate sensing and pacing. A combination dual-chamber pacemaker/ICD pulse generator is attached to the atrial and ventricular leads, and both the pulse generator and leads are placed in the pacemaker pocket. Sensing, pacing, and impedance characteristics of both the atrial and ventricular leads are again assessed through the new generator. Several episodes of ventricular fibrillation are then induced to make certain the arrhythmia is properly detected and terminated by the ICD, and the defibrillation threshold is determined. The defibrillation lead may require repositioning to ensure an adequate defibrillation threshold. The incision is then closed and the wound is dressed. The physician documents these services, generates a report, and communicates with the referring physician, the patient, and the patient's family.

Postservice

After monitoring the vital signs and obtaining and reviewing a chest X ray and electrocardiogram, the ICD sensing, pacing, and impedance characteristics are assessed, and final settings for the ICD and dual-chamber pacemaker are determined. The wound is assessed and instruction for postoperative care is given. The patient returns to the pacemaker clinic where appropriate pacemaker sensing and capture are once again determined and the ICD is interrogated. The patient is exercised to assess rate-responsive settings. The wound is assessed with respect to appropriate healing. The dressing is removed. Any required antibiotics or analgesic medications are prescribed.

Combined Arterial-Venous Grafting for Coronary Bypass

⊘ ❺ **33517** Coronary artery bypass, using venous graft(s) and arterial graft(s); single vein graft (List separately in addition to code for arterial graft)

Work Value: 3.61 // Global Period: ZZZ

➲ *CPT Assistant* Fall 91: 5, Winter 92: 13, Nov 99: 18, Apr 01: 7, Feb 05: 14; *CPT Changes: An Insider's View* 2000

Clinical Example

The typical patient is a 64 year old male with one or more of the following risk factors for mortality or prolonged length of stay:

Diabetes	31.4%
Cerebral VD	12.0%
PVD	14.2%
CHF	12.0%

Preservice

Additional discussion regarding the number and location of grafts is performed, compared to the base code.

Additional discussion regarding the leg incisions and the potential for temporary postoperative edema and leg wound healing problems occurs. There is no additional preservice work compared to the base code.

Intraservice

Additional operative time is required to identify an additional coronary target vessel:

Open the artery, tailor the vein end, and construct a hemostatic anastomosis.

Probe the coronary/graft anastomosis to ensure patency:

- Perform a controlled aortotomy in an area of relatively normal aorta
- Construct a hemostatic proximal aortograft anasomsis after tailoring the proximal end of the vein and ensuring that there will be appropriate graft length when the heart is full, beating and working. Carefully inspect both proximal and distal anastomoses for hemostasis, and assess graft inflow and outflow characteristics, before terminating cardiopulmonary bypass and before concluding the operation. Leg and incisions are closed with absorbable suture and drains as needed

Postservice

Post-op same day work through admission to intensive care:

There is no additional physician work related to the add on procedure.

Postoperative Intensive Care:

- Additional intensive care time and ventilator hours occur as a result of patient characteristics associated with additional bypass grafts being indicated, and due to the nature of the add on procedure.

Post-op other hospital work – beginning on post-op day 3 until discharge day:

- Additional hospital length of stay occurs as a result of patient characteristics associated with additional bypass grafts being indicated, and due to the nature of the add on procedure.

Discharge day work:

- No significant additional discharge day work occurs as a result of additional vein bypass grafts.

Post-op office work – After discharge from hospital:

- Additional office work occurs in patient's with vein bypass grafts due to the occurrence of wound healing problems and/or ipsilateral edema in the operated leg. This increases with increasing additional grafts, although both legs may be explored for even one venous add on graft.

Coronary Artery Bypass—Combined Arterial-Venous Grafting 33517

Both venous and arterial grafts are used in these bypass procedures. The appropriate arterial graft codes (33533-33536) must also be reported in conjunction with codes 33517-33530.

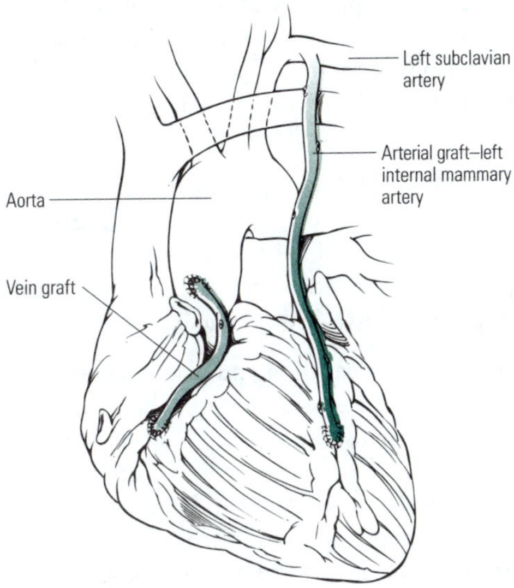

Coronary Artery Bypass—Sequential Combined Arterial-Venus Grafting 33517

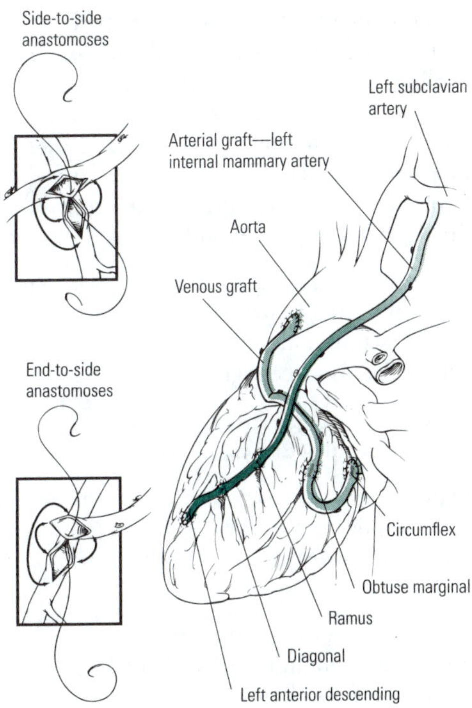

Coding Tip for 33517, 33533

Procurement of the saphenous vein graft is included in the description of the work for code 33517 and should not be reported as a separate service or cosurgery. When a surgical assistant performs an arterial and/or venous graft procurement, modifier 80, *Assistant surgeon,* should be appended to procedure codes 33517 and 33533 as appropriate.

Arterial Grafting for Coronary Artery Bypass

❺ **33533** Coronary artery bypass, using arterial graft(s); single arterial graft

Work Value: 33.64 // Global Period: 090

➲ ***CPT Assistant*** **Winter 92: 12, Nov 99: 18, Apr 01: 7, Feb 05: 14;** ***CPT Changes: An Insider's View*** **2000**

Clinical Example

The typical patient is a 62-year-old male with one or more of the following risk factors for mortality or prolonged length of stay.

Diabetes requiring insulin or oral agents	52%
Peripheral vascular disease	25%
Cerebral Vascular Disease	21%
Prior CVA	12%
Cardiogenic shock	2%
Renal failure	9%
Myocardial infarction within 7 days	51%

Preservice

A complete or interval history and comprehensive physical exam are performed. Special attention is paid to neurologic history, history of lower extremity vein surgery or venous stasis disorders, pre-existing disabilities in the legs or hands and blood pressure equality in both arms. Preoperative orders for perioperative medications are written,review preoperative work-up, prior history and physical examination (if done), office notes from referring and primary physicians, chest x-rays, stress test results, coronary angiogram and echocardiogram (if done), cath report, echo report, laboratory results (CBC, electrolytes, renal and liver function, coagulation), cardiology assessment and pulmonary assessment as indicated. Review planned incision site and procedure, and review the surgical procedure, post-op recovery in and out of the hospital, and expected outcome(s) with the patient and/or family. Patient and/or family questions are answered, paying particular attention to patient and/or family expectations related to the number and location of bypass grafts. Obtain informed consent form, confirm operating room start time and notify the patient and/or family. Make arrangments for a surgical assistant. Change into scrub clothes, identify the patient and mark planned surgical incision site per policy. Answer the patient's concerns that may have arisen and visit with the patient's family if indicated. Check with the laboratory on availability of blood and/or cross match. Review the length and type of anesthesia with the anesthesiologist. Plan invasive monitoring including use of arterial line and pulmonary artery catheter. Review the planned procedure and positioning and draping of the patient.

Verify that perioperative drugs (antibiotics, heparin) have been administered.

Review trans-esophageal echocardiogram with anesthesiologist and/or cardiologist with special attention to quality of ascending aorta and ventricular function. Place the bladder catheter and place the patient in a supine position, carefully pad the extremities to prevent pressure injury.

Scrub, gown and glove. Prep and drape the skin of the chest, abdomen, and legs from the neck to the ankles including both groin areas. Prep and drape the arm if radial artery graft planned.

Intraservice

Make a standard sternotomy skin incision and divide the sternum in the midline with the reciprocating saw. Assess the sternal edges for hemostasis and cauterize; place bone wax or Vancomycin paste if indicated. Retract the left side of the sternum for planned left internal mammary artery (LIMA) harvest and assess LIMA by palpation. Use electrocautery to incise endothoracic fascia and muscle on chest wall, creating a line 1.5-2.0 cm. on each side of LIMA. Dissect LIMA using electrocautery and apply clips to vessel branches on LIMA, continually palpate and assess LIMA integrity and presence of pulse. Open left pleura as necessary, retract lung if necessary with lap pad and assess proximal and distal extent of LIMA dissection when complete. Administer systemic heparin.

Assess chest wall for bleeding and cauterize as necessary. Divide LIMA distally, assess flow, clip end of LIMA to allow continued pulsatile pressure within lumen, wrap LIMA in papaverine-soaked sponge.

Incise the pericardium and place the pericardial retraction sutures. Inspect aorta for signs of atherosclerosis and determine cannulation site. Determine appropriate cannulas to use based on anatomy and patient BSA. Place purse string sutures in aorta and right atrium. Check with the anesthesiologist and/or perfusionist regarding activated clotting time value to assess the level of heparinization. Insert cannulas for cardiopulmonary bypass in the aorta and the right atrium. Prepare LIMA and re-assess flow. Initiate cardiopulmonary bypass and inspect the aorta for signs of dissection. Initiate systemic cooling. Initial inspection of target site on coronary artery and mark with ink. Place antegrade and retrograde (if necessary) cardioplegia cannulas if cardiac arrest planned. Cross clamp the aorta and administer cardioplegia and topical hypothermia.

Assess effectiveness of cardioplegia based on arrest of heart and temperature probe in ventricular septum; maintain septal temperature below 15 degrees centigrade.

Repeat cardioplegia every 20 minutes or as necessary while cross clamp is in place.

Expose the vessel to be grafted and assess vessel quality and locate area for arteriotomy based on knowledge of arteriogram and appearance of vessel.

Perform the coronary arteriotomy.
Incise pericardium to allow LIMA to reach target vessel.

Perform end-to-side LIMA anastomosis to target coronary vessel using fine monofilament suture and optical magnification.

Remove cross-clamp taking care to avoid cerebral air embolus and place tacking sutures to anchor LIMA along target vessel.

Resuscitate the heart by allowing it to beat while unloaded on cardiopulmonary bypass. Ensure that all suture lines are hemostatic, by elevating the heart from the pericardium and placing additional sutures if there are anastomotic leaks.

Place temporary pacing wires and begin atrial, atrio-ventricular, or ventricular pacing if indicated. Discontinue cardiopulmonary bypass by reducing arterial flow and retarding venous return to pump while continuously monitoring hemodynamics with arterial and pulmonary artery lines.

Evaluate the postprocedure, intraoperative echocardiogram specifically examining for ventricular function and regional wall motion abnormalities. When the patient is stable, give protamine and remove the arterial and venous cannulas.

Repair the cannulation, vent, and cardioplegia sites with additional sutures and irrigate the wound with saline with or without antibiotics. Check pleural space(s) for blood as appropriate and assess the chest wall for bleeding at IMA site. When hemostasis is adequate, place pericardial and if necessary, pleural drains through separate small incisions.

Re-approximate the sternum with multiple stainless steel wires twisted to "just tight."

Close the fascia, subcutaneous tissues, and skin in multiple layers with absorbable suture.

Postservice

Postoperative same day work through admission to intensive care: Apply sterile dressings to the incision, remove drapes with close attention to pacing wires (if any), tubes and lines to ensure that none are dislodged or disconnected, this attention continues as the patient is moved to the ICU bed for transfer. In a coordinated team manner, monitor the patient's overall condition as the anesthesia team converts the monitoring equipment (arterial blood pressure, pulmonary artery pressures, ECG) to a portable monitor. Periodically observe chest drainage system to assess interval bleeding and to ascertain that negative pressure is not lost and that the tubes are not obstructed. Accompany the patient to the intensive care unit and direct the team should the patient's condition change en route. Sign operating room forms, indicating pre and postoperative diagnoses, and the operation performed.Obtain and examine postoperative chest Xray to assess expansion of the lungs and placement of the chest and nasogastric tubes (if inserted). Write orders for postoperative labs, films, medications, diet, and patient activity.

Write a brief operative note for the patient's chart documenting in the daily progress notes pre- and postoperative diagnoses, operation performed, findings, blood loss, intraoperative IV fluids administered, complications, and specimens sent to pathology (if any). Review intensive care and medications with staff and establish short term goals for patient with ICU nursing staff. Discuss procedure outcome with family describing procedure performed, the general findings, an initial assessment of the degree of procedural success, and expectations for the remainder of the day of surgery and the longer term. Discuss procedure outcome with the patient after emergence from anesthesia. Dictate the postoperative report. Discuss procedure outcome with the referring physician if any, and coordinate care with other physicians. Dictate procedure outcome and expected recovery letter for referring physician and/or insurance company.

Postoperative Intensive Care: Assess neurological state and monitor emergence from anesthesia. Administer sedatives, paralyzing agents and analgesics as needed.

Evaluate gross neurologic function including level of consciousness, behavioral appropriateness, and presence and nature of focal neurological defect if present. Repeat evaluation until intraoperative neurologic injury is ruled out.

Assess hemodynamic condition and evaluate cardiac rhythm, assess rate and conduction abnormalities.

Consider temporary pacemaker, and initiate temporary pacing as needed. Determine suitable mode, adjust output and sensitivity of device. Repeat assessment of hemodynamic effects. Assess arrhythmias, differentiate atrial extrasytoles or runs from ventricular extrasystoles or runs, correlate with operative events and hemodynamic effects, consider antiarrhythmic therapy (treatment or prophylaxis).

Review 12-lead EKG for signs of ischemia or injury, compare to preoperative tracing. Assess blood pressure, central venous pressure, pulmonary artery pressures, cardiac output and index. Correlate pulmonary artery diastolic pressure, wedge pressure and CVP at baseline, confirm calibration of transducers with zero level at the level of the right heart, assess waveforms. Administer crystalloid fluids or blood products depending on cardiac index, mixed venous oxygen saturation, hemoglobin, and central filling pressures. Adjust inotropic and vasoactive agents given by continuous infusion to optimize O_2 delivery and minimize adverse end-organ effects. Carefully evaluate peripheral perfusion by observation and physical exam, correlating findings with invasive monitoring results. Monitor chest tube bleeding. Assess the character of the mediastinal drainage (rate, amount, tenacity, stability of clot). Assess the patency of the mediastinal tubes, ensure that a cardiac tamponade state is avoided. Correlate bleeding quantity and character with chest x-ray, labs, hemodynamics, urine output and physical exam.

Assess laboratory results, correlate with other findings, and determine the need for blood, blood products including platelets cryoprecipitate and fresh frozen plasma. Consider other adjunctive pharmacologic therapies for coagulopathy. Consider need for re-exploration if chest tube output exceeds acceptable limits or if tamponade is present.

Respiratory System: Examine breath sounds, observe chest mechanics, assure mid-line tracheal position by physical exam. Assess ventilator settings, observe underlying respiratory pattern, observe baseline airway pressures generated and minute gas flow. Reevaluate postoperative chest Xray if necessary. Confirm endo-tracheal tube placement by review of postoperative chest Xray.

Monitor lungs for infiltrate/atalectasis and assess pleural spaces for fluid collection. Assess blood gases and adjust ventilator as needed. Wean the patient from the ventilator. Assess readiness for extubation and extubate patient and assure airway and adequacy of ventilation.

Assess adequacy of urine output, check postoperative creatinine in light of pre-operative renal function. Assess volume status and administer fluids as needed. Decide if diuretic is indicated, determine dose, monitor response. Correlate urine flow with blood pressure compared to preopeative, assess interaction of cardiac output and vasoactive agents with renal function. Monitor distal extremity perfusion, assess peripheral pulses and compare to preoperative findings.

Integrate comprehensive evaluation with patient history, expected status based on conduct of the operation, and response to critical care interventions. Assess extent of inflammatory state, consider treatment with antipyretics or steroids as indicated. Review nursing/other staff patient chart notes and discuss interval plans with nursing staff. Set parameters for interval adjustments in patient treatment and establish interval to next patient evaluation if expected goals met. Answer nursing/other staff questions and answer patient family questions. Write orders and chart patient progress notes.

Other postoperative hospital work, beginning on postoperative day two until discharge day: Perform a directed interval history and physical exam. Inspect all wounds for drainage and underlying hematoma, inflammation. Review nursing and other staff patient chart notes. Assess postoperative pain, use of analgesics, adequacy of response. Assess adequacy of respiration, character of breathing, relationship to surgical pain and intravascular volume status. Assess character of pulmonary secretions and patient's ability to clear airway. Review vital signs, I&O, laboratory results and patient's daily weight. Review chest radiograph; evaluate cardiac monitor for rate, rhythm and presence or absence of arrhythmia; evaluate stored EKG monitoring history, if indicated. Assess progress of system recovery and risk for development of complications.

Encourage patient ambulation and vigorous pulmonary physiotherapy. Carefully assess and monitor postoperative nutritional status as maintained by both enteral (if necessary) and oral feedings. Remove chest tube when appropriate (usually 24-48 hours postoperatively).

Obtain and review chest Xray after tube removal and at least once more before discharge as indicated by patient's condition. Remove the temporary pacemaker wires if present. Answer patient and/or family questions and nursing/other staff questions (verbal and written). Develop an interval plan of care, including drug therapy for underlying conditions (eg, diabetes), surgically induced conditions, actual or anticipated complications (eg, beta blockers for atrial fibrillation, antibiotics for prophylaxis or treatment) or preventive care (eg, statins, ACE inhibitors, beta blockers, antiplatelet agents). Answer questions from insurance staff. Write orders for postoperative labs, films, medications, diet, and patient activity. Discuss the patient's progress with the referring physician (verbal and written). Coordinate care with other physicians and document evaluation, patient progress and plan in medical record.

Discharge day work: Perform detailed interval history and physical exam and check final pathology/lab/film reports and discuss with the patient. Check wounds and the patient's progress. Carefully explain to the patient and a family member dietary management, activities permitted, bathing, handling of wound, and return appointment to office. Outline expectations for recovery, adjusted to specific underlying cardiac state, associated chronic diseases, operative findings and character of postoperative recovery. Describe potential complications, how to recognize them, and what to do if recovery is not as anticipated.

Coordinate care with other physicians and review patient chart notes with nursing and other staff.

Review post-discharge wound care and activity limitations with the patient; answer patient/family questions, nursing/other staff questions and answer insurance staff questions. Write orders for post-discharge labs, films, and medications. Chart patient discharge notes and write prescriptions and discharge instructions. Explain nature, purpose and expected duration of use of new medications. Relate importance of secondary prevention of cardiac disease through risk factor reduction (abstinence from smoking, ideal body weight, glucose control (if indicated), beta blockers, statins, ACE inhibition and antiplatelet agents with the patient.

Review patient's home medications and homeopathic agents, ensure that additional agents are compatible or will not be used. Dictate discharge summary and communicate with patient's primary care physician(s).

Postoperative office work following discharge from hospital: Perform a detailed interval history, physical exam and review medications compliance and interval encounters with other care providers. Check patient wounds and progress; remove sutures and drains and review post-discharge labs/films. Write orders for medications and answer patient/family and insurance staff questions. Discuss the patient's progress with referring physician (verbal and written) and coordinate care with other physicians. Discuss progress with the patient and/or family. Dictate patient progress notes for medical chart and letters to referring physicians.

Coding Tip for 33533

Procurement of the artery for grafting is included in the description of the work for code 33533 and should not be reported as a separate service or cosurgery, except when an upper extremity artery (radial artery) is procured.

Arteries and Veins

Thromboendarterectomy

35371 Thromboendarterectomy, including patch graft, if performed; common femoral

Work Value: 15.23 // Global Period: 090

Clinical Example

A 70-year-old male smoker has disabling right calf pain with ambulation. No pulses are palpable at the right femoral, popliteal, DP, or PT positions. An aortogram reveals diffuse atherosclerosis with complete occlusion of the common femoral artery. The iliac, superficial femoral, and profunda femoris arteries are not severely diseased. Endarterectomy of the common femoral artery is performed through a groin incision.

Preservice

Preservice work begins after the decision to operate is made and may include performing the procedural work-up, reviewing preoperative studies, discussing the procedure with the patient and the patient's family, obtaining informed consent, discussing comorbidities with anesthesia with the patient, dressing for the operating room, ensuring that all necessary equipment is present, positioning the patient, scrubbing, gowning, and prepping and draping the patient.

Intraservice

Intraservice work may include incising the skin in the groin; dissecting the soft tissue to find the common femoral artery, taking care to avoid injury to surrounding nerves; clearing soft tissue from around the artery; gaining proximal and distal arterial control; administering a systemic anticoagulant and waiting for circulation; clamping the artery proximal and distal to the diseased segment; incising the artery longitudinally across the diseased segment; performing endarterectomy by excising plaque, intima, and most of media; irrigating to remove debris; closing the arteriotomy with fine vascular suture; flushing the system once more to remove air and debris; removing clamps and applying additional sutures as needed to control hemorrhage; palpating distal pulses to check for restitution of blood flow; listening with Doppler to ensure normal flow pattern across the repair; reversing the anticoagulant with protamine; irrigating the wound; performing a final check for hemostasis; closing the soft tissue in multiple layers; irrigating the subcutaneous tissue; and closing the skin.

Postservice

Postservice work includes immediate postoperative care starting after skin closure plus all related subsequent in-hospital and outpatient care for 90 days. Postservice in a typical case may include applying sterile dressings; helping to transfer the patient from the operating room table to a gurney; assisting in the transport of the patient to the postanesthesia care unit (PACU) or intensive care unit (ICU); stabilizing the patient; writing postoperative orders and notes; dictating the operative note; communicating with the PACU/ICU nurses and referring physicians; discussing the case with the patient and the patient's family when the patient emerges from anesthesia; performing multiple postoperative checks on the day of surgery; providing daily attention to wounds, reconstruction patency, nutrition, and other patient needs; writing daily orders and progress notes; preparing the discharge documentation, communicating with the patient's primary care physician, referring physician, and rehabilitation and physical therapy personnel; dictating the discharge summary; and performing outpatient visits as required for 90 days.

35372 Thromboendarterectomy, including patch graft, if performed; deep (profunda) femoral

Work Value: 18.50 // Global Period: 090

Clinical Example

A 75-year-old diabetic, female smoker has severe right foot pain at rest. Her right femoral pulse is palpable, but there are no pulses at more distal locations. Doppler studies confirm critical ischemia. An aortogram reveals nearly normal iliac and common femoral arteries. Her profunda femoris is severely stenotic from its origin to the second branch point, but beyond that it is nearly normal. The superficial femoral artery is completely occluded. Endarterectomy of the profunda femoris is performed.

Preservice

Preservice work begins after the decision to operate is made and may include performing the procedural work-up, reviewing preoperative studies, discussing the procedure with the patient and the patient's family, obtaining informed consent, discussing comorbidities with anesthesia with the patient, dressing for the operating room, ensuring that all necessary equipment is present, positioning the patient, scrubbing, gowning, and prepping and draping the patient.

Intraservice

Intraservice work may include incising the skin in the groin; dissecting the soft tissue to find the deep femoral artery, taking care to avoid injury to surrounding nerves; clearing soft tissue from around the artery; gaining proximal and distal arterial control; administering a systemic anticoagulant and waiting for circulation; clamping the artery proximal and distal to the diseased segment; incising the artery longitudinally across the diseased segment; performing endarterectomy by excising plaque, intima, and most of media; irrigating to remove debris; closing the arteriotomy with fine vascular suture; flushing the system once more to remove air and debris; removing clamps and applying additional sutures as needed to control hemorrhage; palpating distal pulses to check for restitution of blood flow; listening with Doppler to ensure normal flow pattern across the repair; reversing the anticoagulant with protamine; irrigating the wound; performing a final check for hemostasis; closing the soft tissue in multiple layers; irrigating the subcutaneous tissue; and closing the skin.

Postservice

Postservice work includes immediate postoperative care starting after skin closure plus all related subsequent in-hospital and outpatient care for 90 days. Postservice in a typical case may include applying sterile dressings; helping to transfer the patient from the operating room table to a gurney; assisting in the transport of the patient to the postanesthesia care unit (PACU) or intensive care unit (ICU); stabilizing the patient; writing postoperative orders and notes; dictating the operative note; communicating with the PACU/ICU nurses and referring physicians; discussing the case with the patient and the patient's family when the patient emerges from anesthesia; performing multiple postoperative checks on the day of surgery; providing daily attention to wounds, reconstruction patency, nutrition, and other patient needs; writing daily orders and progress notes; preparing the discharge documentation, communicating with the patient's primary care physician, referring physician, and rehabilitation and physical therapy personnel; dictating the discharge summary; and performing outpatient visits as required for 90 days.

Thromboendarterectomy
35371-35372

The common femoral artery (35371) or the deep (profunda) femoral artery (35372) is incised and the plaque and lining are removed, enlarging the diameter of the artery.

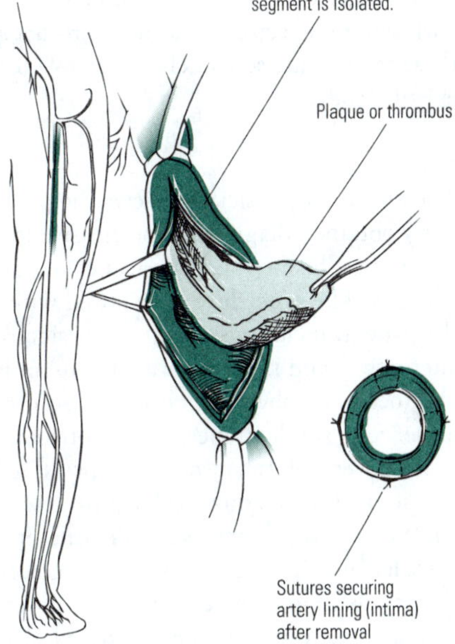

Vascular Injection Procedures

Venous

36475 Endovenous ablation therapy of incompetent vein, extremity, inclusive of all imaging guidance and monitoring, percutaneous, radiofrequency; first vein treated

Work Value: 6.72 // Global Period: 000

➲ *CPT Changes: An Insider's View* 2005

Clinical Example

The patient is a 50-year-old G2P2 female with painful, unilateral leg swelling that increases during the course of the day while at her job that requires that she stands for a significant portion of the day. She has been diagnosed with great saphenous vein insufficiency with resultant superficial varicosities by way of history, physical examination, and noninvasive ultrasound testing, all of which were performed during a previous outpatient office visit. At that time various treatment options were discussed and the patient has decided to undergo percutaneous endovenous radiofrequency ablation therapy of the insufficient saphenous vein. If it is necessary for endovenous ablation therapy to be coupled with stab phlebectomy and/or sclerotherapy, these services are separately reportable using existing codes.

Preservice

The operating physician reviews the previously obtained diagnostic noninvasive imaging studies, history and physical exam, and lab tests. The procedure is reviewed with the patient, including a final discussion of alternatives and risks. Informed consent is obtained. The physician checks to ensure the presence of sterile drapes, sterile ultrasound probe cover, gel, flush solutions, pressure bag and sterile intravenous set, local tumescent anesthetic, scalpel, access needle, dilator, vascular sheath, guidewires, sterile radiofrequency ablation catheter, and other necessary supplies and equipment. The physician changes into surgical scrubs and positions the patient such that target veins are accessible. The patient is prepped and draped.

Intraservice

Set up the operating field. Attach a pressurized heparin saline drip to the sterile radiofrequency ablation catheter. Test actuation, temperature, and impedance to ensure that all components are connected and operating properly. Use ultrasound guidance to find the target greater saphenous vein (GSV) access site. Use ultrasound guidance to map and mark the entire length of the target vein, noting vein depth and diameter. Use ultrasound guidance to map vein tributaries. Instill local anesthesia at the access site. Incise skin over the GSV access site. Perform venotomy. Use the Seldinger technique to introduce a guidewire. Advance the dilator over the guidewire. Exchange the dilator for a sheath of appropriate size. Secure the sheath in place by suture. Remove the guidewire and flush the sheath. Place the radiofrequency (RF) probe through the sheath and advance it to the saphenofemoral junction using ultrasound guidance. Locate the tip of probe just below the superficial epigastric tributary vein. Verify the RF probe's position by ultrasound. Using ultrasound guidance, infiltrate tumescent anesthesia into the perivenous space to create a "halo" of fluid around the GSV from the entry site to the saphenofemoral junction. With the patient in the Trendelenburg position, verify that the target parameters are within the acceptable range. Reconfirm RF position with ultrasound imaging. Apply RF energy. Carefully withdraw the probe, maintaining target vein wall temperature by varying the pullback rate and/or applying compression over the limb. Monitor impedance, power, and vein wall temperature throughout the procedure. Record the total RF application time. Repeat ultrasound of the saphenous to confirm successful ablation.

Postservice

Elevate the extremity and apply sterile dressings. Apply a compression wrap or stocking starting at the foot and ending at the most proximal thigh. Transfer the patient to a stretcher. Ensure the patient's hemodynamic stability and comfort in the recovery area. Write orders. Dictate an operative note. Review the results with the patient's family. Communicate with the referring physician.

Review results with the patient after sedation wears off. Evaluate the patient after the recovery interval for discharge suitability. Provide discharge activity advice to the patient and the patient's family. Arrange for follow-up care as required.

36478 Endovenous ablation therapy of incompetent vein, extremity, inclusive of all imaging guidance and monitoring, percutaneous, laser; first vein treated

Work Value: 6.72 // Global Period: 000

➲ ***CPT Changes: An Insider's View* 2005**

Clinical Example

The patient is a 50-year-old G2P2 female with painful, unilateral leg swelling that increases during the course of the day while at her job that requires that she stands for a significant portion of the day. She has been diagnosed with great saphenous vein insufficiency with resultant superficial varicosities by way of history, physical examination, and noninvasive ultrasound testing, all of which were performed during a previous outpatient office visit. At that time various treatment options were discussed and the patient has decided to undergo percutaneous endovenous laser ablation therapy of the insufficient saphenous vein. If it is necessary for endovenous ablation therapy to be coupled with stab phlebectomy and/or sclerotherapy, these services are separately reportable using existing codes.

Preservice

The operating physician reviews the previously obtained diagnostic noninvasive imaging studies, history and physical exam, and lab tests. The procedure is reviewed with the patient, including a final discussion of alternatives and risks. Informed consent is obtained. The physician checks to ensure the presence of sterile drapes, sterile ultrasound probe cover, gel, flush solutions, pressure bag and sterile intravenous set, local tumescent anesthetic, scalpel, access needle, dilator, vascular sheath, guidewires, laser fiber, safety goggles for all present during the procedure, and any other necessary supplies and equipment. The physician changes into surgical scrubs and positions the patient such that target veins are accessible. The patient is prepped, draped, and fitted with a pair of safety goggles.

Intraservice

Set up the operating field. Attach a pressurized heparin saline drip to the sterile laser ablation catheter. Test the actuation, temperature, and impedance to ensure that all components are connected and operating properly. Use ultrasound guidance to find the target greater saphenous vein (GSV) access site. Use ultrasound guidance to map and mark entire length of target vein, noting vein depth and diameter. Use ultrasound guidance to map vein tributaries. Instill local anesthesia at the access site. Incise the skin over the GSV access site. Perform venotomy. Use the Seldinger technique to introduce a guidewire. Advance the dilator over the guidewire. Exchange the dilator for a sheath of appropriate size. Secure the sheath in place by suture. Remove the guidewire and flush the sheath. Place the laser fiber through the sheath and advance it to the saphenofemoral junction using ultrasound guidance. Locate the tip of fiber just below the superficial epigastric tributary vein. Verify fiber position by ultrasound. Using ultrasound guidance, infiltrate tumescent anesthesia into the perivenous space to create a "halo" of fluid around the GSV from the entry site to the saphenofemoral junction. With the patient in the Trendelenburg position, verify target parameters are within the acceptable range. Reconfirm laser fiber position with ultrasound imaging. Apply laser energy. Carefully withdraw the laser fiber, maintaining target vein wall temperature by varying pullback rate and/or applying compression over the limb. Monitor the impedance, power, and vein wall temperature throughout the procedure. Record the total laser application time. Repeat ultrasound of the saphenous to confirm successful ablation.

Postservice
Elevate the extremity and apply sterile dressings. Apply a compression wrap or stocking starting at the foot and ending at the most proximal thigh. Transfer the patient to a stretcher. Ensure the patient's hemodynamic stability and comfort in the recovery area. Write orders. Dictate an operative note. Review results with the patient's family. Communicate with the referring physician. Review results with the patient after sedation wears off. Evaluate the patient after recovery interval for discharge suitability. Provide discharge activity advice to the patient and the patient's family. Arrange for follow-up care as required.

Central Venous Access Procedures

⊙ **36555** Insertion of non-tunneled centrally inserted central venous catheter; younger than 5 years of age

Work Value: 2.68 // Global Period: 000

➲ *CPT Assistant* Dec 04: 7; *CPT Changes: An Insider's View* 2004

Clinical Example
A 2-year-old male needs a central venous catheter. A percutaneous nontunneled, centrally inserted central venous catheter is inserted.

Preservice
The procedure is explained to the patient's parents and consent is obtained. Prior medical records, including any history of prior central venous catheter placements/attempts, are reviewed. Arrangements are made with the operating room/angio suite staff and the anesthesiologist. The physician assists with patient positioning and scrubs in standard fashion. After gowning, the access site is prepped and draped in usual fashion.

Intraservice
Local lidocaine anesthesia is administered. The subclavian/jugular vein is punctured and a guidewire is passed centrally. The central venous catheter is then placed. The catheter is sutured in position, dressed in standard fashion, and attached to intravenous infusion fluids.

Postservice
Orders are written for catheter care as well as for portable chest X ray. Catheter position is confirmed and no pneumothorax is detected. Catheter and insertion site wound care is prescribed. A note is placed in the patient's chart and a report is dictated.

Insertion of Non-Tunneled Centrally Inserted Central Venous Catheter
36555

During placement of a central venous catheter, a short tract is developed as the catheter is advanced from the skin entry site to the point of venous cannulation. The catheter tip must reside in the subclavian, innominate or iliac veins, the inferior or superior vena cava, or right atruim to be considered a "central venous" catheter.

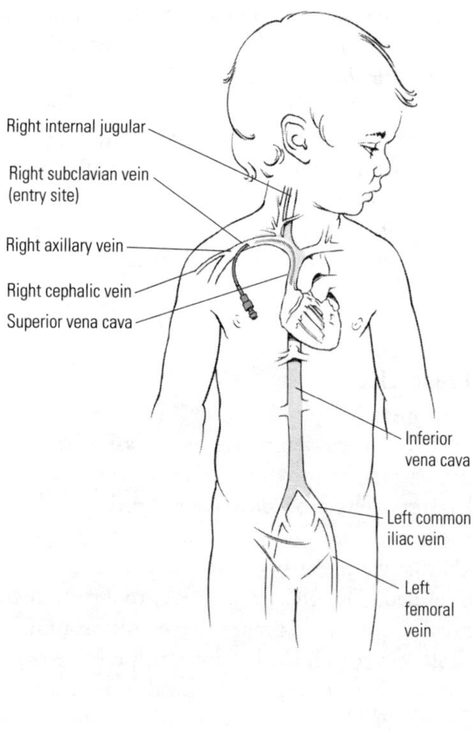

36556 Insertion of non-tunneled centrally inserted central venous catheter; age 5 years or older

Work Value: 2.50 // Global Period: 000

➲ *CPT Assistant* Dec 04: 7; *CPT Changes: An Insider's View* 2004

Clinical Example

A 40-year-old female needs a central venous (CV) catheter. A centrally inserted, non-tunneled, central venous catheter is inserted.

Preservice

The procedure is explained to the patient and consent is obtained. Prior medical records, including any history of prior CV catheter placements/attempts, are reviewed. The physician assists with patient positioning and scrubs in standard fashion. The access site is prepped and draped in standard fashion.

Intraservice

Local lidocaine anesthesia is administered. The subclavian/internal jugular vein is punctured and a guidewire is passed centrally. The venotomy site is dilated to the appropriate size and the CV catheter is placed. The catheter is sutured in position, dressed in standard fashion, and flushed or attached to intravenous infusion fluids.

Postservice

Orders are written for catheter care as well as for a portable chest X ray. The position of the catheter is confirmed and pneumothorax is ruled out. A note is placed in the patient's chart and a report is dictated.

Insertion of Non-Tunneled Centrally Inserted Central Venous Catheter
36556

During placement of a central venous catheter, a short tract is developed as the catheter is advanced from the skin entry site to the point of venous cannulation. The catheter tip must reside in the subclavian, innominate or iliac veins, the inferior or superior vena cava, or right atrium, to be considered a "central venous" catheter.

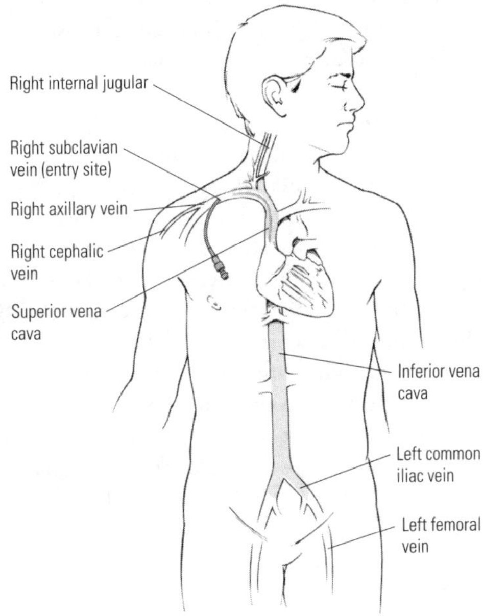

⊙ 36560 Insertion of tunneled centrally inserted central venous access device, with subcutaneous port; younger than 5 years of age

Work Value: 6.26 // Global Period: 010

➲ *CPT Assistant* Dec 04: 7; *CPT Changes: An Insider's View* 2004

Clinical Example

A 3-year-old male is admitted and requires a long-term central venous catheter. A tunneled, centrally inserted central venous catheter with a subcutaneous port is inserted.

Preservice

The procedure is explained to the patient's parents and consent is obtained. Prior medical records, including any history of prior central venous catheter placements/attempts, are reviewed. Arrangements are made with the operating room/angio suite staff and with the anesthesiologist. The physician assists with patient positioning and scrubs in standard fashion. After gowning, the access site is prepped and draped in usual fashion.

Intraservice

Local lidocaine anesthesia is administered. The subclavian/internal jugular vein is punctured and a guidewire is passed centrally. A subcutaneous pocket and tunnel are then created from the anterior chest wall to the venotomy site and a catheter passed though the tunnel. The central venous catheter is then placed. The catheter is connected to the port device and the connection is checked with injection. The port is secured in the chest wall pocket. The skin incisions are sutured. The wounds are dressed in standard fashion.

Postservice

Orders are written for port flushing and portable chest X ray. Wound care is prescribed. Catheter position is confirmed and no pneumothorax is detected. A note is placed in the patient chart and a report is dictated. The patient is seen in the office to check the wounds.

36569 Insertion of peripherally inserted central venous catheter (PICC), without subcutaneous port or pump; age 5 years or older

Work Value: 1.82 // Global Period: 000

➲ *CPT Assistant* Oct 04: 14, Dec 04: 8, May 05: 13; *CPT Changes: An Insider's View* 2004

Clinical Example

A 62-year-old male requires long-term antimicrobial therapy. A PICC is inserted.

Preservice

The procedure is explained to the patient and consent is obtained. Prior medical records, including any history of prior central venous catheter placements/attempts, are reviewed. The physician gowns and gloves. The access site is prepped and draped in standard fashion.

Intraservice

Local lidocaine anesthesia is administered. The basilic vein is punctured and a guidewire is passed centrally. The peripherally inserted central venous catheter is cut to the appropriate length and then placed. The catheter is sutured in position, dressed in standard fashion, and flushed or attached to intravenous (IV) infusion fluids.

Postservice

Orders are written for IV fluids. Wound-site care and catheter management is prescribed. A note is placed in the patient's chart and a report dictated.

⊙ **36571** Insertion of peripherally inserted central venous access device, with subcutaneous port; age 5 years or older

Work Value: 5.31 // Global Period: 010

➲ *CPT Assistant* Dec 04: 9; *CPT Changes: An Insider's View* 2004

Clinical Example

A 30-year-old male requires long-term intravenous therapy. A peripherally inserted central venous access device with a subcutaneous port is inserted.

Preservice

The procedure is explained to the patient and consent is obtained. Prior medical records, including any history of prior central venous catheter placements/attempts, are reviewed. The physician assists with patient positioning and scrubs in standard fashion. After gowning, the access and pocket site is prepped and draped in usual fashion.

Intraservice

Local lidocaine anesthesia is administered. The basilic vein is punctured and a guidewire is passed centrally. A subcutaneous pocket is then created. The catheter is measured to length and then placed. The catheter is connected to the port device and the connection is checked with injection. The port is secured into the pocket. The skin incisions are sutured. The wounds are dressed in standard fashion.

Postservice

Orders are written for port flushing. Once the catheter position is confirmed, wound care is prescribed. A note is placed in the patient chart and a report is dictated. The patient is seen in the office to check the wounds.

Implantable Venous Access Port
36571

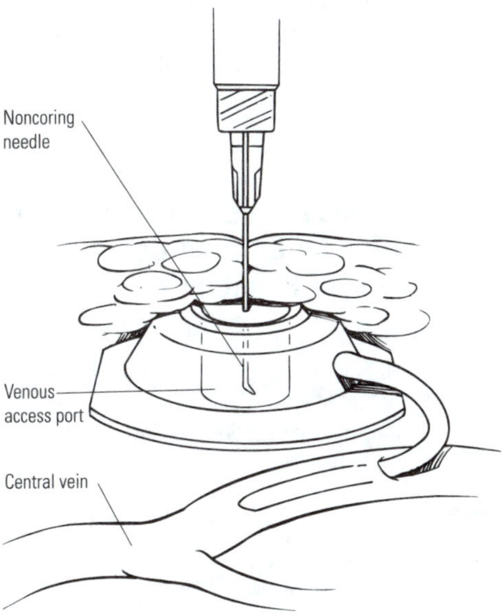

Coding Tip for 36555, 36556, 36560, 36569, 36571

Insertion of a central venous access device requires the placement of the device through a newly established venous access site.

36589 Removal of tunneled central venous catheter, without subcutaneous port or pump

Work Value: 2.27 // Global Period: 010

➲ *CPT Assistant* Dec 04: 11; *CPT Changes: An Insider's View* 2004

Clinical Example

A patient with a previously placed tunneled central venous dialysis catheter no longer needs central venous access. Discussion with the patient and physician confirms the decision to remove the previously placed catheter.

Preservice

The procedure is explained to the patient and/or the patient's family and consent is obtained. The catheter site is prepped and draped.

Intraservice

Local lidocaine anesthesia is injected. The tunneled central venous catheter is surgically removed by cut-down and blunt dissection. Hemostasis is established with manual pressure. The wound is closed and dressed in standard fashion.

Postservice

Wound care is prescribed. The patient is seen in the office for post catheter removal and wound check.

Coding Tip for 36589 and 36590

If an existing central venous access device is removed and a new one is placed using a separate venous access site, both the removal of the old device (codes 36589 and 36590) and insertion of the new device should be separately reported.

⊙ **36590** Removal of tunneled central venous access device, with subcutaneous port or pump, central or peripheral insertion

Work Value: 3.32 // Global Period: 010

➲ *CPT Assistant* Dec 04: 11; *CPT Changes: An Insider's View* 2004

Clinical Example

A patient has completed treatment and no longer needs the previously placed central venous access device with port/pump. Discussion with the patient and the patient's primary physician confirms the decision to remove the previously placed tunneled central venous catheter and port/pump device.

Preservice
The procedure is explained to the patient and/or to the patient's family and consent is obtained. The port site is prepped and draped in usual fashion.

Intraservice
Local lidocaine anesthesia is administered. The skin is surgically incised and the existing port is dissected free. The port and catheter are removed. Hemostasis is established with manual pressure. The port pocket is closed and dressed in standard fashion.

Postservice
Wound care is prescribed and postoperative care is provided. The patient is seen in the office for a wound check and suture removal.

Coding Tip for 36589 and 36590
It is not appropriate to report codes 36589 or 36590 for the removal of a nontunneled central venous catheter.

Arterial

⊘ **36620** Arterial catheterization or cannulation for sampling, monitoring or transfusion (separate procedure); percutaneous

Work Value: 1.15 // Global Period: 000

➲ *CPT Assistant* Fall 95: 7, Apr 98: 3, Nov 99: 32-33, Aug 00: 2, Oct 03: 2

Clinical Example
A 65-year-old female is admitted to the hospital because of pneumonia, fever, septic shock, hypoxemia, and agitation. An arterial catheter is inserted, both to monitor blood pressure and to obtain frequent arterial blood samples.

Preservice
The reason for the procedure is explained to the patient and the patient's family. The patient is informed of the benefits and possible complications and risks of the procedure. Both arms are examined and the radial and ulnar arteries are located.

Intraservice
The puncture site is prepared with the appropriate antiseptic. The radial artery is located and fixed and a needle with intracatheter is inserted into the radial artery. The catheter is threaded into the artery and the needle is withdrawn. A blood sample is taken for an arterial blood gas analysis. The catheter is irrigated with saline. An obturator is inserted into the catheter, which is then fixed to the skin.

Postservice
The catheter and puncture site are inspected and the radial pulse is palpated. The patient is given detailed follow-up instructions regarding the care, future monitoring, and withdrawal of blood samples. (Note that as long as the catheter is in place, daily monitoring and withdrawal of blood samples will take place.)

Hemodialysis Access, Intervascular Cannulation for Extracorporeal Circulation, or Shunt Insertion

⊙ **36870** Thrombectomy, percutaneous, arteriovenous fistula, autogenous or nonautogenous graft (includes mechanical thrombus extraction and intra-graft thrombolysis)

Work Value: 5.17 // Global Period: 090

➲ *CPT Assistant* May 01: 3; *CPT Changes: An Insider's View* 2001

Clinical Example
A male patient on chronic hemodialysis presents for dialysis and is noted to have no flow in his forearm dialysis graft. He is referred to interventional radiology for restoration of flow through his graft. This is done as an emergency, to allow him to return to the dialysis center for dialysis later the same day, so no treatment is missed.

Preservice
The preservice period includes physician services provided from the day before the operative procedure until the time of the operative procedure. The preoperative evaluation may

include performing the procedural work-up; reviewing records; communicating with other professionals, the patient, and the patient's family; and obtaining consent. Other preoperative work may include dressing, scrubbing, and waiting before the operative procedure; preparing the patient and needed equipment for the operative procedure; positioning the patient and other non-"skin-to-skin" work in the operating room.

Intraservice

The intraservice period includes all "skin-to-skin" work that is a necessary part of the procedure, including systematic sedation; intragraft thrombolysis either by bolus injection, infusion, "pulse-spray" techniques, or "lyse-and-wait" techniques; maceration of thrombus and shunt clearance with a thrombectomy device, angioplasty balloons, and/or Fogarty-type catheters; removal of guidewires and catheters with manual compression to achieve hemostasis; and hemostasis monitoring.

Postservice

The postoperative period includes services provided on the day of the procedure and within 90 days of the procedure (for a global period of 90 days) and may include: postoperative care on the day of the procedure and any subsequent visit on the day of the operative procedure; non-"skin-to-skin" work in the operating room; patient stabilization in the recovery room or special unit; communicating with the patient and other professionals (including providing written and oral reports and orders); postoperative visits in the intensive care unit; other in-hospital visits; discharge day management services; and office visits within the assigned global period of 90 days.

Coding Tip for 36870

Do not report code 36870 in conjunction with code 36550.

Transcatheter Procedures

Arterial Mechanical Thrombectomy

⊙ **37184** Primary percutaneous transluminal mechanical thrombectomy, noncoronary, arterial or arterial bypass graft, including fluoroscopic guidance and intraprocedural pharmacological thrombolytic injection(s); initial vessel

Work Value: 8.66 // Global Period: 000

➲ *CPT Changes: An Insider's View* 2006

Clinical Example

The patient is a 75-year-old female with a history of recent stroke who presents with acute onset of lower limb ischemia, which began earlier the same day. At presentation to the emergency room, the patient's foot is cool and pale. The patient does not have pain at rest, but a light hypesthesia of the forefoot is noted. The patient has a history of previous synthetic femoral-popliteal bypass graft in the left leg. A physical exam reveals a normal left femoral pulse, but no pulse is palpable in the bypass graft, the popliteal artery, or pedal or tibial arteries. The emergency room physician refers the patient to the vascular specialist on-call, who orders an emergent diagnostic angiogram (reported separately), which demonstrates a patent common femoral artery and profunda femoral artery, but total occlusion of the femoral popliteal bypass graft is confirmed. There is reconstitution of the popliteal artery below the level of the distal anastomosis, and delayed run-off is identified in the personal and posterior tibial arteries. After considering all treatment options, the physician decides to use an endovascular approach for treatment. Because of the history of recent stroke, the patient is felt to be a poor surgical candidate, and is not a candidate for pharmacologic thrombolysis. Mechanical thrombectomy is offered to try to reestablish flow to the foot.

Preservice

The physician discusses the procedure with the patient, the patient's family, and the referring physician and informed consent is obtained. The physician supervises room setup, including sterile preps and drapes, and proper patient positioning is confirmed. The physician selects the appropriate equipment such as catheters, sheaths, guidewires, and mechanical thrombectomy device, and directs the staff to prepare for the procedure.

Intraservice

The physician orders medications for conscious sedation. The physician punctures the common femoral artery in an antegrade fashion. A wire is used to select the occluded bypass graft (separately reported). The guidewire is positioned, under fluoroscopy, across the occlusion, and an appropriate-sized sheath is placed at the groin. The physician administers heparin and then advances the mechanical thrombolysis device over the wire, into the thrombus, and into the lower limit of the occlusion. The physician positions the device optimally under fluoroscopy and then activates the device, passing it across the site (often several times), macerating the thrombus. All fluoroscopy and angiograms performed to guide the therapy and monitor the progress of the therapy are included. If residual thrombus is documented, the mechanical thrombolytic device is again activated for further thrombus removal. Lytic agent may be administered, as necessary. Fluoroscopy is again used to direct the device. If a small fragment of thrombus is not removed by the thrombectomy device, it may be removed with aspiration through the sheath or through a large-bore catheter placed to the remaining thrombus. The physician then performs a final completion angiogram to confirm that the entire volume of occlusive material has been removed and that flow has been restored. The mechanical thrombectomy device, catheters, and guidewires are removed. Compression is applied for hemostasis.

Postservice

The physician reviews all final fluoroscopic images, dictates and reviews the procedure report, and apprises the referring physician of the outcome of the procedure.

Coding Tip for 37184

Do not report code 37184 for mechanical thrombectomy performed for treatment of thrombus or embolus complicating other percutaneous interventional procedures. Instead, see code 37186 for these procedures.

Other Procedures

⊙ 37215 Transcatheter placement of intravascular stent(s), cervical carotid artery, percutaneous; with distal embolic protection

Work Value: 19.58 // Global Period: 090

➲ *CPT Assistant* May 05: 7;
CPT Changes: An Insider's View 2005

Clinical Example

A 66-year-old male has recurrent episodes of transient right hemiparesis while on aspirin. Neurologic evaluation reveals no fixed neurological deficit. Carotid ultrasound demonstrates an 80-99% stenosis of his left internal carotid artery. Diagnostic cervicocerebral arteriography confirms an 80% focal left internal carotid stenosis (measured using the NASCET method). The patient is ten years post coronary bypass surgery. He had a subendocardial myocardial infarction two months ago with subsequent catheter placement showing diffuse distal disease and an ejection fraction of 30%. He has angina at low levels of exercise. Discussion with a surgeon who performs carotid endarterectomy leads to agreement that the patient is at high risk for open carotid surgery. Carotid stent placement with embolic protection is therefore recommended.

Note: This code includes selective carotid access, all diagnostic imaging for ipsilateral common carotid, bifurcation and cerebral vessels, plus all radiological supervision and interpretation. In addition, when the physician work of the initial ipsilateral carotid arteriogram (including imaging and access) confirms the need for carotid stenting, code 37215 is inclusive of these services. If carotid stenting is not indicated, the appropriate codes for carotid catheterization and imaging would be reported in lieu of code 37215.

Preservice

Review the patient's history and pertinent non-invasive diagnostic studies, paying special attention to cerebrovascular and cardiac symptoms, and other co-morbidities that would place the patient at high risk for surgery. Review the patient's physical exam to ensure that the patient has palpable femoral pulses suitable for percutaneous access. Pay special attention to medications, including antiplatelet agents and anticoagulants that the patient may be taking or should be taking. Review all preprocedural blood tests, focusing on coagulation and renal function studies. If renal insufficiency is present, assess whether the patient has received appropriate renal protective agents and hydration. Based on the review of all previous diagnostic studies, the physician should estimate the range of the guiding catheters and sheaths, guide wires, selective catheters, balloons, stents, and embolic protection devices that may be required, and ensure that all are available for use. (This procedure requires a substantial inventory of equipment, and absence of any single piece can disable the effort. Thus, this task cannot be taken lightly.) Discuss the procedure details, including alternatives and risks, with the patient and the patient's family. Finally, review informed consent with the patient and the patient's family. Perform a careful baseline neurological examination.

Preservice Radiological Supervision and Interpretation Work: Check the interventional suite to ensure the imaging equipment is functioning and configured properly and in compliance with all radiation safety issues. Ensure that all technical personnel have been familiarized with the carotid stent technique and are fully familiar with all required devices, especially the embolic protection system. Select (or supervise the selection of) all equipment, including catheters, wires, balloons, stents, sheaths, protection device, contrast material, and so on, and ensure that all needed equipment is available. Locate and review prior films and studies. Don radiation protection. Position (or supervise the proper positioning of) the patient.

Intraservice

Ensure electrocardiogram and hemodynamic monitors are in place and functioning. Perform all following steps under fluoroscopic guidance. Puncture the common femoral artery for the insertion of the 6F sheath. (All radiological supervision and imaging work are included.) Direct technical personnel throughout the procedure. Interpret the imaging of the vessel being treated, including complete intracranial and extracranial views of the target vessel in all views necessary. Ensure accurate radiological views, exposures, shielding, image size, injection sequences, radiation protection, and management of the patient and staff. Analyze all imaging in real time during the procedure, including pretreatment imaging, fluoroscopic and angiographic imaging throughout the procedure as required, and postprocedure fluoroscopic and angiographic imaging. This includes all imaging done to manipulate the wires, catheters, and devices into position. Ensure the embolic protection system (EPS) is positioned and deployed correctly and that the positioning of the EPS is stable throughout the procedure. Ensure that the the stent and opening balloon are positioned and deployed correctly. Assess the postoperative success and complications of the procedure. Complete the intra- and extracranial study poststent, recapture the protection device, and remove the catheters. Take a quantitative measurement of the lesion, target vessel, and the distal EPS landing zone to determine the appropriate size of the balloon, stent, and the EPS. Take continuous fluoroscopic imaging during all catheter and stent manipulations to assess the proper position of the EPS and adequate EPS performance throughout the procedure.

Baseline Cervical Cerebral Angiography and Quantitative Measurements: Advance a standard .035 guidewire into the aortic arch at the base of the great vessels. Advance a carotid configuration catheter to the aortic arch. Roadmap the common carotid artery origin and proximal segment. Remove a standard .035 wire and replace it with a .035 hydrophilic wire. Insert a carotid-selective reverse curve catheter into the sheath over the hydrophilic wire. Administer heparin intravenously. Reform the shape of the carotid-selective catheter in the aortic arch. Use the carotid catheter to selectively catheterize the origin of the common carotid artery. Inject contrast to perform an initial roadmap arteriogram of the common carotid and bifurcation. Perform a cervical carotid angiography in the anteroposterior (AP) and lateral views. Take quantitative measurements of the vessels including the area of stenosis and the area of the EPS landing zone. Perform a cerebral angiography including at minimum, lateral and AP Towne views. Place a catheter to ensure a continuous heparin flush.

Selection of appropriate Stent and EPS: Choose equipment based on results of the quantitative measurements. Connect the side-arm of a long guiding sheath to the arterial pressure transducer. Perform a focused arteriogram of bifurcation and distal internal carotid through the guiding sheath.

Prep Distal EPS: Prep a .014 wire and ensure the filter is completely air-free. Assemble the delivery system and ensure it is air-free. Assemble the retrieval system and ensure it is air-free.

Exchange for Guiding the Catheter/Sheath: Advance a .035 hydrophilic wire under the roadmap into the external carotid. Advance the catheter into the external carotid. Remove the hydrophilic wire and insert a stiff .035 exchange-length wire. Exchange the long guiding sheath/catheter into the common carotid. Remove the wire and carotid-selective catheter. Check ACT to ensure adequate anticoagulation.

Placement of Distal EPS: Load a .014 wire/EPS/delivery system and advance into the common carotid. Perform high magnification predeployment arteriogram of carotid bifurcation. Check the patient's neurological status and throughout the case at intervals. Advance and maneuver the .014 wire/EPS across the lesion into the distal extracranial internal carotid. Carefully position it using confirmatory angiography and road-mapping. Activate the EPS by opening the filter umbrella in the distal internal carotid. Remove the EPS deployment catheter. Assess the position of the deployed EPS with an angiogram to confirm good flow and filter/wall apposition. Reposition and repeat as necessary until the proper position is attained.

Pre-Stent Carotid Angioplasty: Prepare the angioplasty balloon and ensure it is air-free. Advance a 3 to 4-mm low-profile balloon across the lesion and check the position. Insufflate the balloon to pre-dilate the lesion. Remove the balloon.

Carotid Stent Placement: Prepare the stent delivery system and ensure it is air-free. Load the appropriately sized self-expanding stent into the guiding catheter. Advance the stent delivery catheter carefully across the lesion. Perform a final angiographic check to ensure exact positioning. Deploy the stent. Remove the stent delivery device. Load and advance a 5 to 6-mm balloon. Position the balloon within the stent and inflate the balloon for post dilatation. Check the electrocardiogram for bradycardia or other arrhythmia and treat as needed with intravenous medications.

EPS Removal: Advance the EPS retrieval system through the stent to the distal EPS position. Deactivate the EPS. Remove the .014 wire and EPS.

Final Carotid and Cerebral Angiography: Perform the completion bifurcation arteriogram. Check carefully for residual stenosis, dissection, and vasospasm and treat if present (eg, use nitroglycerin for vasospasm). Perform completion intra-cerebral arteriogram in anteroposterior and lateral Towne views. Review the cerebral images in detail for emboli, vasospasm, and cross-filling. Insert a soft-tip 035 guidewire into a long guiding sheath/catheter. Remove the guiding sheath/catheter from the common carotid. Remove the guiding sheath and guidewire from the puncture site and attain hemostasis. Conduct a final neurological check prior to transferring the patient to the recovery area.

Postservice

Ensure the patient's blood pressure and heart rate are stable and normal upon arrival in the recovery area. Conduct thorough neurological exams at frequent intervals. Write postoperative orders. Communicate with the patient's family and the referring physicians.

Review the results of the procedure with the patient when the patient's sedation wears off. Review and interpret all images. Postprocess all radiologic images and convert them to archived form for permanent record. Review and record the patient's fluoroscopic exposure time and contrast volume. Dictate the procedure notes, including an interpretation of the diagnostic and therapeutic imaging. Review, revise, and sign the final report. Send a formal report to the patient's primary care physician and referring providers. Daily, conduct in-hospital visits, write orders and notes, and communicate with the patient. Conduct discharge day management including communicating with the patient's family and primary care physician. Conduct all postprocedure outpatient office visits within the global period.

Coding Tip for 37215

Code 37215 includes all ipsilateral selective carotid catheterization; all diagnostic imaging for ipsilateral, cervical, and cerebral carotid arteriography; and all related radiological supervision and interpretation.

Ligation

37765 Stab phlebectomy of varicose veins, one extremity; 10-20 stab incisions

Work Value: 7.63 // Global Period: 090

➲ *CPT Assistant* Aug 04: 6; *CPT Changes: An Insider's View* 2004

Clinical Example

A 70-year-old male with a lifelong history of slowly enlarging left lower extremity varicose veins complains of pain and heaviness in the leg when trying to participate in the daily exercise routine recommended by his primary care physician. He failed a trial of using medical-grade graduated compression stockings. Stab phlebectomy is performed.

Preservice

Obtain and review the previous work-up, paying special attention to potential cardiovascular risk factors. Review the peripheral vascular exam and the preoperative noninvasive studies. Discuss informed consent, citing potential risks of the procedure, with the patient and the patient's family. Communicate with the anesthesiologist to determine the anesthetic of choice. Communicate with the operating room nurses about the appropriate draping to expose all of the symptomatic veins.

Unique to stab phlebectomy is the vein marking that must be performed immediately before the operation. Because even very large varicosities collapse when a patient is supine, the target veins must be marked with the patient erect. This is typically performed with the patient on a small pedestal in the preoperative holding area. The surgeon uses a large magic marker, or Sharpie, placing a mark over each varicosity that will be excised. Each vein is marked individually in what oftentimes looks like a topographical map when completed. Other routine preoperative work includes dressing, scrubbing, supervising patient positioning, waiting for the anesthetic to become effective, prepping, and draping the patient.

Intraservice

Incise the skin over one of the marked veins using a very small scalpel blade. This is often performed by the surgeon wearing optical magnifying loupes. Gently dissect subcutaneous tissue to find the vein. Pass the instrument or crochet hook around the vein. Using a gentle traction and twisting motion, extract the vein through the skin incision. Use a Kitner or other soft pad instrument to bluntly dissect the soft tissue from the vein. Evert as much of the vein as possible through the incision. Perform a final phlebectomy of the everted vein with a snapping motion. Hold pressure over the phlebectomy site. When hemostasis is achieved, move to the next site. Close the incisions with a single subcuticular dissolving suture or a steri-strip. Repeat the procedure for up to 20 individual skin incisions.

Postservice

Apply dressings, transfer the patient to a stretcher, accompany the patient to the recovery area, write orders, dictate an operative note, communicate with the patient's family, communicate with the referring and consulting physicians, and participate with the anesthesiologist in the recovery area to ensure the patient emerges smoothly from anesthesia. Discuss the results of the procedure with the patient once the patient is fully awake. This service is most often performed as a same-day surgery. Conduct discharge management once the anesthetic has resolved completely. Discharge day management includes the surgeons final examination of the patient, discussing the hospital stay, providing instructions for continuing care, and preparing the discharge records. All related postdischarge care for remainder of the global period (90 days) is included in this service.

Coding Tip for 37765

Do not report code 37765 if fewer than 10 incisions are performed. If fewer than 10 incisions are performed, report code 37799.

37766 Stab phlebectomy of varicose veins, one extremity; more than 20 incisions

Work Value: 9.58 // Global Period: 090

➲ ***CPT Assistant* Aug 04: 6; *CPT Changes: An Insider's View* 2004**

Clinical Example

A 70-year-old male with a lifelong history of slowly enlarging left lower extremity varicose veins complains of pain and heaviness in the leg when trying to participate in the daily exercise routine recommended by his primary care physician. He has failed a trial of using medical-grade graduated compression stockings. Stab phlebectomy is performed.

Preservice

Obtain and review the previous work-up, paying special attention to potential cardiovascular risk factors. Review the peripheral vascular exam and the preoperative noninvasive studies. Discuss informed consent, citing potential risks of the procedure, with the patient and the patient's family. Communicate with the anesthesiologist to determine the anesthetic of choice. Communicate with the operating room nurses about the appropriate draping to expose all of the symptomatic veins.

Unique to stab phlebectomy is the vein marking that must be performed immediately before the operation. Because even very large varicosities collapse when a patient is supine, the target veins must be marked with the patient erect. This is typically performed with the patient on a small pedestal in the preoperative holding area. The surgeon uses a large marker, placing a mark over each varicosity that will be excised. Each vein is marked individually in what oftentimes looks like a topographical map when completed. Other routine preoperative work includes dressing, scrubbing, supervising patient positioning, waiting for the anesthetic to become effective, prepping, and draping the patient.

Intraservice

Incise the skin over one of the marked veins using a very small scalpel blade. This is often performed by the surgeon wearing optical magnifying loupes. Gently dissect subcutaneous tissue to find the vein. Pass the instrument or crochet hook around the vein. Using a gentle traction and twisting motion, extract the vein through the skin incision. Use a Kitner or other soft pad instrument to bluntly dissect the soft tissue from the vein. Evert as much of the vein as possible through the incision. Perform a final phlebectomy of the everted vein with a snapping motion. Hold pressure over the phlebectomy site. When hemostasis is achieved, move to the next site. Close the incisions with a single subcuticular dissolving suture or a steri-strip. Repeat the procedure for the 21+ individual skin incisions.

Postservice

Apply dressings, transfer the patient to a stretcher, accompany the patient to the recovery area, write orders, dictate an operative note, communicate with the patient's family, communicate with the referring and consulting physicians, and participate with the anesthesiologist in the recovery area to ensure the patient emerges smoothly from anesthesia. Discuss the results of the procedure with the patient once the patient is fully awake. This service is most often performed as a same-day surgery. Conduct discharge management once the anesthetic has resolved completely. Discharge day management includes the surgeons final examination of the patient, discussing the hospital stay, providing instructions for continuing care, and preparing the discharge records. All related post-discharge care for remainder of the global period (90 days) is included in this service.

Hemic and Lymphatic Systems

Lymph Nodes and Lymphatic Channels

Excision

38500 Biopsy or excision of lymph node(s); open, superficial

Work Value: 3.76 // Global Period: 010

➲ *CPT Assistant* **Jun 97: 5, Jul 99: 7, Oct 05: 23;** *CPT Changes: An Insider's View* **2001**

Clinical Example

A 60-year-old female is referred with persistently enlarged superficial axillary nodes. Preoperatively, once a decision has been made to operate, the surgeon reviews laboratory and x-ray/imaging studies to plan the operative approach, discusses the procedure with the patient, and obtains informed consent. At operation, under local anesthesia, an incision is made, the nodes are mobilized, and vessels ligated. After discharge, the patient is seen for suture removal. In addition, the final pathology report is reviewed, discussed with the patient, the patient's family, and other health care providers, especially with respect to further care of the patient.

Preservice

Write preoperative orders for perioperative medications. Review the preoperative work-up, paying particular attention to pathology reports and mammogram, chest x-ray, and other films. Review the planned incisions and procedure. Change into scrub clothes. Review the surgical procedure, postoperative recovery in and out of the hospital, and the expected outcome(s) with the patient and the patient's family. Answer the patient's and familys questions and obtain informed consent. Review the length and type of anesthesia with the patient and the nursing staff. Review the planned procedure and the positioning and draping of the patient. Verify that all necessary surgical instruments and supplies are readily available in the operative suite. Ensure compliance with universal precautions relating to body substance isolation policies as required by the Joint Commission on Accrediation of Healthcare Organizations and the Occupational Safety and Health Administration. Monitor patient positioning and draping, and assist with positioning as needed. Scrub and gown.

Intraservice

Inject lidocaine with epinephrine along the proposed skin incision to provide hemostasis and local anesthesia. Make a skin incision and carefully incise the subcutaneous tissues. Place a self-retaining retractor to maintain exposure. Carefully incise the clavipectoral fascia overlying the pathological lymph node. By careful blunt, sharp, monopolar/bipolar electrocautery dissection, dissect the pathological lymph node free circumferentially. Carefully dissect the small lymphatics and bridging blood vessels out and ligate them with fine ties or cautery. Remove and bisect the pathological lymph node and submit a portion for cultures. Deliver the remainder to the pathologist for histological examination. Carefully inspect the wound for hemostasis. Perform additional ligation or cautery. Irrigate the wound. (No drain is placed.) Carefully reapproxmiate the subcutaneous tissue using individual sutures. Separately reapproximate the skin.

Postservice

Apply dressings. Write orders for postoperative labs, films, medications, diet, and patient activity. Review recovery room care and medications with the staff. Discuss the outcome of the procedure with the patient's family. Discuss the outcome of the procedure with the patient after the patient emerges from anesthesia. Dictate the postoperative report. Discuss the outcome of the procedure with the referring physician. Dictate a letter describing the outcome of the procedure and the expected recovery for the referring physician and/or insurance company. Examine and talk with the patient. Check the patient's wounds and the patient's progress. Discuss the patient's progress with the referring physician (verbal and written). Review the patient chart notes from the nursing and/or other staff. Answer the patient's and family's questions. Answer the nursing and/or other staff's questions (verbal and written). Answer the insurance staff's questions. Review post-discharge wound care and activity limitations with the patient. Review postdischarge labs and films. Discuss progress with the patient and the patient's family. Remove sutures and drains. Dictate patient progress notes for the patient's medical chart.

Coding Tip for 38500

The axilla lymph are divided into Levels I through III. Level II and III are deep. Level I may be deep or superficial depending upon where in Level I and the patient's body habitus. Superficial nodes at most sites are easily palpable.

38510 Biopsy or excision of lymph node(s); open, deep cervical node(s)

Work Value: 6.69 // Global Period: 010

➲ ***CPT Assistant*** **May 98: 10, Jul 99: 6;** ***CPT Changes: An Insider's View*** **2001**

Clinical Example

A 68-year-old male with an enlarged deep cervical node and a prior fine needle aspirate suspicious for lymphoma is referred by an oncologist. Preoperatively, once a decision has been made to operate, the surgeon reviews laboratory and x-ray/imaging studies to plan the operative approach, discusses the procedure with the patient, and obtains informed consent. The patient undergoes complete excision of the lymph node, which is located in the internal jugular lymph node chain. Frozen section confirms abnormal cells consistent with lymphoma. He has a routine postoperative course and is discharged to be followed up in-office through the 90-day global period, which includes a check the wound for signs of infection and fluid accumulation. In addition, the final pathology report is reviewed, discussed with the patient, the patient's family, and other health care providers, especially with respect to further care of the patient.

Preservice

Write preoperative orders for perioperative medications. Review the preoperative work-up, paying particular attention to pathology reports and films. Review the planned incisions and procedure. Change into scrub clothes. Review the surgical procedure, post-operative recovery in and out of the hospital, and expected outcome(s) with patient and the patient's family. Answer the patient's and family's questions and obtain informed consent. Review the length and type of anesthesia with the anesthesiologist. Review the planned procedure and the positioning and draping of the patient. Verify that all necessary surgical instruments and supplies are readily available in the operative suite. Monitor patient positioning and draping, and assist with positioning as needed. Scrub and gown.

Intraservice

Inject lidocaine with epinephrine along the proposed skin incision to provide hemostasis. Make a skin incision and carefully incise platysma. Use sharp dissection to develop flaps beneath the platysma. Identify the marginal mandibular branch of the facial nerve. Place a self-retaining retractor to maintain exposure. Carefully incise the deep cervical fascia overlying the pathological lymph node. By careful blunt, sharp, monopolar/bipolar electrocautery dissection, dissect the pathological lymph node free circumferentially. Identify and protect the hypoglossal (CNN XII) and spinal accessory (CNN XI) nerves. Carefully dissect the small lymphatics and bridging blood vessels out and ligate them with fine ties or cautery. Remove and bisect the pathological lymph node and submit a portion for cultures. Deliver the remainder to the pathologist for histological examination. Carefully inspect the wound for hemostasis. Perform additional ligation or cautery. Irrigate the wound. (No drain is placed.) Carefully reapproximate the platysma using individual sutures. Reapproximate the skin separately.

Postservice

Apply dressings. Write orders for postoperative labs, films, medications, diet, and patient activity. Review recovery room care and medications with the staff. Discuss the outcome of the procedure with the patient's family. Discuss the outcome of the procedure with the patient after the patient emerges from anesthesia. Dictate the postoperative report. Discuss the outcome of the procedure with the referring physician. Dictate a letter describing the outcome of the procedure and the expected recovery for the referring physician and/or insurance company. Examine and talk with the patient. Check the patient's wounds and the patient's progress. Discuss the patient's progress with the referring physician (verbal and written). Review the patient chart notes from the nursing and/or other staff. Answer the patient's and family's questions. Answer the nursing and/or other staff's questions (verbal and written). Answer the insurance staff's questions. Review postdischarge wound care and activity limitations with the patient. Review postdischarge labs and films. Discuss progress with the patient and the patient's family. Remove sutures and drains. Dictate patient progress notes for the patient's medical chart.

Radical Lymphadenectomy (Radical Resection of Lymph Nodes)

⑤ **38724** Cervical lymphadenectomy (modified radical neck dissection)

Work Value: 23.72 // Global Period: 090

➲ *CPT Assistant* **Jan 01: 13, Aug 02: 8**

Clinical Example

A 45-year-old male with a previously excised melanoma of the left neck presents with a 2-cm neck mass in left Level III. At operation, a modified radical neck dissection is performed.

Preservice

Write preadmission orders for preoperative medications. Review medical history, pathology, and radiology reports. Review radiographic images of the head and neck and surveillance for distant metastases. Review the results of preadmission testing (lab, electrocardiogram, and chest X ray). Meet with the patient and the patient's family to review the planned procedure and postoperative management. Reexamine the patient to make sure the physical findings have not changed and update the patient's medical chart. Obtain informed consent. Review airway and medical management with the anesthesiologist. Review the planned airway management and procedure with the operating room staff. Verify that all required instruments and supplies are available. Change into scrub clothes. Monitor/assist with the positioning of the patient, including placing a transverse shoulder roll to provide neck extension. Review radiographic images on view box. Mark patient (outline the planned resection). Inject the planned incision with topical vasoconstrictor. Monitor/assist with prepping and draping. Scrub and gown. Perform surgical time out with operating surgical team.

Intraservice

Make a skin incision to optimize the exposure of the neck: an apron flap design that extends from the mastoid tip to the mandibular symphysis, a hockey stick incision, two parallel (McFee) incisions, or other design. Elevate the subplatysmal flap superiorly to the mandibular border, inferiorly to the supraclavicular region, and posteriorly to the trapezius, taking care not to injure the XIth cranial nerve, which may run immediately subcutaneous. Preserve the marginal mandibular nerve by elevating the submandibular gland fascia as part of the flap and by elevating the flap deep to the common facial vein after dividing it. Elevate the contents of the submental triangle (level Ia) from the inferior border of the mandible and the opposite digastric muscle off of the mylohyoid muscle. (Retraction of the mylohyoid muscle anteriorly allows for identification of the lingual nerve.) Identify branches to the submandibular ganglion as is the submandibular duct, and ligate and divide them. (Alternatively, the submandibular gland may be spared while meticulously removing nodal tissue that accompanies the facial vein and artery. Care is required to identify and avoid the marginal branch of VII during this maneuver). Elevate the dissected contents of levels Ia and Ib over the digastric muscle in continuity with the nondissected portion of the neck.

At this time, intraoperative assessment is necessary to determine the proximity and/or fixation of lymph node metastases to the internal jugular vein (IJV), spinal accessory nerve (SAN), and sternocleidomastoid muscle (SCM). Sacrifice or preservation of the nonlymphatic structures usually depends on the size and extent of lymph node metastases at level II, the upper jugular lymph nodes. Dissection and retraction of the posterior belly of the digastric exposes the IJV. Identification of the SAN is performed anterior and posterior to the SCM. Examination of anterior portion typically determines whether to sacrifice or preserve the nerve. The external jugular vein and great auricular nerves are ligated and divided. If the SCM is to be sacrificed while sparing XI, posterior to anterior nerve dissection bisects the SCM. If the muscle can be spared, elevation of the fascia from the undersurface of the SCM parallel to the SAN can be used to isolate the nerve. Posterior to the SCM, the nerve is identified cephalad to the greater auricular nerve as it wraps around the SCM. The SCM is degloved along anterior and posterior boundaries from clavicle to mastoid, then reflected laterally while the undersuface is dissected, creating a bridge of muscle attached at top and bottom with XI entering posteriorly along its mid portion and exiting to the skull base from its deep surface several centimeters above the entry site. This maneuver requires great care to avoid excessive trauma to the nerve while permitting adequate visualization of underlying nodal tissue. If SAN can be preserved, dissection is then continued from its proximity to the SCM posterocaudally to the trapezius muscle. If the SCM is to be sacrificed, the nerve is traced superiorly while dividing the SCM. A posterior to anterior dissection is then performed beginning at the anterior border of the trapezius muscle. The posterior triangle contents are elevated in an en bloc fashion off the fascia of the deep cervical musculature, preserving the phrenic nerve and the brachial plexus. In this region, the transverse cervical vein and thyrocervical artery trunk are encountered and either ligated or carefully preserved. The SAN must then be freed from the soft tissues of the posterior triangle and can be retracted away from the region of dissection. The posterior triangle contents posterosuperior to the nerve (level Vb) are rotated under the nerve inferiorly. If the SCM is being resected, the muscle is transected at the mastoid and clavicle and elevated in continuity with the posterior triangle contents. Careful dissection of the supraspinal portion of level II, also known as the submuscular triangle (level IIb), anterior to the SCM is extremely important. The soft tissues of this region are also rotated under the SAN, up to the posterior aspect of the IJV. The vagus nerve and lymphatic duct structures are identified. Care is taken particularly in left neck procedures to clamp and ligate all tissues between phrenic and vagus nerves to avoid chyle leakage. The contents of levels II, III, and IV have been elevated after division or inferior retraction of the omohyoid muscle. The IJV is once again evaluated and if uninvolved, it is dissected in a posteroanterior fashion, sharply incising the fascia of the jugular vein with a scalpel blade using a feather-light touch. Branches of the IJV are encountered more anteriorly and must be clamped, divided and ligated individually. The ansa hypoglossae marks the deep boundary of dissection anteriorly avoiding injury to the superior thyroid artery and superior laryngeal nerve. (If the IJV requires sacrifice due to metastatic nodal involvement or tumor thrombosis, the vein is ligated and divided superiorly and inferiorly following identification and preservation of the vagus nerve.)

Dissection is continued anteriorly, elevating the fascia and soft tissues up to the infrahyoid strap muscles and the hyoid-digastric junction. Preservation of a fascial layer superficial to the carotid artery is usually possible, and exposure of the carotid artery should be discouraged unless necessary. It is necessary to identify and preserve the hypoglossal nerve as it crosses the carotid artery. This nerve can be used to mark the floor of dissection as the posterior contents are reflected to meet the submandibular dissection. The neck specimen is then removed and oriented for lymph node level-specific histopathologic evaluation for pathologic staging purposes. The wound is carefully inspected for adequate hemostasis. Suction drains are placed and a layered closure is performed.

Postservice

Apply sterile dressings. Monitor the patient during reversal of anesthesia. Monitor the transport of patient from the operating room to the recovery room. Discuss the postoperative recovery care with the anesthesia and nursing staff. Review the immediate postoperative care with the postanesthesia care unit/ intensive care unit staff. Write postoperative orders. Discuss the outcome of the procedure with the patient's family. Examine the patient to ensure proper drain functioning, marginal mandibular, and lingual and hypoglossal nerve and cranial nerve XI function. Write postoperative note. Dictate an operative report and provide a copy to the referring physician. Write orders for postoperative medications, diet, and patient activity. Check wounds and monitor patient progress. Chart notes. Review patient management with the nursing staff. Monitor the overall medical condition of the patient including fluid and electrolyte balance, blood pressure, respiratory status, and urinary function. Monitor neck incisions for signs of infection, hematoma, seroma, or chyle leakage. Assess shoulder function and arrange for consultation with a physical therapist as indicated. Watch for signs of atelectasis. Advance the diet to liquids and then to a soft diet, as appropriate. Answer the patient's and familys questions. Answer the nursing staffs questions. Discuss the patient's progress with the referring physician (verbal and written). Assure an adequate level of pain control. Monitor closed suction drainage and remove drains prior to discharge if appropriate. Chart discharge instructions. Write orders for follow-up, postdischarge labs, X rays, home care, and physical therapy. Write prescriptions for medications and supplies needed postdischarge. Review postdischarge wound care and activity limitations with the patient and the patient's family. Dictate the discharge summary. Dictate a discharge letter to the referring physician. Examine the patient and remove sutures and staples. Respond to questions from ancillary health care professionals providing care. If suction drains were not removed as an inpatient, monitor output and remove when appropriate. Review pathology report. Monitor shoulder and lower lip functional deficits, if any. Order physical therapy as needed. Assess for adequacy of pain control. Discuss advancing diet and daily activities with the patient. Discuss long-term scar management. Order and review postdischarge labs and films. Begin routine surveillance for recurrent tumor. Discuss the need for postoperative radiation with the patient. Arrange for postoperative radiation therapy consultation as needed. Discuss the case with the radiation oncologist and prepare documents for transmission to that office. Discuss a dental consult. Dictate progress notes for the patient's chart for each follow up visit.

+ 38746 Thoracic lymphadenectomy, regional, including mediastinal and peritracheal nodes (List separately in addition to code for primary procedure)

Work Value: 4.88 // Global Period: ZZZ

Clinical Example

A 60-year-old male with a long smoking history presents with a mass clinically staged as T2NO in the right upper lobe, which was noted on a routine chest X ray. A complete extent of disease work-up is negative and the patient is taken to the operating room where a right upper lobectomy is performed. In order to completely and accurately assess the status of the lymph nodes in the mediastinum, an area not included with the lobectomy specimen, a mediastinal lymphadenectomy is performed, which removes the contents of the superior mediastinum, an area bounded by the subclavian vein superiorly, the right upper lobe bronchus inferiorly, the trachea posteriorly, and the inferior vena anteriorly. The subcarinal space is also included in the dissection. The presence of tumor in any lymph nodes in the mediastinum signifies a significantly worse prognosis and indicates the need for postoperative adjuvant therapy.

Introduction

⊘ **38792** Injection procedure; for identification of sentinel node

Work Value: 0.52 // Global Period: 000

➲ *CPT Assistant* **Nov 98: 15, Jul 99: 6, Dec 99: 8**

Clinical Example

A 55-year-old female, swimming coach recently underwent wide local excision of a pigmented skin lesion of the upper arm. Final pathology returned a 1-mm thick superficial spreading malignant melanoma. There is no palpable axillary adenopathy or evidence for distant metastasis. Sentinel node biopsy is recommended and she elects to proceed. General anesthesia is induced. Approximately 3 cc of isosulfan is injected intradermally at several sites around the wide excision site. A separately billable sentinel node biopsy is then performed. During observation after injection, her hemodynamics remain stable and there is no physical evidence of local histamine release or other anaphylactic manifestation.

Preservice

Seek a history of prior allergic reactions to vital dyes, food coloring, or radioisotopes. Based upon the site of the primary tumor and the location of the anticipated draining nodal basin, choose the site for dye or tracer injection.

Intraservice

Inject the dye or tracer intradermally and elevate the extremity. Take care to inject around the scar tissue to achieve adequate tracer concentration in the local lymphatic spaces.

Postservice

Observe the patient for evidence of local histamine release and other allergic or anaphylactic manifestations. Make dosimetry and/or radioactivity measurements if needed after radionuclide tracer use.

Mediastinum and Diaphragm

Mediastinum

Excision

❺ **39220** Excision of mediastinal tumor

Work Value: 19.47 // Global Period: 090

Clinical Example

A 50-year-old patient complains of chest fullness and a chest computed tomographic scan reveals a 4-cm substernal mass consistent with thymoma. Staging work-up reveals localized disease with no evidence of metastases.

Preservice

Write preoperative orders for perioperative medications. Review the preoperative work-up including: chest X rays, laboratory results (eg, complete blood count, electrolytes, renal and liver function), other laboratory results (eg, human chorionic gonadotropin, alpha-fetoprotein, other studies for myasthenia gravis), chest computed tomographic scan, position emission tomographic scan, and pathology biopsy results. Review cardiac assessment (eg, catheterization, echo, scan) and pulmonary assessment (eg, pulmonary function tests and arterial blood gas). Arrange for surgical assistant. Review prior history and physical. Perform interval history and physical exam. Review the planned incisions and procedure. Change into scrub clothes. Review the surgical procedure, postoperative recovery in and out of the hospital, and expected outcome(s) with the patient and the patient's family. Answer the patient's and family's questions. Obtain and review informed consent. Identify the patient and the correct site. Review the selection of intubation (double-lumen endotracheal tube), intraoperative management, the length and type of anesthesia, and postoperative analgesic strategy (eg, epidural, patient-controlled analgesia, intravenous medications) with the anesthesiologist. Review the planned procedure and the positioning and draping of the patient. Verify that perioperative drugs (antibiotics, heparin) have been administered. Verify the availability of blood products and/or crossmatch. Perform a time out as required by the Joint Commission on the Accreditation of Healthcare Organizations. Place a bladder catheter. Place rolls and towels appropriate to the patient's position to avoid pressure injury. Carefully pad the extremities to prevent pressure injury. Prep and drape the chest, abdomen, and neck. Check for and prepare appropriate operative instruments and imaging equipment. Monitor or assist with prepping and draping the patient.

Intraservice

Throughout the operation communicate and consult with the anesthesiologist and circulating nurse. Review the intraoperative laboratory studies with the anesthesiologist including the levels of blood gases, electrolytes, and hemoglobin or hematocrit. Make adjustments as necessary to the ventilator settings or selective ventilation of one or both lungs. Assess the extent of blood or fluid loss and the need for replacement. Review the selection and titration of amounts of vasoactive pressors to maintain the patient's hemodynamic stability. Assess the need for blood or other volume expanders. Request appropriate additional intraoperative consultants when the patient's condition necessitates their involvement.

Make a median sternotomy incision. Divide the soft tissues in the middling using cautery dissection. Divide the sternum with the sternal saw. Explore the chest for metastatic disease, paying particular attention to the contents of the mediastinum. Examine the relationship of the tumor to the anterior mediastinum including the thymus, heart, great vessels, phrenic nerves, pericardium, and sternum. Determine the potential for a complete resection, the anticipated extent of the resection, and the need for reconstruction of chest wall, pericardium, or great vessels. Mobilize the thymus beginning inferiorly with careful dissection of the thymus off the pericardium. (If pericardial involvement is identified, that portion of the pericardium must be resected.) Monitor intra-arterial blood pressure carefully during the dissection of the tumor off the anterior and lateral extent of the pericardium. (Excessive pressure on or cauterization of the pericardium will cause hypotension and arrhythmias.) Continue dissection superiorly to the level of the innominate vein. Perform a right lateral dissection by dividing the parietal pleura and entering the right chest. Explore the right chest. Pay attention to the lung parenchyma, visceral pleura, and parietal pleura, and look for occult metastatic disease. Identify, protect, and preserve the right phrenic nerve throughout the course of the right lateral dissection. Dissect the mediastinal fat and thymic tissues, leaving approximately a 1-cm margin anterior to the right phrenic nerve. Continue the dissection superiorly to the innominate vein. Identify, dissect, doubly ligate, and divide the veins draining the mediastinal tumor and thymus into the innominate vein.

Perform a left lateral dissection by dividing the parietal pleura and entering the left chest. Explore the left chest. Pay attention to the lung parenchyma, visceral pleura, and parietal pleura and look for occult metastatic disease. Identify, protect, and preserve the left phrenic nerve throughout the course of the left lateral dissection. Dissect the mediastinal fat and thymic tissues, leaving approximately a 1-cm margin anterior to the left phrenic nerve. Continue the dissection superiorly to the innominate vein. With the tissue mobilized inferior to the innominate vein, dissect free en bloc that portion of the thymus extending behind the innominate vein. Divide the investing fascia over the right lateral aspect of the thymic tissue extending into the neck. Expose, grasp, and gently dissect away the cervical thymic tissue from the upper mediastinal and lower neck structures so as to completely remove the right superior horn (cervical extent of thymus tissue). Address the investing fascia over the left lateral aspect of the thymic tissue extending into the neck. Expose, grasp, and gently dissect away the cervical thymic tissue from the upper mediastinal and lower neck structures so as to completely remove the left superior horn (cervical extent of thymus tissue). Remove the tumor completely. Orient the tumor with its attached tissues for subsequent examination by the pathologist. Confer with the pathologist in the operating room to ensure the pathologist has the appropriate knowledge of the patient, the operation, the tissues removed, and the orientation of the tissues. Request a frozen section examination of close margins. Wait for the frozen section report before deciding upon additional tissue to be resected and or reconstructed.

Irrigate mediastinum after a careful inspection for hemostasis. Irrigate both chest cavities with warm saline. Place right and left chest tubes. Place the mediastinal tube. Fix all chest and mediastinal drainage tubes to the skin with fixation sutures. Connect all drainage tubes to the chest drainage unit. Ensure that appropriate drainage of each thoracic cavity and the mediastinum will occur. Perform four layers of closure for chest incision. Perform the sternal closure, facial closure, subcutaneous closure, and cutaneous closure. Examine the chest drainage device for bleeding or air leak and decide if amount of leak present is acceptable. Reopen if bleeding, hypotension, or air leak is unexpectedly large and attempt further repair of this problem. Re-close chest incision in four layers.

Postservice

Apply sterile dressings. Conduct postoperative debriefing with the operating room team (nurses, anesthetist, anesthesiologists, scrub nurse, circulator nurse, assistant, and others). Assist/monitor the repositioning of the patient to supine. Monitor the patient's stabilization. Await extubation. Write operative note for the patient's chart documenting the pre- and postoperative diagnoses, operation performed, findings, blood loss, intraoperative intravenous fluids administered, complications, and specimens sent to pathology. Sign operating room forms, indicating pre- and postoperative diagnoses and the operation performed. Sign pathology, microbiology and pharmacy forms. Assist/monitor the transfer of the patient to a gurney. Accompany the patient during transport to the recovery room/intensive care unit. Write postoperative orders (care, labs, films, medications, diet, and activity). Review the recovery room care and medications with staff. Write orders for a postoperative chest X ray to assess the expansion of the lungs and the placement of the chest and nasogastric tubes. Discuss the outcome of the procedure with the patient's family. Discuss the outcome of the procedure with the patient after the patient emerges from anesthesia. Dictate the official operative note. Call and discuss the outcome of the procedure with the referring primary physician. Call and discuss the outcome of the procedure with the referring specialist physician. Coordinate care with other physicians. Dictate a letter describing the outcome of the procedure and the expected recovery for the referring physician and/or insurance company. Revisit the patient to assess postoperative chest X ray and clinical status.

Postoperative Same Day Work (After Discharge From Recovery): Conduct an interval history. Assess the patient's cardiovascular state. Assess the patient's blood pressure. (The patient's hemodynamic state can be quite labile during the first postoperative day.) Administer crystalloid fluids or blood products depending on the patient's arterial tracings, pulse rate, hemoglobin, and urine output. Assess the need for inotropic therapy. Assess the patient's neurological state. Monitor the patient's emergence from anesthesia. Administer sedatives and analgesics as needed. Evaluate the patient's gross neurologic function including level of consciousness, behavioral appropriateness, and presence and nature of focal neurologic defect if present. Assess the adequacy of the patient's fluid status and urine output. Assess the volume status and administer fluids as needed. Decide if diuretic is indicated. If so, administer and monitor. Monitor respiratory status and plan extubation to the patient if not already done so in the operating room. Re-evaluate the postoperative chest

X ray if necessary. Confirm the placement of the endotracheal tube by reviewing the postoperative chest X ray. Monitor the patient's lungs for infiltrate/atelectasis. Assess the pleural spaces for fluid collection. Assess blood gases and adjust ventilator as needed. Wean the patient from the ventilator. Assess the patient's readiness for extubation. Extubate patient and assure airway and adequacy of ventilation. Titrate FiO2 and pain regimen to minimize carbon dioxide elevation. Check the patient's wound dressings. Check the output of the chest tubes to decide on the proper level of suction based on severity of the leak. Monitor the output to rule out bleeding. Review the patient chart notes left by the nursing and/or other staff. Revise orders, as needed. Answer the patient's and familys questions. Answer the nursing and/or other staffs questions. Write orders for the following days labs, films, medications, diet, and patient activity. Chart patient progress.

Other Postoperative Hospital Work (Postoperative Day 1 Until Discharge Day): Daily rounds (morning) include critical care (cardiovascular, respiratory, neuro, renal) as noted in the previous section until the patient is stable in the intensive care unit. Once the patient is transferred to the floor or stepdown unit, conduct daily rounds (morning) that include: examinations and interviews with patient, interval histories, the assessment and management of cardiovascular status (eg, arterial tracings, pulse, blood pressure, telemetry tracings), volume status, intake and output, neurologic status, respiratory status (eg, bronchodilators, oxygen, percussion, postural drainage, pulse oximetry, incentive spirometry), nutritional status (oral and or enteral), wound dressings, and chest tube drainage. Encourage ambulation and vigorous pulmonary physiotherapy. Remove chest tube(s) on the appropriate day. Monitor the patient for postoperative complications and treat as indicated. Discuss patient progress with the referring physician (verbal and written). Coordinate care with other physicians. Review the patient chart notes left by the nursing and/or other staff. Answer the patient's questions. Answer the nursing and/or other staffs questions (verbal and written). Answer the ancillary staffs (respiratory, pharmacy, dietary, physical therapy) questions. Write orders for postoperative labs, films, medications, diet, and patient activity. Chart patient progress notes. Assess cardiovascular, respiratory, and nutritional status. Check the lab and test results. Communicate the results and the patient's progress to the patient and the patient's family. Answer the familys questions. Answer the hospital staffs questions.

Discharge Day Work: Conduct final predischarge assessment. Check respiratory status. Check wounds. Review nutrition/diet. Review patient chart notes left by the nursing and/or other staff. Check the final pathology/lab/film reports. Discuss the pathology results and ramifications with the patient and the patient's family. Fill out discharge forms and orders for outpatient labs and X rays. Fill out prescriptions. Explain to the patient and the patient's family the suggested home activities regarding dietary management, activities that are permitted/restricted, the management of wound sites, the management of drains and tubes, and the need for a return appointment in the office. Coordinate care with other physicians. Coordinate home health needs with a home health service. Answer the patient's and familys questions. Answer the nursing and/or other staffs questions. Answer the insurance staffs questions. Write the discharge day note. Dictate the clinical resume.

Postoperative Office Work (Postdischarge From the Hospital): Conduct interval histories and physical exams. Review the postdischarge labs/films. Check the patient's wounds and tubes and the patient's progress. Remove sutures and drains. Discuss with the patient management of analgesics and other medications. Write prescriptions for new medications/doses. Discuss the patient's progress with the patient and the patient's family. Answer the patient's and familys questions regarding further perioperative care as well as potential need for additional therapy. Answer the insurance staffs questions. Discuss patient progress with the referring physician (verbal and written). Coordinate care with other physicians. Dictate/write patient progress notes for the patient's medical chart.

Diaphragm

Repair

39560 Resection, diaphragm; with simple repair (eg, primary suture)

Work Value: 12.97 // Global Period: 090

➲ *CPT Assistant* Nov 99: 21, Nov 00: 3; *CPT Changes: An Insider's View* 2000

Clinical Example

A 20-year-old female was diagnosed with a right hepatic lobe mass using a computed tomography (CT) scan. A tentative diagnosis of adenoma was made. The patient continued to have follow-up CT scans and the hepatic mass enlarged. The patient underwent surgery, at which time the right hepatic lobe, segment seven, was noted to be adherent to the right mid-lateral diaphragm and could not be dissected away. Therefore, the diaphragmatic mass was taken en bloc with the liver segment. It was repaired primarily with two running sutures. The hepatic lobe was taken off with an ultrasonic dissector with successive cutting and clipping and the use of cautery. Abdominal fascia and skin were reapproximated without complication. The specimen was noted at pathology to contain a purulent whitish discharge.

Preservice

The surgical contact with the patient starts with a preoperative history and physical and immediate past history within 24 hours of the operation to reassess the patient's condition prior to taking the patient to the operating room. Medical decision-making involves assessing the patient's immediate surgical risk. In patient's with abdominal masses involving vital organs, this entails a high level of judgment, intensity, and risk on the part of the surgeon.

Intraservice

The patient undergoes a thoracoabdominal incision. A primary tumor invading both the diaphragm and the liver is noted. The right hepatic lobe, segment seven, which was noted to be adherent to the right mid-lateral diaphragm could not be dissected away. Therefore, the diaphragmatic mass must be taken en bloc with the liver segment. It is repaired primarily with two running 0-Prolene sutures. Abdominal fascia and skin are reapproximated after removal of the hepatic tumor.

Postservice

With the surgical team in attendance, the patient is transported to the intensive care unit. Management of bleeding and wound drainage occur. The patient's respiratory status is carefully monitored as are hemodynamics and vital signs. The patient is then transferred to the step-down unit where monitoring of drains and drips is required. The patient is then transferred to the step-down unit where monitoring of drains and drips is required. The patient is transferred to the floor where the patient receives daily visits to assess the wound and the patient's respiratory and hemodynamics status. The surgeon and his team then follow the patient in the office, monitoring pain, infection, would healing, and respiratory status.

39561 Resection, diaphragm; with complex repair (eg, prosthetic material, local muscle flap)

Work Value: 19.75 // Global Period: 090

➲ *CPT Assistant* Nov 99: 21, Nov 00: 3; *CPT Changes: An Insider's View* 2000

Clinical Example

A 62-year-old male with a left lower lobe lung cancer is found at thoracotomy to have a malignant focal invasion of the left diaphragm. The diaphragm is incised 2 to 3 cm away from the cancer and the incision is continued circumferentially around the neoplasm, resecting a patch of involving diaphragm with a free margin. The residual defect is closed with graft material. The lower lobe and attached diaphragm are resected en bloc.

Preservice

The surgical contact with the patient starts with a preoperative history and physical and immediate past history within 24 hours of the operation to reassess the patient's condition prior to taking the patient to the operating room. Medical decision-making involves assessing the patient's immediate surgical risk. In patient's with invasive cancer, this entails a high level of judgment, intensity, and risk on the part of the surgeon.

Intraservice

The patient undergoes a left thoracotomy. A primary tumor invading the diaphragm from the left lower lung is noted. In the excision of primary diaphragmatic tumors, the pleural and peritoneal layers are excised en bloc along with that portion of the diaphragmatic leaf containing the tumor. Smaller defects are closed primarily. If the tumor is located in the periphery of the diaphragm, the adjacent portion of the diaphragm and part of the chest wall are removed in continuity. The diaphragm is incised 2 to 3 cm away from the cancer and the incision is continued circumferentially around the neoplasm, resecting a patch of involved diaphragm with a free margin. In general, the defect is closed with a prosthetic soft tissue patch of Gore-tex or other suitable material such as Dacron-Silastic sheeting, preserved dura mater, or Marlex mesh reinforced with woven Dacron. The prosthetic material is secured to the cut edges of the diaphragm or to the chest wall, as necessary.

Postservice

With the surgical team in attendance, the patient is transported to the intensive care unit. Management of bleeding and wound drainage occur. The patient's respiratory status is carefully monitored as are the patient's hemodynamics and vital signs. The patient is then transferred to the step-down unit where monitoring of drains and drips required. The patient is transferred to the floor where the patient receives daily visits to assess the wound and the patient's respiratory and hemodynamic status. The surgeon and his team then follow the patient in the office, monitoring pain, infection, wound healing, and respiratory status.

Digestive System

Esophagus

Endoscopy

⊙ ❺ **43235** Upper gastrointestinal endoscopy including esophagus, stomach, and either the duodenum and/or jejunum as appropriate; diagnostic, with or without collection of specimen(s) by brushing or washing (separate procedure)

Work Value: 2.39 // Global Period: 000

➲ *CPT Assistant* Spring 94: 4, Dec 97: 11, Jun 03: 11, Sep 03: 3

Clinical Example

A 72-year-old male with weight loss and epigastric pain refractory to pharmacological therapy is referred for esophagogastroduodenoscopy. An esophagogastroduodenoscopy is performed.

Preservice

Review with the patient any symptoms and ascertain if dysphagia has been a problem. Review the patient's history to assess the need for preprocedure antibiotics. Review the patient's allergies and medications, specifically noting the use of antiplatelet or anticoagulation medications. Perform a preanesthetic exam with an airway assessment and cardiopulmonary evaluation. Review the patient's laboratory studies as they relate to coagulation status and platelet count. Review the patient's X rays. Review the risks and benefits of the procedure with the patient and obtain informed consent.

Intraservice

Start intravenous access and administer conscious sedation. Insert a standard upper endoscope into the mouth and advance it through the esophagus and stomach and through the pylorus into the duodenum. Examine the duodenal mucosa. Withdraw the endoscope into the stomach and retroflex it to allow the examination of the gastric fundus. Straighten the endoscope to allow the examination of the remainder of the gastric mucosa. Withdraw the endoscope. Measure the gastro-esophageal junction from the incisors. Assess for the presence of a hiatal hernia, and then examine the esophageal mucosa. Withdraw the endoscope.

Postservice

Transfer the patient to the recovery suite. Assess postprocedure vital signs. Dictate a procedure report. When stable for discharge, review the findings with the patient and the patient's family.

Upper Gastrointestinal Endoscopy
43235

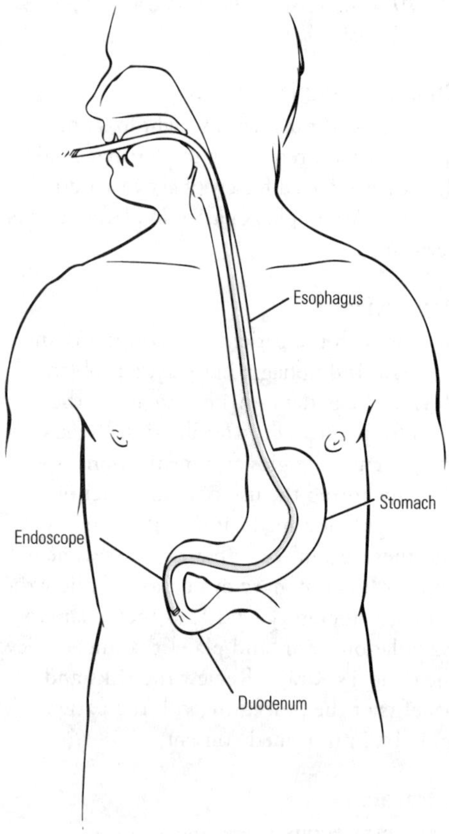

⊙ **43239** Upper gastrointestinal endoscopy including esophagus, stomach, and either the duodenum and/or jejunum as appropriate; with biopsy, single or multiple

Work Value: 2.87 // Global Period: 000

➲ *CPT Assistant* **Spring 94: 4, Apr 98: 14, Feb 99: 11, Oct 01: 4**

Clinical Example

A middle-aged male with persistent dyspepsia and mild anemia undergoes esophagogastroduodenoscopy. A 1-cm antral ulcer is found. Multiple biopsies are taken for histology and a Helicobacter pylori urease screen test is performed.

⊙ ❺ **43246** Upper gastrointestinal endoscopy including esophagus, stomach, and either the duodenum and/or jejunum as appropriate; with directed placement of percutaneous gastrostomy tube

Work Value: 4.32 // Global Period: 000

➲ *CPT Assistant* **Spring 94: 4, Feb 97: 10**

Clinical Example

A 68-year-old female on chronic anticoagulation for atrial fibrillation with congestive heart failure has recently suffered a stroke. A swallowing study shows impaired swallowing with aspiration. Esophagogastroduodenoscopy with percutaneous endoscopic gastrostomy tube placement is performed.

Preservice

Review with the patient any symptoms. Review the patient's allergies and medications, specifically noting the use of antiplatelet or anticoagulation medications. Perform a pre-anesthetic exam including an airway assessment and cardiopulmonary evaluation. Review the patient's laboratory studies as they relate to coagulation status and the platelet count. Review the patient's X rays. Review the risks and benefits of the procedure with the patient and obtain informed consent.

Intraservice

Start intravenous access and administer antibiotics. Administer conscious sedation. Insert a standard upper endoscope into the mouth and advance it through the esophagus and stomach and through the pylorus into the duodenum. Examine the duodenal mucosa.

Withdraw the endoscope into the stomach and retroflex it to allow for the examination of the gastric fundus. Straighten the endoscope to allow for the examination of the remainder of the gastric mucosa. Insuflate the stomach with air until transillumination allows external visualization on the upper abdominal wall of the endoscope light. Prep the abdomen site with bactericidal solution. Press a finger on the abdominal wall site to endoscopically confirm the apposition of the stomach against the abdominal wall. Infiltrate local anesthetic into the subcutaneous and intramuscular portions of the abdomen site. Use a scalpel to make an incision in the abdominal wall. Introduce a gastrostomy introducer catheter through the incision into the stomach. Introduce a snare through the endoscope and loop it around the catheter. Withdraw the catheter introducer needle and pass a guide wire externally through the introducer into the stomach. Tighten the snare around the guide wire and then withdraw the endoscope, snare, and guidewire through the mouth. Remove the guide wire from the endoscope. Pass a percutaneous gastrostomy over the guide wire through the mouth and push it until it exits through the abdominal wall incision. Gently pull the gastrostomy until resistance is felt. Introduce the endoscope through the mouth into the stomach to confirm the positioning of the internal bolster of the gastrostomy against the stomach wall. Slip an external bolster over the guidewire and introducer to position the gastrostomy in place. Remove the guide wire. Suction air from the stomach and remove the endoscope. Clean, bandage, and dress the abdominal site.

Postservice

Transfer the patient to the recovery suite. Assess postprocedure vital signs. Dictate a procedure report. When the patient is stable for discharge, review the findings with the patient and the patient's family.

⊙ **43260** Endoscopic retrograde cholangiopancreatography (ERCP); diagnostic, with or without collection of specimen(s) by brushing or washing (separate procedure)

Work Value: 5.95 // Global Period: 000

➲ *CPT Assistant* Spring 94: 5, Oct 04: 13

Clinical Example

An elderly patient with a history of pancreatitis undergoes diagnostic endoscopic retrograde cholangiopancreatography to rule out choledocholithiasis and a pancreatic duct anomaly.

Endoscopic Retrograde Cholangiopancreatography (ERCP)
43260

Examination of the hepatobiliary system (pancreatic ducts, hepatic ducts, common bile ducts, duodenal papilla [ampulla of Vater] and gallbladder [if present]) performed through a side-viewing flexible fiberoptic endoscope.

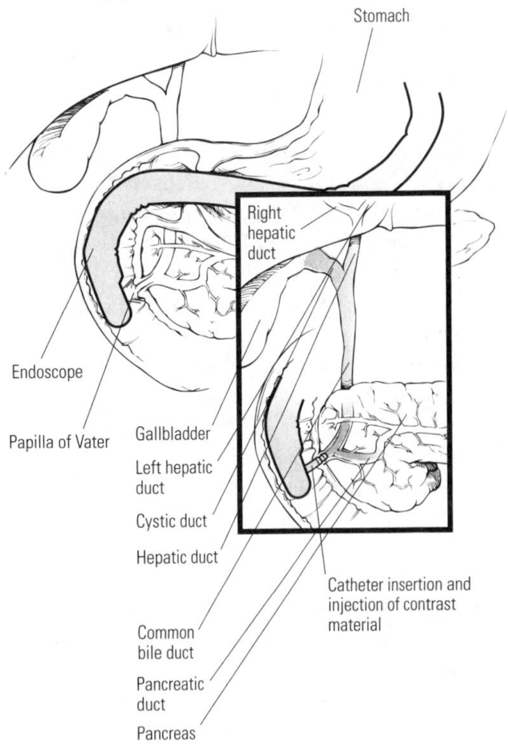

Stomach

Laparoscopy

43644 Laparoscopy, surgical, gastric restrictive procedure; with gastric bypass and Roux-en-Y gastroenterostomy (roux limb 150 cm or less)

Work Value: 29.24 // Global Period: 090

➲ *CPT Assistant* May 05: 3; *CPT Changes: An Insider's View* 2005

Clinical Example

A 44-year-old male who is 5 ft 11 in tall, weighs 390 lbs, and has a body mass index of 55, presents with a history of Type II diabetes controlled with three oral hypoglycemic medications and hypertension controlled with two medications. A recent sleep study showed severe obstructive sleep apnea for which he was placed on continuous positive airway pressure (CPAP) with subjective improvement, but he complains of poor tolerance of the mask. His gastroesophageal reflux is controlled with an H2-blocker, but his mobility is compromised due to severe arthritis of his lower back and right knee. Family and diet history confirm morbid obesity began at age 9. The patient underwent multiple weight loss programs, losing up to 75 lbs three times. However, the weight loss was never maintained for more than 6 months, and each weight regain was more than what was originally lost. Weight-loss programs attempted included very low calorie diets, Weight Watchers, exercise, appetite suppressants, and meal replacements. At operation, he undergoes a laparoscopic gastric restrictive procedure with gastric bypass and Roux-en-Y gastroenterostomy.

Preservice

Review preoperative hospital admission work-up, paying special attention to the patient's cardiopulmonary status including the management of CPAP and oximetry, skin care with antiseptic showers and antibiotics, and thromboembolic prophylaxis. Review films, cardiogram, and laboratory studies. Review planned procedure. Write preoperative orders for perioperative medications. Change into scrub clothes. Review the surgical procedure, postoperative recovery, and expected outcome(s) with the patient and the patient's family. Answer the patient's and familys questions and obtain informed consent. Verify that all necessary instruments and supplies are readily available in the operating room, including a special stretcher. Monitor the patient's positioning and draping, and assist with positioning as needed to prevent neuropraxias and pressure necrosis of skin. Scrub and gown.

Intraservice

Under general anesthesia, enter the abdomen under direct vision or using a Veress needle technique to obtain access for pneumoperitoneum. Pump carbon dioxide into the abdominal cavity through tubing connected to an insufflator to expand the abdominal cavity. Introduce a laparoscopic camera into the abdomen to allow visualization of the internal organs. Place four to six trocar ports in the anterior abdominal wall above the umbilicus. Retract the liver to expose the upper stomach. (Because the liver is typically fatty, it must be handled with extra care to avoid tearing, puncture, or cracking.) Identify the gastroesophageal junction and make a 2-cm incision in the gastrohepatic ligament along the edge of the lesser curve between the first and second vessel caudad to the gastroesophageal junction. Using blunt and ultrasonic dissection, create a retrogastric tunnel cephalad, toward the angle of His. Create a small (15 to 20 cc) gastric pouch after the stomach is transected with repeated firings of an endoscopic linear stapler. (An orogastric tube may be used to calibrate the size of the pouch.) Control minor bleeding from the staple lines with hemoclips. Identify the Ligament of Treitz. Measure the small intestine distally for a short distance and transect it with a linear stapler. Bring the distal limb up to the proximal gastric pouch, either anterior to the transverse colon (antecolic) or posterior to the transverse colon (retro-colic). The omentum may be divided longitudinally with an ultrasonic scalpel or endoscopic stapler, to allow for decreased tension for passage of the Roux limb in an ante-colic position. Incise the transverse mesocolon to create a tunnel for a retro-colic Roux limb position, as indicated. (Care must be taken to avoid twisting of the Roux limb to avoid obstruction or ischemia of the intestine.) Close the mesenteric defect to prevent internal herniation. Perform a gastrojejunal anastomosis between the Roux limb and the gastric pouch, by using either a hand-sewn technique, stapled technique, or a combination of both. Measure the Roux limb up to 150 cm distal from the gastrojejunal anastomosis and mark it. Perform a jejunojejunostomy between the bypassed biliopancreatic limb and the marked segment of the Roux limb. Perform this anastomosis using either a hand-sewn technique, stapled technique, or combination of both. (Intraoperative testing for anastomotic leak may be performed as clinically indicated, utilizing air, intraoperative endoscopy, or methylene blue.) Place drains(s) and/or perform distal gastrostomy as indicated. Close fascia and skin.

Postservice

Apply dressings. Check the patient's vital signs and transfer the patient to the recovery room and then to the intensive care unit. Write the postoperative note in the patient's chart. Dictate the procedure report. Dictate the outcome of the procedure and expected recovery letter for the referring physician and/or insurance company. Consult with the patient and the patient's family regarding the surgery. Write orders for CPAP and continuous oximetry and strip recording and blood gases. Stress the importance of vigorous pulmonary reinflation measures due to marked intra-abdominal obesity and high diaphragms. Monitor thromboembolic prophylaxis, drain(s), and tube losses at wound checks and dressing changes. Review the postoperative upper gastrointestinal radiograms for absence of leak(s) from and progression of contrast through the anastomosed elements. Monitor the patient for signs of complications (eg, airway obstruction, hemorrhage, intestinal leak or obstruction, pulmonary embolus, atelectasis, and so on). Remove drain(s) as appropriate. Start oral fluids when appropriate. Discuss the special dietary instructions with the patient regarding the patient's markedly altered intake/gastric physiology, including a 30-mL stomach capacity. (Take care to discuss the patient's inability to take food and fluids at the same time, and instruct the patient to avoid true solids for several weeks). Confer with a nutritionist and the patient regarding postoperative food preparation and caloric goals. Review the instructions for postdischarge diet and home care with the patient and the patient's family. Write orders for postdischarge medications. Prepare discharge records. Discuss the outcome of the procedure with the referring physician.

Bariatric Surgery

LAPAROSCOPY

43770 Laparoscopy, surgical, gastric restrictive procedure; placement of adjustable gastric band (gastric band and subcutaneous port components)

Work Value: 17.85 // Global Period: 090

➲ *CPT Changes: An Insider's View* 2006

Clinical Example

A 44-year-old female presents with a body mass index of 48, hypertension, and poorly controlled diabetes. She has failed nonoperative obesity interventions and has elected gastric banding instead of gastric bypass surgery. She undergoes laparoscopic placement of an adjustable gastric band and subcutaneous port.

Preservice

The patient's history and physical are reviewed. The preoperative work-up, labs, X rays, cardiac evaluation, and the sleep study report are reviewed. Orders for perioperative medications. vitamin/mineral supplements, antibiotics, heparin, and bowel prep are written. Planned incisions and procedure are reviewed. The physician changes into scrub clothes. The surgical procedure, postoperative recovery in and out of the hospital, and expected outcome(s) are reviewed with the patient and the patient's family. Questions from the patient and the patient's family are answered and informed consent is obtained. The length and type of anesthesia are reviewed with the anesthesiologist. The physician verifies that all necessary surgical instruments and supplies are readily available in the operative suite, monitors the patient positioning and draping, and assists with positioning as needed. All extremities are checked for proper positioning and padding to avoid neuropathy.

Intraservice

Under general anesthesia, surgical laparoscopy is performed. Pneumoperitoneum is established to distend the abdomen, and the laparoscope is introduced. Gas flow and intra-abdominal pressure are carefully monitored so as not to impair ventilation or venous return. Four to six trocar ports are sited through the anterior abdominal wall above the umbilicus. The viscera are inspected. An orogastric tube may be placed to decompress the stomach. The liver is retracted to expose the gastroesophageal junction. A path is made behind the upper stomach 2 cm below the gastroesophageal junction. The dissection plane may be guided by use of a per-oral gastric balloon catheter, which defines the location of the gastroesophageal junction, or by anatomical landmarks from the right crus of the diaphragm to the Angle of His. Excess visceral fat covering the upper stomach may need to be excised to prevent incorporation within the band, which would cause external compression and subsequent obstruction. The adjustable gastric band is introduced into the abdomen and pulled through the prepared retro-gastric path and around the upper stomach, just below the gastroesophageal junction. The band is locked. The band position is secured with strategically placed gastro-gastric sutures to prevent band slippage or gastric prolapse. The tubing attached to the band is tunneled through the abdominal wall. It is connected to an access port that is secured in or on the abdominal rectus muscle or other secure subcutaneous location. Hemostasis is obtained. The trocars are removed and all fascial and skin openings are closed as appropriate.

Postservice

Sterile dressings are placed. Orders for postoperative labs, films, medications, diet, and patient activity are written. Recovery room care and medications are reviewed with staff. The outcome of the procedure is discussed with the patient's family and then with patient after the patient emerges from anesthesia. The postoperative report is dictated. A letter describing the outcome of the procedure and expected recovery is dictated for the patient's primary care physician and/or insurance company. The patient is examined and wounds are checked. Nursing/staff chart notes are reviewed. Questions from the patient and the patient's family are answered. Questions from the nursing and other staff are answered. Orders for the floor nurse are written and summarized. The patient's fluid and electrolyte status is checked. Orders for labs, films, medications, diet, and patient activity are written. A confirmatory contrast upper gastrointestinal radiograph is ordered and reviewed to exclude gastric prolapse, perforation, or obstruction. When the contrast study and patient's status are acceptable, a clear liquid diet is instituted and the patient is discharged. Home restrictions (ie, diet, activity, bathing, return visits) are discussed with the patient, nutritionist, and the patient's family. All appropriate medical records are completed, including day of discharge progress notes, discharge summary, and discharge instructions, prescriptions, and insurance forms.

Postoperative Work in the Office: The patient is examined and the wounds assessed. All patient and family questions are answered. Sutures are removed when appropriate. At each visit, the patient's blood pressure, heart sounds, breath sounds, lower extremities, and weight are checked and details of diet, supplements, and activity are reviewed. The patient is evaluated for weight loss, appetite, hunger, nausea, vomiting, or complications. The patient is evaluated for diet and food intolerance or non-compliance. The band is inflated, as needed, based on hunger, weight loss, and restriction. (This is performed in the office under sterile technique, by percutaneously accessing the subcutaneous port with a non-coring needle connected to a syringe filled with saline. Saline is injected into the port, aspirated back to ensure successful puncture, and a predetermined amount of saline is injected into the port. The needle is then removed. It is estimated by survey that band adjustments would typically be performed twice during the postoperative period.) Any additional or adjuvant treatment that may be required and other specialist referrals are discussed. Evaluation and management components are rescored and pertinent information is forwarded to the patient's primary care physician.

Intestines (Except Rectum)

Excision

⑮ **44120** Enterectomy, resection of small intestine; single resection and anastomosis

Work Value: 20.74 // Global Period: 090

➲ *CPT Assistant* Mar 04: 3

Clinical Example

A 67-year-old female status post multiple abdominal operations presents with clinical and X-ray evidence of small bowel obstruction. She fails to respond to nasogastric (NG) decompression and intravenous hydration. At operation, a segment of bowel is found that requires resection.

Preservice

Write orders for preoperative medications including beta blockers if indicated. Select and order the appropriate antibiotic(s) and confirm timing and administration. Ensure appropriate selection, timing, and administration of deep vein thrombosis (DVT) prophylaxis. Review and document the results of preoperative testing (eg, labs, electrocardiogram, chest X ray, availability of blood products). Review the preoperative work-up, paying particular attention to imaging information and reports. Meet with the patient and the patient's family to review the planned procedure and postoperative management. Mark the site and side of the proposed skin incision and confirm the location with the patient. Review and obtain informed consent from the patient and a witness. Review the length and type of anesthesia with the anesthesiologist. Verify that all required instruments and supplies are available. Assist in transferring the patient from the emergency room gurney to the operating table. Monitor/assist with the positioning of the patient. Assist the anesthesia team with line placement and induction of anesthesia and intubation. Insert or supervise the insertion of a Foley catheter. Review radiographic images. Indicate areas surrounding the skin incision that are to be prepped and draped. If present, clip hair from the area surrounding the surgical site. Scrub and gown. Perform surgical time out with operating surgical team and anesthesia team.

Intraservice

Excise the skin and subcutaneous tissue of the old incision. Secure hemostasis by ligature or cautery. Identify the site of the previous closure and clear the subcutaneous tissue from it with a scalpel. Extend the incision cephalad and/or caudad so as to enter the abdomen in an area free of adhesions. Identify the linea alba, grasp it with toothed instruments, and open it with a scalpel, carefully avoiding injury to the underlying bowel. Enter the peritoneum and dissect the bowel adherent to the previous incision to avoid injury. Repair serosal tears with a fine nonabsorbable suture. Dissect the adherent bowel until the bowel is free of adhesions from the ligament of Treitz to the ileocecal valve. Carefully place a mechanical self-retraining retractor to avoid injury to abdominal contents. Conduct a visual and manual complete exploration of the abdominal cavity and its contents. Confirm the position of the NG tube. Inspect and palpate the stomach for pathology. Locate and palpate the duodenum. Inspect and palpate the gallbladder for the presence of stones. Palpate the liver bimanually to detect potential hepatic metastases, as is the porta hepatis. Inspect the pancreas through the hepaticogastric ligament and palpate for possible masses. Inspect and palpate the small bowel from the ligament of Treitz to the ileocecal valve. Inspect and palpate the cecum and appendix, and ascending, transverse, and descending colon. Inspect and palpate the cul-de-sac and pelvic contents. Place laparotomy pads to wall off the segment of nonviable bowel. Identify the nonviable bowel, apply two clamps 2-cm proximal to the nonviable bowel, and divide the bowel between the clamps. Apply two more clamps 2-cm distal to the nonviable bowel and divide the bowel between the clamps. Resect and ligate the mesentery containing the blood supply to this segment, retaining as much blood supply as possible. Carry out a two-layered anastomosis. Inspect the abdomen for injury and the presence of any instruments or lap-pads (ie, conduct a count). Remove and account for the retractor components. Return the abdominal organs to normal anatomical position. Drape the omentum over the abdominal contents. Close the fascia with running suture. Conduct a second instrument, needle, sponge, and lap-pad count. Irrigate and approximate the subcutaneous tissues and close the skin.

Postservice

Apply elastic skin closures and sterile dressings. Monitor the patient during the reversal of anesthesia, protecting the wound with a hand so that wound disruption does not occur with an unrestrained cough. Assist in transferring the patient from the operating table to a gurney. Monitor the transport of the patient from the operating room to the recovery room. Discuss postoperative recovery care with the anesthesia and nursing staff. Instruct the nursing staff in the care of drains, tubes, and other devices. Review postoperative labs. Check chest X ray to confirm the location of the NG tube and assess pulmonary status. Discuss the procedure and its outcome with the patient's family in the waiting area. Write a brief operative note. Write a postoperative note in the recovery room. Dictate an operative report and supply a copy to the referring physician(s). Call the referring physician(s). Discharge the patient from the recovery room. Write orders for transferring to general surgical floor and discuss ongoing care with nursing staff. Examine the patient, including reviewing vital signs and confirming as necessary. Auscultate the patient's heart, lungs, and abdomen for bowel sounds. Manage dressings to wounds daily and monitor the status of the incision looking for signs of infection. Continue prophylaxis for DVT. Monitor daily for adequacy. Assess the need for beta-blockers and order as required. Assess the need for antibiotics and order as required. Monitor and document the patient's progress. Evaluate the patient for sepsis, bowel function, and cardiorespiratory function. Assess the patient's pain scores and the adequacy of analgesia. Monitor the patient's fluid and electrolyte status and renal function. Review the patient chart notes from the nursing and other staff. Write orders for labs, films, medications, diet, and patient activity. Chart patient progress notes daily. Answer the patient's and familys questions. Answer the nursing and other staffs questions. Prior to discharge, review the pathology with the patient. Manage the NG tube. Remove when appropriate and advance the patient's diet. Discuss home restrictions (ie, diet, activity, bathing) with the patient, the patient's family, and the discharging nurse. Write prescriptions for medications needed postdischarge. Complete all appropriate medical records, including day of discharge progress notes, discharge summary, discharge instructions, and insurance forms. Discharge the patient when there is a return of bowel function, adequate nutrition intake, and adequate pain control with oral analgesics.

Postservice Office Work: Examine and talk with the patient. Remove sutures and staples, when appropriate. Check the wound. Monitor the patient's diet caloric intake by weight. Arrange for dietary consultation as needed. Review the pathology report in response to the patient's and familys questions. Answer the patient's and familys questions. Write medication prescriptions. Order and review postdischarge labs and films, as necessary. Discuss the patient's progress with the referring physician(s) (verbal and written). Dictate progress notes for the patient's medical record.

Coding Tip for 44120

It is appropriate to append modifier 63, *Procedure Performed on Infants,* less than 4 kg, to code 44120.

44145 Colectomy, partial; with coloproctostomy (low pelvic anastomosis)

Work Value: 28.45 // Global Period: 090

➲ *CPT Assistant* Fall 92: 24

Clinical Example

A 70-year-old male with hypertension and cardiac history presents with a mid-rectal adenocarcinoma. An endorectal ultrasound reveals a T2 lesion with no evidence of metastatic disease. At operation, a low anterior resection with colorectal anastomosis

Preservice

Select and order the appropriate antibiotic(s) and confirm timing and administration.

Assure appropriate selection, timing, and administration of DVT prophylaxis. Write preadmission orders for preoperative medications, including beta-blockers as required. and review results of preadmission testing (lab, EKG, chest x-ray, availability of blood products). Review preoperative work-up, with particular attention to pathology and imaging information and reports. Reexamine the patient to make sure that physical findings have not changed and update history and physical exam. Meet with the patient and family to review planned procedure and postoperative management. Mark the site and side of proposed skin incision and confirm with the patient. Review and obtain informed consent, including witness. Review the length and type of anesthesia with anesthesiologist. Verify that all required instruments and supplies are available. Assist in the transfer of the patient from gurney to the operating table andmonitor and assist with positioning of the patient. Assist the anesthesia team with line placement and induction of anesthesia and intubation. Insert or supervise insertion of Foley catheter. Place 3-way irrigating rectal catheter, inflate balloon. Indicate areas surrounding the skin incision to be prepped and draped. If present, clip hair from area surrounding surgical site. Scrub and gown and perform surgical time-out with operating surgical team and anesthesia team.

Intraservice

Skin incision is made using sharp dissection. Hemostasis is achieved using electrocautery and small ligatures, as necessary. The linea Alba is identified and carefully divided. The peritoneum is grasped, elevated, and carefully incised to avoid injury to bowel. The peritoneal cavity is entered under direct vision. Adhesions are cleared by sharp dissection in order to expose all of the abdominal viscera. A visual and manual complete exploration of the abdominal cavity and its contents is carried out. The NG tube is placed and its position is confirmed. The stomach is inspected and palpated for pathology. The duodenum is visualized and palpated. The gallbladder is inspected and palpated for the presence of stones. The liver is palpated bimanually in order to detect potential hepatic metastases, as is the porta hepatis. The pancreas is inspected through the hepatico gastric ligament and palpated for possible masses. The tail of the pancreas is palpated for possible lymphadenopathy. The small bowel is inspected and palpated from the ligament of Treitz to the ileocecal valve. The small bowel mesentery is inspected and palpated for the presence of lymphadenopathy. The cecum and appendix, ascending, transverse, and descending colon are inspected and palpated. The cul-de-sac and pelvic contents are inspected and palpated. Any suspicious finding(s) are noted and appropriate biopsies taken and sent to pathology for frozen section. A self-retaining retractor is carefully inserted, while avoiding injury or entrapment of abdominal contents. The location and extent of the primary lesion is confirmed. The abdominal contents, to the exclusion of the sigmoid colon, are packed away using laparotomy pads and additional retractors are placed for optimal exposure. Umbilical tapes are placed, using fine dissection, and ligated, proximal and distal to the lesion, in order to prevent suture line implantation. The left colon is mobilized toward the splenic flexure by opening the retroperitoneum along the white fascial line of Toldt. (Mobilization of the splenic flexure is performed, and billed separately.) The distal margin of resection is dissected below the peritoneal reflection. The left ureter is identified and a vessel loop is placed for continual identification and protection of the ureter. The inferior mesenteric artery is ligated at its origin to include all of the regional lymph nodes. The inferior mesenteric vein is identified and ligated at the base of the pancreas. The mobilization of the rectum begins with posteriorly posterior to the presacral fascia to the level of the coccyx bone, in order to perform a total mesorectal excision. The lateral attachments of the rectum are sharply dissected to the level of the pelvic floor, with isolation and ligation of the middle hemorrhoidal artery. The anterior dissection of the rectum is carried posterior to the prostate. At this time the rectum is divided with a linear stapler at least two centimeters distal to the tumor. The proximal colon is divided at in the mid descending colon between two clamps. A purse string suture is placed around the proximal colon (usually a 0 proline), and the anvil of the circular stapler is placed into the colon and the purse string is tightened. Then the cartridge is placed transanally and the anvil is secured and the instrument is fired. After the low colorectal anastomosis is completed, the pelvis is filled with sterile fluid and air is injected into the rectum, in order to check for any leakage of air. The colon and rectal "donuts" are checked for continuity. The anastomotic segment is inspected for viability, absence of tension, and patency. The specimen is oriented and sent to pathology. The abdominal cavity is irrigated copiously with antibiotic solution. Hemostasis is obtained. The abdomen is inspected for injury and the presence of any instruments or lap-pads (ie, count is made). The retractor components are removed and accounted for. The abdominal organs are returned to normal anatomical position. The omentum is draped over the abdominal contents. The fascia is closed with running suture. A second instrument, needle, sponge, and lap-pad count is conducted. The subcutaneous tissues are irrigated and approximated and the skin is closed.

Postservice

Hospital Work: Apply Steri-Strips and sterile dressings. Remove the rectal catheter. Monitor the patient during reversal of anesthesia, protecting the wound with a hand so that wound disruption does not occur with an unrestrained cough. Assist in transfer of patient from the operating table to the gurney. Monitor transport of the patient from operating room to recovery room. Discuss postoperative recovery care with anesthesia and nursing staff. Instruct nursing staff in care of drains, tubes and other devices. Review postoperative labs. Check chest X ray to confirm location of NG tube and assess pulmonary status. Discuss procedure and outcome with family in waiting area. Write brief operative note. Write postoperative note in the recovery room. Dictate operative report and copy referring physician(s). Call referring physician(s). Patient is discharged from recovery room. Write the patient care orders and discuss floor care with the nursing staff. Examine the patient, including reviewing vital signs and confirming as necessary. Auscultate heart, lungs, and abdomen for bowel sounds and manage dressings to wounds daily, monitoring status of incision, looking for signs of infection. Continue prophylaxis for deep venous thrombosis and monitor daily for adequacy. Assess the need for beta-blockers and the need for antibiotics, order as required.

Monitor and document the patient's progress including evaluating for sepsis, bowel function; cardiorespiratory function. Assess pain scores and adequacy of analgesia. Monitor fluid and electrolyte status and renal function. Review nursing and other staff patient chart notes. Write orders for labs, films, medications, diet, and patient activity. Chart patient progress notes daily. Answer patient, family and nursing/other staff questions. Prior to discharge, review the pathology with the patient. Manage nasogastric tube, remove when appropriate and advance diet. Obtain oncology consultations. Write prescriptions for medications needed post-discharge. Discuss home restrictions (i.e., diet, activity, bathing) with the patient, family members, and discharging nurse. Discharge the patient when there is return of bowel function, adequate nutrition intake, and adequate pain control with oral analgesics. Complete all appropriate medical records, including day of discharge progress notes, discharge summary and discharge instructions, and insurance forms.

Office Work: Examine and talk with the patient. Monitor healing of incision with appropriate physical examination, including answering questions from patient and family. Remove sutures and staples, when appropriate. Monitor diet caloric intake by weight andarrange for dietary consultation as needed. Review pathology report in response to family and patient questions Answer patient and family questions. Write medication prescriptions. Post discharge labs/films are ordered and reviewed, as necessary. Begin routine surveillance for recurrent tumor. Discuss schedule of tumor marker and imaging surveillance. Discuss the need for postoperative chemotherapy with patient and offer referral to cancer support groups. Discuss progress with referring physician(s) (verbal and written).Discuss case with oncologist and prepare documents for transmission to that office. Dictate progress notes for medical record.

Coding Tip for 44145

A coloproctostomy is an anastomosis between the colon and the rectum.

Rectum

Endoscopy

❺ **45330** Sigmoidoscopy, flexible; diagnostic, with or without collection of specimen(s) by brushing or washing (separate procedure)

Work Value: 0.96 // Global Period: 000

➲ *CPT Assistant* Spring 94: 9, May 05: 3

Clinical Example

A 64-year-old male underwent colonoscopy 6 months earlier at which time a 2-cm sessile adenomatous polyp was removed from the descending colon. Flexible sigmoidoscopy is performed.

Preservice

Symptoms are reviewed with the patient. The patient's history is reviewed to assess the need for preprocedure antibiotics. The patient's allergies and medications are reviewed and any use of antiplatelet or anticoagulation medications are noted. The patient's laboratory studies as they relate to coagulation status and the platelet count are reviewed. The patient's X rays are reviewed. The risks and benefits of the procedure are reviewed with the patient and informed consent is obtained.

Intraservice

A standard flexible sigmoidoscope is inserted into the rectum and advanced through the sigmoid colon to the splenic flexure. The sigmoidoscope is withdrawn to allow examination of the colon mucosa. In the rectum, the sigmoidoscope is retroflexed to allow examination of the rectal mucosa, and then straightened and withdrawn.

Postservice

The patient is transferred to the recovery suite. Postprocedure vital signs are assessed. A procedure report is dictated. When patient is stable for discharge, the findings are reviewed with the patient and the patient's family.

Coding Tip for 45330

If a flexible instrument is used, codes for flexible sigmoidoscopy should be used, as described in the 45330-45345 code series.

⊙ ❺ **45378** Colonoscopy, flexible, proximal to splenic flexure; diagnostic, with or without collection of specimen(s) by brushing or washing, with or without colon decompression (separate procedure)

Work Value: 3.69 // Global Period: 000

➲ *CPT Assistant* Spring 94: 9, Aug 99: 3, Jan 02: 12, Jan 04: 4, May 05: 3

Clinical Example

A 67-year-old female is found to have heme positive stool with a hemoglobin of 11.5 gms/dL and a mean corpuscular volume (MCV) of 78. She denies any abdominal symptoms. A colonoscopy is performed.

Preservice

Symptoms are reviewed with the patient. The patient's history is reviewed to assess the need for preprocedure antibiotics. The patient's allergies and medications are reviewed and any use of antiplatelet or anticoagulation medications are noted. A preanesthetic exam with airway assessment and cardiopulmonary evaluation is performed. The patient's laboratory studies as they relate to coagulation status and the platelet count are reviewed. The patient's X rays are reviewed. The risks and benefits of the procedure are reviewed with the patient and informed consent is obtained.

Intraservice

Intravenous access is started and conscious sedation is administered. A standard colonoscope is inserted into the rectum and advanced to the cecum. The ileocecal valve is identified and the terminal ileum is intubated. The colonoscope is withdrawn through the ascending colon, hepatic flexure, transverse colon, splenic flexure, and sigmoid colon to allow examination of the colon mucosa. In the rectum, the colonoscope is retroflexed to allow examination of the rectal mucosa, and then straightened and withdrawn.

Postservice

The patient is transferred to the recovery suite. Postprocedure vital signs are assessed. A procedure report is dictated. When stable for discharge, the findings are reviewed with the patient and the patient's family.

Colonoscopy
45378

A colonoscope is inserted in the anus and moved through the colon past the splenic flexure in order to visualize the lumen of the rectum and colon.

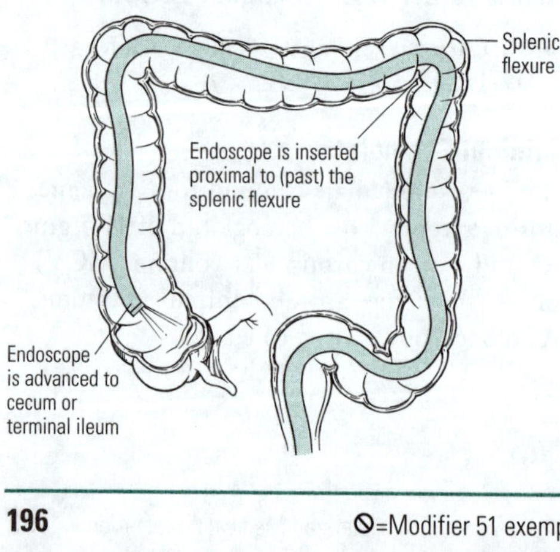

⊙ **45380** Colonoscopy, flexible, proximal to splenic flexure; with biopsy, single or multiple

Work Value: 4.43 // Global Period: 000

➲ *CPT Assistant* Spring 94: 9, Jan 96: 7, Feb 99: 11, Aug 99: 3, Jan 04: 7, Jul 04: 15

Clinical Example

A 40-year-old male with diarrhea, anemia, and intermittent rectal bleeding is evaluated with colonoscopy. Diffuse inflammation is found, and multiple biopsies are taken in several regions of the colon for diagnosis.

⊙ **45383** Colonoscopy, flexible, proximal to splenic flexure; with ablation of tumor(s), polyp(s), or other lesion(s) not amenable to removal by hot biopsy forceps, bipolar cautery or snare technique

Work Value: 5.86 // Global Period: 000

➲ *CPT Assistant* Spring 94: 9, Aug 99: 3, Jan 04: 4

Clinical Example

An elderly patient, who has a high surgical risk, undergoes laser treatment to ablate a bulky villous adenoma with severe atypia located at the hepatic flexure.

⊙ **45384** Colonoscopy, flexible, proximal to splenic flexure; with removal of tumor(s), polyp(s), or other lesion(s) by hot biopsy forceps or bipolar cautery

Work Value: 4.69 // Global Period: 000

➲ *CPT Assistant* Spring 94: 9, Jul 98: 10, Feb 99: 11, Aug 99: 3, Jan 04: 6, Jul 04: 15

Clinical Example

A middle-aged patient undergoes colonoscopy and has three diminutive polyps scattered throughout the colon. The polyps are cauterized and removed by application of a hot biopsy forceps.

Coding Tip for 45378, 45380, 45383, 45384, and 45385

Colonoscopy is the examination of the entire colon from the rectum to the cecum and may include an examination of the terminal ileum.

⊙ **45385** Colonoscopy, flexible, proximal to splenic flexure; with removal of tumor(s), polyp(s), or other lesion(s) by snare technique

Work Value: 5.30 // Global Period: 000

➲ *CPT Assistant* **Spring 94: 9, Jan 96: 7, Jul 98: 10, Aug 99: 3, Jan 04: 5, Jul 04: 15**

Clinical Example

A middle-aged patient undergoes a colonoscopy and is found to have two polyps, 6–12 mm in diameter. The polyps are removed by snare and retrieved.

Colonoscopy
45383, 45385
Removal of tumor(s), polyp(s), or other lesion(s), by snare technique.

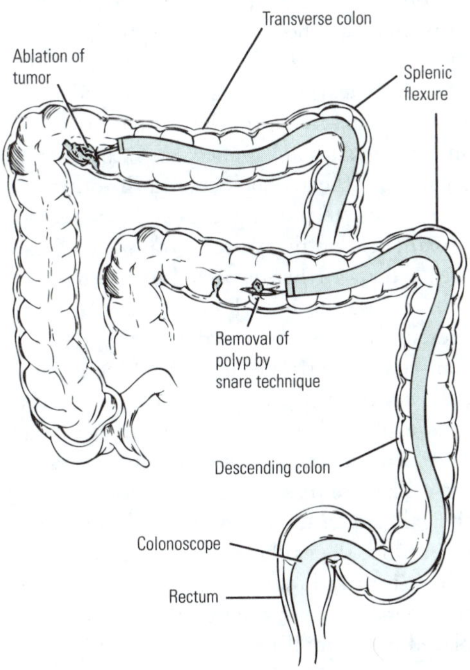

Coding Tip for 45378, 45380, 45383, 45384, and 45385

Codes 45378, 45380, 45383, 45384, and 45385 describe an endoscopy in which a colonoscope is inserted into the anus and moved through the colon proximally past the splenic flexure (ie, the examiner is able to advance the colonoscope beyond the splenic flexure) to visualize the lumen of the transverse and ascending (right side) to the cecum and/or terminal ileum.

Biliary Tract

Laparoscopy

❺ **47562** Laparoscopy, surgical; cholecystectomy

Work Value: 11.63 // Global Period: 090

➲ *CPT Assistant* **Nov 99: 23, Mar 00: 9, Sep 03: 3;** ***CPT Changes: An Insider's View*** **2000**

Clinical Example

A 27-year-old female presents with repeated episodes of right quadrant pain with radiation to the back and right shoulder. Abdominal examination reveals slight tenderness in the right upper quadrant. Ultrasound confirms two stones in the gallbladder. Liver chemistries are normal. Elective laparoscopic cholecystectomy is performed.

Preservice

- Select and order the appropriate antibiotic(s) and confirm timing and administration.
- Assure appropriate selection, timing, and administration of DVT prophylaxis.
- Assess need for beta-blockers, order as required.
- Review preadmission work-up, with particular attention to imaging information and reports.
- Reexamine patient to make sure that physical findings have not changed and update history and physical.
- Review results of preadmission testing (lab, EKG, chest x-ray, availability of blood products).
- Meet with patient and family to review planned procedure and post-operative management.
- Mark site and side of proposed skin incision and confirm with patient.

- Review and obtain informed consent, including witness.
- Review length and type of anesthesia with anesthesiologist.
- Verify that all required instruments and supplies are available, including laparoscopic equipment.
- Assist in transfer of patient from gurney to operating table.
- Monitor/assist with positioning of patient.
- Install or supervise installation of Foley catheter.
- Assist anesthesia team with line placement and induction of anesthesia and intubation.
- Indicate areas of skin to be prepped and mark surgical incisions.
- Scrub and gown.
- Perform surgical "time out" with operating surgical team.

Intraservice

A skin incision is made and carried through the subcutaneous tissues and hemostasis is obtained with suture or cautery. The midline fascia, usually below the umbilicus, is exposed to either side of the midline, and incised vertically in the midline. Stay sutures of Vicryl or similar material are then placed in the fascia on either side of the midline. The peritoneum is opened under direct vision and a 10 mm trocar is placed. The side stay sutures are then attached to the winding posts of the 10 mm trocar. The abdomen is then insufflated with carbon dioxide. Physiologic changes are monitored at this time. The appropriate camera is inserted, and the assistant is instructed as to how to hold the camera, where the focus is, and to make certain of the orientation of the camera. A thorough exploration of the abdominal cavity is undertaken visually prior to placing the other trocars. Under direct vision, with the camera viewing placement of the other ports, local anesthesia is injected and a trocar is placed in the right upper quadrant immediately adjacent to the midline. Two additional 5 mm ports are then placed on the anterior axillary line of the right upper quadrant. The liver is retracted appropriately, and the other trocars are used to perform as detailed an exploratory laparoscopy as possible, viewing the small bowel, colon, stomach, spleen where possible, and pelvic organs. At this time, adhesions may be lysed sharply and/or bluntly. The gallbladder is grasped at the superior fundus with a Babcock or ratcheted grasper, and this is fixed in place with a towel clip. The dissection of the cystic duct and the identification of its junction with the common duct are undertaken with a variety of instruments, including blunt dissection instruments and a right-angle clamp. The triangle of Calot is further dissected to identify the cystic artery or other anomalous vessels. After the cystic duct has been appropriately identified, variations in anatomy are identified or ruled out and the junction of the cystic duct with the common hepatic duct is confirmed. Clips are placed just below the infundibulum of the gallbladder on the cystic duct. Clips are then placed proximally on the cystic duct as well, and the duct is transected. The identity and location of the cystic artery is then reconfirmed and it is dissected free from the surrounding tissue. Three clips are applied, one immediately adjacent to the gallbladder, and the other two as close to this clip as possible more proximally and this vessel is transected. The area is then further inspected to ensure a second posterior branch of the artery is not present. If one is identified, it is clipped and transected in a similar fashion. Placing the gallbladder on traction and maneuvering it to ensure adequate exposure of the tissues being dissected, the cautery and suction devices are utilized to dissect the gallbladder free of the gallbladder mesentery and its fossa in the liver. Once the gallbladder has been dissected free, it is placed over the liver. The camera is then removed from the umbilical port and placed in the midline port close to the liver. A grasping forceps is introduced through the umbilical trocar and is utilized to grasp the cystic duct end of the gallbladder, and the gallbladder is maneuvered under direct visualization to the trocar, and removed through or with the umbilical trocar the stay sutures having been released from the trocar first.

Alternatively an Endobag is used to remove the gallbladder utilizing the same technique. The umbilical trocar is replaced reattaching the fascial stay sutures. Full pneumoperitoneum is reestablished. The right upper quadrant is then irrigated and aspirated removing all debris and blood clot. The gallbladder fossa is then inspected for hemostasis. If bleeding is encountered, electrocautery or hemostatic agents are utilized to achieve hemostasis. The cystic artery and cystic duct stumps are then inspected to make certain that all the clips remain securely in place. A drain may be placed in the right upper quadrant at the surgeon's discretion if there is a small amount of bleeding or if there is any bile drainage seen from the gallbladder fossa which cannot be controlled. The drain is introduced through the upper abdominal trocar and delivered, with a grasping forceps, through a lateral trocar and delivered through the abdominal wall with removal of that port. The drain is then secured in place with a suture. The other individual trocars are then withdrawn under direct laparoscopic vision, making certain that there is no bleeding. The umbilical trocar is removed, carbon dioxide is allowed to escape from the abdomen, and the fascial defect at the umbilicus, and possibly the upper midline, are closed with interrupted sutures. The fascial stay sutures are either removed or tied to each other. Local anesthetic is injected once again to all four trocar sites. The subcutaneous tissue is approximated with interrupted sutures to eliminate a dead space. The skin incisions are closed in subcuticular fashion. Sponge, needle, and instrument counts are obtained and confirmed prior to closure.

Postservice

Post-operative Work – Hospital:

- Apply Steristrips and sterile dressings. Monitor patient during reversal of anesthesia, protecting the wound with a hand so that wound disruption does not occur with an unrestrained cough. Assist in transfer of patient from operating table to gurney. Monitor transport of patient from operating room to recovery room. Discuss postoperative recovery care with anesthesia and nursing staff. Instruct nursing staff in care of drains, tubes and other devices. Review post-operative labs. Discuss procedure and outcome with family in waiting area. Write brief operative note. Write postoperative note in the recovery room. Dictate operative report and copy referring physician(s). Call referring physician(s). Patient is discharged from recovery room.
- Write orders for transferring to general surgical floor and discuss ongoing care with floor nurses.
- Examine patient, including reviewing vital signs and confirming as necessary.
- Auscultate heart, lungs, and abdomen for bowel sounds.
- Manage dressings to wounds daily, monitoring status of incision, looking for signs of infection.
- Continue prophylaxis for DVT. Monitor daily for adequacy.
- Assess need for beta-blockers, order as required.
- Assess need for continued antibiotics, order as required.
- Monitor and document patient progress.
- Assess pain scores and adequacy of analgesia.
- Monitor fluid and electrolyte status and renal function.
- Review nursing/other staff patient chart notes.
- Write orders for labs, films, medications, diet, and patient activity.
- Chart patient progress notes, daily.
- Answer patient and family questions. Answer nursing/other staff questions.
- Advance diet, as appropriate.
- Manage drain, if installed, and remove when appropriate.
- Write orders for follow-up, post-discharge labs, x-rays, home care, and physical therapy.

- Write prescriptions for medications needed post-discharge.
- Home restrictions (i.e., diet, activity, bathing) are discussed with the patient, family members and discharging nurse.
- The patient is discharged when there is return of bowel function, taking adequate nutrition, and adequate pain control with oral analgesics.
- All appropriate medical records are completed, including day of discharge progress notes, discharge summary and discharge instructions, and insurance forms.

Postoperative Work – In Office:

- Examine and talk with patient.
- Remove staples or sutures, when appropriate.
- Review activity and restrictions.
- Monitor healing of incision with appropriate physical examination, including dealing with questions of patient and family.
- Monitor diet caloric intake by weight.
- Answer patient/family questions.
- Write medication prescriptions.
- Post discharge labs/films are ordered and reviewed.
- Discuss progress with referring physician(s) (verbal and written).
- Dictate progress notes for medical chart.

Laparoscopic Cholecystectomy
47562

The gallbladder is dissected and removed from the liver bed under laparoscopic guidance.

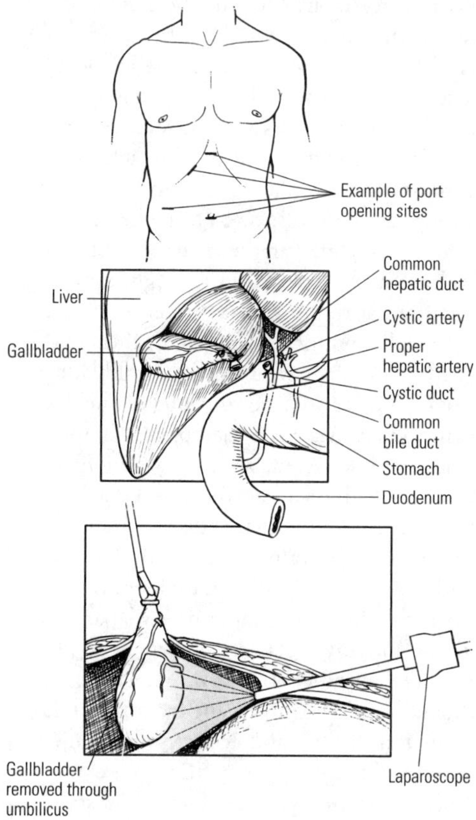

Abdomen, Peritoneum, and Omentum

Incision

49000 Exploratory laparotomy, exploratory celiotomy with or without biopsy(s) (separate procedure)

Work Value: 12.44 // Global Period: 090

➲ *CPT Assistant* Fall 92: 23, Mar 01: 10

Clinical Example

A 19-year-old male presents to the emergency department with a stab wound to the left flank. An abdominal X ray reveals no free air. He is hemodynamically stable. He subsequently develops abdominal tenderness over 6 hours of observation. The attack weapon was allegedly a 12-in butcher knife. Computed tomography scan reveals fluid in the cul-de-sac. He is taken to the operating room, where a thorough exploration reveals a stab wound of the left retroperitoneum with minimal bleeding. All other structures are normal. The incision is closed. The patient had an uneventful postoperative course and is discharged on the third postoperative day.

Preservice

Preservice work begins after the decision to operate is made and includes assessing the patient in the emergency department; taking a history regarding the incident; obtaining and reviewing emergency department admission imaging and laboratory studies, paying special attention to cardiopulmonary, gastrointestinal, and hematologic status; communicating with other health care professionals; ordering preoperative antibiotics and tetanus prophylaxis; and arranging for an adequate supply of intraoperative blood products. Preservice, which is frequently performed under adverse circumstances due to uncooperative patients (secondary to drug or alcohol ingestion), also includes trying to obtain consent from the patient or responsible family member. Other preoperative services include dressing, scrubbing, and waiting to begin the operation; supervising the positioning, prepping, and draping of the patient; and ensuring that the necessary surgical instruments and supplies are present and available in the operative suite.

Intraservice

An abdominal incision is made that is large enough to allow evaluation of the entire abdominal cavity. The peritoneal surfaces are inspected for the site of violation. Hematomas, crepitus, and bile staining are sought and excluded, including all appropriate maneuvers to inspect the retroperitoneum, such as mobilization of the duodenum, ascending colon, and descending colon, and mobilization of the gastrocolic ligament to inspect the pancreas. The solid viscera are evaluated by inspection and palpation. The gastrointestinal tract from the esophagogastric junction to the peritoneal reflection of the rectum in the pelvis is evaluated and injury excluded. The grat vessels of the abdomen and the urinary tract are examined and injury excluded. All other intra-abdominal organs are systematically inspected and the absence of injury is confirmed. The abdomen is closed in layers.

Postservice

Postservice work begins after skin closure in the operating room and includes the application of sterile dressings. Postservice work also includes monitoring the patient's stability in the recovery room; writing orders; communicating with the patient's family and other health care professionals (including providing written and oral reports and orders); and all hospital visits and services performed by the surgeon, including monitoring cardiopulmonary status; monitoring and caring for the incisions; and managing antibiotic and pain medication. Discharge management includes the surgeons final examination of the patient, providing instructions for continuing care, and preparing the discharge records. In addition, all postdischarge office visits for this procedure are considered part of the postoperative work for this procedure, including removing sutures; ordering and evaluating periodic laboratory reports, if needed; and making antibiotic and pain medication adjustments.

Laparoscopy

49320 Laparoscopy, abdomen, peritoneum, and omentum, diagnostic, with or without collection of specimen(s) by brushing or washing (separate procedure)

Work Value: 5.09 // Global Period: 010

➲ ***CPT Assistant*** **Nov 99: 24, Mar 00: 9;** ***CPT Changes: An Insider's View*** **2000, 2001**

Clinical Example

A 35-year-old female with a known history of endometriosis presents with right lower quadrant pain with direct rebound tenderness and an elevated white blood cell count. The following day, her white blood cell count returns to normal, but she still has direct and rebound tenderness. She is taken to the operating room and undergoes laparoscopy. There is no evidence of acute appendicitis, mesenteric lymph adenitis, or obvious endometriosis. The entire intraperitoneal inspection is normal and nothing surgically is indicated. Postoperatively she improves and is subsequently discharged from the hospital on the third postoperative day.

Preservice

Preservice work includes taking a comprehensive history; performing a comprehensive examination to determine the patient's current medical status; reviewing the indications for the procedure and its appropriateness; obtaining informed consent; admitting the patient to the hospital; preparing the hospital records and the patient's chart in accordance with hospital policy; checking on the patient; reviewing records prior to the surgery; scrubbing for the procedure; waiting for the induction of anesthesia; and preparing the patient.

Intraservice

Intraservice work includes performing a bimanual pelvic examination to assess uterine size, position, and mobility before a uterine cannula is inserted; obtaining exposure of the cervix; grasping the anterior lip of the cervix with a tenaculum attached to an intrauterine cannula; achieving pneumoperitoneum by inserting a Veress or Touhy needle at the inferior rim of the umbilicus through a 2-mm incision; insufflating the peritoneal space with carbon dioxide gas to a pressure of 10 mm Hg; extending the 2-mm incision to 1 cm once satisfactory displacement of organs is achieved; inserting the laparoscope trocar and sleeve through the rectus fascia; removing the trocar from the sleeve; documenting the proper placement as the operating laparoscope is advanced down the trocar sleeve into the pelvis; connecting the gas hose to the trocar (once the laparoscope has been inserted a second trocar may be placed for ancillary instruments); viewing the entire abdomen and pelvis systematically and noting and/or photodocumenting the pathology; removing secondary trocars under direct vision and observing the sites for bleeding; deflating the abdomen; closing the fascia separately; closing the skin wounds; transferring the patient to a stretcher; and escorting the patient to the recovery room.

Postservice

Postservice work includes writing orders for postoperative care; accompanying the patient to the recovery room; talking with the patient's family; evaluating the patient in the recovery room; dictating the operative procedure and making periodic checks on the patient's condition; removing any drainage catheters on postoperative day 1; monitoring the patient for normal voiding; visiting the patient in the hospital for 3 days; discharging the patient on postoperative day 3 with instructions for follow-up care; and reevaluating the patient once postoperatively.

Laparoscopy
49320

The physician inserts a fiberoptic laparoscope to observe the necessary organs in these procedures.

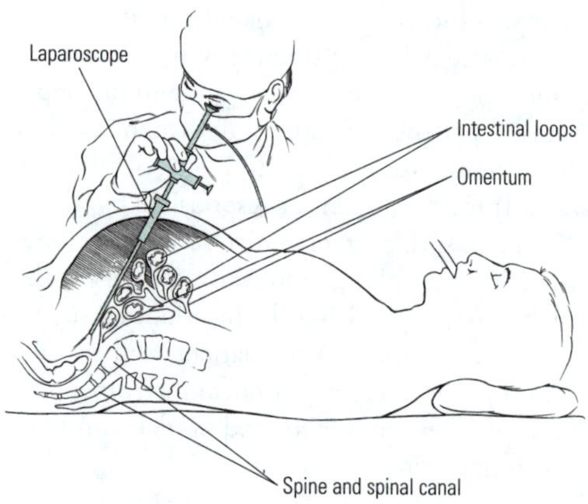

Repair

Hernioplasty, Herniorrhaphy, Herniotomy

49560 Repair initial incisional or ventral hernia; reducible

Work Value: 11.84 // Global Period: 090

➲ *CPT Assistant* Winter 93: 6, Winter 94: 14, Nov 97: 19

Clinical Example

A 67-year-old female presents with a bulge in the lateral aspect of her cholecystectomy incision. In the supine position, the bulge goes away and the fascial defect is 4 cm.

+ 49568 Implantation of mesh or other prosthesis for incisional or ventral hernia repair (List separately in addition to code for the incisional or ventral hernia repair)

Work Value: 4.88 // Global Period: ZZZ

➲ *CPT Assistant* Winter 94: 14, Nov 97: 19, Sep 01: 11, Nov 05: 15

Clinical Example

A 75-year-old male with a history of previous partial gastrectomy for peptic ulcer disease presents with a 10-cm midline fascial defect (ie, incisional hernia). In repairing the hernia, it becomes apparent that the repair will require the use of mesh.

Coding Tip for 49568

The implantation of mesh or other prosthesis is reported separately only with the incisional or ventral hernia repair codes 49560-49566.

Urinary System

Kidney

Laparoscopy

50545 Laparoscopy, surgical; radical nephrectomy (includes removal of Gerota's fascia and surrounding fatty tissue, removal of regional lymph nodes, and adrenalectomy)

Work Value: 24.93 // Global Period: 090

➲ *CPT Assistant* Oct 01: 8; *CPT Changes: An Insider's View* 2001

Clinical Example

A 32-year-old female is found to have a 3-cm renal cell carcinoma in the lower pole of the left kidney discovered on computed tomography scan for suspected gallbladder disease. The gallbladder was found to be normal. The patient wishes to avoid a large scar and elects a laparoscopic radical nephrectomy.

Preservice

Appropriate preoperative studies are obtained and reviewed. The patient is seen by the operating surgeon before being given an anesthetic. Procedure specific equipment is checked. The patient is taken to the operating room and given either general or spinal anesthesia. The patient is appropriately positioned for the procedure and prepped and draped.

Intraservice

An intra- or extraperitoneal approach is used. The abdomen is insufflated with carbon dioxide and four operating ports are placed. The left colon is taken down at the white line and reflected medially. The kidney is mobilized without opening Gerota's fascia (leaving a layer of fat over the kidney). The ureter and renal vessels are identified and ligated. (Lymph node bearing tissue along the aorta may be removed as a separate specimen.) The upper pole of the kidney is carefully dissected off of the spleen and the kidney is now entirely free within the abdomen. Two of the laparoscopic ports are connected by a 5-cm incision and the kidney is removed. The wound is closed and the laparoscopic incisions are closed.

Postservice

The surgeon waits in the operating room and assists the anesthesiologist in transferring the patient to a recovery room stretcher. The patient is transferred to the recover room. Postoperative orders are written. A detailed operative report is dictated. The surgeon talks with the patient's family about the procedure, diagnosis, and postoperative care. The patient is admitted to the hospital from the recovery room. Postoperative care for the global period is included. Hospital by-laws require that a detailed discharge summary must be dictated.

Laparoscopic Radical Nephrectomy
50545

Radical nephrectomy (includes removal of Gerota's fascia and surrounding fatty tissue, removal of regional lymph nodes, and adrenalectomy).

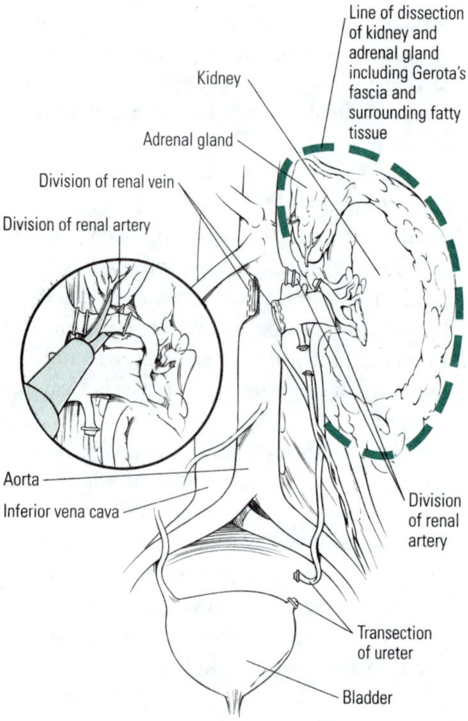

Bladder

Introduction

❺ 51720 Bladder instillation of anticarcinogenic agent (including retention time)

Work Value: 1.50 // Global Period: 000

➲ ***CPT Assistant*** **Nov 02:11;** ***CPT Changes: An Insider's View*** **2007**

Clinical Example

A 72-year-old man is four weeks postoperative transurethral resection of a noninvasive transitional carcinoma of the bladder. He is a candidate for intravesical bacille Calmette-Guerin (BCG) therapy. BCG is reconstituted and placed in the bladder per BCG protocol. Possible side effects of the BCG treatment are carefully reviewed with the patient.

Preservice

Work day prior to surgery:

Check to be sure the chemotherapeutic drug is available (BCG is the most common, less commonly used are Thiotepa, Interferon and Mitomycin). Check the schedule for the following day. Check with scheduling staff to see if the patient was notified, as drug has been ordered. Review the laboratory studies (eg complete blood cell count (CBC) if Thiotepa).

Work day of surgery:

Review procedure and post-procedure recovery with the patient and family. Answer patient and family questions; be sure informed consent is in record. Review voiding after BCG is instilled. Review urinalysis result to ensure it is infection free. Follow OSHA guidelines when the drug is mixed and prepared.

Intraservice

The patient is placed supine on the exam table and the genitalia are prepped. Local anesthetic is instilled into the urethra and a 16 French straight catheter is placed. Follow OSHA guidelines. Any residual urine is drained. The drug (most commonly BCG) is allowed to flow from a syringe by gravity slowly into the bladder. The catheter is removed and all items are carefully disposed of in a zip-lock bag per OSHA guidelines and then placed into a special chemotherapy waste container.

Postservice

Assist patient off of the exam table. Carefully record drug lot number in the medical record. Discuss the planned retention time (2 hours for BCG). Meet with the patient and family and discuss the immediate expected symptoms and signs. Conduct a postoperative pain assessment. Write orders and prescriptions. Dictate detailed office note.

Urodynamics

51726 Complex cystometrogram (eg, calibrated electronic equipment)

Work Value: 1.71 // Global Period: 000

➲ *CPT Assistant* Sep 02: 6

Clinical Example

A 66-year-old female complains of urinary frequency, and urgency with residual urine of 120 mL.

Preservice

Preservice includes the services provided from the day before the surgery or diagnostic procedure until the time of the procedure and may include obtaining and reviewing records, previous history, laboratory studies, and urologic X rays before the procedure; communicating with other health professionals (eg, the family physician and anesthesiologist); communicating with the patient to explain the procedure, operative risks and benefits, and to obtain informed consent; dressing for surgery; waiting for anesthesia (the administration of general or spinal anesthesia); positioning, prepping, and draping the patient; scrubbing; preparing and checking needed equipment for the surgery or procedure; and performing any other non-skin-to-skin work in the operating room or procedure suite. Preservice may also include calibrating electronic equipment; inserting a urodynamic catheter and measuring postvoid residual urine; connecting the catheter to an infusion pump and pressure transducer and zero transducer to atmospheric pressure; and purging air from the tubing. Preservice does not include the consultation or evaluation at which time the decision to provide the procedure is made. Calibrate electronic equipment. Insert urodynamic catheter and measure post-void residual urine. Connect catheter to infusion pump and pressure transducer and zero transducer to atmospheric pressure. Purge air from tubing.

Intraservice

This is an interactive examination between the patient and examiner. The procedural steps vary considerably depending upon the cystometric findings. Infuse fluid into bladder and record bladder sensations and bladder volume at predefined physiologic landmarks. Each rise in vesical pressure must be accounted for by careful observations. If involuntary detrusor contractions are not demonstrated, assist the patient to a sitting and/or standing position and repeat infusion. Check the patient for stress incontinence.

Postservice

Postservice may include all of the postprocedure care on the day of the procedure; monitoring patient stabilization; writing postoperative orders; communicating with the patient and/or the patient's family and referring physician (including providing written and telephone reports); other nonskin-to-skin work in the procedure suite; other follow-up care including writing prescriptions before the patient is discharged, if applicable, and interpreting results.

51784 Electromyography studies (EMG) of anal or urethral sphincter, other than needle, any technique

Work Value: 1.53 // Global Period: 000

➲ *CPT Assistant* Sep 02: 6

Clinical Example

A child (any sex, any age) presents with a voiding dysfunction. Self-adhesive electrodes are placed perianally to determine whether the muscles are coordinated during filling and voiding. The urologist reads the graphic recordings measuring EMG activity during a series of filling and voiding trails. The urologist ensures the signal is reliable at all times by replacing electrodes as necessary. The urologist interprets the level of activity and determines whether the muscle activity is increasing and decreasing at appropriate times.

51795 Voiding pressure studies (VP); bladder voiding pressure, any technique

Work Value: 1.53 // Global Period: 000

➲ *CPT Assistant* Dec 01: 7, Sep 02: 6

Clinical Example

A 69-year-old male complains of urinary frequency, urgency, weak stream, and a postvoid residual urine of 210 mL.

Preservice

Preservice includes the services provided from the day before the surgery or diagnostic procedure until the time of the procedure and may include obtaining and reviewing records, previous history, laboratory studies, and urologic X rays before the procedure; communicating with other health professionals (eg, the family physician and anesthesiologist); communicating with the patient to explain the procedure, operative risks and benefits, and to obtain informed consent; dressing for surgery; waiting for anesthesia (the administration of general or spinal anesthesia); positioning, prepping, and draping the patient; scrubbing; preparing and checking the needed equipment for the surgery or procedure; and any other nonskin-to-skin work in the operating room or procedure suite. Preservice may also include calibrating the electronic equipment, inserting a urodynamic catheter, measuring postvoid residual urine, connecting the catheter to an infusion pump and pressure transducer and zero transducer to atmospheric pressure, and purging air from the tubing. Preservice does not include the consultation or evaluation at which time the decision to provide the procedure is made. Calibrate electronic equipment. Insert urodynamic catheter and measure post-void residual urine. Connect catheter to infusion pump and pressure transducer and zero transducer to atmospheric pressure. Purge air from tubing.

Intraservice

This is an interactive examination between the patient and examiner. The procedural steps vary considerably depending upon the cystometric findings. Infuse fluid into the bladder and record bladder sensations and bladder volume at predefined physiologic landmarks. Ask the patient to try to void when he feels full. Each rise in vesical pressure must be accounted for by careful observations to distinguish detrusor contractions from rises in abdominal pressure. If detrusor contractions are not demonstrated, assist the patient with provocative maneuvers such as turning on running water or helping him relax. If the patient is still unable to void, terminate the examination.

Postservice

Postservice may include all of the postprocedure care on the day of the procedure; monitoring patient stabilization; writing postoperative orders; communicating with the patient and/or the patient's family and referring physician (including providing written and telephone reports); other non skin-to-skin work in the procedure suite; and other follow-up care, including writing prescriptions before the patient is discharged, if applicable, and interpreting results.

51798 Measurement of post-voiding residual urine and/or bladder capacity by ultrasound, non-imaging

Work Value: 0.00 // Global Period: XXX

➲ *CPT Assistant* Dec 05: 3;
CPT Changes: An Insider's View 2003

Clinical Example

A 70-year-old male complains of progressive decrease in the force of his urinary flow, urgency, frequency, and nocturia times five. As a part of his urologic evaluation, a residual urine volume needs to be determined. With the patient supine on the exam table, a dedicated ultrasound machine is used to measure the residual urine immediately after the patient voids. The residual urine volume is measured at 655 mL; therefore, the patient is asked to go to the bathroom again to try to empty more completely. He is then rescanned and the urine volume is measured at 608 mL.

Preservice

Ask the patient to empty his bladder completely in the bathroom. Have the patient disrobe to allow examination of pubic area. Position and drape the patient in a supine position on the exam table. Turn on the ultrasound machine and select the gender-appropriate mode.

Intraservice

Palpate the abdominal area to identify the pubic bone. Apply ultrasound jelly to the suprapubic area. Scan the suprapubic area repeatedly, typically three to six times. If the volume is high, as in the vignette, ask the patient to void again and repeat the procedure. Clean off the jelly from the patient's abdominal area.

Postservice

The machine notes the scan with the largest volume. Print the bladder image along with the volume of urine in milliliters.

51798

Measurement of post-voiding

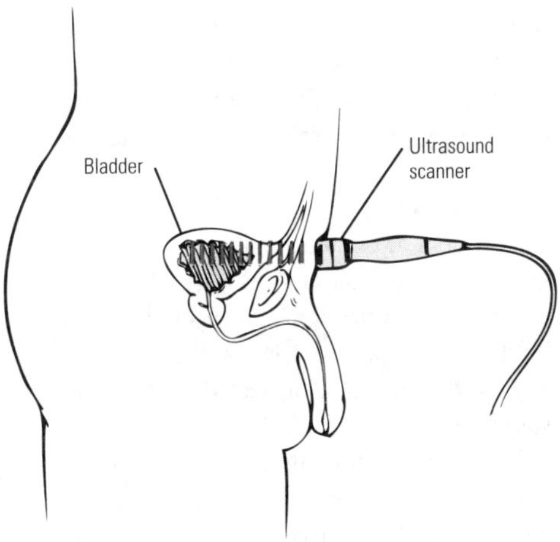

Laparoscopy

51990 Laparoscopy, surgical; urethral suspension for stress incontinence

Work Value: 13.26 // Global Period: 090

➲ ***CPT Assistant*** **Nov 99: 26, May 00: 4;** ***CPT Changes: An Insider's View*** **2000**

Clinical Example

A 55-year-old female with genuine stress urinary incontinence has failed medical therapy and wears four to five pads a day. Urodynamic testing demonstrates a compliant bladder without uninhibited contractions and good detrusor activity. She has tried Kegel exercises without success. When offered open surgery and laparoscopic repair, she chooses the laparoscopic urethral suspension. Following discharge, the patient receives normal follow-up care in the office.

Preservice

Preservice work may include obtaining and reviewing hospital admission laboratory studies and urologic X rays before the procedure; communicating with other health care professionals (eg, family physician, anesthesiologist); communicating with the patient to explain the operative risks and benefits and to obtain informed consent; dressing for surgery; waiting for anesthesia (eg, placing the central arterial and venous lines and administering general, spinal, and/or epidural anesthesia); positioning, prepping, and draping the patient; scrubbing; and preparing and checking the needed equipment for surgery and any other non–"skin-to-skin" work in the operating room.

Intraservice

Intraservice work includes placing the patient in a low lithotomy position; employing an extraperitoneal or transperitoneal approach using 4 trocar-sheath units placed in a diamond configuration to access the pelvic organs; determining the bladder neck region and exposing the periurethral tissue and Cooper's ligament; placing two stitches of 2-0 nonabsorbable suture laparoscopically into the endopelvic fascia at the bladder neck region on each side and securing them to the ipsilateral Cooper's ligament; tying the sutures with extracorporeal or intracorporeal knots so as to create a hammock-type suspension of the bladder neck; and removing the ports and closing the sites in the usual fashion.

Postservice

Postservice work includes all postoperative care on the day of the procedure, including stabilizing the patient; writing postoperative orders; communicating with the patient's family and referring physician (including providing written and telephone reports); and performing other non–"skin-to-skin" work in the operating room. Postservice work also includes all postoperative hospital visits and discharge day management and all postdischarge office visits for this procedure for 90 days after the day of the operation (which includes evaluating periodic laboratory reports and making medication adjustments).

Laparoscopic Sling Suspension
Urinary Incontinence
51990

Nonabsorbable sutures are placed laparoscopically into the endopelvic fascia at the bladder neck region on each side and secured to the ipsilateral pectineal ligament. The sutures are tied using extra vaginal-urethral knots so as to create a hammock type suspension of the bladder neck, without urethral occlusion.

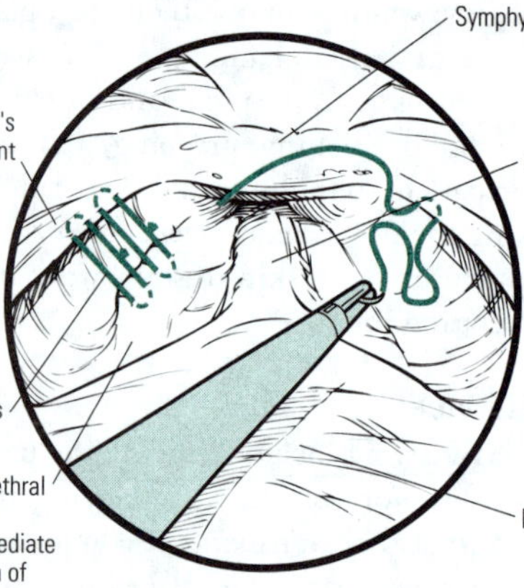

Coding Tip for 51990

If an open sling operation for stress incontinence is performed, code 57288 should be reported.

Endoscopy—Cystoscopy, Urethroscopy, Cystourethroscopy

⑤ **52000** Cystourethroscopy (separate procedure)

Work Value: 2.23 // Global Period: 000

➲ *CPT Assistant* Oct 00: 7, May 01: 5, Sep 04: 11, Oct 05: 23

Clinical Example

A 67-year-old male with a 50-pack-per-year history of cigarette smoking has had gross hematuria for the past year. Cystourethroscopy is explained to the patient and then performed to evaluate the bladder. The findings are discussed with the patient.

Preservice

The day before the procedure, check the video equipment. Check the schedule for the following day and confirm that the necessary instruments and personnel will be available. Check with the scheduling staff to see if the patient was notified. Review the laboratory studies. Confirm that the necessary imaging studies are available for review at the time of the planned procedure.

On the day of the surgery, change into scrub clothes. Discuss the procedure with the anesthesiologist, if appropriate. Review the surgical procedure and the postoperative recovery with the patient and the patient's family. Answer the patient's and family's questions. Confirm that informed consent is in the patient's record. Evaluate the patient's need for antibiotics. Take time out for patient identification. Position the patient on the cystoscopy table. Prep and drape the patient.

Intraservice

Inject local anesthetic jelly into the urethra and apply a penile clamp. Assemble the endoscopic equipment, connect the video system, and apply defogger to the lenses and video source. Connect the irrigation source. Connect the light source and white balance. Insert the endoscope into the urethra. Inspect the external meatus and fossa navicularis. Inspect the urethra (pendulous and bulbar in male). Inspect the external urinary sphincter. Inspect the prostatic urethra including the presence/absence of hypertrophy, veru montanium, prostatic utricle, and lateral lobes. Assess the bladder neck (median bar and median lobe). Inspect the trigone. Identify the ureteral orifices (size and location). Check for efflux of urine from each ureter. Inspect the bladder mucosa (trabeculation, cellules, diverticuli, lesions, and stones). Assess the bladder's capacity, compliance, and sensation. Retroflex the scope if flexible (or if using a rigid scope change lenses) to inspect the dome of the bladder with suprapubic manual compression. Drain the bladder. Disconnect the video equipment and light source. Remove the endoscope.

Postservice
Assist in transferring the patient from the cystoscopy table. Assist in transferring the patient to the recovery area. Conduct a postoperative pain assessment. Write postoperative orders and prescriptions. Discuss the procedure and findings with the patient. Discuss the outcome of the procedure with the referring physician, noting any unusual aspects of postoperative care (eg, cardiac disease, diabetic management). Fill out and complete a bladder mapping diagram. Dictate a detailed operative narrative. Schedule the patient's next appointment.

Coding Tip for 52000
Code 52000 is designated as a separate procedure and is not reported when performed with another procedure of which it would be considered an integral component.

Vesical Neck and Prostate

52647 Laser coagulation of prostate, including control of postoperative bleeding, complete (vasectomy, meatotomy, cystourethroscopy, urethral calibration and/or dilation, and internal urethrotomy are included if performed)

Work Value: 11.15 // Global Period: 090

➲ ***CPT Assistant*** **Nov 97: 20, Mar 98: 11, Apr 01: 4;** ***CPT Changes: An Insider's View*** **2006**

Clinical Example
A 70-year-old male has severe, obstructive symptoms secondary to benign prostatic hypertrophy (BPH).

Preservice
Preservice work includes consulting with the anesthesia staff; making sure the laser has been tested and calibrated; positioning the patient; making sure the video system is working; waiting for the spinal or general anesthetic to take effect; prepping the patient; and testing the fire laser.

Intraservice
During cystoscopic examination under anesthesia, a 25-g obstructive prostate is noted. A right-angle laser fiber is passed into the prostatic fossa through a continuous-flow resectoscope and laser energy is delivered for 90 seconds to each of four quadrants and to the median lobe. The procedure is approximately 30 minutes in duration. A suprapubic tube may be inserted prior to the procedure or a Foley catheter inserted following the procedure. The procedure is performed on an ambulatory basis or for a 1-day stay. The patient returns to the office on the fifth postoperative day and the Foley catheter is removed or the patient is instructed to turn the valve on the suprapubic tube to initiate a voiding trail. He may be placed on an intermittent catheter until successful voiding begins, a process that may take up to 2 weeks. Though not common for all, some patients may also require placement of a suprapubic tube.

Postservice
Postservice may include all of the postprocedure care on the day of the procedure; monitoring patient stabilization; writing postoperative orders; communicating with the patient and/or the patient's family and referring physician (including providing written and telephone reports); and explaining to the patient the use of the suprapubic tube or Foley catheter.

Coding Tip for 52647
Code 52647 describes noncontact laser coagulation of the prostate. This code is intended to describe laser procedures that primarily heat the prostate and require sloughing for the treatment to be complete.

52648 Laser vaporization of prostate, including control of postoperative bleeding, complete (vasectomy, meatotomy, cystourethroscopy, urethral calibration and/or dilation, internal urethrotomy and transurethral resection of prostate are included if performed)

Work Value: 12.00 // Global Period: 090

➲ ***CPT Assistant*** **Mar 98: 11, Apr 01: 5, Jul 05: 15;** ***CPT Changes: An Insider's View*** **2006**

Clinical Example
A 75-year-old male has severe, obstructive symptoms secondary to benign prostatic hypertrophy (BPH).

Preservice
Preservice includes consulting with the anesthesia staff; making sure the laser has been tested and calibrated; positioning the patient; making sure the video system is working; waiting for the spinal or general anesthetic to take effect; prepping the patient; and testing the fire laser.

Intraservice
During cystoscopic examination under anesthesia, a 65-g obstructive prostate is noted. A right-angle laser fiber is passed into the prostate fossa through a continuous-flow resectoscope with the delivery of laser energy for 45 seconds at a time. Prostate tissue is vaporized at 20 different points within the prostatic fossa, ultimately creating a resected cavity similar to a transurethral resection of the prostate. After completion of the laser procedure, a resectoscope sheath may be inserted transurethrally to resect debris and remaining prostate tissue. The procedure is approximately an hour in duration. A catheter is placed and the patient is discharged on the second postoperative day. He returns to the office on the fifth postoperative day and his catheter is removed with a voiding trail. Though not common for all, some patients may also require placement of a suprapubic tube.

Postservice
Postservice may include all of the postprocedure care on the day of the procedure; monitoring patient stabilization; writing postoperative orders; communicating with the patient and/or the patient's family and referring physician (including providing written and telephone reports); and explaining to the patient the use of the suprapubic tube or Foley catheter.

Contact Laser Vaporization of Prostate
52648

A laser is used to vaporize the prostate.

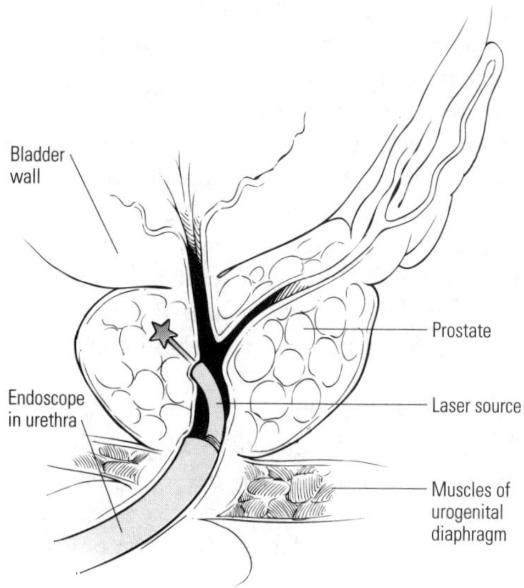

Coding Tip for 52648
Code 52648 describes contact laser vaporization with or without transurethral resection of the prostate. This code is used to report laser procedures that use a contact tip or high-power density.

Male Genital System

Prostate

Incision

⑤ 55700 Biopsy, prostate; needle or punch, single or multiple, any approach

Work Value: 2.58 // Global Period: 000

➲ *CPT Assistant* May 96: 3

Clinical Example
A 65-year-old male has a persistent elevation of his prostate-specific antigen. Multiple sector biopsies of the prostate under local anesthesia are performed. Expectations and potential finding of the biopsies are discussed.

Preservice
The day before the procedure, check the schedule for the following day and confirm that the necessary instruments and personnel will be available. Confirm that the ultrasound machine is available and working. Check with the scheduling staff to see if the patient was notified. Review the laboratory studies. Confirm that the necessary imaging studies are available for review at the time of the planned procedure. On the day of the surgery, change into scrub clothes. Review the procedure and postoperative recovery with the patient and the patient's family. Answer the patient's and family's questions. Make sure informed consent is in the patient's record. Confirm that the patient has taken enema and preoperative antibiotics. Confirm that the patient is off of anticoagulants and/or nonsteroidal anti-inflammatory medications. Position the patient on the exam/ultrasound table.

Intraservice
Take time out for patient identification. Position the patient on his left side with knees flexed (for a right-handed urologist). Repeat the digital rectal exam and dilate the anus. Introduce the transrectal probe into the rectum. Infiltrate local anesthetic (usually 10 ccs of 1% lidocaine) into the base of each seminal vesicle, around both sides of the prostatic capsule, and at both apices of the prostate. (Usually a total of 12 sector biopsies are taken from the apex, base, peripheral zone, central zone, and specific hypoechoic areas on both the right and left sides of the prostate.) After each individual biopsy, remove the biopsy gun from the transrectal probe (which remains in the rectum). Remove each specimen from the biopsy needle and place them on the telfa pad. Recock the gun and reinsert it through probe for the next biopsy. Place each of the 12 prostate biopsy samples in a formalin-filled container and label each container with the patient's identification information and the location of the biopsy. Remove the rectal probe. Apply rectal pressure for an appropriate amount of time.

Postservice
Assist in transferring the patient from the operating table to the postoperative stretcher. Review the recovery area care and medications with staff. Meet with the patient and the patient's family and discuss the procedure, expected outcome, and planned postoperative care. Conduct a postoperative pain assessment. Discuss with the patient what the pathologist will do with the tissue and when the biopsy result will be available. Call the referring physician regarding the outcome of the procedure and any unusual aspects of postoperative care (eg, cardiac disease, diabetic management). Dictate an operative report.

Coding Tip for 55700
If imaging guidance is performed, code 76942 may be reported.

Laparoscopy

55866 Laparoscopy, surgical prostatectomy, retropubic radical, including nerve sparing

Work Value: 32.25 // Global Period: 090

➲ *CPT Assistant* Jun 03: 8;
CPT Changes: An Insider's View 2003

Clinical Example
A 48-year-old male with a prostate-specific antigen of 3.5 undergoes a prostate biopsy that reveals Gleason 7 adenocarcinoma of both lobes. He is counseled on the risks and benefits of surgery versus radiation and has chosen laparoscopic radical prostatectomy.

Preservice
The day before surgery, review the preoperative lab results. Review the patient's medical record. Write the preoperative orders (to be faxed to hospital).

On the day of the surgery, change into scrub clothes. Review the surgical procedure and the postoperative recovery in and out of hospital with the patient and the patient's family. Answer the patient's and family's questions and be sure informed consent is in the patient's record. Speak to the anesthesiologist about the expected length of the procedure and any special concerns about this particular patient (eg, teeth, positioning, unusual medical problems). Position the patient on the operating table. Verify that all necessary instruments are available.

Intraservice

Transport the patient to the operating room and place the patient in the modified lithotomy position. Prep and drape the lower abdomen in standard fashion. Achieve a pneumoperitoneum in standard fashion and place four trocars. Introduce the laparoscope and dissect the seminal vesicles and vas deferens. Incise the peritoneum at the reflection point of the anterior rectum and posterior bladder. Identify and then divide the vas deferens on each side. Carefully dissect the seminal vesicles out using the harmonic scalpel to divide all bleeding vessels until the structures are completely freed. Dissect the space just posterior to the seminal vesicles to open the Denonvilliers fascia, thereby revealing a prerectal fat plane. Completely mobilize the opening of the peritoneum and the bladder. Divide the median umbilical ligaments and urachus close to the umbilicus. Using careful blunt dissection, reflect the bladder away from the abdominal wall to expose the endopelvic fascia. Clear away the fat overlying the endopelvic fascia and incise the endofascia bilaterally to free the prostate away from the lateral pelvic side wall. Develop and then suture ligate the dorsal vein complex with a 2-0 absorbable surgical suture. Open the bladder neck. Remove the Foley and place a curved urethral sound to aide in traction of the prostate. (This allows identification of the posterior bladder neck, which is then carefully dissected away from the base of the prostate.) Take down the area of the pedicles of the prostate. Open the tissue overlying the seminal vesicles and then withdraw these structures into the area of dissection and use them as traction. Take down both lateral pedicles, up to the level near the apex. Divide the dorsal vein complex. Use careful sharp dissection around the apex of the prostate. Rock the prostate back and forth and continue dissecting along the lateral pedicle plane to define the apex of the prostate posteriorly. Identify the urethra and use sharp dissection to divide the anterior and posterior urethra and the rectourethralis muscle. Undo the final attachments and withdraw the specimen in the endocath sac. Ensure hemostasis. Perform the vesicourethral anastomosis with an interrupted 2-0 absorbable sterile suture. Place a 20-French Foley catheter through the anastomosis. Place a 19-French JP drain through one of the abdominal side ports. Inspect all of the four trocar sites, then inspect all surgical sites at 5-mmHg pressure before removing the trocars under direct vision.

Postoperative Same Day Work Through Discharge From Recovery: Apply dressings. Assist in transferring the patient from the operating table to the postoperative stretcher. Accompany the anesthesiologist and the patient to the recovery area. Assist in transferring the patient to the recovery area bed. Write postoperative orders. Review recovery area care and medications with the staff. Meet with the patient's family and discuss the procedure, expected outcome, and the planned postoperative care in hospital and out of the hospital. Discuss the procedure with the patient as necessary in the recovery area when the patient is awake. Call the referring physician regarding the outcome of the procedure and any unusual aspects of postoperative care (eg, cardiac disease, diabetic management). Dictate a detailed operative narrative.

Postservice

Examine the patient. Check the wound and the patient's progress. Review all of the patient's hospital medical record notes (eg, nursing, pharmacy, dietary, discharge planner). Answer the patient's and family's questions. Answer the nursing and other staff's questions. Write any further necessary orders. Write a note in progress note section of the patient's medical record.

Postoperative Other Hospital Work; Postoperative Day 1 Until Discharge Day: Examine and talk to the patient. Check wounds and dressings. Discuss the patient's progress with the patient and the patient's family. Review all of the patient's hospital medical record notes. Discuss with the patient postoperative care of the wound at home. Answer the nursing and other staff's questions. Answer the patient's and family's questions. Write orders in the patient's medical record. Write progress notes.

Discharge Day Work: Examine and talk with the patient and the patient's family. Check wounds and the patient's progress. Review all of the patient's hospital medical record notes. Answer the patient's and family's questions. Write orders for postdischarge care. Write prescriptions for postoperative medications. Discuss the postoperative care of the wound with the patient and the patient's family. Dictate a detailed hospital discharge summary.

Postoperative Office Work; After Discharge From Hospital: Examine the patient and check vital signs. Talk with the patient and the patient's family. Review with the patient bladder control exercises after the catheter is removed. Answer questions from the patient and the patient's family. Write necessary prescriptions. Remove sutures. Schedule the next office visit. Mark the appropriate diagnosis and CPT code on the superbill. Dictate patient progress notes for the office medical record. Dictate a letter to the referring physician.

Other Procedures

55873 Cryosurgical ablation of the prostate (includes ultrasonic guidance for interstitial cryosurgical probe placement)

Work Value: 20.25 // Global Period: 090

➲ *CPT Assistant* **Apr 01: 4, Sep 02: 9, Jun 03: 8;** *CPT Changes: An Insider's View* **2001**

Clinical Example

A 62-year-old male with clinically localized prostate cancer, having considered all available treatment options, has elected to have cryosurgical ablation of the prostate.

Preservice

Appropriate preoperative studies are obtained and reviewed. The patient is seen by the operating surgeon before being given an anesthetic. Procedure-specific equipment is checked. The patient is taken to the operating room and given either general or spinal anesthesia. The patient is appropriately positioned for the procedure and then prepped and draped.

Intraservice

The patient is placed in the doral lithotomy position. The skin of the perineum and suprapubic area is prepped and draped and the bladder palpated. The bladder is filled in a retrograde fashion using a syringe or catheter. A trocar puncture is made into the bladder. A guidewire is introduced into the bladder through the sheath once the trocar itself is removed. A skin incision is made to facilitate catheter advancement over the guidewire. A suprapubic tube is placed. This accomplished, the guidewire is removed, the balloon inflated, return checked through the catheter port, and the catheter is sutured to the skin. A guidewire is then placed into the bladder through the urethra and a urethral warming device is advanced into the bladder over the guidewire. The guidewire is then removed. The transrecatal ultrasound probe is positioned in the rectum. (See the separate CPT descriptor, Ultrasonic guidance for interstitial cryosurgical probe placement.) Multiple needle passes are made into the prostate through the perineum. The stylet of each needle is removed and an angle tipped wire advanced through the needle into the prostate. The needle sheath is then removed. The process is repeated multiple times until all needles have been replaced with angle-tipped wires. A small incision is made on the perineum where each guidewire enters the skin to facilitate passage of a series of sequential dilators. Using these dilators, a tract is made through the perineum and pelvic floor into the prostate. Finally, multiple cryosurgical probes are placed over the guidewires and into the prostate under ultrasonic guidance. The cryoprobes are cooled to the appropriate setting. The iceballs growth and regression is monitored with ultrasound. A second freeze is routinely done. A third freeze may be done in the area of the urethral diaphragm and prostatic apex by withdrawing the posterior probes. After all areas are treated, the cryoprobes are thawed and removed. The cryoprobe sheath sites in the perineum may be closed with sutures. A compression dressing is applied.

Postservice

The surgeon waits in the operating room and assists the anesthesiologist in transferring the patient to a recovery room stretcher. The patient is transferred to the recovery room. Postoperative orders are written. A detailed operative report is dictated. The surgeon talks with the patient's family about the procedure, diagnosis, and postoperative care. The patient is either admitted to the hospital or dismissed home later that day after being assessed by the surgeon. Hospital by-laws require that a detailed discharge summary must be dictated. All postoperative care for 90 days is included.

Coding Tip for 55873

Ultrasonic guidance is an inclusive component of code 55873 and therefore, should not be reported separately.

Other Procedures

55875 Transperineal placement of needles or catheters into prostate for interstitial radioelement application, with or without cystoscopy

Work Value: 13.31 // Global Period: 090

➲ *CPT Assistant* Apr 04: 6; *CPT Changes: An Insider's View* 2007

Clinical Example

A 60-year-old male presents with localized stage A1-B2 prostate cancer without evidence of metastatic disease. Previous biopsy confirmed cancer.

Preservice

Preservice work begins with assessing the patient, taking a history, reviewing current prescriptions, obtaining and reviewing current imaging and laboratory studies, communicating with other health care professionals, and communicating with the patient and/or the patient's family to explain the operative risks and benefits and obtain informed consent. Other preoperative services include dressing, scrubbing, and waiting to begin the operation; supervising the positioning, prepping, and draping of the patient; and ensuring that the necessary surgical instruments and supplies are present and available in the operative suite.

Intraservice

The patient is placed under general or spinal anesthesia. Under ultrasound guidance, the urologist positions the template for the exact coordinates as was done in the preoperative ultrasound study. The urologist transperineally stabilizes the prostate to the bladder with sutures or needles. The urologist transperineally inserts approximately 30–45 needles into the prostate according to the coordinates. The radioactive seeds are inserted through the needles and placed (maximum tolerance allowed: 12 mm) to allow for the entire prostate field to be irradiated. The urologist performs a cystoscopy to ensure that no seeds were misdirected into the bladder. The prostate stabilization needles are removed and a Foley catheter is placed.

Postservice

The patient is observed as an outpatient for 24 hours and then discharged. The patient returns to urologist in 1 week, 1 month, and 3 months after the procedure for postoperative evaluation.

Female Genital System

Vulva, Perineum, and Introitus

Excision

56605 Biopsy of vulva or perineum (separate procedure); one lesion

Work Value: 1.10 // Global Period: 000

➲ *CPT Assistant* Sep 00: 9

Clinical Example

A 60-year-old female reports a vulvar lesion. An examination of the vulva and perineum discloses a 0.5-cm dysplastic-appearing lesion. A vulvar biopsy is warranted to evaluate the etiology of this lesion to determine the appropriate treatment.

Preservice

The example assumes the procedure is done on the same day as the complaint was noted. The procedure and potential complications are explained in detail and informed consent is obtained.

Intraservice

The vulva is prepared with an antiseptic solution. Local anesthesia is injected surrounding the site to be biopsied. Using a scalpel or punch biopsy instrument, the lesion is incised or completely excised. Simple suturing may be required.

Postservice

The biopsy site is observed for bleeding. Prescriptions for analgesics and instructions for perineal care are given to the patient. As this procedure has a 0 day global period, this completes the postservice work. The patient is asked to return for reevaluation in 1 to 2 weeks. The pathology report is reviewed and discussed with the patient at that time.

Vagina

Introduction

57150 Irrigation of vagina and/or application of medicament for treatment of bacterial, parasitic, or fungoid disease

Work Value: 0.55 // Global Period: 000

Clinical Example

A 31-year-old G2 P2 female comes into the office for the treatment of resistant monilial vaginitis. The vagina is swabbed with gentian violet.

Preservice

Once the diagnosis is confirmed, the procedure is explained to the patient and informed consent is obtained.

Intraservice

Intraservice includes an examination of the vagina and swabbing the inside of the vagina with gentian violet.

Postservice

The patient is observed for possible side effects to the procedure and is sent home with instructions about sexual activity.

---

❺ **57160** Fitting and insertion of pessary or other intravaginal support device

Work Value: 0.89 // Global Period: 000

➲ *CPT Assistant* Nov 96: 9, Oct 98: 11, Jun 00: 11

Clinical Example

A 74-year-old G4 P4 postmenopausal female presents with cystocele and uterine prolapse. In addition, she suffers from chronic obstructive pulmonary disease, which makes her a poor candidate for surgical intervention. Pelvic examination reveals that her prolapse is reducible and that she has no evidence of laceration or ulceration of her vaginal mucosa. The insertion of a pessary or intravaginal support device is recommended.

Preservice

Preservice work includes explaining the procedure to the patient, obtaining informed consent, and placing the patient in the proper position.

Intraservice

Intraservice work includes examining the patient to determine the proper type and size of pessary, fitting the pessary into the vagina (often multiple sizes have to be tried), examining the patient for incontinence, providing instruction to the patient on inserting and removing the pessary, observing the patient inserting and removing the pessary, and then re-examining the patient for fit of the pessary after the patient walks around.

Postservice

Postservice work includes providing the patient with instructions for care of the pessary as well as follow-up procedures, consulting with the patient's family, dictating the procedure report, and completing the patient report.

Repair

❺ 57240 Anterior colporrhaphy, repair of cystocele with or without repair of urethrocele

Work Value: 11.42 // Global Period: 090

➲ *CPT Assistant* Winter 90: 7, Jan 97: 3, Jun 02: 5

Clinical Example

A 68-year-old G3 P3 female presents with a mass bulging from her vagina that is made worse by standing for long periods of time or coughing. She had a hysterectomy 20 years ago and denies stress urinary incontinence. On exam she has an anterior midline defect that protrudes to the introitus with valsalva. She has good lateral, apical, and posterior support. An anterior colporrhaphy is recommended.

Preservice

Preservice work includes taking a comprehensive history and performing a comprehensive examination to determine the patient's current medical status; reviewing the indications for the procedure and its appropriateness; obtaining informed consent; admitting the patient to the hospital; preparing the hospital records and chart in accordance with hospital policy; checking on the patient and reviewing labs, X rays, and records before the surgery; scrubbing for the procedure, and waiting for the induction of anesthesia and the preparation of the patient.

Intraservice

Intraservice work includes making an incision in the anterior vagina from beneath the urethral meatus to the vaginal apex; dissecting the pubourethral and pubocervical tissue from the vaginal apex; closing the pubourethral tissue to complete the repair of the urethrocele; closing the pubocervical tissue to complete the repair of the mid-line cystocele; excising excess vaginal epithelium; draining the bladder; obtaining hemostatsis; closing the wound; applying dressings and packing; and removing manipulators, probes and packs.

Postservice

Postservice work includes completing the operating room record; evaluating and stabilizing the patient; writing postoperative orders; dictating the operative report; consulting with the patient's family; assessing the patient's status; removing packs, drains, catheters, sutures, and staples; performing discharge care (eg, reviewing laboratory reports, providing patient instructions, completing discharge summary/medical records); and conducting follow-up visits (eg, reviewing pathology and laboratory reports, removing packs, catheters, drains, sutures, and staples).

---

❺ 57260 Combined anteroposterior colporrhaphy;

Work Value: 14.36 // Global Period: 090

➲ *CPT Assistant* Jun 02: 5

Clinical Example

A 72-year-old G2 P2 female who underwent a hysterectomy 25 years ago presents for evaluation of worsening vulvar pressure and a mass that protrudes from the vagina when she coughs or stands for a long period of time. She denies stress urinary incontinence but does have problems emptying with defecation. On examination she has an anterior midline defect and a posterior midline defect with good apical and lateral support of the vaginal cuff. An anterior and posterior colporrhaphy is recommended.

Preservice

Preservice includes taking a comprehensive history and performing a comprehensive examination to determine the patient's current medical status; reviewing the indications for the procedure and its appropriateness; obtaining informed consent; admitting the patient to the hospital; preparing the hospital records and chart in accordance with hospital policy; checking on the patient and reviewing labs, X rays, and records before the surgery; scrubbing for the procedure, and waiting for the induction of anesthesia and the preparation of the patient.

Intraservice
Intraservice includes making an incision in the posterior vaginal epithelium; dissecting the vaginal epithelium from the underlying rectovaginal septum; carrying out the dissection to the vaginal apex superiorly and bilaterally to the levator musculature; conducting a rectal examination to delineate the extent of the defect; closing the rectovaginal septum from the apex of the vagina to the distal vagina incorporating some of the lavator musculature bilaterally; closing the transverse perineal musculature to re-establish the perineal body; attaching the distal rectovaginal septum to the perineal body; draining the bladder; making an incision in the anterior vagina from beneath the urethral meatus to the vaginal apex; dissecting the pubourethral and pubocervical tissue from the vaginal apex; closing the pubourethral tissue to complete the repair of the urethrocele; closing the pubocervical tissue to complete the repair of the midline cystocele; excising the excess vaginal epithelium; obtaining hemostasis; closing the wound; packing the vagina; applying dressings and packings; and removing manipulators, probes, and packs.

Postservice
Postservice includes completing the operating room record; evaluating and stabilizing the patient; writing postoperative orders; dictating the operative report; consulting with the patient's family; assessing the patient's status; removing packs, drains, catheters, sutures, and staples; performing discharge care (eg, reviewing laboratory reports, providing patient instructions, completing discharge summary/medical records); and performing follow-up visits (eg, reviewing the pathology and laboratory reports, removing packs, catheters, drains, sutures, and staples).

---

⑤ **57288** Sling operation for stress incontinence (eg, fascia or synthetic)

Work Value: 14.01 // Global Period: 090

➲ *CPT Assistant* Nov 99: 28, May 00: 4, Oct 00: 7, Apr 02: 18, Jun 02: 7; *CPT Changes: An Insider's View* 2000

Clinical Example
A 66-year-old female has documented urinary incontinence and urethral dysfunction. After suitable counseling on the various treatment options, she elects to undergo a sling operation for stress incontinence (eg, fascia or synthetic material).

Preservice
The day before surgery, review the preoperative lab results, review the medical record, and write the preoperative orders to be emailed or faxed to the hospital. On the day of surgery, change into scrub clothes. Review the surgical procedure and the postoperative recovery in and out of the hospital with the patient and the patient's family. Answer the patient's and familys questions and be sure informed consent is in the patient's record. Speak to the anesthesiologist about the expected length of the procedure and any special concerns about this particular patient (eg, teeth, positioning, unusual medical problems). Take time out for patient identification. Wait for the anesthesiologist to administer the anesthetic.

Intraservice
Position the patient in the lithotomy position. Prep the lower abdomen and vagina. Place the Foley catheter and drain the bladder. Make vaginal incision (s). Develop perivesical space bilaterally. Perforate the endopelvic fascia bilaterally. Make suprapubic incision(s). Appropriately place the fascial ligature carrier. Properly position the sling (fascia or synthetic). Suture the sling in place under the proper tension. Close the abdominal and vaginal incisions. Place the vaginal pack.

Postservice

Postoperative Same Day Through Discharge from Recovery: Wait for the anesthesiologist to awaken the patient. Transfer the patient off the operating table. Place the Foley catheter to the drainage system. Go with the patient and anesthesiologist to the recovery area bed. Assist in transferring the patient to the recovery bed. Review recovery area care with staff. Meet with the patient's family and discuss the procedure, expected outcome, planned postoperative care in and out of the hospital. Discuss the procedure with the patient as necessary in the recovery area when the patient is awake. Conduct a postoperative pain assessment. Write the postoperative orders. Call the referring physician regarding the outcome of the procedure and any unusual aspects of postoperative care (eg, cardiac disease, diabetic management). Dictate a detailed operative report.

Postoperative Other Hospital Work; Beginning on Postoperative Day 1 Until Discharge Day: Examine the patient. Conduct a postoperative pain assessment. Remove the vaginal pack. Check the lab values. Check the catheter. Review the medical record. Answer the patient's and familys questions. Answer the nursing and other staffs questions. Write any further necessary orders. Write a progress note.

Discharge Day Work: Examine and talk with the patient and the patient's family. Discuss postoperative care of the catheter with the patient and the patient's family. Review all patient hospital medical records. Review the patient's diet (avoid constipation). Write the discharge orders. Write prescriptions for postoperative medications. Dictate the discharge summary.

Postoperative Office Work; After Discharge From Hospital: Examine the patient and the patient's incisions. Check vital signs. Talk with the patient and the patient's family. Remove the Foley catheter in the office. Conduct a voiding trial at the appropriate postoperative visit. Reinsert the Foley catheter if the patient is unable to void. Write necessary prescriptions. Dictate an office note. Dictate a letter to the referring physician.

Cervix Uteri

Endoscopy

57454 Colposcopy of the cervix including upper/adjacent vagina; with biopsy(s) of the cervix and endocervical curettage

Work Value: 2.33 // Global Period: 000

➲ *CPT Assistant* Apr 00: 5, Feb 03: 5, Jun 03: 10; *CPT Changes: An Insider's View* 2003

Clinical Example

A 30-year old woman with an abnormal Pap smear is advised to undergo colposcopic visualization of the cervix. She is advised that a biopsy will be obtained if a lesion is identified.

Preservice

Preservice work includes the review of the patient's chart, Pap smear and other relevant reports. Obtain informed consent and confirm that colposcopic instruments are present and functioning properly.

Intraservice

The cervix including upper/adjacent vagina is cleaned several times with 3% acetic acid. After adequate time for acetic acid effect the cervix and vagina fornices are examined with a colposcope at several magnifications. The transformation zone (area at risk for cervical cancer) is seen completely and abnormal aceto white areas are noted at 12 o'clock extending into the endocervical canal. An endocervical curettage and a cervical biopsy at 12 o'clock is performed. The biopsy site is treated with Monsel's solution or Silver Nitrate for hemostasis.

Postservice

Postservice work includes the the documentation of the procedure, instructions to the patient for follow-up, and precautions to control bleeding. Review the pathology report and formulate plan for follow-up treatment.

Coding Tip for 57454

Code 57454 is reported only one time, whether one or multiple cervical biopsies are performed.

Corpus Uteri

Excision

58100 Endometrial sampling (biopsy) with or without endocervical sampling (biopsy), without cervical dilation, any method (separate procedure)

Work Value: 1.53 // Global Period: 000

Clinical Example

A 63-year-old female presents for a scheduled endometrial and endocervical sampling. She was seen yesterday for evaluation of several recent episodes of unexplained vaginal bleeding. You review with her the purpose and the risks and benefits and then perform the procedure.

Preservice

An explanation of the procedure is provided and informed consent is obtained. Appropriate laboratory studies are reviewed. The patient is placed in the proper position and appropriate prepping and draping are performed.

Intraservice

A pelvic exam is performed to ascertain the position of the uterus. The speculum is inserted. Anesthesia is utilized on the cervix and a tenaculum is applied if needed. Sampling of the endometrium with or without endocervical sampling is performed by any method. The instruments are removed and hemostasis is obtained.

Postservice

The patient is allowed to recover in the procedure room. Once she has recovered, she is discharged and appropriate instructions and follow-up are given. The procedure note is dictated. When available, the pathology report is reviewed and the patient is notified and appropriate follow-up is established.

Hysterectomy Procedures

❺ **58150** Total abdominal hysterectomy (corpus and cervix), with or without removal of tube(s), with or without removal of ovary(s);

Work Value: 17.21 // Global Period: 090

➲ ***CPT Assistant*** **Dec 96: 10, Apr 97: 3, Nov 97: 21, Sep 00: 9, Aug 01: 11**

Clinical Example

A 52-year-old G0 female has been evaluated for a large pelvic mass. Ultrasound demonstrated bilateral complex solid and cystic adnexal masses and a leiomyomatous uterus. CA-125 is elevated. She now undergoes surgery. Exploratory laparotomy reveals bilateral endometriomas densely adherent to the pelvic sidewalls and total cul-de-sac obliteration, as well as myomata enlarging the uterus to 10–12 weeks size. Total abdominal hysterectomy and bilateral salpingo-oophorectomy are performed.

Preservice

A comprehensive history is obtained and a comprehensive examination is performed to determine the patient's current medical status. Indications for the procedure and its appropriateness are reviewed. Informed consent is obtained. The physician admits the patient to the hospital, prepares the hospital records and chart in accordance with hospital policy, checks on the patient, and reviews records prior to the surgery. The physician scrubs for the procedure and waits for anesthesia induction and the preparation of the patient.

Intraservice

Under general anesthesia, the abdomen is entered through a midline incision. An exploratory laparotomy is performed. At exploration the patient is found to have bilateral endometriomas densely adherent to the pelvic sidewalls and total cul-de-sac obliteration. Total abdominal hysterectomy and bilateral salpingo-oophorectomy are performed. The supporting pedicles containing the tubes, ligaments, and arteries are clamped and cut free. The uterus and cervix are removed along with a narrow rim or cuff of vaginal lining. The vaginal defect is sutured closed. The abdomen is closed in layers. The abdominal incision is closed by suturing.

Postservice

Following the procedure, the physician writes orders for postoperative care, accompanies the patient to the recovery room, and talks with the patient's family. The patient is then evaluated in the recovery room. The physician dictates the operative procedure and makes periodic checks on the patient's condition. Any drainage catheters are normally removed when the patient is ambulatory and she is monitored for normal voiding. The physician visits the patient in the hospital for 4 days. The patient is discharged on postoperative day 4 with instructions for follow-up care. The patient is reevaluated twice postoperatively.

Laparoscopy/Hysteroscopy

58558 Hysteroscopy, surgical; with sampling (biopsy) of endometrium and/or polypectomy, with or without D & C

Work Value: 4.74 // Global Period: 000

➲ ***CPT Assistant*** **Nov 99: 28, Mar 00: 10, Sep 02: 10, Jan 03: 7, May 03: 19;** ***CPT Changes: An Insider's View*** **2000**

Clinical Example

A 55-year-old postmenopausal female presents with abnormal bleeding on combined continuous hormone replacement therapy. An endometrial biopsy was attempted, but yielded inadequate tissue for diagnosis. An endovaginal ultrasound revealed an endometrial thickness greater than 1 cm with the suggestion of an intrauterine filling defect. Under adequate anesthesia, a pelvic examination is performed that documents a normal-sized anteflexed uterus. The cervix is dilated and the diagnostic hysteroscope is introduced into the endometrial cavity. An irregular polypoid mass is identified. The cervix is further dilated to admit the resectoscope and the entire lesion is resected. The cavity is then curetted with a sharp curette.

Preservice

Preservice begins after the decision to operate is made and continues until the time of the procedure. Preservice includes reviewing the previous work-up, including consulting with the referring physician, if necessary, and other health care professionals, such as the anesthesiologist; taking a comprehensive history and performing a comprehensive examination to determine the patient's current medical status; and communicating with the patient and/or the patient's family to explain the indications for the procedure, as well as the operative risks and benefits, and to obtain informed consent. The physician admits the patient to the hospital (or surgery center) and prepares the hospital records and chart in accordance with hospital policy. Other preoperative services include scheduling the procedure, dressing, scrubbing, and waiting to begin the procedure. The physician must personally ensure that all necessary equipment and supplies are available and compatible, including confirmation and mixing of solution for visualization (eg, 50% glycine or saline). The physician must also confirm the proper positioning of the patient and grounding of electrical equipment.

Intraservice

Following induction of appropriate anesthesia, a bimanual pelvic examination is performed to assess uterine size, position, and mobility. The adnexa and posterior cul de sac are palpated for the presence of masses or nodularity. The bladder is drained with a catheter. The cervix is exposed, grasped, and dilated slightly larger than the scope. The uterine sound is passed. The scope is inserted and the physician confirms the proper pressure setting of the pump or gravity flow to adequately distend the endometrial cavity. The entire endometrial cavity is examined, including the anterior, posterior, fundal, and lateral walls. The endocervical canal is examined. An irregular polypoid mass is identified. The cervix is further dilated to admit the resectoscope and the entire lesion is resected. Bleeding points are coagulated. The cavity is then curetted with a sharp curette. The hysteroscope is removed from the uterus. The cervix is checked for bleeding from a puncture site or laceration. If found, bleeding is controlled by suture, pressure, or fulguration. All instruments are removed from the vagina and cervix. The patient is transferred to a stretcher and escorted to the recovery room.

Postservice

Postservice includes monitoring the patient's stability in the recovery room; writing orders and dictating an operative report; communicating with the patient, the patient's family and other health care professionals (including providing written and oral reports and orders); ordering and reviewing postoperative radiographs and laboratory studies; paying careful attention to fluid-volume and electrolyte status; monitoring and caring for the incision; monitoring, maintaining, and removing all tubes, catheters, and drains; managing antibiotic and pain medication; and all other visits and services performed by the surgeon. Discharge management includes the physicians final examination of the patient, providing instructions for continuing care, and preparing discharge records. The physician must also review the pathology report.

Coding Tip for 58558

Code 58558 describes surgical hysteroscopy, with sampling (biopsy) of the endometrium and/or polypectomy, with or without a dilation and curettage (D&C). A D&C is commonly performed with a hysteroscopy; thus, both of these procedures are described in a single code. The code is worded in this way to make it clear that when sampling (biopsy or curetting) of the endometrium and/or polypectomy is performed, the D&C should not be reported separately.

58563 Hysteroscopy, surgical; with endometrial ablation (eg, endometrial resection, electrosurgical ablation, thermoablation)

Work Value: 6.16 // Global Period: 000

➲ **_CPT Assistant_ Nov 99: 28, Mar 00: 10, Mar 02: 11, Apr 02: 19, Jan 03: 7; _CPT Changes: An Insider's View_ 2000, 2002**

Clinical Example

A 44-year-old obese female was referred by another physician for the management of menorrhagia to the point of significant anemia. Attempts to control her bleeding with cyclic progestins and antiprostaglandins have been unsuccessful. She is a heavy smoker and therefore not a candidate for oral contraceptives. An endometrial biopsy revealed no abnormality. The patient wants to avoid hysterectomy. She is taken to the operating room. After adequate anesthesia is obtained, a pelvic examination is performed. No obvious abnormality is appreciated, but the examination is compromised by the patient's size. The cervix is progressively dilated and a vigorous curettage is performed. The resectoscope is then introduced into the uterine cavity. A diagnostic hysteroscopy demonstrates a normal uterine cavity. The entire cavity is then meticulously coagulated.

Preservice

Preservice work begins after the decision to operate is made and continues until the time of the procedure. Preservice work includes reviewing the previous work-up, including consulting with the referring physician, if necessary, and other health care professionals, such as the anesthesiologist; taking a comprehensive history and performing a comprehensive examination to determine the patient's current medical status; and communicating with the patient and/or the patient's family to explain the indications for the procedure, as well as the operative risks and benefits, and to obtain informed consent. The physician admits the patient to the hospital (or surgery center) and prepares the hospital records and chart in accordance with hospital policy. Other preoperative services include scheduling the procedure, dressing, scrubbing, and waiting to begin the procedure. The physician must personally ensure that all necessary equipment and supplies are available and compatible, including confirmation and mixing of solution for visualization (eg, 50% glycine or saline). The physician must also confirm the proper positioning of the patient and grounding of electrical equipment.

Intraservice

Following induction of appropriate anesthesia, a bimanual pelvic examination is performed to assess uterine size, position, and mobility. The adnexa and posterior cul de sac are palpated for the presence of masses or nodularity. No obvious abnormality is appreciated, but the examination is compromised by the patient's size. The cervix is progressively dilated, the bladder is drained with a catheter, and vigorous curettage is performed. The scope is inserted and the physician confirms the proper pressure setting of the pump or gravity flow to adequately distend the endometrial cavity. The entire endometrial cavity is examined, including the anterior, posterior, fundal, and lateral walls. The endocervical canal is examined. The entire cavity is then meticulously coagulated by rollerball, resectoscope, or laser. The hysteroscope is removed from the uterus. The cervix is checked for bleeding from a puncture site or laceration. If found, bleeding is controlled by suture, pressure, or fulguration. All instruments are removed from the vagina and cervix. The patient is transferred to a stretcher and escorted to the recovery room.

Postservice

Postservice includes monitoring the patient's stability in the recovery room; writing orders and dictating an operative report; communicating with the patient, the patient's family, and other health care professionals (including providing written and oral reports and orders); ordering and reviewing postoperative radiographs and laboratory studies; paying careful attention to fluid-volume and electrolyte status; monitoring and caring for the incision; monitoring, maintaining, and removing all tubes, catheters, and drains; managing antibiotic and pain medication; and all other visits and services performed by the surgeon. Discharge management includes the physicians final examination of the patient, providing instructions for continuing care, and preparing discharge records. The physician must also review the pathology report.

Hysteroscopy
58563

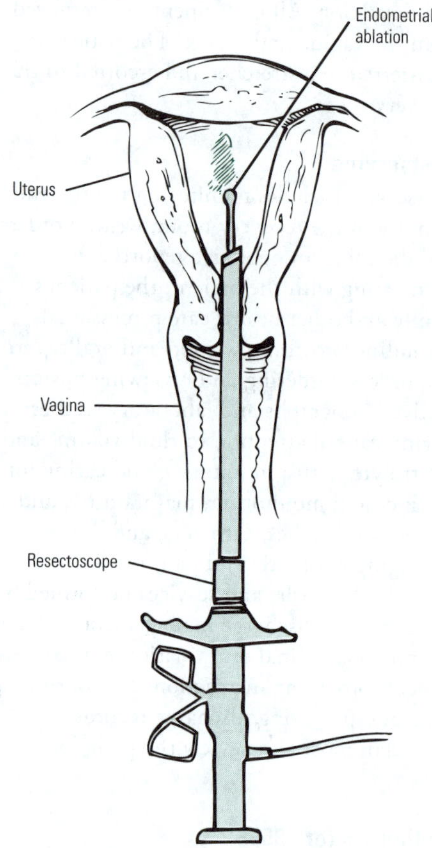

Oviduct/Ovary

Laparoscopy

58661 Laparoscopy, surgical; with removal of adnexal structures (partial or total oophorectomy and/or salpingectomy)

Work Value: 11.30 // Global Period: 010

➲ ***CPT Assistant*** **Nov 99: 28, Mar 00: 10, Jan 02: 11;** ***CPT Changes: An Insider's View*** **2000**

Clinical Example

A 52-year-old postmenopausal female has been evaluated for an adnexal mass palpated on routine exam. She had a vaginal hysterectomy 15 years ago for benign disease. Ultrasound documents a 5-cm simple cystic mass arising from the left adnexa. Color Doppler flow analysis shows a normal resistive index and CA-125 is 5. Diagnostic laparoscopy confirms a benign-appearing cystically enlarged left ovary. Additional operating ports are placed and the left tube and ovary are excised laparoscopically and placed in a bag. If possible, they are removed from the abdominal cavity in the bag. Frozen section confirms a benign cystadenoma. The right tube and ovary are free of apparent abnormality and are left in place. The patient is observed in the hospital for 8-24 hours and discharged home with instructions. The patient receives routine office follow-up care during the 10-day global period.

Preservice

A comprehensive history is obtained and a comprehensive examination is performed to determine the patient's current medical status. Indications for the procedure and its appropriateness are reviewed. Informed consent is obtained. The physician admits the patient to the hospital, prepares the hospital records and chart in accordance with hospital policy, checks on the patient, and reviews the records prior to the surgery. The physician scrubs for the procedure, and waits for anesthesia induction and the preparation of the patient.

Intraservice

A bimanual pelvic examination is done to assess uterine size, position, and mobility before a uterine cannula is inserted. Exposure of the cervix is obtained. The anterior lip of the cervix is grasped with a tenaculum attached to an intrauterine cannula. Pneumoperitoneum is achieved by inserting a Veress or Touhy needle at the inferior rim of the umbilicus through a 2-mm incision. The peritoneal space is insufflated with carbon dioxide (CO_2) gas to a pressure of 10 mm Hg. Once satisfactory displacement of organs is achieved, the 2-mm incision is extended to 1 cm and the laparoscope trocar and sleeve are inserted through the rectus fascia. The trocar is removed from the sleeve and proper placement is documented as the operating laparoscope is advanced down the trocar sleeve into the pelvis. The gas hose is then connected to the trocar. Once the laparoscope has been inserted, a second trocar may be placed for ancillary instruments. The entire abdomen and pelvis are viewed systematically and pathology noted. It may be photodocumented. Upon completion of the exploration, additional trocars are placed under direct vision as needed. The infundibulopelvic ligament is isolated and the ureter is protected while the ovarian pedicle is controlled using staples, suture, electrocoagulation or clips. The adnexal structures are separated from the round ligament and any other adhesions or attachments are divided. The structures are now free and must be removed from the abdomen either via a colpotomy incision or by extending one of the abdominal incisions. If the ovary contains a cyst, it may be placed in a sterile bag, allowing the cyst to be aspirated and deflated without spilling its contents intra-abdominally. The pelvis is then carefully observed under water or low CO_2 pressure to ensure hemostasis. Ancillary trocars are then removed under direct vision and the insertion sites are observed for bleeding. The abdomen is deflated. The fascia may be closed separately, then the skin wounds are closed. The patient is transferred to a stretcher and escorted to the recovery room.

Postservice

Following the procedure, the physician writes orders for postoperative care, accompanies the patient to the recovery room, and talks with the patient's family. The patient is then evaluated in the recovery room. The physician dictates the operative procedure and makes periodic checks on the patient's condition. Any drainage catheters are normally removed when the patient is ambulatory and she is monitored for normal voiding. The physician visits the patient in the hospital for 1 day. The patient is discharged on postoperative day 1 with instructions for follow-up care. The patient is reevaluated twice postoperatively.

58662 Laparoscopy, surgical; with fulguration or excision of lesions of the ovary, pelvic viscera, or peritoneal surface by any method

Work Value: 12.08 // Global Period: 090

➲ *CPT Assistant* Nov 99: 28, Mar 00: 10; *CPT Changes: An Insider's View* 2000

Clinical Example

A 34-year-old G0 female presents with progressively severe dysmenorrhea, pelvic pain, and dysparunia. She had previously taken oral contraceptives which helped, but did not completely relieve the pain. She stopped oral contraceptives 9 months ago to begin trying to conceive. She misses 12 days of work with each menses. The patient is taken to the operating room. After induction of general anesthesia, a pelvic examination under anesthesia is performed and a uterine manipulator is placed on the cervix. Laparoscopy is performed, revealing multiple implants of endometriosis in the anterior and posterior cul de sac with scarring along both uterosacral ligaments. There are several implants on both the left and right posterior broad ligament. Both ovaries are free, but each has surface implants of endometriosis. The fallopian tubes appear normal and chromotubation is performed, which demonstrates bilateral tubal patency. All of the lesions of endometriosis are vaporized, excised, or cauterized.

Preservice

Preservice work begins after the decision to operate is made and continues until the time of the procedure. Preservice work includes reviewing the previous work-up, including consulting with the referring physician, if necessary, and other health care professionals, such as the anesthesiologist; taking a comprehensive history and performing a comprehensive examination to determine the patient's current medical status; and communicating with the patient and/or the patient's family to explain the indications for the procedure, as well as the operative risks and benefits, and to obtain informed consent. The physician admits the patient to the hospital (or surgery center) and prepares the hospital records and chart in accordance with hospital policy, checks on the patient, and reviews the records prior to the surgery. Other preoperative services include scheduling the operation, dressing, scrubbing, and waiting to begin the operation; supervising the positioning, prepping, and draping of the patient; and ensuring that the necessary surgical instruments and supplies are present and available in the operating suite.

Intraservice

After induction of anesthesia, a bimanual pelvic examination is done to assess uterine size, position, and mobility before a uterine cannula is inserted. The adnexa and posterior cul de sac are palpated for the presence of masses or nodularity. Exposure of the cervix is obtained and the cervix is dilated, if necessary. The anterior lip of the cervix is grasped with a tenaculum attached to an intrauterine cannula. The bladder is drained with a catheter. An intraumbilical incision is made. A Veress needle is inserted and appropriate placement is checked. Pneumoperitoneum is achieved with insufflation of carbon dioxide (CO_2) gas. Once satisfactory displacement of organs is achieved, the laparoscopic trocar and sleeve are inserted through the abdominal wall. The trocar is removed from the sleeve and proper placement is documented as the operating laparoscope is advanced down the trocar sleeve. The pelvis and the viscera are inspected to check for evidence of trauma. The CO_2 tubing is connected to the trocar. Gas flow and intra-abdominal pressure are carefully monitored so as not to impair ventilation and venous return. Once the laparoscope has been inserted, a second trocar may be placed for ancillary instruments. The entire abdomen and pelvis are viewed systematically and pathology noted. It may be photodocumented. Upon completion of the exploration, additional trocars are placed under direct vision as needed. The lesions of endometriosis in the anterior cul de sac are excised, vaporized, or cauterized taking care not to damage the ureter, pelvic vessels, or colon. Lesions on the ovaries are excised, vaporized, or cauterized. Any specimens obtained are removed from the abdomen. Chromotubation is performed to assess tubal patency. Meticulous hemostasis is maintained and the peritoneal cavity is irrigated. Ancillary trocars are then removed under direct vision to ensure that an abdominal wall vascular injury or hemorrhage occurs. The pneumoperitoneum is evacuated. The fascia may be closed separately, then the skin wounds are closed. The instruments are removed from the vagina. The patient is transferred to a stretcher and escorted to the recovery room.

Postservice

Postservice begins in the operating room after skin closure with the application of sterile dressings. Postservice includes monitoring the patient's stability in the recovery room; communicating with the patient's family and other health care professionals (including providing written and oral reports and orders); ordering and reviewing postoperative radiographs and laboratory studies; paying careful attention to fluid-volume and electrolyte status; monitoring and caring for the incision; monitoring, maintaining, and removing all tubes, drains, and catheters; managing antibiotic and pain medication; and all other hospital visits and services performed by the surgeon. Discharge management includes the surgeons final examination of the patient, providing instructions for continuing care, and preparing discharge records. Additionally, all postdischarge visits for this procedure for 90 days after the day of the operation are considered part of the postservice, including removing the sutures; ordering and evaluating periodic imaging and laboratory studies, if needed; obtaining and reviewing all final surgical histopathology results; coordinating care with a referring physician, and making antibiotic and pain medication adjustments.

Maternity Care and Delivery

Antepartum Services

59001 Amniocentesis; therapeutic amniotic fluid reduction (includes ultrasound guidance)

Work Value: 3.00 // Global Period: 000

➲ *CPT Assistant* **Feb 02: 7, Aug 02: 2;** *CPT Changes: An Insider's View* **2002**

Clinical Example

A female presents at 22 weeks' gestation with a rapidly increasing uterine size. Ultrasound reveals the presence of a twin gestation. One twin is small for gestational age and had oligohydramnios. The other twin is appropriate for gestational age and has severe polyhydramnios. Twin-twin transfusion syndrome is diagnosed. The patient is counseled about the available therapies. She elects amniotic fluid reduction. The physician performs therapeutic amniotic fluid reduction under continuous, real-time ultrasound guidance with appropriate postprocedure monitoring.

Preservice

The physician reviews previous ultrasound and lab studies, confirms the availability of all necessary personnel and equipment, and communicates with the referring obstetrician, as needed. The physician explains the risks and benefits of the procedure to the patient and obtains informed consent. The patient is prepped and positioned for the procedure.

Intraservice

Real-time ultrasound scanning is performed to identify the sac with increased amniotic fluid. The area is draped and prepped and a needle insertion site is identified. Under real-time ultrasound guidance, a 22-gauge needle is inserted into the amniotic sac. The needle is then attached to tubing by an assistant while the physician holds the needle in place. The assistant attaches the needle to a drainage system. Utilizing continuous ultrasound guidance, fluid is removed until a normal amount of fluid is seen on ultrasound. The physician remains in constant communication with the ultrasound technician regarding the status of both fetuses and the fluid level. (Continual monitoring of the needle location is required to avoid injury to the fetus or placenta because the uterine shape is altered by the removal of fluid.) Once a normal fluid level is obtained, the needle is removed.

Postservice

The patient remains in the facility for approximately 1 hour following the procedure. The physician monitors uterine activity and fetal heart tones. The physician provides discharge instructions, including the signs and symptoms of preterm labor and the possibility of fluid leakage. The physician documents the procedure.

Amniocentesis, Therapeutic Amniotic Fluid Reduction
59001

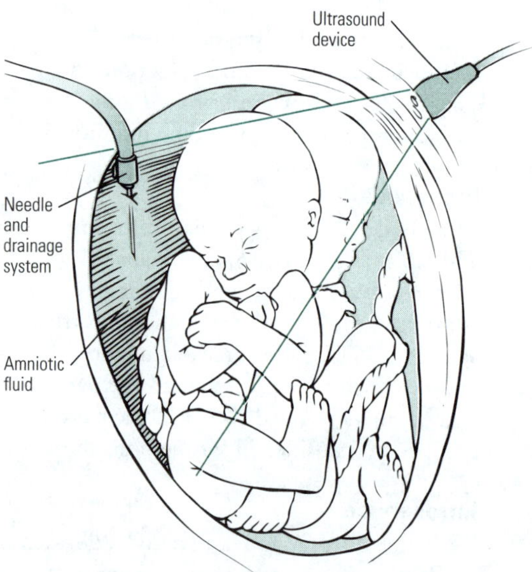

Vaginal Delivery, Antepartum and Postpartum Care

59409 Vaginal delivery only (with or without episiotomy and/or forceps);

Work Value: 13.48 // Global Period: MMM

➲ ***CPT Assistant*** **Feb 96: 1, Mar 96: 11, Jul 96: 11, Sep 96: 4, Feb 97: 11, Apr 97: 1, Aug 02: 3**

Clinical Example

A 22-year-old primigravida presents to the emergency room at 40 weeks' gestation in active labor. The physician has not seen this patient before. Labor progresses normally and she delivers a healthy infant.

Vaginal Delivery
59409

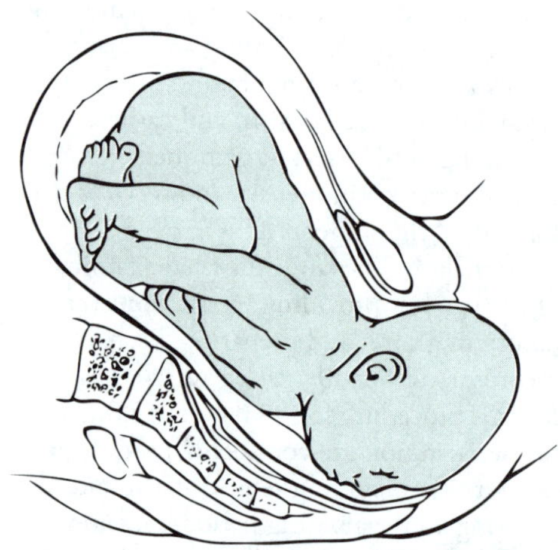

59425 Antepartum care only; 4-6 visits

Work Value: 6.22 // Global Period: MMM

➲ ***CPT Assistant*** **Fall 94: 21, Apr 97: 11, Aug 02: 3**

Clinical Example

A 22-year-old primigravida comes to the office for her first antenatal visit at 8 weeks' gestation. She returns for routine antenatal visits at 12, 16, 20, and 24 weeks, then transfers her care to another physician.

59426 Antepartum care only; 7 or more visits

Work Value: 11.04 // Global Period: MMM

➲ *CPT Assistant* **Fall 94: 21, Apr 97: 11, Aug 02: 3**

Clinical Example

A 22-year-old primigravida transfers her care to the physician at 24 weeks' gestation. (She was previously seen by another physician.) She returns for routine antenatal visits at 28, 30, 32, 34, 36, 37, 38, 39, and 40 weeks. Another physician performs the delivery.

Coding Tip for 59425 and 59426

Codes 59425 and 59426 are available for reporting antepartum care only. If four to six antepartum visits are provided, code 59425 is reported. Seven or more antepartum visits are reported with code 59426. If the physician provides one to three antepartum visits, they are individually reported with the appropriate evaluation and management codes.

Cesarean Delivery

59514 Cesarean delivery only;

Work Value: 15.95 // Global Period: MMM

➲ *CPT Assistant* **Oct 96: 10, Feb 97: 11**

Clinical Example

A 22-year-old primigravida presents to the emergency room at 40 weeks' gestation in active labor. The physician has not seen this patient before. While monitoring her in labor, the physician notes acute fetal distress, necessitating an emergency cesarean delivery, which the physician performs.

Cesarean Delivery
59514

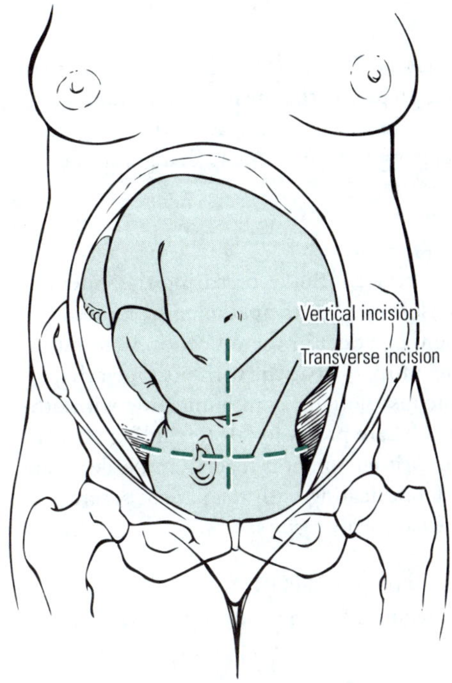

Endocrine System

Thyroid Gland

Excision

60001 Aspiration and/or injection, thyroid cyst

Work Value: 0.97 // Global Period: 000

Clinical Example

A 65-year-old female, taking digoxin for control of atrial fibrillation and a history of congestive heart failure, presents with a 2-cm palpable and visible thyroid nodule that is solitary and cystic by sonography. The trachea is somewhat deviated by the nodule. Aspiration is performed for cytologic exam and the nodule resolves. The cytology results are benign.

Preservice

Preservice includes reviewing records, including diagnostic studies; consulting with the referring physician regarding the treatment plan; counseling the patient and the patient's family; and obtaining informed consent.

Intraservice
Intraservice includes positioning the patient and preparing the operative site; administering local anesthetic; aspirating the cyst; applying pressure; and applying a sterile dressing.

Postservice
Postservice includes preparing the slide; consulting with the pathologist; monitoring the patient in the office for 30 minutes; providing the patient with postoperative care instructions; communicating with other health care professionals (including providing written and oral reports and orders); and communicating with the patient regarding the pathology results.

Coding Tip for 60001
To report a fine-needle aspiration, see codes 10021 and 10022 as appropriate.

60100 Biopsy thyroid, percutaneous core needle

Work Value: 1.56 // Global Period: 000

➲ *CPT Assistant* Jun 97: 5

Clinical Example
A 50-year-old male presents with a 3-cm mass in the lower pole of the right lobe of the thyroid. Percutaneous core biopsy of this mass has been requested.

Preservice
The patient's history is reviewed for potential risk factors and etiologies for the mass. Previous imaging studies, which may have prompted the request for a biopsy, are reviewed along with any potential contraindications. The procedure is discussed with the patient including risks, complications, and alternatives.

Intraservice
The mass is localized for biopsy and a core of tissue is obtained. A frozen section may be obtained for adequacy of tissue. If imaging guidance is used, it is coded separately.

Postservice
A procedure report is dictated. The patient is observed for complications. Postprocedure care is discussed with the patient, including how the patient will obtain the biopsy results.

60210 Partial thyroid lobectomy, unilateral; with or without isthmusectomy

Work Value: 11.15 // Global Period: 090

Clinical Example
A 37-year-old female presents with dysphagia and a 1.5-cm palpable thyroid nodule in the lower pole of the right lobe that is cold on radionuclide scan, solid by sonography, and nondiagnostic by fine needle aspiration cytology. The esophagus is deviated by the nodule on barium swallow. The intraoperative findings are consistent with benign colloid nodule. The lower half of right lobe, including the nodule, is removed. The frozen section confirms benign colloid nodule.

Preservice
Preservice includes preparing the hospital admission work-up; reviewing the roentgenograms and laboratory studies; communicating with other health care professionals; consulting with the referring physician, if necessary; communicating with the patient and the patient's family; and obtaining informed consent.

Intraservice
Intraservice includes positioning, prepping, and draping the patient; partially excising the thyroid; reviewing the frozen section with the pathologist; closing the incision with a layered closure; and applying a sterile dressing.

Postservice
Postservice includes stabilizing the patient and then communicating with the patient, the patient's family, and other health care professionals (including providing written and oral reports and orders). Discharge day management includes the surgeons final examination of the patient, discussing the hospital stay, providing instructions for

continuing care, and preparing the discharge records. Additionally, all hospital visits and postdischarge office visits for this problem for 90 days after the day of the operation are considered part of the postoperative work for this procedure, including evaluating lab reports and adjusting medication.

60220 Total thyroid lobectomy, unilateral; with or without isthmusectomy

Work Value: 12.29 // Global Period: 090

Clinical Example

A 37-year-old female presents with dysphagia and a 1.5-cm palpable thyroid nodule in the lower pole of the right lobe that is cold on radionuclide scan, solid by sonography, and nondiagnostic by fine needle aspiration cytology. The esophagus is deviated by the nodule on barium swallow. Preoperatively, once a decision has been made to operate, the surgeon reviews laboratory and X-ray/imaging studies to plan the operative approach, discusses the procedure with the patient, and obtains informed consent. During surgery, a neck exploration is performed, with exposure and examination of both sides of the thyroid. The right lobe is carefully dissected and appropriate nerves and parathyroid glands are identified and preserved. The right lobe of the thyroid and a portion of the isthmus is resected. Frozen section reveals thyroid adenoma. The neck is closed in a standard fashion, with drainage of the neck included as indicated. Postoperatively, the patient is advanced to a diet and intravenous fluids and injectable pain medications are tapered as tolerated. The patient is discharged from the hospital when the calcium level is stable, phonating well, tolerating a diet, and comfortable on oral pain medications. Office visits are conducted as necessary during the 90-day global period to ensure that no wound complications or infections occur. In addition, the final pathology report is reviewed, discussed with the patient, the patient's family, and other health care providers, especially with respect to further care of the patient.

Preservice

Write preoperative orders for admission to the Ambulatory Surgery Unit and for preoperative medications. Review the preoperative work-up, paying particular attention to cytopathology reports. Review the preoperative work-up regarding laryngotracheal or esophageal compression. Review the preoperative work-up, paying attention to adequate thyroid function. Review the planned incisions and procedure. Change into scrub clothes. Review the surgical procedure, postoperative recovery in and out of the hospital, and expected outcome(s) with the patient and the patient's family. Answer the patient's and familys questions and obtain informed consent.

Intraservice

Open the neck through a collar incision. Palpate both thyroid lobes through the strap muscles and confirm the presence of a single right-sided nodule. Elevate and rotate the strap muscles laterally to expose the right lobe and isthmus. (The gross features of the nodule are consistent with colloid nodule.) Dissect the lobe free from its attachments, using a ligature to control the branch vessels near the lobe to preserve the parathyroid blood supply. Identify the recurrent laryngeal nerve near its intersection with the inferior thyroid artery, and trace the nerve carefully to its laryngeal entry. Look for the external branch of the superior laryngeal nerve while dividing the superior pole vessels. Free the isthmus from the trachea and divide it near its junction with the left lobe. Send the lobe and isthmus to surgical pathology, where frozen section discloses a right colloid nodule. Reconfirm parathyroid viability and assure hemostasis. Suture the strap muscles in layers, close the platysma, and reapproximate the skin. Apply a sterile dressing.

Postservice

Apply dressings. Write a brief operative note. Write orders for postoperative medications, diet, and patient activity. Review recovery room care and medications with the staff. Discuss the procedure outcome with the patient's family. Discuss the procedure outcome with the patient after the patient emerges from anesthesia. Dictate the operative report. Discuss the procedure findings and outcome with the referring physician. Dictate the procedure outcome and expected recovery letter for the referring physician and/or the insurance company. Examine the patient and check the wound and the patient's progress, paying particular attention to airway and voice. Write orders for the following days medications, diet, and patient activity. Chart patient progress notes. Advance the patient's diet and stop parenteral analgesics. Discharge the patient with wound care, activity, and follow-up instructions. Examine and talk with the patient. Check wounds and the patient's progress. Review the nursing and other staffs patient chart notes. Review postdischarge wound care and activity limitations with the patient. Review the follow-up plans with the patient and the patient's family. Answer the patient's and familys questions. Answer the nursing and other staffs questions. Answer the insurance staffs questions. Write orders for post-discharge medications. Chart the patient's discharge notes. Examine and talk with the patient. At the first postoperative visit, review the final pathology report with the patient and the patient's family. See the patient one or two more times to ensure that neck range of motion, phonation, respiration, and swallowing have returned to their pre-morbid state. Periodically update the patient's primary care physician about the operative findings and the patient's status. Dictate patient progress notes for the medical chart.

Thyroid Lobectomy
60220

The thyroid is exposed via a transverse cervical incision. The superior and inferior thyroid vessels serving the lobe are ligated, the isthmus is severed, and the entire thyroid lobe is resected.

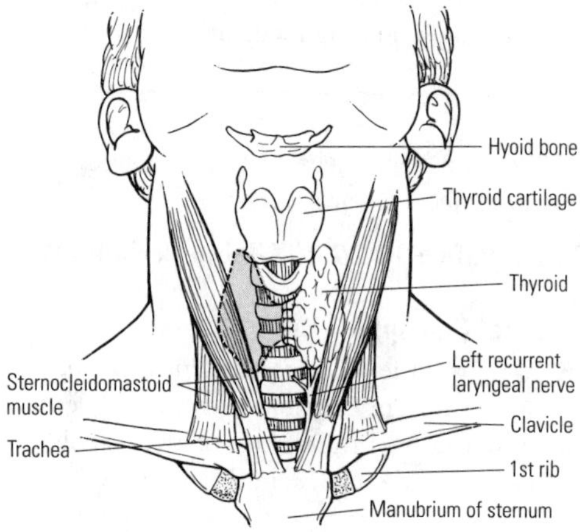

Parathyroid, Thymus, Adrenal Glands, Pancreas, and Carotid Body

Excision

+ 60512 Parathyroid autotransplantation (List separately in addition to code for primary procedure)

Work Value: 4.44 // Global Period: ZZZ

Clinical Example

A 50-year-old male with hypertension and on hemodialysis for end-stage renal disease has secondary hyperparathyroidis and suffers from intractable pruritis. He has sustained a pathologic humerus fracture in the recent past due to hyperparathyroid bone disease. Four hyperplastic parathyroid glands are identified in the neck and are removed. Approximately 60 mg of parathyroid tissue is diced and reimplanted in muscle pockets in the forearm; muscle implantation is difficult due to scarring from prior hemodialysis vascular access operations in the arm.

Intraservice

Intraservice work includes prepping and draping the implantation site (eg, arm or leg); preparing the back table for the parathyroid tissue to be used for reimplantation; waiting for frozen section confirmation of the parathyroid tissue; implanting multiple segments of parathyroid tissue into individual muscle pockets; closing the incision; applying a sterile dressing; and preparing the remaining parathyroid tissue for cryopreservation.

Parathyroid Autotransplantation
60512

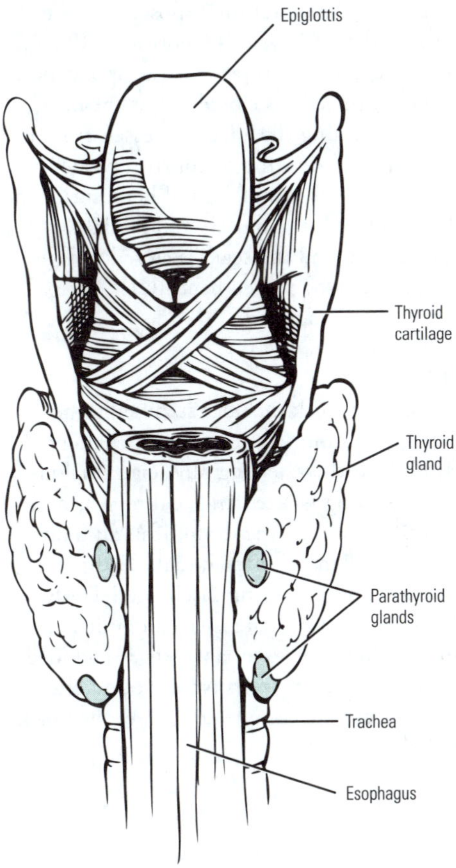

Posterior view of pharynx

Nervous System

Skull, Meninges, and Brain

Twist Drill, Burr Hole(s), or Trephine

⊘ **61210** Burr hole(s); for implanting ventricular catheter, reservoir, EEG electrode(s), pressure recording device, or other cerebral monitoring device (separate procedure)

Work Value: 5.83 // Global Period: 000

➲ *CPT Changes: An Insider's View* 2007

Clinical Example

A 45-year-old male presents with a severe closed head injury that has a Glasgow Coma Scale of 6 and no focal or lateralizing signs. Admitting computed tomography scan shows no hematomas or shift but obliteration of the basal cisterns. Intracranial pressure monitoring with capability for drainage of ventricular fluid is desired. A frontal ventriculostomy catheter is implanted and attached to an external monitoring and collection system.

Preservice

Preservice includes reviewing the imaging studies; reviewing the patient's past medical history and appropriate lab studies; and obtaining informed consent. Preservice also includes the day-of-service work of preoperative preparation, including scrubbing, positioning the patient, and setting up the equipment.

Intraservice

A frontal scalp is made under local anesthesia. A twist drill hole is made, and a ventriculostomy catheter is introduced into the anterior horn of the lateral ventricle. The catheter is tunneled beneath the scalp for approximately 12 cm and then brought to the surface via a small stab wound. The catheter is connected to a pressure transducer and drainage tubing system. The system is calibrated to ensure patency of the catheter. The scalp is then closed and dressings are applied.

Postservice

Postservice includes stabilizing the patient; communicating with the patient's family and referring physician (including providing written and oral reports and orders); and monitoring for signs of leakage of ventricular fluid or infection. No postoperative services are included in the 000-day global period assigned.

Coding Tip for 61210

Code 61210 describes the implantation of a ventricular catheter, reservoir, electroencephalogram electrode(s), pressure recording device, or other cerebral monitoring device by burr hole technique, and because of its separate procedure designation, may not be reported when these procedures are considered inherent in the larger or major procedure performed.

Surgery for Aneurysm, Arteriovenous Malformation or Vascular Disease

❺ **61700** Surgery of simple intracranial aneurysm, intracranial approach; carotid circulation

Work Value: 50.44 // Global Period: 090

➲ ***CPT Assistant*** **Jun 99: 11, Jul 99: 10;** ***CPT Changes: An Insider's View*** **2001**

Clinical Example

A 42-year-old female presents with a sudden onset of severe headache with a brief period of unconsciousness. A computed tomography scan shows diffuse subarachnoid hemorrhage in the basal cisterns, and an angiogram shows a 0.8-cm aneurysm of the anterior communicating artery. The patient undergoes a craniotomy for clipping of the intracranial aneurysm. Postoperative hospital care and office visits are conducted as necessary through the 90-day global period.

Preservice

Preservice work includes reviewing the angiogram, imaging studies, and appropriate lab studies and obtaining informed consent. Preservice work also includes the day-of-service work of preoperative preparation, including scrubbing, positioning the patient, and setting up the equipment. Positioning is lengthy due to stabilization of the patient's head in a pin fixation device.

Intraservice

A scalp flap is outlined and reflected over the frontotemporal region. After the overlying muscles are divided and the bone is exposed, the bone is removed to expose the sphenoid ridge and orbital roof. The dura is opened and retracted, exposing the frontal and temporal lobes. The aneurysm is exposed by dissection and opening the Sylvian fissure. The vessels are carefully exposed and the neck of the aneurysm is identified. When the neck is exposed and permits the application of a clip, the clip is closed across the neck while excluding the adjacent vessels from the clip. After examining to confirm proper clip placement and completion of hemostasis, the dura is closed, the muscle and fascial layers secured, and the scalp is closed in layers. A drain may be placed beneath the scalp. Dressings are applied.

Postservice

Postservice work includes stabilizing the patient; communicating with the patient's family and the referring physician (including providing written and oral reports and orders); removing the drain, if used; monitoring for signs of intracranial bleeding or seizures; and preparing discharge records. All hospital visits, intensive care unit visits, and discharge day management is included. Postdischarge office visits for wound and general care are completed during the 90-day global period.

Intracranial Aneurysm, Intracranial Approach
61700

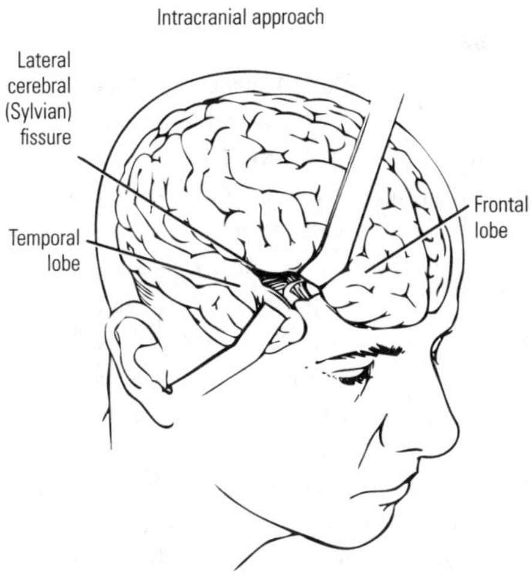

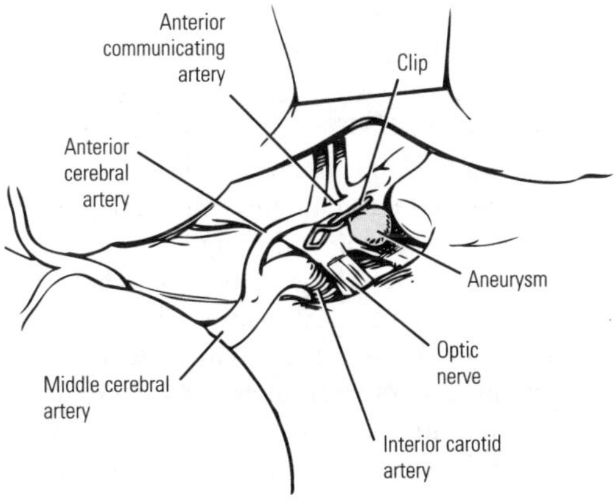

Stereotaxis

61793 Stereotactic radiosurgery (particle beam, gamma ray or linear accelerator), one or more sessions

Work Value: 17.75 // Global Period: 090

➲ *CPT Assistant* Nov 97: 23, May 03: 19, Apr 04: 15, Jan 06: 46

Clinical Example

A 75-year-old male presents with a history of renal cell carcinoma, now present in the right cerebellum. He has headaches, dizziness, and compression of the fourth ventricle as seen on a magnetic resonance imaging (MRI) scan. No other lesions are evident, and the chest exam reveals normal lesion enhances 2 cm in diameter. Stereotactic radiosurgery is delivered using the gamma knife system.

Preservice

Preservice includes reviewing previous medical records, evaluating the imaging studies and appropriate lab and screening studies, and obtaining informed consent.

Intraservice

Intraservice begins with the application of the stereotactic head frame under local anesthesia. The patient is then transported to the radiology department where sterotactic imaging studies are obtained through MRI or angiography. (Radiology procedures are reported separately.) The neurosurgeon positions and secures the patient on the imaging table and attaches an appropriate stereotactic localizer. The neurosurgeon then works with a radiologist or technician to identify the precise areas to be imaged by adjusting the scanning geometry and by timing the contrast injection(s). Finally, the neurosurgeon verifies that the target is optimally imaged. Dosimetry planning follows in conjunction with radiation oncology and a radiation physicist as well a computer programmer. The programmer processes all of the stereotactic images into the dose planning computer during this phase. This dose planning involves use of a computer-based planning module to achieve an optimal dosimetry plan for the patient. A test is then done using the radiosurgical device to ensure correct targeting and dosimetry. The patient is placed in the device while still in the frame. (Positioning is more complex due to the use of a stereotactic frame that requires coordinate indexing to the patient table.) The treatment is then delivered. For each isocenter treated, the neurosurgeon sets the stereotactic coordinates, verified by other team members. The frame is removed at the end of the service period.

Postservice

Postservice includes stabilizing the patient, communicating with the patient's family and referring physician (including providing written and oral reports and orders), and monitoring for signs of complications. The recovery room visit and discharge day management are included. Discharge records are prepared and postdischarge office visits for wound and general care are completed during the 90-day global period.

Neurostimulators (Intracranial)

61885 Insertion or replacement of cranial neurostimulator pulse generator or receiver, direct or inductive coupling; with connection to a single electrode array

Work Value: 7.37 // Global Period: 090

➲ *CPT Assistant* Sep 99: 5, Nov 99: 30, Jun 00: 3, Apr 01: 8, Sep 03: 3; *CPT Changes: An Insider's View* 2000, 2005

Clinical Example

A 45-year-old male presents with essential tremor that has become quite severe and is disabling. He has had the disease for 8 years and has failed to obtain tremor relief through various oral medications and physical therapy. He is not a candidate for direct brain resection or an ablative brain procedure because of the severity of his tremor and the length of symptoms. His history also includes implantation of a deep brain stimulator electrode array, which upon stimulation, eliminated 80% of the patient's tremor. He undergoes internalization of the tail of the electrode array and placement and connection of a subcutaneous stimulator generator for long-term brain stimulation.

Preservice

Preservice work includes reviewing the patient's records and any pertinent imaging studies, including previous deep brain stimulation procedures; examining the tail of the stimulation electrode array for any disconnections or other technical problems (if this is a two-stage operation); communicating with other professionals, the patient, and the patient's family; obtaining informed consent; dressing; scrubbing; preparing the needed equipment for the procedure; and supervising the prepping and draping of the patient. (This implies that the tail of the array was available for such an exam before going into surgery, and then had been externalized to the scalp for testing after its initial placement.)

Intraservice

Intraservice work includes recovering the cranial lead from the subgaleal space under general anesthesia; making a linear incision just below the clavicle over a distance of approximately 3 cm; creating a subcutaneous pocket under this incision; reopening the cephalic wound where the electrode array had been placed; making a small incision at approximately the level of the mastoid and passing the electrode extension passer from the cephalic wound down a subgaleal tract and out the mastoid wound; pulling the lead through the subcutaneous tract using this passer; passing the same passer from the mastoid wound down another subcutaneous tract and out the clavicular wound; pulling the electrode tail and extension wire through this subcutaneous tract; placing a sleeve on the distal tail of the electrode array; inserting the array tail into the proximal end of the extension wire and tightening it; placing the sleeve over the connection and tying it in place with 0-silk suture; placing the boot and connector in the subgaleal space while securing the proximal end of the extension wire to the skull; inserting the distal end of the extension wire into the generator and tightening it; coiling the excess extension wire behind the stimulator generator; suturing the stimulator generator into place in the subcutaneous tissue; testing the stimulator using a sterile technique to determine the impedance of the connections and to rule-out an electrical short; and closing the skin and subcutaneous tissues of all wounds with deep sutures and skin staples.

Postservice

Postservice work includes applying sterile dressings; checking the entire stimulator system for proper function; communicating with the patient's family and other health care professionals (including providing written and oral reports and orders); monitoring the patient's neurological condition for any deficits; monitoring the patient for infection; and managing the patient's antibiotic and pain medication. Discharge day management includes performing a final examination of the patient, reviewing the postdischarge continuing care and instructions with the patient and the patient's family, and preparing the discharge records. Additionally, all postdischarge office visits for this procedure for 90 days after the day of the operation are considered part of the postoperative work for this procedure, including removing staples and sutures, monitoring wound healing, and examining the patient in the office at appropriate postoperative intervals to ensure adequate healing of all wounds and functioning/effectiveness of the stimulator system.

Coding Tip for 61885

Code 61885 describes deep brain stimulation. Deep brain stimulation is used in the treatment of functional disorders such as movement problems from Parkinson's disease, essential tremor, multiple sclerosis, head trauma, drug-induced hyperkinesias, vascular malformations, cerebral hemorrhage, or intractable pain.

Spine and Spinal Cord

Injection, Drainage, or Aspiration

62287 Aspiration or decompression procedure, percutaneous, of nucleus pulposus of intervertebral disc, any method, single or multiple levels, lumbar (eg, manual or automated percutaneous discectomy, percutaneous laser discectomy)

Work Value: 8.88 // Global Period: 090

➲ ***CPT Assistant*** **Nov 99: 34, Mar 02: 11;** ***CPT Changes: An Insider's View*** **2000**

Clinical Example

A 25-year-old male athlete has had low back pain with sciatica, an absent ankle reflex, and weakness of the posterior calf muscle for 5 weeks. He has not responded to anti-inflammatory drugs and restricted activities. He has a history of a previous similar episode that cleared in 3 weeks. A magnetic resonance imaging scan shows a diffuse bulging annulus and disk at L5-S1. The patient refuses to accept a laminotomy but agrees to a percutaneous discectomy, which is done in the operating room using a C-arm guidance system.

Preservice

Preservice includes reviewing previous medical records from the earlier episode, and evaluating the imaging, lab, and screening studies. Preservice also includes obtaining informed consent plus the day-of-service work of preoperative preparation, scrubbing, positioning the patient, and setting up the equipment. (Positioning is more complex due to the use of a decubitus position and accommodation for the C-arm fluoroscope.)

Intraservice

The discectomy probe is introduced through the flank and guided into the region of the foramen where it is pushed through the annulus into the disc interspace. Fluoroscopic guidance is required during the insertion and following subsequent adjustments in position of the instrument while aspirating and removing disc tissue from the interspace. The probe is removed when no further disc material can safely be removed.

Postservice

Postservice includes stabilizing the patient, communicating with the patient's family and referring physician (including providing written and oral reports and orders), and monitoring for signs of bleeding. All subsequent visits, including discharge day management, are included during the 90-day global period.

Coding Tip for 62287

For fluoroscopic guidance, report code 77002.

62310 Injection, single (not via indwelling catheter), not including neurolytic substances, with or without contrast (for either localization or epidurography), of diagnostic or therapeutic substance(s) (including anesthetic, antispasmodic, opioid, steroid, other solution), epidural or subarachnoid; cervical or thoracic

Work Value: 1.91 // Global Period: 000

➲ *CPT Assistant* Nov 99: 32-35, Jan 00: 2, Dec 00: 15, Sep 04: 5; *CPT Changes: An Insider's View* 2000

Clinical Example

A 45-year-old male presents with severe pain (rated 8/10) involving both arms and the neck after multiple neck operations over a 10-year period. Various systemic medications (oral narcotic and non-narcotic) and physical therapy have failed to provide significant long-term pain relief. The patient is given a single subarachnoid or epidural narcotic injection in the cervical or thoracic space.

Preservice

Preservice includes reviewing the records and any pertinent imaging studies; communicating with other professionals, the patient, and the patient's family; and obtaining consent. The preoperative work also includes dressing, scrubbing, preparing the patient and needed equipment for the procedure, positioning the patient on the x- ray table, and draping the injection site.

Intraservice

An injection needle is directed into the subarachnoid or epidural space at the proper vertebral level, possibly under X ray fluoroscopy. Care is taken to avoid damaging any nerve roots or the spinal cord. A contrast injection is performed as necessary to confirm the location of the needle tip or catheter and to determine the degree of free flow of liquid in the space to assure both safety and accuracy. The therapeutic injection(s) is performed through the same needle. The injection needle is removed and a sterile dressing is applied.

Postservice

The patient is closely observed for 2-8 hours postprocedure in a monitored setting for any new, unexpected neurologic defects and/or any change in vital signs (eg, respiratory depression, bradycardia, altered mental status). The physician communicates the findings with the patient and other professionals (including providing written and oral reports and orders).

Coding Tip for 62310, 62311, and 62319

Codes 62310, 62311, and 62319 are not reported for each substance injected on one side at a particular spinal level. The injection procedure codes are considered unilateral procedures. Therefore, these codes are reported once per level, per side (right or left) regardless of the number or types of injections performed on the right or left side at a specific spinal level. If both sides are injected at a specific spinal level, the appropriate injection code should be reported with modifier 50, *Bilateral procedure,* appended.

62311 Injection, single (not via indwelling catheter), not including neurolytic substances, with or without contrast (for either localization or epidurography), of diagnostic or therapeutic substance(s) (including anesthetic, antispasmodic, opioid, steroid, other solution), epidural or subarachnoid; lumbar, sacral (caudal)

Work Value: 1.54 // Global Period: 000

➲ *CPT Assistant* Nov 99: 32-35, Jan 00: 1, Dec 00: 15, Sep 04: 5; *CPT Changes: An Insider's View* 2000

Clinical Example

A 45-year-old male presents with severe pain (rated 8/10) involving both legs and the lower back after multiple back operations over a 10-year period. Various systemic medications (oral narcotic and non-narcotic) and physical therapy have failed to provide significant long-term pain relief. The patient is given a single subarachnoid or epidural narcotic injection in the lumbar or sacral space.

Preservice

Preservice work includes reviewing the records and any pertinent imaging studies; communicating with other professionals, the patient, and the patient's family; and obtaining consent. The preoperative work also includes dressing, scrubbing, preparing the patient and needed equipment for the procedure, positioning the patient on the x-ray table, and draping the injection site.

Intraservice

An injection needle is directed into the subarachnoid or epidural space at the proper vertebral level, under x-ray fluoroscopy, as necessary. Care is taken to avoid damaging any nerve roots, cauda equina, or the spinal cord. A contrast injection is performed as necessary to confirm the location of the needle tip or catheter and to determine the degree of free flow of liquid in the space to assure both safety and accuracy. The therapeutic injection(s) is performed through the same needle. The injection needle is removed and a sterile dressing applied.

Postservice

The patient is closely observed for 2-8 hours postprocedure in a monitored setting for any new, unexpected neurologic defects and/or any change in vital signs (eg, respiratory depression, bradycardia, altered mental status). The physician communicates the findings with the patient and other professionals (including providing written and oral reports and orders).

62319 Injection, including catheter placement, continuous infusion or intermittent bolus, not including neurolytic substances, with or without contrast (for either localization or epidurography), of diagnostic or therapeutic substance(s) (including anesthetic, antispasmodic, opioid, steroid, other solution), epidural or subarachnoid; lumbar, sacral (caudal)

Work Value: 1.87 // Global Period: 000

➲ *CPT Assistant* Nov 99: 32-35, Jan 00: 2, Dec 00: 15, Oct 01: 9; *CPT Changes: An Insider's View* 2000

Clinical Example

A 45-year-old male presents with severe pain (rated 8/10) involving both legs and the back after multiple neck operations over a 10-year period. Various systemic medications (oral narcotic and non-narcotic) and physical therapy have failed to provide significant long-term pain relief. A catheter (subarachnoid or epidural) is placed in the lumbar or sacral space and an intermittent bolus of a narcotic is injected.

Preservice

Preservice work includes reviewing the records and any pertinent imaging studies; communicating with other professionals, the patient, and the patient's family; and obtaining consent. The preoperative work also includes dressing, scrubbing, preparing the patient and needed equipment for the procedure, positioning the patient on the x-ray table, and draping the catheter puncture site.

Intraservice

An injection needle is directed into the subarachnoid or epidural space at the proper vertebral level, under x-ray fluoroscopy, as necessary. Care is taken to avoid damaging any nerve roots or the spinal cord. A contrast injection is performed as necessary to confirm the location of the needle tip or catheter and to determine the degree of free flow of liquid in the space to assure both safety and accuracy. An infusion catheter is threaded through the needle in the subarachnoid or epidural space. The therapeutic injection(s) is performed through the same catheter. The injection catheter is removed and a sterile dressing is applied, with detailed attention given to wound care to prevent infection, which may lead to meningitis or epidural abscess.

Postservice

The patient is closely observed for 2-8 hours postprocedure in a monitored setting for any new, unexpected neurologic defects and/or any change in vital signs (eg, respiratory depression, bradycardia, altered mental status). The physician communicates the findings with the patient and other professionals (including providing written and oral reports and orders).

Coding Tip for 62319

Procedures commonly used in the management of postoperative pain include code 62319 for continuous epidural analgesia and the series of codes for somatic nerve blocks (codes 64400-64450).

Catheter Implantation

62350 Implantation, revision or repositioning of tunneled intrathecal or epidural catheter, for long-term medication administration via an external pump or implantable reservoir/infusion pump; without laminectomy

Work Value: 8.04 // Global Period: 090

➲ *CPT Assistant* Nov 99: 36; *CPT Changes: An Insider's View* 2000, 2001

Clinical Example

A 65-year-old male presents with bilateral leg and pelvic bone pain (rated 8/10) due to prostate cancer and metastases to multiple bone sites in the lower body. Because of the multiple sites of bone involvement and lack of response to chemotherapy, no radiation therapy or further chemotherapy is planned for him. His expected survival time is 9 months due to cancer. Although his pain has been lessened with the use of oral opiates, the patient is experiencing intolerable side effects, even at relatively low doses. After successful screening, an intrathecal catheter is inserted and its position verified. The catheter is anchored for connection to an implanted pump. No laminectomy is required for catheter insertion in this patient because the catheter is introduced percutaneously into the subarachnoid space via a needle inserter. Only a small skin incision is needed to connect the catheter to the implanted pump catheter.

Preservice

Preservice work includes reviewing the hospital admission workup; preparing the equipment required for surgery; and obtaining informed consent. The patient is placed in a lateral recumbent position on a radiolucent table, prepped, draped, and marked for catheter placement.

Intraservice

A Touhy needle is inserted in the midlumbar region, such as L3-L4, until the dura is penetrated. The catheter is advanced using fluoroscopy to the desired placement level and patency is verified by injection of nonionic contrast. With the Touhy needle in place, a vertical incision (3-5 cm) is made to expose the supraspinous ligament to provide tissue to secure the catheter segment. The Touhy needle and guide are withdrawn. The catheter is secured with a purse string suture around the catheter. An anchoring sleeve to prevent tension and angulation of the catheter is sutured to the tissue and the catheter is inserted into the sleeve. The skin is closed after the catheter is connected to the reservoir or pump.

Postservice

Postservice work includes stabilizing the patient and communicating with the patient, the patient's family, and other health care professionals (including providing written and oral reports and orders). Discharge day management includes the surgeons final examination of the patient, discussing the hospital stay, providing instructions for continuing care, and preparing the discharge records. Additionally, all hospital visits and postdischarge office visits for care of the wound for 90 days after the day of the operation are considered part of the postoperative work for this procedure.

Coding Tip for 62350

Code 62350 is reported when an intrathecal or epidural catheter is connected to an external pump, an implantable reservoir, or an implantable infusion pump not requiring a laminectomy.

Reservoir/Pump Implantation

62368 Electronic analysis of programmable, implanted pump for intrathecal or epidural drug infusion (includes evaluation of reservoir status, alarm status, drug prescription status); with reprogramming

Work Value: 0.75 // Global Period: XXX

➲ *CPT Assistant* Nov 02: 10

Clinical Example

A 65-year-old male presents for an electronic analysis of an implanted infusion pump that delivers opiates to control pain because he has begun to experience increasing pain that has become quite severe (rated 6/10) after several months of good control. The patient has prostate cancer and metastases to multiple bone sites in the lower body and resultant bilateral leg and pelvic bone pain. Because of the multiple sites of bone involvement and lack of response to chemotherapy, no radiation therapy or further chemotherapy is planned. His expected survival time is 9 months due to cancer. Analysis of the pump function via external electronic analysis verifies the infusion rate. The pump is then reprogrammed to increase the rate of infusion and control the increased level of pain.

Preservice

Preservice work includes reviewing the patient's medical chart, paying special attention to the patient's response to drug delivery via an implanted infusion pump.

Intraservice

Electronic analysis is performed to determine reservoir status, alarm status, and the drug prescription status. Electronic analysis of the pump function verifies the infusion rate. The pump is reprogrammed to increase the rate of infusion and to control the increased level of pain.

Postservice

Postservice work includes communicating with the patient, the patient's family, and other health care professionals (including providing written and oral reports and orders), and reprogramming the pump as needed.

Posterior Extradural Laminotomy or Laminectomy for Exploration/ Decompression of Neural Elements or Excision of Herniated Intervertebral Discs

⑤ **63047** Laminectomy, facetectomy and foraminotomy (unilateral or bilateral with decompression of spinal cord, cauda equina and/or nerve root(s), (eg, spinal or lateral recess stenosis)), single vertebral segment; lumbar

Work Value: 15.22 // Global Period: 090

➲ ***CPT Assistant*** **Jan 99: 11, Jan 01: 12, Feb 01: 10, Nov 02: 11**

Clinical Example

A 72-year-old female presents with 5 months of neurogenic claudication that is unresponsive to physical therapy or epidural cortisone injections. Imaging studies reveal L4-L5 spinal stenosis. She undergoes L4-L5 decompressive laminectomy with medial facetectomies and bilateral L5 foraminotomies. Postoperative hospital care and office visits are conducted as necessary through the 90-day global period.

Preservice

Review the preoperative lab work-up. Write preoperative orders for perioperative medications. Locate, review, and place magnetic resonance imaging and/or other spinal imaging studies on the view box in the operating room. Review the planned incisions and procedure. Greet the patient in the holding area and review the surgical procedure, postoperative recovery in and out of the hospital, and expected outcome(s) with the patient and the patient's family. Sign and mark the operative site. Obtain informed consent. Verify that all necessary surgical instruments, supplies, and devices are available in the operative suite. Review the length and type of anesthesia with the anesthesiologist. Monitor initial patient positioning for the induction of anesthesia. Following the induction of anesthesia, assist with repositioning of patient, and verify/assist with padding the patient to prevent pressure on neurovascular structures. Scrub and gown. Mark the incisions and supervise the prepping/draping of the patient.

Intraservice

Make a midline incision in the skin and subcutaneous tissue. Expose the L4 spinous process and lamina with subperiosteal dissection. Remove the spinous process and lamina of L4 with a drill or bone-biting instruments. Remove the ligamentum flavum, exposing the thecal sac and nerve roots. Remove the medial L4-L5 facets with a drill or bone-biting instruments, exposing the L5 nerve roots. Perform a foraminotomy for the L5 nerve root. Perform a diskectomy to complete the foraminotomy, as needed. Irrigate the wound and close it in layers (over a drain, if placed). Apply sterile dressings.

Postservice

Turn the patient into the supine position. When anesthesia is reversed, transfer the patient to the recovery room. Write an operative note for the patient's record. Examine the patient, checking wound(s) and the patient's progress. Monitor for abnormal neurological findings. Sign operating room forms, including pre- and postoperative diagnosis and the operations performed. Discuss the outcome of the procedure with the patient's family. Dictate the postoperative report. Discuss the outcome of the procedure with the referring physician. Dictate the procedure outcome and expected recovery in a letter for the referring physician and/or insurance company. Order and review films to check the alignment of the lumbar spine. Write orders daily, as necessary, for medications, diet, and patient activity. Examine the patient daily, checking wounds and the patient's progress. Review the nursing and/or other staffs patient chart notes. Write patient progress notes. Discuss the patient's progress with the referring physician (verbal and written). Answer the patient's and family's questions, the nursing and/or other staffs questions (verbal and written), and the insurance staffs questions. At discharge, review the post-discharge wound care, use and proper fit of the brace, and activity limitations, including planned physical therapy, with the patient. Answer the patient's and family's questions and the nursing and/or other staff's questions. Write orders for post-discharge films, and medications. Write patient discharge notes. In the office, write orders for medications and follow-up films. Review post discharge films. Examine the patient, performing periodic neurological exams. Monitor the patient's wounds and remove sutures/staples. Review the use and proper fit of the brace with the patient. Review the progress of the patient's physical therapy and revise orders as needed. Dictate patient progress notes for the patient's medical chart. Answer the patient's and family's questions and the insurance staff's questions. Discuss the patient's progress with the referring physician (verbal and written).

✚❺ 63048 Laminectomy, facetectomy and foraminotomy (unilateral or bilateral with decompression of spinal cord, cauda equina and/or nerve root(s), (eg, spinal or lateral recess stenosis)), single vertebral segment; each additional segment, cervical, thoracic, or lumbar (List separately in addition to code for primary procedure)

Work Value: 3.47 // Global Period: ZZZ

➲ ***CPT Assistant*** **Fall 91: 8, Jan 99: 11, Jan 01: 12**

Clinical Example

A 72-year-old female presents with 5 months of neurogenic claudication unresponsive to physical therapy or epidural cortisone injections. Imaging studies reveal L3-L4 and L4-L5 spinal stenosis. She undergoes L3-L4 and L4-L5 decompressive laminectomies, medial facetectomies, and bilateral L4 and L5 foraminotomies.

Intraservice

After completion of the first vertebral level treated, the physician proceeds to the next level. The incision and subperiosteal dissection is carried rostrally, exposing the L3 spinous process and lamina. The spinous process and lamina of L3 is removed with a drill or bone-biting instruments exposing the dura and ligamentum flavum of the L3-L4 interspace. The ligamentum flavum is removed, exposing the lateral recess of the spinal canal. Medial facetectomy (unilateral or bilateral) is performed with a drill, osteotome, or bone-biting instruments. The L3 nerve root is exposed and decompressed via foraminotomy and diskectomy (if necessary).

Coding Tip for 63047 and 63048

Code 63048 is an add-on code that may be reported only when code 63047 has been reported for the first lumbar vertebral segment procedure, and it is necessary to report procedures for one or more additional segments. For coding purposes, a segment is defined as a single complete vertebral bone with associated articular processes and laminae.

Anterior or Anterolateral Approach for Extradural Exploration/Decompression

⑤ **63075** Discectomy, anterior, with decompression of spinal cord and/or nerve root(s), including osteophytectomy; cervical, single interspace

Work Value: 19.47 // Global Period: 090

➲ ***CPT Assistant* Nov 98: 18, Jan 01: 12, Feb 02: 4; *CPT Changes: An Insider's View* 2002**

Clinical Example

A 47-year-old male presents with 3 months of right cervicobrachial pain radiating into the hand and gait difficulty. Examination shows mild triceps weakness with an absent right triceps reflex and decreased pinprick sensation in the right long finger. The patient has an extensor plantar response and mild hyperpathia in the lower limbs. A magnetic resonance imaging (MRI) scan reveals a right anterolateral spondylotic disc herniation at C6-C7 with compression of the C7 nerve root and anterolateral surface of the spinal cord. An anterior C6-C7 diskectomy with osteophytectomy and C7 foraminotomy is performed. Postoperative hospital care and office visits are performed as necessary through the 90-day global period.

Preservice

Review the preoperative lab work-up. Write preoperative orders for perioperative medications. Locate, review, and place MRI and/or other spinal imaging studies on the view box in the operating room. Review the planned incisions and procedure. Greet the patient in the holding area and review the surgical procedure, postoperative recovery in and out of the hospital, and expected outcome(s) with the patient and the patient's family. Sign and mark the operative site. Obtain informed consent. Verify that all necessary surgical instruments, supplies, and devices are available in the operative suite. Review the length and type of anesthesia with the anesthesiologist. Monitor initial patient positioning for the induction of anesthesia. Following the induction of anesthesia, assist with repositioning of patient and verify/assist with padding the patient to prevent pressure on neurovascular structures. Scrub and gown. Mark the incisions and supervise the prepping/draping of the patient.

Intraservice

A transverse incision is made anteriorly over the level of the proposed arthrodesis. The platysma muscle is cut inline with the skin incision. The interval between the sternocleidomastoid and carotid sheath laterally and the trachea and esophagus medially is developed and the prevertebral fascia is cleared from the front of the spine. The disc between the vertebrae to be fused is identified and the level confirmed by X ray. The longus colli muscles are mobilized along their medial edges. Lateral and longitudinal self-retaining traction devices are inserted. The anterior longitudinal ligament and anterior anulus are removed by sharp dissection. The disc space is distracted and an operating microscope is used to visualize the posterior portion of the disc. Additional disc material and osteophytes are removed to decompress the spinal canal and nerve root(s). A drain is placed in the wound as desired. The platysma muscle, subcutaneous tissue, and skin are sutured. Sterile dressings and a collar or brace are applied.

Postservice

When anesthesia has been reversed, transfer the patient to the recovery room. Write an operative note in the patient's record. Examine the patient, checking wound(s) and patient progress. Monitor for abnormal neurological findings. Sign operating room forms, including the pre- and postoperative diagnosis and the operations performed. Discuss the outcome of the procedure with the patient's family. Dictate the postoperative report. Discuss the outcome of the procedure with the referring physician. Dictate the procedure outcome and expected recovery in a letter for the referring physician and/or the insurance company. Order and review films to check the alignment of the cervical spine. Write orders daily, as necessary, for medications, diet, and patient activity. Examine the patient daily, checking wounds and patient progress. Review the nursing and/or other staff's patient chart notes. Write patient progress notes. Discuss the patient's progress with the referring physician (verbal and written). Answer the patient's and family's questions, the nursing and/or other staff's questions (verbal and written), and the insurance staffs questions. At discharge, review post-discharge wound care, use and proper fit of the collar, and activity limitations, including planned physical therapy, with the patient. Answer the patient's and family's questions and the nursing and/or other staffs questions. Write orders for post-discharge films, and medications. Write patient discharge notes. In the office, write orders for medications and follow-up films. Review post-discharge films. Examine the patient, performing periodic neurological exams. Monitor the patient's wounds and remove sutures/staples. Review the use and proper fit of the brace with the patient. Review the progress of the patient's physical therapy and revise orders as needed. Dictate patient progress notes for the patient's medical chart. Answer the patient's and family's questions and the insurance staffs questions. Discuss the patient's progress with the referring physician (verbal and written).

Extracranial Nerves, Peripheral Nerves, and Autonomic Nervous System

Introduction/Injection of Anesthetic Agent (Nerve Block), Diagnostic or Therapeutic

64470 Injection, anesthetic agent and/or steroid, paravertebral facet joint or facet joint nerve; cervical or thoracic, single level

Work Value: 1.85 // Global Period: 000

➲ *CPT Assistant* Nov 99: 33, 37, Feb 00: 4, Sep 04: 3; *CPT Changes: An Insider's View* 2000

Clinical Example

A 67-year-old female presents with a long history of cervical spine pain in her neck that radiates into her shoulders. She has no pain into her fingertips, no weakness in her arms, and denies any bowel or bladder symptoms. She has failed to obtain relief using various oral medications and physical therapy. A recent X-ray showed cervical spondylosis between C5-C6. The patient undergoes cervical facet joint injection with corticosteriod (eg, betamethasone sodium phosphate) into the cervical facet joint at C5-C6.

Preservice

Preservice work includes reviewing records and any pertinent imaging studies; communicating with other professionals, the patient, and the patient's family; and obtaining consent. Preservice work also includes dressing, scrubbing, preparing the patient and needed equipment for the procedure, positioning the patient on the X-ray table for appropriate fluoroscopic view, and draping the injection site.

Intraservice

Under intravenous anesthetic, the affected joint/joint nerve is identified and the skin is infiltrated with a local anesthetic. A needle is directed into the cervical or thoracic facet joint or along the facet joint nerve at the proper vertebral level with X-ray fluoroscopic guidance. Contrast injection is performed to confirm the location of the needle tip. Once this is completed, an anesthetic agent and/or steroid is injected. The injection needle is removed and a sterile dressing is applied.

Postservice

After the procedure, the patient is observed for any new and unexpected neurological defects. The physician reviews the procedure and results with the patient and other professionals (including providing written and oral reports and orders).

Coding Tip for 64470

Code 64470 is a unilateral procedure. When injections are performed at both the right and left paravertebral facet joints or paravertebral facet joint nerves, append modifier 50, *Bilateral procedure,* to the code.

64483 Injection, anesthetic agent and/or steroid, transforaminal epidural; lumbar or sacral, single level

Work Value: 1.90 // Global Period: 000

➲ ***CPT Assistant*** **Nov 99: 33, 37, Feb 00: 4;** ***CPT Changes: An Insider's View*** **2000**

Clinical Example

A 71-year-old male with coronary artery disease and moderate heart failure presents with recurrent right leg pain, the ability to stand for only 10 minutes and walk less than 1 block, and minimal problems sitting. The patient's history includes a previous laminectomy at L4-L5; a magnetic resonance imaging scan with gadolinium, showing a small recurrent herniation between L4-L5 with scar tissue; and neurodiagnostic studies compatible with an acute L5 radiculopathy. He has failed to obtain relief using various oral medication, physical therapy, and traction. He undergoes a transforaminal epidural injection of an anesthetic agent and/or steroid at the L5-S1 level.

Preservice

Preservice work includes reviewing records and any pertinent imaging studies; communicating with other professionals, the patient, and the patient's family; and obtaining consent. Preservice work also includes dressing, scrubbing, preparing the patient and needed equipment for the procedure, positioning the patient on the X-ray table for appropriate fluoroscopic view, and draping the injection site.

Intraservice

Under intravenous anesthetic, the affected foramen is identified and the skin is infiltrated with a local anesthetic. A needle is directed lateral to midline under fluoroscopic guidance into the foramen. Both anteroposterior and oblique or lateral views are needed to get depth as well as an anterior and posterior position. Contrast injection is performed to confirm the location of the needle tip. Once this is completed, an anesthetic agent and/or steroid is injected. The injection needle is removed and a sterile dressing is applied.

Postservice

After the procedure, the patient is observed for any new and unexpected neurological defects. The physician reviews the procedure and results with the patient and other professionals (including providing written and oral reports and orders).

Coding Tip for 64483

A transforaminal epidural spinal injection technique is a technically different approach from central epidural injection. Because the vertebral artery as well as the spinal cord is close to the nerve root, this procedural technique is more difficult than a central epidural injection. Codes 64483 and 64484 identify the spinal anatomy, the substances injected, and the spinal level or levels involved.

+ 64484 Injection, anesthetic agent and/or steroid, transforaminal epidural; lumbar or sacral, each additional level (List separately in addition to code for primary procedure)

Work Value: 1.33 // Global Period: ZZZ

➲ ***CPT Assistant*** **Nov 99: 33, 37, Feb 00: 4, Feb 05: 14;** ***CPT Changes: An Insider's View*** **2000**

Clinical Example

A 71-year-old male with coronary artery disease and moderate heart failure presents with recurrent right leg pain, the ability to stand for only 10 minutes and walk less than 1 block, and minimal problems sitting. The patient's history includes previous laminectomy at L3-L4 and L4-L5; a magnetic resonance imaging scan with gadolinium, showing a small recurrent herniation between L4-L5 with scar tissue; and neurodiagnostic studies compatible with an acute L4 and L5 radiculopathy. He has failed to obtain relief using various oral medications, physical therapy, and traction. He undergoes a transforaminal epidural injection of an anesthetic agent and/or steroid at the L4-L5 and L5-S1 levels.

Intraservice

Under intravenous anesthetic, the affected additional foramen is identified and the skin is infiltrated with a local anesthetic. A needle is directed lateral to midline under fluoroscopic guidance into the foramen. Additional anteroposterior and oblique or lateral views are needed to get depth as well as anterior and posterior position. Contrast injection is performed to confirm the location of the needle tip. Once this is completed, an anesthetic agent and/or steroid is injected. The injection needle is removed and a sterile dressing is applied.

Coding Tip for 64484

Code 64484 is an add-on code reported for each additional spinal level injected and is always reported in addition to code 64483.

Neurostimulators (Peripheral Nerve)

64573 Incision for implantation of neurostimulator electrodes; cranial nerve

Work Value: 8.15 // Global Period: 090

➲ *CPT Assistant* Sep 99: 4, Nov 99: 38, Apr 01: 8; *CPT Changes: An Insider's View* 2000

Clinical Example

A 31-year-old male with a 21-year history of partial complex epilepsy is experiencing 10–12 seizures per month and considerable side effects from maximal doses of carbamazepine and sodium valproate. His history includes previous single-drug and polypharmacy drug regimens, but in each case, the number, intensity, and duration of seizures were intolerable. His history also indicates no evidence for nonepileptic seizures under video electroencephalogram recording. He undergoes an open operation to implant a neurostimulator electrode on the vagal nerve.

Preservice

Preservice work includes reviewing the patient's records and any pertinent imaging studies, including previous treatments for seizure disorder; communicating with other professionals, the patient, and the patient's family; obtaining informed consent; dressing; scrubbing; preparing the needed equipment for the procedure; and supervising the prepping and draping of the patient.

Intraservice

Intraservice work includes making a curvilinear incision on the side of the neck over the sternocleidomastoid (SCM) muscle after the induction of anesthesia; retracting the wound edges with a self-retaining retractor; obtaining hemostasis; dissecting the external jugular vein and SCM muscle; exposing the carotid sheath and carefully opening it; exposing the vagus nerve, being careful not to damage either the jugular vein, carotid artery, and laryngeal nerve; carrying out the dissection along the posterior carotid sheath and vagus nerve to expose approximately 6 cm of the nerve; placing the stimulator electrode coil by spiraling it around the vagus nerve; testing the electrode array for good contact with the nerve by measuring electrode impedance; repositioning the electrode array as necessary; obtaining absolute hemostasis; irrigating the wound with antibiotic solution; testing the electrode placement and efficacy; inspecting the wound for any bleeding or damage to nerves, veins, and/or arteries; tunneling the tail of the electrode subcutaneously to enable it to be connected to a neurostimulator generator; irrigating the wound; and closing it in layers.

Postservice

Postservice work includes applying sterile dressings; checking the entire stimulator system for proper function; communicating with the patient's family and other health care professionals (including providing written and oral reports and orders); monitoring the patient's neurological condition for any deficits; monitoring the patient for infection; and managing the patient's antibiotic and pain medication. (Frequently during the postoperative period, the patient's neurological condition is monitored for any deficits from either electrode placement and/or the stimulation itself and/or from carotid artery, jugular vein, or vagal nerve damage.)

Discharge day management includes performing a final examination of the patient, reviewing the postdischarge continuing care and instructions with the patient and the patient's family, and preparing the discharge records. Additionally, all postdischarge office visits for this procedure for 90 days after the day of the operation are considered part of the postoperative work for this procedure, including removing staples and sutures, monitoring wound healing, and examining the patient in the office at appropriate postoperative intervals to ensure adequate healing of all wounds and functioning/effectiveness of the implant.

Implantation Neurostimulator Electrodes, Cranial Nerve (Vagal Nerve Stimulation)
61885, 64573

Open incision for implantation of a neurostimulator electrode (64573) on the vagus nerve (a cranial nerve) with connection of the electrode to an implanted programmable pulse generator (61885) in the infraclavicular area.

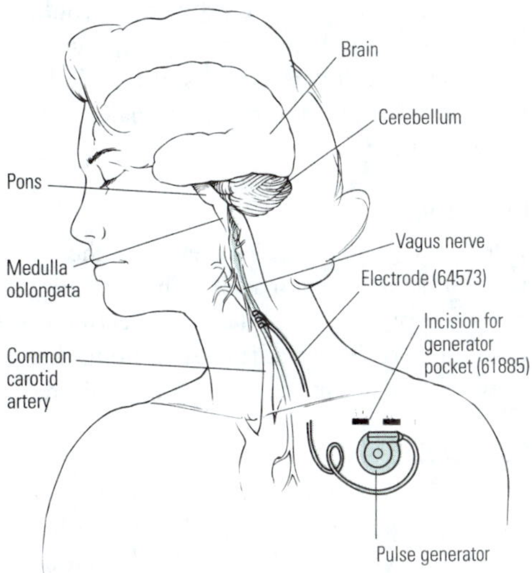

Destruction by Neurolytic Agent (eg, Chemical, Thermal, Electrical or Radiofrequency)

Somatic Nerves

64614 Chemodenervation of muscle(s); extremity(s) and/or trunk muscle(s) (eg, for dystonia, cerebral palsy, multiple sclerosis)

Work Value: 2.20 // Global Period: 010

➲ ***CPT Assistant*** **Apr 01: 2, Feb 05: 14, Aug 05: 13;** ***CPT Changes: An Insider's View*** **2001**

Clinical Example

A 36-year-old, right-handed male complains of severe cramping of his right hand when trying to write or print. This began several years ago but has worsened considerably to the point where his writing is now illegible. Examination shows flexion of the fingers. Based on available clinical and electrodiagnostic information, involuntary overactivity at the flexor digitorum sublimis, flexor carpi ulnaris, and flexor digitorum profundus was identified. The specific muscles were identified, and targeted injections using optimal doses of botulinum toxin were administered. The cramping was relieved and the patient could subsequently write legibly for long periods of time.

Preservice

Preservice work includes the work completed to confirm whether botulinum toxin would be of benefit and identify the appropriate injection sites. Preservice work also includes discussing the procedure, its rationale, and risks, with the patient.

Intraservice

Intraservice work includes preparing the region for injections, marking the location of each appropriate muscle, and injecting the botulinum toxin in multiple sites along the muscle. (Several muscles are usually injected.)

Postservice

Postservice work includes dictating the postoperative report and communicating with the referring physician. Additionally, the physician reviews the potential complications and again gives the patient guidelines for calling or returning. The value of repeat injection, the timing of that injection, and the long-term prognosis are reviewed.

Chemodenervation of Extremity
64614

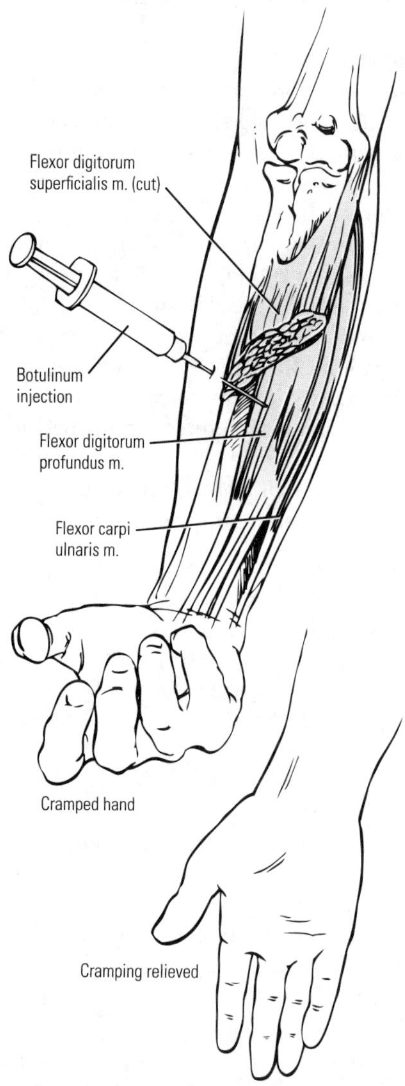

Coding Tip for 64614

Codes 64612-64614 are reported once even though multiple injections are performed in sites along a particular muscle. (Several muscles are typically injected.)

Neuroplasty (Exploration, Neurolysis or Nerve Decompression)

⑤ 64721 Neuroplasty and/or transposition; median nerve at carpal tunnel

Work Value: 4.84 // Global Period: 090

➲ *CPT Assistant* **Fall 92: 17, Sep 97: 10, Jun 01: 11**

Clinical Example

A 50-year-old female with carpal tunnel syndrome undergoes an open carpal tunnel release.

Preservice

Write the preadmission orders for preoperative medications. Review the results of preadmission testing including labs, X rays, computed tomogrpahy scans, and/or magnetic resonance imaging scans. Complete the consultation with the referring physician and other healthcare professionals. Reexamine the patient to make sure that physical findings have not changed. Meet with the patient and the patient's family to review the planned procedure and postoperative management. Review informed consent with the patient. Verify that all required instruments and supplies are available. Monitor/assist with positioning the patient, padding the bony prominences, and applying thermal regulation drapes. Assess the position of the extremities and head and adjust as needed. Place the patient's arm on the hand surgery table. Indicate the areas of the skin to be prepped and mark the surgical incisions. Apply a tourniquet to the proximal arm. Prep and drape the arm and hand. Elevate and exsanguinate the arm. Inflate the pneumatic tourniquet. Scrub and gown. Perform a surgical time out with the operating surgical team.

Intraservice

Make an incision along the ulnar border of the carpal tunnel in the palm. Carry out careful dissection. Identify and protect the branches of the palmar cutaneous branch of the median nerve, as well as the palmar cutaneous branch of the ulnar nerve. Identify the transverse carpal ligament. Identify the proximal and distal edges of the transverse carpal ligament. Place a groove director in the carpal tunnel along its ulnar border. Use a #15-blade to incise the transverse carpal ligament along its ulnar border. Take care not to injure the underlying flexor tendons or the branches of the median or ulnar nerve. Take care to protect the superficial palmar arch and the communicating sensory branches between the median and ulnar nerves, which course just distal to the transverse carpal ligament. Once the transverse carpal ligament is released, examine the contents of the carpal tunnel, including the flexor tendons and the median nerve. If needed, carry out an external neurolysis of the median nerve. Thoroughly irrigate the wound. Approximate the skin with an interrupted suture.

Postservice

Apply sterile dressing and splint. Monitor patient stabilization in the recovery room. Consult with the patient and the patient's family regarding the surgery and postoperative regimen. Communicate with health care professionals including providing written and oral reports and orders. Coordinate postoperative care with the recovery room nursing staff. Check the patient's vital signs. Assess the circulation, sensation, and motor function of the operated extremity. Discuss home restrictions (ie, activity, bathing) with the patient and the patient's family. Write prescriptions for medications needed post-discharge. Complete all appropriate medical records, including the discharge summary, discharge instructions, and insurance forms. Dictate the operative report. Write a procedure note in the patient chart. In the office, examine and talk with the patient. Answer the patient's and familys questions. Remove the splint/dressings. Assess the surgical wound. Remove sutures. Assess the circulation, sensation, and motor function of the operated extremity. Redress the wound. Order occupational therapy. Supervise the patient's rehabilitation. Discuss the patient's progress with the primary care physician (verbal and written). Write medication prescriptions. Dictate progress notes for the medical record.

Eye and Ocular Adnexa

Anterior Segment

Anterior Chamber

Incision

65855 Trabeculoplasty by laser surgery, one or more sessions (defined treatment series)

Work Value: 3.90 // Global Period: 010

➲ *CPT Assistant* Mar 98: 7, Mar 03: 23

Clinical Example

A 65-year-old, African-American male presents with uncontrolled intraocular pressure on maximally tolerated medical therapy. He has had progressive visual field loss and optic disc cupping. The patient has early cataracts. He states he is faithful with his medical regimen because he is very afraid of going blind.

Preservice

Pre-operative laser history is filled out; the chart is reviewed; the laser is tuned; the eye is pre-treated with miotic drops and the pressure is checked; the procedure and technique is explained to the patient and the patient is positioned at the laser and the appropriate laser settings are determined; and topical anesthetic drops are applied.

Intraservice

The laser goniolens is placed on the cornea and gonioscopy is performed. The aiming beam is focused on the anterior trabecula and tests are fired until pigment blending occurs. Between 60 and 100 beams are placed circumferentially. The lens is rinsed and the eye is irrigated and post-treated with anticoagulants and anti-inflammatory drops.

Postservice

Case is discussed with patient and family; arrangements are made for a follow-up visit within 24 hours; and patient is seen, as appropriate, over next three months to ensure that normal inflammations subside. Visits typically occur at 1 day, 1 week, and 2 months. Operative notes are dictated and discussion with family takes place.

Iris, Ciliary Body

Destruction

❺ **66761** Iridotomy/iridectomy by laser surgery (eg, for glaucoma) (one or more sessions)

Work Value: 4.87 // Global Period: 090

➲ *CPT Assistant* Mar 98: 7

Clinical Example

A 67-year-old female, who is at risk for acute angle closure glaucoma, presents with occludable narrow angles.

Preservice

A careful history is taken with special reference to anticoagulants, which may increase bleeding associated with the iridotomy. If a diathesis for bleeding is detected or the patient is on a high risk anticoagulant, the method of laser therapy may have to be modified by using both an argon and/or YAG laser. Prior to laser surgery, topical pilocarpine (cholinergic drug or parasympathomimetic) is instilled to achieve miosis. The patient waits. This drug takes a minimum of 30-45 minutes to achieve miosis. A topical alpha agonist is instilled to blunt the intraocular pressure (IOP) rise typically associated with laser iridotomy and to decrease bleeding. Following topical instillation of an anesthetic drop, the patient is seated at the laser.

Intraservice

A coupling gel is placed on the iridotomy contact lens. The lens is placed on the eye to stabilize the globe and allow maximal magnification of the iris. After the appropriate laser settings are configured, a hole is made in the iris using a variety of techniques. The position of the hole varies according to surgeon preference. The degree of difficulty of completing the iridotomy depends on patient cooperation, chamber depth, corneal clarity, and inflammation. After completing the iridotomy, the contact lens is removed, the eye is irrigated profusely to remove the coupling gel. A second drop of alpha agonist is instilled to decrease the IOP spike. A mild topical corticosteroid is applied.

Postservice

The IOP is rechecked 30-45 minutes after laser therapy to look for an acute rise. The physician also checks for the patency of the iridotomy. If IOP is markedly elevated, further antiglaucoma medications are instilled and the IOP rechecked. If the IOP is acceptable, the patient returns for repeat IOP and further evaluation at 1-2 weeks, depending on the level of preoperative glaucoma damage.

Lens

Incision

⑤ 66821 Discission of secondary membranous cataract (opacified posterior lens capsule and/or anterior hyaloid); laser surgery (eg, YAG laser) (one or more stages)

Work Value: 3.32 // Global Period: 090

Clinical Example

Eight months after surgery, a 70-year-old female complains of diminished vision in her operated eye. An eye examination reveals posterior capsular opacification that interferes with normal daily activity.

Preservice

The patient history and examination is reviewed to confirm that the patient has decreased visual acuity and opacification of the posterior capsule. Careful examination of the macula including use of the potential acuity meter is required to rule out macular diseases that cause visual loss. Informed consent is obtained. The patient's chart, past history and last ocular examination are reviewed. Topical steroids, antiglaucoma medications, and topical anesthetic are instilled.

Intraservice

The patient is seated at the laser and a contact lens is applied. Multiple applications of laser energy are delivered, caution being taken not to damage the intraocular lens implant or other structures. Test burns are applied to confirm the adequacy of the YAG energy, the burst mode and the power are adjusted to achieve optimal vaporization.

Postservice

The patient is monitored approximately two hours after the procedure for elevated intraocular pressure (IOP), which is a recognized complication of YAG laser capsulotomy. In the case of elevated IOP, medical treatment is usually sufficient for control. The patient is seen one to two weeks following the procedure for a refraction, IOP measurement, dilated fundus examination, and evaluation of the results of treatment. The patient is seen again at 1 month and 2 months following the procedure for a dilated retinal examination to look for evidence of retinal hole formation or retinal detachment.

Removal Cataract

⑤ 66984 Extracapsular cataract removal with insertion of intraocular lens prosthesis (one stage procedure), manual or mechanical technique (eg, irrigation and aspiration or phacoemulsification)

Work Value: 10.36 // Global Period: 090

➲ ***CPT Assistant*** **Fall 92: 5, 8, Feb 01: 7, Nov 03: 10, Mar 05: 11**

Clinical Example

A 70-year-old female complains of vision problems. Examination reveals that a cataract in her right eye has progressed to the point of visual impairment. She has difficulty reading and recently failed a driving test.

Preservice

Preparation of the patient begins in the surgical holding area. The eye for surgery is identified by the surgeon. The eye is briefly examined to rule out any changes since the last examination. The adequacy of pupillary dilation is checked. Preoperative topical antibiotics may be administered to the operative eye. The patient is greeted and any final questions or concerns are addressed. The surgeon checks pertinent aspects of the patient's chart and notes vital signs, laboratory, radiologic, and electrocardiographic data. If not previously performed, an appropriate history and physical is performed. The ophthalmic surgeon may then perform aneshtesia. This may be a topical, peribulbar, or retrobulbar anesthetic block. This may be performed while short-acting intravenous neuroleptic anesthesia is given. The patient's vital signs are closely monitored to guard against respiratory arrest or other such potential emergency. The surgeon may then elect to place an ocular compressive device on the eye to reduce intraorbital pressure. This may remain in place for several minutes during which time the patient's vital signs are monitored.

Intraservice

The patient is positioned for intraocular microsurgery. The surgeon preps and drapes the operative site. The adequacy of the anesthetic block must be checked. If a peribulbar or retrobulbar anesthetic block is not used, the application of a topical or subconjunctival anesthetic is carried out. Cataract extraction devices such as phacoemulsification units must be checked to assure that the proper irrigation, aspiration, and phacoemulsification parameters are entered and that the machine operates properly. The microscope then is positioned. The surgeon places a lid speculum and a bridle-suture(s) to assure proper position of the eye. A flap of conjunctiva might be raised to lend access to the surgical limbus. Hemostasis is accomplished with a proper cautery instrument. A precise side-port incision is made away from the surgical incision. The manner of surgical incision varies: It may be a clear-corneal incision performed with a diamond keratome; a surgical limbus incision; or a scleral-tunnel incision, which requires a partial thickness scleral incision with forward tunneling into clear cornea with a crescent knife. In the case of the latter incision, the actual configuration of the incision may be arcuate, tangential, or parallel to the limbus. A viscoelastic substance is employed to insufflate the anterior chamber. The anterior chamber is then entered with a sharp blade to a precise incision size of 3.2 mm. A sharp bent needle and forceps are used to fashion an opening in the anterior capsule of the cataract. This is done in a circular fashion to ensure strength and integrity. Its diameter routinely measures 5-8 mm. The cataractous lens is loosened by injecting fluid between the lens and its capsule, a process known as hydrodissection. The surgeon may choose to inject fluid between the lamella of the lens material itself. Additional viscoelastic material may is injected into the anterior chamber prior to phacoemulsification. The function of the phacoemulsification handpiece is checked again. If satisfactory, the tip is inserted into the eye. Phacofragmentation with simultaneous aspiration of the lens material is carried out. The lens must be rotated and disassembled to avoid inadvertent trauma to intraocular structures. The side-port incision is used to allow access to a second instrument. The dense cataractous lens material is removed from the eye. The phacoemulsification tip is removed from the eye. An irrigation-aspiration tip is introduced into the eye to commence cleanup of the residual cortical lens material. The thin, transparent lens capsule is then carefully vacuumed and polished in an attempt to avoid future secondary membrane formation.

At this point, the anterior segment is ready for the intraocular lens. Depending on the lens style deemed appropriate by the surgeon, the incision may need to be opened to a slightly larger chord-length to allow an injector to enter the anterior chamber. The lens is placed in the eye using an injection device. Once in the eye, the lens is properly positioned and centered. This is accomplished by ensuring that the prosthesis is located in the empty lenticular capsule. The integrity of this fragile, transparent membrane is of paramount importance. Some surgeons elect to create a peripheral iridectomy in the iris. The surgeon must now evacuate the viscoelastic substance from the eye to prevent postoperative complication. This is generally accomplished with the irrigation and aspiration handpiece. The anterior chamber must be properly pressurized and the incisional site must be assessed for the need of sutures to guarantee a water-tight closure. A miotic drug is injected into the eye to produce pupillary miosis. If a conjunctival flap was prepared, it must be securely fastened at its point of insertion. The bridle suture(s) and lid speculum are removed. It is common to inject an antibiotic and steroid in the subtenons space. An antibiotic ointment may be placed on the eye. A soft patch and a rigid shield is then positioned on the operative eye by the surgeon. The patient is prepared to leave the operative suite.

Postservice

The surgeon will commonly speak with the patient and the patient's family. Instructions are given and explained, questions are addressed, and a prognosis is given. The patient is seen the next day in the ophthalmic office. All postoperative examinations include a history of the postoperative course, an examination of the operative eye including vision, intraocular pressure, and ophthalmic evaluation of the anterior and posterior segment. Further instructions are given for medication use, patient activity, and future follow-up. Corneal keratometry and topography are commonly performed postoperatively to ascertain surgical stigmatism. The global surgical period for code 66984 is 90 days. The patient is examined four times during the postoperative period as well as on the day of the procedure for discharge management. At least on two occasions a dilated exam of the retina is performed. A postoperative examination with a refraction is usually performed between weeks three and six and a spectacle prescription is dispensed if the refraction is stable.

Posterior Segment

Vitreous

67027 Implantation of intravitreal drug delivery system (eg, ganciclovir implant), includes concomitant removal of vitreous

Work Value: 11.43 // Global Period: 090

➲ *CPT Assistant* Nov 97: 23, Nov 98: 1

Clinical Example

A 40-year-old, HIV-positive male presents with cytomegalovirus (CMV) retinitis in one eye. After a discussion of available treatment options, the patient chooses the ganciclovir implant for treatment of his disease. His medical history is reviewed, his case is discussed with his primary care provider, and laboratory tests are reviewed to ensure that surgery would indeed be appropriate. The patient is taken to the operating room where the procedure is performed using a retrobulbar block and intravenous (IV) sedation (supplied by the anesthesiologist or certified registered nurse anesthetist). A partial vitrectomy is performed through a pars plana incision and a ganciclovir implant is placed into the eye and sutured into position. The patient requires frequent postoperative evaluation, including monthly evaluations for the status of his CMV retinitis both in the involved eye and for disease elsewhere.

Preservice

The patient's history and examination findings are reviewed. Written informed consent for the procedure is obtained. The benefits and significant risks of the procedure, including retinal detachment, are explained to the patient. Laboratory test results are obtained and reviewed to confirm that the patient is a surgical candidate. Similarly, physical exam results from the primary care physician are reviewed to be certain the patient remains a candidate for this procedure. The patient is taken to the operating room and placed in the supine position. A retrobulbar injection is given and IV sedation is administered. Routine sterile prepping and draping is performed.

Intraservice

On a side table the ganciclovir implant is prepared. It is removed from the sterile package, a small hole is placed through the strut with a 30-gauge needle, the excess strut is trimmed, and the hole threaded with a double-armed 8-0 nylon suture. A lid speculum is placed between the eyelids, and the operating microscope is positioned over the eye to perform the procedure. The conjunctiva is opened inferotemporally for approximately three clock hours. Hemostasis is maintained with bipolar cautery. A stab incision into the eye is made 4 mm from the limbus and continued circumferentially for 5 to 6 mm.

The choroid is opened to a similar length. The vitreous cuter is placed inside the wound and a partial vitrectomy is performed. The Ganciclovir implant is inserted through the wound and sutured into position using the double-armed 8-0 nylon suture. Prolapsed vitreous is removed using the vitreous cutter. The wound is then closed with 8-0 nylon suture. The eye is filled to a normal pressure with a balanced salt solution on a 30-gauge needle. The pressure of the eye is confirmed with gentle palpation of the globe. The conjunctiva is closed with a 6-0 plain suture. The retina is inspected with the indirect ophthalmoscope (ophthalmoscopy) to ensure that there have been no retinal breaks. The ophthalmoscopic exam will also confirm that the implant is well positioned outside of the visual axis. Subconjunctival antibiotics are administered. After an appropriate recovery period, the patient is discharged home, usually on the same day. At the time of the discharge, the physician discusses the warning symptoms of retinal detachment and endophthalmitis with the patient. The physician also reviews with the patient the use of topical antibiotics and corticosteroids the patient will be administering at home.

Postservice

Patients are evaluated on postoperative day 1, day 7, 1 month, and then monthly thereafter. Each exam consists of vision, slit lamp evaluation, intraocular pressure determination, and retinal ophthalmoscopy of the operated eye. Specific attention is directed to the status of the CMV retinitis in the eye and to the retina for evidence of retinal tears or detachment. At each exam, recommendations regarding management of systemic anti-CMV medications are often made and communicated with the patient's primary care provider. Follow-up during the 90-day period is more frequent than with most other forms of ocular surgery due to the necessity to continue monitoring the infectious disease, even after the surgical wounds are well healed.

Intravitreal Drug Delivery System
67027

A drug delivery system that releases medication into the vitreous is implanted into the vitreous by pars plana incision.

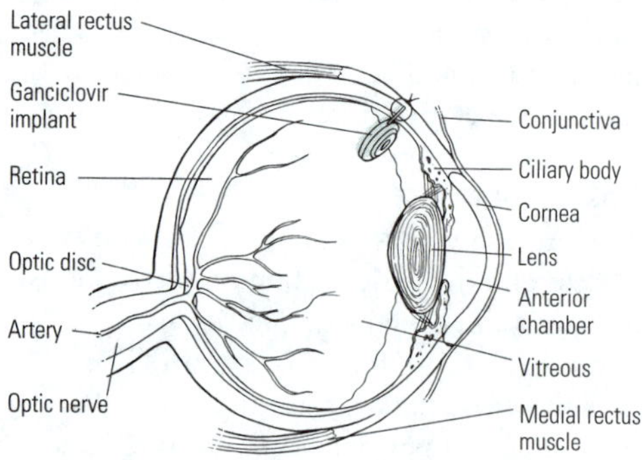

Retina or Choroid

Destruction

67210 Destruction of localized lesion of retina (eg, macular edema, tumors), one or more sessions; photocoagulation

Work Value: 9.35 // Global Period: 090

➲ *CPT Assistant* Mar 98: 7, Nov 98: 19

Clinical Example

A 56-year-old male with longstanding type II diabetes mellitus has noted decreased vision. Clinically significant macular edema is present. Focal photocoagulation is administered to the macula. Recovery is monitored during laser photocoagulation treatment.

Preservice

The patient's vision is measured, pupils are dilated, and anesthesia (topical or retrobulbar) is applied. Flourescein angiograms are reviewed with stereoscopy and placed in position to be continuously monitored during laser photocoagulation treatment.

Intraservice

Laser photocoagulation is performed, using projection of fluorescein angiogram as a guide. Each leaking microaneurysm with respect to papillomacular bundle and foveal avascular zone is closed. After closing each individual microaneurysm demonstrating leaking, attention is directed to areas of capillary dropout and areas of diffuse leakage where photocoagulation is applied in a "grid fashion". For each burn, the surgeon assesses the response to patient's motion, anterior segment opacity affecting the intensity of laser reaching lesion, thickness of lesion, and tissue reaction to treatment. The surgeon pauses frequently between burns to ensure continued steadiness of both patient and surgeon.

Postservice

Follow-up begins immediately after treatment. The surgeon assesses adequacy of treatment and checks for signs of complication such as bleeding, retinal tears, breaks in Bruch's membrane, or physician error. The patient is counseled regarding postoperative care of treated eye. The patient is counseled regarding the fact the treated eye will be blurred for a period of time and great care should be taken in performing various tasks, including driving. Follow-up visits are scheduled generally at six and 12 weeks following treatment, and additional laser therapy is administered in approximately 20 percent of patients during the global period.

---

❺ 67221 Destruction of localized lesion of choroid (eg, choroidal neovascularization); photodynamic therapy (includes intravenous infusion)

Work Value: 3.45 // Global Period: 000

➲ ***CPT Assistant*** **Feb 01: 8, Sep 01: 10, Jun 02: 10**
CPT Changes: An Insider's View **2001**

Clinical Example

A 77-year-old male notes decreased vision and metamorphopsia in his left eye. Past medical history is remarkable for hypertension and smoking. Visual acuity is 20/30 in the right eye and 20/100 in the left eye. Slit lamp biomicroscopy reveals pseudophakic anterior segments. Dilated retinal examination with indirect ophthalmoscopy and slit lamp biomicroscopy reveals subretinal fluid and hemorrhage in the left macula. Fluorescein angiography demonstrates a predominantly classic subfoveal choroidal neovascular membrane. Ocular coherence tomography (OCT) demonstrates subretinal fluid and intraretinal edema.

Preservice

The patient's history is reviewed. Photographs, fluorescein angiogram, and OCT results are re-examined. On the angiogram, an appropriate frame is chosen for lesion measurement. The greatest linear dimension is measured, and the laser spot size diameter is calculated. The treatment procedure is explained to the patient and the patient's family. The necessity of staying out of the sun for 5 days is stressed to all. The laser and slit lamp are confirmed to be in good working order.

Intraservice

The physician oversees the placement of an intravenous access, which is flushed, and an individually calculated dose of verteporfin is infused over ten minutes, followed by a flush of the line. A timer is set for 5 minutes. The physician places a contact lens on the surface of the patient's appropriate eye. The red-free beam is used to visualize the macula. The fundus is compared with the angiographic image (either an 8 or 10 print or a computer-monitor image), and landmarks are selected for safe and effective placement of the laser beam. At five minutes the macula is treated for 83 cumulative seconds. The laser beam is stopped and removed as necessary to insure safety. At completion the contact lens is removed.

Postservice

Staying out of sunlight is reiterated with the patient and the patient's family. The operative note is dictated. The importance of a follow-up visit is emphasized with the patient and scheduled. The patient's status is communicated to the referring physician. The physician reminds the patient to cease smoking. The patient is made aware to call if he has any problems, and that there will be a follow-up phone call from a nurse in two days.

Ocular Adnexa

Eyelids

Excision, Destruction

❺ 67820 Correction of trichiasis; epilation, by forceps only

Work Value: 0.71 // Global Period: 000

➲ *CPT Assistant* Jul 98: 10

Clinical Example

A 68-year-old female presents with excessive pain and tearing in the left eye.

Preservice

The patient records are reviewed.

Intraservice

The procedure is explained to the patient and informed consent is obtained. Topical anesthetic is applied to the eye. The patient is properly positioned at the slit lamp. Under the slit lamp magnification, the aberrant lashes are identified and epilated with forceps. Following removal, an antibiotic drop is instilled in the eye. The patient is provided with postoperative instructions.

Postservice

The operative report is dictated and the results are communicated to the referring physician as appropriate.

Trichiasis
67820

When the eyelashes are ingrown or misdirected (trichiasis), the physician uses a biomicroscope and forceps to remove the offending eyelashes. Report 67825 when cryosurgery or electrosurgery is used to destroy the follicles.

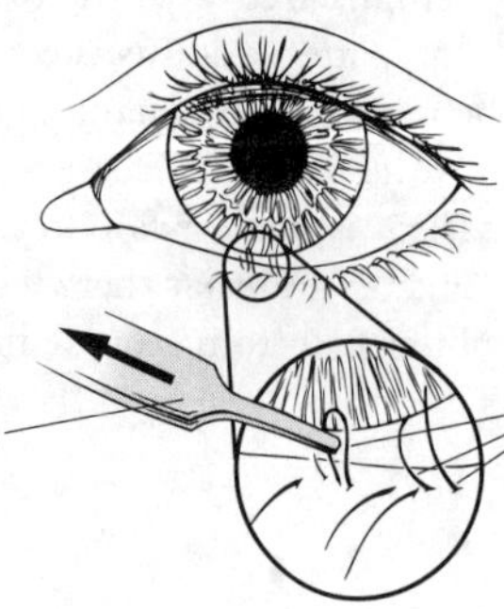

Conjunctiva

Lacrimal System

Probing and/or Related Procedures

68815 Probing of nasolacrimal duct, with or without irrigation; with insertion of tube or stent

Work Value: 3.24 // Global Period: 010

➲ *CPT Assistant* Nov 02: 11

Clinical Example

A 4-year-old presents with a 3-year history of crusting, tearing, and frequent episodes of conjunctivitis. The patient is taken to the operating room, where general anesthesia is begun. The superior and inferior puncta are dilated with a lacrimal dilator. A lacrimal probe is introduced into a punctum; passed through the canaliculus, the lacrimal sac, and the nasolacrimal duct; and saline is irrigated through the duct into the nasopharynx. A second probe with silicone tubing is passed through the inferior canaliculus and through the lacrimal drainage system and retrieved from the nasopharynx. The other end of the tube is passed through the superior canaliculus to the nasopharynx. The tubes are tied together.

Preservice

Although the example describes a child under general anesthesia, this procedure is commonly used in conjunction with other lacrimal and/or eyelid reconstructive procedures in adults under local anesthesia or monitored anesthetic care. The insertion of a tube or stent in the lacrimal system is to maintain patency of the system during the healing process of the surrounding diseased or reconstructed tissues. Justification for this procedure is first determined by an appropriate examination typically reported under a separate evaluation and management CPT code. A nasal examination is also performed. The tubing or stent must be available at the time of the procedure. If not, it must be ordered. Decongestion of the nasal mucosa with or without anesthetic (eg, phenylephrine hydrochloride or cocaine) is performed before the tube or stent is inserted. Before the tube or stent is inserted, the lacrimal punctate are dilated. If not done under general anesthesia, topical and local anesthesia are given around the punctate and lacrimal sac areas.

Intraservice

Usually, a commercially available silicone tubing with metal rods attached to either end is passed through the dilated puncta, canaliculus, nasolacrimal sac, and nasolacrimal duct into the nose under the inferior turbinate. The end of the metal rod is retrieved in the nose and the length of tubing is withdrawn. The procedure is performed in both the upper and lower canalicular systems. The tubing is knotted inside the nostril. The knotted ends are sometimes sutured to the inside of the alae of the nose for easy retrieval at a later date.

Postservice

Postservice evaluations are typically performed once or twice during the first week after the procedure (eg, 1 day and/or 1 week postoperative). The next postoperative visit is a predetermined time when the tube or stent is scheduled to be removed. If the tube or stent is left in for 3 months or more, then periodic visits are required to make sure that the tubing is not cheese-wiring the puncta.

Probing of Nasolacrimal Duct
68815
A balloon catheter is in the nasolacrimal duct.

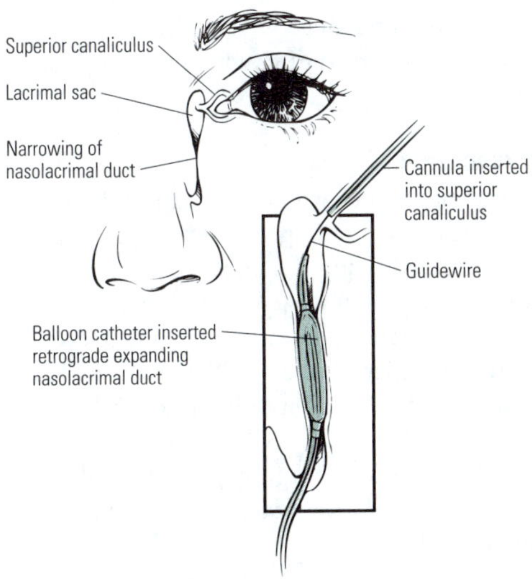

Coding Tip for 68815

Nasolacrimal duct probing is included in the descriptor for code 68815. It is not appropriate to separately report codes 68810 and 68811 for probing the nasolacrimal duct and inserting a tube or stent.

Auditory System

External Ear

Removal

69200 Removal foreign body from external auditory canal; without general anesthesia

Work Value: 0.77 // Global Period: 000

Clinical Example

The patient is a 18-month-old child who placed a plastic round bead in the external auditory meatus. The patient was referred by a family physician. The decision to remove the foreign body without general anesthesia was discussed fully with the parents.

Preservice

The child is prepared for the procedure, which includes positioning the patient supine for examination of the ear. The child is usually crying hysterically. Nursing assistance is required for placing the child in a papoose (restraint) and to immobilize the childs head. The ear is carefully examined with an operating otoscope head or otomicroscope for adequate illumination and exposure. A favorably located foreign body in the outer one-half of the ear canal may be successfully approached if it does not occlude the canal completely, local irritation is minor, and is not painfully lodged in the canal. Otologic operating instruments properly configured for controlling foreign bodies are required.

Intraservice

The operator positions the speculum light source and instrument with physical effort related to the uncontrollable and unpredictable movement of the child, knowing that the epithelial lining of the external auditory meatus is thin and easily damaged, and abrasion or hematoma is easily produced following attempted instrumentation to remove the foreign body. When the operator is confident that the circumstances are favorable, the physician can make an attempt at removal under the optimal circumstances without general anesthesia. Successful removal of the foreign body often concludes the encounter.

Postservice

Following the procedure, the child usually cries hysterically and requires consolation and comforting from the staff and parents immediately following the procedure. Failure to remove the foreign body after one or two skillful attempts may lead to the decision to rethink the need for general anesthesia.

---

❺ **69210** Removal impacted cerumen (separate procedure), one or both ears

Work Value: 0.61 // Global Period: 000

➲ *CPT Assistant* Apr 03: 9, Jul 05: 14

Clinical Example

A 69-year-old male presents with worsening hearing with a sudden change in the left ear over a several day period. He is found to have a massive cerumen impaction filling the entire external auditory canal. The physician physically removes the cerumen from the canal with instrumentation.

Preservice

The patient's records are reviewed, paying particular attention to any medications that might promote bleeding and any abnormality of the pinna, external auditory canals, tympanic membranes, balance, and hearing. The procedure is explained and questions of the patient and/or the patient's family are answered. The patient is positioned, instrumentation is checked, and hands are cleaned.

Intraservice

The pinna and external auditory canal are examined. The pinna is grasped and the external auditory canal exposed and opened. The cerumen is removed using a variety of instrumentation, including cerumen curettes, spoons, suctions, and micro forceps. Occasionally concurrent irrigations are required along with the suction. Extreme care is taken not to injure the external auditory canal or tympanic membrane. After the removal is completed, the external auditory canal and tympanic membrane are examined and status noted. If needed, the same procedure is performed on the opposite ear.

Postservice

The patient is counseled regarding future cerumen management strategies and any medications necessary are given. The appropriate procedure note and referral letter is dictated.

Coding Tip for 69210

If the use of an operating microscope is necessary when performing the procedure (code 69210), it is appropriate to separately report code 69990 for the use of the operating microscope.

Inner Ear

Introduction

69930 Cochlear device implantation, with or without mastoidectomy

Work Value: 17.60 // Global Period: 090

Clinical Example

A bilateral, profoundly deaf adult (18 years of age or older) or child (2–18 years of age); subject does not achieve significant open-set word understanding with an appropriate hearing aid.

Preservice

Preservice work includes evaluating the patient's audiology, speech, and psychology reports; evaluating the patient's computed tomography scan to determine whether cochlea is patent; discussing the procedure with the patient (if an adult) and the patient's family (if a child); obtaining informed consent; selecting the CTS for the operating room; and positioning, prepping, and draping the patient after cranial nerve monitors are placed.

Intraservice

Intraservice work includes performing an intact canal wall mastoidectomy, which provides entrance into the middle ear space; performing a cochleostomy into the inner ear; drilling a seat into the occipital cortex to provide a place for the implanted hardware; placing the cochlear implant into the inner ear (this requires significant expertise to manipulate the electrode into the inner ear without damaging the electrode); securing the electrode in the inner ear with a fascia patch; securing electrodes to the mastoid cortex; suturing the wound; and performing electrophysiologic testing of the implant.

Postservice

Postservice work includes dictating the operative report; writing orders; and talking to the patient and the patient's family. Postoperative care requires changing the mastoid dressing and removing the drain on the first or second postoperative day; checking on the patient approximately four times while the patient is in the hospital; and removing stitches approximately 1 week after the procedure is performed. (This care is similar to the care following an intact canal wall or revision mastoid surgery.) The patient then returns 1 month after implantation for programming of the speech processor. This requires 6–8 hours of time in an adult and 16–36 hours in a child. (The time commitment is more extensive than a revision mastoidectomy because of the speech processor programming.)

Cochlear Device Implantation
69930

An internal coil is attached to the temporal bone and the ground wire attached to the internal coil is connected to the temporalis muscle.

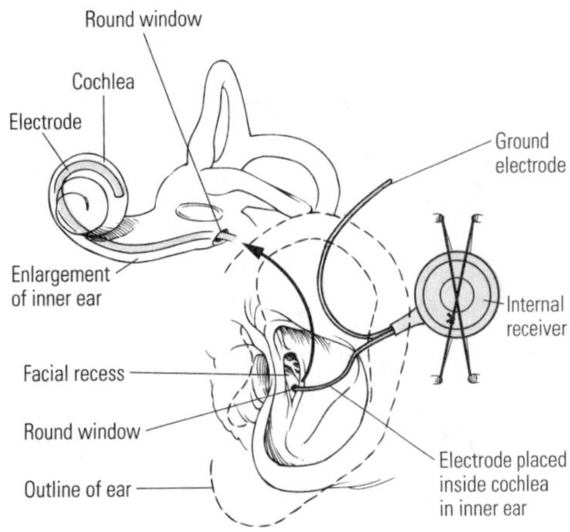

Radiology

It is essential to review the basic guidelines of the CPT® codebook when reporting from the Radiology section. In doing so, the user will gain an understanding to apply the appropriate code logic in selecting the most accurate radiology code(s). Some of the basic guidelines include:

Supervision and Intrepretation

Administration and Supply of Contrast Material(s)

Written Report(s)

Diagnostic Radiology (Diagnostic Imaging),
including Mammography Interventional Radiology

Diagnostic Ultrasound

Radiation Oncology

Nuclear Medicine

Diagnostic Radiology (Diagnostic Imaging)

Chest

⑤ 71010 Radiologic examination, chest; single view, frontal

Work Value: 0.18 // Global Period: XXX

Clinical Example

A 65-year-old male with unstable angina and pulmonary edema underwent emergency coronary artery bypass grafting. Immediately postoperatively the patient is hypoxemic with decreased breath sounds on the left. A portable anteroposterior chest radiograph is ordered in the recovery room.

Preservice

Review the reason for the exam and any pertinent clinical history. Review any prior applicable plain film or imaging studies.

Intraservice

Supervise the technologist performing the examination. Interpret the exam and compare the exam findings to previous studies. Dictate a report for the patients medical record.

Postservice

Review and sign the final report. Discuss the findings with the referring physician.

---

⑤71020 Radiologic examination, chest, two views, frontal and lateral;

Work Value: 0.22 // Global Period: XXX

➲ *CPT Assistant* Sep 03: 3, Mar 05: 11

Clinical Example

A 70-year-old female with stage 4 breast cancer and known pleural and pulmonary metastases presents to her physician with new onset dyspnea and fever. Postero-anterior and lateral chest radiographs are ordered.

Preservice

Review the reason for the exam and any pertinent clinical history. Review any prior applicable plain film or imaging studies.

Intraservice

Supervise the technologist performing the examination. Interpret the exam and compare the exam findings to previous studies. Dictate a report for the patients medical record.

Postservice

Review and sign the final report. Discuss the findings with the referring physician.

71275 Computed tomographic angiography, chest (noncoronary), without contrast material(s), followed by contrast material(s) and further sections, including image postprocessing

Work Value: 1.92 // Global Period: XXX

➲ *CPT Assistant* Jul 01: 4, Jun 05: 11, Dec 05: 7
CPT Changes: An Insider's View 2001, 2007;
Clinical Examples in Radiology Spring 05:7

Clinical Example

A 34-year-old female presents with chronic arm pain, paresthesia, and muscle wasting. She is evaluated for possible thoracic outlet obstruction.

Preservice

Describe the procedure to the patient and obtain informed consent where applicable. Review any prior applicable studies.

Intraservice

Obtain/interpret scout views of the area to be imaged. Obtain/review noncontrast computed tomography (CT) images to localize the vascular phase sequence and to screen those patients who are not candidates for the arterial phase component of the study. Supervise the low- or iso-osmolar contrast injection. Obtain the arterial phase CT images and review to ensure adequate anatomic coverage. Obtain and review delayed parenchymal phase CT images. Create and/or supervise 2D reconstructions of the vasculature and associated organs. Interpret and annotate the reconstructions. Supervise and/or create 3D reconstructions of the vasculature and associated organs. Adjust the projection of the 3D reconstructions to optimize visualization of anatomy or pathology. Interpret the axial source images of the precontrast sequence, arterial phase sequence, and parenchymal phase sequence, as well as the 2D and 3D reformatted images resulting from the study, which often includes a cine review. Compare the results to all pertinent available prior studies.

Postservice

Dictate, audit, and sign the final report.

Spine and Pelvis

72275 Epidurography, radiological supervision and interpretation

Work Value: 0.76 // Global Period: XXX

➲ *CPT Assistant* Nov 99: 40, Jan 00: 2, Aug 00: 7; *CPT Changes: An Insider's View* 2000

Clinical Example

1) A 45-year-old male presents with extensive rectal carcinoma involving the left lumbosacral plexus. He has intractable left perirectal pain and has lost much of his control of bladder and bowel functions. Various systemic medications (oral narcotic and non-narcotic), physical therapy, radiation therapy, and chemotherapy have all failed to provide significant long-term pain relief. There are no further operative resections possible for the tumor. This patient is a good candidate for a neurolytic injection because of the severity of the pain and the diminished control of bladder and bowel function. A neurolytic injection to ablate the left S2-S4 nerve roots is recommended. The injection could be performed subarachnoid or epidural and an epidural approach is selected. A diagnostic epiduragram is performed to define the anatomic extent of the epidural space in this patient, and exclude adhesions or other reasons that the neuroloytic substance cannot be delivered to the selected nerve roots.

2) A 62-year-old female, who is status post multiple lumbar surgeries, presents with chronic low back pain and a left L4 radiculopathy. She has had a prior epidural steroid injection without significant response. She is referred for a diagnostic epiduragram to exclude epidural adhesion/fibrosis, and a possible repeat therapeutic injection.

Preservice

The patient's prior imaging examinations (eg, radiographs, computed tomography scans, magnetic resonance imaging scans) of the level to be studied are reviewed so that the patient's anatomy, anatomic variants, history of prior surgery, and pathology are familiar.

Intraservice

The patient is placed on an X-ray table in the prone, oblique, or decubims position. Preliminary fluoroscopy is performed to identify the appropriate level and approach for the initial needle placement, and the skin entry site marked. During the needle/catheter placement (the needle/catheter placement is a separate procedure and separately reported and should not be considered in the assessment of physician work or practice of this code), intermittent fluoroscopy is used to confirm the correct position. A small test dose of radiographic contrast is injected to confirm the proper position. If position is not correct (eg, subarachnoid or venous opacification), additional fluoroscopic guidance is provided during respositioning until proper position is achieved. If a catheter is to be placed, additional fluoroscopic guidance is provided during and after the catheter placement to confirm the proper position for injection of the full diagnostic dose of contrast. Following the epidural space injection of appropriate radiographic contrast (separately codeable and not included in the physician work for this code), multiple radiographic images are obtained from different angles. These images are formally interpreted. The results are discussed with the physician performing the injection procedure (if different from the interpreting physician) to determine if there is any abnormality of the epidural space that would limit the desired distribution of therapeutic substances to be injected.

Postservice

A report is dictated for the patient's medical record. The findings are discussed with the referring physician and the patient.

Epidurography
72275

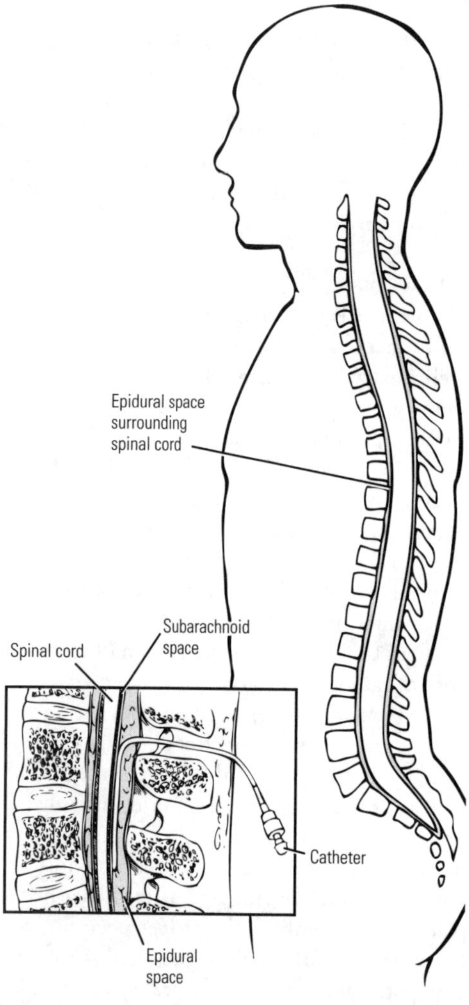

Coding Tip for 72275

Code 72275 should be reported only when an epidurogram is performed, images are documented, and a formal radiologic report is issued.

Other Procedures

76376 3D rendering with interpretation and reporting of computed tomography, magnetic resonance imaging, ultrasound, or other tomographic modality; not requiring image postprocessing on an independent workstation

Work Value: 0.20 // Global Period: XXX

➲ ***CPT Assistant*** **Dec 05: 1, 7;** ***CPT Changes: An Insider's View*** **2006;** ***Clinical Examples in Radiology*** **Winter 06:17**

Clinical Example

A 27-year-old female patient G2P1 has previously delivered an infant with a cleft lip and palate. The obstetrician performs a pelvic exam and concludes that the uterine size appears consistent with a 20-22 weeks gestation. The patient is scheduled for a 2D ultrasound examination to confirm fetal dating of the pregnancy and to evaluate for possible fetal abnormalities including a possible facial cleft malformation. An ultrasound technologist scans a patient in a conventional ultrasound unit that has 2D ultrasound capabilities. Sagittal and transverse images of the pregnant uterus are obtained in 2D ultrasound (coded separately). The attending physician evaluates the images and concludes that the images generated from the 2D ultrasound are not able to confidently exclude or identify a facial cleft anomaly. A 3D ultrasound is ordered to better visualize the facial structures in 3D shaded surface rendering.

Preservice

Discuss the need for 3D imaging with technologist to assure adequate source data. Review any prior imaging studies. Describe the procedure to the patient and obtain consent as needed. Review the source imaging data.

Intraservice

Supervise the technologist in creating the 3D images, interpret the images, and dictate a report for the patient's medical record.

Postservice

Review and sign the report. Discuss findings with the referring physician.

76377 3D rendering with interpretation and reporting of computed tomography, magnetic resonance imaging, ultrasound, or other tomographic modality; requiring image postprocessing on an independent workstation

Work Value: 0.79 // Global Period: XXX

➲ *CPT Assistant* Dec 05: 1 *CPT Changes: An Insider's View* 2006; *Clinical Examples in Radiology* Winter 06:17

Clinical Example

A 50-year-old male presented to his physician with hematuria. Renal ultrasound (coded separately) identified a 3 cm lower pole right renal mass consistent with renal cell carcinoma, previously diagnosed with ultrasound. The patient is a possible candidate for nephron-sparing partial nephrectomy and a computerized tomographic (CT) scan of the abdomen is ordered by the patient's urologist. Three-dimensional rendering is requested for further evaluation. A computed tomography examination of the abdomen, both before and after the use of contrast media, is performed (coded separately). Subsequent postprocessing and 3D reconstruction are performed, demonstrating that the patient is a candidate for partial nephrectomy.

Preservice

Review protocol with the technologist. Review any prior imaging studies. Describe the procedure to the patient and obtain consent as needed. Review the source imaging data.

Intraservice

The physician supervises and/or creates 3D reconstructions of the organs of interest using an independent workstation. He or she adjusts the projection of the 3D reconstructions to optimize visualization of the anatomy or pathology. The physician interprets the 3D-reformatted images resulting from the study, which typically includes a cine review. The images are compared to all pertinent available prior studies, and a report is dictated for the patients medical record.

Postservice

Review and sign the report. Discuss findings with the referring physician.

Coding Tip for 76377

Code 76377 should be used in conjunction with the code(s) for base imaging procedure(s).

Diagnostic Ultrasound

Abdomen and Retroperitoneum

❺ **76700** Ultrasound, abdominal, real time with image documentation; complete

Work Value: 0.81 // Global Period: XXX

➲ *CPT Assistant* Fall 93: 13, Oct 01: 3, Dec 05: 3; *CPT Changes: An Insider's View* 2002, 2007; *Clinical Examples in Radiology* Winter 05:9,11

Clinical Example

A 65-year-old male alcoholic has developed increasing abdominal distention, decreased urine output, and jaundice. A complete ultrasound examination of the abdomen is ordered for further evaluation.

Preservice

Review the reason for the exam and any pertinent clinical history. Review any prior applicable plain film or imaging studies.

Intraservice

Supervise the sonographer performing the exam. Interpret the ultrasound exam and evaluate the liver, gallbladder, biliary tree, spleen, pancreas, kidneys, abdominal aorta, and inferior vena cava. Compare the exam results and correlate the findings to previous studies. Dictate a report for the patient's medical record.

Postservice

Review and sign the final report. Discuss findings with the referring physician.

Coding Tip for 76700

A complete ultrasound examination of the abdomen (code 76700) consists of B mode scans of the liver, gall bladder, common bile duct, pancreas, spleen, kidneys, and upper abdominal aorta and inferior vena cava, including any demonstrated abdominal abnormality.

Pelvis

Obstetrical

76805 Ultrasound, pregnant uterus, real time with image documentation, fetal and maternal evaluation, after first trimester (< or = 14 weeks 0 days), transabdominal approach; single or first gestation

Work Value: 0.99 // Global Period: XXX

➲ **_CPT Assistant_ Apr 97: 2, Nov 97: 25, Oct 01: 3, Aug 02: 2, Mar 03: 7; _CPT Changes: An Insider's View_ 2002, 2003; _Clinical Examples in Radiology_ Winter 05:3-4**

Clinical Example

A 35-year-old pregnant female with a menstrual age of 24 weeks is large for dates. An ultrasound is ordered to evaluate the gestational age and assess the fetus. Ultrasound determinations of gestational age are consistent with 28-week gestation. Fetal evaluation including a survey of intracranial, spinal, and abdominal anatomy, 4-chamber view of the heart, and umbilical cord insertion is normal. The placenta location is anterior and away from the cervical os, and the amniotic fluid is normal. Both ovaries are visualized and normal.

Preservice

Review clinical information. Review pertinent prior imaging studies.

Intraservice

Supervise the sonographer performing the examination. Interpret the examination including determining the number of fetuses and amniotic/chorionic sacs. Survey the intracranial, spinal, and abdominal anatomy. Evaluate the 4-chamber heart view. Assess the umbilical cord insertion site. Assess the amniotic fluid volume. Evaluate the maternal adnexa when visible. Prepare the report for the patient's medical record.

Postservice

Discuss findings with the patient and the referring physician when appropriate. Review and sign the prepared report.

Nonobstetrical

❺ **76830** Ultrasound, transvaginal

Work Value: 0.69 // Global Period: XXX

➲ **_CPT Assistant_ Aug 96: 10, Jul 99: 8, Aug 02: 2, Mar 03: 7, Dec 05: 3; _CPT Changes: An Insider's View_ 2002; _Clinical Examples in Radiology_ Inaugural 04:6-7**

Clinical Example

A 25-year-old female was diagnosed with a complex right ovarian cyst 6 weeks ago by transabdominal pelvic ultrasound. The lesion was presumed to represent a benign hemorrhagic cyst. After 6 weeks the patient has a persisting right adenexal mass on physical examination. A transvaginal examination ultrasound of the pelvis is ordered for further evaluation and characterization.

Preservice

Review the reason for the exam and any pertinent clinical history. Review any prior applicable imaging studies.

Intraservice

Supervise the sonographer performing the exam. Interpret the ultrasound exam, evaluating the uterus, including the endoetrium; the ovaries; and cul de sac. Compare the exam and correlate the findings to previous studies. Dictate the report for the patient's medical record.

Postservice

Review and sign the final report. Discuss findings with the referring physician.

Coding Tip for 76830

If a trasvaginal examination is performed in addition to a transabdominal nonobstetrical ultrasound exam, code 76830 should be reported in addition to the appropriate transabdominal exam code.

Ultrasonic Guidance Procedures

+ 76937 Ultrasound guidance for vascular access requiring ultrasound evaluation of potential access sites, documentation of selected vessel patency, concurrent realtime ultrasound visualization of vascular needle entry, with permanent recording and reporting (List separately in addition to code for primary procedure)

Work Value: 0.30 // Global Period: ZZZ

➲ ***CPT Assistant*** **Dec 04: 13;** ***CPT Changes: An Insider's View*** **2004;** ***Clinical Examples in Radiology*** **Inaugural 04:1-2, Winter 05:5-6**

Clinical Example

A patient requires internal jugular central venous catheter placement. The physician decides that ultrasound guidance is necessary for safe internal jugular venous access.

Intraservice

Potential access sites are examined with ultrasound and an acceptable patent access site is selected. Permanent documentation of sites examined is recorded. After a sterile field has been established, the ultrasound probe is covered with a sterile sleeve. Ultrasound transmission gel is applied and real-time ultrasound is performed. The advancement of the access needle into the lumen of the selected vessel is monitored. This position is also recorded. Description of the guidance process is included in the final procedure report.

Postservice

Review and sign the guidance report. Communicate results to the referring physician when appropriate.

Coding Tip for 76937

Code 76937 should not be reported in addition to code 76942.

76942 Ultrasonic guidance for needle placement (eg, biopsy, aspiration, injection, localization device), imaging supervision and interpretation

Work Value: 0.67 // Global Period: XXX

➲ ***CPT Assistant*** **Fall 93: 12, Fall 94: 2, May 96: 3, Jun 97: 5, Oct 01: 2, May 04: 7, Dec 04: 12, Apr 05: 15-16;** ***CPT Changes: An Insider's View*** **2001;** ***Clinical Examples in Radiology*** **Summer 05:1, 2, 6, Fall 05:1**

Clinical Example

A 42-year-old pregnant female requests prenatal testing for genetic disorders. A transcervical chorionic villus (CVS) sampling is performed at 10 weeks gestation using ultrasonic guidance.

Preservice

CVS is performed between 9 and 12 weeks gestation to obtain placental tissue for fetal karyotyping. CVS is performed by either the transcervical or transabdominal route. Transcervical CVS involves passing a pliable plastic catheter through the uterine cervix into the placental tissue. Transabdominal CVS is performed by placing a percutaneous needle through the maternal abdominal and uterine walls into the placenta. Ultrasonic guidance and interpretation is required to appropriately place the catheter/needle during a CVS procedure. Preservice consists of verifying that the appropriate equipment and transducers are available and in working order. Counseling and informed consent are done as part of the decision to do CVS, and the patient is informed about the reasons for the ultrasonic guidance.

Intraservice

After a complete sonogram performed as a separate procedure demonstrates the viability of the fetus, number of fetuses, gestational age, and placental location, the patient is placed in the lithotomy position. The uterine cervix and vagina are prepared with antiseptic solution. The ultrasound transducer is placed on the maternal abdomen and the plastic catheter is directed using ultrasonic guidance (second operator) through the cervix into the placental tissue. The stylet is withdrawn and placental tissue is aspirated into a syringe as the catheter is withdrawn. The transabdominal CVS is performed with the patient in the supine position. The maternal abdomen is prepared in sterile fashion. The ultrasound transducer is placed on the abdomen and a spinal needle is directed by ultrasonic guidance through the abdominal and uterine walls into the placental tissue. Tissue is aspirated in a syringe and the needle is removed under sonographic guidance.

Postservice

Postservice consists of writing or dictating a procedural report describing the ultrasonic guidance and interpretation.

Coding Tip for 76942

Code 76942 should be reported for each distinct lesion that requires separate needle placement. Therefore, if several passes are made into two separate lesions in the same organ (ie, two lesions in the same breast), code 76942 would be reported twice.

Radiologic Guidance

Flouroscopic Guidance

+ 77001 Fluoroscopic guidance for central venous access device placement, replacement (catheter only or complete), or removal (includes fluoroscopic guidance for vascular access and catheter manipulation, any necessary contrast injections through access site or catheter with related venography radiologic supervision and interpretation, and radiographic documentation of final catheter position) (List separately in addition to code for primary procedure)

Work Value: 0.38 // Global Period: ZZZ

➲ *CPT Changes: An Insider's View* 2007

Clinical Example

A patient is referred for placement of a tunneled central venous catheter. To facilitate the advancement of the catheter and ensure accurate placement, fluoroscopy is used.

Intraservice

When venous access is obtained (if fluoroscopic guidance is used for venous access, this is included), fluoroscopy is used to insert the guidewire. The catheter is then inserted into a central venous position. Any contrast injection through the access site (via a needle, catheter, or sheath) for venographic evaluation and mapping of the appropriate path is included. Spot film or other radiographic confirmation of final catheter position is performed. A description of all aspects of fluoroscopic guidance are reported with the procedure.

Postservice

The report is reviewed and signed. Results of the procedure are communicated to the referring physician when appropriate.

Coding Tip for 77001

It is not appropriate to report code 77001 in conjunction with code 77002.

77003 Fluoroscopic guidance and localization of needle or catheter tip for spine or paraspinous diagnostic or therapeutic injection procedures (epidural, transforaminal epidural, subarachnoid, paravertebral facet joint, paravertebral facet joint nerve or sacroiliac joint), including neurolytic agent destruction

Work Value: 0.60 // Global Period: XXX

➲ *CPT Changes: An Insider's View* 2007

Clinical Example

A 45-year-old male presents with severe pain (rated 8/10) involving both legs and the lower back after multiple back operations over a 10-year period. Various systemic medications (oral narcotic and nonnarcotic) and physical therapy have all failed to provide significant long-term pain relief. There are no further operations on his spine that are felt likely to provide further relief. The physician provides fluoroscopic guidance during the performance of any one of a series of possible needle/catheter procedures described as follows to confirm the proper position of the needle/catheter.

Code 62310: This patient is a good candidate for a subarachnoid narcotic injection because of the severity of the pain and the lack of other treatment options. A test subarachnoid injection of morphine is recommended to determine whether a long-term infusion (using and external or implanted infusion pump) could provide significant pain relief for this patient.

Codes 62310 and 62318: This patient is a good candidate for an epidural narcotic injection because of the severity of the pain and the lack of other treatment options. A test epidural injection of morphine is recommended to determine whether a long-term infusion (using an external or implanted infusion pump) could provide significant pain relief for this patient. Code 62310 would be appropriate for cervical or thoracic epidural injection if the patient's pain were in the neck, arms, chest, or high back area. Code 62318 would be appropriate for a lumbar or caudal injection if the pain were in the legs and/or lower back/buttock area.

Codes 62311 and 62319: This patient is a good candidate for an epidural narcotic infusion or series of intermittent bolus injections. A continuous infusion of narcotic and local anesthetic could be used for several days during aggressive physical therapy to try and break a cycle of sympathetic dysfunction (eg, from reflex sympathetic dysfunction or, by its new term, complex regional pain syndrome). Many physicians feel that a continuous infusion of narcotic (as compared to a single injection) is a better predictor of long-term pain relief. The catheter could also be used for a series of single injections over several hours or 1-2 days to test for narcotic pain relief versus pain relief from saline injections. Code 62310 would be appropriate for a cervical or thoracic epidural injection if the patient'ss pain were in the neck, arms, chest, or high back area. Code 62318 would be appropriate for a lumbar or caudal injection if the pain were in the legs and/or lower back/buttock area.

Code 62319: The patient is a good candidate for a subarachnoid narcotic infusion or series of intermittent bolus injections. A continuous infusion could be used for several days during aggressive physical therapy to try and break a cycle of sympathetic dysfunction (eg, from reflex sympathetic dysfunction or, by its new term, complex regional pain syndrome). The continuous infusion of narcotic also is used by physicians as a better test for pain relief than a single injection. The catheter could also be used for a series of single injections over several hours or one to two days to test for narcotic pain relief versus pain relief from alternating, blinded saline injections.

Preservice

The physician reviews the patient's prior imaging studies (eg, radiographs, computed tomography scans, magnetic resonance imaging scans) to be familiar with the patient's spine anatomy (eg, numbering of levels, anatomic variants, prior surgery, pathology).

Intraservice

The patient is placed on an x-ray table in the prone, decubitus, or prone oblique position, depending on the type of injection to be performed. Preliminary fluoroscopy is performed to identify the appropriate level and approach for initial needle placement, and the skin entry site is marked. During the needle/catheter placement, intermittent fluoroscopy is used to confirm the correct approach and the need for needle repositioning or realignment. When the needle position appears correct, radiographic contrast may be injected to confirm the proper position. If the position is not correct, additional fluoroscopy is provided during repositioning until the proper position is achieved. If a catheter is to be placed, additional fluoroscopic guidance is provided during and after the catheter positioning to confirm proper positioning. Additional contrast injection may be performed. If a different physician is performing the needle/catheter placement, continuous consultation occurs with that physician regarding the placement and positioning.

Postservice

A report describing the guidance procedure, including the final position of the needle/catheter is dictated, proofread, and submitted for the patient record.

Coding Tip for 77003

Injection of contrast during fluoroscopic guidance and localization is included in codes 22526, 22527, 62263, 62264, 62270-62282, 62310-62319, and 0027T.

Breast Mammography

+ 77052 Computer aided detection (computer algorithm analysis of digital image data for lesion detection) with further physician review for interpretation, with or without digitization of film radiographic images; screening mammography (List separately in addition to code for primary procedure)

Work Value: 0.06 // Global Period: ZZZ

➲ *CPT Changes: An Insider's View* 2007

Clinical Example

A screening mammogram has been performed on an asymptomatic female who is at least 40 years of age. The radiographic images are further processed using computer-aided detection (CAD).

Preservice

The screening mammogram is reviewed and a preliminary interpretation is performed prior to reviewing the CAD data. There is no physician work for CAD in the preservice period, as this service is performed and reported with the screening mammogram.

Intraservice

Compare and correlate the result of the CAD analysis with the screening mammogram. Determine the significance of potential abnormalities indicated by CAD and formulate recommendations. Integrate the result of the CAD analysis with the interpretation of the screening mammogram.

Postservice

No additional postservice is performed. The result of the CAD is integrated with the report of the screening mammogram and not reported separately.

Coding Tip for 77052

It is not appropriate to report code 77052 in conjunction with code 77057.

77055 Mammography; unilateral

Work Value: 0.70 // Global Period: XXX

➲ *CPT Changes: An Insider's View* 2007

Clinical Example

A 55-year-old female recently had a screening mammogram. An asymmetrical density was identified in the left breast and further mammographic evaluation was recommended. Further supplemental mammographic views were recommended to clarify the features, location, and reality of this suspected lesion. After reviewing the screening mammogram, it was determined that diagnostic views in a craniocaudal spot compression/magnification, medial lateral spot compression/magnification and 90-degree lateral view were necessary. At the completion of the examination, the radiologist conveys the findings of the examination to the patient. Report was dictated and the results were discussed with the referring physician.

Preservice

The screening mammogram is reviewed. Often the screening examination is from another institution. A decision as made as to which diagnostic views would further elucidate the asymmetric density.

Intraservice

The requested diagnostic views are reviewed and are compared with the screening study. Additional views of the breast may be necessary based on the review of the initial diagnostic views. When the asymmetric density has been completely evaluated an interpretation of the examination is rendered and a report is dictated for the referring physician. Per federal legislative requirement (MQSA) the exam is coded using

BIRADS terminology and a separate report in lay language is dictated and sent to the patient.

Postservice

Due to the patient's anxiety typically associated with this service, the findings are usually called to the referring physician at the completion of the examination. The findings are typically discussed with the patient at the completion of the examination.

77056 Mammography; bilateral

Work Value: 0.87 // Global Period: XXX

➲ *CPT Assistant* Jul 96: 6; *CPT Changes: An Insider's View* 2007

Clinical Example

A 57-year-old patient has a history of a palpable mass in the right breast. Previous mammograms, the last performed two years earlier, are available for review and comparison. The current mammogram of both breasts is reviewed. The mass in the right breast is identified as a new mass and further mammographic evaluation is necessary to clarify the features of this mass. After reviewing the initial diagnostic views, it was determined that additional diagnostic views in a craniocaudal spot compression/magnification, medial lateral spot compression/magnification and 90-degree lateral views were necessary. At the completion of the examination, the radiologist conveys the findings of the examination to the patient. A report was dictated and the results were discussed with the referring physician.

Preservice

Patient history is reviewed. Previous mammograms are reviewed.

Intraservice

Current mammogram is evaluated and additional diagnostic views of the right breast are then obtained to further evaluate the characteristics of the palpable mass. All of these findings are then interpreted in comparison with the previous studies. A report is dictated for the referring physician. Per federal legislative requirement (MQSA) the exam is coded using BIRADS terminology and a separate report in lay language is dictated and sent to the patient.

Postservice

Due to the patient's anxiety typically associated with this service, the findings are usually called to the referring physician at the completion of the examination. The findings are typically discussed with the patient at the completion of the examination.

Coding Tip for 77056

Report code 77056 in conjunction with code 77051 for computer-aided detection applied to a diagnostic mammogram.

77057 Screening mammography, bilateral (2-view film study of each breast)

Work Value: 0.70 // Global Period: XXX

➲ *CPT Changes: An Insider's View* 2007

Clinical Example

An asymptomatic 45-year-old woman presents for a screening mammography.

Preservice

The preservice period includes all clinical activities performed by the physician prior to image interpretation and may include review of clinical information provided by the referring physician or obtained from the patient including age, parity, estrogen replacement status, availability of prior mammograms or any history of breast disease that would necessitate converting the screening mammogram to a diagnostic mammogram; discussions with the patient prior to the examination may be required to clarify clinical information or to answer the questions patients frequently have regarding the risk of radiation exposure, the risk of compression and potential injury to breast implants.

Intraservice

The intraservice period includes all clinical activities related to image interpretation and rendering the radiological report and may include initial review of images for technical quality, proper positioning and complete anatomic coverage (need for additional views); interpretation of images including image magnification and "hot light" viewing and comparison with two prior examinations when available; determine significance of abnormal findings and formulate recommendations; code each examination using BIRADS terminology; dictate report to referring physician documenting findings, BIRADS classification and follow-up recommendations. Complete a second review of images by a different or the same physician (double reading) prior to submission of the final report.

Postservice

The postservice period includes all clinical activities that occur after image interpretation (many of which are federally mandated by MQSA) and multiple quality assurance, patient notification and tracking activities related to compliance with federally mandated quality assurance programs. These activities may include the following:

Clinical Activities: Because of patient anxiety, findings are often discussed with the patient; review and authentication of the dictated report; complete second interpretation of some studies when prior mammograms that were unavailable initially become available for comparison at a later date; review of films and discussion with referring physician as needed.

Federally Mandated Clinical Activities Related to MQSA and Screening Mammography may include: Preparation of separate report to the patient explaining her results in lay language; abnormal results suspicious for cancer are personally communicated by telephone with the referring physician.

Federally Mandated Non-clinical Activities Related to MQSA and Screening Mammography may include: Re-review of images on all patients who undergo biopsy and correlation with pathology report; regular review of personal and practice statistics for call-back rate, false positive rate and false negative rate; regular review of quality assurance data including densitometry, sensitometry and processing problems including troubleshooting problems with the physicist; mammography dedicated CME required by MQSA (15 hours every 3 years); oversee initial entry and full Mammography Accreditation/Certification application including selection of phantom and clinical images; supervision of assembly of update application; radiologist time spent preparing for and during annual MQSA inspection; documentation of physician compliance with MQSA.

Screening Mammography
76092

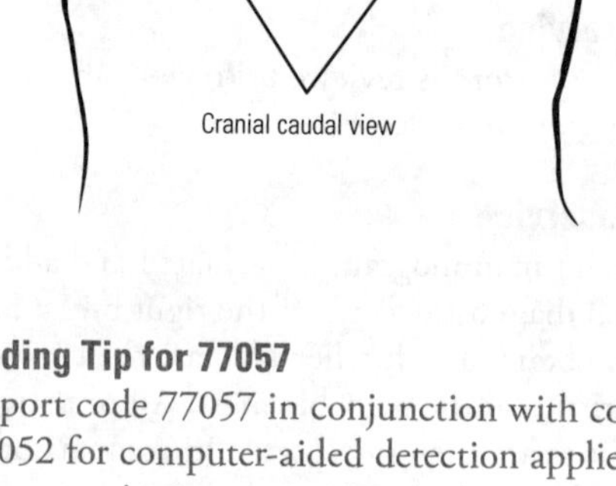

Coding Tip for 77057

Report code 77057 in conjunction with code 77052 for computer-aided detection applied to a screening mammogram.

⑤ 77080 Dual energy X-ray absorptiometry (DXA), bone density study, 1 or more sites; axial skeleton (eg, hips, pelvis, spine)

Work Value: 0.20 // Global Period: XXX

➲ *CPT Changes: An Insider's View* 2007

Clinical Example

A 66-year-old female had previous bone density demonstrating severe osteoporosis. The patient has been on hormone replacement therapy for one year and a follow-up DXA scan is ordered.

Preservice

Preservice work includes reviewing the reason for the exam and any pertinent clinical history, and reviewing any prior DXA studies.

Intraservice

Intraservice work includes reviewing scout images to assure scanning technique was satisfactory, interpretation of the DXA scan data and comparing it to established norms, comparing the results of the DXA scan to previous studies and dictating a report for the medical record.

Postservice

Postservice work includes reviewing and and signing the final report, and discussing findings with the referring physician.

77081 Dual energy X-ray absorptiometry (DXA), bone density study, 1 or more sites; appendicular skeleton (peripheral) (eg, radius, wrist, heel)

Work Value: 0.22 // Global Period: XXX

➲ *CPT Changes: An Insider's View* 2007

Clinical Example

1) A 35-year-old female presents with kidney stones secondary to hyperparathyroidism. Family history is positive for her father having osteoporosis.

2) A 40-year-old female marathon runner presents with recurrent tibial stress fractures. Her history reveals a low calcium diet and amenorrhea.

3) A 58-year-old male presents with corticosteroid-dependent rheumatoid arthritis and rib fractures from playing golf.

4) A 73-year-old female presents with a recent hip fracture.

5) A 70-year-old female, who is undergoing estrogen replacement therapy for osteoporosis, is referred for therapy progress/disease-monitoring purposes.

6) A 62-year-old female presents with a height loss and a family history of osteoporosis.

7) A 70-year-old female is concerned about the possibility of osteoporosis. She has never taken estrogen. Her mother had a hip fracture. She is healthy and has not lost height.

8) A 50-year-old early menopausal woman who has a family history of breast cancer is debating whether or not to initiate estrogen replacement therapy.

Preservice

Review history and physical exam. Discuss the procedure with the patient.

Intraservice

Interpret the results of relevant studies. Compare study results in relation to current diagnosis and future treatment, if appropriate.

Postservice

Dictate, correct, and sign the report. Discuss and communicate the report/findings with the referring physician(s).

Nuclear Medicine

Diagnostic

Cardiovascular System

+⑤78478 Myocardial perfusion study with wall motion, qualitative or quantitative study (List separately in addition to code for primary procedure)

Work Value: 0.50 // Global Period: XXX

➲ *CPT Assistant* Mar 99: 10, Oct 04: 10; *Clinical Examples in Radiology* Inaugural 04:3-5

Clinical Example

A 64-year-old male smoker with a history of peripheral vascular disease, hypertension, and myocardial infarction 7 years ago presents with advancing dyspnea on exertion and occasional chest discomfort. His general internist refers him for myocardial perfusion stress test.

Preservice

The physician reviews the existing information, request for exam, and relevant clinical data, to clarify the indications for the procedure and to determine the clinical questions to be answered.

Intraservice

The physician assesses the patient's cardiac rhythm. He/she directs the technologist in lead placement for optimal gating signal and any necessary adjustments in gating acquisition parameters based on individual rhythm assessment. The gated portion of the acquisition is frequently performed on both parts of a stress and rest perfusion study (twice) for comparison. The physician may verify the completeness and adequacy of the data prior to completion of the study. The physician views the completed gated tomographic display data for technical adequacy of interpretation. The images are viewed in multiple display formats, including 3D reconstruction. The cine image information includes datasets in three views for both the stress and rest portions of the study. The heart motion is qualitatively scored independently for the two parameters of wall motion and endocardial thickening. This occurs in a standardized segment model for each dataset with each segment scored as normal, mildly hypokinetic, moderately hypokinetic, severely hypokinetic, akinetic, or dyskinetic. Attention is paid to the assessment of regional myocardial function and to the percent of myocardium that is regionally dysfunctional to elucidate the amount of underlying myocardial scar (or severe ischemia post stress). Quantitative tools of wall motion and wall thickening may be generated and reviewed for each image after the qualitative assessment for refinement of the analysis. The segmental wall motion data are compared to the static flow perfusion images to generate a clinically relevant wall motion analysis for the individual patient. Comparison to previous studies may occur to detect changes. A formal report commenting on regional wall motion and regional thickening is dictated for the medical record. The data are placed into the clinical context of the myocardial perfusion in these regions.

Postservice

The findings are discussed with the referring physician and may be discussed with the patient. The formal report is reviewed and edited as necessary and signed.

Coding Tip for 78478

Code 78478 should be reported in conjunction with codes 78460, 78461, 78464, and 78465.

Other Procedures

78811 Tumor imaging, positron emission tomography (PET); limited area (eg, chest, head/neck)

Work Value: 0.00 // Global Period: XXX

➲ *CPT Assistant* Dec 05: 7; *CPT Changes: An Insider's View* 2005; *Clinical Examples in Radiology* Spring 05:13, 15

Clinical Example

A 42-year-old female presents with a history of invasive ductal carcinoma of the left breast. The initial tumor was 4.5 cm in largest diameter by mammography. She has now completed neoadjuvant chemotherapy and an assessment of treatment response is requested prior to surgical resection. A limited PET scan of the chest is performed.

Preservice

The physician reviews the clinical request, pertinent medical records, and prior imaging studies. The physician interviews the patient. A decision is made whether the appropriate study has been requested. The physician reviews the results of the finger-stick blood glucose level (included in the procedure). The physician discusses with the technologist the patient positioning and other specifics of the examination including hydration, imaging time after injection, the need for Foley a catheter, and so on.

Intraservice

An appropriate dose of radiopharmaceutical is prescribed by the physician. The physician supervises a certified technologist who assays the dose of the radiopharmaceutical, instructs the patient on the procedure, and in a designated injection room injects the radiopharmaceutical where the patient remains during the uptake period. The physician supervises the technologist in the acquisition and reconstruction of the data in multiple planes including transmission scans, and for the nonattenuation-corrected and attenuation-corrected emission scans. The physician reviews the study for adequacy and the need for additional acquisitions. All images are interpreted by the physician with correlation with prior imaging studies. Quantification of an abnormality is made by the calculation of the standardized uptake value when clinically indicated. The physician dictates a report for the patient's medical record.

Postservice

The physician reviews and signs the report for the medical record. The physician discusses the results with the referring physician, the patient, and the patient's family. Regulatory review and oversight is provided by the physician throughout the procedure.

Coding Tip for 78811

Codes 78811-78816 differentiate the three levels of work associated with PET and PET/CT imaging.

78812 Tumor imaging, positron emission tomography (PET); skull base to mid-thigh

Work Value: 0.00 // Global Period: XXX

➲ ***CPT Assistant*** **Dec 05: 7;** ***CPT Changes: An Insider's View*** **2005;** ***Clinical Examples in Radiology*** **Spring 05:13, 15**

Clinical Example

A 59-year-old male with a long history of smoking presents with a new 2-cm nodule on chest X ray. A chest computed tomography scan is performed and demonstrates an indeterminate solitary pulmonary nodule. A transthoracic needle aspiration biopsy demonstrates a non-small cell lung cancer. A PET scan is performed from the skull base to mid thigh for initial staging of lung cancer.

Preservice

The physician reviews the clinical request, pertinent medical records, and prior imaging studies. The physician interviews the patient. A decision is made whether the appropriate study has been requested. The physician reviews the results of the finger-stick blood glucose level (included in the procedure). The physician discusses with the technologist the patient positioning and other specifics of the examination including hydration, imaging time after injection, the need for a Foley catheter, and so on.

Intraservice

An appropriate dose of radiopharmaceutical is prescribed by the physician. The physician supervises a certified technologist who assays the dose of the radiopharmaceutical, instructs the patient on the procedure, and in a designated injection room injects the radiopharmaceutical where the patient remains during the uptake period. The physician supervises the technologist in the acquisition and reconstruction of the data in multiple planes including transmission scans, and for the nonattenuation-corrected and attenuation-corrected emission scans. The physician reviews the study for adequacy and the need for additional acquisitions. All images are interpreted by the physician with correlation with prior imaging studies. Quantification of an abnormality is made by the calculation of the standardized uptake value when clinically indicated. The physician dictates a report for the patient's medical record.

Postservice

The physician reviews and signs the report for the medical record. The physician discusses the results with the referring physician, the patient, and the patient's family. Regulatory review and oversight is provided by the physician throughout the procedure.

78813 Tumor imaging, positron emission tomography (PET); whole body

Work Value: 0.00 // Global Period: XXX

➲ *CPT Assistant* Dec 05: 7; *CPT Changes: An Insider's View* 2005; *Clinical Examples in Radiology* Spring 05:13, 15

Clinical Example

A 33-year-old male presents with a history of a malignant melanoma resected from his back, inferior to the right scapula, 8 months previously. A small, nonpainful left axillary lymph node has developed in the previous month. All recent laboratory and imaging studies have been unremarkable. He is referred for staging prior to left axillary resection. A whole-body PET scan is performed.

Preservice

The physician reviews the clinical request, pertinent medical records, and prior imaging studies. The physician interviews the patient. A decision is made whether the appropriate study has been requested. The physician reviews the results of the finger-stick blood glucose level (included in the procedure). The physician discusses with the technologist the patient positioning and other specifics of the examination including hydration, imaging time after injection, the need for a Foley catheter, and so on.

Intraservice

An appropriate dose of radiopharmaceutical is prescribed by the physician. The physician supervises a certified technologist who assays the dose of the radiopharmaceutical, instructs the patient on the procedure, and in a designated injection room injects the radiopharmaceutical where the patient remains during the uptake period. The physician supervises the technologist in the acquisition and reconstruction of the data in multiple planes including transmission scans, and for the nonattenuation-corrected and attenuation-corrected emission scans. The physician reviews the study for adequacy and need for additional acquisitions. All images are interpreted by the physician with correlation with prior imaging studies. Quantification of an abnormality is made by the calculation of the standardized uptake value when clinically indicated. The physician dictates report for the patient's medical record.

Postservice

The physician reviews and signs the report for the medical record. The physician discusses the results with the referring physician, the patient, and the patient's family. Regulatory review and oversight is provided by the physician throughout the procedure.

Pathology and Laboratory

This chapter provides clinical examples within the Pathology and Laboratory section of the Current Procedural Terminology (CPT®) codebook. Services in the Pathology and Laboratory section are provided by a physician or by a technologist under responsible supervision of a physician.

The following is a brief overview of the codes provided in this chapter.

Cytopathology, 88172

Code 88172 is used to report the evaluation of the fine needle aspirate specimen. The material aspirated is frequently examined microscopically by a physician immediately to ensure that diagnostic material is present. Often times this is performed to render a preliminary diagnostic assessment, so that a repeat operative procedure is not necessary.

Surgical Pathology, 88309 and 88325

Understanding the pathology service definition is necessary for proper use of the surgical pathology codes. The unit of service for the code series, 88300-88309 is the specimen. A *specimen* is defined as tissue or tissues that is (are) submitted for individual and separate attention, requiring individual examination and pathologic diagnosis. When material received for pathologic examination comprises multiple specimens, each specimen is considered a single unit of service and is to be reported using a single code.

88309

Code 88309 is used to report surgical pathology. When this code is reported, services include accession, examination, and reporting. It is important to note that the services reported by codes 88311-88399 are not inclusive to code 88309. Rather, they are reported in addition to code 88309 when provided.

88325

Consultations on slides, referred material, and record and specimen review should be reported using codes 88321-88325. Code 88325 is reported per unit of service or surgical case. A unit of service for code 88325 is considered the surgical pathology case or cytopathology case, which can include multiple specimens for review.

Cytopathology

88172 Cytopathology, evaluation of fine needle aspirate; immediate cytohistologic study to determine adequacy of specimen(s)

Work Value: 0.60 // Global Period: XXX

➲ *CPT Assistant* Fall 93: 26, Fall 94: 2, Dec 98: 8; *CPT Changes: An Insider's View* 2001

Clinical Example

A fine needle aspiration is being performed for the evaluation of a 1-cm lung nodule in a 56-year-old male with chronic obstructive pulmonary disease. The physician is asked to immediately evaluate the smears to determine whether the specimen is adequate to make a definitive diagnosis.

Preservice

Preservice work includes obtaining and reviewing the history and diagnostic studies, including examining previous slides or reports; reviewing literature or research; and communicating with other professionals prior to examining the specimen.

Intraservice

Intraservice work includes performing the gross examination, handling, and processing; microscopic examination; and any required photography or research as necessary to make a final diagnosis. Intraservice also includes any dictation or report preparation performed during the specimen examination and communicating with other professionals during the examination.

Postservice

Postservice work includes preparing and finalizing the report; communicating with other professionals, the patient, and the patient's family (providing written and oral reports and orders); obtaining and reviewing the results of other diagnostic studies, including examining previous slides or reports after examining the specimen; and arranging for further studies or other services.

Coding Tip for 88172

Code 88172 should not be reported in conjunction with codes 88333 and 88334 for the same specimen.

Surgical Pathology

❺ **88309** **Level VI** – Surgical pathology, gross and microscopic examination

Bone resection

Breast, mastectomy – with regional lymph nodes

Colon, segmental resection for tumor

Colon, total resection

Esophagus, partial/total resection

Extremity, disarticulation

Fetus, with dissection

Larynx, partial/total resection – with regional lymph nodes

Lung – total/lobe/segment resection

Pancreas, total/subtotal resection

Prostate, radical resection

Small intestine, resection for tumor

Soft tissue tumor, extensive resection

Stomach – subtotal/total resection for tumor

Testis, tumor

Tongue/tonsil – resection for tumor

Urinary bladder, partial/total resection

Uterus, with or without tubes and ovaries, neoplastic

Vulva, total/subtotal resection

Work Value: 2.80 // Global Period: XXX

➲ *CPT Assistant* Winter 91: 18, Spring 91: 2, Fall 93: 2, 26, Jul 00: 4, Sep 00: 10, Dec 03: 11

Clinical Example

A 67-year-old male presents with rectal bleeding. He undergoes low anterior resection of an adenocarcinoma of the rectum. The pathologist performs the gross and microscopic examination of the specimen and issues a written report of the results.

Intraservice

Intraservice work includes obtaining and reviewing the clinical history and diagnostic studies, including examining previous study reports and communicating with professionals. Intraservice work also includes performing the examination of the specimen; interpreting the test results; comparing the results to previous study reports; considering relevant statistical variations; identifying clinically meaningful findings; reviewing literature or research during the examination of the test results; dictating and preparing the pathology report; and communicating the results to other professionals.

Coding Tip for 88309

The unit of service for code 88309 is the specimen.

---

❺ 88325 Consultation, comprehensive, with review of records and specimens, with report on referred material

Work Value: 2.50 // Global Period: XXX

➲ *CPT Assistant* Winter 91: 19, Apr 97: 9, Dec 02: 10

Clinical Example

A 65-year-old female presents with atypical breast calcifications on a screening mammogram. She undergoes needle localization with excisional biopsy. The pathologists differential diagnosis is ductal carcinoma-in-situ versus invasive ductal carcinoma. Slides including immunohistochemical stains for p63 and calponin, and medical records including the operative report and the mammogram and mammography report, are referred for consultation.

Intraservice

Intraservice work includes obtaining and reviewing the clinical history and referral information, including the referral letter; reviewing the radiographic reports and results of additional clinical testing. Intraservice work also includes reviewing the gross examination report; communicating as necessary with the referring pathologist on the gross findings and block designations; interpreting the test results; comparing the results to previous study reports; considering relevant statistical variations; identifying clinically meaningful findings; reviewing submitted radiographs and correlating them with block and section designations; determining whether additional workup is necessary; reviewing literature or research during the examination of the test results; dictating and preparing the pathology report; and communicating the results with other professionals.

Coding Tip for 88325

Code 88325 is reported when a more comprehensive consultative service is required for the referred material that involves review of records and specimens.

Medicine

This chapter provides clinical examples within the Medicine section of the Current Procedural Terminology (CPT®) codebook. The Medicine section contains a variety of listings for reporting procedures and services provided by many different types of health care providers. In addition, many services and procedures provided by non-physician practitioners can be found in the Medicine section. Several of the clinical examples provided in this chapter represent services provided by physical therapists, occupational therapists, audiologists, and speech pathologists.

Immunization Administration for Vaccines/Toxoids

90465 Immunization administration younger than 8 years of age (includes percutaneous, intradermal, subcutaneous, or intramuscular injections) when the physician counsels the patient/family; first injection (single or combination vaccine/toxoid), per day

Work Value: 0.17 // Global Period: XXX

➲ *CPT Assistant* Apr 05: 1-3, Aug 05: 15, Nov 05: 1; *CPT Changes: An Insider's View* 2005

Clinical Example

An 18-month-old girl is seen for a well-child visit. In accordance with national recommendations for childhood immunizations, the pediatrician determines that the child should receive a diphtheria, tetanus, and pertussis (DTaP) vaccination.

Intraservice

The physician reviews the patient's previous experience with the vaccine and determines whether there are any contraindications prior to proceeding. A vaccine information sheet (VIS) is given to the patient's parent/guardian for the DTaP vaccine, and in keeping with state and federal laws, the information—including risks and benefits of the DTaP vaccine—is discussed with the parent/guardian in detail. The vaccine and the diseases it protects against are also discussed. Appropriate documentation is entered into the patient record. The documentation for the vaccine includes which VIS was given; the date of the publication of the VIS; the date the VIS was given; the name, address, and title of the person who administered the vaccine; the date of administration; the vaccine manufacturer; and the vaccine lot number. Additionally, the appropriate types and doses of medications to alleviate fever and pain at the injection site are discussed. Because the physician participates in the Vaccines for Children program, the nurse obtains the vaccine from the appropriate inventory, making sure to document which supply of vaccines was used for this particular patient. Although federal law does not mandate separate vaccine inventories, the Centers for Disease Control and Prevention strongly recommends them for reasons of accountability. Informed consent is obtained by the physician who then orders the nurse to prepare the vaccine. The nurse prepares the DTaP vaccine using a safe, sharp syringe and administers the vaccine. The patient is observed in the office for an immediate allergic reaction and then is discharged home by the nurse. The immunization tracking number is entered into a computerized statewide registry.

Coding Tip for 90465

The codes for immunization administration (codes 90464 and 90465) must be reported in addition to the vaccine and toxoid codes 90476-90749.

+ 90466 Immunization administration younger than 8 years of age (includes percutaneous, intradermal, subcutaneous, or intramuscular injections) when the physician counsels the patient/family; each additional injection (single or combination vaccine/toxoid), per day (List separately in addition to code for primary procedure)

Work Value: 0.15 // Global Period: ZZZ

➲ *CPT Assistant* Apr 05: 1-3, Aug 05: 15, Nov 05: 1; *CPT Changes: An Insider's View* 2005

Clinical Example

An 18-month-old girl is seen for a well-child visit. In accordance with national recommendation for childhood immunizations, the pediatrician determines that the child should receive a diphtheria, tetanus, and pertussis (DTaP) vaccination.

Intraservice

The physician reviews the patient's previous experience with the vaccine and determines whether there are any contraindications prior to proceeding. A vaccine information sheet (VIS) is given to the patient's parent/guardian for the DTaP vaccine, and in keeping with state and federal laws, the information—including risks and benefits of the DTaP vaccine—is discussed with the parent/guardian in detail. The vaccine and the diseases it protects against are also discussed. Appropriate documentation is entered into the patient record. The documentation for the vaccine includes which VIS was given; the date of the publication of the VIS; the date the VIS was given; the name, address and title of the person who administered the vaccine; the date of administration; the vaccine manufacturer; and the vaccine lot number. Additionally, the appropriate types and doses of medications to alleviate fever and pain at the injection site are discussed. Because the physician participates in the Vaccines for Children program, the nurse obtains the vaccine from the appropriate inventory, making sure to document which supply of vaccines was used for this particular patient. Although federal law does not mandate separate vaccine inventories, the Centers for Disease Control and Prevention strongly recommends them for reasons of accountability. Informed consent is obtained by the physician who then orders the nurse to prepare the vaccine. The nurse prepares the DTaP vaccine using a safe, sharp syringe and administers the vaccine. The patient is observed in the office for an immediate allergic reaction and then is discharged home by the nurse. The immunization tracking number is entered into a computerized statewide registry.

90471 Immunization administration (includes percutaneous, intradermal, subcutaneous, or intramuscular injections); one vaccine (single or combination vaccine/toxoid)

Work Value: 0.17 // Global Period: XXX

➲ ***CPT Assistant*** **Nov 98: 31, Jan 99: 2, Apr 99: 10, Oct 99: 9, Nov 99: 47-48, Nov 00: 10, Feb 01: 5, Jul 01: 2, Nov 02: 11, Mar 04: 11, Apr 04: 14, Apr 05: 1-3, 5, Nov 05: 1;** ***CPT Changes: An Insider's View*** **2002, 2005**

Clinical Example

A 17-year-old patient is seen for a preventive medicine visit. In accordance with national recommendations for immunizations, the physician determines that the patient should receive a hepatitis B vaccination.

Intraservice

The patient and the patient's parent and/or guardian are asked about any previous immunization reactions and are given the Centers for Disease Control and Prevention vaccine information sheet on hepatitis B. The physician reviews the benefits and risks of providing the hepatitis B vaccination with the patient and the patient's parent and/or guardian. After consent, the patient is given the hepatitis B immunization as an injection. The immunization tracking number is entered into a computerized statewide registry.

+ 90472 Immunization administration (includes percutaneous, intradermal, subcutaneous, or intramuscular injections); each additional vaccine (single or combination vaccine/toxoid) (List separately in addition to code for primary procedure)

Work Value: 0.15 // Global Period: ZZZ

➲ ***CPT Assistant*** **Nov 98: 31, Jan 99: 2, Apr 99: 10, Oct 99: 9, Nov 99: 47-48, Nov 00: 10, Feb 01: 5, Jul 01: 2, Nov 02: 11, Mar 04: 11, Apr 04: 14, Apr 05: 1-3, Nov 05: 1;** ***CPT Changes: An Insider's View*** **2000**

Clinical Example

A 17-year-old patient is seen for a preventive medicine visit. In accordance with national recommendations for immunizations, the physician determines that the patient should receive hepatitis B and meningococcal vaccinations.

Intraservice

The patient and the patient's parent and/or guardian are asked about any previous immunizations reactions and are given the Centers for Disease Control and Prevention vaccine information sheets on both the hepatitis B and meningococcal vaccines. The patient is first given the hepatitis B immunization as an injection. During the same visit, the patient receives a meningococcal vaccination as an additional injection. The immunization tracking numbers for each vaccine are entered into a computerized statewide registry.

Hydration, Therapeutic, Prophylactic, and Diagnostic Injections and Infusions (Excludes Chemotherapy)

Hydration

90760 Intravenous infusion, hydration; initial, up to 1 hour

Work Value: 0.17 // Global Period: XXX

➲ *CPT Assistant* Nov 05: 1; *CPT Changes: An Insider's View* 2006

Clinical Example

A 49-year-old female has a diagnosis of viral gastroenteritis. Intravenous (IV) hydration is prescribed. A peripheral IV line needs to be established.

Preservice

The physician provides and confirms the orders. The physician interacts and reviews the plan with the staff.

Intraservice

The physician provides direct supervision and is immediately available in the office. The patient and the patient's response to treatment is periodically assessed by the physician. This assessment is typically done through communication with the nurse.

Postservice

The physician provides appropriate instructions regarding immediate care. The physician provides minimal instructions regarding ongoing care. The physician conducts appropriate interactions with the staff regarding patient monitoring.

+90761 Intravenous infusion, hydration; each additional hour (List separately in addition to code for primary procedure)

Work Value: 0.09 // Global Period: ZZZ

➲ *CPT Assistant* Nov 05: 1; *CPT Changes: An Insider's View* 2006, 2007

Clinical Example

A 49-year-old female with a diagnosis of viral gastroenteritis has 2 liters of intravenous (IV) hydration prescribed. At the end of the first hour, another 1500 cc remain to be infused and the infusion is continued.

Intraservice

The physician provides direct supervision and is immediately available in the office. The physician periodically assesses the patient and the patient's response to treatment. This assessment is typically done through communication with the nurse.

Coding Tip for 90761

Code 90761 is intended to identify hydration if provided as a secondary or subsequent service after a different initial service (eg, codes 90760, 90765, 90774, and/or 96413) is provided.

Therapeutic, Prophylactic, and Diagnostic Injections and Infusions

90765 Intravenous infusion, for therapy, prophylaxis, or diagnosis (specify substance or drug); initial, up to 1 hour

Work Value: 0.21 // Global Period: XXX

➲ *CPT Assistant* Nov 05: 1; *CPT Changes: An Insider's View* 2006

Clinical Example

A 69-year-old male presents with a history of a left olecranon bursitis due to oxacillin-resistant *Staphylococcus aureus*. He is receiving daily infusions on an outpatient basis and has been clinically improving. A peripherally inserted central catheter (PICC) line has been previously established.

Preservice
The physician provides and confirms the orders. The physician interacts and reviews the plan with the staff.

Intraservice
The physician provides direct supervision and is immediately available in the office. The physician periodically assesses the patient and the patient's response to treatment. This assessment is done typically through communication with the nurse.

Postservice
The physician provides appropriate instructions regarding immediate care. The physician provides minimal instructions regarding ongoing care. The physician conducts appropriate interactions with the staff regarding patient monitoring.

Coding Tip for 90765
It is not appropriate to report code 90765 with codes for intravenous push or infusion if code 90765 is an inherent part of the procedure (eg, the administration of contrast material for a diagnostic imaging study).

+ 90767 Intravenous infusion, for therapy, prophylaxis, or diagnosis (specify substance or drug); additional sequential infusion, up to 1 hour (List separately in addition to code for primary procedure)

Work Value: 0.19 // Global Period: ZZZ

➲ *CPT Assistant* Nov 05: 1; *CPT Changes: An Insider's View* 2006

Clinical Example
A 70-year-old female, who is status post a ruptured colonic diverticula, presents for infusion of two drugs. She has a single lumen peripherally inserted central catheter line in place.

Preservice
The physician confirms the orders.

Intraservice
The physician provides direct supervision and is immediately available in the office. The physician periodically assesses the patient and the patient's response to treatment. This assessment is done typically through communication with the nurse.

+ 90768 Intravenous infusion, for therapy, prophylaxis, or diagnosis (specify substance or drug); concurrent infusion (List separately in addition to code for primary procedure)

Work Value: 0.17 // Global Period: ZZZ

➲ *CPT Assistant* Nov 05: 1; *CPT Changes: An Insider's View* 2006

Clinical Example
A 73-year-old patient with a diabetic ulcer and osteomyelitis presents for infusion. His wound culture was positive for several bacteria, including oxacillin-resistant *Staphylococcus aureus*. He is to receive an infusion of two antibiotics simultaneously through his previously established two-lumen central catheter.

Preservice
The physician provides and confirms the orders.

Intraservice
The physician provides direct supervision and is immediately available in the office. The physician periodically assesses the patient and the patient's response to treatment. This assessment is done typically through communication with the nurse.

Coding Tip for 90768
Code 90768 is reported only once per encounter.

90772 Therapeutic, prophylactic or diagnostic injection (specify substance or drug); subcutaneous or intramuscular

Work Value: 0.17 // Global Period: XXX

➲ *CPT Assistant* Nov 05: 1; *CPT Changes: An Insider's View* 2006

Clinical Example

A 19-year-old male presents with severe dysuria. A urethral swab is performed and found to be consistent with gonorrhea.

Preservice

The physician provides and confirms the orders. The physician interacts and reviews the plan with the staff.

Intraservice

The physician provides direct supervision and is immediately available in the office. The physician assesses the patient's response to treatment.

Postservice

The physician provides appropriate instructions regarding immediate care. The physician provides minimal instructions regarding ongoing care. The physician conducts appropriate interactions with the staff regarding patient monitoring.

Coding Tip for 90772

Code 90772 is reported for nonantieoplastic hormonal injection therapy.

90774 Therapeutic, prophylactic or diagnostic injection (specify substance or drug); intravenous push, single or initial substance/drug

Work Value: 0.18 // Global Period: XXX

➲ *CPT Assistant* Nov 05: 1; *CPT Changes: An Insider's View* 2006

Clinical Example

A 58-year-old female with no major underlying health problems presents for evaluation of nausea and vomiting. She is diagnosed with gastroenteritis with mild dehydration. An intravenous (IV) anti-emetic is prescribed, along with 1 liter of IV hydration.

Preservice

The physician provides and confirms the orders. The physician interacts and reviews the plan with the staff.

Intraservice

The physician provides direct supervision and is immediately available in the office. The physician periodically assesses the patient and the patient's response to treatment. The assessment is done typically through communication with the nurse.

Postservice

The physician provides appropriate instructions regarding immediate care. The physician provides minimal instructions regarding ongoing care. The physician conducts appropriate interactions with the staff regarding patient monitoring.

+ 90775 Therapeutic, prophylactic or diagnostic injection (specify substance or drug); each additional sequential intravenous push of a new substance/drug (List separately in addition to code for primary procedure)

Work Value: 0.10 // Global Period: ZZZ

➲ *CPT Assistant* Nov 05: 1; *CPT Changes: An Insider's View* 2006

Clinical Example

A 58-year-old female with no major underlying health problems presents for evaluation of nausea and vomiting and is diagnosed as having gastroenteritis with mild dehydration. An intravenous anti-emetic is prescribed, along with 1 liter of intravenous (IV) hydration. The nausea persists and the physician prescribes a benzodiazepine by IV push.

Preservice

The physician provides and confirms the orders.

Intraservice
The physician provides direct supervision and is immediately available in the office. The physician periodically assesses the patient and patient's response to treatment. This assessment is done typically through communication with the nurse.

Coding Tip for 90775
Report code 90775 to identify the intravenous push of a new substance/drug if provided as a secondary or subsequent service after a different initial service is provided. In addition, code 90775 must always be reported in conjunction with codes 90765, 90774, 96409, and 96413 as appropriate.

Psychiatry

Psychiatric Diagnostic or Evaluative Interview Procedures

90801 Psychiatric diagnostic interview examination

Work Value: 2.80 // Global Period: XXX

➲ ***CPT Assistant*** **Summer 92: 12, Nov 97: 39-40, Mar 01: 5, Mar 02: 4, May 05: 1**

Clinical Example
1) An evaluation session in the office for a 24-year-old male who says he heard voices coming out of a wall and was threatening to harm the neighbors.

2) The parents of a 15-year-old boy ask for an evaluation for their son, who was brought home by police after violating curfew and perhaps breaking and entering. They tell the physician he has a history of attention-deficit hyperactivity disorder, has been suspended from school, and has refused to take medicine for the past 6 months.

Preservice
Preservice work depends on how the patient was referred. At a minimum, preservice requires a phone discussion with the person who initiated the referral (eg, the physician, the patient's family, law enforcement, employer). Preservice also involves reviewing the records from the referral source and the lab or consultation reports.

Intraservice
Intraservice work includes obtaining a complete psychiatric history, including present illness, past history, and family history; performing a complete mental status examination and a selected physical examination; making arrangements for laboratory tests; establishing a definitive diagnosis or at least a narrow enough differential to warrant a treatment plan; decision making concerning the need for and degree of supervision (eg, hospitalization); counseling the patient concerning the diagnosis and treatment options and the patient's proposed options.

Postservice
Postservice work includes arrangement for further studies and further care; report or discussion with referral source; arrangement for getting additional information; dictating results of examination; and frequently involves additional communication with patient and/or family after results of studies are known or to deal with side effects of instituted treatment. This would probably require information from collateral sources regarding patient's compliance, accuracy of prediction that patient might remain on out-patient status, etc. Report and consultation with third party utilization manager to arrange for payment and funding for proposed treatment.

Coding Tip for 90801
For a Mini-Mental Status Examination performed by a physician, see the evaluation and management service codes.

Psychiatric Therapeutic Procedures

Office or Other Outpatient Facility

Insight Oriented, Behavior Modifying and/or Supportive Psychotherapy

90804 Individual psychotherapy, insight oriented, behavior modifying and/or supportive, in an office or outpatient facility, approximately 20 to 30 minutes face-to-face with the patient;

Work Value: 1.21 // Global Period: XXX

➲ *CPT Assistant* Nov 97: 39, Jul 99: 10, Mar 01: 5, Mar 02: 4, Oct 02: 11, May 05: 1

Clinical Example

1) Approximately 20 to 30 minutes psychotherapy with an obsessive-compulsive 29-year-old female on chlomipramine, last seen 6 weeks ago, who begins to uncontrollably pull her hair out after she is fired from her job.

2) Approximately 20 to 30 minutes psychotherapy with a 12-year-old boy, major depression, single episode, who has been seen in outpatient psychotherapy for 9 months, and is stable. Improvement on antidepressants.

Preservice

Preservice work includes preparing to see patient, reviewing records, and communicating with other professionals and the patient's family.

Intraservice

Intraservice work includes obtaining (or updating) a history, performing an evaluation, counseling the patient, and writing notes.

Postservice

Arranging for further services; reviewing results of studies; communicating further with patient, family, and other professionals, including written or telephone reports; documenting the services provided; providing written or telephone reports to Medicare or other third party payers.

Coding Tip for 90804

It is appropriate to report code 90887 in conjunction with code 90804 on the same date of service when both services are performed.

90805 Individual psychotherapy, insight oriented, behavior modifying and/or supportive, in an office or outpatient facility, approximately 20 to 30 minutes face-to-face with the patient; with medical evaluation and management services

Work Value: 1.37 // Global Period: XXX

➲ *CPT Assistant* Nov 97: 39, Jul 99: 10, Mar 01: 5, Mar 02: 4, May 05: 1

Clinical Example

1) Approximately 20 to 30 minutes psychotherapy with an obsessive-compulsive 29-year-old female on chlomipramine, last seen 6 weeks ago, who begins to uncontrollably pull her hair out after she is fired from her job. Consider strategy for augmenting medication regimen.

2) Approximately 20 to 30 minutes psychotherapy with a 12-year-old boy, major depression, single episode, who has been seen in outpatient psychotherapy for 9 months, and is stable. Improvement on antidepressants. Patient beginning to ask about stopping medications. Consider altering medication and evaluating compliance.

Preservice

Preservice work includes preparing to see patient, reviewing records, and communicating with other professionals and the patient's family.

Intraservice

Intraservice work includes obtaining (or updating) a history, performing an evaluation, counseling the patient, and writing notes.

Postservice

Postservice work includes arranging for further services; reviewing the results of studies; communicating further with the patient, the patient's family, and other professionals (including providing written or oral reports);

documenting the services provided; providing written or oral reports to Medicare or other third-party payers; conducting a medical diagnostic evaluation (eg, evaluating comorbid medical conditions, drug interactions, and physical examinations); managing drugs, when indicated, and physician orders; and interpreting laboratory or other medical diagnostic studies and observations.

90807 Individual psychotherapy, insight oriented, behavior modifying and/or supportive, in an office or outpatient facility, approximately 45 to 50 minutes face-to-face with the patient; with medical evaluation and management services

Work Value: 2.02 // Global Period: XXX

➲ *CPT Assistant* Nov 97: 39, Jul 99: 10, Mar 01: 6, May 05: 1

Clinical Example

1) Approximately 45 to 50 minutes individual psychotherapy in office for a 72-year-old female with dysthymic disorder and dependent personality disorder, with chronic obstructive pulmonary disease and congestive heart failure, on antidepressant medication, who made an overdose attempt 4 months ago but has been stable since. Consideration of comorbid medical diagnoses, interaction of medication, and laboratory screening and interpretation.

2) Approximately 45 to 50 minutes individual psychotherapy in office for a 16-year-old girl with panic disorder. Treated with cognitive behavioral therapy. Consider medication adjustments with tricyclic and alprazolam.

Preservice

Preservice includes preparing to see patient, reviewing records, and communicating with other professionals and the patient's family.

Intraservice

Intraservice includes obtaining (or updating) a history, performing an evaluation, counseling the patient, and writing notes.

Postservice

Postservice includes arranging for further services; reviewing the results of studies; communicating further with the patient, the patients family, and other professionals (including providing written or oral reports); documenting the services provided; providing written or oral reports to Medicare or other third-party payers; conducting a medical diagnostic evaluation (eg, evaluating comorbid medical conditions, drug interactions, and physical examinations); managing drugs, when indicated, and physician orders; and interpreting laboratory or other medical diagnostic studies and observations.

Inpatient Hospital, Partial Hospital or Residential Care Facility

INSIGHT ORIENTED, BEHAVIOR MODIFYING AND/OR SUPPORTIVE PSYCHOTHERAPY

90816 Individual psychotherapy, insight oriented, behavior modifying and/or supportive, in an inpatient hospital, partial hospital or residential care setting, approximately 20 to 30 minutes face-to-face with the patient;

Work Value: 1.25 // Global Period: XXX

➲ *CPT Assistant* Nov 97: 39-40, Mar 01: 6-7, Mar 02: 4, May 05: 1

Clinical Example

1) Approximately 20 to 30 minutes psychotherapy in a hospital on the third day of detoxification admission for a 24-year-old male with a year-long history of cocaine dependence and alcohol.

2) Approximately 20 to 30 minutes individual psychotherapy in a residential treatment center for a 14-year-old boy with conduct disorder who periodically requires seclusion for aggression.

Preservice

Preservice work includes obtaining (or updating) a history, counseling the patient, and writing notes.

Intraservice

Intraservice work includes obtaining (or updating) a history, counseling the patient, and writing notes.

Postservice

Postservice work includes arranging for further services; communicating further with other professionals and the patient's family; obtaining and/or reviewing the results of diagnostic and other studies; documenting the services provided; and providing written and oral reports.

90817 Individual psychotherapy, insight oriented, behavior modifying and/or supportive, in an inpatient hospital, partial hospital or residential care setting, approximately 20 to 30 minutes face-to-face with the patient; with medical evaluation and management services

Work Value: 1.41 // Global Period: XXX

➲ *CPT Assistant* Nov 97: 39-40, Mar 01: 6-7, Mar 02: 4, May 05: 1

Clinical Example

1) Approximately 20 to 30 minutes individual psychotherapy in a nursing home with an 85-year-old female with carcinoma metastatic to lung and adjustment disorder with anxiety. Consider prescribing medication.

2) Approximately 20 to 30 minutes individual psychotherapy in a residential treatment center for a 14-year-old boy with schizophrenia on a typical neuroleptic requiring laboratory monitoring who periodically requires seclusion for aggression.

Preservice

Preservice work includes communicating with other professionals and the patient's family; obtaining and/or reviewing the results of diagnostic and other studies; reviewing the patient's chart; and providing written and oral reports.

Intraservice

Intraservice work includes obtaining (or updating) a history, counseling the patient, and writing notes.

Postservice

Postservice work includes arranging for further services; communicating further with other professionals and the patient's family; obtaining and/or reviewing the results of diagnostic and other studies; documenting the services provided; providing written and oral reports; conducting a medical diagnostic evaluation (eg, evaluating comorbid medical conditions, drug interactions, and physical examinations), managing drugs, when indicated, and physician orders; and interpreting laboratory or other medical diagnostic studies and observations.

90818 Individual psychotherapy, insight oriented, behavior modifying and/or supportive, in an inpatient hospital, partial hospital or residential care setting, approximately 45 to 50 minutes face-to-face with the patient;

Work Value: 1.89 // Global Period: XXX

➲ *CPT Assistant* Nov 97: 39-40, Mar 01: 6-7, Mar 02: 4, May 05: 1

Clinical Example

1) Approximately 45 to 50 minutes individual psychotherapy in a hospital with a 35-year-old female with postpartum depression responding to medication, who is about to be discharged.

2) Approximately 45 to 50 minutes individual psychotherapy in a hospital with a 15-year-old boy hospitalized for detoxification, preparing for transfer to partial hospitalization program.

Preservice

Preservice work includes communicating with other professionals and the patient's family; obtaining and/or reviewing the results of diagnostic and other studies; reviewing the patient's chart; and providing written and oral reports.

Intraservice

Intraservice work includes obtaining (or updating) a history, counseling the patient, and writing notes.

Postservice

Postservice work includes arranging for further services; communicating further with other professionals and the patient's family; obtaining and/or reviewing the results of diagnostic and other studies; documenting the services provided; and providing written and oral reports.

Other Psychotherapy

90853 Group psychotherapy (other than of a multiple-family group)

Work Value: 0.59 // Global Period: XXX

➲ *CPT Assistant* Summer 92: 15, Nov 97: 40-41, Mar 01: 8, Mar 02: 4, May 05: 1

Clinical Example

1) Group psychotherapy in the office with eight men and women with a dual diagnosis of substance abuse and personality disorders.

2) Group psychotherapy in a residential treatment facility for six adolescent females. Diagnosis unspecified.

Preservice

Preservice work includes reviewing the patients records, including reviewing medication and lab studies; consulting with collateral sources from half of the patients; communicating with houseparents, nursing staff, and parents concerning the patients; reviewing the records and results of studies since the last session; and reviewing the chart.

Intraservice

Intraservice work includes obtaining an observed mental status of each patient; observing and interpreting patterns of interaction among the patients in the group; and interpreting the effects of personality patterns and substance abuse behavior on group interactions and on reported behavior outside the group.

Postservice

Postservice work includes dictating records; arranging for the next group service and for other individual services these patients require; communicating with third-parties for coverage; arranging for follow-up care, including drug screenings, appropriate lab studies for medication, and individual psychiatric and other medical services; supervising the co-therapist, if applicable; reporting to employee assistant managers and/or law enforcement agencies, if applicable; obtaining and reviewing results of studies; and communicating with other third parties, as necessary (eg, schools). Documenting services is done afterwards. (Telephone communication with the patients families is much greater in this type of group. As opposed to the usual hospital setting, writing notes and communicating with other professionals, third parties, and family is done after the session.)

Other Psychiatric Services or Procedures

90862 Pharmacologic management, including prescription, use, and review of medication with no more than minimal medical psychotherapy

Work Value: 0.95 // Global Period: XXX

➲ *CPT Assistant* Summer 92: 16, Nov 97: 40-41, Mar 01: 5, Mar 02: 4, May 05: 1

Clinical Example

1) A 72-year-old male with bipolar disorder, or lithium with familial benign tremor, comes in for treatment because his tremor has suddenly become worse.

2) An 8-year-old boy on methylphenidate HCl for attention-deficit hyperactivity disorder is developing tics and comes in for medication management.

Preservice

Preservice work includes preparing to see the patient; reviewing records; ordering laboratory services; reviewing the results of lab tests; communicating with the neurologist concerning the patient's tremor; and communicating with the patient's family.

Intraservice

Intraservice work includes conducting a mental status examination with a special assessment of mood disorder and cognitive examination; obtaining a history of present illness; reviewing the patient's history of taking medication; examining the tremor and conducting a brief neurological assessment; and regulating medication.

Postservice

Postservice work includes arranging for a follow-up visit; arranging for lab studies after medicine change; communicating with the neurological consultant; documenting services; providing reports to necessary third parties; and communicating with the patient's family.

Biofeedback

90901 Biofeedback training by any modality

Work Value: 0.41 // Global Period: 000

➲ *CPT Assistant* Sep 97: 11, Apr 98: 14, Jun 98: 10, Jun 99: 5, May 02: 18, Sep 04: 13, Mar 05: 16

Clinical Example

A 47-year-old male has a chronic history of muscle spasms in the neck and shoulders, and tension-type diagnosed headaches. He has not responded well to a prior history of treatment with anti-anxiety medication and physical therapy. The patient is monitored with surface EMG-electrodes placed bilaterally on the trapezius, frontalis, and sternocleidomastoid muscle areas, given specific instruction as to how to interact with biofeedback information (visual and/or auditory signals meaningfully related to amplitude of EMG) and provided with directions of appropriate reduction of tension in the targeted muscle group. Possible factor precipitating tension-type headaches discussed. Pain levels reviewed from charts supplied by patient; session changes reviewed with patient and recommendation made for follow-up training during the week plus additional recommendations for monitoring, 45-60 minutes session length, with one-on-one interaction with treating therapist. A brief session could be 30 minutes. The sample note may be a computerized printout of changes in EMG values over time, plus comments of treating practitioner, patient's responses, compendium pain values as well as recording of medication type and usage during the interval since last session.

Preservice

Preservice work includes preparing to see the patient; preparing biofeedback equipment, and reviewing the patient's records.

Intraservice

Intraservice work includesincludes placement of electrodes; the reading of responses (including galvanic skin responses); and working with the patient to monitor and control/change muscle responses.

Postservice

Postservice work includes disposal or cleaning of electrodes, and documentation of services and results.

Coding Tip for 90901

If biofeedback training and behavior modification, supportive psychotherapy, and/or the development of insight or affective understanding are performed during the same encounter during the same session, codes 90875-90976 should be reported to identify the services rendered. If the services are not performed during the same session, psychophysiological therapy incorporating biofeedback training is not performed, and separate codes should be used to identify the specific services performed.

90911 Biofeedback training, perineal muscles, anorectal or urethral sphincter, including EMG and/or manometry

Work Value: 0.89 // Global Period: 000

➲ *CPT Assistant* Sep 97: 11, Nov 97: 41, Jun 98: 10, Jun 99: 5

Clinical Example

A 40-year-old female with postpartum incontinence receives anorectal biofeedback with anal manometry (45 minutes) for initial sensory training to decreasing volumes of rectal distension. Requires extensive patient counseling and reassurance.

Gastroenterology

91034 Esophagus, gastroesophageal reflux test; with nasal catheter pH electrode(s) placement, recording, analysis and interpretation

Work Value: 0.97 // Global Period: 000

➲ *CPT Assistant* May 05: 3; *CPT Changes: An Insider's View* 2005

Clinical Example

A 54-year-old female presents with a 3-year history of heartburn, regurgitation, and throat soreness. She has no dysphagia, weight loss, or gastrointestinal (GI) bleeding. She has not improved with over-the-counter medications. Her diagnostic testing, including an upper GI and esophagogastroduodenoscopy, was normal. She is suspected to have gastroesophageal reflux disease and was placed on pharmacological agents with initial improvement, but continues to have breakthrough regurgitation symptoms despite adjusting pharmacological management.

Preservice

The patient's history, including prior studies, is reviewed. The procedure and its purpose is explained to the patient. The patient is counseled to maintain normal activity and food consumption during the test. The patient's questions are answered and informed consent is obtained. Confirmation is obtained that all necessary instruments and supplies are readily available. Patient positioning and prepping is supervised.

Intraservice

Following nasal spray administration of 2% lidocaine, a thin plastic catheter is passed through one nostril, down the back of the throat, and into the esophagus as the patient swallows. The tip of the catheter contains a sensor that is positioned in the esophagus so that it is just above the lower esophageal sphincter. In this position the sensor records each reflux of acid. The catheter protruding from the nose is connected to a recorder that registers each reflux of acid. The patient is counseled again to go about his or her usual activities, for example, eating, sleeping, and working. Meals, periods of sleep, and symptoms are recorded by the patient in a diary and/or by pushing buttons on the recorder. The patient is discharged with the catheter and recorder in place. The patient returns to the site of service, typically the next day, and the catheter is removed.

Postservice

Staff downloads the recorder data into a computer, where it is summarized and put into graphic form. The computer tracings are analyzed by the physician for the presence of acid pH in the distal esophagus and correlation with symptoms as recorded by the patient. Treatment recommendations and decisions are made based on the data, including the potential need for additional medical, pharmacologic, endoscopic, and/or surgical intervention. A report and outcome letter is dictated for the referring physician and/or insurance company.

Esophageal Acid Reflux Test
91034

A catheter with a pH electrode is placed into the esophagus, either through the nares or swallowed, to measure intraesophageal pH (an indicator of gastric reflux).

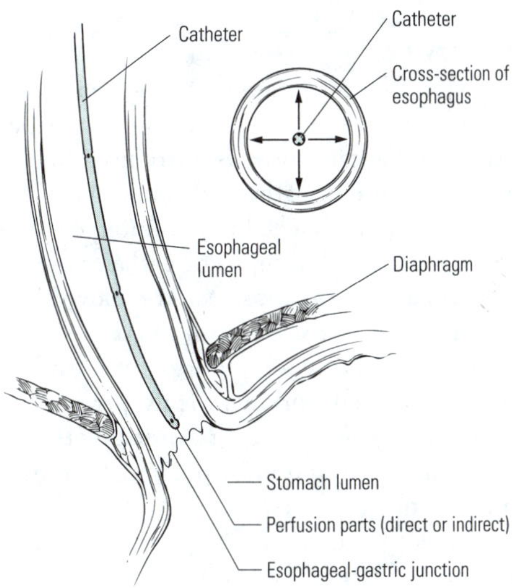

91035 Esophagus, gastroesophageal reflux test; with mucosal attached telemetry pH electrode placement, recording, analysis and interpretation

Work Value: 1.59 // Global Period: 000

➲ *CPT Assistant* May 05: 3; *CPT Changes: An Insider's View* 2005

Clinical Example

A 40-year-old male presents with severe chest pain. A thorough cardiac evaluation suggested no cardiac abnormality. The patient was placed on pharmacological agents, but symptoms have persisted. An esophagogastroduodenoscopy revealed mild distal esophageal erythema, otherwise unremarkable.

Preservice

The patient's history, including prior studies, is reviewed. The procedure and its purpose is explained to the patient. The patient is counseled to maintain normal activity and food consumption during the test. The patient's questions are answered and informed consent is obtained. Confirmation is obtained that all necessary instruments and supplies are readily available. Patient positioning and prepping is supervised.

Intraservice

Following administration of 2% lidocaine, a capsule that contains an acid sensing probe, a battery, and a transmitter is introduced into the esophagus on a catheter through the nose or mouth and is attached to the lining of the esophagus with a clip. The catheter then is detached from the capsule and removed. The patient is counseled again to go about his or her usual activities, for example, eating, sleeping, and working. Meals, periods of sleep, and symptoms are recorded by the patient in a diary and/or by pushing buttons on the recorder. The patient is discharged with a recorder in place. The patient returns to the site of service, typically the next day, to return the recorder.

Postservice

Staff downloads the recorder data into a computer, where it is summarized and put into graphic form. The computer tracings are analyzed by the physician for the presence of acid pH in the distal esophagus and correlation with symptoms as recorded by the patient. Treatment recommendations and decisions are made based on the data, including the potential need for additional medical, pharmacologic, endoscopic, and/or surgical intervention. A report and outcome letter is dictated for the referring physician and/or insurance company.

91038 Esophageal function test, gastroesophageal reflux test with nasal catheter intraluminal impedance electrode(s) placement, recording, analysis and interpretation; prolonged (greater than 1 hour, up to 24 hours)

Work Value: 1.10 // Global Period: 000

➲ *CPT Assistant* May 05: 3; *CPT Changes: An Insider's View* 2005

Clinical Example

A 44-year-old male presents with a complaint of frequent heartburn. The patient has tried a variety of pharmacologic agents without relief of symptoms. An esophagogastroduodenoscopy was unremarkable. An esophageal pH test failed to elucidate the etiology of the patients symptoms.

Preservice

The patient's history, including prior studies, is reviewed. The procedure and its purpose is explained to the patient. The patient is counseled to maintain normal activity and food consumption during the test. The patient's questions are answered and informed consent is obtained. Confirmation is obtained that all necessary instruments and supplies are readily available. Patient positioning and prepping is supervised.

Intraservice

Following nasal spray administration of 2% lidocaine, a multichannel catheter with impedance sensors is inserted via the nose to a depth of 60 cm. After the catheter is positioned, it is taped securely at the nares to prevent movement over the prolonged monitoring period. The patient is then instructed on the use of a recording device to monitor symptom occurrences, body position, and meal periods. After completing the patient instructions, the recording is started and the patient is discharged from the laboratory. The patient is instructed to keep a log book of symptoms. Upon completion of the monitoring period, the patient returns to the lab, the catheter is withdrawn, and the patient is discharged.

Postservice

Staff downloads the recorder data into a computer, where it is summarized and put into graphic form. The computer summary is analyzed by the physician, who considers correlations with symptoms as recorded by the patient. Treatment recommendations and decisions are made based on the data, including the potential need for additional medical, pharmacologic, endoscopic, and/or surgical intervention. A report and outcome letter is dictated for the referring physician and/or insurance company.

Coding Tip for 91038

Code 91038 includes a specific time range in its descriptor to clearly define what constitutes a prolonged period for monitoring intraluminal impedance testing.

91110 Gastrointestinal tract imaging, intraluminal (eg, capsule endoscopy), esophagus through ileum, with physician interpretation and report

Work Value: 3.64 // Global Period: XXX

➲ *CPT Assistant* Oct 04: 15, Aug 05: 14; *CPT Changes: An Insider's View* 2004

Clinical Example

A 57-year old male has a history of obscure gastrointestinal (GI) bleeding. He is referred for wireless capsule endoscopy. After a 12-hour fast, the patient presents for capsule endoscopy. After informed consent is obtained, the patient's abdomen is cleaned and shaved for proper placement of the sensor array. The belt assembly, including the data recorder and battery pack, is adjusted to fit the patient and attached to the sensor array. The battery pack has been completely charged the previous evening. The patient is instructed on the ingestion technique and swallows the capsule endoscope. The patient is observed for immediate signs of complications; if none are observed, the patient is discharged. The patient is instructed not to resume eating for 4 hours. The capsule advances by peristalsis through the GI tract. After 8 hours, the patient returns and is assessed for signs or symptoms of complications. The data recorder belt and sensor array are removed and disinfected. The physician discusses relevant procedural feedback with the patient. The patient is discharged. Numerous video images and diagnostic information from the data recorder are downloaded to the workstation for processing. Once the download information is complete, the physician reviews the capsule images at a 15 frames/second base rate with frequent stops to evaluate potential diagnostic abnormalities. During the review, the physician activates the localization software to input the esophagogastric junction, pylorus, and ileocecal valve locations. After completing the analysis of the images and diagnostic information, the physician makes a diagnosis and generates a report.

Preservice

Possible contraindications are assessed, such as the presence of a pacemaker, an active bowel obstruction, or a swallowing disorder. The patient is counseled on the nature of the procedure, why it is being performed, and possible complications. Instructions are provided to the patient on preparing for the procedure (eg, fasting, clothing to wear). Informed consent is obtained.

Intraservice

Staff performs all needed functions for procedure including obtaining and entering needed data into recorder, placing sensor array on the patient's abdomen, and attaching the battery pack to the recorder. The patient is given the capsule to swallow, which is observed by the physician, and the patient is provided instructions for activities, meals, and return time. The patient returns after 89 hours, at which time the sensor array is removed and data are downloaded from the recorder to the workstation by staff. The physician then proceeds to review 50,000-60,000 images. The entire study is scanned and key anatomic landmarks are annotated (eg, esophagogastric junction, duodenum, ileocecal valve), permitting the identification of potentially positive findings and the determination of gastric and small bowel emptying times. Once the landmarks (thumbnails) have been determined, all of the images are viewed. When an abnormality is identified, a thumbnail is created. Key findings or abnormalities are noted and recorded on a localization drawing that may also be used to guide subsequent tests.

Postservice

Upon completing the review of all images and formulating an interpretation, a report is prepared and dictated. The findings are communicated to the patient and a copy of the report is sent to the referring physician. The referring physician may also be contacted to discuss the findings.

91120 Rectal sensation, tone, and compliance test (ie, response to graded balloon distention)

Work Value: 0.97 // Global Period: XXX

➲ *CPT Assistant* May 05: 3; *CPT Changes: An Insider's View* 2005

Clinical Example

A 35-year-old female presents with 3-year history of constipation. She has no desire to defecate and manually disimpacts her bowel once every 2 to 3 weeks. On examination, the abdomen was distended. Rectal exam showed impaired rectal sensation and hard stools, of which patient was completely unaware.

Preservice

The patient's history, including prior studies, is reviewed. The procedure and its purpose is explained to the patient. The patient is counseled to maintain normal activity and food consumption during the test. The patient's questions are answered and informed consent is obtained. Confirmation is obtained that all necessary instruments and supplies are readily available. Patient positioning and prepping is supervised.

Intraservice

After informed consent is obtained, the patient undergoes rectal cleansing. The patient is placed in the left lateral position. A 5-mm diameter probe, with a 10-cm, highly compliant balloon is placed into the rectum and taped in position. The balloon is connected to a computerized distending device. Stepwise graded balloon distentions are performed to assess the intraoperating pressure (IOP). Baseline rectal tone is assessed over a 30-minute period. Intermittent balloon distensions are performed at 4 mm Hg increments until the patient reports sensation, desire to defecate, and urgency to defecate. Pain on maximum tolerable volume is recorded. While being monitored, the patient is asked to defecate the balloon. After a 15-minute rest, the balloon is reinserted into the rectum and inflated to IOP. The patient is fed a standardized 1000-kcal meal. Rectal tone and sensory changes are recorded for a subsequent 60-minute period. At the conclusion of the test, the balloon is deflated, and the balloon and probe are removed.

Postservice

The physician discharges the patient. The physician calculates and interprets the rectal sensory thresholds, rectal pressure, compliance, and rectal tone changes at rest and after provocation. Treatment recommendations and decisions are made based on the data, including the potential need for additional medical, pharmacologic, endoscopic, and/or surgical intervention. A report and outcome letter is dictated for the referring physician and/or insurance company.

Coding Tip for 91120

Code 91120 describes a comprehensive assessment of sensory, motor, and biomechanical function of the rectum in patients with irritable bowel syndrome, constipation, and/or fecal incontinence, for example. Testing is performed at rest and after provocative stimuli.

91122 Anorectal manometry

Work Value: 1.77 // Global Period: 000

Clinical Example

A 66-year-old female is becoming reluctant to leave her home because of fecal soiling. She is continent of solid stool, but has had slowly worsening incontinence of liquid stool for 3 years. She frequently has rectal urgency. She has had 4 vaginal deliveries. Recent flexible sigmoidoscopy was normal. The physician performs and interprets an anorectal manometry study.

Preservice

Preservice work includes explaining the procedure to the patient and reviewing indications.

Intraservice

Intraservice work includes performing a digital rectal exam; inserting a lubricated multichannel catheter into the patient's rectum 15–20 cm; performing a station pull-through at 1/2-cm increments (pausing 10–15 seconds between manipulations) to identify the location of the internal anal sphincter and basal pressure; repeating the procedure; repeating the procedure again while the patient squeezes the anal sphincter to determine augmented squeeze pressure; repeating the procedure; having the patient squeeze as hard and as long as possible to determine maximal squeeze pressure and duration; testing sensation with pinpricks in four quadrants of the anus; measuring baseline pressure for 5 minutes and then gradually inflating/deflating a balloon to and from 5, 10, 15, 20, 25, 30, 40, 50, 75, 100, 125, and 150 cc to determine sensing threshold; and looking for relaxation response to the balloon distention.

Ophthalmology

General Ophthalmological Services

New Patient

92002 Ophthalmological services: medical examination and evaluation with initiation of diagnostic and treatment program; intermediate, new patient

Work Value: 0.88 // Global Period: XXX

➲ ***CPT Assistant*** **Feb 97: 6, Aug 98: 3, Jun 05: 11, Dec 05: 10**

Clinical Example

A 42-year-old white male presents with a 3-day history of a red, painful left eye and blurred vision.

Preservice

Preservice work includes examining and reviewing intake medical history provided by optometric technician; in those cases where this is an interval examination of a patient not seen in 3 years, a review of past medical and ocular history; review of correspondence by other medical providers regarding the individual case.

Intraservice

A comprehensive medical and ocular history is obtained. The ocular structures related to the patient's chief complaint are examined and evaluated. The examination includes an external examination, ophthalmoscopy, biomicroscopy of the related structures of the eye, and an ocular neurological assessment when indicated. A microbiological culture may be taken. The condition is assessed and a treatment plan is described to the patient, including information about medication, instructions, and follow-up visits.

Postservice

Postservice work includes completion of medical record and transmittal of information to the patient's general practitioner or others as indicated.

Coding Tip for 92002, 92004, 92012, and 92014

When reporting ophthalmologic visits, be sure to confer with the physician to select code 92002, 92004, 92012, or 92014 or the appropriate evaluation and management (E/M) services codes, depending on the specific services provided to the patient at that visit. As indicated in the definitions of ophthalmology services, the ophthalmology codes are more specific to the services and examination rendered during a visit related to the ocular system. However, E/M codes may be more appropriate when there are many eye problems, when counseling and/or coordination of care dominates the visit, or when an underlying medical condition(s) of the patient is the primary reason for the visit. The code that most accurately describes the services performed should be the code reported, whether it is an E/M code or an ophthalmology visit code.

92004 Ophthalmological services: medical examination and evaluation with initiation of diagnostic and treatment program; comprehensive, new patient, one or more visits

Work Value: 1.67 // Global Period: XXX

➲ *CPT Assistant* **Feb 97: 6, Aug 98: 3, Jun 05: 11, Dec 05: 10**

Clinical Example

A 32-year-old with a 12-year history of insulin-dependent diabetes presents with blurred vision and a sudden onset of floaters in the left eye.

Preservice

Examine and review the patient's intake medical history provided by the optometric technician. In those cases where this is an interval examination of a patient not seen in three years, conduct a review of past medical and ocular history, and review correspondence by other medical providers regarding the individual case.

Intraservice

Conduct an evaluation of the eye and ocular adnexa that includes a comprehensive medical and ocular history, external examination of the eye, ophthalmoscopy, and biomicroscopy; examine the gross visual fields; conduct a neurological evaluation and when applicable, a dilated funduscopic evaluation; initiate a diagnostic and treatment plan, which may include other special ophthalmological testing, consultations, laboratory, and radiological services; prescribe medication and/or corrective lenses; counsel the patient and provide detailed instructions on the treatment plan.

Postservice

Complete the medical record and communicate the information to the patient's general practitioner or others as indicated.

Established Patient

92012 Ophthalmological services: medical examination and evaluation, with initiation or continuation of diagnostic and treatment program; intermediate, established patient

Work Value: 0.67 // Global Period: XXX

➲ *CPT Assistant* **Feb 97: 6, Aug 98: 3, Jun 05: 11, Dec 05: 10**

Clinical Example

A 63-year-old female with congestive heart failure and mild chronic obstructive pulmonary disease and increasing shortness of breath presents for an interval exam for evaluation of her chronic open-angle glaucoma. She is currently being treated with 0.1% dipirefrin and 0.25% timolol maleate twice a day.

Preservice

Examine and review intake medical history provided by optometric technician; in those cases where this is an interval examination of a patient not seen in three years, a review of past medical and ocular history; review of correspondence by other medical providers regarding the individual case.

Intraservice

A comprehensive medical and ocular history is obtained. The ocular structures related to the patient's chief complaint are examined and evaluated. The examination includes an external examination, ophthalmoscopy, biomicroscopy of the related structures of the eye, and an ocular neurological assessment when indicated. A microbiological culture may be taken. The condition is assessed and a treatment plan is described to the patient, including information about medication, instructions, and follow-up visits.

Postservice

Complete medical record; transmit information to the patient's general practitioner or others as indicated and update transmittals to other providers of care.

92014 Ophthalmological services: medical examination and evaluation, with initiation or continuation of diagnostic and treatment program; comprehensive, established patient, one or more visits

Work Value: 1.10 // Global Period: XXX

➲ *CPT Assistant* **Feb 97: 6, Aug 98: 3, Dec 99: 10, Jun 05: 11, Dec 05: 10**

Clinical Example

The patient is a 64-year-old with a recent onset of decreased vision and a past history of cataracts and macular drusen.

Preservice

Include history of previous records; and review correspondence by other medical providers regarding the individual case.

Intraservice

Examine and evaluate the eye and ocular adnexa. Obtain a comprehensive medical and ocular history. Perform an external examination of the eye, ophthalmoscopy, and biomicroscopy. Perform a gross visual fields and neurological evaluation. Perform a dilated funduscopic evaluation if indicated. Initiate a treatment plan, which may include other special ophthalmological testing, consultations, and laboratory and radiological services. Prescribe medication and/or corrective lenses as indicated. Counsel the patient and provide the patient with detailed instructions about the treatment plan.

Postservice

Complete medical record and transmittal of information to the patient's general practitioner or others as indicated.

Coding Tip for 92014

There is no separate code in the CPT codebook for reporting corneal topography. When performed, corneal topography is considered an inherent part of the visit code reported for that encounter.

Special Ophthalmological Services

92020 Gonioscopy (separate procedure)

Work Value: 0.37 // Global Period: XXX

➲ *CPT Assistant* **Feb 97: 6, Aug 98: 3**

Clinical Example

A 53-year-old hyperopic female with a family history of angle closure glaucoma was previously noted to have an intraocular pressure of 22. She returns for further diagnostic evaluation by gonioscopy.

Preservice

The previous record and charts are reviewed.

Intraservice

The history of the patient's ocular hypertension is explained to the patient along with the familial incidence of angle closure glaucoma. The need to assess the status of the angle to determine whether it was open or closed is explained to the patient and the implications of that. She is also explained the nature of the procedure. At this point a drop of topical anesthetic is placed in the inferior cul-de-sac of each eye. The patient's head is placed in the slit lamp and the patient is given a fixation target to look at. The gonioscopy lens is carefully placed on the cornea. It is slowly rotated 360 degrees so that the angle can be viewed in its entirety. The lens is rotated on the patient's eye and the patient is occasionally asked to look in different directions of gaze with the lens on the eye to better facilitate the view of the angle. When the angle structures are narrow, compression is performed with the lens against the cornea to diagnostically push the iris away from the angle to see if they can be opened manually. The gonioscopy lens is then removed from the eye. The hydroxypropyl methylcellulose ophthalmic solution is irrigated from the patient's eye and the patient is given topical drops for the subsequent irritation. The patient is then explained the nature of the findings and the symptoms of angle closure.

Postservice

Arrangement is made to see the patient in follow up in six months. Because of the familial nature of the problem, telephone calls are usually fielded within the first six months on the implications of angle closure in the patient.

---

❺ **92083** Visual field examination, unilateral or bilateral, with interpretation and report; extended examination (eg, Goldmann visual fields with at least 3 isopters plotted and static determination within the central 30°, or quantitative, automated threshold perimetry, Octopus program G-1, 32 or 42, Humphrey visual field analyzer full threshold programs 30-2, 24-2, or 30/60-2)

Work Value: 0.50 // Global Period: XXX

➲ *CPT Assistant* Feb 97: 6, Aug 98: 3

Clinical Example

The patient is a 69-year-old with a 3-year history of primary open-angle glaucoma.

Preservice

The patient's name and date of birth are confirmed in the database of the automated perimeter. The refractive error is determined from the past record, refraction, or a neutralization of the current spectacles. The refractive error for perimetry is calculated.

Intraservice

The extensive test results for each eye are reviewed by the physician to assess the reliability and consistency of the responses. Multiple data points are then compared with previous visual fields to determine the extent, distribution, and pattern of the visual field loss. An interpretation and report is generated for the patient record. Prior visual fields are also reviewed and compared with the current field. Interpretation of the visual field results including reliability, normality, abnormality, change, or artifact is recorded by the physician in the chart.

Coding Tip for 92083

Gross visual field testing (eg, confrontation testing) is part of general opthalmological services and is not reported separately.

92135 Scanning computerized ophthalmic diagnostic imaging (eg, scanning laser) with interpretation and report, unilateral

Work Value: 0.35 // Global Period: XXX

➲ *CPT Assistant* Aug 98: 3, Nov 98: 33, Mar 99: 10, Apr 99: 10

Clinical Example

A 65-year-old female presents with elevated intraocular pressure. A complete eye examination is performed. Particular attention is paid to an evaluation of the optic nerves, looking for evidence of glaucomatous optic neuropathy. Visual field examination reveals no evidence of visual field loss attributable to glaucoma. Examination of the nerve fiber layer by scanning laser polarimetry is indicated to look for evidence of tissue loss consistent with glaucoma.

Preservice

The examination is performed with a scanning laser polarimeter controlled by a computer system. The computer must be booted-up and have adequate storage capacity. Occasionally the existing patient database must be backed up and prior scans that are temporarily stored on the hard disk archived to make room for the patient's data. Once the machine is prepared for the examination, the patient's data are entered into the database (or an existing folder is opened for patients that have been previously examined). The patient is examined to ensure the ability to fixate with the eye not being scanned.

Intraservice

The scanning head is aligned with the eye to be examined. The patient is instructed to follow a fixation light with the other eye to bring the optic nerve of the eye being examined into position. Focus and brightness are then properly adjusted. Three scans are obtained. Once the images have been processed by the computer and examined for quality by the physician, they are stored to the hard disk. A mean image is displayed. The operator uses the computer pointing device to mark the edge of the optic nerve so that the nerve fiber layer parameters may be determined and compared with the age-corrected normative database. The mean image is then stored to the disk. A printout is obtained. The physician evaluates the printout, looking for areas of nerve fiber layer loss, significance of differences from the normal database, and the clinical correlation with the patients other data. If the current study is a follow-up of a previous one, evaluation and change over time and correlation with the new clinical course is done.

Postservice

A report is dictated.

Ophthalmoscopy

92225 Ophthalmoscopy, extended, with retinal drawing (eg, for retinal detachment, melanoma), with interpretation and report; initial

Work Value: 0.38 // Global Period: XXX

➲ *CPT Assistant* **Feb 97: 6, Aug 98: 2, Dec 99: 10**

Clinical Example

A 61-year-old Caucasian male, who is noted to have a pigmented choroidal lesion, is referred for evaluation and documentation. The dilated examination shows a 5-mm × 6-mm pigmented choroidal mass in the right eye, which is slightly elevated.

Preservice

The referring letters are reviewed. Previous records are also reviewed at this time. The patient just had his vision checked previously and has been widely dilated.

Intraservice

The patient is placed on a flat surface. The physician places the drawing materials in an inverted position on the patients chest. Using the indirect ophthalmoscope and an indirect lens held in one hand, the lesion is viewed. The retinal vasculature is then drawn to scale. The retinal arterial and venous crossings over and in proximity to the pigmented mass are carefully sketched. Any overlying pigmenture abnormalities are documented, as are any overlying vitreous pathology. The time of the retinal drawings itself is 20 minutes. It is a monocular procedure. The patient is then placed in a sitting position and the retinal drawing is shown to the patient. The patient is counseled about the possibility of growth and the need for close follow-up care. Growth will be documented by showing extension of the pigmented mass in relation to the carefully drawn vascular landmarks.

Postservice

The patient is instructed to arrange any further diagnostic tests necessary (ie, fluorescein angiography, ultrasound). The referral letter is sent. Follow-up visits are scheduled.

---

⑤ **92226** Ophthalmoscopy, extended, with retinal drawing (eg, for retinal detachment, melanoma), with interpretation and report; subsequent

Work Value: 0.33 // Global Period: XXX

➲ *CPT Assistant* **Feb 97: 6, Aug 98: 2**

Clinical Example

A 66-year-old female had a posterior vitreous detachment evaluated 2 months ago. At that time no retinal tear was found. She returns with increased floaters in the same eye. She does not note a visual field defect.

Preservice

The physician reviews the patients chief complaint, past ocular history, and family history. The patient is informed of the need for a repeat extended retinal reexamination.

Intraservice

In a darkened room, the fundus of one eye is examined in detail. Scleral depression with topical anesthesia around the circumference of the eye is employed to detect a retinal break(s) or other retinal abnormalities. The findings are transferred with colored pencils to a fundus drawing. An interpretation is prepared.

Postservice

A report is written in the patient's medical record.

Opthalmoscopic Appearance of Retina

92225, 92226

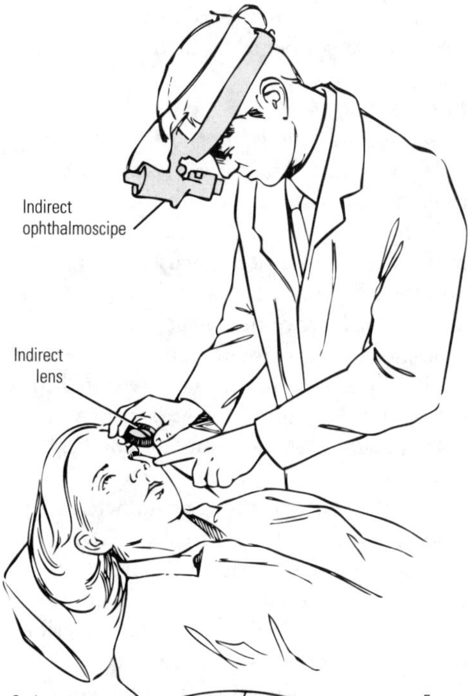

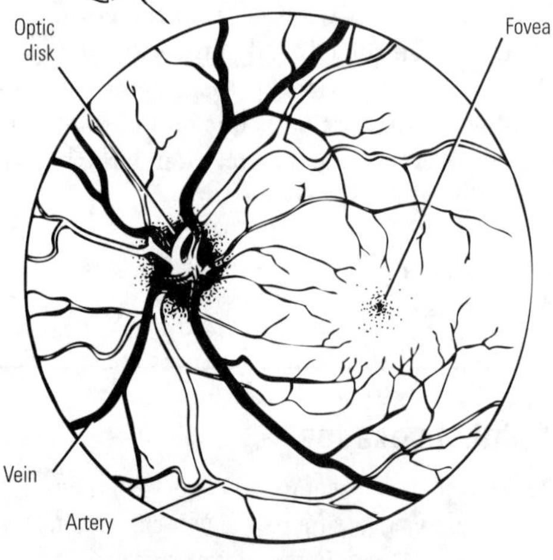

Ophthalmoscopic appearance of retina

---

❺ 92235 Fluorescein angiography (includes multiframe imaging) with interpretation and report

Work Value: 0.81 // Global Period: XXX

➲ ***CPT Assistant*** **Feb 97: 6**

Clinical Example
An 82-year-old female with age-related macular degeneration noted blurred vision and on examination was found to have a hemorrhage in the macula. Fluorescein angiography is ordered to determine the cause.

Preservice
The patient's history is reviewed. Previous and current fundus photos are evaluated. Previous retinal fluorescein angiograms are reviewed. The patient and family are informed of the value of an angiographic fundus evaluation, and the risks and benefits are explained. The nurse starts the intravenous line for administration of the intravenous dye.

Intraservice
The transit, mid-phase, and late-phase angiographic frames are studied and an interpretation is developed. Angiographic findings are compared with previous studies. A report is prepared.

Postservice
The report is dictated. The referring physician is informed of the outcome.

Fluorescein Angiography
92235
Fluorescein dye is injected in a peripheral vein to enhance imaging. Serial multiframe angiography is performed to evaluate choroidal and retinal circulation. In this illustration, arteries display an even fluorescence, while veins appear striped from the laminar dye flow.

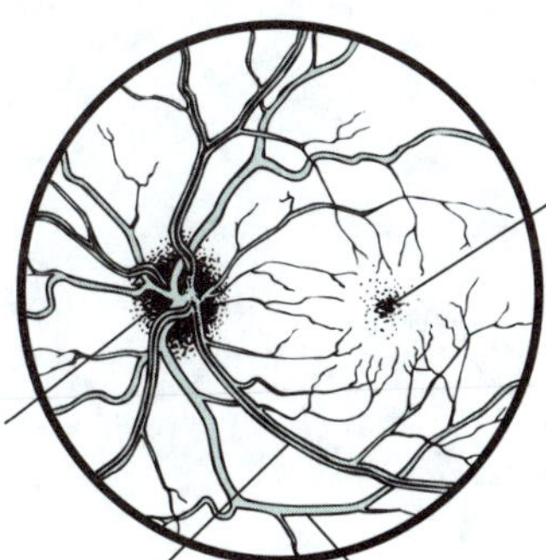

---

⑤ **92250** Fundus photography with interpretation and report

Work Value: 0.44 // Global Period: XXX

➲ *CPT Assistant* Feb 97: 6, Apr 99: 10

Clinical Example
A 35-year-old male with type I diabetes mellitus of 20 years duration with early renal failure and controlled hypertension presents with decreased vision associated with clinically significant macular edema in both eyes, disc neovascularization in the right eye, and neovascularization elsewhere in the left eye. Color fundus photographs are obtained.

Preservice
The physician reviews the patients history, any previous photographic studies, and lab tests.

Intraservice
The physician evaluates the stereoscopic fundus photographs of each fundus to determine the presence of lesions that could benefit from treatment (eg, clinically significant macular edema, presence of high risk characteristics). The physician prepares a report that details the abnormalities present.

Postservice
The report is written into the patients medical record. The referring physician is informed of the results.

Coding Tip for 92225, 92226, 92235 and 92250
Routine opthalmoscopy is part of general and special ophthalmologic services whenever indicated. It is a nonitemized service and is not reported separately.

Cardiovascular

Therapeutic Services and Procedures

⊙ 92980 Transcatheter placement of an intracoronary stent(s), percutaneous, with or without other therapeutic intervention, any method; single vessel

Work Value: 14.82 // Global Period: 000

➲ *CPT Assistant* **Aug 96: 2, Dec 96: 11, Apr 98: 9, Aug 98: 3, Aug 00: 11, Mar 01: 11, Apr 01: 10, Mar 02: 2, Aug 03: 10, Apr 05: 14**

Clinical Example

The decision is made to place a stent and this is discussed fully with the patient/family. Note: An intracoronary stent is used for treatment of acute closure of a coronary artery following another catheter intervention (balloon angioplasty, atherectomy or laser angioplasty). Stents may also be used in the management of complex coronary lesions where acute closure may be anticipated. The physician work value of this service should reflect all work involved as if the service is provided as a stand-alone procedure. If stents are placed at the time of another coronary intervention such as balloon angioplasty, the multiple procedure rule will be applied resulting in full payment for the more highly valued service and 50 percent payment for the additional service.

Preservice

The decision is made to place a stent and this is discussed fully with the patient/family.

Intraservice

The patient is prepared for the procedure, which includes sterilization of the access site and cannulation with an indwelling sheath (typically the femoral artery is used). A guide catheter is positioned in the appropriate coronary ostium and baseline arteriograms are obtained. A guidewire is passed down the target vessel across the target stenosis. The stent is loaded on a carrying catheter (which has an expandable balloon.) which is inserted into the guiding catheter and advanced using fluoroscopic guidance. The operator positions the stent in the target vessel and confirms the location by fluoroscopy and comparison to previous contrast injections. When the operator is confident the stent is in the correct location, the balloon is inflated to expand and secure the stent. The carrying catheter balloon is deflated and the catheter removed over the guidewire. Then a larger or less compliant balloon is passed over the guidewire into the stent, expanded until the stent is fully dilated, and then removed.

Postservice

After the completion of the procedure, the arterial sheath remains in place for 4 to 24 hours as Heparin and other anticoagulants used to prevent thrombosis of the newly placed stent often cause bleeding at the groin site requiring transfusion. Twenty-four hour follow-up care is included in this procedure.

Cardiography

93000 Electrocardiogram, routine ECG with at least 12 leads; with interpretation and report

Work Value: 0.17 // Global Period: XXX

➲ *CPT Assistant* Aug 97: 9, Feb 05: 9, Mar 05: 1, 11

Clinical Example

A 69-year-old male is seen in the office for evaluation of chest tightness and palpitations. A 12-lead electrocardiographic (ECG) tracing is obtained by technical personnel along with clinical and drug therapy data. The tracing is reviewed by the physician, appropriate measurements are made (including axis, intervals, and voltages), and an overall interpretation is made. The tracing is compared with previous ECG tracings when available. Potential etiologies for any electrocardiographic findings observed, such as myocardial infarction, hypokalemia, or digoxin toxicity, are proposed. A report is prepared, signed, and transmitted to the patient's medical record.

Preservice

The rationale for the ECG request is reviewed along with any pertinent patient history.

Intraservice

The tracing is reviewed by the physician, appropriate measurements are made (including axis, intervals, and voltages), and an overall interpretation is made. The tracing is compared to previous ECG tracings when available. Potential etiologies for any electrocardiographic findings observed, such as myocardial infarction, hypokalemia, or digoxin toxicity, are proposed.

Postservice

A report is prepared, signed and transmitted to the patient's medical record.

---

❺ **93010** Electrocardiogram, routine ECG with at least 12 leads; interpretation and report only

Work Value: 0.17 // Global Period: XXX

➲ *CPT Assistant* Aug 97: 9, Mar 05: 1

Clinical Example

A 55-year-old male presents to his internists office with complaints of exertional chest pain for 1 month. After a focused visit and examination, the patient is sent to the laboratory for an electrocardiogram (ECG). The ECG is performed by the technician and held for the cardiologist to interpret and complete a report of his/her findings.

Preservice

The patients medical records and chart are reviewed. Clinical questions to be answered are determined.

Intraservice

The physician obtains the ECG results directly from the technician and/or goes to the ECG reading room to acquire the 12-lead ECG information. The physician reviews and compares one or more previous ECGs with the current ECG results. The physician reviews and compares the ECG reading, adjusting for age, weight, known cardiac diagnosis, and presence or absence of electronic cardiac devices. The ECG is inspected for rhythm, which includes a diagnosis of atrial rhythm, a diagnosis of ventricular rhythm, and the summation of those two rhythms as the patients intrinsic rhythm as it relates to the ECG. Primary intervals are visually inspected and compared with computer-generated intervals and the previous ECG intervals (eg, PR, QRS duration, QT duration, and others). The physician compares and analyzes the P-wave morphology and P-wave axis, and the QRS morphology and associated axis. The physician analyzes the QRS morphology in relation to the previous infarction, recent infarction, a change in morphology in comparison to previous ECG, and criteria for hypertension and hypertrophy. The physician carefully inspects each tracing for the presence or absence of pacemaker artifacts. The physician then identifies and describes the presence or absence of atrial and/or ventricular. The physician then compares his ECG diagnosis with that obtained from the computer ECG diagnosis, and deletes and or includes the appropriate diagnosis. The physician dictates, writes, and/or confirms his interpretation with that of the computer-generated interpretation.

Postservice

The findings are discussed with the referring physician and the patient. The report is reviewed, edited as necessary, and signed. The ECG results are reviewed and stored for future reference.

Coding Tip for 93010

If ECG monitoring is performed, see codes 99354-99360.

93268 Patient demand single or multiple event recording with presymptom memory loop, 24-hour attended monitoring, per 30 day period of time; includes transmission, physician review and interpretation

Work Value: 0.52 // Global Period: XXX

➲ *CPT Assistant* Jun 96: 2, Nov 99: 49-50, Oct 05: 14; *CPT Changes: An Insider's View* 2003

Clinical Example

A 56-year-old female presents with mitral valve prolapse and multiple episodes of syncope and presyncope. Neurologic workup had been negative. The cardiac evaluation is essentially negative. Holter monitor studies have been negative for any malignant arrhythmias. Normal sinus rhythm is found with occasional premature ventricular contractions. The patient is given an event recording device. This is applied by the patient and is patient-activated when symptoms occur. At home, the patient experiences a presyncopal episode and activates the recorder. She then transmits the recording transtelephonically to a receiving center. Ventricular tachycardia is noted during the period of symptoms.

Echocardiography

93307 Echocardiography, transthoracic, real-time with image documentation (2D) with or without M-mode recording; complete

Work Value: 0.92 // Global Period: XXX

➲ *CPT Assistant* Dec 97: 5, Sep 05: 11

Clinical Example

A 75-year-old male with chest pressure and shortness of breath is admitted with cardiomegaly and pulmonary congestion on chest X ray and electrocardiogram changes of left bundle branch block.

Preservice

The physician reviews existing information (eg, request for a consult) and relevant clinical data to clarify the indications for the procedure and to determine the clinical questions that need to be answered.

Intraservice

A sequence of tomographic images from multiple views is obtained and recorded. The physician may verify the suitability of the images prior to the completion of the study and obtain additional views if necessary. Videotaped or digitally recorded views of the heart are reviewed. The structure and dynamics of the heart chambers, valves, and great vessels are analyzed and measured, and a complete interpretation is developed. Evaluations of quantitative, anatomic, and functional measures such as left-ventricular size, wall thickness, ejection fraction, regional wall motion, left-ventricular mas, and atrial and aortic root dimensions, are made. Multiple sets of tomographic views are evaluated and compared with previous studies for quantitative and qualitative changes.

Postservice

A report is dictated and the findings may be reviewed in detail with the referring physician.

Coding Tip for 93307

When the interpretation and report (professional component) are performed separately, the use of modifier 26, *Professional component,* becomes necessary.

+93320 Doppler echocardiography, pulsed wave and/or continuous wave with spectral display (List separately in addition to codes for echocardiographic imaging); complete

Work Value: 0.38 // Global Period: ZZZ

➲ *CPT Assistant* Nov 97: 44, Dec 97: 5

Clinical Example

A 65-year-old male with a history of angina and a recent syncopal spell presents with a long systolic murmur, electrocardiographic changes compatible with left ventricular hypertrophy, and a chest X ray showing mild cardiomegaly.

Preservice

The physician reviews the existing information (eg, request for a consult), including relevant clinical data to clarify the indications for the procedure and to determine the clinical questions that need to be answered by the echo exam. In conjunction with an ultrasonic imaging study (coded separately as code 93307) of the cardiac chamber(s) valves and great vessels, blood flow velocities are recorded at those sites. The physician may verify the suitability of the data prior to the completion of the study and obtain additional measurements if necessary.

Intraservice

In conjunction with an ultrasonic imaging study of the cardiac chamber(s) valves and great vessels (coded separately as code 93307), blood flow velocities are recorded at those sites. The physician may verify the suitability of the data prior to the completion of the study and obtain additional measurements if necessary. Videotaped or digitally recorded flow velocity data are reviewed and multiple functional measurements are made, including pressure gradients, stenotic valve areas, quantitation of regurgitation (eg, regurgitant volume, fraction, and effective orifice area), global left ventricular systolic performance, and diastolic function. The findings are frequently compared to previous studies to determine whether there has been improvement or deterioration in these measures.

Postservice

A report is dictated and the findings are frequently reviewed in detail with the referring physician.

Coding Tip for 93320

Code 93320 is reported in conjunction with codes 93303, 93304, 93307, 93308, 93312, 93314, 93315, 93317, and 93350.

93350 Echocardiography, transthoracic, real-time with image documentation (2D), with or without M-mode recording, during rest and cardiovascular stress test using treadmill, bicycle exercise and/or pharmacologically induced stress, with interpretation and report

Work Value: 1.48 // Global Period: XXX

➲ *CPT Assistant* Aug 02: 11

Clinical Example

A 48-year-old male with hypertension and a history of cigarette smoking describes occasional exertional chest discomfort that is thought to be possible, but not definite, angina pectoris. His resting electrocardiogram demonstrates left ventricular hypertrophy with QRS widening and secondary repolarization changes. A treadmill stress echocardiogram is requested to evaluate for inducible myocardial ischemia and to aid in risk-stratification.

The physician reviews the referral information (eg, request for the procedure) and relevant clinical data with the patient to clarify the indications for the procedure and to determine the clinical questions that need to be answered. A sequence of baseline tomographic images from apical and precordial windows is recorded on videotape and into computer memory in a cine-loop format. The physician may verify the suitability of the baseline images and consider the need for border enhancement using echocardiographic contrast material.

The patient then undergoes conventional treadmill exercise using a symptom-limited protocol. Immediately upon completion of the treadmill exercise, the patient is again imaged and a sequence of poststress tomographic images is recorded from apical and precordial windows, again using both videotape and digital recording techniques.

The interpreting physician reviews the videotaped and digitally recorded views of the heart, analyzing global and regional left ventricular function both at rest and following stress. Regional changes are evaluated carefully. Other cardiac causes of chest pain (such as valvular disease or cardiomyopathy) are also assessed. Where appropriate, geometric measures of cardiac structure and function are made. A diagnostic interpretation is developed, and a report is dictated, edited, and signed. The findings may be reviewed in detail with the requesting physician.

Intraservice

The physician reviews existing information and relevant clinical data to clarify the indications for the procedure, refines the clinical questions that need to be addressed, and determines the suitability of stress echocardiography and the most appropriate testing method. A sequence of tomographic images, recorded both at a baseline and again immediately following the completion of a treadmill exercise, is reviewed in both videotape and digital cine-loop formats. Global and regional ventricular performance is evaluated carefully. Other cardiac causes of chest pain are also assessed. Where appropriate, geometric measures of cardiac structure and function are made. A diagnostic interpretation is developed. A report is dictated, edited, and signed. The findings may be reviewed in detail with the requesting physician.

Coding Tip for 93350

The appropriate stress testing code from the 93015-93018 code series should be reported in addition to code 93350 to capture the exercise stress portion of the study.

Noninvasive Physiologic Studies and Procedures

93733 Electronic analysis of dual chamber internal pacemaker system (may include rate, pulse amplitude and duration, configuration of wave form, and/or testing of sensory function of pacemaker), telephonic analysis

Work Value: 0.17 // Global Period: XXX

➲ *CPT Assistant* Summer 94: 23

Clinical Example

An 80-year-old female with a DDD pacemaker implanted 6 years earlier for an atrioventricular block calls for routine transtelephonic assessment of the permanent pacemaker. After the patient is identified and the appropriate patient data are made available (ie, previous transmission, D type of generator, date of implant), the patient is asked to transmit a free-running (non-magnet) electrocardiogram (ECG). If the ECG is of good quality, the patient is then asked to transmit a 30-second ECG with a magnet placed over the pacemaker. At times it is difficult for the patient to remember the necessary sequence and has to repeat the magnet sequence to obtain an ECG that is interpretable. Strips are then analyzed and the information is recorded.

Preservice

Preservice work includes identifying the patient and retrieving the patient's prior record for comparison. Often with elderly patients it is also necessary to help with the transmission with coaching over the phone.

Intraservice

Intraservice work includes receiving the magnet, non-magnet, and ECG strips; analyzing the information for normalcy; gathering all pressure transtelephonic monitoring data (ie, rate, pulse width); and comparing the data to expected indicators.

Postservice
Postservice work includes preparing the report for the patient and/or the referring physician and storing the data.

Noninvasive Vascular Diagnostic Studies

Extremity Arterial Studies (Including Digits)

93922 Noninvasive physiologic studies of upper or lower extremity arteries, single level, bilateral (eg, ankle/brachial indices, Doppler waveform analysis, volume plethysmography, transcutaneous oxygen tension measurement)

Work Value: 0.25 // Global Period: XXX

➲ ***CPT Assistant*** **Jun 96: 9, Dec 05: 3**

Clinical Example
A 65-year-old male, status post left femoral angioplasty, complains of increasing recurrent claudication. There is diminished posterior tibial pulse. Ankle/brachial indices are obtained to compare with the immediate postprocedure ankle/brachial indices.

93923 Noninvasive physiologic studies of upper or lower extremity arteries, multiple levels or with provocative functional maneuvers, complete bilateral study (eg, segmental blood pressure measurements, segmental Doppler waveform analysis, segmental volume plethysmography, segmental transcutaneous oxygen tension measurements, measurements with postural provocative tests, measurements with reactive hyperemia)

Work Value: 0.45 // Global Period: XXX

➲ ***CPT Assistant*** **Jun 96: 9, Jun 01: 10, Dec 05: 3**

Clinical Example
A 30-year-old female complains of cold, painful fingers, especially during winter months. Her fingers are pale with slow capillary refill. Upper extremity arterial Doppler studies and segmental volume plethysmography with cold stimulation is performed.

Coding Tip for 93923
The language in the descriptor for code 93923 states, "Noninvasive physiologic studies of upper or lower extremity arteries," indicating that if both the upper and the lower extremity arteries are studied in this fashion, code 93923 should be reported twice: once for the upper extremities and once for the lower extremities.

Pulmonary

Other Procedures

⑤ **94010** Spirometry, including graphic record, total and timed vital capacity, expiratory flow rate measurement(s), with or without maximal voluntary ventilation

Work Value: 0.17 // Global Period: XXX

➲ ***CPT Assistant*** **Summer 91: 16, Summer 95: 4, Feb 96: 9, Nov 97: 45, Nov 98: 35, Feb 99: 9, Aug 03: 15, Jul 05: 11**

Clinical Example
A 45-year-old female complains of shortness of breath and occasional wheezing. Spirometry is performed.

Preservice
Spirometry is performed in a separate room from an E/M service. Data are input into the computer to identify the patient. The technologist calibrates the equipment and prepares the supplies, greets the patient, verifies that inhaled medications have been withheld, obtains vital signs, positions the patient, and provides instructions to the patient on how to perform the spirometry test. The test is repeated a minimum of three times, and up to eight times, to achieve at least two acceptable and repeatable sets of values (in accordance with the ATS/ERS Consensus Statement).

Intraservice
The physician evaluates the data to ensure accuracy. The physician reviews

the mid-maximal flow rates, examines the flow-time curves, and compares the results with the results of the previous studies available for significant interval change according to the ATS/ERS Consensus Statement. The physician interprets the results and writes a report.

Postservice
The physician documents the results in the patient's medical record. The physician discusses the results with the patient and the patient's family and communicates the results to the referring physician.

Coding Tip for 94010
Maximal voluntary ventilation is included when code 94010 is reported.

94060 Bronchodilation responsiveness, spirometry as in 94010, pre- and post-bronchodilator administration

Work Value: 0.31 // Global Period: XXX

➲ *CPT Assistant* Summer 95: 4, Feb 96: 9, Feb 97: 10, Nov 98: 34, Jan 99: 8, Feb 99: 9, Jul 05: 11; *CPT Changes: An Insider's View* 2005

Clinical Example
1) A 60-year-old man with a history of chronic obstructive pulmonary disease (COPD) with chronic cough and shortness of breath is being evaluated as a new patient.

2) A 30-year-old woman with a history of intermittent wheezing is being evaluated because symptoms of shortness of breath.

Preservice
1) Explanation of procedure to patient and sometimes other family members.

2) Explanation of the indications for doing the procedure.

3) Explanation of potential complications.

Intraservice
Work includes performing and monitoring the procedure.

Postservice
1) Review and interpret result of procedure.

2) Explain implication of results to patient and sometimes other family members.

3) Discuss follow-up treatment options with patient and sometimes other family members.

4) Observation for the side effects from the bronchodilator.

Coding Tip for 94060
The supply of the bronchodilator may be separately reported with code 99070 and the appropriate Healthcare Common Procedure Coding System (HCPCS) supply code for the bronchodilator used.

94240 Functional residual capacity or residual volume: helium method, nitrogen open circuit method, or other method

Work Value: 0.26 // Global Period: XXX

➲ *CPT Assistant* Summer 95: 4, Feb 96: 9, Jul 05: 11

Clinical Example
1) A 60-year-old male with a history of chronic obstructive pulmonary disease with chronic cough and shortness of breath is being evaluated as a new patient.

2) A 30-year-old female with a history of intermittent wheezing is being evaluated because of symptoms of shortness of breath.

Preservice
Preservice work includes explaining the procedure to the patient and patient's family, explaining the indications for doing the procedure, and explaining the potential complications.

Intraservice
Intraservice work includes performing and monitoring the procedure.

Postservice
Postservice work includes reviewing and interpreting the results of the procedure; explaining the implication of the results to the patient and the patient's family; and discussing follow-up options with the patient and the patient's family.

94360 Determination of resistance to airflow, oscillatory or plethysmographic methods

Work Value: 0.26 // Global Period: XXX

➲ *CPT Assistant* Summer 95: 4, Feb 96: 9, Jul 05: 11

Clinical Example

1) A 60-year-old male with a history of chronic obstructive pulmonary disease with chronic cough and shortness of breath is being evaluated as a new patient.

2) A 30-year-old female with a history of intermittent wheezing is being evaluated because of symptoms of shortness of breath.

Preservice

Preservice work includes explaining the procedure to the patient and patient's family, explaining the indications for doing the procedure, and explaining the potential complications.

Intraservice

Intraservice work includes performing and monitoring of the procedure.

Postservice

Postservice work includes reviewing and interpreting the results of the procedure; explaining the implication of the results to the patient and the patient's family; and discussing follow-up options with the patient and the patient's family.

94620 Pulmonary stress testing; simple (eg, 6-minute walk test, prolonged exercise test for bronchospasm with pre- and post-spirometry and oximetry)

Work Value: 0.64 // Global Period: XXX

➲ *CPT Assistant* Summer 95: 4, Feb 96: 9, Nov 98: 35, Jan 99: 8, Mar 04: 10, Jul 05: 11, 13; *CPT Changes: An Insider's View* 2007

Clinical Example

1) A 65-year-old female is seen because of dyspnea and cough after walking several city blocks. She has a normal physical examination and her spirogram is normal.

2) A 65-year-old female with documented chronic obstructive pulmonary disease is evaluated for entrance into a pulmonary rehabilitation program.

Preservice

A simple exercise test is performed with baseline spirogram. The physician performs a brief history and physical to determine if patient is fit to do test. Time is taken to answer questions about the test. A simple exercise test is performed with a baseline spirogram.The patient walks on a treadmill until dyspnea occurs and a repeat spirogram is obtained to evaluate for exercise induced bronchospasm. Or, a six minute walk is performed to evaluate distance, dyspnea, oxyhemoglobin desaturation and heart rate. The test is usually repeated after a rest period to eliminate learning bias.

Intraservice

The physician analyzes the data and prepares a written interpretation of the test results.

Postservice

The physician discusses the findings with the patient and devises plans for therapy and further testing, then communicates the results with the referring physician.

Coding Tip for 94620

In CPT 2007, code 94620 was editorially revised to include a 6-minute walking test and oximetry in the code descriptor. The 6-minute walking test is the most common test performed in pulmonary stress testing.

94720 Carbon monoxide diffusing capacity (eg, single breath, steady state)

Work Value: 0.26 // Global Period: XXX

➲ *CPT Assistant* Summer 95: 4, Feb 96: 9, Jul 05: 11; *CPT Changes: An Insider's View* 2002

Clinical Example

1) A 60-year-old male with a history of chronic obstructive pulmonary disease with chronic cough and shortness of breath is being evaluated as a new patient.

2) A 30-year-old female with a history of intermittent wheezing is being evaluated because of symptoms of shortness of breath.

Preservice
Preservice work includes explaining the procedure to the patient and patient's family, explaining the indications for doing the procedure, and explaining the potential complications.

Intraservice
Intraservice work includes performing and monitoring the procedure.

Postservice
Postservice work includes reviewing and interpreting the results of the procedure; explaining the implication of the results to the patient and the patient's family; and discussing follow-up treatment options with the patient and the patient's family.

Allergy and Clinical Immunology

Allergy Testing

95010 Percutaneous tests (scratch, puncture, prick) sequential and incremental, with drugs, biologicals or venoms, immediate type reaction, specify number of tests

Work Value: 0.15 // Global Period: XXX

➲ *CPT Assistant* Summer 91: 15

Clinical Example
A 65-year-old male inpatient with a history of skin rash, possibly urticarial, after taking penicillin and worsening of asthma after being given cefuroxime, developed subacute bacterial endocarditis. Patient is seen by infectious disease consultant who recommends penicillin as the most suitable drug. The physician is asked to evaluate the patient for penicillin allergy.

Preservice
Determine which antibiotic is to be tested. Determine the risk factors for safe testing (eg, cardiac disease, beta blocker presence). Order the appropriate test materials, including the appropriate dilutions of drugs. Obtain informed consent from the patient and explain all risks, including anaphylaxis and the treatment for anaphylaxis. Prepare materials for the treatment of anaphylaxis.

Intraservice
Apply prick/puncture type tests (usually three) sequentially every 20 minutes. Observe the patient for the development of a positive skin test and possible anaphylaxis. If the test is positive, prepare a schedule for oral desensitization. If the test is negative, write orders for the administration of penicillin. The physician should be present in room for the entire intraservice period to observe for the presence of anaphylaxis.

Postservice
Write or dictate a procedural report.

Allergen Immunotherapy

❺ **95144** Professional services for the supervision of preparation and provision of antigens for allergen immunotherapy, single dose vial(s) (specify number of vials)

Work Value: 0.06 // Global Period: XXX

➲ *CPT Assistant* Fall 91: 19, Spring 94: 30, Summer 95: 4, May 96: 11, Nov 98: 35, Feb 05: 10-11; *CPT Changes: An Insider's View* 2002

Clinical Example
A 12-year-old male is seen on referral by his primary care physician for symptoms of progressively more severe rhinorrhea, sneezing, wheezing, and coughing. Allergy tests showed positive reactions to cat and dog danders, six different genera of mold spores, and dust mites. A decision is made to start allergen immunotherapy. The physician orders the preparation of immunotherapy, identifying the specific amount of each antigen; establishes the dosage schedule; and supervises the preparation of the vials. Because the patient will be receiving his immunotherapy injections at an outside

clinic, single-dose vials are ordered to ensure accuracy of dosing.

Intraservice

The physician determines which antigens are to be used for immunotherapy and at what concentrations. The physician determines the dosage schedule. The physician provides direct supervision for sterile preparation of vials and needed quality control of the product through testing or other means.

Coding Tip for 95144

A single-dose vial contains a single dose of antigen administered in one injection.

Neurology and Neuromuscular Procedures

Sleep Testing

95810 Polysomnography; sleep staging with 4 or more additional parameters of sleep, attended by a technologist

Work Value: 3.52 // Global Period: XXX

➲ ***CPT Assistant*** **Feb 98: 6, Nov 98: 35, Sep 02: 2-3**

Clinical Example

An elderly male presents with complaints of heavy snoring and daytime sleepiness. He undergoes polysomnography. Recording occurs for 7–8 hours of 1–4 channel electroencephalogram, electro-oculography, and submental electromyography for sleep staging, and electrocardiogram, airflow, respiratory effort, oximetry, and extremity muscle activity while attended by a technologist, to determine the severity and confirm the diagnosis of obstructive sleep apnea syndrome, and to look for other sleep disorders that may be contributing to the daytime sleepiness.

95811 Polysomnography; sleep staging with 4 or more additional parameters of sleep, with initiation of continuous positive airway pressure therapy or bilevel ventilation, attended by a technologist

Work Value: 3.79 // Global Period: XXX

➲ ***CPT Assistant*** **Nov 97: 46, Feb 98: 6, Nov 98: 35, Sep 02: 2-3**

Clinical Example

An elderly male with severe obstructive sleep apnea confirmed on previous testing undergoes polysomnography, with recording of 6 or more hours of 4-channel electroencephalogram, electro-olfactogram, and submental electromyography for sleep staging, and electrocardiogram, airflow, respiratory effort, and oximetry, while attended by a technologist who initiates positive airway pressure treatment and titrates the inspiratory and expiratory pressures upwards using continuous or bilevel positive airway pressure (BiPAP) to control the abnormal respiratory events during sleep.

Preservice

Review the pretest consultation and data. Provide instruction to the night technician who will be hooking up the patient to the equipment, including starting pressures, the sequence of pressures tested, and the use of BiPAP. Provide instruction on the use of drugs, including oxygen, by the patient during the day prior to the test and during the night of the test.

Intraservice

Review the sleep technicians notes. Open the sleep record (hard copy or computer file). Analyze the recording and identify and analyze abnormal events. Compile abnormal events separately for each CPAP pressure used.

Postservice

Prepare the report and communicate the results to the patient and referring physician.

Routine Electroencephalography (EEG)

⑤ 95816 Electroencephalogram (EEG); including recording awake and drowsy

Work Value: 1.08 // Global Period: XXX

➲ *CPT Assistant* Sep 96: 11, Nov 98: 35, Nov 99: 51, Jul 00: 1; *CPT Changes: An Insider's View* 2000, 2003

Clinical Example

A 75-year-old female has developed memory complaints and word finding difficulty, which fluctuates markedly from day to day. Examination is notable for occasional paraphasic errors and poor short-term memory recall. Head computed tomography scan is normal. An EEG is ordered.

Preservice

Determine which type of EEG study is the most appropriate for the patient based on the referral question being asked.

Intraservice

Supervise patient preparation and performance of the test by the technician. Review the recorded data, assess the normal and abnormal findings, review the activation procedures performed including hyperventilation and photic stimulation, interpret the data, and provide clinical correlation of the findings based on the patient's history.

Postservice

Generate the report and make recommendations for further management.

---

⑤ 95819 Electroencephalogram (EEG); including recording awake and asleep

Work Value: 1.08 // Global Period: XXX

➲ *CPT Assistant* Nov 98: 35, Nov 99: 51, Jul 00: 1; *CPT Changes: An Insider's View* 2000, 2003

Clinical Example

A 40-year-old male has complaints of recurrent episodes of a strange epigastric rising feeling followed by a strange taste in his mouth and then a sense of unreality where he is not fully able to interact with others around him. The episode lasts 1 minute and leaves him feeling tired afterward. An EEG is ordered.

Preservice

Determine which type of EEG study is most appropriate for the patient based on the referral question being asked.

Intraservice

Supervise patient preparation and performance of the test by the technician. Review the recorded data, assess the normal and abnormal findings, review the activation procedures performed including hyperventilation and photic stimulation, interpret the data, and provide clinical correlation of the findings based on the patient's history.

Postservice

Generate the report and make recommendations for further management.

Electromyography and Nerve Conduction Tests

⑤ 95861 Needle electromyography; two extremities with or without related paraspinal areas

Work Value: 1.54 // Global Period: XXX

➲ *CPT Assistant* Nov 97: 46, Jul 00: 2, Apr 02: 2, May 03: 20, Jun 03: 3, Feb 04: 4, Jul 04: 6, Oct 04: 15, Jun 05: 9; *CPT Changes: An Insider's View* 2003

Clinical Example

A 75-year-old female with a 5-month history of marked pain and proximal left lower limb weakness now presents with 3 weeks of severe pain and weakness in the proximal right lower limb. Physical examination shows a cachectic elderly female with disproportionate wasting of the left thigh muscles. Needle electromyography of two limbs is indicated.

Preservice

The physician reviews the medical records, takes a brief history, and performs a brief examination to establish the questions to be addressed as part of the electromyography. The physician considers the potential anatomic lesions that could cause the clinical manifestations and considers the questions being posed by the referring physician. The appropriate muscles to be studied and then determined.

Intraservice

The physician participates in patient preparation, focusing on discussing the test with the patient and answering questions regarding the pain associated with the procedure. The physician places the ground surface electrode, cleans the skin overlying anticipated muscle puncture sites, and dons gloves prior to the examination. Prior to inserting the needle electrode in to each muscle to be examined, the electromyographer must perform a focused physical examination to determine surface anatomic landmarks and identify structures to avoid during the needle insertion. Under minimal voluntary contraction of the muscle, several voluntary motor unit potentials are analyzed along multiple passes through the muscle, noting duration, amplitude, configuration, and other diagnostic variables both visually and by sound that allow the waveform to be classified as normal or abnormal. The patient is examined after the needle is withdrawn from each puncture site to assure hemostasis and to apply any needed manual pressure or bandage where minor bleeding may be observed.

Postservice

The physician grades the insertional, spontaneous, and voluntary motor unit potential activity from each muscle examined; summarizes the clinical and electrodiagnostic data; and interprets the findings.

⊘❻ 95900 Nerve conduction, amplitude and latency/velocity study, each nerve; motor, without F-wave study

Work Value: 0.42 // Global Period: XXX

➲ ***CPT Assistant*** **Jan 96: 2, Nov 99: 51-52, Jan 00: 10, Jul 00: 3, Apr 02: 2, Apr 03: 4, May 03: 20, Jul 04: 13, Mar 05: 17, Dec 05: 9;** ***CPT Changes: An Insider's View*** **2000**

Clinical Example

A 55-year-old female presents to the clinic with weakness of the right quadriceps muscle and pain over the right hip. These symptoms began following a motor vehicle accident where she was pinned by the steering wheel for several minutes. A traumatic femoral neuropathy is suspected. A motor nerve conduction study without f-wave of the right femoral nerve is indicated.

Preservice

The physician reviews the medical records, takes a brief history and performs a brief examination to establish the questions to be addressed as part of the nerve conduction study, Specifically the physician considers available recording and stimulating sites for the nerve, and determining the appropriate sites based on the possible sites of nerve injury. The appropriate muscles to be studied are then determined.

Intraservice

Intraservice work includes physician performance or supervision of patient preparation, placement of ground, stimulating and recording surface electrodes, stimulation of nerves and recording of the waveform of the resulting compound muscle action potentials. The waveform is analyzed with respect to latency, amplitude and configuration. Interelectrode distances are measured and recorded. Test design changes during the course of the study in response to the information obtained.

Postservice

Postservice work involves calculation of nerve conduction velocities, comparison to normal values, summarization of clinical and electrodiagnostic data, physician interpretation, generation of a differential diagnosis and sometimes suggestions for further work-up.

Coding Tip for 95900

Code 95900 is reported only once when multiple sites on the same nerve are stimulated or recorded.

⊘ **95903** Nerve conduction, amplitude and latency/velocity study, each nerve; motor, with F-wave study

Work Value: 0.60 // Global Period: XXX

➲ *CPT Assistant* **Jan 96: 2, Nov 99: 51-52, Jan 00: 10, Jul 00: 3, 12, Apr 02: 2, Apr 03: 4, May 03: 20, Mar 05: 17, Dec 05: 9**

Clinical Example

A 50-year-old female complains of weakness and numbness of her arms and legs for 3 months. Physical examination shows weakness of distal upper and lower limb muscles, areflexia, and stocking-glove sensory loss. Differential diagnostic considerations included axonal or demyelinating polyneuropathies. Electrophysiologic findings included normal sensory potentials, only slightly prolonged motor condution velocities, and markedly prolonged F-wave latencies recorded from both the hand and foot muscles. The F-wave testing results indicate that she has a generalized primarily proximal demyelinating radiculoneuropathy. After a course of prednisone fails, she receives intermittent infusions of human immune globulin, which result in marked clinical improvement. Most primarily demyelinating neuropathies are diagnosable only by electrodiagnostic techniques, not blood or imaging tests. Omission of F-wave testing will greatly decrease the sensitivity of the motor nerve conduction studies in detecting neuropathies and will decrease the ability of these tests to differentiate between primarily axonal and demyelinating neuropathies which have different etiologies and treatments.

Preservice

Preservice work involves the examiner determing which nerves are to be studied based on the referring physician's questions and the available clinical information.

Intraservice

The physician performs or supervises patient preparation; the placement of ground, stimulating, and recording surface electrodes; the stimulation of nerves; and the recording of the waveform of the resulting compound muscle action potentials. The waveform is analyzed with respect to latency, amplitude, and configuration. Interelectrode distances are measured and recorded. F-wave studies involve changing the electromyograph's gain, time base, and filter settings (sometimes); reorienting the stimulating electrode (sometimes); and stimulating motor nerves enough times to generate more than 10 F-waves, which are recorded and analyzed. Test design changes are made during the course of the study in response to the information obtained.

Postservice

Postservice work involves calculation of nerve conduction velocities, sometimes calculation of certain F-wave indices that are more sensitive than raw F-wave latencies, comparison to normal values, summarization of clinical and electrodiagnostic data, physician interpretation, generation of a differential diagnosis and sometimes suggestions for further work-up.

⊘ ❺ **95904** Nerve conduction, amplitude and latency/velocity study, each nerve; sensory

Work Value: 0.34 // Global Period: XXX

➲ *CPT Assistant* **Jan 96: 2, Sep 99: 11, Nov 99: 51-52, Jul 00: 12, Apr 02: 2, Apr 03: 4, May 03: 20, Mar 05: 17, Dec 05: 9; *CPT Changes: An Insider's View* 2002**

Clinical Example

A 45-year-old female with no significant past medical history presents with 3 months of tingling asleep numbness in both lower limbs distally and in the left more than right hand. Physical examination shows normal strength, loss of pin prick, and vibration over the feet, lower legs, and fingers bilaterally, as well as absent ankle reflexes. Differential diagnostic considerations include sensorimotor peripheral neuropathy, sensory peripheral neuropathy, sensory neuronopathy, and central nervous system disorders. Nerve conduction studies show normal distal lower and upper limb motor nerve conduction values. Sensory nerve conduction studies are indicated.

Preservice

The physician reviews the medical records, takes a brief history, and performs a brief examination to establish the questions to be addressed as part of the nerve conduction study. The physician considers available recording and stimulating sites for the nerve and determines the appropriate sites based on the possible sites of nerve injury. The appropriate muscles to be studied are then determined.

Intraservice

The physician performs or supervises patient preparation, focusing on discussing the test with the patient and answering questions regarding the pain associated with the procedure. After identifying anatomic landmarks, the physician (and/or the technologist) cleans the skin overlying the anticipated nerve stimulation and recording sites and places the recording electrodes and ground surface electrodes. Electrical stimuli are delivered via the surface stimulating electrode prongs; this includes searching for the optimal site by the obtained response, rotating the prongs to secure the proper shape of waveform on the electromyography machine screen, and constantly communicating with the patient in an effort to reduce muscle artifact. Reporting procedures are explained to the patient.

Postservice

The waveforms from each sensory nerve tested are assessed. Clinical and electrodiagnostic data are summarized. The physician interprets the data, generates a differential diagnosis, and provides suggestions for further investigations, as necessary.

Evoked Potentials and Reflex Tests

⑤ 95925 Short-latency somatosensory evoked potential study, stimulation of any/all peripheral nerves or skin sites, recording from the central nervous system; in upper limbs

Work Value: 0.54 // Global Period: XXX

➲ *CPT Assistant* Nov 98: 35-36, Apr 02: 2

Clinical Example

A 35-year-old female complains of numbness in the right arm. Physical examination, MRI of the brain, needle EMG and nerve conduction studies are normal. Median somatosensory evoked potentials are indicated.

Preservice

The physician reviews the medical records, takes a brief history and performs a brief examination to establish the questions to be addressed as part of the somatosensory evoked potential (SEP) Specifically the physician considers the potential anatomic lesions that could cause the clinical manifestations and considers the questions being posed by the referring physician. The appropriate muscles to be studied are then determined.

Intraservice

Intraservice work includes physician supervision of patient preparation, placement of ground, stimulating and recording surface electrodes, stimulation of nerves and/or dermatomes and recording the resulting evoked potentials at several sites from periphery to cerebral cortex. Multiple trials are averaged since the signals are very small. Test design changes during the course of the study in response to the information obtained.

Postservice

Postservice work involves determination of the latency and amplitude of the evoked potentials, comparison to normal values, summarization of clinical and electrodiagnostic data, physician interpretation, generation of a differential diagnosis and suggestions for further work-up.

⑤ 95926 Short-latency somatosensory evoked potential study, stimulation of any/all peripheral nerves or skin sites, recording from the central nervous system; in lower limbs

Work Value: 0.54 // Global Period: XXX

➲ *CPT Assistant* May 01: 11, Apr 02: 2

Clinical Example

Over the last two months, a 45-year-old male has noted progressive difficulty in gait, urinary urgency and numbness in his feet. Physical examination is remarkable for diffuse mild (4/5) weakness in the lower limbs (right side worse), hyperactive knee and ankle muscle stretch reflexes with a right Babinski sign and equivocal loss of vibration sense in the feet. The referral diagnoses include cervical spondylosis, motor neuron disease or intracranial pathology (eg, hydrocephalus or stroke). Bilateral tibial nerve somatosensory evoked potentials are indicated.

Preservice

The physician reviews the medical records, takes a brief history and performs a brief examination to establish the questions to be addressed as part of the SEP. Specifically the physician considers the potential anatomic lesions that could cause the clinical manifestations and considers the questions being posed by the referring physician. The appropriate muscles to be studied are then determined.

Intraservice

Intraservice work includes physician supervision of patient preparation; placement of ground, stimulating and recording surface electrodes; stimulation of nerves and/or dermatomes, and recording the resulting evoked potentials at several sites from periphery to cerebral cortex. Multiple trials are averaged since the signals are very small. Test design changes during the course of the study in response to the information obtained.

Postservice

Postservice work involves determination of the latency and amplitude of the evoked potentials, comparison to normal values, summarization of clinical and electrodiagnostic data, physician interpretation, generation of a differential diagnosis and suggestions for further work-up.

95937 Neuromuscular junction testing (repetitive stimulation, paired stimuli), each nerve, any one method

Work Value: 0.65 // Global Period: XXX

➲ *CPT Assistant* **Nov 98: 35-36, Apr 02: 2**

Clinical Example

A 25-year-old female has noted intermittent ptosis of the eyelids and double vision for 3 months. Physical examination is normal except she develops ptosis of the eyelids after 60 seconds of sustained upgaze. A primary diagnostic consideration is myasthenia gravis. Acetylcholine receptor antibody titers and a Tensilon test are normal. Repetitive nerve stimulation studies of a hand and shoulder muscle are normal. Repetitive nerve stimulation studies of the inferior orbicularis oculi and nasalis muscles innervated by the facial nerve are abnormal, showing a decrement-increment pattern on 2 Hz and 3 Hz stimulation. The abnormal facial repetitive nerve stimulation studies demonstrate abnormal neuromuscular transmission and support the clinical diagnosis of myasthenia gravis.

Preservice

The examiner determines which nerve-muscle pairs are to be studied based on the referring physicians questions and the available clinical information.

Intraservice

The physician performs or supervises patient preparation; setting the electromyographys gain, time-base, and filter settings; the placement of ground, stimulating, and recording surface electrodes; the stimulation of nerves; and recording the waveforms of the resulting compound muscle action potentials. If possible, the body part receiving the stimulation is immobilized to minimize motion artifacts that often interfere with reliable data collection. This is much more easily done if a distal limb nerve is stimulated. The compound muscle action potential waveforms are analyzed with respect to amplitude, configuration, and, sometimes, area, following one or more trains of repetitive nerve stimulation.

Different numbers and rates of stimuli are delivered depending on the clinical situation. The test design changes during the course of the study in response to the information obtained.

Postservice

The compound muscle action potential amplitude and configuration change is calculated during the course of the trains of repetitive nerve stimulation. (Sometimes the compound muscle action potential area change is calculated during the course of the trains of repetitive nerve stimulation.) The data are compared with normal values. Clinical and electrodiagnostic data are summarized. The physician interprets the data, generates a differential diagnosis, and makes suggestions for further work-up, as necessary.

Special EEG Tests

95951 Monitoring for localization of cerebral seizure focus by cable or radio, 16 or more channel telemetry, combined electroencephalographic (EEG) and video recording and interpretation (eg, for presurgical localization), each 24 hours

Work Value: 0.00 // Global Period: XXX

➲ *CPT Assistant* **Nov 98: 35, Mar 03: 21, Dec 04: 18**

Clinical Example

A 25-year-old female has a 15-year history of partial and grand mal seizures, which are still poorly controlled despite all medication regimens tried. Her seizures, occurring two to three times per week, have made her unable to work. The results of her magnetic resonance imaging scan are normal. She is referred for long-term video-EEG monitoring. The patient is monitored for 4 days, during which time eight partial complex seizures were recorded. After cortical resection at the seizure focus, identified by the video-EEG monitoring, the patient is seizure-free and eventually stops all medication and returns to work.

Preservice

The risks of withdrawing medication, grand mal status, restrictions on behavior, the procedure itself, outcomes, and why the procedure has been recommended are explained to the patient. In addition, technicians are instructed as to the specific monitoring techniques that should be used for the patient.

Intraservice

During and after each seizure during a 24-hour period (typically several), the nursing notes are reviewed and the video and EEG recordings from before are reviewed and interpreted. For each 24-hour period, a note is written of the behavioral and EEG findings for seizures that day.

Postservice

For each admission (typically several days to 1 week), a summary of the video behavior and EEG information recorded with the seizures is dictated. The separate types of seizures found are analyzed, compared, and contrasted. The patients suitability for surgery, which part of the brain to resect, and what risks are involved are determined. Findings are reviewed with the surgeon and the test results are discussed with the referring physician, the patient, and/or the patients family.

EEG Monitoring
95951

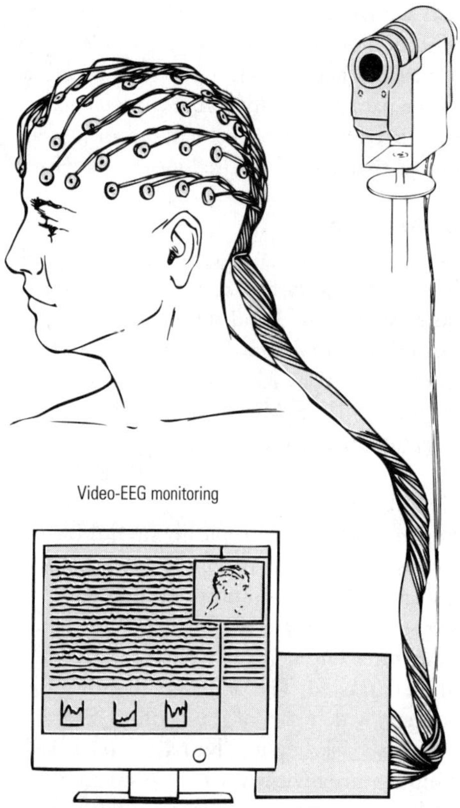

Video-EEG monitoring

Coding Tip for 95951

Video-EEG monitoring is used for prolonged monitoring of seizures. Usually, the coded procedure lasts 24 hours. Sometimes the monitoring is shorter, such as when the patient is off monitoring to undergo magnetic resonance imaging. When monitoring is less than 15 hours but more than 8 hours, append modifier 52, *Reduced services.*

Other Procedures

95990 Refilling and maintenance of implantable pump or reservoir for drug delivery, spinal (intrathecal, epidural) or brain (intraventricular);

Work Value: 0.00 // Global Period: XXX

➲ *CPT Assistant* Nov 02: 4, Nov 05: 1; *CPT Changes: An Insider's View* 2003

Clinical Example

A 45-year-old female presents with severe cancer-related pain. She has failed to obtain adequate pain relief without intolerable side effects from multiple trials of systemic medications, both narcotic and non-narcotic, as well as various blocks and injections. It is judged that the pain would not be improved by any further surgical resection, radiation therapy, and/or chemotherapy. A trial of an intrathecal infusion of morphine gave 80% pain relief at low-dose rates. A permanent, implanted, subcutaneous programmable infusion pump was placed as well as an implanted, intrathecal, infusion catheter for a long-term intrathecal infusion of narcotic.

Preservice

The solution to be injected into the pump/reservoir is ordered by the physician from the appropriate pharmacy. The order must specify the name of the drug, the volume of the solution, the concentration of the solution, and the nature of the drug (preservative-free).

Intraservice

The center of the implanted subcutaneous continuous infusion pump or reservoir is palpated and identified. This center point is marked on the skin. The entire area over the pump or reservoir is then carefully prepped with iodine or alcohol. Throughout this procedure, sterile technique is meticulous to prevent infection in the infusion solution, which would cause life-threatening meningitis. A special pump refill kit is then opened and an extra 20-cc syringe, 20-gauge needle, and 4 × 4 sponge are added to the kit. Sterile gloves are donned and a sterile drape with an open center area is taken from the refill kit and placed over the pump, being sure that all skin in the exposed center area has been prepped with iodine or alcohol. Using sterile technique, the previously prepared drug to be injected into the pump or reservoir is then drawn from its transport or commercially-prepared vial into one of the 20-gauge needles. The solutions container is checked to be sure that the drug, the drug volume, and the drugs concentration are all correct according to what was ordered.

The 22G Huber needle in the refill kit is then attached to the overpressurization T-tubing in the kit and the tubings stopcock closed. The Huber needle is carefully, under sterile conditions, punctured through the skin over the center of the pump or reservoir. The needle is advanced and probed to find the actual center of the pump or reservoir, and then the needle is advanced through the injection septum of the pump or reservoir to the proper depth. Once the needle has been positioned in the pump/reservoir, an empty 20-cc (or other appropriate volume) syringe is attached to the needles tubing, stopcock opened, and the pump/reservoir emptied of its contents. The volume of the solution removed from the pump/reservoir is measured and checked against the medical records and/or pump status printout to be sure that the entire volume of the pump/reservoir has been removed. Failure to remove all of the fluid can result in overfilling the pump/reservoir with the new solution and damaging the pump/reservoir or even causing a pump/reservoir malfunction, which would cause a potentially life-threatening intrathecal overdose of narcotic or baclofen. The stopcock is closed and the syringe is removed. The syringe containing the new solution is attached to the tubing and the stopcock is re-opened. The solution is then slowly injected into the pump/reservoir over several minutes. It is double-checked that the correct volume has been injected into the pump/reservoir and then any possible overpressurization of the pump/reservoir is checked by turning the stopcock to allow the pump solution to flow into the tubings T-piece. (This step of checking to avoid injecting too much solution and checking for overpressurization are critical to prevent overfilling the pump, which again could cause pump malfunction and/or sudden intrathecal overdosage of the drug that could be life-threatening.)

Postservice

Once the T-tubing overpressurization check has been completed, the needle and tubing assembly are withdrawn from the pump and the skin. A sterile sponge is used to dry the skin and seal the puncture area. Sterile dressing is placed over the puncture spot. Excess iodine or alcohol is wiped from the surrounding skin. The contaminated needles, tubing, syringes, sponge, and gloves are properly disposed.

Coding Tip for 95990

Refer to the parenthetic notes that identify the appropriate codes to use to identify analysis and/or reprogramming of implantable infusion pumps (codes 62367 and 62368), as well as the code for refilling and maintaining implanted infusion pumps or reservoirs for systemic drug therapy (code 96530).

Central Nervous System Assessments/Tests (eg, Neuro-Cognitive, Mental Status, Speech Testing)

96101 Psychological testing (includes psychodiagnostic assessment of emotionality, intellectual abilities, personality and psychopathology, eg, MMPI, Rorschach, WAIS), per hour of the psychologist's or physician's time, both face-to-face time with the patient and time interpreting test results and preparing the report

Work Value: 1.86 // Global Period: XXX

➲ *CPT Changes: An Insider's View* 2006

Clinical Example

A 35-year-old female is referred by her primary care physician due to significant changes in behavior. A series of tests (standardized and/or projective) is administered to evaluate emotionality, intellectual abilities, personality, and psychopathology. The administration of the tests is completed by the provider for the purposes of a mental health diagnosis.

Preservice

The qualified health care professional speaks with the referring source (eg, physician, institution, patient) to ascertain the nature of the referral question(s) to be addressed by the assessment. In addition, the qualified health care professional finds out any special factors or limitations that might affect the testing itself (eg, language limitations, educational deficits, possible resistance to the testing). The qualified health care professional then typically speaks with the patient to set an appointment and to explain the procedures. Prior to meeting with the patient, the qualified health care professional makes a preliminary selection of which tests to be used. This selection depends upon the nature of the clinical questions to be answered as well as certain patient variables (eg, reading level, visual impairment, language proficiency).

Intraservice

The qualified health care professional meets with the patient and conducts an interview, including a comprehensive history. In particular, the qualified health care professional focuses on the patients own questions for the assessment to shape the assessment process. The health care professional attempts to establish a rapport with the patient to ensure maximum involvement and cooperation on the part of the patient with the testing procedures. On the basis of the information gathered from the interview, the health care professional may modify the selection of testing instruments. For example, if the patient raises a question that had not been part of the initial referral, additional instruments may be added to the battery to address this.

The qualified health care professional administers all of the face-to-face or performance-based tests, carefully following appropriate administration procedures to ensure valid test results. The health care professional carefully records the patients responses verbatim during the testing to have an accurate record of the test results for later analysis.

The qualified health care professional explains fully the procedures for the paper-and-pencil or self-report inventories that have been selected. The patient is then left alone to complete the inventories; however, the qualified health care professional checks in on the patient periodically to ensure that the inventories are being completed correctly.

The qualified health care professional meets again with the patient to answer any last questions about the procedures and to inform the patient about the timetable for the results.

Postservice

The qualified health care professional scores all of the test protocols according to the latest methods for each test. The self-report inventories are either hand-scored with templates or are entered into a computer. Once the tests are fully scored, the results are analyzed and interpreted. The interpretations from each of the tests are integrated with data from all of the other tests as well as from the clinical interview and whatever collateral information is available (eg, hospital records, prior assessments) to develop a comprehensive picture of the patients personality, psychopathology, coping strengths and weaknesses, and cognitive functioning, as well as to answer any specific referral questions. The qualified health care professional then writes a report for the referring professional and/or for the patient. The qualified health care professional may then also communicate with either or both orally to discuss the results of the testing.

96102 Psychological testing (includes psychodiagnostic assessment of emotionality, intellectual abilities, personality and psychopathology, eg, MMPI and WAIS), with qualified health care professional interpretation and report, administered by technician, per hour of technician time, face-to-face

Work Value: 0.50 // Global Period: XXX

➲ *CPT Changes: An Insider's View* 2006

Clinical Example

A 35-year-old female is referred by her primary care physician due to significant changes in behavior. A series of tests (standardized and/or projective) is administered to evaluate emotionality, intellectual abilities, personality, and psychopathology. The administration of the tests is completed by a technician for the purposes of a mental health diagnosis.

Preservice

The qualified health care professional speaks with the referring source (eg, physician institution, patient) to ascertain the nature of the referral question(s) to be addressed by the assessment. In addition, the qualified health care professional finds out any special factors or limitations that might affect the testing itself (eg, language limitations, educational deficits, possible resistance to the testing). The qualified health care professional then typically speaks with the patient to set an appointment and to explain the procedures. Before meeting with the patient, the qualified health care professional makes a preliminary selection of which tests to be used. This selection depends upon the nature of the clinical questions to be answered as well as certain patient variables (eg, reading level, visual impairment, language proficiency).

Intraservice

The qualified health care professional meets with the patient and conducts a diagnostic interview, including a comprehensive history. In particular, she/he focuses upon the patient's own questions for the assessment in order to shape the assessment process. She/he attempts to establish rapport in order to ensure maximum involvement and cooperation on the part of the patient with the testing procedures. On the basis of the information gathered from the interview, the qualified health care professional may modify the selection of testing instruments (eg, if the patient raises a question that had not been part of the initial referral, additional instruments may be added to the battery to address this). The qualified health care professional introduces the patient to the technician who conducts the remainder of the assessment. The qualified health care professional meets again with the patient in order to answer any last questions about the procedures and to inform him or her about the timetable for the results.

Postservice

The qualified health care professional scores all of the test protocols according to the latest methods for each test. The self-report inventories are either hand-scored with templates or are entered into a computer. Once the tests are fully scored, the results are analyzed and interpreted. The interpretations from each of the tests are integrated with data from all of the other tests as well as from the clinical interview and whatever collateral information is available (eg, hospital records, prior assessments) to develop a comprehensive picture of the patients personality, psychopathology, coping strengths and weaknesses, and cognitive functioning, as well as to answer any specific referral questions. The qualified health care professional then writes a report for the referring professional and/or for the patient. The qualified health care professional may then also communicate with either or both orally to discuss the results of the testing.

96103 Psychological testing (includes psychodiagnostic assessment of emotionality, intellectual abilities, personality and psychopathology, eg, MMPI), administered by a computer, with qualified health care professional interpretation and report

Work Value: 0.51 // Global Period: XXX

➲ *CPT Changes: An Insider's View* 2006

Clinical Example

A 35-year-old female is referred by her primary care physician due to significant changes in behavior. A series of tests (standardized and/or projective) is administered to evaluate emotionality, intellectual abilities, personality, and psychopathology. The administration of the tests is completed by a computer for the purpose of a mental health diagnosis.

Preservice

The qualified health care professional speaks with the referring source (eg, physician institution, patient) to ascertain the nature of the referral question(s) to be addressed by the assessment. In addition, the qualified health care professional finds out any special factors or limitations that might affect the testing itself (eg, language limitations, educational deficits, possible resistance to the testing). The qualified health care professional then typically speaks with the patient to set an appointment and to explain the procedures. Before meeting with the patient, the qualified health care professional makes a preliminary selection of which tests to be used. This selection depends upon the nature of the clinical questions to be answered as well as certain patient variables (eg, reading level, visual impairment, language proficiency).

Intraservice

The qualified health care professional meets with the patient and conducts an interview, including a comprehensive history. In particular, she/he focuses upon the patient's own questions for the assessment in order to shape the assessment process. S/he attempts to establish rapport in order to ensure maximum involvement and cooperation on the part of the patient with the testing procedures. On the basis of the information gathered from the interview, the psychologist may modify the selection of testing instruments (eg, if the patient raises a question that had not been part of the initial referral, additional instruments may be added to the battery to address this). The qualified health care professional sets up the computer program and instructs the patient on the use of the computer. The psychologist then checks frequently with the patient to ensure that she/he is completing the test correctly. The psychologist then sets up the next instrument and continues as before until all tests are completed. The qualified health care professional meets again with the patient in order to answer any last questions about the procedures and to inform him or her about the timetable for the results.

Postservice

The qualified health care professional scores all of the test protocols according to the latest methods for each test. The self-report inventories are either hand-scored with templates or are entered into a computer. Once the tests are fully scored, the results are analyzed and interpreted. The interpretations from each of the tests are integrated with data from all of the other tests as well as from the clinical interview and whatever collateral information is available (eg, hospital records, prior assessments) to develop a comprehensive picture of the patients personality, psychopathology, coping strengths and weaknesses, and cognitive functioning, as well as to answer any specific referral questions. The qualified health care professional then writes a report for the referring professional and/or for the patient. The qualified health care professional may then also communicate with either or both orally to discuss the results of the testing.

96105 Assessment of aphasia (includes assessment of expressive and receptive speech and language function, language comprehension, speech production ability, reading, spelling, writing, eg, by Boston Diagnostic Aphasia Examination) with interpretation and report, per hour

Work Value: 0.00 // Global Period: XXX

➲ *CPT Assistant* **Jul 96: 8, May 05: 1**

Clinical Example

A 45-year-old male presents who is 3 months status post cerebrovascular accident in the distribution of the left middle cerebral artery. A careful language evaluation is required to determine the nature and extent of aphasia deficits and to make recommendations for rehabilitation.

Preservice

Preservice work includes reviewing the medical records as necessary to plan the appropriate standardized assessment procedures for aphasia (eg, Boston Diagnostic Aphasia Examination).

Intraservice

Intraservice work includes administering the assessment procedures and making clinical observations of the patients behavior during the actual testing process.

Postservice

Postservice work includes scoring the test procedures, interpreting the various test findings, formulating a diagnosis, developing treatment recommendations, obtaining a written report of the patient history, making behavioral observations, and making recommendations.

96111 Developmental testing; extended (includes assessment of motor, language, social, adaptive and/or cognitive functioning by standardized developmental instruments) with interpretation and report

Work Value: 2.60 // Global Period: XXX

➲ *CPT Assistant* Jul 96: 9, May 05: 1; *CPT Changes: An Insider's View* 2005

Clinical Example

An 8-year-old male with impulsive, overly active behavior and previously assessed "average" intelligence was referred for evaluation of "attention deficit disorder." He had reading and written expression skills at the end of first grade level. The patient received speech and language therapy during his attendance at Head Start when he was four-years-old.

Preservice

Prior to the initial appointment with the pediatric developmental and behavioral subspecialist, when the child's mother called to make the appointment, she mentioned that he had early chronic ear infections and tube placement. Since then, he has seemed to have difficulty hearing what is being said. The pediatric subspecialist called the mother to discern if this had been assessed by the child's primary care physician. She denied any further assessment as the primary care physician reassured her "this may be a sign of his attention deficits." After explaining to the mother that it could be very helpful to have the primary care physician see the patient again before an appointment with the pediatric subspecialist and then obtaining her permission to contact the primary care physician, the pediatric subspecialist called the primary care physician and suggested a hearing evaluation would be appropriate prior to the requested current assessment. The primary care physician agreed. Several weeks later, the primary care physician called the pediatric subspecialist and reviewed the results of the child's hearing evaluation and asked if the referral was still acceptable. The pediatric subspecialist accepted the referral and the appointment was scheduled.

Intraservice

The pediatric subspecialist chose the Woodcock–Johnson Test of Cognitive Abilities, Third Edition, as this instrument allows the assessment of 'verbal abilities,' 'visual-spatial' abilities, processing speed, short-term and long-term memory composite scores. Identification of large differences in these individual areas can identify comorbid cognitive processing areas impacting the child's ability to maintain focused selective attention. The testing session began with the subtests emphasizing auditory and verbal memory and knowledge (Memory for Words, Auditory Working Memory, Verbal Ability, General Information). Visual processing was assessed next (Picture Recognition, Spatial Relations, Planning). Processing rates for verbal information (Retrieval Fluency) and then visual/fine motor skills (Visual Matching, Decision Speed) were assessed. Finally, 'fluid processing' was observed (Concept Formation). Throughout the 75 minute session (included three 5 minute break periods for the child to go to the restroom, obtain a snack with the physician, and check with his mother while in the company of the physician), the physician noted the child's expressive discourse language skills, seated posture, fidgetiness, signs of external and internal distractibility, apparent mental effort, mood and preferences for certain tasks. Hand position during the pencil and paper tasks and fine motor control used while opening the snack packages and "juice box "; were specifically noted. After the testing, the responses were scored and the physician reviewed the results with the patient and his mother. The explanations were directed at the child and the mother individually so that each understood the testing results. The results indicated a significant difference between Verbal Ability and

Concept Formation and the Visual/Spatial Composite score. A formal assessment of receptive and expressive language was suggested. The patient's awkward pencil grip and notably slow speed during the pencil and paper tasks, taken in the context of the history provided, supported a suggested referral to an occupational therapist for consultation. Observations made during the testing confirmed the 'hyperactivity' scale observations made by the patient's teacher and mother on the rating scales obtained by the primary care physician prior to the referral.

Postservice

After the evaluation testing appointment, the physician wrote a report (included in the work of the 96111 code) describing the results of the testing and recommendations reflective of the results. The mother called two-weeks later and said the school psychologist would not schedule a meeting to review the results for eight weeks. She gave permission for full communication with all pertinent school personnel. The physician called the school psychologist to explain the need for prompt review of the test results as the patient's current classroom modifications were minimal and exacerbating his weak auditory attention. The school psychologist said the classroom teacher could make interim changes, but the physician would have to talk with her directly. The physician contacted the teacher by telephone and described the rationale for the utility of the classroom modifications. The teacher said she would implement them if the school speech pathologist agreed. Two days later the school speech pathologist called the physician directly about the recommendation for an assistive technology device (FM trainer). She said the physician would have to write a separate letter requesting this device for the patient. The physician wrote the letter.

96116 Neurobehavioral status exam (clinical assessment of thinking, reasoning and judgment, eg, acquired knowledge, attention, language, memory, planning and problem solving, and visual spatial abilities), per hour of the psychologist's or physician's time, both face-to-face time with the patient and time interpreting test results and preparing the report

Work Value: 1.86 // Global Period: XXX

➲ *CPT Changes: An Insider's View* 2006

Clinical Example

A 68-year-old female is referred by her neurologist because of family reports of changes in her behavior, including attention difficulties, memory problems, and difficulties with problem solving. A neurobehavioral status exam is completed for the purpose of making a medical diagnosis.

Preservice

Review the referral and accompanying records. Select the methods to use to evaluate the patients neurobehavioral status.

Intraservice

Meet with the patient and, if appropriate, the patients family to perform a neurobehavioral status exam, which includes screening for impairments in acquired knowledge, attention, language, learning, memory, problem solving, and visual-spatial abilities. Observe the patients behavior and record responses.

Postservice

Review the findings from the neurobehavioral status examination. Develop a clinical impression and produce a written summary of the findings, including recommendations for further assessment, treatment, and/or follow-up. Arrange for additional services as needed.

96118 Neuropsychological testing (eg, Halstead-Reitan Neuropsychological Battery, Wechsler Memory Scales and Wisconsin Card Sorting Test), per hour of the psychologist's or physician's time, both face-to-face time with the patient and time interpreting test results and preparing the report

Work Value: 1.86 // Global Period: XXX

➲ *CPT Changes: An Insider's View* 2006

Clinical Example

A 23-year-old male is referred by his neurologist because of postconcussion symptoms secondary to a motor vehicle accident. A series of neuropsychological tests is administered by a provider for the purpose of making a medical diagnosis.

Preservice

Consult with the referring clinician regarding referral questions. Review the patients history. Select the appropriate procedures needed to address the referral question, and select the appropriate neuropsychological test instruments.

Intraservice

Administer the standardized test procedures. Observe the patients test-taking behavior and record observations. Create a record of the patients responses to the test questions and procedures.

Postservice

Score and compare the test procedures. Interpret individual tests and aggregate battery of tests to formulate a clinical and diagnostic impression. Create a written report that includes a summary of the observations of the patients test behavior and an interpretation of the test results. Develop a clinical impression and produce a written summary of findings, including recommendations for further assessment, treatment, and/or follow-up. Provide feedback to the patient.

96119 Neuropsychological testing (eg, Halstead-Reitan Neuropsychological Battery, Wechsler Memory Scales and Wisconsin Card Sorting Test), with qualified health care professional interpretation and report, administered by technician, per hour of technician time, face-to-face

Work Value: 0.55 // Global Period: XXX

➲ *CPT Changes: An Insider's View* 2006

Clinical Example

A 23-year-old male is referred by his neurologist because of postconcussion symptoms secondary to a motor vehicle accident. A series of neuropsychological tests is administered by a technician for the purpose of making a medical diagnosis.

Preservice

The qualified health care professional reviews the complete medical and developmental records provided by the referring physician and selects a comprehensive battery of neuropsychological tests.

Intraservice

The patient arrives for the appointment and meets with the qualified health care professional, who conducts a comprehensive clinical interview. The qualified health care professional gathers additional information from the patient about the nature of the complaint and the history of the presenting problems. Based on the clinical history, a final selection of tests to be administered is made. The procedures are explained to the patient, and the patient is introduced to the technician, who administers the objective tests. During testing, the qualified health care professional frequently checks with the technician to monitor the patients performance and to make any necessary modifications to the test battery or assessment plan. When all tests have been administered, the qualified health care professional meets with the patient again to answer any questions.

Postservice

After completion of the assessment, all standardized test procedures are reviewed and scored. Scoring tests that require a verbal responses requires reviewing the responses (which are recorded verbatim during the examination as part of the intraservice activity) and comparing the responses with the standardization sample responses and assigning a score. Because there is virtually an infinite combination of possible responses, the assignment of an accurate score requires judgment and experience on the part of the examiner. After all tests are scored, the results are reviewed to identify the areas in which the patient demonstrated intact performance or clinically significant impairments. Taking into account the patients history and clinical information, a diagnostic impression is formed, and a written report is prepared. A follow-up session is scheduled with the patient to provide feedback about the test results, and recommendations for follow-up that may include referral to another medical specialist or working with the referring physician to develop a rehabilitation plan.

96120 Neuropsychological testing (eg, Wisconsin Card Sorting Test), administered by a computer, with qualified health care professional interpretation and report

Work Value: 0.51 // Global Period: XXX

➲ *CPT Changes: An Insider's View* 2006

Clinical Example

A 23-year-old male is referred by his neurologist because of postconcussion symptoms secondary to a motor vehicle accident. A series of individualized neuropsychological tests is administered by a computer for the purpose of making a medical diagnosis.

Preservice

The qualified health care professional reviews the complete medical and developmental records provided by the referring physician or party and selects a comprehensive battery of neuropsychological tests.

Intraservice

The patient arrives for the appointment and meets with the qualified health care professional who conducts a comprehensive clinical interview and review of the presenting complaints. The qualified health care professional explains the computerized testing procedures as part of a more comprehensive test battery that also includes face-to-face testing. The computer test is explained to the patient, and a practice trial is administered to ensure adequate understanding of the test and response requirements. The computer test is administered under the supervision of the qualified health care professional who monitors performance to ensure continued engagement in the task. Upon completion, the next test is introduced and the procedures are repeated until all tests are administered.

Postservice

After all computer-administered tests are completed, the qualified health care professional obtains the results from the computer and integrates the findings with the results of other tests. After all tests are scored, the results are reviewed to identify the areas in which the patient demonstrated intact performance or clinically significant impairments. Taking into account the patients history and clinical information, a diagnostic impression is formed, and a written report is prepared. A follow-up session is scheduled with the patient to provide feedback about the test results, and recommendations for follow-up that may include referral to another medical specialist or working with the referring physician to develop a rehabilitation plan.

Coding Tip for 96101-96120

For the development of cognitive skills, report codes 97532 and/or 97533.

Health and Behavior Assessment/ Intervention

96150 Health and behavior assessment (eg, health-focused clinical interview, behavioral observations, psychophysiological monitoring, health-oriented questionnaires), each 15 minutes face-to-face with the patient; initial assessment

Work Value: 0.50 // Global Period: XXX

➲ *CPT Assistant* **Mar 02: 4, Feb 04: 11, Mar 04: 10, May 05: 1, Jun 05: 10;** ***CPT Changes: An Insider's View*** **2002**

Clinical Example

A 5-year-old boy undergoing treatment for acute lymphoblastic leukemia is referred for assessment of pain, severe behavioral distress, and combativeness associated with repeated lumbar punctures and intrathecal chemotherapy administration. Previously unsuccessful approaches had included pharmacologic treatment of anxiety (lorazepam), conscious sedation (midazolam), and finally, chlorohydrate, which only exacerbated the childs distress as a result of partial sedation. General anesthesia was ruled out because the childs asthma increased the anesthesia respiratory risk to unacceptable levels.

The patient was assessed using standardized questionnaires (eg, the Information Seeking scale, Pediatric Pain Questionnaire, Coping Strategies Inventory) which, in view of the childs age, were administered in a structured format. The medical staff and childs parents were also interviewed. On the day of a scheduled medical procedure, the child completed a self-report distress questionnaire. Behavioral observations were also made during the procedure using the CAMPIS-R, a structured observation scale that quantifies child, parent, and medical staff behavior.

Preservice

Review the patients records and the results of health and assessment instruments. Select and prepare the behavioral health instruments. Select and prepare the equipment.

Intraservice

Assess the patients condition. Administer the health and behavior assessment instruments.

Postservice

Narrate a report of the patients condition, a description of the services provided, and the results and interpretation of the health and behavior assessment instruments and tests.

Coding Tip for 96150

This service does not represent preventive medicine counseling and risk factor reduction intervention.

96151 Health and behavior assessment (eg, health-focused clinical interview, behavioral observations, psychophysiological monitoring, health-oriented questionnaires), each 15 minutes face-to-face with the patient; re-assessment

Work Value: 0.48 // Global Period: XXX

➲ *CPT Assistant* **Mar 02: 4, Feb 04: 11, Mar 04: 10, May 05: 1, Jun 05: 10;** ***CPT Changes: An Insider's View*** **2002**

Clinical Example

1) A 35-year-old female, diagnosed with chronic asthma, hypertension, and panic attacks was originally seen 10 months ago for assessment and follow-up treatment. Original assessment included an extensive interview regarding the patients emotional, social, and medical history, including her ability to manage problems related to the chronic asthma, hospitalizations, and treatments. Test results from original assessment provided information for treatment planning, which included health and behavior interventions involving a combination of behavioral cognitive therapy, relaxation response training, and visualization. After 4 months of treatment interventions, the patients hypertension and anxiety were significantly reduced and the patient was discharged. Now 6 months following discharge, the patient has injured her knee

and has undergone arthroscopic surgery with follow-up physical therapy.

The patient was seen to reassess and evaluate her psychophysiological responses to these new health stressors. A review of the records from the initial assessment, testing, and treatment intervention, as well as current medical records, was made. The patients affective and physiological status, compliance disposition, and perceptions of efficacy of relaxation and visualization practices utilized during previous treatment intervention were examined. The administration of an anxiety inventory/ questionnaire (eg, Burns Anxiety Inventory) was used to quantify patients current level of response to present health stressors and compared with original assessment levels. Need for further treatment is evaluated.

2) A 5-year-old male has returned for treatment of acute lymphoblastic leukemia. He is being referred for a reassessment of behavioral distress and combativeness associated with repeated lumbar punctures and intrathecal chemotherapy administration. He was initially seen for several sessions and improved with effective management strategies used by his parents and medical staff. His distress and combativeness have suddenly worsened to the extent that treatment is difficult.

Preservice

Review the patients records and the results of health and assessment instruments. Select and prepare the behavioral health instruments. Select and prepare the equipment. Prepare for the interview. Review the patients medical records. Consult with the staff.

Intraservice

Reassess the patients condition via an interview and behavioral health instruments. Administer the behavior health instruments. Review the interview and reassessment of the patient. Observe the staff working with the patient. Counsel the patient and explore behavior modification options.

Postservice

Narrate the patients condition, a description of the services provided, and the results and interpretation of the behavioral health instruments. Prepare a written report and collaborate with the medical staff, the patients family, community, and other resources.

96152 Health and behavior intervention, each 15 minutes, face-to-face; individual

Work Value: 0.46 // Global Period: XXX

➲ *CPT Assistant* **Mar 02: 4, Feb 04: 11, Mar 04: 10, May 05: 1, Jun 05: 10;** ***CPT Changes: An Insider's View*** **2002**

Clinical Example

A 55-year-old executive has a history of cardiac arrest, high blood pressure and cholesterol, and a family history of cardiac problems. He is 30 lbs overweight, travels extensively for work, and reports to be a moderate social drinker. He currently smokes approximately one-half pack of cigarettes a day, although he has periodically attempted to quit smoking for up to 5 weeks at a time. The patient is considered by his physician to be a Type A personality and at high risk for cardiac complications. He experiences angina pains one or two times per month.

Results from the health and behavior assessment are used to develop a treatment plan, taking into account the patients coping skills and lifestyle. Subsequently, weekly intervention sessions focus on psychoeducational factors impacting his awareness and knowledge about his disease process, and the use of relaxation and guided imagery techniques that directly impact his blood pressure and heart rate. Cognitive and behavioral approaches for cessation of smoking and initiation of an appropriate physician-prescribed diet and exercise regimen are also employed.

Preservice

Review the patients records and the results of health and assessment instruments. Select and prepare the health and behavior assessment instruments and equipment.

Intraservice

Perform the cognitive and behavioral intervention treatment approaches for the health risk factors of the patient. Administer the health and behavior instruments.

Postservice

Narrate a description of the patients condition, progress notes, a description of services provided, and the results and interpretation of the health and behavior assessment instruments.

96153 Health and behavior intervention, each 15 minutes, face-to-face; group (2 or more patients)

Work Value: 0.10 // Global Period: XXX

➲ *CPT Assistant* Mar 02: 4, Feb 04: 11, Mar 04: 10, May 05: 1, Jun 05: 10; *CPT Changes: An Insider's View* 2002

Clinical Example

A 45-year-old female is referred for smoking cessation secondary to chronic bronchitis, with a strong family history of emphysema. She smokes two packs per day. The health and behavior assessment reveals that the patient uses smoking as a primary way of coping with stress. Social influences contributing to her continued smoking include several friends and family members who also smoke. The patient has made multiple previous attempts to quit on her own. When treatment options are reviewed, she is receptive to the recommendation of an eight-session group cessation program. The program components include educational information (eg, health risks, nicotine addiction), cognitive-behavioral treatment (eg, self-monitoring, relaxation training, behavioral substitution), and social support (eg, group discussion, social skills training).

Preservice

Review the patients records and the results of the health and assessment instruments. Select and prepare the health and assessment instruments and equipment.

Intraservice

Perform the cognitive and behavioral intervention treatment approaches for the health risk factors of the patient. Administer the health and behavior assessment instruments.

Postservice

Narrate a description of the patients condition, progress notes, a description of the services provided, and the results and interpretation of the health and behavior assessment instruments.

96154 Health and behavior intervention, each 15 minutes, face-to-face; family (with the patient present)

Work Value: 0.45 // Global Period: XXX

➲ *CPT Assistant* Mar 02: 4, Feb 04: 11, Mar 04: 10, May 05: 1, Jun 05: 10; *CPT Changes: An Insider's View* 2002

Clinical Example

A 9-year-old girl was diagnosed with insulin-dependent diabetes 2 years ago. Her mother reports great difficulty with morning and evening insulin injections and blood glucose testing. The patient whines and cries, delaying the procedures for 30 minutes or more. She refuses to give her own injections or conduct her own blood glucose tests, claiming they hurt. Her mother spends many minutes pleading for her cooperation. The patients father refuses to participate, saying he is afraid of needles. Both parents have not been able to go to a movie alone, because they know of no one who can care for their child. The patients 10-year-old sister claims she never has any time with her mother, because her mother is always occupied with the patients illness. The patient and her sister have a very poor relationship and are always quarreling. Her parents frequently argue; her mother complains that she gets no help from her husband. Her father complains that his wife has no time for anyone except the patient.

A family-based approach is used to address the multiple components of the patients problem behaviors. Relaxation and exposure techniques are used to address her fathers fear of injections, which he has been inadvertently modeling for his daughter. She is taught relaxation and distraction techniques to reduce the tension she experiences with finger sticks and injections. Both parents are taught to shape her behavior, praising and rewarding successful diabetes management behaviors, and ignoring delay tactics. Her parents are also taught judicious use of time-out and response-cost procedures. Family roles and responsibilities are clarified. Clear communication, conflict resolution, and problem-solving skills are taught. Family members practice applying these skills to a variety of problems so that they will know how to successfully address new problems that may arise in the future.

Preservice

Review the patients records and review the results of health and assessment instruments. Prepare and select the health and behavior assessment instruments and equipment.

Intraservice

Perform the cognitive and behavioral intervention treatment approaches for the health risk factors of the patient. Administer the health and behavior assessment instruments. Use the health and behavior equipment.

Postservice

Narrate a description of the patients condition, progress notes, a description of the services provided, and the results and interpretation of the health and behavior assessment instruments.

Chemotherapy Administration

Injection and Intravenous Infusion Chemotherapy

96401 Chemotherapy administration, subcutaneous or intramuscular; non-hormonal anti-neoplastic

Work Value: 0.21 // Global Period: XXX

➲ *CPT Assistant* Nov 05: 1, Jan 06: 47; *CPT Changes: An Insider's View* 2006

Clinical Example

A 34-year-old patient with testicular cancer presents with the appropriate indications for chemotherapy.

Preservice

The physician provides and confirms the orders. The physician interacts and reviews the plan with staff. The physician confirms and reviews the lab results as necessary.

Intraservice

The physician provides direct supervision and is immediately available in the office. The physician assesses the patients response to the treatment.

Postservice

The physician provides appropriate instructions regarding immediate care. The physician provides minimal instructions regarding ongoing care. The physician conducts appropriate interactions with the staff regarding patient monitoring.

Coding Tip for 96401

If a significant, separately identifiable evaluation and management (E/M) service is performed, the appropriate E/M service code should be reported with modifier 25 in addition to code 96401.

96402 Chemotherapy administration, subcutaneous or intramuscular; hormonal anti-neoplastic

Work Value: 0.19 // Global Period: XXX

➲ ***CPT Assistant*** **Nov 05: 1;** ***CPT Changes: An Insider's View*** **2006**

Clinical Example

A 72-year-old male with prostate cancer presents with the appropriate indications for luteinizing hormone-releasing hormone agonist therapy.

Preservice

The physician provides and confirms the orders. The physician interacts and reviews the plan with staff.

Intraservice

The physician provides direct supervision and is immediately available in the office. The physician assesses the patients response to the treatment.

Postservice

The physician provides appropriate instructions regarding immediate care. The physician provides minimal instructions regarding ongoing care. The physician conducts appropriate interactions with the staff regarding patient monitoring.

96405 Chemotherapy administration; intralesional, up to and including 7 lesions

Work Value: 0.52 // Global Period: 000

➲ ***CPT Assistant*** **Sep 96: 5, Aug 97: 19, Feb 01: 10, Jul 01: 2, Nov 05: 1;** ***CPT Changes: An Insider's View*** **2006**

Clinical Example

A 60-year-old female presents with a well-defined biopsy-proven primary solid basal cell carcinoma of the nose and normal cardiac, liver, and renal status.

96406 Chemotherapy administration; intralesional, more than 7 lesions

Work Value: 0.80 // Global Period: 000

➲ ***CPT Assistant*** **Sep 96: 5, Aug 97: 19, Feb 01: 10, Jul 01: 2, Nov 05: 1;** ***CPT Changes: An Insider's View*** **2006**

Clinical Example

A 65-year-old male presents with a multiple biopsy-proven primary superficial basal cell carcinoma of the torso. The patient is not a surgical candidate but otherwise has normal cardiac, renal, and liver status.

96409 Chemotherapy administration; intravenous, push technique, single or initial substance/drug

Work Value: 0.24 // Global Period: XXX

➲ ***CPT Assistant*** **Nov 05: 1;** ***CPT Changes: An Insider's View*** **2006**

Clinical Example

A 67-year-old male with bladder cancer presents for an intravenous (IV) push administration. The patient does not have a venous access device and requires an IV initiation.

Preservice

The physician provides and confirms the orders. The physician interacts and reviews the plan with staff. The physician confirms and reviews any appropriate lab results as necessary. The physician calculates the dose.

Intraservice

The physician provides direct supervision and is immediately available in the office. The physician assesses the patients response to the treatment.

Postservice

The physician provides appropriate instructions regarding immediate care. The physician provides minimal instructions regarding ongoing care. The physician conducts appropriate interactions with the staff regarding patient monitoring.

+ 96411 Chemotherapy administration; intravenous, push technique, each additional substance/drug (List separately in addition to code for primary procedure)

Work Value: 0.20 // Global Period: ZZZ

➲ *CPT Assistant* Nov 05: 1; *CPT Changes: An Insider's View* 2006

Clinical Example

A 67-year-old male with bladder cancer is to receive the second drug for the days treatment. The patient has just finished receiving an intravenous (IV) push of a first drug (reported separately under 96408) as part of the chemotherapy course.

Preservice

The physician provides and confirms the orders. The physician calculates the dose.

Intraservice

The physician provides direct supervision and is immediately available in the office. The physician assesses the patients response to the treatment.

96413 Chemotherapy administration, intravenous infusion technique; up to 1 hour, single or initial substance/drug

Work Value: 0.28 // Global Period: XXX

➲ *CPT Assistant* Nov 05: 1; *CPT Changes: An Insider's View* 2006

Clinical Example

This procedure is initiated for a 64-year-old female with ovarian cancer or rheumatoid arthritis. The patient has a venous access device in place.

Preservice

The physician provides and confirms the orders. The physician interacts and reviews the plan with staff. The physician confirms and reviews any appropriate lab results as necessary. The physician calculates the dose.

Intraservice

The physician provides direct supervision and is immediately available in the office. The physician periodically assesses the patient and the patients response to the treatment. This assessment is typically done through communication with the nurse.

Postservice

The physician provides appropriate instructions regarding immediate care. The physician provides minimal instructions regarding ongoing care. The physician conducts appropriate interactions with the staff regarding patient monitoring.

+ 96415 Chemotherapy administration, intravenous infusion technique; each additional hour (List separately in addition to code for primary procedure)

Work Value: 0.19 // Global Period: ZZZ

➲ *CPT Assistant* Nov 05: 1; *CPT Changes: An Insider's View* 2006, 2007

Clinical Example

A previously started infusion is continued for a 64-year-old female with ovarian cancer or rheumatoid arthritis. The patient has a venous access device in place.

Intraservice

The physician provides direct supervision and is immediately available in the office. The physician periodically assesses the patient and the patients response to the treatment. This assessment is typically done through communication with the nurse.

96416 Chemotherapy administration, intravenous infusion technique; initiation of prolonged chemotherapy infusion (more than 8 hours), requiring use of a portable or implantable pump

Work Value: 0.21 // Global Period: XXX

➲ *CPT Assistant* Nov 05: 1; *CPT Changes: An Insider's View* 2006

Clinical Example

A 58-year-old female presents for one of several periodic prolonged infusions of fluorouracil therapy.

Preservice

The physician provides and confirms the orders. The physician interacts and reviews the plan with staff. The physician confirms and reviews any lab results as necessary. The physician calculates the dose.

Intraservice

The physician provides direct supervision and is immediately available in the office. The physician periodically assesses the patient and the patients response to treatment. This assessment is typically done through communication with the nurse.

Postservice

The physician provides appropriate instructions regarding immediate care. The physician provides minimal instructions regarding ongoing care. The physician conducts appropriate interactions with the staff regarding patient monitoring.

+ 96417 Chemotherapy administration, intravenous infusion technique; each additional sequential infusion (different substance/drug), up to 1 hour (List separately in addition to code for primary procedure)

Work Value: 0.21 // Global Period: ZZZ

➲ *CPT Assistant* Nov 05: 1; *CPT Changes: An Insider's View* 2006

Clinical Example

A 64-year-old female with ovarian cancer presents for infusion. She has completed infusion of one chemotherapy drug and is now infused with a second drug through her implanted venous access device.

Preservice

The physician confirms the orders. The physician conducts a reassessment of the patients status prior to commencing the new drug infusion. The physician calculates the dose.

Intraservice

The physician provides direct supervision and is immediately available in the office. The physician periodically assesses the patient and the patients response to treatment. This assessment is typically done through communication with the nurse.

Coding Tip for 96417

Code 96417 is reported only once per sequential infusion. Code 96415 is reported for additional hour(s) of sequential infusion.

Other Chemotherapy

96521 Refilling and maintenance of portable pump

Work Value: 0.21 // Global Period: XXX

➲ *CPT Assistant* Nov 05: 1; *CPT Changes: An Insider's View* 2006

Clinical Example

A 58-year-old female having a prolonged infusion of fluorouracil presents to have her portable infusion pump refilled.

Preservice

The physician provides and confirms the orders. The physician interacts and reviews the plan with staff. The physician confirms and reviews any lab results as necessary. The physician calculates the dose.

Intraservice

The physician provides direct supervision and is immediately available in the office. The physician assesses the patients response to the treatment.

Postservice

The physician provides appropriate instructions regarding immediate care. The physician provides minimal instructions regarding ongoing care. The physician conducts appropriate interactions with the staff regarding patient monitoring.

96522 Refilling and maintenance of implantable pump or reservoir for drug delivery, systemic (eg, intravenous, intra-arterial)

Work Value: 0.21 // Global Period: XXX

➲ *CPT Changes: An Insider's View* 2006

Clinical Example

A 66-year-old male patient with metastatic colorectal carcinoma with disease limited to the liver returns for treatment. A hepatic artery catheter has previously been placed by a surgeon with an attached implanted pump (eg, Infusaid pump). The pump is refilled.

Preservice

The physician provides and confirms the orders. The physician interacts and reviews the plan with staff. The physician confirms and reviews any lab results as necessary.

Intraservice

The physician provides direct supervision and is immediately available in the office. The physician calculates and recalculates the dosage and the infusion rate.

Postservice

The physician provides appropriate instructions regarding immediate care. The physician provides minimal instructions regarding ongoing care. The physician conducts appropriate interactions with the staff regarding patient monitoring.

96523 Irrigation of implanted venous access device for drug delivery systems

Work Value: 0.04 // Global Period: XXX

➲ *CPT Changes: An Insider's View* 2006

Clinical Example

A 72-year-old male with lung carcinoma has an implanted venous access device for drug delivery and returns to the clinic for flushing and maintenance of the device on a day when chemotherapy or other treatments are not planned.

Preservice

The physician provides the orders.

Intraservice

No physician intraservice is required. Clinic staff complete the required device maintenance.

Coding Tip for 96523

Codes 96521-96523 may be reported when these devices are used for therapeutic drugs other than chemotherapy.

Photodynamic Therapy

96567 Photodynamic therapy by external application of light to destroy premalignant and/or malignant lesions of the skin and adjacent mucosa (eg, lip) by activation of photosensitive drug(s), each phototherapy exposure session

Work Value: 0.00 // Global Period: XXX

➲ *CPT Assistant* Aug 03: 15; *CPT Changes: An Insider's View* 2002

Preservice

Clinical Labor Activities:

Encounter 1: Review of pertinent test results. Education on treatment requirements, risks and scheduling.

Encounter 2: Review treatment requirements, any reactions or complaints regarding photosensitizing agent.

Intraservice

Clinical Labor Activities:

Encounter 1: Patient is gowned and positioned. Assist physician during assessment of lesions for size, location, functional risks, depth. Preparation of aminolevulinic acid HCI for Topical Solution, 20%. Application of prepared photo-sensitizing agent in topical solution form directly to individual lesions.

Encounter 2: Patient returns within strict 14 to 18 hour treatment parameter for photodynamic agent treatment. Patient is gowned and positioned. The patient receives irradiation of the affected area with the BLU-U Photodynamic Therapy Illuminator for approximately 17 minutes. Patient must be observed and this process must be monitored by a healthcare professional to provide intervention to any adverse reaction. The time period for light exposure remains the same regardless of the number of lesions. Exposure to the BLU-U light generates a photodynamic reaction with the topical agent. The reaction is a cytotoxic process, preventing further reproduction and growth of the keratotic cells while destroying the existing cells of the lesion.

Postservice

Encounter 1: Instruct patient regarding continued duration of photosensitivity, functional risks, and mandatory follow-up period and care. Communicate with patient and family on intra-procedural care.

Encounter 2: Instruct patient regarding continued duration of photosensitivity, functional risks, follow-up period and care. Communicate with patient and family on post-procedural care.

Coding Tip for 96567

If ocular photodynamic therapy is performed, code 67221 is reported.

+ 96570 Photodynamic therapy by endoscopic application of light to ablate abnormal tissue via activation of photosensitive drug(s); first 30 minutes (List separately in addition to code for endoscopy or bronchoscopy procedures of lung and esophagus)

Work Value: 1.10 // Global Period: ZZZ

➲ ***CPT Assistant*** **Nov 99: 54, Sep 00: 5;** ***CPT Changes: An Insider's View*** **2000**

Clinical Example

A 63-year-old caucasian, male patient with a history of smoking and some alcohol use, complains of extreme difficulty with swallowing. Endoscopic examination is performed and reveals a diagnosis of esophageal cancer. A computed tomography scan shows adjacent lymph node and celiac involvement. A determination is made that the patient is not a candidate for surgical resection. The patient receives radiation therapy and chemotherapy. Subsequently, the patient develops recurrent complaints of dysphagia. Reassessment reveals that the tumor has progressed and is surgically nonresectable. Palliative therapy of the patients dysphagia using photodynamic therapy for 30 minutes has been proposed.

Preservice

The patient receives an intravenous injection of the photoactive drug. The patient is monitored for adverse reaction to the drug.

Intraservice

The patient is sedated with intravenous meperidine, midazolam hydrochloride, or diazepam. An endoscope is passed through to the esophagus and the 5-cm tumor is localized. The endoscope is passed distal to the tumor. A diffuser tip is inserted and the laser light source is activated and applied to the tumor. The endoscopic laser light is applied for 12.5 minutes using a 2.5-cm cylindrical diffusing fiberoptic endoscope, which is required for every 2.5 cm of tumor length. During each application, the light source is periodically turned off so that the position of both the endoscope and the diffuser may be checked. With sedation and pauses to recheck position, the treatment session takes 30 minutes.

Postservice

The patient is re-examined 2-3 days after the procedure. The patient is counseled to remain out of reflected or direct sunlight for one month because of increased risk of serious sunburn. A procedure report is dictated and checked.

+ 96571 Photodynamic therapy by endoscopic application of light to ablate abnormal tissue via activation of photosensitive drug(s); each additional 15 minutes (List separately in addition to code for endoscopy or bronchoscopy procedures of lung and esophagus)

Work Value: 0.55 // Global Period: ZZZ

➲ *CPT Assistant* Nov 99: 54, Sep 00: 5; *CPT Changes: An Insider's View* 2000

Clinical Example

A 63-year-old caucasian, male patient with a history of smoking and some alcohol use, complains of extreme difficulty with swallowing. Endoscopic examination is performed and reveals a diagnosis of esophageal cancer. A computed tomography scan shows adjacent lymph node and celiac involvement. A determination is made that the patient is not a candidate for surgical resection. The patient receives radiation therapy and chemotherapy. Subsequently, the patient develops recurrent complaints of dysphagia. Reassessment reveals that the tumor has progressed and is surgically nonresectable. Palliative therapy of the patients dysphagia using photodynamic therapy for 30 minutes has been proposed. (An additional 15 minutes beyond the original 30 minutes is spent assessing this patient.)

Preservice

The patient receives an intravenous injection of the photoactive drug. The patient is monitored for adverse reaction to the drug.

Intraservice

The patient is sedated with intravenous meperidine, midazolam hydrochloride, or diazepam. An endoscope is passed through to the esophagus and the 5-cm tumor is localized. The endoscope is passed distal to the tumor. A diffuser tip is inserted and the laser light source is activated and applied to the tumor. The endoscopic laser light is applied for 12.5 minutes using a 2.5-cm cylindrical diffusing fiberoptic endoscope, which is required for every 2.5 cm of tumor length. During each application, the light source is periodically turned off so that the position of both the endoscope and the diffuser may be checked. With sedation and pauses to recheck position, the treatment session takes 30 minutes.

Postservice

The patient is re-examined 2-3 days after the procedure. The patient is counseled to remain out of reflected or direct sunlight for one month because of increased risk of serious sunburn. A procedure report is dictated and reviewed.

Special Dermatological Procedures

96913 Photochemotherapy (Goeckerman and/or PUVA) for severe photoresponsive dermatoses requiring at least four to eight hours of care under direct supervision of the physician (includes application of medication and dressings)

Work Value: 0.00 // Global Period: XXX

Clinical Example

A 38-year-old female presents with a 14-year history of generalized psoriasis. Previous topical therapy has included various topical corticosteroids, tars, and anthralin preparations. In addition, she has previously had courses of phototherapy. One year ago, she was placed on 15 mgs of methotrexate, weekly. This was discontinued 1 month ago, because of persistently abnormal liver function tests. Evaluation reveals generalized, indurated plaques of psoriasis affecting 50% of her body surface area with confluent plaque involvement of her scalp. She is otherwise in good general health with a minor degree of associated psoriatic arthritis of her hands and feet. She is admitted for an intensive course of Photochemotherapy (Goeckerman) with an expected duration of treatment of 18 days.

Preservice

A general medical history is obtained, including current medications and a history of arthritis, possible sensitivities to topical medications (eg, tars), and a history of photosensitivity disorders. The patients duration of psoriasis is evaluated and all previous therapies are reviewed. A skin evaluation of total body surface area including scalp, genitalia, and nails, is performed, and the percentage of body surface involvement is assessed. An evaluation of individual lesions stressing erythema, induration, and scaling, is also performed. An examination is conducted to detect any existing skin cancers and/or assess nevi, and to evaluate any photoaging and detect other signs of cutaneous disease. Appropriate diagnostic tests are ordered. Also, a basic general medical evaluation is performed specifically relating to cardiac status. The patient is referred for an ophthalmological consult if PUVA is contemplated. Medical decision making is of high complexity. All aspects of the Goeckerman regimen including risks, expected duration of therapy, and compliance with chosen treatments, is discussed with the patient. Alternative treatment options are also discussed including topical, phototherapy, and photochemotherapy (PUVA), and systemic medications. Potential side effects of methoxsalen are explained. A preservice report is dictated for the referring physician.

Intraservice

The physician evaluates the patient daily. The physician discusses with the nurses the progress and daily treatments of the patient. The physician discusses issues relating to disease, education, remissions, prognosis, and future care with the patient. The general regimen of the patient involves: phototherapy and/or PUVA, one to two times daily; the application of topicals (eg, tars, anthralin), one to two times daily to all affected areas including the scalp; the application of dressings (eg, gauze, saran wrap, appropriate occlusive dressings); and daily baths/showers including shampooing the scalp and removing all medications.

Postservice

The physician performs a full skin discharge examination and counsels the patient regarding the patients immediate postdischarge treatment (eg, topicals, phototherapy and/or photochemotherapy). The physician also discusses future management and follow-up as necessary. The medical record is completed and a postdischarge summary dictated. A note to the referring physician is dictated as to the course and outcome of treatment and future management.

96920 Laser treatment for inflammatory skin disease (psoriasis); total area less than 250 sq cm

Work Value: 1.15 // Global Period: 000

➲ *CPT Changes: An Insider's View* 2003

Clinical Example

A 35-year-old Caucasian male presents with a 10-year history of stable moderate plaque psoriasis, which worsens during the winter months. There is a family history of psoriasis. Physical findings include inflamed, scaly, somewhat tender lesions present on the extensor surfaces of elbows and knees, hips, sacrum, and scalp involving 10% of the body surface area, or about 1500 sq cm. Current therapies include daily use of both moderate-potency topical corticosteroid ointment and calcipotriene ointment. A corticosteroid lotion is used daily on the scalp; topical tar preparations are added when necessary. These therapies have produced a partial improvement response of approximately 80% plaque clearance, leaving less than 250 sq cm of chronic plaques resistant to topical therapy. The patient continues to suffer from significant erythema, induration, pruritus, and desquamation of thick scales from these nonresponsive areas. The severity of the disease is documented and the decision is made to utilize laser treatment for recurrent psoriatic plaques. Activities of daily living and quality of life are negatively impacted by the presence of symptomatic lesions.

Preservice

The physician reviews the treatment options including systemic therapy, phototherapy, additional topical therapy, and laser treatment. The physician reviews the chart, confirms the area of treatment with the patient, and obtains informed consent for the laser treatment. The physician verifies the positioning of the patient and checks the laser equipment.

Intraservice

The affected area is draped and the lesion site(s) is prepped with a clarifying agent such as mineral oil or other moisturizing agent. The physician assesses the redness of the lesions and any erythema. Pain or blistering from previous therapy or treatment methodology is also assessed. The physician determines the laser dosage level from an assessment of the minimum erythema dosage of laser light on normal skin. The physician treats the area of inflamed lesions or plaque with the laser. The physician monitors for pain as well as skin surface reaction throughout the process.

Postservice

The physician discusses follow-up treatment with the patient. The physician also discusses with the patient pain management, dressings if required, and care of the treated area.

96921 Laser treatment for inflammatory skin disease (psoriasis); 250 sq cm to 500 sq cm

Work Value: 1.17 // Global Period: 000

➲ *CPT Changes: An Insider's View* 2003

Clinical Example

A 35-year-old Caucasian male presents with a 10-year history of stable moderate plaque psoriasis, which worsens during the winter months. There is a family history of psoriasis. Physical findings include inflamed, scaly, somewhat tender lesions present on the extensor surfaces of elbows and knees, hips, sacrum, and scalp involving 10% of the body surface area, or about 1500 sq cm. Current therapies include daily use of both moderate-potency topical corticosteroid ointment and calcipotriene ointment. A corticosteroid lotion is used daily on the scalp; topical tar preparations are added when necessary. These therapies have produced a partial improvement response of approximately 80% plaque clearance, leaving 250-500 sq cm of chronic plaques resistant to topical therapy. The patient continues to suffer from significant erythema, induration, pruritus, and desquamation of thick scales from these nonresponsive areas. The severity of the disease is documented and the decision is made to utilize laser treatment for recurrent psoriatic plaques. Activities of daily living and quality of life are negatively impacted by the presence of symptomatic lesions.

Preservice

The physician reviews the treatment options including systemic therapy, phototherapy, additional topical therapy, and laser treatment. The physician reviews the chart, confirms the area of treatment with the patient, and obtains informed consent for the laser treatment. The physician verifies the positioning of patient and checks the laser equipment.

Intraservice

The patient is positioned, the affected area is draped, and the lesion site(s) is prepped with a clarifying agent such as mineral oil or other moisturizing agent. The physician assesses the redness of the lesions and any erythema. Pain or blistering from previous therapy or treatment methodology is also assessed. The physician determines the laser dosage level from an assessment of the minimum erythema dosage of laser light on normal skin. The physician treats each lesion or plaque with the laser. The physician monitors for pain as well as skin surface reaction throughout the process.

Postservice

The physician discusses follow-up treatment with the patient. The physician also discusses with the patient pain management, dressings if required, and care of the treated area.

96922 Laser treatment for inflammatory skin disease (psoriasis); over 500 sq cm

Work Value: 2.10 // Global Period: 000

➲ *CPT Changes: An Insider's View* 2003

Clinical Example

A 35-year-old Caucasian male presents with a 10-year history of stable moderate plaque psoriasis, which worsens during the winter months. There is a family history of psoriasis. Physical findings include inflamed, scaly, somewhat tender lesions present on the extensor surfaces of elbows and knees, hips, sacrum, and scalp involving 10% of the body surface area, or about 1500 sq cm. Current therapies include daily use of both moderate-potency topical corticosteroid ointment and calcipotriene ointment. A corticosteroid lotion is used daily on the scalp; topical tar preparations are added when necessary. These therapies have produced a partial improvement response of approximately 80% plaque clearance, leaving over 500 sq cm of chronic plaques resistant to topical therapy. The patient continues to suffer from significant erythema, induration, pruritus, and desquamation of thick scales from these nonresponsive areas. The severity of the disease is documented and the decision is made to utilize laser treatment for recurrent psoriatic plaques. Activities of daily living and quality of life are negatively impacted by the presence of symptomatic lesions.

Preservice

The physician reviews the treatment options including systemic therapy, phototherapy, additional topical therapy, and laser treatment. The physician reviews the chart, confirms the area of treatment with the patient, and obtains informed consent for the laser treatment. The physician verifies the positioning of patient and checks the laser equipment.

Intraservice

The patient is positioned, the affected area is draped, and the lesion site(s) is prepped with a clarifying agent such as mineral oil or other moisturizing agent. The physician assesses the redness of the lesions and any erythema. Pain or blistering from previous therapy or treatment methodology is also assessed. The physician determines the laser dosage level from an assessment of the minimum erythema dosage of laser light on normal skin. The physician treats each lesion or plaque with the laser. The physician monitors for pain as well as skin surface reaction throughout the process.

Postservice

The physician discusses follow-up treatment with the patient. The physician also discusses with the patient pain management, dressings if required, and care of the treated area.

Physical Medicine and Rehabilitation

97001 Physical therapy evaluation

Work Value: 1.20 // Global Period: XXX

➲ *CPT Assistant* Nov 97: 47, Feb 00: 11, Sep 01: 10, Oct 02: 11, Dec 03: 4, Feb 04: 5, Apr 05: 13

Clinical Example

A 56-year-old female presents with right shoulder adhesive capsulitis (initial visit). She has painful and limited range of motion with the inability to use the arm for the majority of her activities at work. Medical history is significant for hypertension. She has had shoulder complaints for less than 1 month. The examination includes but is not limited to: a range of motion examination; a joint integrity and mobility examination; a muscle performance examination (including strength, power, and endurance), comparing left to right; a respiration, heart rate, and blood pressure assessment; and an environmental, home, or work barriers examination.

Preservice

Preservice work includes obtaining patient intake information, gathering or preparing equipment and materials that will be used during the procedure, and coordinating with other team members.

Intraservice

Intraservice work includes examining the patient, which includes obtaining a patient history, performing relevant systems reviews, and using tests and measures to elicit additional information; evaluating the patient based on data gathered from the examination; organizing and interpreting the data and establishing and/or obtaining such additional information as may be necessary; developing a plan of care including a prognosis for functional improvement; selecting interventions to produce improvement in the patients condition; and providing instruction regarding the cause, prognosis, and plan of care for the patients condition, which may include prevention and health promotion information.

Postservice

Postservice work includes documenting the entire evaluation process and the results of the evaluation, as well as performing administration functions (such as patient and family communication and scheduling) relative to the patient's care.

97002 Physical therapy re-evaluation

Work Value: 0.60 // Global Period: XXX

➲ *CPT Assistant* Nov 97: 47, Feb 00: 11, Sep 01: 10, Oct 02: 11, Dec 03: 4, Feb 04: 5

Clinical Example

Re-evaluation of an 18-year-old female who had an anterior cruciate ligament repair 8 weeks ago. She has been undergoing conservative management and is now at the appropriate stage for the progression of an open and modified closed-chain rehabilitation program. Joint effusion continues to be a problem with irritation from the prescribed brace the patient is wearing. Examination would include but not be limited to the following: a range of motion examination; a gait examination; a joint integrity and mobility examination; girth measurement and a muscle performance examination; and a functional assessment.

Preservice

Preservice work includes reviewing the patients chart or history, gathering or preparing equipment or materials to be used during the procedure, and coordinating with other team members.

Intraservice

Intraservice work includes re-examining the patient, which includes verifying the patient history or chart, performing relevant system reviews, and using appropriate tests and measures of patient progress; re-evaluating the patient based on the data gathered in the re-examination; organizing and interpreting the data and establishing and obtaining such additional information as may be necessary; modifying the plan of care as appropriate to the results of the re-evaluation; and providing instruction to the patient as appropriate to the results of the re-evaluation.

Postservice

Postservice work includes documenting the entire evaluation process and the results of the evaluation, as well as performing administration functions (such as patient and family communication and scheduling) relative to the patient's care.

Modalities

Supervised

97010 Application of a modality to one or more areas; hot or cold packs

Work Value: 0.06 // Global Period: XXX

➲ *CPT Assistant* Summer 95: 5, Apr 96: 11, Nov 97: 47, Dec 98: 1, Nov 01: 5, Aug 02: 11

Clinical Example

A 55-year-old male presents following right total knee arthroplasty with stiffness and inability to fully extend his knee. Hot packs are applied around the knee for 20 minutes prior to other therapeutic procedures. The provider checks the patient 5 minutes after the initiation of treatment to determine skin sensitivity and the appropriateness of thermal reaction from the modality.

Preservice

Preservice work includes reviewing the patients chart for medical treatment, setting up the equipment area, reviewing previous documentation as needed, communicating with other health care professionals (eg, social worker, nurse), discussing the patients status with family members, and communicating with the referring physician for additional information/clarification.

Intraservice

Intraservice work includes checking the patients range of motion, skin integrity, and sensation. (Additional intraservice work is detailed in the example.)

Postservice

Postservice work includes writing up a report/documentation of treatment, communicating with the referring physician to report the patients progress, and communicating with other team members.

97012 Application of a modality to one or more areas; traction, mechanical

Work Value: 0.25 // Global Period: XXX

➲ ***CPT Assistant*** **Summer 95: 5, Apr 96: 11, Nov 97: 47, Dec 98: 1, May 99: 11, Nov 01: 5, Aug 02: 11, Dec 03: 4, Oct 04: 9**

Clinical Example

A 48-year-old female presents with lumbar radiculopathy. She has pain and muscle guarding in the lumbar region. Lumbar traction is applied using pelvic and stabilization belts with the patient in the supine position. The traction is intermittent. It takes the provider 10-15 minutes to set up the treatment and establish the position and poundage. At the end of a 15-20 minute application, the provider takes approximately five minutes to disassemble the treatment and assist the patient.

Preservice

Preservice work includes reviewing the patients chart for medical treatment, setting up the equipment area, reviewing previous documentation as needed, communicating with other health care professionals (eg, social worker, nurse), communicating with family members, and communicating with the referring physician for additional information/clarification.

Intraservice

Intraservice work includes checking the patient's pain level, sensory distribution, and muscle guarding. (Additional intraservice work is detailed in the example.)

Postservice

Postservice work includes writing up a report/documentation of treatment, communicating with the referring physician to report the patients progress, and communicating with other team members.

97014 Application of a modality to one or more areas; electrical stimulation (unattended)

Work Value: 0.18 // Global Period: XXX

➲ ***CPT Assistant*** **Summer 95: 5, Apr 96: 11, Nov 97: 47, May 98: 10, Nov 01: 5, Jan 02: 11, Apr 02: 18, Aug 02: 11, Dec 03: 4**

Clinical Example

Patient is 20-year-old male who sustained a traumatic sprain to the acromioclavicular joint. Electrical stimulation at sensory level is applied using two electrodes, one anterior and one posterior, to the shoulder. Electrical stimulation is performed for pain control prior to range-of-motion activity. Unit set up requires 5-10 minutes for electrode placement and patient positioning. Electrical stimulation left in place for approximately 15 minutes.

Preservice

Preservice work includes reviewing the patients chart for medical treatment, setting up the equipment area, reviewing previous documentation as needed, communicating with other health care professionals (eg, social worker, nurse), communicating with family members, and communicating with the referring physician for additional information/clarification.

Intraservice
Intraservice work includes checking the patient's pain level, sensory distribution, and muscle guarding. (Additional intraservice work is detailed in the example.)

Postservice
Postservice work includes writing up a report/documentation of treatment, communicating with the referring physician to report the patients progress, and communicating with other team members.

Coding Tip for 97010, 97012, and 97014
A modality is any physical agent applied to produce therapeutic changes to biologic tissue; includes but not limited to thermal, acoustic, light, mechanical, or electric energy.

97016 Application of a modality to one or more areas; vasopneumatic devices

Work Value: 0.18 // Global Period: XXX

➲ ***CPT Assistant*** **Summer 95: 6, Apr 96: 11, Dec 98: 1, Nov 01: 5, Aug 02: 11, May 05: 14**

Clinical Example
A 55-year-old male presents with a crush injury to the left hand he sustained 7 days ago while at work. He has swelling and loss of motion. Intermittent compression is applied using a short compression sleeve. The patient is first measured via volumetrics to determine the amount of swelling in the hand objectively. Then a stockinet is applied to the hand, the vasopneumatic cuff is applied, the hand is elevated, and the pressure is determined. The vasopneumatic device is left in place for at least 30 minutes with the provider removing the device to check the hand at least two times during the 30-minute period. At the termination of treatment, the provider then repeats the volumetric measure to determine the effect of the treatment.

Preservice
Preservice work includes reviewing the patients chart for medical treatment, setting up the equipment area, reviewing previous documentation as needed, communicating with other health care professionals (eg, social worker, nurse), communicating with family members, and communicating with the referring physician for additional information/clarification.

Intraservice
Intraservice work includes checking the patients range of motion, sensation, and volumetric measurement. (Additional intraservice work is detailed in the example.)

Postservice
Postservice work includes writing up a report/documentation of treatment, communicating with the referring physician to report the patients progress, and communicating with other team members.

Constant Attendance

97032 Application of a modality to one or more areas; electrical stimulation (manual), each 15 minutes

Work Value: 0.25 // Global Period: XXX

➲ ***CPT Assistant*** **Summer 95: 6, Dec 98: 1, Nov 01: 5, Apr 02: 18, Jul 04: 14**

Clinical Example
The patient is a 52-year-old male who had a reconstruction procedure for patellar femoral dysfunction. Electrical stimulation is used for neuromuscular reeducation during stepping and climbing activities. The provider works with the patient for proper electrode placement and stimulus parameter adjustment during the exercise session. The provider uses manual probe stimulation to find motor points of quadriceps to obtain good muscle contraction. The session most likely lasts up to 30 minutes with 15 minutes of direct therapist time.

Preservice
Preservice work includes reviewing the patients chart for medical treatment, setting up the equipment area, reviewing previous documentation as needed, communicating with other health care professionals (eg, social worker, nurse), communicating with family members, and communicating

with the referring physician for additional information/clarification.

Intraservice

Intraservice work includes checking the patients sensation, skin integrity, and range of motion. (Additional intraservice work is detailed in the example.)

Postservice

Postservice work includes writing up a report/documentation of treatment, communicating with the referring physician to report the patients progress, and communicating with other team members.

Coding Tip for 97032

The application of this modality requires direct (ie, one-on-one) patient contact by the provider.

97035 Application of a modality to one or more areas; ultrasound, each 15 minutes

Work Value: 0.21 // Global Period: XXX

➲ **_CPT Assistant_ Summer 95: 7, Sep 96: 10, Dec 98: 1, Nov 01: 5**

Clinical Example

Patient has acute shoulder joint capsulitis. Provider has determined that the restriction of motion is coming from the anterior inferior glenohumeral joint capsule. Ultrasound is applied, using a coupling gel, first to the anterior joint capsule for 5 minutes then to the inferior joint capsule for 5 minutes using direct contact techniques and careful positioning of the patient. The provider is with patient for the entire time.

Preservice

Preservice work includes reviewing the patients chart for medical treatment, setting up the equipment area, reviewing previous documentation as needed, communicating with other health care professionals (eg, social worker, nurse), communicating with family members, and communicating with the referring physician for additional information/clarification.

Intraservice

Intraservice work includes checking the patient's skin integrity, sensation, level of pain, and range of motion. (Additional intraservice work is detailed in the example.)

Postservice

Postservice work includes writing up a report/documentation of treatment, communicating with the referring physician to report the patients progress, and communicating with other team members.

Coding Tip for 97032 and 97035

The application of this modality requires direct (ie, one-on-one) patient contact by the provider.

Therapeutic Procedures

97110 Therapeutic procedure, one or more areas, each 15 minutes; therapeutic exercises to develop strength and endurance, range of motion and flexibility

Work Value: 0.45 // Global Period: XXX

➲ **_CPT Assistant_ Summer 95: 7, Feb 97: 10, Nov 98: 37, Dec 99: 11, Mar 05: 11, Apr 05: 14, Aug 05: 11, Dec 05: 8, Mar 06: 15**

Clinical Example

A 60-year-old male, status post total knee replacement, presents with loss of motion and strength. The patient and the patient's health care provider work one-on-one through an exercise program of passive range of motion and progressive resistive exercises as tolerated. The patient requires feedback and verbal queues for proper performance of some exercises.

Preservice

Chart reviews for medical treatment; pre set up of activities, equipment, area; review of previous documentation as needed; communicating with other health care professionals (eg, social worker, nurse); discussions with family members; calls to referring MD for additional information/clarification.

Intraservice
The patient's range of motion, muscle strength, and muscle flexibility are assessed. The health care provider initiates or modifies one-on-one activities of the exercise program. The health care provider uses direct manual contact to elicit the appropriate movements of the patient's knee joint.

Postservice
Writing up report/documentation of treatment; calls to referring physician to report progress; communicating with other team members.

Coding Tip for 97110
Code 97110 is a therapeutic procedure that identifies a manner of effecting change through the application of clinical skills and/or service that attempts to improve function. When reporting code 97110, the provider is required to have direct (ie, one-on-one) patient contact.

97112 Therapeutic procedure, one or more areas, each 15 minutes; neuromuscular reeducation of movement, balance, coordination, kinesthetic sense, posture, and/or proprioception for sitting and/or standing activities

Work Value: 0.45 // Global Period: XXX

➲ ***CPT Assistant*** **Summer 95: 7, Feb 97: 10, Apr 05: 14, Aug 05: 11, Mar 06: 15;** ***CPT Changes: An Insider's View*** **2002**

Clinical Example
A female has a right cerebral vascular accident resulting in a left spastic hemiplegia. Although she can move her left arm, she has no functional use of it, as her increased muscle tone results in a flexion synergy in which she adducts her shoulder, flexes her elbow, and pulls her hand into a tight fist. To diminish the spasticity during her daily activities, the provider applies deep pressure to the patients biceps. The provider then internally rotates the patients upper arm, extends the elbows, pronates the forearm, and extends the patients fingers and thumb. This combination of movements releases the spasm, and with manual guiding from the provider, the patient is able to practice grasping, holding, and releasing large objects.

Preservice
Preservice work includes reviewing the patients chart for medical treatment, setting up the equipment area, reviewing previous documentation as needed, communicating with other health care professionals (eg, social worker, nurse), communicating with family members, and communicating with the referring physician for additional information/clarification.

Intraservice
Intraservice work includes checking the patients muscle tone, sensation, active movement patterns, and ability to reach, grasp, and release an object. The provider uses direct manual contact to elicit the appropriate movement of the knee joint. (Additional intraservice work is detailed in the example.)

Postservice
Postservice work includes writing up a report/documentation of treatment, communicating with the referring physician to report the patients progress, and communicating with other team members.

97113 Therapeutic procedure, one or more areas, each 15 minutes; aquatic therapy with therapeutic exercises

Work Value: 0.44 // Global Period: XXX

➲ ***CPT Assistant*** **Summer 95: 7, Feb 97: 10, Apr 05: 14, Mar 06: 15**

Clinical Example
A 42-year-old male who underwent an S/P lumbar fusion presents unable to tolerate a progressive therapeutic exercise program on land. He is limited by pain during functional activities, and experiences restricted dynamic truck and hip motion secondary to lumbar dysfunction and adhesions. The patient needs to return to work in 4 weeks. The patient will require at least 30 minutes of one-on-one skilled care in the aquatic environment utilizing simultaneously specific hydrodynamics and ongoing progressive therapeutic exercise

that is carefully integrated, when appropriate, with land therapeutic exercise.

Preservice
Preservice work includes reviewing the patient's chart for medical treatment, setting up the equipment area, reviewing previous documentation as needed, communicating with other health care professionals (eg, social worker, nurse), communicating with family members, and communicating with the referring physician for additional information and/or clarification.

Intraservice
Intraservice work includes checking the patient's level of pain, trunk range of motion, and activity level. The provider uses direct feedback and/or manual contact to guide the patient to achieve the desired movement pattern to increase ability to perform functional activities.

Postservice
Postservice work includes writing up a report and documenting treatment, communicating with the referring physician to report the patient's progress, and communicating with other team members

---

97116 Therapeutic procedure, one or more areas, each 15 minutes; gait training (includes stair climbing)

Work Value: 0.40 // Global Period: XXX

➲ ***CPT Assistant*** **Summer 95: 8, Sep 96: 7, Feb 97: 10, Jun 03: 3, Apr 05: 14, Mar 06: 15**

Clinical Example
An 18-year-old post–anterior cruciate ligament arthroscopic repair patient presents for gait training to eliminate gait deviations affecting normal swing and stance phase (ie, stride length and cadence symmetry).

Preservice
Preservice work includes reviewing the patient's chart for medical treatment, setting up the equipment area, reviewing previous documentation as needed, communicating with other health care professionals (eg, social worker, nurse), communicating with family members, and communicating with the referring physician for additional information and/or clarification.

Intraservice
Intraservice work includes checking the patient's range of motion, muscle strength, balance, and weight shifting ability. Gait training is initiated. The provider uses verbal cues and direct manual contact to elicit the appropriate movement pattern.

Postservice
Postservice work includes writing up a report/documentation of treatment, communicating with the referring physician to report the patient's progress, and communicating with other team members.

Coding Tip for 97116
If gait training is performed, it is appropriate to report code 97116.

97124 Therapeutic procedure, one or more areas, each 15 minutes; massage, including effleurage, petrissage and/or tapotement (stroking, compression, percussion)

Work Value: 0.35 // Global Period: XXX

➲ ***CPT Assistant*** **Summer 95: 8, May 96: 10, Feb 97: 10, Dec 99: 7, Apr 05: 14, May 05: 14, Mar 06: 15**

Clinical Example
A 60-year-old female with a "frozen shoulder" and altered glenohumeral rhythm presents for therapeutic massage to the middle trapezius and rhomboid muscles to release scapular tightness.

Preservice
Chart reviews for medical treatment; pre setup of activities, equipment, area; review of previous documentation as needed; communicating with other health care professionals (eg, social worker, nurse); discussions with family members; calls to referring physician for additional information/clarification.

Intraservice

The patient's range of motion, level of pain, and tissue extensibility are assessed. The health care provider uses manual contact to increase circulation and promote tissue relaxation to the scapular muscles.

Postservice

Postservice work includes writing up the report/documentation of treatment; calls to referring physician to report progress; and communicating with other team members.

Coding Tip for 97124

It is not appropriate to report code 97124 for mechanical massage therapy.

97140 Manual therapy techniques (eg, mobilization/ manipulation, manual lymphatic drainage, manual traction), one or more regions, each 15 minutes

Work Value: 0.43 // Global Period: XXX

➲ *CPT Assistant* Nov 98: 37, Feb 99: 10, Mar 99: 1, Jul 99: 11, Aug 01: 10, Dec 03: 5

Clinical Example

A 36-year-old male presents with neck, shoulder, and upper back pain, and severe muscle guarding with limited range of motion, which has developed gradually over the past 2 months and became more severe recently after lifting his child. Testing identified segmental hypomobilities at the facet joints of C4-C5, C5-C6, and C7-T1, and in the anterior glenohumeral joint with hypomobilities of inferior glide of the glenohumeral joint, along with myofascial trigger points palpated along the left cervical paraspinal region, upper trapezius, levator scapula, and infraspinatus muscles.

Preservice

The patient's medical records are reviewed for prior treatment. The treatment area and patient are prepared. The therapist communicates with other health care professional team members and with the patient's family. The therapist contacts the referring physician to exchange information.

Intraservice

The therapist places the patient in a supine position. The therapist conducts passive testing of soft tissue extensibility; gross and segmental range of motion; capsular restrictions; the level of muscle guarding; and the level of pain in the lower cervical, upper thoracic, and glenohumeral regions. Level and type of restrictions are identified. The therapist initiates treatment that incorporates isolated spinal and peripheral manual joint and soft tissue techniques to the cervical, scapular, and shoulder areas. This includes myofascial release, muscle energy, and passive stretch; manual traction, passive intervetebral mobilization/ manipulation, glenohumeral inferior glide; as well as capsular oscillations and stretch. The goal of this intervention is to activate pain-free lower cervical/upper thoracic range of motion, increase extensibility of the myofascial tissue of the cervical and upper quarter region, and facilitate the return to functional activities.

Postservice

Treatment and the components of the care provided are documented, along with any changes in the patient's status and future plan of care. The referring physician, other health care professionals, and the patient's family are contacted to discuss the patient's progress.

97530 Therapeutic activities, direct (one-on-one) patient contact by the provider (use of dynamic activities to improve functional performance), each 15 minutes

Work Value: 0.44 // Global Period: XXX

➲ *CPT Assistant* Summer 95: 9, Dec 01: 6, Apr 03: 26, Jul 03: 15, Aug 05: 11

Clinical Example

A carpenter, who sustained multiple trauma from an automobile accident, experiences decreased strength and coordination of both upper extremities and poor standing tolerance. The health care provider designs a series of woodworking projects that require the patient to stand for periods of time and make use of upper extremity coordination. The difficulty of each project requires progressively increased strength, coordination, endurance, and standing tolerance.

Preservice

Preservice work includes chart reviews for medical treatment; pre set-up of activities, equipment area; review of previous documentation as needed; communicating with other health care professionals (eg, social worker, nurse); discussions with family members; calls to referring physician for additional information/clarification.

Intraservice

Design an activity based on the patient's functional and motivational needs. Assess the patient's muscle strength, movement coordination, and standing activity level. Modify the activity based on the patient's progress. Use verbal and direct manual contact to elicit the appropriate movement pattern.

Postservice

Postservice work includes writing up report/documentation of treatment; calls to referring physician to report progress; and communicating with other team members.

97532 Development of cognitive skills to improve attention, memory, problem solving, (includes compensatory training), direct (one-on-one) patient contact by the provider, each 15 minutes

Work Value: 0.44 // Global Period: XXX

➲ *CPT Assistant* Dec 01: 1; *CPT Changes: An Insider's View* 2001

Clinical Example

An older adult has a combination of depression and organic brain syndrome. Although she lives with her daughter's family, she is alone during the day at their home. She has difficulty remembering when to take her medicines and frequently forgets to eat the meals her daughter prepares for her. At times she exhibits disconnected language that impairs her conversational abilities. By analyzing the patient's home environment and daily routine, the practitioner develops a structured system that may include exercises to enhance attention, memory, and social interaction skills, by which the patient incorporates taking her medication and eating her meals into her daily activities.

Preservice

Preservice work includes preparing to see the patient, reviewing records, and communicating with other professionals.

Intraservice

Intraservice work includes the services provided while the health care provider is with the patient and/or the patient's family.

Postservice

Postservice work includes arranging for further services, reviewing the results of studies, and communicating further with the patient, the patient's family, and other professionals, including providing written and oral reports.

Active Wound Care Management

97597 Removal of devitalized tissue from wound(s), selective debridement, without anesthesia (eg, high pressure waterjet with/without suction, sharp selective debridement with scissors, scalpel and forceps), with or without topical application(s), wound assessment, and instruction(s) for ongoing care, may include use of a whirlpool, per session; total wound(s) surface area less than or equal to 20 square centimeters

Work Value: 0.58 // Global Period: XXX

➲ *CPT Assistant* Jun 05: 1,10; *CPT Changes: An Insider's View* 2005

Clinical Example

A 68-year-old female presents with a pressure ulcer on the sacrum and reports of pain from the ulcerated area. Examination reveals that the wound is covered with black eschar and is surrounded by chronic inflammation with dark pigmentation. It is determined that the patient is not a candidate for surgery due to several comorbidities, however the patient would benefit from sharp debridement of the necrotic tissue. The wound is lightly cleansed and then measured. The sacral wound measures 6.5 cm × 2 cm with 100% black wound bed and no obvious drainage. The surrounding tissue is palpated with the wound margin observed as being inflamed and indurated. The wound is wiped with an antimicrobial solution, followed by sharp debridement using scissors, scalpel, and forceps to remove the devitalized tissue and facilitate subsequent wound healing. An enzymatic agent, saline gauze, and a composite dressing are placed directly on the wound bed. The last component related to this intervention is instruction to the patient/caregiver regarding the application of dressings, frequency of dressing change, and signs of wound deterioration.

Preservice

Review the patient's chart/referral. Remove existing dressings.

Intraservice

Measure and cleanse the wound. Palpate the surrounding tissue. Perform a thorough cleaning and debridement as described in the example.

Postservice

Instruct the patient and/or caregiver on proper wound care, the dressing change schedule, and the proper positioning of the body area containing the wound.

97598 Removal of devitalized tissue from wound(s), selective debridement, without anesthesia (eg, high pressure waterjet with/without suction, sharp selective debridement with scissors, scalpel and forceps), with or without topical application(s), wound assessment, and instruction(s) for ongoing care, may include use of a whirlpool, per session; total wound(s) surface area greater than 20 square centimeters

Work Value: 0.80 // Global Period: XXX

➲ *CPT Assistant* Jun 05: 1,10; *CPT Changes: An Insider's View* 2005

Clinical Example

A 72-year-old male presents with a pressure ulcer on the left hip and a venous ulcer of the left medial lower leg just proximal to the ankle. The wounds are lightly cleansed and then measured. Examination of the left hip wound reveals a stage III ulcer measuring 5 cm × 4.4 cm × 3.2 cm. The wound bed is obscured with semiadherent, yellow necrotic tissue. The wound margin is indurated with nonblanchable redness noted. Moderate amounts of serosanguineous drainage is noted. The left lower leg wound measures 10 cm × 6.8 cm × 1.5 cm. This is a full-thickness wound. Seventy-five percent is covered with adherent yellow necrotic tissue. Twenty-five percent is dull pink tissue. The wound margins are irregular and macerated. Copious serosanguineous drainage is evident. Circumferential measurements taken at the calf and ankle reveals 2 cm of measurable edema on the left compared to the right lower extremity. A more thorough cleansing of the left hip wound is performed utilizing high pressure waterjet with suction to facilitate loosening of the tissue. The wound is then wiped with an antimicrobial solution followed by sharp debridement with scissors, scalpel, and forceps to remove devitalized tissue. The wound is then dressed with saline moistened gauze, lightly packed, and a composite dressing is applied. The ankle wound is wiped with an antimicrobial solution followed by sharp debridement utilizing scissors, scalpel, and forceps to remove the devitalized tissue. A barrier cream is applied to protect the tissue around the wound and to prevent further breakdown. The wound is dressed with an absorbent dressing that promotes further autolytic debridement and covered with a composite dressing.

The last component related to this intervention is instruction to the patient/caregiver regarding appropriate exercise and limb elevation.

Preservice

Review the patient's chart and/or referral. Remove existing dressings.

Intraservice

Measure and cleanse the wound. Palpate the surrounding tissue. Perform a thorough cleaning and debridement as described in the example.

Postservice

Instruct the patient and/or caregiver on proper wound care, the dressing change schedule, the proper positioning of the body area containing the wound, and exercise.

Coding Tip for 97598

It is not appropriate to report codes 97597-97598 in conjunction with codes 11040-11044.

97605 Negative pressure wound therapy (eg, vacuum assisted drainage collection), including topical application(s), wound assessment, and instruction(s) for ongoing care, per session; total wound(s) surface area less than or equal to 50 square centimeters

Work Value: 0.55 // Global Period: XXX

➲ *CPT Assistant* Apr 05: 13, Jun 05: 1,10; *CPT Changes: An Insider's View* 2005

Clinical Example

A 73-year-old male presents with a stage III pressure ulcer of the sacrum. The base of the wound is clean and red and presents with heavy amount of serous drainage. There is also significant induration of the entire wound periphery with 1.5 cm of undermining proximally. The wound measures 8.5 × 5 × 3.2 cm.

Before applying the negative pressure therapy, the wound is thoroughly cleansed. The wound is assessed to assure that no sinus tracts and/or fistulas are present. The skin around the wound is cleansed thoroughly and prepared for the application of transparent film. The foam sponge is cut to fit the size and depth of the wound as well as the undermined areas.

The foam is secured in the wound using an adhesive transparent film. The film is applied with an ample border to assure a tight seal. The suction feet and tubing are then inserted into the foam. Additional transparent film is placed around the suction feet to secure the seal. The tubing is then connected to the negative pressure therapy pump. The negative pressure parameters are set on intermittent application at 100 mm Hg. The pump is activated and the dressing is inspected for appropriate negative pressure suction and no evidence of leaks.

Preservice

Review the patient's chart/referral. Remove existing dressings.

Intraservice

Thoroughly clean the wound and assess the wound to assure that no sinus tracts and/or fistulas are present. Clean the skin around the wound and prepare for the application of transparent film. Insert the tubing and connect the tubing to the negative pressure therapy pump. Set the pump parameters and activate the pump. Inspect the pump for leaks and clogs and the need for canister replacement.

Postservice

Instruct the patient/caregiver on the maintenance of the pump, the technique for canister replacement, the proper inspection of the dressing, and signs or symptoms of wound deterioration.

97606 Negative pressure wound therapy (eg, vacuum assisted drainage collection), including topical application(s), wound assessment, and instruction(s) for ongoing care, per session; total wound(s) surface area greater than 50 square centimeters

Work Value: 0.60 // Global Period: XXX

➲ *CPT Assistant* Apr 05: 13, Jun 05: 1,10; *CPT Changes: An Insider's View* 2005

Clinical Example

The patient is a 68-year-old female who underwent gastric surgery. Four days after surgery, the abdominal postoperative site dehisced, revealing a proximal wound measuring 4 cm × 6.2 cm × 2.5 cm and a distal wound measuring 8.4 cm × 4.6 cm × 3.5 cm. The proximal wound has a 100% red granulating wound bed with indurated wound margins and moderate amounts of serosanguineous drainage. The distal wound presents with a 25% yellow necrotic wound bed, indurated wound margins, localized redness, and copious amounts of purulent drainage.

The wounds are cleansed. The wounds are then assessed to assure that no sinus tracts and/or fistulas are present. The skin around the wound is cleansed thoroughly and prepared for the application of transparent film. The foam sponges are cut to fit the size and depth of each wound.

The foam is secured in the wounds using an adhesive, transparent film. The film must be applied with an ample border to assure a tight seal. The suction feet and tubing are then inserted into the foam at each site. Additional transparent film is placed around the suction feet to secure the seal. The tubing of both wounds is joined to the negative pressure therapy pump by a "Y" connector. The pump parameters are set at continuous pressure of 125 mm Hg. The pump is activated and the dressing is inspected for appropriate negative pressure suction and no evidence of leaks.

The patient continues to be monitored for tolerance, and the tubing and film monitored for leaks, clogs, and the need for canister replacement.

Preservice

Review the patient's chart/referral. Remove existing dressings.

Intraservice

Thoroughly clean the wound and assess the wound to assure that no sinus tracts and/or fistulas are present. Clean the skin around the wound and prepare for the application of transparent film. Insert the tubing and connect the tubing to the negative pressure therapy pump. Set the pump parameters and activate the pump. Inspect the pump for leaks and clogs and the need for canister replacement.

Postservice

Instruct the patient/caregiver on the maintenance of the pump, the technique for canister replacement, the proper inspection of the dressing, and signs or symptoms of wound deterioration.

Tests and Measurements

97750 Physical performance test or measurement (eg, musculoskeletal, functional capacity), with written report, each 15 minutes

Work Value: 0.45 // Global Period: XXX

➲ ***CPT Assistant*** **Summer 95: 5, Feb 97: 10, Aug 98: 11, Mar 00: 11, Nov 01: 5, May 02: 18, Apr 03: 28, Dec 03: 7, Feb 04: 5**

Clinical Example

The physician refers the patient, a data entry operator, for evaluation and treatment of suspected carpal tunnel syndrome. Nerve conduction studies were negative; however, the patient complains of numbness in the median nerve distribution and pain in the proximal palm while on the job and often at night. Assessments are made of pinch grip strengths using computerized instruments that are calibrated before each evaluation. Sensibility tests of touch pressure threshold and vibration are also performed on the patient to detect early development of carpal tunnel syndrome. Computerized instruments are preferred and hand-held instruments are subject to reliability. Test results are negative, and work simulation is set up for the patient to perform keyboard entry for 30 minutes. Upon retest, vibration detection and touch pressure threshold have decreased from normal to diminished light touch in the dominant hand. Pinch and grip strengths have also diminished because of the pain. Conservative treatment is initiated, which includes ergonomic changes in equipment and job pacing in conjunction with the physician's application of anti-inflammatory medication.

Preservice

Preservice work includes reviewing the patient's chart for medical treatment, setting up the equipment area, reviewing previous documentation as needed, communicating with other health care professionals (eg, social worker, nurse), discussing the patient's status with family members, and communicating with the referring physician for additional information and/or clarification.

Intraservice

Intraservice work includes checking the patient's level of pain, sensation, pinch and grip strength, and functional job titles abilities. The provider develops program to address the instruction/practice of accommodated work-related activities. The provider also educates the patient about safe job performance, job pacing, and self management of the program. (Additional intraservice work is detailed in the example.)

Postservice

Postservice work includes writing up a report/documentation of treatment, communicating with the referring physician to report the patient's progress, and communicating with other team members.

Coding Tip for 97750

Code 97750 requires direct one-on-one patient contact.

Orthotic Management and Prosthetic Management

97760 Orthotic(s) management and training (including assessment and fitting when not otherwise reported), upper extremity(s), lower extremity(s) and/or trunk, each 15 minutes

Work Value: 0.45 // Global Period: XXX

➲ *CPT Assistant* Dec 05: 8, 11; *CPT Changes: An Insider's View* 2006

Clinical Example

A patient with a 6-week-old median and ulnar nerve injury is referred to splinting to improve hand use. Through a combination of gross impairment assessment and clinical reasoning, the therapist designs a splint that stabilizes the thumb for three jaw chuck prehension and facilitates the finger extension required to place the hand around large objects. During the fitting process, the patient is instructed in splint application, uses and frequency of wear, how to check for pressure areas and care of the splint.

Preservice

Preservice work includes reviewing the patient's history/chart, communicating with other team members, and gathering/preparing materials to be used in the procedure.

Intraservice

Direct patient time may include assessing splint for proper fit and function (optimal components/position); making necessary modification to splint; training patient in use of splint, wearing schedule, care and precautions, tolerance issues, adjustments; having patient practice functional activities while wearing splint.

Postservice

Postservice work includes writing notes/documentation, charting, communicating with other team members, and communicating with the patient and the patient's family.

Coding Tip for 97760

It is not appropriate to report code 97760 in addition to code 97116.

97761 Prosthetic training, upper and/or lower extremity(s), each 15 minutes

Work Value: 0.45 // Global Period: XXX

➲ *CPT Assistant* Dec 05: 8, 11; *CPT Changes: An Insider's View* 2006

Clinical Example

(Upper Extremity) A patient with a below-elbow amputation is referred for training in the use of a body-powered B/E prosthesis that has both a Dorrance hook and functional hand terminal devices (TDs). After determining that the patient understands how to activate the muscles used to power the TDs, control training begins with practice opening and closing the TDs and performing graded, repetitive tasks. Treatment culminates in training the patient to use the prosthesis as a functional assist. (Lower Extremity) A patient with a below-knee amputation is referred for training in the use and care of a below-knee prosthesis with a molded socket and SACH foot. Following instruction in the purpose and use of the various components of the device itself, the patient is trained in the application and removal of the prosthetic device, and the proper alignment and fit of the prosthetic device with observation of related changes in skin condition during stance and gait activities.

Preservice
Preservice work includes reviewing the patient's chart and communicating with other team members on the patient's status/progress.

Intraservice
Intraservice work includes checking the fit and componentry of the prosthetic; instructing the patient in care of the prosthetic characteristics, precautions, and wear; assessing the level of function while wearing the prosthetic; instructing the patient on home program–based training techniques learned in the clinic.

Postservice
Postservice work includes writing notes/documentation and communicating with other team members.

97762 Checkout for orthotic/prosthetic use, established patient, each 15 minutes

Work Value: 0.25 // Global Period: XXX

➲ ***CPT Assistant*** **Dec 05: 8, 11;** ***CPT Changes: An Insider's View*** **2006**

Clinical Example
A 56-year-old female with a diagnosis of rheumatoid arthritis is seen for a follow-up checkout subsequent to a metacarpal phalangeal flexible implant arthroplasty. The therapist has previously fitted the patient with a dorsal dynamic orthosis that provides correction of residual deformity and permits metacarpal flexion and extension in desired plane and range. The patient's edema has decreased and she complains of pressure on the ulnar styloid. The therapist reassesses the fit and makes adjustments to the orthosis.

Preservice
Preservice work includes reviewing the patient's history, chart, and last notes; communicating with the physician and insurance carrier; and assembling supplies and tools.

Intraservice
Intraservice work includes assessing hand/wrist problems, wound status, wound care, and bandaging; assessing the splint for alignment and fit; adjusting/repairing components of the orthotic/prosthetic; adding, deleting, and/or padding the orthotic/prosthetic; reinstructing the patient regarding the patient's wearing schedule, application, and care of the orthotic/prosthetic; and having a patient practice the proper technique.

Postservice
Postservice work includes writing notes/documentation; providing the patient's family with information about the home program; communicating with other therapists, physicians, and the insurance carrier; and cleaning up tools, splinting supplies, and the bandaging area.

Medical Nutrition Therapy

97802 Medical nutrition therapy; initial assessment and intervention, individual, face-to-face with the patient, each 15 minutes

Work Value: 0.45 // Global Period: XXX

➲ ***CPT Assistant*** **Apr 03: 10, Nov 03: 1;** ***CPT Changes: An Insider's View*** **2001**

Clinical Example
A 66-year-old female with preexisting osteoporosis has been diagnosed with type II diabetes and hyperlipidemia. Initial medical nutrition therapy (MNT) assessment and intervention is being initiated, in addition to oral medication for treatment of diabetes.

Intraservice

Thoroughly review the patient's medical record for a medical diagnosis, past medical history, history of present illness, and pertinent lab data. Obtain a nutrition history from the patient and evaluate the patient's nutrient intake and use of nutrition supplements. Identify nutrition problems. Obtain physical measurements and perform calculations related to body size. Conduct a nutrition assessment to evaluate the patient's nutrient requirements, appropriateness of weight in relation to the patient's desirable body weight and goal weight, the adequacy of the patient's present diet, potential drug-nutrient interactions, exercise patterns, psychosocial food patterns, and the patient's knowledge of and willingness to implement nutrition interventions. Review clinical data and lab information and evaluate the patient's ability to perform self-monitoring. Formulate a complex nutrition prescription specific to the patient's diagnosis. Translate the nutrition prescription into an individualized meal plan and menu guidelines. Provide self-management training. Review with the patient the techniques for self-monitoring. Identify with the patient self-management goals and the barriers to adhering to those goals. Discuss strategies to overcome barriers and schedule a follow-up appointment(s). Document the nutrition assessment, nutrition prescription, and self-management training provided in the patient's medical record, making note of communication with other health care providers and any referrals made.

97803 Medical nutrition therapy; re-assessment and intervention, individual, face-to-face with the patient, each 15 minutes

Work Value: 0.37 // Global Period: XXX

➲ ***CPT Assistant*** **Apr 03: 10, Nov 03: 1;** ***CPT Changes: An Insider's View*** **2001**

Clinical Example

A 67-year-old male with congestive heart failure, decreased cardiac output, and edema who has received prior nutrition self-management training is receiving follow-up and more detailed self-management training to address comorbidities.

Intraservice

Review the patient's medical record. Obtain a nutrition history from the patient. Identify changes in the physician orders and nutrition problems. Conduct a nutrition assessment to evaluate the patient's adherence to the nutrition prescription and meal plan and identify barriers to adherence. Review the effectiveness of dietary modifications in the medical management of the patient's diagnoses, changes in weight status, and need for additional nutrition interventions. Provide reinforcement self-management training on the patient's nutrition prescription, menu guidelines, and self-monitoring procedures. Discuss with the patient the schedule for follow-up. Document the patient's nutrition history and nutrition assessment, the reinforcement instructions provided, collaboration with other health care providers, and referrals made in the patient's medical record.

97804 Medical nutrition therapy; group (2 or more individual(s)), each 30 minutes

Work Value: 0.25 // Global Period: XXX

➲ ***CPT Assistant*** **Apr 03: 10, Nov 03: 1;** ***CPT Changes: An Insider's View*** **2001**

Clinical Example

A 55-year-old male with hyperlipidemia and obesity who has received prior face-to-face self-management training is receiving follow-up self-management training in a small group setting.

Intraservice

Review the patient's medical record. Obtain a nutrition history from the patient. Identify changes in the physician orders and nutrition problems. Conduct a nutrition assessment to evaluate the patient's adherence to the nutrition prescription and meal plan, the effectiveness of dietary modifications in the medical management of the patient's diagnosis, changes in weight status, and need for additional nutrition interventions. Provide skill development/self-management training in a small group setting on nutrition prescription, menu guidelines, and self-monitoring procedures. Discuss with the patient the schedule for follow-up. Document the patient's nutrition history and nutrition assessment, and the instructions provided in the patient's medical record.

Coding Tip for 97802, 97803, and 97804

MNT includes nutritional diagnostic therapy and counseling services provided by a registered dietician or licensed nutrition professional for the purpose of managing disease.

Acupuncture

97810 Acupuncture, 1 or more needles; without electrical stimulation, initial 15 minutes of personal one-on-one contact with the patient

Work Value: 0.60 // Global Period: XXX

➲ *CPT Assistant* Jan 05: 16-17, Jun 05: 5; *CPT Changes: An Insider's View* 2005

Clinical Example

A 17-year-old male presents for repeat treatment of nontraumatic cervicalgia of 3-days duration. The patient reports cervical pain and limited range of motion.

Preservice

The practitioner reviews the chart, greets the patient, and obtains a brief account of the results of the previous treatment and any significant changes that have occurred since the last visit. Points are selected for today's treatment.

Intraservice

The practitioner locates three points and selects the appropriate needle lengths and gauges for this treatment. The practitioner then inserts and mildly stimulates the needles. The patient is instructed to rest for 20 minutes while the needles are retained. The practitioner returns periodically to monitor the patient and to restimulate the needles and to inquire about patient comfort and treatment response. When the desired effect is achieved, the practitioner removes the needles and presses on the points with a cotton ball to prevent bruising or bleeding.

Postservice

The needles are disposed in accordance with Occupational Safety and Health Administration guidelines. The practitioner then assists the patient to an upright position, making sure that the patient does not feel faint. Follow-up instructions are given to the patient. Final documentation is recorded in the patient chart.

Acupuncture, Needle
97810

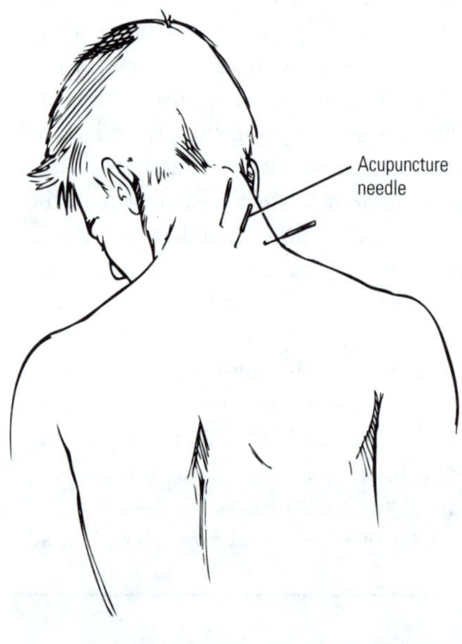

97813 Acupuncture, 1 or more needles; with electrical stimulation, initial 15 minutes of personal one-on-one contact with the patient

Work Value: 0.65 // Global Period: XXX

➲ *CPT Assistant* Jan 05: 16-18, Jun 05: 5; *CPT Changes: An Insider's View* 2005, 2006

Clinical Example

A 49-year-old female receiving chemotherapy for breast cancer was previously referred for acupuncture to relieve postchemotherapy nausea. This treatment is part of an ongoing series of treatments for this condition. The patient is weak but not faint and has not vomited since chemotherapy was received earlier in the day.

Preservice

The practitioner reviews the chart, greets the patient, and obtains a brief account of the results of the previous treatment and any significant changes that have occurred since the last visit. The appropriate four points are selected for today's treatment.

Intraservice

The patient is placed in the supine position and the points are located. The practitioner selects the appropriate needles before inserting and mildly stimulating them. Electrodes are then attached to the shafts of the needles and an appropriate frequency (Hz) and waveform is selected. The practitioner then slowly increases the amplitude of the signal until patient tolerance is reached. The patient is instructed to rest for 20 minutes while the needles are retained.

The practitioner returns periodically to monitor the patient, re-adjust the electrical stimulation and to inquire about patient comfort and treatment response. When the desired effect is achieved, the practitioner removes the electrodes and needles, and presses on the points with a cotton ball to prevent bruising or bleeding.

Postservice

The needles are disposed in accordance with OSHA guidelines. The practitioner then assists the patient to an upright position, making sure that the patient does not feel faint. Follow-up instructions are given to the patient. Final documentation is recorded in the patient chart.

Coding Tip for 97810 and 97813

Only one initial code is reported per date of service.

+ 97814 Acupuncture, 1 or more needles; with electrical stimulation, each additional 15 minutes of personal one-on-one contact with the patient, with re-insertion of needle(s) (List separately in addition to code for primary procedure)

Work Value: 0.55 // Global Period: ZZZ

➲ *CPT Assistant* Jan 05: 16, Jun 05: 5; *CPT Changes: An Insider's View* 2005, 2006

Clinical Example

A 65-year-old male returns for a repeat visit to treat lumbalgia.

Preservice

Following removal of needles from the initial acupuncture service provided (97813), the practitioner assists the patient to his feet and asks him to walk around the room to test the effectiveness of treatment. The pain has reduced but is still significant, so the practitioner selects four additional points, palpates to locate them, and then marks and cleans those points.

Intraservice

The practitioner inserts the four additional needles and manipulates them to produce a deep, aching sensation. Electrodes are attached to the shafts of the needles and an appropriate frequency (Hz) and waveform is selected. The practitioner then slowly increases the amplitude of the signal until patient tolerance is reached. The patient is instructed to rest. The practitioner remains in the room and continues to stimulate the needles during this phase of treatment by adjusting the electrical stimulation until the pain and dysfunction are improved to an acceptable level. At the conclusion of this service the electrodes and needles are removed.

Postservice

Follow-up instructions are given to the patient. The needles are disposed in accordance with Occupational Safety and Health Administration guidelines. Final documentation is recorded in the patient chart.

Chiropractic Manipulative Treatment

98940 Chiropractic manipulative treatment (CMT); spinal, one to two regions

Work Value: 0.45 // Global Period: 000

➲ *CPT Assistant* Jan 97: 7, 11, Feb 99: 10, Dec 00: 15, Mar 06: 15

Clinical Example

CMT service on two spinal body regions, thoracic and lumbar, of an established patient previously scheduled for this service. The previous initial examination of the patient revealed a 32-year-old female with mid-back pain, stiffness, and persistent low back pain of 2-weeks duration.

Preservice

A brief evaluation of the patient, including a review of symptoms and a focused examination of the problem and related reason, reveals that chiropractic spinal manipulative treatment is clinically indicated in two regions: the thoracic (T5) region and the lumbar (L4) region.

Intraservice

Diversified Manipulation to T5: Following the premanipulation assessment and preparation, with the patient positioned prone on the treatment table, the physician applies brief myofascial treatment of existing trigger points in the thoracic paravertebral musculature. The appropriate segmental level is identified in the adjusting position (T5). The physician makes a pisiform contact on the left transverse process of T5. Breathing instructions are given to the patient. The physician prestresses the periarticular soft tissues. An articular (osseous) adjustive procedure is applied to the determined manipulatable spinal lesion at T5 utilizing a short lever, low amplitude, high velocity thrust in a posterior to anterior direction. Postadjustment procedures and interactive reassessments are made.

Diversified Manipulation to L4: A supportive cushion (half-Dutchman's roll) is placed under the patient's pelvis at the appropriate position. The patient's ankles are cuffed, the locking levers of the table are released, and the table is gently extended (axial distraction). A palmar contact is made on the spinous process of L4 with the physician's cephalad hand. With the other hand the physician grasps the table or appropriate handle at the caudal end of the table. The patient is advised to take in a deep breath and let it out. A slow, controlled flexion maneuver is applied within patient tolerance and safety to the caudal portion of the table with multiple (5–8) repetitions. This process is repeated through three cycles. Following this treatment the locking levers are secured, the caudal end of the table is returned, the patient's ankles are un-cuffed, and the cushion is removed. Postadjustment procedures and interactive reassessments are made. The patient is then turned onto her side and positioned for a side-posture manipulation/adjustment. A brief stretch is applied to the lumbar-pelvic musculature and a long lever, low amplitude, high velocity thrust is applied to the L4/L5 joint complex. Postadjustment procedures and interactive reassessments are made. The patient is then returned to a comfortable position for a brief rest.

Postservice

Chart entry and documentation, including documentation of appropriate subjective and objective assessments as well as the procedural components of this patient visit, are completed.

98941 Chiropractic manipulative treatment (CMT); spinal, three to four regions

Work Value: 0.65 // Global Period: 000

➲ *CPT Assistant* Jan 97: 7, 11, Mar 97: 10, Feb 99: 10, Dec 00: 15, Mar 06: 15

Clinical Example

CMT service on four spinal body regions; cervical, head, lumbar, and pelvic—of an established patient previously scheduled for this service. The previous initial examination of the patient revealed a 44-year-old male with complaints of a persistent tension-type headache noted daily for the last 6 months. Regular use of muscle relaxants decreased the pain temporarily, but he developed gastrointestinal irritation from the medication and is seeking a different approach to treatment. Secondarily, he described low-back pain that was noted intermittently for the past 2 years, but was most recently aggravated by a long bike ride. The ride aggravated his back pain to the point that he can no longer get a full night's rest due to his right-sided pelvic pain and lumbar aching.

Preservice

A brief evaluation of the patient, including a review of symptoms and a focused examination of the problem and related areas, reveals that chiropractic spinal manipulative treatment is clinically indicated in four regions: head (occiput), upper cervical (C2), lumber (multiple lumbar segments), and pelvic (right innominate).

Intraservice

Diversified Manipulation of C2: With the patient properly placed in the supine position during the premanipulation period, and with the premanipulative interactive assessments completed, an index contact with the right hand is taken at the predetermined manipulable segment in the right cervical region (C2). The left hand cradles the head, with appropriate support to the occiput and ear of the contralateral side. The head is laterally flexed to the right of the isolation prestress of the appropriate articulation. A specific thrust is made straight lateral at right angles to the midsagittal plane of the head within the appropriate paraphysiologic articular range to avoid iatrogenic/clinical risk. Postadjustment procedures and interactive reassessments are made.

Diversified Craniovertebral Adjustment: From the concluding position of the previous procedure, the physician repositions the craniocervical region and completes a premanipulative interactive assessment in the new region. The physician steps to the left of the table and cradles the head with the right hand using the appropriate supportive technique. The contact is made by taking a palmar position of the hand over the patient's ipsilateral mandible and cheek, thumb anterior to ear, and fifth digit under the jaw. With the physician's forearm low and parallel to the sternum, the patient's head is positioned with the manipulable lesion up and a bidirectional, 1-in thrust is made with both hands straight cephalad. Postadjustment procedures and interactive reassessments are made.

Diversified Innominate Adjustment: From the concluding position of the previous procedure, the patient is repositioned in a left recumbent side-posture, and the physician completes a premanipulative interactive assessment in the new region. The patient's lower shoulder is placed anterior with the hand under the head. The upper shoulder is posterior with the forearm resting on the lateral thoracic wall. The lower thigh and leg are straight. The upper thigh and leg are flexed with the dorsum of the foot in the popliteal space of the lower knee. The pelvis is vertical or slightly anterior on the upper side. The physician stands on the contralateral side facing cephalad with the cephalad foot on the floor. The caudal foot is off the floor with a thigh-to-thigh contact on the patient's upper thigh. The posterior ilium receives a pisiform contact with the physician's caudal hand, while the physician's cephalad hand makes a palmar contact on the anterior upper shoulder of the patient. With the appropriate articular prestress used, a manipulative thrust is delivered with the pisiform contact anterior and superior. Simultaneously, the physician makes a slight body drop downward with the thigh to open up the articulation. Postadjustment procedures and interactive reassessments are made.

Multisegmental Gonstead Lumbar Adjustments: Using similar positioning as the previous procedure, a similar adjustment is made to the posterior L5 vertebra with a pisiform contact on the L5 transverse process. The patient is then positioned in a right recumbent side-lying position and a similar adjustment is made to the L4 vertebra. A premanipulative interactive assessment is made prior to the application of the procedure, and postadjustment interactive assessments are made following the procedure.

Postservice

Chart entry and documentation, including documentation of appropriate subjective and objective assessments as well as the procedural components of the patient visit, are completed. A brief telephone consultation or written summary with the patient's insurance company or referring provider to supply an update of patient progress is also conducted.

98942 Chiropractic manipulative treatment (CMT); spinal, five regions

Work Value: 0.87 // Global Period: 000

➲ *CPT Assistant* Jan 97: 7, 11, Feb 99: 10, Dec 00: 15, Mar 06: 15

Clinical Example

CMT service on six spinal body regions—cervical, head, thoracic, lumbar, pelvic, and sacral—of an established patient previously scheduled for this service. This previous initial examination of the patient revealed a 38-year-old male who sustained injuries to multiple body parts from a fall off an extension ladder. While trying to prevent the fall, he twisted and strained his upper and lower back and struck his head. He landed on his side on the collapsed ladder injuring his pelvis, hip, and lower extremities. Complaints of 5-days duration include neck, mid- and lower-back pain and stiffness, headache, and pelvic and hip pain and stiffness. He also suffered multiple contusions of various body regions including the head, shoulders, ribs, hip, buttocks, thigh, leg, and ankle.

Preservice

A brief evaluation of the patient, including a review of symptoms and focused examination of the problem and related areas reveals that chiropractic spinal manipulative treatment is clinically indicated in six regions; cervical (C5), head (occiput), thoracic (T3, T6), lumbar (L5), pelvic (left innominate), and sacral (sacrum).

Intraservice

Diversified Manipulation of C5: The patient is placed in a seated position during the premanipulation period, and the premanipulation interactive assessments are completed. With the physician standing on the left side of the patient, a middle finger contact with the right hand is taken at the predetermined manipulable segment in the left mid-cervical region (left C5). While the right middle finger is in contact with the segment described, the right hand simultaneously cradles the left laterally flexed head of the patient. A specific clockwise, very short amplitude, high velocity thrust is made, not exceeding the paraphysiologic range of motion to avoid iatrogenic/clinical risk. Postadjustment procedures and interactive reassessments are made.

Diversified Occipital Adjustment: From the concluding position of the previous procedure, the physician repositions the patient supine and completes a premanipulation interactive assessment in the new region. The physician then steps to the right of the table and cradles the head with the left hand, while simultaneously taking a specific middle finger contact to the patient's lower left occiput. With the physician's right arm low and parallel to the patient's sternum in cephalad direction, and the palmar surface across the patient's right jaw for stabilization, a short amplitude, high velocity lift of the left occiput is administered by the physician's left hand/middle finger with the patient's reassessments are made.

Diversified Manipulation of T3 and T6: From the concluding position of the previous procedure, the physician repositions the patient prone with the head in central position and completes a premanipulation interactive assessment in the new region. A contact is made at the right transverse process of T3 with the physician's left hand. The right hand takes a soft tissue traction by pushing slightly cephalad at the right occiput. The patient is then instructed to take a deep breath and exhale. At the point of full expiration, a straight arm body drop thrust is executed, with the line of drive slightly in the caudal direction. Next, contact is made at the right transverse process of T6 with the physician's left hand. The right hand contacts the patient's left transverse process of T6. A soft tissue traction is taken, and the patient again is instructed to inhale and exhale fully. At the point of full expiration, a straight arm body drop thrust is executed with the line of drive at a 90-degree angle to the dorsal spine. Postadjustment procedures and interactive reassessments are made.

Gonstead Adjustment of L5: From the concluding position of the previous procedure, the patient is repositioned in right recumbent side-posture, and the physician completes a premanipulative interactive assessment of the new region. The patient's lower shoulder is placed anterior, with both hands interlocked. The upper shoulder is posterior, the lower thigh and leg are straight, and the upper thigh and leg are flexed with the dorsum of the foot in the popliteal fossa of the lower knee. The pelvis is vertical or slightly anterior on the upper side. The physician stands with feet slightly apart. The physician makes a pisiform contact on the left transverse process of the L5 with the caudal hand, a palmar contact on the upper anterior shoulder with the cephalad hand, and the upper thigh contact with one thigh. An appropriate articular prestress is used and a high velocity, low amplitude manipulative thrust with the thigh contact. Postadjustment procedures and interactive reassessments are then performed.

Diversified Innominate Adjustment: A premanipulative interactive assessment is performed. Using similar positioning as the previous procedure, a similar adjustment is executed on the left posterior innominate, directing the line of drive more cephalad to open the joint space of the sacrailiac joint. A post adjustment interactive assessment is completed following the procedure.

Diversified Manipulation of the Sacrum: The patient is repositioned from the concluding position of the previous procedure to the prone position, and a premanipulation assessment of the new region is performed. Contact is made at the base of the subluxated sacrum, with the physician's right hand placed just to the left of the median line and the physician's left hand clockwise. A straight-arm body drop is made with the line of drive posterior to anterior at 90 degrees to the procedures. Interactive reassessments are made.

Postservice

Chart entry and documentation including documentation of appropriate subjective and objective assessments as well as the procedural components of this patient visit, are completed. The physician will follow up with the patient's general internist to confirm the patient's progress and to confirm that there are no signs of a closed head injury.

98943 Chiropractic manipulative treatment (CMT); extraspinal, one or more regions

Work Value: 0.40 // Global Period: XXX

➲ ***CPT Assistant*** **Jan 97: 7, 11, Mar 97: 10, Feb 99: 10, Dec 00: 15, Mar 06: 15**

Clinical Example

CMT service on two extraspinal body regions—the upper extremities and the abdomen—as a portion of the manipulative treatment provided within a more complex chiropractic manipulative treatment service involving both spinal and extraspinal manipulation procedures on an established patient previously scheduled for this service. The previous initial examination revealed a 52-year-old patient who suffered a severe motor vehicle accident over 7 years ago. She has since been diagnosed with fibromyalgia and mild clinical depression. Prior to the accident, she had been very active and now is only able to be employed in relatively sedentary positions. As a secretary, she has developed moderate right-sided carpal tunnel syndrome for which surgery was unsuccessful. Besides right-hand weakness and numbness, she also complains of forearm and elbow pain that worsens as the day goes on. She complains of neck stiffness with associated "pressure type-headaches" on a regular basis. Moderate low-back pain and right buttock pain prevent her from sitting for more than 30 minutes before needing to change positions. She describes significant abdominal bloating after meals, which does not seem to respond to medication.

Preservice

A brief evaluation of the patient, including a review of symptoms and a focused examination of the problem and related areas reveals that a chiropractic extraspinal manipulation treatment is clinically indicated in two regions: the upper extremities (elbow and hand), and the abdominal region.

Intraservice

Manipulation to the Elbow: The patient is positioned into a sitting posture and the physician completes a premanipulation interactive reassessment of the region. The physician stands behind the patient and extends the patient's arm out to the side at 90 degrees. The physician's outside hand grasps the patient's wrist from above while the physician's inside hand make a thumb and supported index contact on the posterior head of the radius. The patient's arm is placed into an extended position, and a high-velocity, low amplitude posterior to anterior thrust is delivered on the radial head. Postadjustment procedures and interactive reassessments are made.

Manipulation to the Hand and Wrist: With the patient still in the sitting position, the physician comes to the front of the patient and completes a premanipulative interactive assessment of the new region. The patient's hand is pronated and the physician places both thumbs on the lunate of the patient's wrist. The patient's wrist is then placed into an extended position to the point of joint tension, and a high velocity, low amplitude thrust is delivered through both thumbs on the lunate in a dorsal to a palmar direction. Postadjustment procedures and interactive reassessments are made.

Manipulation to the Abdomen: For complaints related to hiatal hernia, the patient is placed in a seated position. Premanipulative interactive assessments are completed. The physician sits behind the patient and places the fingers slightly below and to the left of the xiphoid, and then moves the fingers in deeply in an anterior to posterior direction. The patient is asked to lean forward slightly to allow a greater penetration of the fingers, which will enable the physician to feel the rectus abdominous relax. At maximum penetration, the physician's fingers will move superiorly and the left. The patient is asked to take a full inspiration and expiration, after which the physician quickly releases pressure. The procedure is repeated, except that on the second pass, instead of moving the fingers superiorly and to the left, the physician moves the fingers anteroinferiorly. This relaxes the pressure of the gastroesophageal junction in the thorax.

Postservice

Chart entry and documentation, including documentation of appropriate subjective and objective assessments as well as the procedural components of this patient visit are completed.

Coding Tip for 98940, 98941, 98942, and 98943

CMT is a form of manual treatment to influence joint and neurophysiologic function and can be accomplished through the use of a variety of techniques.

Education and Training for Patient Self-Management

98960 Education and training for patient self-management by a qualified, nonphysician health care professional using a standardized curriculum, face-to-face with the patient (could include caregiver/family) each 30 minutes; individual patient

Work Value: 0.00 // Global Period: XXX

➲ *CPT Changes: An Insider's View* 2006

Clinical Example

A 60-year-old male with a symptomatic established illness or disease (eg, diabetes or asthma) or the desire to delay disease comorbidities (eg, cardiovascular comorbidities) is referred by a physician to a qualified, nonphysician health care professional (eg, RD or RN) for individual education/training.

Coding Tip for 98960

For education provided as genetic counseling services, report code 96040. For education to a group regarding genetic risks, report codes 98961 and/or 98962 as appropriate.

98961 Education and training for patient self-management by a qualified, nonphysician health care professional using a standardized curriculum, face-to-face with the patient (could include caregiver/family) each 30 minutes; 2-4 patients

Work Value: 0.00 // Global Period: XXX

➲ *CPT Changes: An Insider's View* 2006

Clinical Example

A 60-year-old male with asymptomatic established illness or disease (eg, diabetes or asthma), or the desire to delay disease comorbidities (eg, cardiovascular comorbidities), is referred by a physician to a qualified, nonphysician health care professional (eg, RD or RN), for group education/training.

98962 Education and training for patient self-management by a qualified, nonphysician health care professional using a standardized curriculum, face-to-face with the patient (could include caregiver/family) each 30 minutes; 5-8 patients

Work Value: 0.00 // Global Period: XXX

➲ *CPT Changes: An Insider's View* 2006

Clinical Example

A 60-year-old male with asymptomatic established illness or disease (eg, diabetes or asthma), or the desire to delay disease comorbidities (eg, cardiovascular comorbidities), is referred by a physician to a qualified, nonphysician health care professional (eg, RD or RN) for group education/training.

Moderate (Conscious) Sedation

⊘ **99143** Moderate sedation services (other than those services described by codes 00100-01999) provided by the same physician performing the diagnostic or therapeutic service that the sedation supports, requiring the presence of an independent trained observer to assist in the monitoring of the patient's level of consciousness and physiological status; younger than 5 years of age, first 30 minutes intra-service time

Work Value: 0.00 // Global Period: XXX

➲ *CPT Assistant* Feb 06: 9; *CPT Changes: An Insider's View* 2006; *Clinical Examples in Radiology* Winter 06:18

Clinical Example

A 2-year-old patient undergoes a procedure that requires moderate sedation to complete safely and with minimal emotional trauma. The physician will supervise and direct an independent trained observer who will assist in monitoring the patient's level of consciousness and physiologic status throughout the procedure.

Preservice

The procedural/sedating physician performs and documents a thorough patient assessment to assure that moderate sedation can be safely provided outside of an operating room setting. This assessment includes a review of the patient's current and past medical history (eg, concurrent acute illness or chronic diseases, current medications, allergy history, immunization status, prior medical and surgical history, response to any previous sedative or analgesic agents). The timing of the patient's last meal must also be determined. A physical exam is completed with an emphasis on underlying pathology that might negatively impact the induction or recovery from the sedative. Based upon this assessment, and the sedation and/or analgesia requirements of the procedure, the physician must then determine the appropriate pharmacologic agent(s) to be

used, including
dosing and route of administration. The sedation process, including the risks and benefits, are explained to the parent(s) or legal guardian and consent is obtained. The patient is verbally prepared for the procedure and the appropriate monitoring equipment (eg, heart rate, respiration, pulse oximetry, intermittent blood pressure) is connected to the patient. The physician confirms that the independent observer has assured the availability and the appropriate functioning of oxygen, suctioning equipment, artificial airways, masks, and resuscitation bags.

Intraservice

The physician supervises the administration and induction of the sedating agent, with or without an analgesic, initiated by the independent trained observer. The patient is assessed continuously until an effective and safe level of moderate sedation and/or analgesia is achieved. Additional doses of sedating and/or analgesic agent(s) are ordered by the physician as needed. The physician's intraservice time ends when the procedure is complete, the patient is physiologically stable, and face-to-face physician time is no longer required.

Postservice

Upon completion of the procedure, the independent observer continues to monitor the patient. The physician returns and reassesses the patient until the patient reaches a presedation level of consciousness. The physician then establishes whether predetermined discharge criteria have been met. These assessments and the final assessment are documented in the procedural records and discharge instructions are provided to the parent(s) or legal guardian.

Coding Tip for 99143

Moderate sedation does not include minimal sedation (anxiolysis), deep sedation, or monitored anesthesia care (codes 00100-01999).

⊘ **99144** Moderate sedation services (other than those services described by codes 00100-01999) provided by the same physician performing the diagnostic or therapeutic service that the sedation supports, requiring the presence of an independent trained observer to assist in the monitoring of the patient's level of consciousness and physiological status; age 5 years or older, first 30 minutes intra-service time

Work Value: 0.00 // Global Period: XXX

➲ *CPT Assistant* Feb 06: 9; *CPT Changes: An Insider's View* 2006; *Clinical Examples in Radiology* Winter 06:18

Clinical Example

A patient 5 years of age or older presents with a complaint necessitating performance of some procedure or service (ie, the "supported procedure"), in support for which moderate sedation is deemed clinically appropriate. The treating physician will perform both the supported procedure and the moderate sedation service.

Preservice

The sedation process, including risks and benefits, is explained to the patient, the patient's family, and/or legal guardian, and consent is obtained. The physician performs and documents a patient assessment to assure that moderate sedation can be safely provided outside of an operating room setting. This assessment involves a medical history review (eg, current medications, allergies, prior medical and surgical history, response to any previous sedative or analgesic agents, time since the most recent meal), as well as a physical exam with an emphasis on underlying pathology that might negatively impact the induction with or recovery from sedating agents. Based upon the patient's age, presenting problem(s), medical history, examination, and the type of sedation-supported procedure and its projected duration, the physician determines the appropriate sedating agent(s), route of administration, and respective dosage to be used. The patient is verbally prepared for the sedation procedure. The physician directs that monitoring technology be implemented as needed, and that an independent trained observer be available to assist the physician in monitoring the patient's level of consciousness and physiological status. The availability and appropriate functioning of any materiel necessary for cardiorespiratory intervention are confirmed.

Intraservice

The physician supervises the administration and induction of the sedating agent, with or without an analgesic, initiated by the independent trained observer. The patient is observed until a safe and effective level of moderate sedation is achieved. The physician, assisted by the independent trained observer, continually assesses the patient's level of consciousness and physiological status throughout the performance of the supported procedure. Additional doses of sedating agent are ordered by the physician, as needed, to maintain the achieved level of sedation for the supported procedure.

Postservice

Upon completion of the supported procedure, the independent trained observer continues to monitor the patient. If there are any untoward reactions resulting from conscious sedation, the physician determines the appropriate patient care management. The physician reassesses the patient's clinical condition to assure that the patient has returned to the presedation level of consciousness. This assessment is documented in the medical record, and discharge instructions are provided for the patient, family, and/or legal guardian.

+ 99145 Moderate sedation services (other than those services described by codes 00100-01999) provided by the same physician performing the diagnostic or therapeutic service that the sedation supports, requiring the presence of an independent trained observer to assist in the monitoring of the patient's level of consciousness and physiological status; each additional 15 minutes intra-service time (List separately in addition to code for primary service)

Work Value: 0.00 // Global Period: ZZZ

➲ *CPT Assistant* Feb 06: 9; *CPT Changes: An Insider's View* 2006; *Clinical Example in Radiology* Winter 06:18

Clinical Example

A patient five years of age or older presents with a complaint necessitating performance of some procedure or service (ie, the "supported procedure"?), in support for which moderate sedation is deemed clinically appropriate. The treating physician will perform both the supported procedure and the moderate sedation service.

Intraservice

The physician, assisted by the independent trained observer, continually assesses the patient's level of consciousness and physiological status throughout the performance of the supported procedure. Additional doses of sedating agent are ordered by the physician, as needed, to maintain the achieved level of sedation for the supported procedure.

Coding Tip for 99145

Code 99145 should be reported in conjunction with codes 99143 and 99144 as appropriate.

⊘ 99148 Moderate sedation services (other than those services described by codes 00100-01999), provided by a physician other than the health care professional performing the diagnostic or therapeutic service that the sedation supports; younger than 5 years of age, first 30 minutes intra-service time

Work Value: 0.00 // Global Period: XXX

➲ *CPT Assistant* Feb 06: 9; *CPT Changes: An Insider's View* 2006; *Clinical Examples in Radiology* Winter 06:18

Clinical Example

A 3-year-old patient undergoes a procedure that requires moderate sedation for safety reasons and to minimize emotional trauma. The physician performing the procedure requests that the sedation be delivered and monitored by a second physician.

Preservice

The sedating physician performs and documents a thorough patient assessment to assure that moderate sedation can be safely provided outside of an operating room setting. This assessment includes a detailed review of the patient's current and past medical history (eg, historical factors necessitating the procedure, concurrent acute illness or chronic diseases, current medications, allergy history, immunization status, prior medical and surgical history, and response to any previous sedative or analgesic agents). The timing of the patient's last meal must also be determined. A physical exam is completed with an emphasis on underlying pathology that might negatively impact the induction or recovery from the sedative. Based upon this assessment, and the sedation and/or analgesia requirements of the procedure, the sedating physician must then determine the appropriate pharmacologic agent(s) to be used, including dosing and route of administration. The sedation process, including the risks and benefits, are explained to the parent(s) or legal guardian and consent is obtained. The patient is verbally prepared for the procedure and the appropriate monitoring equipment (eg, heart rate, respiration, pulse oximetry, intermittent blood pressure) is connected to the patient. The availability and the appropriate functioning of oxygen, suctioning equipment, artificial airways, masks, and resuscitation bags are confirmed.

Intraservice

The sedating agent(s) with or without an analgesic agent is administered and the patient is assessed continuously until an effective and safe level of moderate sedation and/or analgesia is achieved. The patient is closely monitored by the sedating physician and additional doses of sedating and/or analgesic agent(s) are delivered as needed. The sedating physician's intraservice time ends when the procedure is complete, the patient is physiologically stable, and face-to-face time with the sedating physician is no longer required.

Postservice

Upon completion of the sedation and when the patient is physiologically stable, patient monitoring is returned to the procedural physician and/or clinical staff. The sedating physician returns and reassesses the patient until the patient reaches a presedation level of consciousness. The sedating physician then establishes whether predetermined discharge criteria have been met. These assessments and the final assessment are documented in the procedural records and postsedation instructions are provided to the parent(s) or legal guardian. This information is then communicated to the procedural physician.

⊘ 99149 Moderate sedation services (other than those services described by codes 00100-01999), provided by a physician other than the health care professional performing the diagnostic or therapeutic service that the sedation supports; age 5 years or older, first 30 minutes intra-service time

Work Value: 0.00 // Global Period: XXX

➲ *CPT Assistant* Feb 06: 9; *CPT Changes: An Insider's View* 2006; *Clinical Examples in Radiology* Winter 06:18

Clinical Example

A patient 5 years of age or older presents with a complaint necessitating performance of some procedure or service (ie, the "supported procedure"), in support for which moderate sedation is deemed clinically appropriate. One health care professional will perform the supported procedure while a different physician will provide the moderate sedation service.

Preservice

The sedation process, including risks and benefits, is explained to the patient, the patient's family, and/or legal guardian, and consent is obtained. The physician providing sedation performs and documents a patient assessment to assure that moderate sedation can be safely provided outside of an operating room setting. This assessment involves a medical history review (eg, current medications, allergies, prior medical and surgical history, response to any previous sedative or analgesic agents, time since the most recent meal), as well as a physical exam with an emphasis on underlying pathology that might negatively impact the induction with or recovery from sedating agents. Based upon the patient's age, presenting problem(s), medical history, examination, and the type of sedation-supported procedure and its projected duration, the physician determines the appropriate sedating agent(s), route of administration, and respective dosage to be used. The patient is verbally prepared for the sedation procedure. The physician directs that monitoring technology be implemented as needed. The availability and appropriate functioning of any materiel necessary for cardiorespiratory intervention are confirmed.

Intraservice

Administration of the sedating agent, with or without an analgesic, is initiated. The patient is observed until a safe and effective level of moderate sedation is achieved. During this face-to-face time, the physician continuously assesses the patient's level of consciousness and physiological status throughout performance of the supported procedure. Additional doses of sedating agent are ordered by the physician, as needed, to maintain the achieved level of sedation for the supported procedure.

Postservice

If, following cessation of continuous face-to-face assessment of the patient's level of consciousness and physiological status, there are any untoward reactions resulting from sedation, the physician providing sedation determines the appropriate patient care management. The physician reassesses the patient's clinical condition to assure that the patient has returned to the presedation level of consciousness. This assessment is documented in the medical record, and discharge instructions are provided for the patient, the patient's family, and/or legal guardian.

Other Services and Procedures

99170 Anogenital examination with colposcopic magnification in childhood for suspected trauma

Work Value: 1.75 // Global Period: 000

➲ *CPT Assistant* Nov 99: 55

Clinical Example

A 3-year-old girl, who has disclosed to her mother that her stepfather has been sexually abusing her by performing penile-vaginal and digital-vaginal penetration, presents for evaluation of suspected child abuse.

Note: The physician performs two services:

1) A comprehensive physical exam, which reveals an enlarged vaginal opening with a hymenal notch at 6:00 and possible scarring of the posterior fourchette;

2) An anogenital exam with colposcopic magnification. Physician work may include alleviating the child's fears about the examination; viewing the anogenital area through the colposcope with the child in the supine position and then in the knee-chest position; and measuring the hymenal orifice diameter and noting abnormal findings. It also may include taking and reviewing slides/photos to

ensure that the findings seen on the photographs are consistent with what was seen on the initial examination and that no abnormalities were missed. Documentation of finding is also part of the anogenital exam.

Preservice

Prior to the examination process, the colposcope is set up for the procedure. The 35 mm camera or videocamera is placed on the colposcope. Identifying information on the patient is placed on an identifying card and on the databack on the camera. Before the anogenital examination, the physician must address the child's anxiety and fears, especially in females, because of the necessity for relaxation in conducting an adequate genital examination. Time is necessary for such calming activities as showing the light from the colposcope on the wall with the examiner alternating between the two shades of light, so that the child can view the light and see that it will not hurt. It is appropriate to drape the older child; however, the younger child may be more frightened by a sheet or gown and may actually want to see what is happening during the examination.

Intraservice

The child is typically examined first in supine, frog-legged position, which offers relative comfort for the child and provides the physician with a clear view of the genitalia and anus. This position may be done in the lap of a parent or caretaker on the examination table if the child is too apprehensive. The child lies in a frog-legged position with her legs in full abduction and the feet in apposition. The anogenital area is closely inspected with the aid of the magnification provided by the colposcope, which enhances the ability of the examiner to visualize small and delicate tissues, which would otherwise be inadequately observed. The colposcope is slowly and gradually taken close to the genital to get out of focus; thereby, increasing the amount of time involved in inspecting the genital area.

The separation technique consists of separating the labia majora with slight downward traction. The other examination technique that must be performed is traction, which consists of gently pulling the labia majora towards the examiner, which assists in viewing the hymenal edges, especially when redundant hymenal tissue is present. The labia minora, posterior fourchette, periurethral arc, and hymen are all closely inspected to detect any erythema, edema, ecchymoses, petechiae, tears, or any other signs of acute trauma. In addition, signs of healed or chronic trauma, such as scarring, notches, clefts, and hymenal narrowing, must be assessed. All suspicious lesions, which may represent veneral warts or herpes, must be closely examined. The hymenal orifice diameter should also be measured using an intraocular scale or an external measuring device placed within the field of vision. The child often does not remain relaxed, causing the hymenal orifice to decrease in size and making it difficult to obtain a accurate measurement. Visualization of the vascular pattern and any interruption of the mucosal surface can be enhanced via the use of the red-free filter, which casts a green light. In addition, scar tissue may become evident due to its avascular appearance. Varying magnification levels are employed throughout the examination, separation, and traction, so as to obtain closer detail of noted findings.

The child is then placed in prone, knee-chest position, to view the anus and any redundant hymenal tissue in the inferior quadrants of the hymen. The colposcope is again brought closer to the child and maneuvered so as to bring the anal and genital areas in focus. The labia majora are separated upward in an effort to visualize the hymenal tissue. Again, any abnormalities of the genital area are noted. The prone, knee-chest position also has the advantage of facilitating visualization of the cervix if the hymenal orifice is of sufficient diameter because the anterior wall of the vagina falls forward. Any foreign bodies in the vaginal canal can be detected and often removed with the child in this position. The perianal region is closely examined to detect fissures, scarring, skin tags, or suspicious lesions, such as venereal warts or herpes. In addition, any dilatation of the anus should be measured vertically and horizontally. It should be noted whether or not stool is present in the rectal vault if anal diatation is noted. The perineum should also be attached to the colposcope; photographs are attained during all of the various anogenital examination techniques and positions of the child.

Before photographing, time is necessary for the physician to discuss with the child such issues as the doctor taking pictures of her with her clothing off only with permission of her parent; that the camera is not the type of camera used at home; the pictures from the colposcope can only be interpreted by medical personnel; and that the child's name is not on the photograph, only identifying numbers (ie, medical record number). When the colposcopic slides or photographs are developed, they must be reviewed by the physician and documented to note that the findings that were present during the examination can be seen. Care is necessary to objectively document evidence and establish base line information for future reference in the event of continued victimization and/or legal proceedings. Accurate and complete photodocumentation is also necessary if second opinions are required through review by another physician, so that the child is not subjected to another examination.

Postservice

Following the procedure, review of the 35-mm slides/photographs must be done to document that the findings noted during the examination process can still be visualized. In addition, any findings seen on the slides/photographs that were not noted at the time of the initial examination must be documented.

Coding Tip for 99170

If conscious sedation is performed, codes 99143-99150 should be reported.

Appendix—List of CPT® Codes

Evaluation and Management (E/M) Services

Office or Other Outpatient Services

Hospital Observation Services

Hospital Inpatient Services

Consultations

Emergency Department Services

Pediatric Critical Care Patient Transport

Critical Care Services

Inpatient Pediatric Critical Care

Inpatient Neonatal Critical Care

Continuing Intensive Care Services

Musculoskeletal System

Respiratory System

Male Genital System

Female Genital System

Maternity Care and Delivery

Endocrine System

Nervous System

Eye and Ocular Adnexa

Auditory System

Radiology

Diagnostic Radiology (Diagnostic Imaging)